THE OXFORD HISTORY OF
AUSTRALIAN LITERATURE

THE OXFORD HISTORY OF AUSTRALIAN LITERATURE

Edited by

LEONIE KRAMER

with contributions by Adrian Mitchell, Terry Sturm
Vivian Smith, Joy Hooton

Melbourne
OXFORD UNIVERSITY PRESS
Oxford   Wellington   New York

Oxford University Press

OXFORD LONDON GLASGOW
NEW YORK TORONTO MELBOURNE AUCKLAND
KUALA LUMPUR SINGAPORE JAKARTA HONG KONG TOKYO
IBADAN NAIROBI DAR ES SALAAM CAPE TOWN
DELHI BOMBAY CALCUTTA MADRAS KARACHI

First published 1981
Reprinted in paperback with corrections 1981

NATIONAL LIBRARY OF AUSTRALIA CATALOGUING IN
PUBLICATION DATA

The Oxford history of Australian literature

Index
Bibliography
ISBN 0 19 554335 1

1. *Australian Literature—History and criticism.*
I. *Kramer, Leonie Judith, 1924—, ed. II. Mitchell,
Adrian Christopher William.*

820'.9

Designed by Arthur Stokes

Computer photocomposed and printed at
Griffin Press Limited, Netley, South Australia.

PUBLISHED BY OXFORD UNIVERSITY PRESS,
7 BOWEN CRESCENT, MELBOURNE

PREFATORY NOTE

The idea of an Oxford History of Australian Literature was conceived many years ago by the late Professor Grahame Johnston. Much of his scholarly work for Australian literature was editorial, and issued in publications for which others have earned credit. I hope that he would have approved this History, and felt that his expectations for it had been fulfilled.

The History was originally intended to be a single-author work, highly selective and critical. The latter objective has been retained, but the former has yielded to the rapid expansion of the subject. It seemed better to divide the responsibility between scholars and critics who had developed a special but not exclusive interest in the three main fields— fiction, drama and poetry. In doing so we ran the risk of clashes of opinion and internal inconsistencies. In the event, though working on such diverse material, the contributors, while sustaining their individual arguments, have, I believe, demonstrated a common purpose—to see their material steadily and to see it whole, to look afresh at the beginnings of our literary history with the detachment that temporal distance makes possible, and to reassess the achievement of individual authors.

All have had to make difficult choices. Our space is limited, and we have been forced to take stock of our assets, and be firm—but I hope just—in our critical decisions. These are, of course, debatable, and we hope they will be debated. The introduction is intended to provide an overview of the subject, and to draw attention to some of the main movements of ideas in both literature and criticism.

Our most difficult decision was to omit a section on non-fictional prose. Documentary writing, memoirs, essays, diaries, letters and general prose have a special importance in Australian literary history, because of their quality and their influence upon other literary forms. But in the space available we could not have included this material without serious distortion. Its significance is made clear in various ways in the text, especially in the section on fiction. Another unavoidable omission is popular literature, which often embodies the attitudes and interests of the reading public. Serious writers tend to mould opinion, popular ones to reflect it, and their works are a rich source of information about social trends and aspirations. Perhaps, however, this history may stimulate further studies by its omissions.

Each contributor owes much to the past—to such pioneering works as H. M. Green's *A History of Australian Literature*, and Leslie Rees's *A History of Australian Drama*, and to innumerable shorter studies, articles and bibliographies. The presence of much of this material in our bibliography is an acknowledgment of indebtedness, especially to those who have alone attempted what we have produced as a team. Our debt to earlier critics and historians of Australian writing is clear. In the preparation of this history many other people were also helpful. We have been fortunate in having the manuscript edited by Frank Eyre, whose experience, advice and criticism have been invaluable to us and we acknowledge with special gratitude the research assistance provided over a long period by Mrs Betty Briggs.

Leonie Kramer
January 1980

CONTENTS

Prefatory Note   *page* v

Introduction   *Leonie Kramer*   1

FICTION   *Adrian Mitchell*   27

DRAMA   *Terry Sturm*   173

POETRY   *Vivian Smith*   269

BIBLIOGRAPHY   *Joy Hooton*   429

Notes   491

Index   497

INTRODUCTION

This history is written only a decade before the bicentenary of the establishment of the first settlement at Sydney Cove in 1788. In reviewing poetry and fiction one senses the end of an age, since a whole generation of poets who began writing in the late thirties and forties have now taken on the dignity of elder statesmen. Further, the figure who has dominated fiction for over twenty years—Patrick White—has now produced so large a body of work that critics are increasingly being tempted into statements which have an air of finality. In the last decade drama has flourished and now occupies a more secure place in literary history than it has commanded hitherto. Precisely because of a particular conjunction of events—the growth of drama and the ageing of a group of leading poets and prose writers—one's awareness of the passing of an age is matched by a sense that a process of revaluation may be about to begin. The large number of younger writers, some of whom might produce their best work in the coming decade, pose a special problem for the historian. This is particularly so in drama, whose flowering is so recent. Young dramatists, like young poets, demand attention, yet resist all but the most tentative judgments.

The work of the senior generation of poets—Kenneth Slessor, R. D. FitzGerald, A. D. Hope, Douglas Stewart, James McAuley, David Campbell and Judith Wright has attracted a considerable body of criticism in the form of monographs and essays in literary and scholarly journals. These latter, for the most part, are concerned with particular aspects of their work, or with analysis and explication. There has been remarkably little discussion of their stature, either relative to each other, or to modern poetry in English. Sometimes, for better or worse, their poetic status has been taken for granted, and in consequence criticism does not inspect too closely the premises upon which it rests. Encouragement of an interest in Australian literature has been a strong motivating impulse for most serious and scholarly critics of the

I

subject. In this they may be subscribing to a view which was established and promoted in the nineteenth century, namely that Australian writing is a delicate plant, which needs nurturing and sheltering, and cannot be expected to withstand the rough and unpredictable winds from the outside world.

A partial explanation of this protective impulse may be found in history, and in the mixed feelings of the early settlers about their chances of survival. Some comparisons have been made by critics between American and Australian literature in terms of their similar experiences of frontier life. But there is a striking difference in the origins of the two literary cultures. The first attempt at a full-length study of American culture was Samuel Lorenzo Knapp's *American Cultural History 1607-1829*. Knapp was approximately the same distance from the literary beginnings of America as we are from those of Australia. He is able to say—as we are not—that

> our ancestors were not, like some colonists, disgorged from the mother country to keep the remaining population sound and pure; they were not a surplus mass thrown off to prevent national apoplexy, or political spasms...[1]

Knapp, having shown other motives for colonizing to be inappropriate to the history of America, is able to locate the beginnings of a national culture in the thrift, enterprise and passion for freedom of the earliest colonists, and to begin his analysis of American literature with a description of the intellectual qualities of the individuals who were its architects.

Stern dedication to freedom of thought and belief drove the Pilgrim Fathers to America. The settlement at Port Jackson in 1788 was a prison. It was not without its men of intellect and distinction, as the early records testify. But these men were obliged to adapt themselves to a situation not of their own choosing. They tried to reconcile their awareness of cultural dislocation with their sense of responsibility to the task imposed upon them. In the early years the physical hardships of the colony, its dependence upon the erratic dispensations of a remote authority and the accidents which threatened its survival, hardly provided congenial conditions for literary expression. They did, however, produce documentary writings which have continued to provide themes and subjects up to the present day.

From the beginning, for annalists, as for settlers, there were difficult adjustments to make. The sheer excitement of discovery which men like Cook, Banks, Leichhardt, Darwin, Mitchell, von Mueller, and so many others experienced, is powerfully transmitted in the various journals, memoirs and letters of the first one hundred years. But the countervailing realities were inescapable. The early colony which was so nearly wiped out by famine was a desperate place, a struggling witness to the injustice of justice and to the brutality of enlightened beings. The contrast between unspoiled nature and degraded humanity would have provided a powerful subject for a poet, had there been one equal to the task. Charles Darwin, on his journey through the Blue Mountains in 1836, came across a large farm employing some forty convicts. He saw a brilliant sunset illuminating the peacefulness of an unspoiled land:

> The sunset of a fine day will generally cast an air of happy contentment on any scene; but here, at this retired farmhouse, the brightest tints in the surrounding woods could not make me forget that forty hardened, profligate men, were ceasing from their daily labours, like the slaves from Africa, yet without their just claim for compassion.[2]

Many years later, in *His Natural Life,* Marcus Clarke found a fictional form for the kind of vista Darwin annotated; but he radically revised the insight that Darwin expressed.

To account for the struggles of nineteenth century writers to reflect their experiences of life in Australia in literary, as distinct from documentary forms, one must go back to the beginnings of settlement. From the literary point of view, the colony chose the wrong time to be born. The great figures of the English neoclassical tradition were dead. In English literary history the 1760s saw a withdrawal from Augustan principles and attitudes, and the beginnings of that elevation of 'consistent imagination' (in the words of Richard Hurd) which became central to the theory and practice of the Romantics. The dying years of the Augustan period, like those of the metaphysical tradition, were marked by a gradual debilitation of forms and language, especially in poetry. The lines in Blake's early poem 'To the Muses', 'The languid strings do scarcely move. The sound is forc'd, the notes are few.' accurately capture the feelings of strain.

The chronological accident which brought Australian settlement into existence in the dying years of one literary tradition and on the eve of another might have contributed to the uncertainty and tentativeness of its early attempts at literary expression. Yet the

3

formal traditions inherited by writers and artists provided a means of ordering new experiences. Notions of the picturesque, for example, inform both early paintings and descriptive accounts of the landscape. Non-fictional prose—essays, reports, arguments, histories—provided models for the first observers; and in another vein, inherited satirical verse conventions met the needs of early poetic critics of colonial life.

Eighteenth century thought and artistic conventions affected the formation of Australian literature in ways which have still not been systematically examined. In *The Legend of the Nineties* (1954) Vance Palmer speculates that

> It is possible that the eighteenth century tradition hampered the efforts of our early writers to accept the life about them. It almost imposed an attitude of detachment.[3]

On the other hand, Palmer sees as a virtue of eighteenth century influence that respect for civilization and rationality which motivated exploration and the recording of discoveries 'in a lucid commonsense way'. Only the writing 'which has a solid factual base' (that is, journals, records and memoirs) is memorable, he argues. Most of the rest—'essays, verse and pseudo-novels'—would be 'no loss'. In short, 'from such a closed society one would not expect poetry, or anything springing from the feelings and imagination.'

It is possible, however, to take a different view of certain aspects of the eighteenth century tradition. The poet's public role—as observer, moralist, philosopher and critic—was better suited to the conditions of a new society than the more private and subjective concerns of the romantic writer. The neo-classical preoccupation with the taming of the wilderness and the cultivation of civilized virtues was peculiarly appropriate to the hopes of the early settlers. It can be argued that eighteenth century literary modes—the ode, elegy, satire and narrative poem—were also well suited to the needs, as well as the aspirations, of early writers. The English tradition of landscape poetry, for example, proved readily adaptable to local subjects and provided a bridge between the old world and the new.

The usefulness of the tradition is exemplified in the work of the minor though prolific poet Charles Tompson. In 1824 he wrote a poem called 'Black Town', an elegy on the death of a settlement which had been established ten years earlier 'for the purpose of civilizing the aboriginal Native of Australia'. A chapel and college were built, and a few Aboriginals were taught farming and other skills, an enterprise itself conformable to eighteenth century aspirations. But they deserted the place. Tompson found the model for his lament in Goldsmith's 'The Deserted Village'. 'Black Town' is a modest imitation lacking the strength and ease of its parent. But it is a genuine attempt to present a real situation, and a subject of local interest and importance, in the context of a view of the rise and fall of civilization which, though a contemporary common-place, is far from irrelevant to the actual events which are the subject of the poem.

In a word, the question of eighteenth century influence is not nearly as straightforward as Palmer and other commentators have suggested. It is true that Tompson uses a standard poetic diction which is thoroughly English. It is also true that, especially in the nineteenth century, 'Australian verse piously continued to follow long outdated models'.[4] Yet the minor English landscape poets of the eighteenth century (especially Thomson and Cowper) provided models for Australian nature poetry, by showing how landscape, feeling and moralizing could be brought together. Themes such as the differences in the seasons, the virtues of country life, the awesomeness of wild and primitive nature and the feelings induced by being alone in the presence of natural forces were readily transferable to a new environment. Such models allowed the possibility of precise description, together with that generalized comment about the natural world, found in the work of Harpur and Kendall, and later Judith Wright. 'Furnley Maurice' (Frank Wilmot) writing in the early 1920s about the poetry of the period described it as 'the last word in conventional English verse production ... done to worn-out patterns discarded in the land of their origin'. In suggesting that Australian poets be Australian he argued that

> A gleam of real independence, a flash of inherent light, some national tone in our word music—little things like these will count for more than the enormous odes of affected nobility written in the calm of a borrowed security.[5]

It is one thing, as he recognised, to prescribe a measure of independence and a 'national tone', another to define the target of the prescription. The important criticism to make of Tompson's efforts to adapt Goldsmith's 'The Deserted Village' to 'Black

5

Town' and, later, of Adam Lindsay Gordon's Byronic and Swinburnian imitations is not that they do not represent Australia and Australians, but that they adopt a poetic manner without putting upon it the imprint of their individual style. Eighteenth century diction, reinforced by the rhetorical effects of romantic and Victorian poetry, encouraged resonant abstractions and elevated sentiments. The reason for the lameness of much nineteenth century verse is not so much the intractability of the subject matter, or the poets' feelings of exile or dislocation, as their lack of originality and inventiveness. To compare Tompson's diction with the language of A. B. (Banjo) Paterson's ballads is to see at once the gulf between the former's imitative style and the latter's lively, local speech rhythms.

Most of Tompson's work exemplifies Blake's criticism of the monotony and artificiality of minor English poetry of the later eighteenth century. Charles Harpur's verse, however, is more attentive to poetic forms and their possibilities. He is a discriminating borrower from eighteenth century and romantic models, and the formal features of his verse are appropriate to his subjects and observations. He was a serious student of poetry and he recognised that forms were not mere containers, but expressed the structure of poetic thought. His verse shows the difficulties under which 'the bards in the wilderness' laboured, but also the value to them of the traditions upon which they were able to draw.

In fiction, the influence of romantic and melodramatic adventure stories—such as the novels of Scott and Dickens—was strong. The complex plot which relied more on a connected train of events complicated by shifts in time, place and concealed relationships, than on a central character whose moral development was the main subject, was favoured by novelists throughout the nineteenth century. This kind of plot was employed by Henry Kingsley, Rolf Boldrewood and Marcus Clarke, but was also typical of the many lesser works which were serialized in newspapers and journals, and of early dramatic writing. Melodrama, passion, villainy and danger were curiously entangled with facts about landscape, the people, the convict system and the hardships of life in the land of hopeful dream and actual nightmare.

It is important to recognize the effort made by the novelists to grapple with the facts of colonial life. Before the middle of the century novels were often fictionalized accounts of colonial life intended for the information of migrants. But from the 1850s on

6

the impulse to fiction was differently based. Thus Henry Kingsley's novels *The Recollections of Geoffry Hamlyn* and *The Hillyars and the Burtons* together present a record, admittedly haphazard and imperfect, of two distinct phases in colonial settlement. In the former Kingsley looks at the pastoralists who made what they could from the land and then returned to the familiar comforts of English country life, materially enriched by their colonial adventures. In the latter he brings to Australia a family of Chelsea blacksmiths, who, representing a lower class in the English hierarchy with more to gain from emigrating, have no intention of returning to the crowded life of London. *The Recollections of Geoffry Hamlyn* has been criticized for its romanticizing of pastoral life, its depiction of English gentlemen, its melodrama and exaggerated local colour. It is certainly something of an extravaganza, but in its description of place and landscape it is exact. This was recognised by Arthur Patchett Martin, who in his *The Beginnings of Australian Literature* (1898) commended Kingsley for his accuracy. In both novels Kingsley tried to marry four worlds, the old and the new, the literary and the observed. Dickens could have supplied the model (*Martin Chuzzlewit* was one of Kingsley's favourite books), but the humour, inventiveness and talent for credible fantasy which Dickens had in abundance, Kingsley totally lacked.

Patchett Martin's generally favourable view of nineteenth century novelists was displaced in the twentieth century by Vance Palmer's more influential opinions. His early criticism rests on an assumption about the failure of nineteenth century novelists to be Australian. Marcus Clarke's *His Natural Life* is 'brilliant and unsatisfactory ... written with one eye on Balzac and the other on the convict records'. Kingsley's *The Recollections of Geoffry Hamlyn* is

> ... full of charming, idyllic pictures, but is, for our purposes, useless'. Mrs. Campbell Praed 'is a clever woman with a genuine talent for romance, but she is not in harmony with the spirit of her country...'⁶

Only Boldrewood's *Robbery Under Arms* is accorded unstinted praise. While acknowledging all these and other works as constituting 'a precious heritage', Palmer goes on to qualify this statement by predicting that 'our coming writers will hardly find sources of inspiration in them'. From a perspective seventy years later, one can acknowledge the weaknesses in these works, but at the same time see them as evidence of the ways in which novelists

7

tried to accommodate their observations within the forms of fiction then popular. Later novelists might not owe them a specific debt, but these early works established themes and expressed attitudes which have continued to be influential. Writers as different in intention and accomplishment as Eleanor Dark, Hal Porter, Thomas Keneally, R. D. FitzGerald and Alexander Buzo have gone back to the historical records for their basic material. Some of them have found a fruitful subject in the contradiction between the eighteenth century's admiration for rationality and the irrationalities of the convict system which that century condoned.

Only modest claims can be made for the achievements of colonial writers, but their work has a special interest for the historian as evidence of the ways in which they tried to find forms which would contain their experience. Even the most minor talents made a genuine attempt to give literary expression to a variety of experiences for which there was no precedent. They were sometimes fluent and prolific, but often infelicitous, and their historical interest frequently outweighs their literary value. In their work one recognises the attempt to reconcile the actualities of experience with the formal demands of literary modes evolved within the English tradition. The models available to them, both in prose and verse, were not ideal for their purposes. But they served as necessary constraints within which the newness, strangeness and excitement of their world could be ordered, and which, at the very least, provided some links with a literary tradition to which the English language gave access. There is some truth in Judith Wright's view that it is necessary for the poet to assimilate the landscape before being able to write with ease and conviction, but it is not a satisfactory explanation of the short-comings of the colonial poets. The fact is that, in general, the more talented recorders of early Australia were not first of all literary men, but explorers, surveyors, scientists, visitors and adminis-trators.

There are, no doubt, complex historical and cultural reasons for the characteristic (and often repetitive) attitudes to the growth and development of Australian literature. After the middle of the nineteenth century it had many advocates. In the 1860s, 70s and 80s critics, notably G. B. Barton (*Literature in New South Wales,* 1866) were on the whole content to describe, rather than to evaluate the state of Australian writing. Barton's work is a survey in the nineteenth century manner. In the 1890s commentaries take on a more polemical note, and there is debate between those whose premise is that there is an identifiable, though small, body of Australian literature, and those who question that premise. In their *The Development of Australian Literature* (1898), Turner and Sutherland pose the question '... how is a national literature to be expressed that has no nation behind it?' This question, or some other form of it, preoccupied critics and writers to such an extent that they did not easily, or at all, come to define the problems faced by Australian writers, and so were unable to perceive what progress they had made towards solving them. Looked at from one aspect the history of Australian literature is characterized by pious hopes. The notion that there is a definable community whose character a properly national literature would express has haunted critics from the beginnings to the present day. Turner and Sutherland felt it necessary to define the contributors to such a literature. They argued with themselves as to whom to include, apart from the native-born. Such arguments have persisted, and have influenced both the purposes of writers and the judgments of critics.

The aspiration to produce a literature which would accurately reflect the character of Australia was, for some writers, realised in the last decade of the nineteenth century. So strong was the desire to identify national characteristics, and later, to endorse the identification, that only recently have the literary complexities of the period begun to be acknowledged. *The Bulletin*'s preference for sketches, succinct short stories and scenes from rural life was balanced, within its own pages, and certainly outside them, by a continuing awareness of literary developments in England, Europe and the United States. The aesthetic movement in England and the symbolist movement in France and Germany were represented alongside the 'Australian material'. The complexities may briefly be summarized by noting that one aspect of the reality of the nineties is embodied in the work of Lawson, and another in the poems of Christopher Brennan. While Lawson was recording the hardships of country life in stories such as 'The Drover's Wife' and 'The Bush Undertaker', Brennan was finding in the city of Sydney images of Baudelaire's vision of decadence, and aspiring towards a symbolic representation of a cosmic vision of a lost Eden, located in the heart of man. The melancholy realism of Lawson, and the yearning, frustrated romanticism of Brennan are contemporaneous, and an account of literary history which accords the one more significance than the other is over-simplified. At the same time, the literary historian is bound to acknowledge that it is Lawson's view and not Brennan's more private, learned vision which at the time and later was widely thought of as more truly representing authentic Australian experience.

The political and literary momentum of the nineties, which culminated in Federation in 1901, now seems to be enshrined in the work of Joseph Furphy, notably in *Such is Life*. The words Furphy used to describe his novel in his covering letter to Archibald, the editor of *The Bulletin*,—'Temper democratic, bias offensively Australian'—have themselves become part of the national literary legend, as has its title, derived from the supposed dying words of Ned Kelly. Yet, in spite of its egalitarian claims, this novel presents a world which is hierarchical, class-conscious, and populated by characters of many nationalities. It purports to be the work of an 'annalist' who despises the romances of Henry Kingsley, yet it depends (albeit surreptitiously) upon the tricks and convolutions of a romantic plot. It is one of the many works in Australian literature curiously ambiguous in its approach to being representatively Australian. It is as though the assertion of nationalism itself raises doubts about the possibility of making such a claim.

The complexities of *Such is Life* and its self-conscious parade of popular wisdom and literary and general knowledge do not, however, undermine its portrayal of the details of the life of settlers and itinerant workers in the 1880s in the Riverina district on the border of New South Wales and Victoria. In one sense it is related to the many documentary accounts of life in the colony; in another it is an ancestor of the many novels of social realism which succeed it (though none displays its literary sophistication). At the same time, it flouts the conventions of the nineteenth century novel of character, and in its digressions, comedy of intellectual life, and journey of the road owes a debt to English novels of the eighteenth century. It is self-consciously preoccupied with the problem of transforming life into fiction. To compare it with Henry Handel Richardson's *The Fortunes of Richard Mahony* (1917–29), which treats the years from 1852 to 1879, is to remark the difference between, in Furphy's case, a novel which, in form and manner, tries to meet the peculiar requirements of its material, and one which is shaped by a concept of the novel derived from nineteenth century European methods of naturalism and realism.

The story of *The Bulletin*'s influence on attitudes to Australian literature is inseparable from the critical stance of its 'Red Page' editor (from 1896) A. G. Stephens. His judgments were and continue to be influential. His encouragement of individual writers, particularly of John Shaw Neilson, and his battle on behalf of *Such is Life* are alone sufficient to earn him a lasting reputation. He has been described by the recent editor of a selection of his writings as 'Australia's most outstanding literary critic'.[8] But Stephens was not, in fact, a critic at all. He was an editor and reviewer. He never formulated a theory of literature or exercised his mind systematically on questions of critical principles. His most sustained comments are on Henry Lawson, but even these are fragmentary. His contribution to the definition of Australian literature is an exhortation to writers to resign themselves to the fact that they cannot escape the examples of the past. This means that while not being able to improve on what Horace told Lydia

> they can make it clear that Lydia's name is Mary Ann, and that she lives at Cow Flat. Thus poetry will be re-created for the generation of Mary Ann and the country of Cow Flat.[9]

Stephens' persistent flippancy, and his considerable prejudices, give rise to the suspicion that his views are superficial. He avoids judgments which might conflict with his general support for the local product. Stephens assumed, without seriously confronting the problem, the possibility of defining literary nationality.

The preoccupation with national identity is itself imitative. It is a common notion, pursued at certain stages of their history, by many countries. Even in a country with a long cultural tradition, it resists definition. In Australia, whose literary history is less than two hundred years old, any attempt to define national characteristics is bound to be more an expression of hopes and possibilities than an historical statement. When Vance Palmer in *The Legend of the Nineties* set out those qualities of Australian nationalism which seemed to him definitive he was, in fact, not so much describing the characteristics of the nineties, as selecting those aspects of the period which best exemplified his view of the real Australia. His literary career, as critic and writer, was an expression of his belief in certain values. Early in his career he wrote that 'it is in the country that the individuality of a people best asserts itself, therefore the bush for the present must be the mainspring of our national literature'.[10] At the centre of his thinking were ideas of character and ways of life which, at the time he was writing, were only part—and a diminishing one—of a much more complex whole. The values of rural life, small communities, and individual qualities of independence, fortitude and egalitarianism, are aspects of the Australian legend which have been particularly influential in the way literature presents Australia. The unreliability of literature as a representation of the realities of life, and its influence on the way countries come to regard themselves, is well illustrated by his work. The legend of the nineties is both a legend and a reality. It is a reality in that the work of Paterson, Lawson, and later Furphy is distinctive in its representation of place and people, and in its cultivation of the idiom of Australian speech. It is legendary in that, while representing a part of the reality, the part in turn has been represented as the whole, or at least as the essence of the whole.

Palmer's definition of the real Australian tradition is the most extensive statement of a position taken by many other commentators. Critics and literary historians have demonstrated again and again that their view of writers up to the time at which they are writing is conditioned more by their hopes for the future than by the facts of the past and present. A national literature it is implied, will be recognisable by its treatment of local subjects, themes and landscape. It will not be derivative, and the sign that it has grown to maturity will be its independence of foreign influences, and unself-conscious expression of its own sense of place and identity.

This general style of argument is common, and versions and fragments of it come to the surface even now. The Jindyworobak school of poets which was active in the 1930s worked from the assumption that writers must rid themselves of all influences from European culture. Their chief spokesman, Rex Ingamells, writing in 1938, expressed it thus:

> The Jindyworobaks ... are those individuals who are endeavouring to free Australian art from whatever alien influences trammel it, that is, to bring it into proper contact with its material.[11]

Nearly thirty years later Judith Wright claimed some progress along the path mapped out by Ingamells:

> We are beginning to write, no longer as transplanted Europeans, nor as rootless men who reject the past and put their hopes only in the

future, but as men with a present to be lived in and a past to nourish us.[12]

She has, nevertheless, expressed herself strongly on the subject of the nationalist and reformist writers of the turn of the century who

> ... by so drastically simplifying the issues for us, left us a dubious legacy that it seems we may take another century to outgrow.

> The proliferation of political demagogy and the cult of the unreal bush-hero nationalist hid the beginning of the twentieth century in a kind of mist of bad writing.[13]

Yet her comments on the novels of Martin Boyd reflect her preoccupation with the notion of what is authentically Australian. In considering the movement of his characters between Australia and England she concludes that 'this strain in our writing may seem to us now outdated'. Literary values are made to depend upon notions as to the proper subjects and attitudes for an Australian writer to take.

A further specific consequence of nationalist doctrines is ill-founded criticism of imitation, and indeed an imperfect notion of its function, and even of the way poets learn their craft. Judith Wright's view of the poets of the nineteenth century is coloured by the conviction expressed in her essay on Charles Harpur that it would have been impossible for him (and other writers) at this time to have had the kind of appreciation of the Australian land-scape that comes naturally to later generations. She acknowledges the inescapability of English models for the early poets, while regretting, especially in the case of Kendall, that the models were frequently Tennyson and Swinburne. Throughout her argument runs the assumption that the development of an Australian consciousness is what matters. Similarly, Rex Ingamells bluntly asserts that 'Kendall is practically valueless as an Australian poet'.[14] Yet the poets of the English Renaissance found models for their lyrics in the work of Italian poets. Spenser's consciousness of him-self as an English poet appealing to an English audience by reviving the legend of King Arthur is not diminished by his drawing on classical and foreign traditions of epic and romance in the context of *The Faerie Queene*. Why, then, should Australian poets be taken to task for learning their craft from Pope, Cowper, Thomson, Byron, Swinburne, Baudelaire and Verlaine?

One answer to this question is simply that the Australian poets of the nineteenth century were minor talents. Their achievement was limited by their capacities, both intellectual and artistic. There is really no reason to suppose that they would have written better in a different cultural environment. There is no reason why exile, or a sense of dislocation or of being alien should not produce good poetry; indeed one of the curious features of the colonial period is its failure to deal adequately with such subjects. Would Kendall, whom Ingamells accuses of 'writing about Australia in an English way', have been a better poet had he been born later or written elsewhere? Would Adam Lindsay Gordon have been a better poet had he remained in England? Hindsight cannot provide the answers to these questions, but reason would suggest that the failure of such poets to meet the test of highly developed poetic talent is more important than their failure to satisfy the requirements of nationalist critical theory. If Australian writers are thought by some critics to have suffered from inherited models, it might be because those critics have themselves imported ideas about literature, and too readily made assumptions about such important matters as the nature of originality. Victor Daley succinctly comments on this question in his poem 'Correggio Jones', a comic comment on the supposed 'tyranny of the Old World'.

One could suggest, however, that insisting upon the supposedly correct direction for Australian writers to take, insisting—as the Jindyworobaks did—that landscape and environment were essential ingredients of poetry, is so severely to limit a writer's range as to restrict interest in his work to all but a handful of patriots. The point was well made by E. A. Badham in 1895. Commenting on the notion that the English language should confine itself to the level of popular usage in Australia she wrote:

> We have to choose between the language of the Bible, of Shakespeare, and of Milton, and that of the comic penny-a-liners. By adopting the latter we should, no doubt, considerably hasten the birth of our National Literature, and when it came it would have the further advantage of being distinctly Australian for the Australians, for it is quite certain that no civilized nation would condescend to notice its existence.[15]

A prediction of a similar kind was made by Sid Long, the artist, in 1905. Amongst other possibilities for Australian painting he foresaw that with the shearer and the man on the land we could develop a fine realistic school of painters, also <u>pot boilers, to the great delight of that section of the public which always loves the obvious.</u>[16]

Frederick Sinnett, writing in 1856 had already made a similar point. His essay 'The Fiction Fields of Australia' remains one of the most intelligent commentaries on nineteenth century Australian prose, because it recognises that lack of talent, not the circumstances of colonial life, explains the deficiencies of the writing of that period. Sinnett remarks that

> most of us have had more than enough of positive Australian dialogue but we have never read an Australian dialogue artistically reported.

He rightly points out that a verbatim report of the conversation of Brown, Jones, and Robinson, in the old world, would be just as uninteresting as a similar report of the squatter, and bullock driver, and digger. And he goes on to argue that

> genius can report it so as to be interesting ... The first genius that performs similar service in Australia will dissipate our incredulity, as to this matter, for ever.[17]

No doubt Sinnett would have recognised that in the matter of language particularly, the passage of time, as well as talent is required. It was not until the end of the century that writers (such as Lawson and Paterson) used local idiom with the ease of familiarity. A further stage is reached in the work of the contemporary poet Bruce Dawe, where one can recognise a formal poetic rhetoric constructed from the rhythms, sounds, expressions and intonations of the Australian vernacular. Contemporary Australian drama exploits local idiom to the full.

Early attempts to document the life of the new colony resulted in some curious amalgams of fact and fiction, of informative detail and melodramatic romance, and awkward combinations of poetic diction and local colour. These were succeeded, later in the nineteenth century, by a lively interest in developments in European and American literature, and by an attempt to establish as the Australian tradition sets of images which were predominantly rural, proletarian and vernacular. The desire for independence from other cultures—and particularly from the English tradition—might be seen as a reaction against the political dependence of Australia's formative years. That an understandable political attitude should flow over into cultural matters in general and literary ones in particular is a sign of the poverty of critical thinking, especially in the 1890s.

Much writing on literary history and criticism both then and now, has been pre-occupied with the growth to maturity. Implicitly or explicitly, critics and commentators have assumed that there is an analogy between the growth to maturity of an individual and of a literary tradition. The principal condition for the maturing process is time. There is an assumption that the mere process of growth guarantees maturity, whereas it is only too easy to see that the one is not a necessary consequence of the other. Because of the persistence of this theory of inevitable progress it is difficult to talk about observable stages in the history of Australian literature without seeming to subscribe to it. But to argue that there is a discernible difference between the characteristics of colonial literature, the realities and legends of the nineties, and the features of certain contemporary writers, is not to imply even a theory of development, let alone an achieved literary condition.

The literary activity of the turn of the century was not sustained. Perhaps it was in some respects the fulfilment of an early hope, rather than the herald of a long summer. However that may be, it is not until the late 1930s (in fiction) and the early 1940s (in poetry) that one finds concentrated activity comparable with that of the end of the nineteenth century. It is not (as the detailed accounts of the main literary forms show) that there was a cessation of activity in the first thirty years of the twentieth century; rather that the volume and quality of writing which marks a period as significant did not begin to accumulate until the decade before the Second World War. The revival begins in the late 1930s, with the first novels of Christina Stead and Patrick White. It continues into the 1940s and 1950s, with first volumes of poetry by R. D. FitzGerald, Judith Wright, James McAuley, Douglas Stewart, A. D. Hope and David Campbell, and takes a new direction with the flourishing of drama in the 1960s and 70s. In short, since the Second World War it has become increasingly difficult to generalize about the features of the literary landscape, such is the range and diversity of subjects and forms. Nevertheless, there are certain shared interests and preoccupations of particular importance.

When one reaches this period, one is struck by the persistence, in prose and verse, of a known or imagined past. Both prose writers and poets of the 1940s and later step into the modern period but they do not announce this by any obvious gestures towards literary experimentation. Australian fiction is not significantly indebted to the work of James Joyce; and poetry, at least until the sixties, was scarcely touched by the more extreme forms of modernism. Yet modern Australian writers convey a sense of present time, even while dwelling remarkably often on the past. In the nineteenth century, the past meant convicts, bush-rangers, and gold rushes. From the 1940s onwards the past is seen as both remoter and more pressing. There is interest in exploration and discovery, the origins of the country, and personal history.

In both poetry and prose there is an impulse to reinterpret the history of Australia. In 1960 Douglas Stewart was able to gather together a collection of 'Voyager Poems'. Leichhardt, Cook, Tasman, and de Quiros are the focus for sentiments about Australia. The excitement and dangers of exploration, the qualities of character it demands and elicits, and the mystery of the impulse towards heroic endeavour are central preoccupations. The many forms of these themes in Stewart's own works and Patrick White's *Voss*, demonstrate the persistent and deep interest in the positive aspects of Australian development—the virtues which are countervailing influences to the suffering, violence and brutality associated with the prison settlement. Contradictions are inherent in the very origins of Australian society. The spirit of adventure was opposed by the practice of oppression; aspirations for future prosperity met despair of surviving the present; excitement at the curious novelties of nature yielded to the monotony of a landscape which, to eyes accustomed to the northern hemisphere, had no seasons and little colour. Modern works based on themes of exploration and discovery re-create a past which might serve as grounds for belief in a future.

The poetic and fictional preoccupation with personal history is marked in the last thirty to forty years. Perhaps it, too, might be seen as a development from the many memoirs, diaries and accounts of experience that were written in the nineteenth century. The history of exploration and discovery situates Australia in time and place, and the many autobiographical works give substance to the shapes of the past. A study of the intellectual history of Australia would find much of its material in this area. Family life, economic circumstances, schooling, nourishment (or the lack of it) for developing artistic impulses, together establish for those born before the Second World War a fund of shared experience; so that the sense of a common life marks the prose of

Hal Porter and the autobiographical poems of James McAuley, different though their intentions and intellectual interests are. The diversification of personal histories that one would expect to result from the influx of migrants from many countries of the world has not yet become a marked feature of Australian writing.

Interest in discovery and exploration, both of the country's and the individual writer's history, might provide some substitute for the weight of accumulated experience which is found in the literary traditions of older countries. The desire to explain how one arrived where one is, to search the memory for clues to one's sense of identity and for the moulding and defining conditions which have produced it, seems to be as much a historian's as a writer's impulse. Yet Hal Porter's autobiographies and Martin Boyd's Australian novels, which draw so heavily on their personal and family history, are shaped much more by artistic than by factual considerations. The boundaries between autobiography, biography and fiction in works such as these are not at all easy to draw; and personal experiences and knowledge, even in Hal Porter's idiosyncratic style, can be recognised as having a significance both particular and general.

Writers who draw heavily on personal and family history in general define the qualities of Australian experience in a more significant way than do those who, like many of the so-called 'social realists', present their observations with the appearance of greater objectivity. There is one obvious reason for this. A writer who starts with social groups (such as those singled out by Katharine Susannah Prichard for special attention) or with a strong view to propound about the nature and shortcomings of society (as Xavier Herbert does), or with a desire to examine the machinery of politics and social life (as has Vance Palmer in his political novels) arrives at the quality of life and experience, if at all, indirectly. Other things, such as the relations between workers and bosses, or black and white, or rich and poor, become more important (especially for writers in pursuit of a social or political theory). The predominance of the mode of social realism in fiction (and in much modern Australian drama) is not at all easy to account for. Its causes may lie deep in history, in notions of equality, and in a sometimes naive faith in the virtues of the underdog. But its consequences are the sacrifice of artistry to mundane detail, of the exploration of character to assertions about stereotypes, of style to what Patrick White called 'dun-coloured' journalism or to lively but brittle colloquialisms.

It is largely because of the predominance of this mode of fiction, notably in the thirties, forties and fifties, that Australian poets of those decades offer more nourishment to the imagination. Their work varies in substance and quality, but much of it shows freshness of vision, liveliness of imagination and the stamp of individual minds confronting experience. The poets provide a richer and more comprehensive account of the world than, with rare exceptions, the novelists of the last forty years have been able to supply. By a curious trick of history the strengths and weaknesses of the nineteenth century seem to have been largely reversed in the twentieth. The colonial poets who struggled to produce the very few poems which have any permanent claim on our attention were succeeded one hundred years later by poets who are notable not for their experimental modernity, but for the confidence with which they adapt and handle a variety of traditional verse forms, and for the precision and concreteness of their language. That precision and concreteness is, however, not infrequently qualified by a tendency to moralistic generalization. The pedagogic and homiletic tone is common in Australian writing, and might suggest some insecurity in the writer as to the kind of audience being addressed.

Interpretation of the past is one dominant aspect of Australian literature since the Second World War; another is the mythologizing of aspects of Australian development. This process is evident even in the writing of history, notably in the work of Manning Clark, who sees Australian history in terms of the interaction and conflict between forces which, under the pressure of his style, take on cosmic dimensions. His *A History of Australia* has some of the elements of the historical novel, particularly in its emphasis upon the character and motivation of its leading figures, such as Macquarie and William Charles Wentworth. In his study of Henry Lawson, Clark creates a figure who is larger than life, a victim of his society, a man grappling with forces more powerful than himself.

In literature the tendency towards mythologizing is present in a number of writers, such as Judith Wright, Les Murray, Patrick White, and Randolph Stow, and also in painters such as Sidney Nolan and Arthur Boyd. In Judith Wright's poetry, (as in Eleanor Dark's *The Timeless Land*), the period before the arrival of white settlers is seen as an age of innocence, in which aboriginal man lived in harmony with himself and nature, governed by mystic rituals of kinship and primal unity. Even those colonists who, like her own ancestors, endured hardship and displayed courage and tenacity in their pioneering of the land, become ravagers of nature and torturers of the land and its people. That there is some historical truth in this account, does not invalidate the claim that a legend is here substituted for reality. The legend itself acquires, through repetition, the status of myth. Judith Wright's poetic practice has affinities with the manner of a poem such as Charles Harpur's 'Creek of the Four Graves', but there is a clear difference between Harpur's effort to dramatise and interpret a story of early days, and Judith Wright's reading of history as the interplay of large forces whose battleground is nature. A more recent manifestation of the mythologizing tendency may be seen in the poetry of Les Murray, who populates the countryside with events and figures in what seems an attempt to give it something of the flavour of the rich mythological landscape of Yeats's Ireland.

The work of Patrick White best exemplifies the transformation of the 'materials of common life' into the substance of myth. So much critical attention has been directed to the philosophical implications of his novels, that their representation (not always ironically) of Australian themes and attitudes has been understated. His major novels begin with *The Aunt's Story*, and together they examine all the main preoccupations of Australian life from the third decade of the nineteenth century to the present day. Theodora Goodman's journey in *The Aunt's Story* takes her from the childhood images of an Australian country house and its dry surroundings, through Europe to America—an allegory, perhaps, of the experience of the Australian making contact with the challenging civilizations far beyond his rural origins. *The Tree of Man* takes up the theme of pioneering, and the struggle to sustain life in the face of natural disasters. Its chief protagonists create order out of chaos; their story is the myth of creation re-enacted in the hinterland of Sydney, a rural area which, within the novel's time, begins to be eroded by suburbia. *Voss* revives the theme of exploration. Its dependence on the actual expeditions of Leichhardt is slight, and is explicitly minimized by the author. Whereas Marcus Clarke relied on convict records to provide the authenticating substance of *His Natural Life,* White eschews the historical facts in the interests of transforming *Voss* into a mental traveller, whose outlandish pride is humbled by the physical and mental hardships of exploration. The actual scenery takes on an allegorical meaning comparable to that of the changing scenes in *A Pilgrim's Progress*.

With *Riders in the Chariot* White begins his exploration of Australian suburban and city life and of the various ingredients in the Australian population—the Jewish refugee from the gas ovens of Germany, the aboriginal artist, the working-class English migrant and the Australian-born inheritor of a decaying colonial folly. Here White also presents an image of monotonous middle-class suburban life, a comfortable, stereotyped man-made desert. His exploration of urban and suburban life continues in *The Solid Mandala*, *The Vivisector* and *The Eye of the Storm*. In *A Fringe of Leaves,* like so many of his contemporaries and predecessors, White goes to an historical event for his story—one which gives him access to the themes of aboriginal and convict life. It is as though, in returning to the nineteenth century, he has wanted to recapture echoes of the country's origins in the English gentleman in exile in Van Diemen's Land, the primitive squalor of aboriginal life and the brutalities of the convict system. In important ways White's work extends the legendary tendencies of the nationalists of the turn of the century. His countryside is a place where reality must be faced, and truth might be found. There is much in common between this picture and what has been called 'the old radical-nationalist discontent with the bourgeois character of Australian society'.[18]

To draw attention to White's connections with some aspects of Australian literary and social history is, however, to omit an aspect of his work which has as yet received little attention. In all his work there is a strong flavour of the foreign. His novels do not move as clearly or restlessly as Martin Boyd's do, between Australia, England and Europe. His characters' journeys away from Australia (except in *The Aunt's Story*) form a smaller part of the whole. But through them and through a wide range of reference to history and literature, White establishes a quality of consciousness in his narrative quite different from that of, say, Furphy, for all the latter's breadth of reference to encyclopaedic knowledge and European literature.

Like White's, Martin Boyd's major Australian novels—*Lucinda Brayford* and the Langton tetralogy—span a long period of Australian life, from the mid-nineteenth century to the end of the

Second World War. Social history, cultural differences and economic fluctuations are accurately observed. But the centre of his fiction is character—the definition of individuality. He shows a discriminating awareness of the influences that bear upon the individual consciousness, and balances the social and cultural values of Europe, England and Australia. He is interested in the interaction of the pagan classical world and the western Christian one; of Anglo-Saxon and Mediterranean attitudes; and of all these with the aspirations of Australians. He offers much implicit social and cultural criticism of both the old world and the new. Like White he examines both the clash between and the merging of European and Australian consciousness, and the seepage of ideas from the past into the present. His talent is enriched by those very influences which enthusiastic nationalists would wish to exclude. His work, however, has been slow to gain critical recognition, in part because he represents a way of life—that of the minor colonial aristocracy—not congenial to notions of egalitarianism.

An examination of the leading figures of Australian writing in relation to their sense of the European tradition would yield valuable information about the nature and quality of Australian experience in modern times. In poetry it would show, for example, that A. D. Hope's imagination was shaped largely by classical and European literature, though his actual experience of Europe (unlike White's) came relatively late in his life. James McAuley absorbed into his close reflection on Australian experience a broad intellectual background in European literature and philosophy. David Campbell married his extensive knowledge of European poetry and poetic forms to his personal experience and observations of Australian country life and family history. At the same time he renewed traditional Australian verse forms and local legends. Any definition of Australian cultural identity and its reflection in literature which does not take account of the enrichment of Australian experience from a variety of sources (including, more recently, Asia) is bound to be inadequate. Indeed, looking back at the history of Australian cultural change since the beginning of settlement, future historians might well see the attempt to establish and perpetuate 'the legend of the nineties' as a retreat from the facts of both pre- and post-Federation Australia. A withdrawal into images of the past, and the espousing of values which, while genuine, were already being challenged, was and is a form of cultural isolationism and protectionism.

So far as literature is concerned, an insistence on the importance of 'Australianness', even if defined as loosely as it was by Stephens, or maturity as envisaged by Judith Wright, at best introduces extra-literary considerations into criticism, at worst proposes a severely limited view of the possibilities of Australian literature. While there is, as has been shown, a considerable body of writing on the need for a national literature, on proposed definitions of its nature, and on why it has or has not come into existence, there is surprisingly little work of an extensive and thorough critical kind either on individual authors, or on literary forms. Since the establishment of literary journals from the 1940s onwards, much detailed expository and analytical work has been done. Yet the relationship between critical and creative writing has been uneasy. Writers have frequently felt that critics lacked understanding and insight. Critics have been over-protective, but not necessarily generous in their attitudes. Protectionism can be prescriptive by laying down conditions in which literary values are less important than social attitudes.

We have therefore come to feel, in writing this history, that what is now needed is a serious critical survey which attempts to place in perspective the successes and failures of Australian writers up to the present. It is inevitable that in attempting such a review in limited space, we should have made debatable decisions as to omissions and inclusions, and that critical opinions formulated in different times and circumstances should now invite challenge. We have tried to take a clear view of the very large body of literature before us, and to expose the critical assumptions upon which our judgments rest. Perhaps we have some slight advantage over our predecessors in the field, in that we have so varied an achievement before us, in all the major literary forms. Even the historical and critical arguments we have tried to refute or replace have enabled us to see that this work itself is subject to the same limitations as they were, and that it too, as part of Australia's cultural history, will in turn come under review in the future.

FICTION

ADRIAN MITCHELL

PART ONE: 1788–1880S

The history of Australian prose begins with the writers of memoirs. In the circumstances, all the first writing is in some fashion a report, providing not just an account of events and discoveries in the new colonies, but also tacitly presenting the self as accountable. Personal experience is hidden by the careful neutrality of the formal report, and that writing has very little direct bearing upon the foundation of an Australian prose tradition. Much more was contributed by those public and private accounts which reveal that the writer has taken up an attitude to the experiences of the new settlement.

Although the despatches of Governor Phillip were promptly collected and published in England, these were intended in the first instance as official reports, and that function determines to a degree both the style and the matters reported. Similarly, the Rev. Richard Johnson's *Address to the Inhabitants of the Colonies established in New South Wales and Norfolk Island* (1794) is dictated more than anything else by his sense of the moral authority of his office. The stance displayed in these official and quasi-official publications persists through much of the non-fictional prose of the colonial period, a prose of public occasion rather than civil discourse, heavily imbued with a sense of its duty to inform, if not instruct. In books of essays, addresses and lectures (such as Woolls's *Miscellanies in Prose and Verse*, 1838), in the early histories and annals, and even in the more vigorous literature of political and social contention and reform (Lang, Ullathorne, Mrs. Chisholm) the prose displays a marked tendency to the rhetoric of moral suasion. Since so many writers of the early and middle colonial period were churchmen, it is not surprising to discover in them some evidence of homiletic mannerisms.

The memoirists set in train an alternative possibility for prose. Several of the officers of the First Fleet had arranged to publish their early experiences and impressions, and sent back to England

27

detailed accounts of the voyage and the new settlement, to a public eager for information and exotic novelty. Clearly, the widespread acquaintance with Cook's voyages had prepared this anticipatory excitement, and no doubt fostered the interest in the natural history rather than in the social experiment of the new colony. Once published, the personal journals ran through several English editions in quick succession, and were promptly translated into French, German, Dutch, and even Swedish. Yet these, though widely received, were not in any sense popular publications; John White's *Journal of a Voyage to New South Wales* (1790), for example, was a very handsome production, with many careful illustrations of birds, animals and plants. Remarkably, these early journals are not overcome by the sense of historical occasion, nor do they appear to be much affected by the circumstances of writing to an audience. They are not exactly informal, but they manage to project a strong sense of personal perspective. They remain attractively individual; that is, they retain the essential virtues of the journal form, the candour of an immediate response to experience. Unlike the cautious detachment of the official style, they reflect the personality of the author. The writing is charming for its enthusiasm and its prejudice, admirable for such detail as it manages to master, and touching for the disappointment it expresses.

Where the history, the statistical survey, or the annals, or such other accounts of the estate and the stewardship to which it was entrusted (such as Wentworth, Field and Lang were subsequently to provide) seek a large, balanced public scale, the journal offers a limited perspective. It does not offer to see steadily, nor whole, nor can it distinguish with much precision between degrees of importance in the details it records. It sees in fragments, and offers sketches of what at the time has seemed eventful. It is, therefore, a suitable form for these first impressions of a settlement that was in its own terms fragmentary, incomplete. And the early fiction takes over some of the features of the journal—they can be discovered in Alexander Harris' *Settlers and Convicts*, for example, and Charles Rowcroft's *Tales of the Colonies*. Similarly, the earliest colonial art has a comparable function, in offering vignettes rather than vistas.

It is a feature of these early memoirs and personal records that, although the voyage out to Botany Bay must have loomed large in their experience, the writers play down the human and practical problems of that long and harrowing journey. Surgeon White laconically notices the various ailments of his charges, and the occasional death of a convict. His journal is livelier when he parades his personal triumphs, as when at the outset he over-ruled and dismissed an incompetent colleague. The interest of his account lies in what he inadvertently reveals about himself, rather than in what he perceives. Captain Watkin Tench, in *A Narrative of the Expedition to Botany Bay* (1789), shows a broader understanding of the venture as a whole, but like White, Hunter and Collins he, too, is oppressed by the tedium of months at sea, and writes much more fully of the ports of call. Tench is not indifferent to what later commentators would extravagantly refer to as the human cargo, and indeed he is the most sympathetic of these early memoirists. Yet he impatiently summarizes the voyage as an unpleasant but necessary service, and his comment is as much an apology for the narrative to that point as it is an expression of his distaste for the job.

Like all the members of the new administration, Tench is inclined by temperament as well as persuaded by rank to separate himself from the activities he describes in his *Narrative* and its sequel, *A Complete Account of the Settlement at Port Jackson* (1793). The role of observer comes naturally to him, and encourages sympathetic and sometimes compassionate reflections on the manners of the convicts, the sailors, the soldiery and the natives. White, on the other hand, taking up the stance of natural historian or scientific observer, impresses us as unpleasantly aloof; his distance is not objectivity but, perhaps, vanity. Collins, whose *Account of the English Colony in New South Wales* (2 vols., 1798–1802) rivals Tench's for historical interest, is much more elaborate and detailed, but in him the individual perception becomes smothered.

Tench is the most literary of these early writers, and his journals are deftly interwoven with references to the classics and graceful rather than learned allusion to English literature. He is a calm, intelligent writer, always alert to the possibilities of narrative effect, and unobtrusively re-arranging the events and details of his entries without distorting the truth of the record. He is at his ease because he is completely enclosed in his cultural tradition. For a man so sensitive to so many new experiences, he may seem remarkably unimpressed by the thought of a new cultural tradition about to be founded. But for him there is no separation from the parent culture. He displays the eighteenth-century conviction that the cultivated mind is at home anywhere; he is a citizen of the world.

One effect of Tench's cast of mind, though a reflection, too, of the actual sequence of events, is that in his account the colony curiously lacks a sense of beginning. When the First Fleet arrived at its destination, that was found to be not yet its destination; and even when the fleet had removed from Botany Bay to Port Jackson there is a strangely subdued sense of arrival. While the memoirists without exception are full of praise for the Harbour itself, there is strangely no sense of the portentousness of the occasion. Additionally, the novelty of remoteness had been immediately disrupted by the appearance of La Perouse's ships just after the First Fleet had regrouped in Botany Bay. Isolation would soon enough become overwhelming, but that first freak of circumstance asserted the sense of continuity with European affairs.

Again and again in these early accounts we find that experience not only qualifies, but almost disqualifies expectation. In particular, the judgment of the great Navigator, Cook, is called into question. The extensive meadows he had reported in Botany Bay, 'some of the finest meadows in the world', turn out to be 'a rotten spungy bog'. Governor Phillip found the location unsuitable for settlement, the soil poor, fresh water scarce; and Port Jackson, though providing superior shelter for shipping, was otherwise not much better. The frustrations of creating some foundation of order, the inadequacy of provisions, and the continuing disappointment with the land—the trees were unfit to use as timber, the landscape was monotonous, and the land infertile—all these led to one inevitable response. Tench is a little more tactful than the others:

> In Port Jackson all is quiet and stupid as could be wished. We generally hear the lie of the day as soon as the beating of the Reveille announces the return of it; find it contradicted by breakfast time; and pursue a second through all its vanities, until night, welcome as to a lover, gives us to sleep and dream ourselves transported to happier climes.[1]

In 1793, after he had completed his tour of duty and returned to London, he reflected a more general scepticism:

> If by any sudden revolution of the laws of nature; or by any fortunate discovery of those on the spot, it has really become that fertile and prosperous land, which some represent it to be . . .[2]

It is a more discreet version of Major Ross's notorious and much testier remark, that 'in the whole world there is not a worse place than what we have yet seen of this', but the same disappointment underlies it.

The Memoirs of James Hardy Vaux (1819) initiates the transition from factual memoirs to fiction. As with Savery, Rowcroft and Harris after him, the rudiments of Vaux's narrative are factual. While there is no imaginative leap clear of the autobiographical details, Vaux's cast of mind is discernibly recreative. The convict writers, Vaux, Savery and Tucker, all set the engaging spectacle of special pleading, although Savery's pose of offended innocence and outraged dignity is eventually distasteful. Vaux is intriguing for his reconstruction of events to show that, whatever crimes he had committed, he has been badly done by on the two occasions which resulted in his sentence of transportation to New South Wales, and further that he has been badly deceived by the authorities from time to time. Yet we have a complete enough account of the particulars to discern the possibility of another reading of his case.

Vaux's memoirs are sometimes seen as in the tradition of the picaresque. Indeed, the original preface by Barron Field alludes to Alemán's *Guzmán de Alfarache,* and Vaux himself refers to Smollett. But the *Memoirs* has neither the energy, nor the rapid sequence of the picaresque novel, nor does it observe the superficies of the world, the contorted manners of men or their distorted morality. James Hardy Vaux is intent on observing himself; this is, in not quite the best sense, a self-seeking book. In it, Vaux records the misfortune which has brought him to his present condition, and parades his superior sensibility. He is contemptuous of the underworld bullies, the London mob, the brutal guards and the depraved convicts in the hulks. He is not of the common cut, and keeps himself separate from his fellow men. The one man with whom he has a sustained professional partnership is increasingly held at a distance. Vaux is not, on his showing, distrustful, but he is so enclosed in his 'adventures' that he has virtually no awareness of others. His interest always turns upon himself—his cleverness, his elegance, his literary sensibility, his style.

The exoneration Vaux hoped for rests on the case that he had not hurt any individual. The theft of property, the various frauds and cheats he had practised were not directed specifically at any victim. By reverse logic, his case is strengthened, it seems, by the many hurts he has endured. Much of this is written with the customary facetiousness of the day, but Vaux has little sense of irony or comedy. Indeed, his taste appears to have been formed by the more ostentatious features of the theatre to which he was so much addicted (as, among other things, a venue where a likely number of pockets may be picked). His *Memoirs* circulated freely enough to create a certain notoriety for him in London, not such as to rival the famous Barrington, but certainly enough to draw comments from the press at the time of his later trial.

His 'Vocabulary of the Flash Language' forms an appendix to the *Memoirs*. Some twenty five years earlier Watkin Tench had wished in a magistrate's court for a means of translating from the idiom of the felonry to plain English. Evidently there was a particular need for such a vocabulary as Vaux supplies; but such glossaries had recurred from time to time in English literature— they can be found incipiently in Greene and Harman, and more fully in Head's *The English Rogue,* for example. Vaux's listing was presumably functional, a practical contribution to the colony; but he uses the flash language on only two or three occasions in his *Memoirs,* when he ensures that the reader understands what is meant. The dictionary has very little direct relevance to his own narrative, and in fact suggests a subterranean colourfulness which he has been careful to suppress. Indeed, Vaux is such an enigmatic figure that it is not impossible he calculated the titillation of this hint into the mysteries of the underworld.

Vaux makes no attempt to describe the new settlement, and he seems to have been remarkably unimpressed by the landscape. He offers only accidental glimpses of small details of early colonial life; as with the early journals, he does not attempt to describe the long sea voyage (though he takes a more sustained interest in his return to England on the *Buffalo*, which was leaking dangerously). His interviews with the Governors and with other famous figures such as Rev. Samuel Marsden do not enlighten us much as to the nature of these men. He has some interest in man in his role in the social system, as judge, banker, bailiff or fence, but is not generally much concerned for the world or human nature, except to take advantage of it. It is Vaux's sustaining vanity that he understands the fine points of the law as well as anyone else, and the whole narrative is in fact a piece of casuistry, in which the acknowledged culpability of the individual is of less occasion than the triumph of tripping up the law by weaknesses in its own procedures.

Self-justification is also the major factor in *Quintus Servinton, a Tale founded Upon Incidents of Real Occurrence* (1830–31), but Henry Savery is more intent than Vaux on proving his credentials as an author. He wishes to display both his learning and his sensibility, as a means of proving his distinction from 'the common herd' of the convicts. *Quintus Servinton* is a long, flaccid novel, distinguished only as the first novel published in Australia. It suits Savery's purpose to be unexceptionable, to demonstrate a steady adherence to the proprieties and to retail the morally estimable. *The Hermit in Van Diemen's Land* (1829) is a much livelier work, collecting a series of thirty sketches published in the Hobart *Colonial Times*, and for which Savery adopted the pen-name Simon Stukeley. In these, Savery examines in detail the relatively close-knit society of Hobart, a very different community in a very different setting from that of Sydney. Like Vaux, he is compulsively fascinated by the procedures of the law, especially where the law offends the individual's innate sense of justice. His social criticism is a more subtle libel on particular individuals, barely disguised, than the much clumsier verse satires of Sydney at this period, but like them the references and the criticism tend to be ephemeral because they are too personal. The early colonial experiences were not all of a piece, and although the professed intention of subsequent writing was to elaborate the homogeneity of Australian experience, the separate foundation and development of each of the colonies accounts for persistent if subtle distinctions and the claim of special loyalties.

Quintus Servinton is a more scrupulously written book, and a more ambitious one. It is a barely concealed autobiography in which Savery may be seen to defend his character, though admitting his culpability in the strict legal sense. If it is a novel, Savery writes in his preface, then it is not fiction: it is a biography, true in its general features. It takes the memoir's account of actuality close to the realm of fiction, for it has patently derived many of its features from the standard expectations of English fiction. A three-decker novel, its first two parts concentrate on Quintus Servinton's career in England, from his schooldays to his marriage and his success in business. Savery has been careful to portray the uniform steadiness of Quintus's character; it is, he insists, beyond suspicion and beyond reproach. But he protests too much. Servinton becomes interesting because the claims Savery makes for him do not quite add up. For example, Quintus is a thoroughly conscientious and dutiful student, and becomes Captain of the school, yet on one important occasion displays an adroitness in interpreting orders to suit his own interests. Savery later acknowledges that there is a fine line between cunning and clever management, but he is so determined to cast Quintus as a gentleman that he resists analysing the moral distinction. In his own mind at least Quintus manages to bridge the gap between commoner and gentleman, and once there, is determined to maintain the social privileges of a gentleman.

This proves difficult when, in the third volume, he is transported to New South Wales. Savery is careful not to specify which settlement Quintus has been transported to. Indeed, Savery gives virtually no details at all of the location of this part of his novel— no particulars of landscape or convict life. Instead *Quintus Servinton* directs its attention to an incipient theme of Australian fiction— the working of authority. In particular, Savery (like Vaux) attempts to determine what levers must be applied where to make the institution attend to the individual case. The well-established pattern of the Newgate novel obviously has some pertinence to Australia's initial circumstances, yet the theme of authority persists: it may be traced in *Robbery Under Arms*, *Such is Life* and *Capricornia*, for example.

Quintus Servinton is offended by having to take his place in the common herd of convicts. He protests against the 'one, sweeping, comprehensive term, CONVICT', because that denies the distinction that, but for the one blemish, he feels he has won by the strict morality of his life. Although he draws the Goldsmithian moral, that through adversity one learns to be content with a little, this is not what the novel really conveys. Rather it shows the danger to an ambitious man of solitariness and misguided independence. One of the first lessons Quintus learned in the world was to keep his own counsel. He has something of the over-reacher in him, an ambition that extends beyond common prudence in what Savery proposes as an otherwise praiseworthy character. His final reform, the necessary self-discipline that had been missing, is accomplished by the rigours of the convict system. The modern reader remains sceptical, not that Quintus has been saved to become a better man, but that this is a vindication of the system.

The formal model of the memoir continues in Charles Rowcroft's *Tales of the Colonies; or, The Adventures of an Emigrant* (1843). This pretends to be the journal of a settler, but is really a disguised instruction manual. Rowcroft's narrator, William Thornley, recounts his experiences from the decision to emigrate from England to some twenty years later when, thoroughly established and respected as one of the Old Settlers, he can review his colonial life and offer it as a model of 'the individual process of emigration', and proof of the success certain to follow prudence, industry and perseverance. Unlike Quintus Servinton, who returned to Devon to live out his last years in retired contentment, Thornley completely adapts himself to life in the colonies, and remains to set down his memoirs. His case, Thornley concludes, is as much a history of Van Diemen's Land as the colony yet has; the growth of the colony is to be measured in terms of the settler's success. But since Rowcroft himself had only four years experience of the colony (though that did not prevent him describing himself as 'a late colonial magistrate') with *Tales of the Colonies* the memoirs have in fact become fiction.

Thornley is a resolutely independent man. He is determined to make his own way in life, and settles with his family in the remote interior, separating himself almost wholly from his fellows. If, as is sometimes said of the book, it sets the pattern for fiction of the next decades, especially as a fictionalized guide book for English readers to the strange and remarkable in Australian life, it should also be noted that it promotes the image of the individual rather than the collective achievement. Even when with the years a comforting sense of community slowly evolves in the colony, Thornley keeps a careful distance from most of his fellows. Temperamentally he is affable, yet he prefers to avoid town and has very little to do with Hobart, apart from one phase of a drawn out, tritely romantic adventure sequence. The values Rowcroft stresses are essentially an amalgam of pastoral retirement and domestic virtue. Thornley does not deny the usefulness of neighbours, but since Rowcroft's purpose is to encourage immigration he needs to make his case in terms of self-sufficiency.

Unlike the original memoirists, who displayed the unperturbed spirit of philosophical enquiry, Rowcroft's habit of mind is to expound. He incorporates information on such diverse topics as how to obtain a land grant and how to milk a wild cow, what the emigrant should bring with him, the expenses of settling, as well as reflections on the transportation system, flogging and the management of convicts (who are not to be called convicts, but 'Government men'), sheep-stealing, bush-ranging and the aborigines. He does not attempt to refine his perceptions, and there is no subtlety to his understanding of the colonial experience.

Nor is there any subtlety of tone. Thornley is either sententious or droll, in that peculiarly distasteful but persistent (distasteful because persistent) facetious manner of much early nineteenth century popular literature. His cheerfulness is of the 'huzzah times three' school, and his adventures have a Boys' Own Paper level of excitement. Rowcroft evidently wrote for immigrants of the lower classes. Thornley is originally a kind of corn-factor, though a chapter heading describes him as 'a sort of half-farmer'. He comes from something a little less than England's yeoman stock, but a little more than Harris's emigrant mechanic. He displays a stubborn vein of common sense, and his ambitions are modest. What he wants from his labours is comfort, security, happiness. The pioneering spirit in him stops there. He has no vain conceit about impressing himself on the future by founding a dynasty. He is not a patriarchal figure, but paterfamilias.

His enthusiasm for the colony (attacks by bushrangers, aborigines and eagles notwithstanding) is countered by Crab, a conventionally comic type who can find nothing to admire in the present. Crab walks into the novel a sour and disbelieving Robinson Crusoe figure, in his costume of skins, and is unable to speak any good of the colony because it is not like Shropshire. ('. . . Why do you come to a new country? Why can't you wait till it's an old one, and fit for Christians to live in?'³) He attaches himself to Thornley, and continues for the next twenty years to predict that this wretched country will kill him at last, and at the end he finds a gloomy satisfaction in proving he was right. Perversely the colony he complains of so persistently makes his fortune for him. He cannot allow himself to speak well of anything, yet his essentially affectionate nature is apparent through his sourness. Rowcroft delights in this figure, the secret sentimentalist; but Crab is useful to him too, for through Crab he can state some of the less pleasant features of colonial experience, and then laugh them away.

Rowcroft's literary manners lead him to the sensationalism of adventure and the recital of triumph over adversity, rather than to the human experience of these events. Thornley, who survives a procession of calamities of various kinds, virtually disappears from the midst of his accounts of these episodes, even when he is the central actor in them, for Rowcroft's imaginative interest is given over entirely to the activity itself. Similarly, his landscape descriptions remain general rather than exact, again in spite of Thornley's situation. Rowcroft's portrait of Australian life is certainly more detailed than anything in Vaux or Savery, yet his characters, both here and in *The Bushranger of Van Diemen's Land* (1846), do not manage to come into any degree of close contact with the bush. They seem to be visiting it rather than living in it.

In certain of the social issues of the time he is likewise disconcertingly remote. The Tasmanian solution to the Aboriginal problem is glanced at right at the end of *Tales of the Colonies*, with Crab recalling 'those sweeping expeditions, and what fun it was'. In fact Rowcroft cannot seriously consider that there is a problem. It was clear to him that had Rousseau known the Australian Aboriginal, he would certainly have been obliged to modify his opinions. The Aboriginals are proposed from time to time as a threat to the settlers, but with the one exception when Thornley in a shepherd's hut defends himself against an attack by an entire tribe, and when their behaviour could equally be that of Red Indians or Zulus or pirates, or even Tucker's bushrangers—the natives are usually shown in retreat, and in any case as both evasive and ultimately unknowable. Their aggression is attributed directly to their leader, Musquito, a Sydney Aboriginal who had been sent to Van Diemen's land to serve his sentence. Rowcroft's imaginary portrait of the historical figure is promising but eventually spoiled by his inability to avoid romantic stereotypes. Musquito, who begins to loom as an interestingly complex figure, is suddenly turned into a type of primitive brooding Napoleon and then abandoned as a mere savage after all.

The other major social problem, the convict system, is dealt with a little more carefully, for Rowcroft arranges a serious conversation between Thornley and a magistrate in which the system itself is defended, but also moderation in the treatment of the Government men is advised. This limited symposium is, however, all too patently imported into the work. For the rest, Rowcroft handles the convict material in two ways, just as he had the Aboriginal. One relates to the *Tales* as memoirs, the rare and all too brief details from what appears to be genuinely perceived, as when Thornley remarks that the convicts all seemed to have a peculiar look. The other presents the convict as a figure from romantic fiction, in this case a gipsy, convicted and escaped and turned bushranger, with a soon-to-be-orphaned daughter. In the figure of the convict and of the Aboriginal, as also with the treatment of landscape, Rowcroft retreats from the problem of coming to terms with his subject, retreats from realism and takes refuge in the conventional, the fanciful and the stereotype.

Incomplete as they are, Rowcroft's reflections on the convict system provide a welcome relief from the internal bias of Vaux and Savery and Tucker, and the more horrifying bias of such passionate public champions of the system as James Mudie (*The Felonry of New South Wales*, 1837). Perhaps Rowcroft had been encouraged in his temperate views by reformists like Ullathorne and Maconochie, yet in terms of the fictional memoirs, these considerations play no very large part. One of Rowcroft's real accomplishments in constructing his image of life in the colonies is to have kept the main issues in a likely perspective. His depiction of the settlement, if not quite impartial, at least attempts some kind of comprehensiveness. The convict system could not be ignored, yet Rowcroft is no immoralist for not being overwhelmed by it. It is his manner that irritates; in his handling of these issues, and in addressing the narrative to a particular class of possible emigrants, Rowcroft reveals himself as just too patronising, and the portrait of the successful and hearty settler rings a little false.

Alexander Harris's *Settlers and Convicts, or Recollections of Sixteen Years' Labour in the Australian Backwoods* (1847) also seeks to correct some of the misrepresentations that are abroad, but in doing so projects a different image of the social relations that had developed in the colonies. His announced intention is 'to convey an idea of facts as they occur in Australian everyday life',[4] and he presents a much more believable account of colonial experience than does Rowcroft. He is not so prone to obvious fabrications, but presents what we are persuaded to accept as actual experience, the memoirs of a working man, perhaps his own.

Harris's phrase 'an idea of facts' is possibly more revealing of his method than he intended, for like Savery's, this 'autobiography' is true in its general features, but they have been re-arranged. It has internal inconsistencies of detail; for example, the settler leaves his sons in charge of his property at the end, yet they cannot be eight years old, and he has only a matter-of-fact interest in his wife, indeed takes only a half a line to marry her, yet before their marriage he had written with some conviction of his love for her. Clearly his family has been invented, though the earlier affection for M ... may not have been, and that point of invention is in terms of human interest one of the weakest sections of the whole.

On the other hand, comparison of *Settlers and Convicts* with Harris's other 'autobiographical' works (*Testimony to the Truth; or, the Auto-biography of an Atheist* 1848, and 'Religio Christi', published in 1858 as a series of articles in the Philadelphia *Saturday Evening Post*) and with his novel, *The Emigrant Family* (1849, and issued again in 1852 as *Martin Beck*), shows considerable re-arrangement of source material which, far from disqualifying, by the revealed com-promise with facts, what he has written serves only to increase admiration for his skill as a writer. In particular, the first half of *Settlers and Convicts*, in which Harris presents a very credible study of timber-cutting in the huge cedar forests, appears to have been a much less substantial part of his own colonial experience, while his actual experiences as a magistrate's clerk are suppressed altogether. Like so many of the early prose writers, Harris has taken over the form of the memoirs, and building on the circumstances of his own experience, re-constituted the details so as to forge the auto-biography of an invented figure, while preserving an idea of the facts.

The alignment is identified in his choice of pen-name. *Settlers and Convicts* was published as by 'An Emigrant Mechanic', and one of its early chapters is a revised version of an article published in *The People's Journal* by 'A Working Hand'. The book is un-ashamedly working class in its orientation, adopting the labourer's perspective on colonial life and approving the values (though deploring the improvidence) of the Australian working popula-tion. Curiously, it combines its incipient democratic temper with a recognition of social stratification, both accepting it and criticising it—again, to a degree, foreshadowing Furphy. Although the narrator of these memoirs eventually owns a property, and prospers, in his career as a settler he is seen most commonly either with his men, or eluding the authorities, or in conflict with wealthier and greedier squatters, and effectively maintains his identification with the labouring man. In his summary reflections Harris continues to concentrate on the conditions of labour rather than the privileges and interest of the landowner, arguing (for example) that in the existing colonial context free and bond labour stood on about level terms. In relation to their employer the settler, they are equally disadvantaged and exploited.

Between bond and free, relations were cautious:

I suppose there is no class of tradesmen or indeed of any men who entertain such a brotherly feeling toward one another as sawyers, yet so strong was the spirit of caste at this period among these that they could not forget that I was a free emigrant.[5]

On some such grounds as this, but also because of the nature of the sawyer's work, the Emigrant Mechanic tends to separate himself from the other men. He had led a more active social life in the Rocks when he first arrived in Sydney, and did not regret leaving it behind him. Yet life in the bush he acknowledges is unnatural and incomplete, because it is a masculine society. He does not elevate the notion of mateship. That is for him most often in the nature of a professional relationship, although as he explains, it can become the basis of a closer bond:

> There is a great deal of this mutual regard and trust engendered by two men working thus together in the otherwise solitary bush; habits of mutual helpfulness arise, and these elicit gratitude, and that leads on to regard. Men under these circumstances often stand by one another through thick and thin; in fact it is a universal feeling that a man ought to be able to trust his own mate in anything.[6]

Yet the relation between the two mates is taken for granted rather than explored, and R . . . , a model of the young Australian, fails to emerge as a character. He makes remarkable exertions for the Mechanic, but as is so often the case in Australian literature, though mateship presupposes mutual obligations and responsibilities the effort seems always to be one-sided. It is not that the Mechanic is selfish but that temperamentally he is independent. In the absence of close personal relationships, our interest lies in his individual perceptions of colonial experience, and not in the facts so much as the shaping ideas which realign those facts. Harris's triumph is in just this—in creating a cast of mind, or shaping consciousness, which suggests a particular kind of man, and provides a steady vantage point from which to make his appraisal of colonial affairs. It is consistent with the kind of man we read of here that he should take a sympathetic but tough-minded and pragmatic view of the Aboriginal problem. And the working man's shudder of outrage at the practice of flogging ('that legalized abomination') is much more telling than the relatively theoretical disapproval of, say, Rowcroft.

The Mechanic has a professional eye on the bush, but he is also responsive to the landscape's grandeur. Harris offers quite a few descriptive set pieces, which seem to repeat the familiar terms (forsaken, ages old, solemn fastnesses), but in these and in his passing observations the naming of separate features combines to release a particular impression; facts again are co-ordinated by a sponsoring idea. Looking up a sheer mountain face from a gorge, he notes, 'I felt my own insignificance in a way I cannot describe; the physical comparison was perfectly extinguishing'; while in another view, of a traveller a mile away, 'the sense of his *conspicuous littleness* is irresistible; and this the next act of reflection can scarcely fail to transfer to yourself'. More consciously than the early memoirists, Harris is aware of the impact of what is perceived upon the perceiver. His procedure is both reflective and reflexive.

Equally, he has an eye, and an ear, for the utterly convincing detail. And Harris carefully places his colloquialisms so as to confirm the authenticity of his account. The special terms of the sawyers and the common idiom of the bush drop with apparently unstudied precision into the narrative—when men are determined to 'get their whack', we have an exact notion of the kind of men they are. And the narrator avoids the literary flourish of Vaux but is capable of some nice turns of thought and phrase, as in the Lawsonian 'unfathomable obscurities of a publican's conscience'. Even towards the end, when the imaginative weave becomes threadbare and the memoirs move patently into a judicial summing up ('remarks at large'), the language is suited to the discursive mode. Harris's style does not call attention to itself, but it is cleverly managed. Informative and thoroughly readable, he is without doubt the most accomplished of the early prose writers.

Harris's novel, *The Emigrant Family, or the Story of an Australian Settler*, together with Rowcroft's *The Bushranger of Van Diemen's Land*, indicates the beginnings of the other dominant mode in Australian fiction, the romance. Both novels are unfortunate, for in each case local detail supplies an attempt at realism which is, however, defeated by the deadening clichés of romantic figures, events and sentiments. Rowcroft's novel is a mish-mash of sensation and local colour, and the only possible defence for him is that the Australian details may have had an exotic interest that in some fashion reconciled *The Tales* with the romance. Harris is again skilful in his presentation of factual detail, but does not manage the sustained integration of *Settlers and Convicts*. He is evidently uneasy with having to 'furnish the tale with sufficient of plot to interest the lovers of romance'. His novel becomes clumsy whenever he turns from the 'simple copy from actual daily life' to character and plot, for neither of which he shows enthusiasm or

41

flair, and which he had avoided in the earlier work. The confirming strengths of the memoir become the tedious weaknesses of his attempt at the romance.

James Tucker's *Ralph Rashleigh* is something of an anomaly in the history of Australian fiction. Written apparently in 1844–45, it was first printed in an abridged and re-written form as a volume of memoirs in 1929, and then published in full in 1952. Since then it has established itself as an impressive early novel, for it is both interesting for the particular light it sheds on convict life, and attractive in its own right.

It is highly entertaining, lively, and not least because it works by a muddle of styles. Tucker's delight in the manufacture of fictions is infectious, and for all the horror and brutality that he describes, the picaresque sequence of Ralph's experiences is most fully confirmed by that narrative zest. It is an uneven work, but its lack of discipline almost amounts to cheerful insubordination, especially for the first half of the novel.

It has a minimal sense of structure. Things happen to Ralph for the most part haphazardly; he is never master of his own fate. After Ralph's brief career in London as an occasional thief, the novel falls into three mains areas of activity: Ralph's experiences as a convict, his enforced participation in bushranging, and his extraordinary life as a member of a tribe of aborigines in northern Queensland. Tucker is not a mere primitive novelist however, for he shows some literary awareness. There are numerous pert literary allusions, the early sequences are in the manner of Fielding and Smollett, and the Newgate novel, while in the final section (which hints obliquely at the topical Eliza Fraser story) Tucker's rendition of the Aboriginals at times seems derived from an acquaintance with the fictional American Indian. 'The world is wide. Dwell where you think fit, but come no more near our hunting-grounds ... I have spoken. Do I say well, my brothers?' says a tribal elder; and Ralph's end comes when, in pursuit of a marauding party, he is ambushed by the sable plunderers: 'the native war-whoop sounded as the prelude to a volley of spears ...' In two highly entertaining chapters describing amateur theatricals by a group of convict players, Tucker changes his mode again, to the mock-bombastic. A sustained interplay of irony and facetiousness co-ordinates all these.

For all the narrative play, and display, the convict experiences are evidently real enough, though no-one else writes of the system quite like this. Tucker is unique. Vaux and Savery, for example, who are like Tucker in writing from within the system, protest their distinction from it, where Ralph accepts as it were the fact of being a convict. Other novels of the convict system, by Caroline Leakey (*The Broad Arrow*, 1859) and John Lang (*The Forger's Wife*, 1855) and later by Marcus Clarke and William Gosse Hay and others, all take an external view. As the subject became increasingly available for historical fiction with the passing of time, so it increasingly became the practice to elaborate the imagined responses of the convict close up to its brutal enormities and moral outrageousness. Tucker is much less sensational, and displays in Ralph a curious mixture of detachment and self-possession, an almost comic impersonality about what happens to him. The effect is only in part explained as a consequence of Tucker's modification of the usual picaresque mode, from first person memoir to third person narrative.

Ralph Rashleigh is two kinds of hero. While he is restrained within the System, he is an anti-hero, and when he is captured by the bush-rangers he is called by them 'a crawler', for he does not share their insane desire for revenge. He is distressed by their blood-lust and revolted by their viciousness, but he can do nothing to prevent them. He makes a sane unheroic appraisal of his circumstances, which leaves him helpless to intervene in the torture, the murder and the rape that take place in front of his eyes, even though it sickens his very soul. If he is no hero, he does not become brutalized; he survives.

The other Rashleigh is the heroic Rashleigh of the second half of the novel, Rashleigh the romantic hero. Once Ralph escapes from the Coal River settlement, he suddenly acquires tremendous strength, drives off hordes of Aboriginals in an amazing display of bravery, courage and physical prowess, and demonstrates a degree of bush-sense, cunning and endurance far beyond anything that could have been expected. We are not prepared for this Tarzan of the antipodes. And while Tucker's facetiousness remains, it is now directed away from Ralph.

The two parts do not reconcile, even when they are considered as a sequence of the convict's lament and the convict's dream. Tucker imitates two different and irreconcilable conventions, and these no doubt reflect his changing ideas about the novel. He begins well in the picaresque yet ends with the romance. In the second half Ralph begins to show evidence of sensibility; from time to time tears appear in his eyes, he develops an affectionate bond with his lubras, and mourns the death of his first aboriginal wife, and he demonstrates an excess of sympathy typical of the popular romance novels of the late eighteenth and early nineteenth century. And his eventual restoration to society, dramatised in a symbolic final apotheosis (he sheds his stained skin to reveal newly-formed cuticle 'more delicate and pure than ever he could recollect it to have been before') is confirmed by public recognition of his sensibility. 'I cannot believe that a person who is amenable to such generous impulses as have prompted Rashleigh can possess a corrupt heart!' But Tucker handles the sentimental mode awkwardly, and he fails to achieve the fluency that this seems to require. He is much more at his ease in the picaresque vein, when he does not need to attend to narrative evenness.

The increasing sensationalism of the events he describes is matched by a change in language. In the early section of the novel Tucker, like the other convict writers, is at pains to demonstrate his familiarity with the flash language. On most occasions this under-world and convict slang is italicized, and sometimes explained. Italics are also persistently used to point a heavy irony or sarcasm, occasionally a pun. In the bushranger chapters, the language changes appropriately. The distinctive feature of convict speech is its esoteric vocabulary (as detailed by James Hardy Vaux); the distinctive feature of the bushrangers' speech is the energetic oaths, the hair-raising, defiant swearing. Here Tucker is writing close to the edge of the barely acceptable. In the third major phase there is rather less dialogue, and that little tends to be an appropriation of an idiom becoming consolidated in fiction of the North American Indian—the novels of Fennimore Cooper were quickly very popular in New South Wales. The different phases in Ralph's life are reflected by different language interests, and Tucker must be given some credit for attempting that.

Although the writing is by turns stilted, arch, flat, and pre-posterous, there is energetic liveliness in his narrative, just as there is weakness and extravagance. Tucker derives his particular charm from the colourful mixture of styles; the book's historical interest, however, lies in the many fascinating insights it permits into convict life, and as evidence of the growing taste for the romance adventure.

Catherine Helen Spence's *Clara Morison: a Tale of South Australia During the Gold Fever* (1854) the first of seven she wrote (only four were published in her lifetime), was highly regarded but not much read. Frederick Sinnett in the earliest important survey of Australian fiction, 'The Fiction Fields of Australia' (1856), praised it as 'decidedly the best Australian novel that we have met with', yet the book had very limited circulation even in Adelaide, and virtually disappeared from sight. In part this is because she refused to write the kind of fiction that was appearing serially in the papers and fiction magazines. She was resolutely opposed to the romance, and in particular the romance of the bush, which was already shaping into a fictional formula. She later summarized this stereotype as a novel about

> the 'deadbeat'—the remittance man, the gaunt shepherd with his starving flocks and herds, the free selector on an arid patch, the drink shanty where the rouseabouts and shearers knock down their cheques, the race meeting...[7]

That was not the Australian reality, but a false impression too often foisted on the outside world, 'and on ourselves'.

In contrast, she determined to write 'a faithful transcript of life in the Colony', hardly an original thought but none the less serious. The effect of such realism in *Clara Morison* is that the colony has more life than the characters. Clara emigrates from Edinburgh to Adelaide but cannot find a position as a governess or lady's companion, and resolutely takes a situation as a servant. She soon discovers that the young people next door are her cousins, and all that is left then is the eventual happy outcome of her love for Mr. Charles Reginald. That rather thin story has to compete with the enfolding portrait of the manners of Adelaide, which are observed astutely and with a deft irony that is from time to time reminiscent of Jane Austen.

The location of the action is for the most part in Adelaide though the climax to Clara's personal affairs takes place in the country. Adelaide is not the whole colony; town and country require their own loyalties, and Spence preserves a careful distinction between the two. She is not at all interested in pastoral romance, and the only point in sending Clara into the country is to isolate her, a more indignant Pamela trapped in a country residence with a more boorish Mr. B., in this case a Mr. Beaufort.

Clara's isolation and vulnerability are stressed throughout the novel. Her circumstances are to an extent a replica of the town's: Adelaide is a separate community, holding itself aloof from and morally superior to the Victorians and the Swan River settlement, suddenly rendered vulnerable by the exodus of almost the entire male population to the goldfields, yet taking practical measures to meet these special circumstances. Although Adelaide is criticised for its provincialism, that criticism comes from a blighting Englishwoman, Miss Withering, contemptuous of all local attempts to imitate genteel manners. Gilbert and Margaret Elliot take a larger, more thoughtful view. Their loyalty is to the colony, and is expressed through carefully reasoned views on political and social reform.

The love story of Clara and Charles Reginald runs a mildly troubled course. It is a rather tame affair, and their mutual attraction is most nearly expressed when they discuss books with each other. This is not quite as artificial as it sounds, for it is Clara's character as much as Catherine Spence's to have an over-mastering passion for books, but it is also the means by which Clara and Reginald declare and understand their essential nature, the means by which each can assess and approve the other's taste. Through these discussions it is revealed that both understand that life consists in a struggle between affection and duty. There are no villains in this novel. Concepts of good and bad character belong to the kind of fiction Catherine Spence rejected. Rather, characters are identified by their opinions, and measured by their behaviour.

Clara Morison is weakest where it is most conventional. The plot is mechanical, and the action is unremarkable. Certainly the sub-title can be misleading. The goldrushes have no bearing at all on the main concerns of the novel, other than to distress the residents of Adelaide as suddenly it is drained of its manpower. The real subject of the novel is the fabric of colonial life, observed as people meet each other in each other's houses—the essential life of the community goes on indoors, not as is customarily proposed, in the great outdoors. In even, unexcited prose, with a quiet, intelligent awareness of the ironic distance between the values of the community and the ambitions of the individual, Spence maps out the character of Adelaide life in the period of the gold fever, 1851–1852.

Her novel works against the grain of what was emerging as the typical matter of Australian fiction but, more than that, it works against the expected patterns of fiction too. The usual main features, plot and character, are subordinate to opinions and what more conventionally is the background, the setting, here moves towards the foreground. That setting is not the visible features of Adelaide, but the cultural context, the very character of the community.

The chapter in which Clara starts work as a servant, begins:

> When young ladies in novels are set to any work to which they are unaccustomed, it is surprising how instantaneously they always get over all the difficulties before them. They row boats without feeling fatigued, they scale walls, they rein in restive horses, they can lift the most ponderous articles, though they are of the most delicate and fragile constitutions, and have never had such things to do in their lives.
>
> It was not so with Clara, however. She found the work dreadfully hard, and by no means fascinating . . .[8]

This is an objection much like Furphy's reaction against the romanticists, especially Kingsley. Catherine Helen Spence is not so caught up in the created world of her fiction that she cannot find an amused detachment from it. On the one hand, as in Furphy, her work of fiction separates itself from the conventions and customs of fiction, and on the other it reminds us that it is nevertheless a fiction itself. Catherine Spence has not written an anti-novel, but it is certainly very different from the prevailing fashion, and taste, and that perhaps accounts for its rather faint reception. The recent revival of interest in her work will no doubt lead to an increased understanding and finer awareness of just how accomplished it is.

Frederick Sinnett's high estimation of *Clara Morison* was published several years before Henry Kingsley's *Recollections of Geoffry Hamlyn* (1859); that judgment was superseded in 1869 when Marcus Clarke asserted that Kingsley's novel was 'the best Australian novel that has been, and probably will be written'.[9] *Geoffry Hamlyn* is almost the complete antithesis of *Clara Morison*. It is a large, sweeping novel, spreading itself at a leisurely pace across generations; it celebrates the masculine accomplishments, the daring and excitement of pioneering life, and admires the ownership of large estates. It elevates its central figures into heroic, almost mythic proportions. Even its politics are directly opposed to Catherine Spence's, for Kingsley distrusts the urge to self-government. Australia, for all its natural advantages, lacks the benefits of social influence; and to migrate from England is to give up

47

an old, well-ordered society, the ordinances of religion, the various give-and-take relations between rank and rank, which make up the sum of English life, for independence, godlessness, and rum![10]

When Rolf Boldrewood declared that *Geoffry Hamlyn* was an immortal work, 'the best Australian novel, and for long the only one',[11] he dismissed in a phrase the published and serial fiction of the preceding half-century. This had amounted to a handful of convict fictions and a sprinkling of emigrant handbooks disguised as novels; and, with the goldrushes in the fifties, an increasing number of elaborated notations of their personal experiences by writers who may be collectively described as literary tourists. Again the basic form is the memoir: the interest is not auto-biographical, but in the recollection of actual experiences as observed and appraised by the individual traveller, and as they happened to him. Most of this literature was designed for the English market, which had developed an interest in Our Colonies, Canadian, Indian, South African, New Zealand, as well as Australian. Some of these publications were by Americans (W. H. Thomes, for example), who compared experiences on the Californian and Australian goldfields, and published their books in the United States.

Geoffry Hamlyn became at once a very popular work, and an influential model for subsequent Australian fiction. Boldrewood's contention that it marks the beginning of the Australian novel is on those grounds defensible. Its success confirmed the romance as the dominant form in Australian fiction, a primacy that lasted until virtually the Second World War, and persisted beyond that— Xavier Herbert's *Poor Fellow My Country* (1975) is the most recent grand romance. But while Kingsley provided the basis for subsequent developments in Australian fiction, he also appropria-ted the other dominant mode, the memoir, and adapted it to the romance: these are Geoffry Hamlyn's recollections.

The practical advantage of using Hamlyn as narrator is that he provides Kingsley with a mask, so that incongruities of style or bluntness of perception can be seen as limitations in Hamlyn rather than in the author. Further, it allows Kingsley to move his narrative from the chronicle of the past, to the present in which Hamlyn calls attention to his difficulties as memoirist. The momentary transfer breaks the pace and changes the tone of the main narrative whenever it begins to grow tedious. This technique is handled quite successfully, and Boldrewood imitated it closely, and to advantage, in *Robbery Under Arms*. But when Kingsley repeated the technique in his subsequent novel of Australia, *The Hillyars and the Burtons* (1865), he forced it into a relentless alternation of first person and third person narrative (as in *Bleak House*, but without Dickens's genius). The Burton sequence is, interestingly, still largely cast in the form of memoirs, with Jim Burton in his old age recalling the past in much the same manner as Hamlyn.

In terms of the development of Australian fiction, the most important feature of Kingsley's novel is not the subject matter or the narrative technique, but the vastness of its scope. This is a pastoral romance on the large scale. The characters are heroic: the men are of enormous stature, or if not enormous then powerful. The women are beautiful, proud, graceful (Mrs. Buckley, we are told, even had 'an imperial sort of way of manoeuvring a frying-pan'). The actions are heroic too: fights with Aboriginals or bush-rangers become a type of military campaign, there are daring rescues, and when the Buckleys are moving their cattle to their new property, that is seen in patriarchal terms. The very landscape is heroic:

> A new heaven and a new earth! Tier beyond tier, height above height, the great wooded ranges go rolling away westward, till on the lofty skyline they are crowned with a gleam of everlasting snow. To the eastward they sink down, breaking into isolated forest-fringed peaks, and rock-crowned eminences, till with rapidly straightening lines they fade into the broad grey plains, beyond which the Southern Ocean is visible by the white sea-haze upon the sky.[12]

The landholdings are vast, the fortunes immense, yet life is relatively effortless. It is all a large slow dream, a dream of ancestral figures, larger than life; a dream in a pleasant summer haze. Kingsley's image of station-life is likewise idealized. The characteristic image is of sitting on the verandah, taking in the view, an image that seems closer to plantation life than to the station. (Indeed, the fact that his grandfather had owned a plantation in the West Indies, and that his books were in the family library, may be just as pertinent as the more commonly proposed view that Kingsley wrote at least part of *Geoffry Hamlyn* while staying at Langi-Willi.) One image only of the real world intrudes, a brief description of the rise of the commercial city, Melbourne; and that is 'Unromantic enough, but beyond all conception wonderful.' That kind of reality is specifically excluded from the novel.

Although there is plenty of action—a bushfire, kangaroo hunts, fights with hostile blacks and bushrangers, escaped convicts, storms, an earthquake, and more orthodox excitements such as branding the cattle—this merely provides an occasion for the display of physical prowess. None of it really tests moral character, because it is in the nature of romance that moral character is unvarying, simplified, and idealized. The good are always good, the brave never doubt, and the wicked are discovered to have a trace of decency in them. George Hawker is a criminal, but he is not damned utterly.

Kingsley's gift lay in re-creation rather than invention. He relied on the conventional for the basis of his characters, though it appears that the enigmatic Dr. Mulhaus was based on von Mueller, the famous botanist. It is not clear that this serves any particular purpose, since Mulhaus is peripheral to the novel's main concerns. There is rather more point to the factual basis of the political skirmishing in *The Hillyars and the Burtons*.

The characters are based in convention, the action merely adventitious, and the life-style idealized. The world of Baroona and Garoopna is separate from Australian society, an enclave of the English landed gentry with virtually no contact with the world outside. A currency lad, 'one of those long-legged, slab-sided, lean, sunburnt, cabbage-tree-hatted lads', makes a brief entrance into Hamlyn's memoirs but is treated with a shade of amused condescension. Indeed, Hamlyn at one point is bluntly critical of Australia in its social aspect, 'Australia, that working man's paradise', because he is frankly contemptuous of the working orders, with their drink, dirt and sloth. Kingsley's accomplishment is in creating, and popularizing, a particular image of the Australian landscape.

The kind of landscape he describes both expresses and demands an emotional response. It expresses a mood, or a feeling, or reflects a character's state of mind; and for the most part, given the genial gloss that Hamlyn's own personality throws over the entire narrative, it is a landscape of blessedness and delight, the golden landscape of pastoral romance. This sets Kingsley at odds with the other conviction about the Australian landscape, that it was in Clarke's phrase a land of weird melancholy, a primitive landscape filled with the strange scribblings of nature learning how to write. Kingsley displays a much more congenial image of Australia, despite the bushfires, the heat and the storms. His descriptions are built up from large general features (valleys, ridges, ranges, forests) but with a few precise or small details carefully placed (e.g. the names of birds or plants). The method is pictorial, and the end product is highly visual. These are appreciative sketches. Yet the effect is deceptive, for the scene is, in fact, not as precisely envisaged as it appears to be: the details are much more evocative than definitive. Kingsley indicates rather than describes a scene, a scene that the reader responds to, just as to a vista; but the sense of extensiveness is also carefully related to the coming action, and all the explicit details contribute to this. And although it is characteristic of Kingsley to take in his views from a height, as was the fashion in topographical painting of the period, that continued elevation contributes its part to the novel's total effect.

One of the curious consequences of choosing Hamlyn as his narrator and chronicler is that Kingsley compromises the achieved heightening of his narrative—or possibly he protects himself against undue inflation. For Hamlyn is the least heroic of the central characters. His own modest history is only tangential to the main story, but temperamentally he is suited to his self-chosen function as chronicler:

> in short, all through my life's dream, I have been a spectator and not an actor, and so in this story I shall keep myself as much as possible in the background, only appearing personally when I cannot help it.[13]

Yet the portrait of himself that Hamlyn allows to emerge through the long pages of his chronicle does not show him as retiring, for he is fond of conversation. He is a cheerful, decent man, approving the values and the sentiments and the ideals of the English landed gentry: but his early obsession with sport (hunting hares, or fishing, or wrestling in the village) and his predisposition to a slightly slangy idiom, the jollity of the sporting man, shows a touch of adolescence in him, and in his *Recollections*, which Kingsley himself does not seem to notice.

In *The Hillyars and the Burtons*, Kingsley writes quite a different, and less accomplished kind of novel. Not only is his handling of point of view obvious and mechanical, and his use of geographical and social divisions clumsy, but his reliance on coincidence and the fortuitous turn of events confesses a shallow story, and the characters are not clearly envisaged. The chief objection, however, is to the over-elaboration of initiating circumstances and subsequent motives and plot. As with the first (serial) version of

Marcus Clarke's *His Natural Life*, there is too much preliminary 'stage business'. Fully one half of the novel elaborates at length the bitter history of the Hillyars, and the reasons for the virtual dispossession of the elder son; as well as an accompanying mystery that involves the Burtons, a Chelsea blacksmith and his family who, with their domestic affections, honesty, industry and sturdy acceptance of their social position, are unmistakably Dickensian in inception.

The Hillyar side of the story, all melodrama and romance (a missing will, step-brothers, exile and revenge ...), reverses the idyllic image of the landed gentry in *Geoffry Hamlyn*, for with all its wealth and property the family is spiritually blighted; the elder son, George, is degenerate, while the beautiful younger son, Erne, is too epicene to be a likely agent of regeneration.

Jim and Joe Burton, in making such a success of their life in Australia, are in marked contrast to Sam Buckley who, having made his fortune, returns with it and Kingsley's approval, to England. The Burtons' future is in Australia. Kingsley may be reflecting changing attitudes to the reasons for immigration in this, for *Geoffry Hamlyn* is a novel of the golden age of the squatters, whereas *The Hillyars and the Burtons* displays an Australia after the goldrushes, an Australia whose interest is now politics and economics, government and investment. The pastoral world is remote from all this. Kingsley has been conscientious about incorporating the chief topics of political debate and public contention of the period, such as land rights and suffrage, and much of the Australian sequence is taken up with discussing the tactics and the goals of the opposing factions. The change of emphasis between the two novels is most aptly dramatized in the day the Burtons arrive in Palmerston (Melbourne). Although Jim is affected at once by the landscape ('more infinitely melancholy than anything we have seen in our strangest dreams'), this impression is quickly subordinated to the political interest. Joe and Jim attend the opening of the House of Assembly, and Jim reflects that the story of the life of eveyone here is 'to some extent mixed up with the course of colonial politics'.

But the transition is also signalled by the 'arrival' of the worthy tradesman. The Burtons in fact repeat and confirm the colonial success of another blacksmith, Dawson, a wealthy man and one of the leading political figures in the colony. The aristocrat withdraws from the colonial experience, and the leading figures in the colonies increasingly come from the common people. In Kingsley's scheme of things, the gentleman will of course return to his proper station in life, in England. Yet Kingsley is not just confirming a prejudice. Other writers were to make the same observation of colonial life, for example Boldrewood in *Robbery Under Arms* and Henry Handel Richardson in her period reconstruction, *The Fortunes of Richard Mahony*. Kingsley's novel is not to be accounted for in terms of its appropriation of historical fact, however discernible the factual basis may be, for that is only one of the strands in this strange and apparently unco-ordinated book. The key lies in the attempted link between the two stories. In his preface, Kingsley proposed as his theme 'the old question between love and duty'. But the expected link between Emma and Erne is not what really binds together the Hillyars and the Burtons. Erne Hillyar also has a very close relationship with Jim, a friend-ship which Jim acknowledges as love. And the value Jim sets on this love is surprising, to say the least. The love of a good woman is acknowledged, but it does not compare with the rarer and finer ideal of men's affection. Kingsley increasingly emphasized this kind of relationship in his fiction. It is present in a subdued form in the friendship of Geoffry Hamlyn and Jim Stockbridge, in their comfortable bachelor quarters, and is much more explicit in *The Boy in Grey* (1871). Yet he does not analyse the special relationship that may exist between men, and his treatment of it can become embarrassing for the cloying sentimentality that gradually adheres to it and because Kingsley is so disconcertingly oblivious to the real nature of the attraction. It remains at the level of boy-friendships and 'boy-dreams'.

In retaining the purity of the ideal, and preserving the relation-ship from passion and intensity, however, Kingsley foreshadows in his celebration of the ideal of male friendship, the code of mate-ship. That convention, so widely held to be one of the distinctive features of the Australian tradition, has to be understood in a much broader context of male loyalties in the nineteenth century. Not all the male relationships are as precious as that between Erne and Jim. A more recognizable version of the mateship pattern is provided in, for example, Tom Williams' care for Erne on the Omeo goldfields, in which we can see love and duty reconciled.

Kingsley's image of Australian life is controlled by his con-ception of fiction. *The Hillyars and the Burtons* is, like *Geoffry Hamlyn*, a romantic novel, and its romanticism is emphasized above all by the persistent dreaminess of everything attaching to Erne Hillyar, and by the cosy recollections of Jim Burton's narration. It is a novel with a strong sense of the past, not a nostalgic past but a past impressed with unhappiness. The novel's romanticism is sufficiently responsive to the harsher realities for the final dreams, by Erne Hillyar and Lesbia Burke, and perhaps James Oxton, to be of sadness and regret, a wish that things might have been otherwise. The kind of imaginative vision Kingsley offers here might be called a discoloured romanticism, a vision somewhere between the 'medieval romance' of Sir Walter Scott and the 'romance of reality' which Marcus Clarke identified in Dickens.

In both novels Kingsley added a special romantic frisson by letting a convict loose in genteel society. George Hawker, as the notorious Touan, alarms the Snowy district in *Geoffry Hamlyn*, while Sam Burton in *The Hillyars and the Burtons* is a much more insidious figure, a study of malice and deviousness. In neither case does Kingsley fully understand the nature of the character. By the 1870s, it was possible to take a much more fully considered view of the convict system; but for Kingsley the convict was ultimately an agent of his fiction, where for Marcus Clarke and later writers such as William Astley ('Price Warung'), there was a conscientious attempt to understand both the meaning of the system and the experience of the convict. The brutal horrors and prolonged suffering of the system were, of course, a temptation to sensationalism not easily resisted. But the impetus to investigate imaginatively and re-assess this aspect of the colonial past came not from an increasingly uncomfortable public conscience, but from the widespread interest in questions of crime and punishment emanating from Europe. Clarke, for example, was influenced by Charles Reade's *It is Never too Late to Mend* (1853), and Balzac's *Splendeurs et Misères des Courtisanes* (1839–47) has also been suggested as one of his models for the novel of convict life. Victor Hugo's *Les Misérables* (1862) had caused a sensation by treating its hero sympathetically and at great length ('The story of a criminal need not necessarily be repulsive—Victor Hugo has made it almost sublime',[14] wrote Clarke); and Alexandre Dumas is another for whom the prison concept held a special fascination. Dostoevsky's *Crime and Punishment* (1866) may have been slow in reaching Australia, but confirms the universality of interest in the theme at this time. Clarke did not rate Dickens' *Great Expectations*

(1860–61) as highly as some of the other novels, but he relished Dickens' low-life characters generally. G. P. R. James based *The Convict* (1847) on the life of the notorious Matthew Brady, the escaped convict who terrorized Tasmania for several years. All these novels appearing at more or less the same time indicate a larger than local interest in the possibilities of convictism for fiction.

When Clarke came to write his powerful novel of the convict system, *His Natural Life*, he had two sets of resources. More thoroughly than any other writer of convict novels, Clarke drew his material from the old convict records, and from diaries and letters and official reports. (He even listed these in an appendix to his novel.) His account of the system is verifiable, that appendix tells us; it is true. However sensational the scenes of prison life, they all actually happened. The other source material is in the various models available in all that recent European activity. There Clarke saw that the convict theme could be treated seriously, that it afforded a special opportunity for examining, in these intensified conditions, questions of good and evil, moral and social responsibility, the problem of accountability, and suffering. They likewise established a new romantic convention of the convict hero, the wronged man who maintains his human integrity in spite of the extreme brutal treatment he must endure. But chiefly from these literary models Clarke learned the moral and psychological interest of his subject.

His Natural Life was written for serial publication in 1870–72. In 1874 it was published as a novel, still with that title but with extensive modifications to the text. (The longer title, *For the Term of His Natural Life*, only appeared on posthumous editions, and it is still not known on whose authority the substitution was made. The change blurs the irony of the original.) Clarke quite properly removed a long, involved and implausible preliminary section that explained why Richard Devine was tried for murder and transported to Van Diemen's Land under the assumed name Rufus Dawes. In its place he substituted a new and briefer Prologue, not entirely satisfactory, but a considerable improvement. Clarke also changed the ending of the original story, by deleting everything after Dawes' escape from Norfolk Island—his life on the gold-fields under yet another name, and his eventual return to England and re-integration with his original life. There was to be no escape, no happy conclusion. His is a life sentence.

In terms of weighting, the effect of these revisions is to concentrate the novel wholly on the convict material. There is no relief from the multiplying horrors of the entire system, the chain-gangs, the floggings, the suicide pacts, the homosexual rape, the cannibalism, the cruelty of the gaolers, the carefully delineated distinctions between the different prisons. By deleting the patently invented material of the first and last sequences of the original version (although his Eureka Stockade sequences clearly owe something to Rafaello Carboni) Clarke avoids impairing the meticulously established authenticity of the convict experiences he describes. Evidently his genius lay in the imaginative trans-formation of the factual, for where he invents he drifts towards the fantastic, the artificial or the conventional. Either by journal-istic habit, or by conscious approximation to what he understood of the current movement to realism in France, he chose to build upon documented evidence.

Rufus Dawes, totally enclosed within the world of the convict system, becomes the focus for all the suffering, the brutal victimization of this unnatural life. And the intensification amounts to a rather sensational heightening of the horrors of the system, compounded by Clarke's highly visual and dramatic presentation of individual scenes. Not every one of the atrocities recounted in the book happens to Dawes, but they all affect him, for he is contained entirely within this special world, and every atrocity contributes towards the definition of it. Yet a further effect is generated by this very intensification: certain of the sequences take on a heightened significance, somewhat in the manner of Melville.

The underlying premise of the novel is that Rufus Dawes is innocent of the crime for which he is convicted. A simple treat-ment of the theme might have ventured to show that virtue would emerge unsullied at the end. But Clarke takes the position that man is a creature of circumstance, and although Dawes is from time to time permitted to re-assert his innate sense of good ('good Mr. Dawes'), every brief resurgence of spirit is crushed, and Dawes is progressively reduced until, well past the point of despair (the suicide takes at least enough interest in life to put an end to it), he lapses into an apathetic indifference to whether he lives or not. Maurice Frere, the tyrant of the system, derides all protestations of innocence: 'Innocent man, be hanged! They're all innocent, if you'd believe their own stories.' Yet so they are, effectively; at another level, no man however guiltless, could emerge untainted from the horrors and the depravities of the convict experience. The system makes short work of Kirkland, the Methodist minister's son; it takes longer to wear down Dawes, but it breaks him at last.

Richard Devine has accepted the sentence of transportation and life imprisonment in order to protect his mother's name. Yet the question of innocence and honourable action is not adequately answered, for Devine is protecting the name of a woman who has committed adultery. He is her illegitimate issue, and so can have no claim on his father's estate; but his disinheritance remains moral rather than legal, for his father dies before the will is altered. From the beginning, it cannot be said that Devine's position is un-ambiguous. Although he has performed no criminal action, he is for all that the product of circumstances, and those circumstances quickly begin to sort against him. Clarke does not analyse the implicit moral complexities in this opening gambit, however, but leaves them unresolved; all that is seen instead is an over-elaborate set of coincidences. Yet it is evident from these opening pages that more is at stake than a novel of protest against the inhumanity of the convict system. It is that, but it is also concerned to look at what is happening to an individual. In terms of the gradual unfolding of Australian literary history, Clarke takes the important step of look-ing at a man, rather than depicting an image of colonial experience, life in its general portraiture. He does not fail to attach his moral vision of the world to an individual. His deepest feelings are humanitarian before social.

The irony of circumstance continues to work against Devine, or Dawes as he now calls himself. At Macquarie Harbor, where he has been sent for instigating the attempted mutiny on the convict ship—in fact he had exposed the plan, and the grim irony of the convicts' revenge in naming him as the ring-leader reinforces the oppressive pattern of his fate—Dawes becomes a pariah among pariahs. Here he loses any residual affiliation with his past. Although he had declared his old identity dead on board the convict ship, the reasons for his action in informing the authorities of the mutiny, and his private views of the other convicts, show that he still preserved much of his former self. At Macquarie Harbor, the transformation takes place, and Dawes becomes embittered, solitary, hostile, hardened in his attitudes, indistinguishable from the other convicts. Such signs of decency as he manages fitfully to show are those of the common man.

Dawes is given his chance at regeneration when he rescues Frere, Sylvia and Mrs. Vickers. The episode becomes a parable, for in this little society of four, stranded on the wild west coast of Tasmania, necessity re-arranges the customary social order. The outcast, the convict, becomes the most indispensable member ('Maurice Frere's authority of gentility soon succumbed to Rufus Dawes' authority of knowledge'). Dawes is won over by Sylvia's simple trust in him, yet he is at once dashed by her innocent reminder of the harsh reality, that even if he were to win a pardon he would always be regarded as less than a full member of society. He can never be rehabilitated. Further, by being so completely competent Dawes incurs Frere's antagonism. His authority of knowledge offers no place to Frere, and consequently his efforts on behalf of the others lead to yet another reversal. In this sequence Clarke clarifies for a moment the real issues underlying the narrative. Here the reality of Dawes's situation is displayed, here his inevitable defeat is recognized.

Dawes's subsequent history is, in Matthew Arnold's sense, painful. By Book IV, the persistent brutalization has started to lose its dramatic edge. The convicts are reduced to listlessness, and to preserve the reader's moral bearings Clarke has to introduce a new character, for the marriage of Sylvia to Frere is likewise a degradation, and becomes durance vile. The Rev. James North, with his own personal conflict and spiritual agonies written down in his diary, serves to enlarge the moral scheme of the novel, by carrying it explicitly beyond the convict system. Yet his is such a different order of character that another effect of his late introduction into the novel is artistic imbalance. He seems to belong to a different mode of fiction, as well as a different world. He has a freedom that even Frere does not have. Frere belongs to the convicts, just as they admire and hate him for his personal authority over them; and his resemblance to them, especially in the coarseness of his nature, is often noticed. And for all his torments, North's freedom allows him a moral and spiritual latitude that is not possible for the prisoners. The difference in character may also emerge from the narrative procedure, however, for by using the device of diary extracts and the first person point of view, Clarke allows the reader a much more detailed knowledge of North's cast of mind, his temperament and his moral nature. North, writing in the first person, is responsible for his destiny. The other characters are accounted for in the third person.

His Natural Life, for all its melodrama and its sensational horrors and far-fetched coincidence, has a brooding intensity unlike any other Australian novel of the nineteenth century. It is remarkable for tracing, with some subtlety and psychological astuteness, shifts in states of mind. It seizes on telling events from the old convict days, it describes authentic features of a limited, specialized community, but it also offers a serious moral vision.

Clarke's other work has faded into relative insignificance. He wrote three other novels, and published two volumes of short stories and sketches in his lifetime; and while these have nothing like the power and moral imagination of *His Natural Life*, some of the stories show Clarke to a degree anticipating Lawson and the *Bulletin* school, both in the range of his subject matter and in some aspects of the narration.

At the beginning of his enthusiastic review of Bret Harte's *The Luck of Roaring Camp*, 'We have always urged upon Australian writers of fiction the importance of delineating the Australian manners which they see around them every day ...'.[15] Clarke's thoroughly enjoyable Bullocktown stories are examples of the realism he had in mind. In these, the manners emerge through the narration itself. The narrator is one with the country town he describes, but he is also wryly amused with it, and with himself. The projected attitude is that his values have been formed in the country, though there is also a degree of sympathetic but critical detachment from it ('the stationary dance of the bush hand is a fearful and wonderful thing ...'). Like so many of Lawson's sketches, these operate as brief anatomies of up-country life.

In a more orthodox style is his set piece, 'Pretty Dick', a story well-received in its day; the excessive pathos and the propriety of the sentiments are, however, no longer tolerable. The story of the child lost in the bush was a commonplace of colonial fiction, yet it was not a theme to take lightly. The subject seems to have exerted an unvarying and compulsive interest, and becomes one of the key images of the colonial experience. Even Furphy broke with his habitual stance to record his version of the lost-in-the-bush story in *Such is Life*, and without criticizing Kingsley's mawkish efforts in *Geoffry Hamlyn*.

The bulk of Clarke's writing was journalism, and Clarke was one of the liveliest journalists in Melbourne. There, he was witty, provocative, facetious, anti-sentimental. His practice was most often to propose only one side of an issue, either to enforce its absurdity or to provoke an argument; it was not cantankerousness on his part, but a means of dramatic heightening, humorous in his sketches and enthusiastic and serious in his essays. This might be the satirical edge of 'The Future Australian Race', or the bemused ironies of the 'Peripatetic Philosopher' series. The heightening sometimes led to extravagance; Clarke is always colourful, always presenting a personal attitude (flippancy, superiority, mockery, impertinence). But his criticisms of materialism, vulgarity and humbug in his sketches of city life are well taken.

Another Melbourne journalist, 'Julian Thomas' (Stanley James) took over the mask of peripatetic philosopher, or roving corres-pondent, popularized by Clarke, and over the signature 'Vagabond' regularly wrote articles and sketches of Melbourne life. These were collected and published in *The Vagabond Papers* (1876–78). They are sensible, readable, and lucid, although their clarity of observation is sometimes overlaid with moral and sentimental orthodoxies.

Melbourne was the real centre of cultural activity at the time. Its prosperity, derived from the goldfields, attracted a large and varied population. Numerous papers, magazines and periodicals emerged to cater for the wide range of interests; and the journalism kept pace with its bustling and lively self-importance ('marvellous Melbourne') as well as its increasing respectability. Literary societies and literary coteries sprang up, such as the Yorick Club and the Cave of Adullam founded by Marcus Clarke. Yet fiction continued to avoid the city, turning as always to the up-country experience for the location of Australian manners and Australian life. City life was essentially the domain of the journalists. Even Boldrewood's reminiscences, *Old Melbourne Memories* (1884), are about country life, the pre-lapsarian 'golden age before the gold'.

'Rolf Boldrewood' (T. A. Browne), author of fourteen novels, was not only prolific but popular. He acknowledged the influence of Henry Kingsley, and followed Kingsley's lead in his novels of the pastoral world. But a greater influence was Sir Walter Scott (the pseudonym 'Boldrewood' comes from Scott's *Marmion*), for Boldrewood's novels of adventure and excitement, romantic action and simplified moral idealism, are all fashioned on some aspect of Scott. In particular, Boldrewood admired the aristocrat and the gentleman, although (again like Scott) he was a local patriot too, and throughout his novels approved the developing colonial virtues.

The one novel for which he is remembered, *Robbery Under Arms* (1888—it appeared as a serial 1882–3), dramatizes that double loyalty clearly, for it offers a choice of hero; Starlight, heroic in the conventional (romantic) sense, brave, a natural leader, a gentleman, and Dick Marston, Sydney-side native, the narrator. The novel was immediately well-received by the public, though Boldrewood was surprised by several rejections when he offered it for serial publication. The success can be accounted for by its topicality, and by the freshness of its narrative manner. Ned Kelly had been hanged only shortly before the serial publication; yet bushranging was increasingly a thing of the past. In Boldrewood's handling of the material, as in the bush ballads, the bushranger is seen as a romantic hero, a fearless and dashing outlaw rather than a criminal, defiant of authority yet abiding by a code of decency. Like Kingsley, Boldrewood has combined the reminiscent narrative with the conventional romance, not pastoral romance this time but romance of adventure. By using a narrator who is not a well-born Englishman, he protects himself against his customary weakness, narrative intervention and the clumsy intrusion of authorial rhetoric. In those other novels in which he uses a narrator, the chosen figures are not as distant from Boldrewood as Dick Marston, and their definition as characters becomes blurred. The narrator in *Robbery Under Arms* is a wholly realized, sustained dramatic creation.

Dick Marston is the making of *Robbery Under Arms*. It is his perspective and his language that shape our response to the novel. The novel begins sensationally, both in language and situation:

> My name is Dick Marston, Sydney-side native. I'm twenty-nine years old, six feet in my stocking soles, and thirteen stone weight. Pretty strong and active with it, so they say. I don't want to blow—not here, any road—but it takes a good man to put me on my back, or stand up to me with the gloves, or the naked mauleys. I can ride anything, anything that ever was lapped in horsehide—swim like a musk-duck, and track like a Myall blackfellow. Most things that a man can do I'm up to, and that's all about it.[16]

Nobody else in Australian fiction announces himself quite like that. This sounds like nothing quite so much as the heroic boast, the vaunt of the American backwoodsman. It is brash, confident, assertive,—and for a moment, self-forgetful. For Dick Marston, 'as

61

strong as a bullock, as active as a rock wallaby, chock-full of life and spirits and health', has been sentenced to death for bush-ranging, and is to be hanged on the gallows in thirty days.

Dick is writing down his story while he awaits his execution, and as his narrative progresses he again and again comments on the foolhardiness of his nature, draws attention to the unwise decisions and lost opportunities, but most of all regrets the suffering he has brought upon those who care for him. The novel is, amongst other things, instruction literature, perhaps the most accomplished in Australia in the nineteenth century, because its intention of moral example and moral reinforcement is wholly integrated with the narrative action, rather than (as is usually the case) drawn from it. The sound advice is in the first instance Dick's self-criticism. Dick hardly has the oblique and reflexive relation of the memoirist to the matter observed and experiences recorded, yet his narrative is not a personal history either, and nothing like an autobiography. For Dick is not the dominant figure in his own life.

Dick truculently insists he is inferior to no man—he is too much the emergent young Australian for that—yet he is also candid about what is not admirable in himself. When in his narrative he disapproves of his actions, it is invariably by comparison with the steady goodness and patient love of the women who wait and weep for him, or with his brother Jim, whom Dick admires as a better man than himself. Jim and Dick, though brothers, are also mates, and Dick is not at all envious that Jim is better liked than he. They understand each other completely in a firm handshake and a searching look; nothing needs to be said. Interestingly, Boldre-wood also notices one of the corollaries of mateship. Jim is led into 'the game' (cattle-duffing) by his loyalty to Dick. Mateship imposes awful responsibilities.

Starlight, by innate superiority of character, is the centre of interest for another part of Dick's narrative, for Dick is both a 'realist' and a romantic. The realist side is expressed through the details of country life, images of the unexceptional—fencing, shearing, mustering, some aspects of the gold-diggings, the early memories of the bush school—but the romantic side of Dick's nature is captivated by Jim's last-minute rescue of Miss Falkland, or by the dashing figure and daring exploits of Starlight. Even Ben Marston admires Starlight, prompting Dick to reflect:

> ... I don't think there's any place in the world where men feel a more real out-and-out respect for a gentleman than in Australia. Every-

body's supposed to be free and equal now; of course, they couldn't be in the convict days. But somehow a man that's born and bred a gentleman will always be different from other men to the end of the world.[17]

Boldrewood does occasionally manage to break through the screen of the projected narrator, it seems, yet if his generalization is rash, the sentiments are not really challenged in the course of the novel.

Robbery Under Arms offers the interesting spectacle, then, of two kinds of hero, one romantic and one 'real', and one contained within the narrative of the other. Boldrewood does not resolve the conflict, because he does not see that the two are in competition. Provided the action is moving forward, he is content; as he is quite unembarrassed in offering Terrible Hollow, isolated in the most inaccessible country, not only as a haven but as park-like, resembling in some details 'the old country'.

Dick's language is general and colloquial, and the thoughts it expresses are uncomplicated. It is highly idiomatic, the idioms serving to colour the descriptive rather than the reflective parts of his narration: Warrigal's horse could kick the eye out of a mosquito, Starlight works the oracle (just as Tom Collins does), and Billy the Boy's eyes were sharp enough to see through a gum tree and out the other side. Although Boldrewood has quite evidently busied himself in collecting colourful expressions, it is credible that Dick Marston would use language in this way. For Dick is a word-conscious narrator, not quite as extravagantly so as Tom Collins, but likely even at the most serious moments to inspect a metaphor for its literal and alluded meaning.

The effect of the language is ultimately to suggest that life is sportive, a game, and the most common terms of measuring experience consolidate this view. 'It was as good as a play,' says Dick, watching Starlight mixing with the swells in Adelaide, and Billy the Boy and Maddie and Bella Barnes use the same formula on several occasions, when recounting how they have mis-informed the police. The outlawry of Starlight and the Marstons is kept to pleasant, exciting adventures. They avoid violence, and while Dick rationalizes that the police must expect to be shot at, they do not shoot to kill. On several occasions they directly oppose their occasional associate, the criminally vicious Moran, because his villainy compromises what Dick presents as the essential fair-mindedness and decency of their scrapes with the law.

Because Dick Marston's is essentially an innocent world, there is no place for Moran in it. Nor, really, is there any place for Ben Marston and Warrigal, grim, threatening, mysterious figures who come and go unexplained through the bush. They are 'other', not known. The mystery of Starlight is quite a different kind of thing. In such an innocent world, there can be no conviction of crime (it is in this sense that one speaks of the increasing secularization of the Australian experience), and Dick's reprieve is inevitable. He is not a bad man, though he has done wrong. What one senses is that Boldrewood, in projecting Dick as a type of the emerging Australian youth, is also projecting a vision of an innocent Australia. He is closer to Kingsley than to Clarke, closer to Paterson than to Lawson.

Mrs. Campbell Praed has no such innocent vision. Like Boldrewood she was a prolific novelist, and as with him her novels inevitably converge towards certain favourite patterns of commentary. Her best work, *Policy and Passion: a novel of Australian life* (1881), was written early in her career before she discovered her formulae, and retains the freshness, charm and confidence of original reflections. It is not free of convention; the love interest of a beautiful young heroine having to decide between two suitors, one an English aristocrat and the other an Australian squatter, is trite. Honoria Longleat, daughter of the Premier of Leichardt's Land (Queensland) is seriously compromised by the Englishman, and the pity is that Rosa Praed allows the clichés of the conventional romantic novel to intrude at this point, for not only is Honoria very deeply shaken indeed, but there are important political repercussions.

Mrs. Praed's interest is in 'the inner workings, the social interests' of Australian life. Her novels are not committed to the exotic and the unusual in colonial experience, nor are they overly pre-occupied with the external narrative of action, of man living against an elaborately described landscape. *Policy and Passion* begins with an 'outside' view, an Englishman looking out at a country town, but the novel is increasingly about exchanges of ideas and revelation of character, whether this takes place in the study, the drawing-room or the House of Assembly.

In the first chapter she rapidly sketches in the look of the township: 'Brassy clouds were gathering slowly in the west, and the sun, beating pitilessly upon the zinc roofs of the verandahs, was mercilessly refracted from the glaring limestone hills ...' But at once she begins to make social distinctions. One of the bars is frequented by the roughs who come down from the bush for a spree, the squatters sit at chairs and tables on the hotel verandah, while idle navvies and rowdies form the admiring mob when Longleat arrives. The reason for starting in this way is apparent; the township, Kooya, is the heart of Longleat's electorate, and these are the people whom he both represents, and of whom he is representative. He is unashamed of his origins as a bullock-driver, and as a land-owner he also has the interests of the squatters at heart. This is a novel about a political figure in which the interest is largely in the personal life of the politician; that is, it is not strictly a political novel. But as the daughter of a Queensland parliamentarian, Mrs. Praed conveys a much more precise acquaintance with the realities of political life than, say, Spence or Kingsley.

Longleat is the novel's most important and original accomplishment. In some of the circumstances of his life and in his political actions he appears to be modelled on a premier of Queensland, A. H. Palmer; but he is also the fore-runner of a number of such figures in later novels of Queensland, by Vance Palmer, or Brian Penton for example, in which one single character overshadows all those around him, and opposes himself to the vastness (or spiritual amorphousness) of the State. Longleat is a powerful figure, a man not only big and strong, but of enormous will and determination, and with a deep commitment to political integrity. The signs of his working-class origins are evident in his appearance and his manners; he is not ashamed of them, and it is a mark of his honesty that he is rough, unpolished. It is also the source of his political strength.

The secret of his past is that he was a convict. His life as Longleat began after he had served his sentence; since then his life has been exemplary. Convictism may have coarsened him, but it has not corrupted him, and the public revelation of his shameful past is essentially irrelevant to him. What corrupts Longleat is his growing passion for the wife of a member of the Opposition. Though his personal actions are no more than socially indiscreet, he is persuaded by her to make an expedient political appointment that compromises his political integrity. The discovery that she has deceived him comes just at the time of the exposure in Parliament of his convict past, and Mrs. Praed succeeds admirably in combining the tensions of the public and private levels of action, the buzz of excitement and anticipation of the Opposition attack, the anxiety of the Government party, the effect of the divergent pressures on Longleat. His collapse is inevitable, but unfortunately Mrs. Praed once again fails to distinguish clearly enough her own particular perception from the sentimental cliché. For Longleat's is a collapse of will; shattered by his own misjudgment of Mrs. Vallancy, he can no longer sustain the world he had been at such pains to create. Yet all is not lost with his suicide, for both his political vision and his daughter's good name are secure with Maddox, the man he had chosen to succeed him as Premier.

Policy and Passion is a better novel than it at first appears. Mrs. Praed's imaginative understanding of Longleat is impressive, and tactfully conveyed. She understands but does not insist upon the nature of his solitariness. With Longleat she is true to her vision, but elsewhere her writing becomes tight and artificial, as in passages of frozen dialogue designed not to express character but to prove that Australians knew about discriminating taste and discerning judgment. Mrs. Praed surrendered her very real talents and her originality to the popular demands of the Home market.

Ada Cambridge, another of the prolific novelists of this period, also yielded to that combination of pressures, to what the English reading public expected and to what was easy for her to write, to custom and convention. She was astute enough to recognize how much 'the laws of the literary romance' are at variance with 'the laws of nature', but her practice led her away from the real to that which could be taken for granted, particularly in action and setting. It would be wrong to describe her work as merely conventional, for throughout her novels she maintains some independence of thought and criticism of social custom; yet that independence amounts to a little rattling of the orthodoxies, and the thought is neither subtle nor profound.

'Tasma' (Mrs. Jessie Couvreur) wrote much less than Ada Cambridge and Mrs. Campbell Praed, but she wrote rather more finely. The range and social vision of her novels is limited, but that becomes her advantage, for all her effects are light, witty, compact. There is nothing fragile about her writing, for there is too much cool sense, too much controlled irony for us to doubt the very pointed intentions of her fiction. Her best novel, an immediate success, is *Uncle Piper of Piper's Hill: An Australian Novel* (1889), and here she displays a charming wit that is quite beyond Ada Cambridge and Mrs. Praed, a sense of humour that Catherine

Helen Spence rarely approaches, a playful narrative irony that is distinctively her own.

The conception of the novel is not very wide ranging, nor is the sense of structure strong. It is a novel of the affluent class of Melbourne, with a slender action in which a group of young people all manage to fall in love with the right partners eventually, despite the opposition of the near-apoplectic Uncle Piper; and yet it is quite unsentimental about love, and that is the source of much of its comic effect. The relationships are confined to one family, so that little of the world outside 'Piper's Hill' is seen, though the description of the decaying country township, Barnesbury, is even more succinct than Mrs. Praed's Kooya. There is nothing of the 'rowdies', 'navvies' and 'roughs' who were about to become the main interest of the *Bulletin* school. Furphy's first article appeared in the *Bulletin* in the same year that *Uncle Piper of Piper's Hill* was published.

Uncle Piper is not at all a bushman, but he is a colonial type recognizable through the caricature. He has been Tom Piper the butcher, and has made his pile in Melbourne, and now he is a blustering, obstinate vulgarian, uncomprehending rather than unkind, a secret sentimentalist, and disguising in affected pragmatism his uneasiness about anything that might require him to think for himself. He is another example of the ascendancy of the working class; and although 'Tasma' deplores his want of social grace she allows some endearing qualities to emerge through the very simplicity of his cantankerousness.

Uncle Piper of Piper's Hill is really about the ironic intelligence which is responsible for the narrating, the undisclosed 'I'. All 'Tasma's' effects flow from the amused detachment of the narrator's stance. In her use of the author-narrator, in her study of the pretensions to refinement and manners, in her awareness of a larger cultural framework in which her own narrative may be set (as for example in the allusions to the great writers and painters), and in concentrating her study on one 'enlarged' family, she anticipates Martin Boyd. Yet her effects are bolder than his, unless in his *Outbreak of Love* mood. Her narrative disconcerts by its mockery yet acceptance of the formulae of romantic fiction, especially the sentimental pretence of concealing interest.

The novels of Mrs. Praed, Ada Cambridge and 'Tasma' most closely resemble each other in choosing to represent a particular level of society. They write of the daughters of men of property, having a fairly limited social life either at the homestead or in the town or, as in *Policy and Passion*, quietly making the transition. The issues that concern them are marriage and inheritance, and the watchful discrimination between the realities of social behaviour and the mere affectation of gentility. Theirs are not necessarily artificial values, for the effort to maintain social standards was as real a part of Australian life as the determination to dispense with them. Kingsley and Boldrewood and Mrs. Praed and the like may have been guilty of treading the flowery pathway of the romancer, but their novels are not to be abruptly dismissed as 'insufferable twaddle'; for while they may not imitate reality with the strict veracity of Furphy's annalist, they reflect the values and aspirations, the point of view, of a considerable portion of the Australian public, as the popularity of the books indicates. The 'Bush' school of writing pretended to do away with such idealism, and claimed to face directly the realities of life in a landscape that was no longer pastoral. This literature too proved to be very popular.

PART TWO: THE 1890S AND THE EDWARDIANS

In most views of Australian literary history, the *Bulletin* is the exclusive forum for the new realism, the spawning ground for a new authentic Australian Literature. The antagonism of the realist towards romance was not just a formal objection, but a reflection of ardent nationalism that welled up as Australia moved towards federation. The novel of manners was not authentic because it recognised English conventions, both in social behaviour and literary accomplishment. The *Bulletin* above all required original writing; there was to be no imitation of the old Anglo-Australian conventions. What resulted was the substitution of one convention for another, the convention of bush realism for that of romance.

Yet it is misleading to suggest that one wholly replaced the other, just as it is misleading to credit the *Bulletin* alone with fostering the new realism. For the romances had increasingly acknowledged local colour, while the emergence of the currency lad to a dominant Australian type may be traced from Kingsley's 'lean, sunburnt, cabbage-tree hatted lads' and Boldrewood's Marston boys, native youth in hue and cry. On the other hand, despite Tom Collins's withering scorn of Kingsley and the romancers expressed

68

in *Such is Life*, most of the fiction that subsequently takes up the bush ethic is itself patently romantic and sentimental—in Miles Franklin, Katharine Susannah Prichard and Frank Dalby Davison, for example. In this respect, the *Bulletin* merely confirmed tendencies already present. What changes is the narrative manner. In encouraging contributors to 'boil it down', the *Bulletin* accomplished a change from the enthusiasms of Kingsley and Boldrewood, and the clever self-possession of Catherine Helen Spence and 'Tasma', to (in the best of the contributors) the dry, laconic understatement of the anecdotal style, and the emergence of an Australian voice, in both the ballad and the short story. Clarke was close to that manner and approach in his Bullocktown stories, but with an edge of indolence, even self-indulgence, that distinguishes him from the *Bulletin* nationalists. His example suggests once more that the *Bulletin* was confirming rather than creating a tradition. It is heard again between the wars, when with the revived interest in the nineties, the legend was consolidated. One of the persistent features of the short stories of this period is that they are very often reminiscent. The life they celebrate belongs to the past, and the ideals they espouse (such as mateship) are based on the fondly remembered. For while Vance Palmer showed in *The Legend of the Nineties* (1954) that the period assumed the proportions of a founding myth for Australian culture, it is also clear that within the literature of that period was much appropriation of the near-mythical, for both humorous and serious effect. The short stories recall again and again the preceding generation, or a distant youthfulness and innocence. The sigh of fatalistic resignation, the 'ah well' of so many of Lawson's stories is endemic.

Henry Lawson was originally esteemed as a poet, though his verses have little to recommend them to the present day reader. He was regarded, it would seem, more for his sympathies than the poetry. He took the side of the down-trodden, the unfortunate, the dispossessed, and his compassion was from fellow feeling and not patronising, yet he sounded the rallying call in a now rather obviously declamatory fashion. Some of his verses catch brief glimpses of the old bush life, with the vantage point being that of the common man rather than the gentle reader.

His natural instinct was for the sketch and short story, for his verses tend to be mechanical. In his stories he mapped out an entire though limited world and whether that world is the real Australia or not is largely beside the point, for it is what Lawson accomplishes with this world of his own creating that matters. Lawson had grown up in the country. He was born on the Grenfell gold-fields and grew up on a selection at Eurunderee, but in the middle 1880s went to Sydney. Despite the famous trek back of Bourke in 1892–93, and his other intermittent experience of the country, Lawson was for most of his writing life essentially a city-dweller; yet his stories are remembered for their image of the bush worker, his desolate country, oppressive circumstances and stubbornly enduring wry humour. The country around Bourke might under-standably lend itself to such sardonic portraiture as 'In a Dry Season', especially since the 1892 expedition coincided with a drought, but Grenfell and Eurunderee are by no means the dreariest country in New South Wales. Lawson chooses to aggravate the conditions of bush experience, to generate a particu-lar effect, sometimes a mood, sometimes an outer landscape to explain, or precipitate, an inner crisis. That is not to challenge his realism, but to point to the concealed skill which creates the illusion.

Some of Lawson's most accomplished stories are to be found in his first published volume, *Short Stories in Prose and Verse* (1894)— 'The Drover's Wife', 'The Union Buries its Dead', 'The Bush Undertaker', and these together with the 'Joe Wilson' stories are the core of his achievement. Each of these early stories is a study of attitudes to experience, not of what happens to an individual but how he accommodates himself to it. And each situation is also seen as a sample of the kind of life the individual leads, and will con-tinue to lead. The drover's wife, for example, keeps watch through the night for a snake; that is all the action amounts to. Yet by the morning we know what her life is, and we have some anticipation of what her life will be (Mrs. Spicer, in 'Water Them Geraniums', confirms it); and the prospect is depressing. There is an exact correspondence with the setting: 'Bush all round—bush with no horizon, for the country is flat. No ranges in the distance ... No undergrowth. Nothing to relieve the eye ...' Because everything is so concentrated upon the one action, it looms as enormous. The psychological pressure does not create any disproportion, and yet the situation discloses terrors that threaten to become inordinate (Alligator the dog 'felt the original curse in common with mankind'). What Lawson offers is not the character of the wife, but the pattern of her existence. This technique repeated through the short stories provides more than a mere portrait of bush life. It is Lawson's conception of plot.

In most of the stories an 'authorial' voice intervenes between the reader and the narrative: 'The Drover's Wife', for example, although presented dramatically and in the present tense, has a barely discernible appraising commentary written into it, an unspecified presence which guides the reader to particular responses, or explains in a narrative aside, as it were, what the significance of some detail is. The watchful presence is not intrusive. Rather, it provides a larger dimension of understanding than the character can envisage.

In 'The Union Buries its Dead', the authorial stance becomes a little clearer, for it is identified with one of the 'mourners'. The story is carefully patterned, taking the reader from a bland outer level of activity (or inactivity) to an increasingly direct personal intimation of the meaning of the experience. It stops short of an exact articulation of it, leaving just an enigmatic hint at the centre, and then returning to the initial torpor and evasive fatalism. It begins with the collective 'we', with the narrator accepting his common identity with the unionists; he is not distinguishable from them or their attitudes. At the graveside he steps back to a personal view of the proceedings, observing the behaviour of the other participants, and drawing attention to the emptiness of the ritual for him: 'It didn't much matter—nothing does'. Yet his indifference seems so studied that we begin to notice the meaning of that meaninglessness for the bushman.

The characteristic Lawsonian twist follows, with the narrator suddenly emerging as story-teller rather than as participant: 'I have left out the wattle ... I have also neglected to mention the heart-broken old mate.' In conducting this catalogue of stereotypes, and in noticing the possibilities for cliché ('A stage priest might have said ...'), Lawson extends his awareness from this particular burial to the customary manner of writing about the 'death in the bush' theme, and so draws attention to his own apparently more honest account—draws attention to it simultaneously as real and as con-trived story. His narrative stance here resembles the participating chronicler, or the memorialist, one might call him, both in and out of the story he records, participant and creator, wryly acknow-ledging his own implication in the values he stands back from.

The tone is laconic, the manner casual, yet the presentation of this image of life, and death, works very much like the isolating pressures in 'The Drover's Wife'. The town seems detached from any wider context, everything is deadened; the language is flattened, the unionists amble through the proprieties, and observe some of the formal procedures of burial but are not much interested in the deceased except that he is deceased. They have only the most casual idle curiosity about him. It doesn't matter who he was or what he was—'it didn't matter much'. The comment has a particular as well as a general bearing. The dead-pan joke, the discovery that the man the union has buried was called James Tyson (Hungry Tyson was a famous pastoralist, and rumoured to be the richest man in Australia) takes the story away from the more sober ramifications of the episode, and returns it to the quiet farce of the narrative surface. It is a criticism of what happens to men in the outback that they seem so devoid of feeling, for what we discern in the narrator is not insensitivity but the pose of insensitivity, as though to guard himself against the impulse of true feeling.

The most effective of Lawson's stories are about fine shades of feeling, and not just what a man feels, but the difficulty he has in admitting his feelings to himself. The Mitchell yarns, assembled together, show Mitchell as a sentimentalist behind his sardonic exterior; indeed, it is basic to the legend of the nineties that the bushman has the right feelings, though there are very few occasions on which he can admit them. Lawson's bushman is not cauterised by his life in the bush, not made insensitive by his troubles. He is still compassionate, but he has learned to be guarded in his expression of compassion or concern, learned to pose as the sceptic or the stoic. When Lawson writes too admiringly of the battlers who have endured, the ever-present danger is that his story will collapse under the weight of sentimentalism.

The 'Joe Wilson' stories, which form a linked set and explore carefully and deliberately the changes in Joe Wilson's attitude to his marriage as a way of measuring changes in Joe himself, are unusually extensive by comparison with Lawson's customary manner. Joe is the narrator, and begins the series as an old man recollecting his courting of Mary. In the familiar comic pattern, he has to be converted from passive to active agent, but it is serious enough to Joe, both then and in the narrative present. Joe's advice to the young chaps is to make the most and best of their courting days 'for they've got a lot of influence on your married life afterwards'. This has a special poignancy in view of Joe's behaviour in

'Drifting Apart'; but Lawson's interest in the subsequent implications of an event marks a difference from his more characteristically abbreviated, documentary procedure. In the 'Joe Wilson' stories he is beginning to build up a personal history. Joe is a more self-conscious, less self-assured narrator, and the distance between the action narrated and the action of narrating allows for Joe's reflections and asides, sombre or gloomy or regretful and doubting.

In comparison with the rest of Lawson's stories, and in the context of the stories of the *Bulletin* school generally, Joe Wilson makes an important qualification of the 'bush type': 'I reckon I was born for a poet by mistake, and grew up to be a bushman, and didn't know what was the matter with me—or the world,' he says at the beginning of 'Joe Wilson's Courtship'. Joe is not at ease with himself or his fellow men, as his mate Jack Barnes is, for example. It is only when he has had a few drinks that he can overcome his sense of constraint. Lawson has not previously come to terms with the separateness of his bush types, their alienation as distinct from their isolation.

Joe differentiates between himself and the typical bushman, Jack, in terms of personal attitudes: 'I was sentimental about other people—more fool I!—whereas Jack was sentimental about himself.' We discover soon enough that this is not quite true. Joe still has to work things out, still has not quite come to understand himself. The essential point, however, is not the exactness of the distinction, but the terms in which Joe feels the distinction ought to be made. For this is not a story about courtship, nor of what a bushman is, or whether Joe is a bushman or poet. It is about a man trying to come to terms with his feelings (the courtship serves to channel some of his confusion), and especially the feeling of *difference*, of not quite belonging, in a social tradition that put a premium on camaraderie and conformity.

In the 'Joe Wilson' stories, Lawson dramatizes a man in the process of getting to know himself, which includes getting to know his own dishonesties. For Joe is at times morally evasive; it is a measure of Lawson's seriousness in these stories that he does not display that evasion for comic effect (as in say the Steelman stories, where the interest lies in the confidence-trick), or for satire, but is both sympathetic and critical. Nothing he wrote afterwards had anything like the candour and subtlety of insight, or control of sentiment. This sequence of stories is the height of his accomplishment. Joe Wilson, chronicling his own history, acknowledging his many doubts and misgivings, and not seeking to excuse himself, is the most completely realized of his many bush studies. In these stories, Lawson set new standards for imaginative realism in Australian fiction.

It is not just Lawson's sympathetic insight, but the mastery of tone and the control of language that impresses. Lawson's is a peculiarly misleading style, for while he seems to be writing in the flat, wry, sardonic manner of the nineties school, and very often in the same simple unaffected yarning fashion, closer reading reveals the delicate shifts of tone, or alteration of perspective, or reverberant image that in part account for the subtle accuracy of his stories—in part, because at his best there is to be found a further fascinating, indefinable touch that issues from somewhere between language and vision.

The other writers of the *Bulletin* school do not fare so well in comparison with Lawson. The effect of Stephens's injunction to 'boil it down' was not simplification so much as reductivism; these stories tend toward farce or melodrama, with the most important ingredient being situational humour. They show little of Lawson's sensitivity, and their place in literary history is now to display the broadening of humour and coarsening of sensitivity that took place in the pages of the *Bulletin* (though to be fair, the *Bulletin* was also encouraging Victor Daley and Shaw Neilson).

'Steele Rudd' (Arthur Hoey Davis), writing sketches of life on the land, quickly discovered that misfortunes can be comic, and turned the woes of Dad and Dave and all the Rudds into sustained farce. At first the sketches managed to express a real affection for them, but they were soon portrayed merely as caricatures. Their actions begin to show them up as clowns. *On Our Selection* (1899) and *Our New Selection* (1903) contrive a loose co-ordination of the individual sketches to form books of reminiscences, written as though by one of the lesser Rudds. The stories became very popular, and the Rudd family began to appear on stage, in cartoons and cartoon strips, and even in the burgeoning Australian film industry, once it got under way. Steele Rudd's later work is more mechanical, the comedy becomes routine, the humour eventually monotonous. Rudd's talent was in the short sketch, the quick definitive action followed by an anti-climactic understatement, laconic or subversive, from one of the boys. His zest in describing Dad exasperated, choked with the overflow of powerful feelings, while the boys slily add a little innocent vinegar, is reminiscent of Norman Lindsay. Rudd and Lindsay have much the same adolescent humour.

Edward Dyson's short stories, of mining or of working life in the city, have little interest now except that they are not stories of bushmen. His attitude to writing was recalled by Norman Lindsay: 'to hell with all that prissy preciousness over the way a man writes.. *What* he writes is more important than how he writes it...'[18] What Dyson writes is variable, none of it is important. These are yarns told with a little elaboration, very simplified characterization, and dialogue in the vernacular (inclining to the demotic) for 'authenticity'. However one might wish to approve his working-class sympathies, his short stories offer only a limited interest as fiction. Barbara Baynton is a much stronger writer, though she wrote only a few short stories and a rather poorly constructed yet vividly written novel, *Human Toll* (1907). Her *Bush Studies* (1902) is a brief but powerful collection, insisting relentlessly on the oppressive and antagonistic in bush life, and demonstrating the vulnerability of those that live in it. Her stories sustain a pressure of mounting uncertainty and dread; yet they are too natural, too alert to the humorous and to the possibilities of incidental satire to be gothic. The dread derives not from apprehensiveness of the bush, but from the sudden ugly attention of various threatening figures who inhabit the bush. She is completely unromantic about the bush itself, but there are frequent sentimental touches (e.g. mother and infant, ewe and lamb, cow and calf) to heighten the impending horror, and she does not always avoid the melodramatic. Yet melodrama can yield some very strong effects, and the intensity of her stories builds upon, rather than suffers adversely from that. Her stories seem to have had very little influence on subsequent writing, unless on some of Vance Palmer's earlier work.

William Astley ('Price Warung') writes a different kind of grotesque in his stories of the old convict days. Unlike Barbara Baynton, his 'realism' is based in historical fact, not imaginative conception. The *Bulletin* considered he was writing social history, not literature, and may have been more precisely discerning than was intended. Astley's stories—*Tales of the Convict System* (1892) *Tales of the Early Days* (1894), *Tales of the Old Regime* (1897) *Tales of the Isle of Death* (1898)—are, like Marcus Clarke's stories from the convict system, drawn from historical records, diaries and papers, and the editors of the *Bulletin* reassured their readers that however scandalous, each narrative was substantially true, even to the conversations, which paraphrase recorded testimony. 'When our contributor has deviated from fact, he has done so in the interests of decency.' But realism is not always well served by a reliance on documentary sources. The details may be true, but the effect is not the kind of truth, the truth of human experience, that we look for.

The kind of truth Astley projects is compelled by a fiercely maintained stance of moral outrage, which to the suspicious may seem a thin justification for sensationalism. Like Frank Hardy and Xavier Herbert, his righteous indignation is more political than moral; the convict material is something to use, to expose. He shows only a limited imaginative identification with it, and little historical perspective despite his information. His accounts are suffused with bitter irony, dictated by a radical contempt for Britain and British law. And the prose is guilty of lurid excesses ('where the vivisectionist gluts the greed of his red-fanged science'). It is all too simply emotive, too fiercely denunciatory. The cruelty of the System is so patent as to pre-empt our responses, and so the tales become burdensome, onerous.

Astley's Riverina tales, collected as *Half-Crown Bob and Tales of the Riverine* (1898), are humorous or sentimental bush yarns, typical of the nineties school. Though these stories are not linked, in them he succeeds in creating a sense of the Riverina, and more particularly of the river-boat people, as an especially cohesive group. In the *Bulletin* manner, he assumes the reader's familiarity with the locale, and his interest in small matters of vocational detail. But that pretence may serve to misdirect the reader. These are Furphy's tactics, on a diminished scale. In one or two of the comic stories Astley approaches the manner, the pace, and the structure of Lawson's humorous stories. But his characteristic mistake is in elaborating the superficial or external aspects of his story, so that it is only an entertainment. Lawson knew what to leave out; Astley did not develop that instinct.

From the midst of a literary climate dominated by the short story, with its emphasis on objectivity and realism, social and political awareness, humour, directness of statement, and 'Australianity', emerged Joseph Furphy's *Such is Life* (1903). While it would of course be unwise to accept his suggestion that his novel is simply a loose federation of yarns, the art of story-telling is central to both its design and its meaning. Furphy had contributed several unremarkable short stories to the *Bulletin*, but for the most of the nineties he was writing and revising his version of 'the vast and ageless volume of human insignificance'. When the novel appeared, pared down from the original massive manuscript, it was welcomed as a classic by a very few, and set aside by virtually everyone else as unreadable. Louis Esson complained 'He writes in the usual style of the badly educated man who has taken as models the articles in the Rationalist press and the penny encyclopedia.' His method is far from direct, and the intricacy of the novel's structure is still incompletely understood, but Furphy is now recognized as one of the important Australian novelists.

Furphy's novel, 'being certain extracts from the diary of Tom Collins', sets out to break with conventional forms, for in Tom's view the novel has become dominated by the need to furnish a plot, and such is not life. If, as he proposes, life is to be depicted as it really is, then the novelist must shun the conventions of fiction—which to Tom means the romantic novel—and find his own procedure for depicting the real. But the other fundamental problem is to decide what life is, or what its meaning is. Tom is bold to propose 'a fair picture of Life, as that engaging problem has presented itself to me'. His terms are instructive. It is the problem, the eternal enigma of life that absorbs him, and the rich detail of his portrait of the bullockies and boundary riders, sundowners and squatters on the black-soil plains of Riverina proper, is of interest to him mainly as the source material for his metaphysical speculations. One of the sustaining ironies of the novel, however, is that Tom's tendency to abstraction is again and again undercut by the very realities from which he takes his point of departure. His philosophizing is a means of evading life.

Where Tom opposes the real to the romantic, life to art, Furphy considers what the relation might be between these. The effect is mostly comic, as when Tom, scathingly denouncing the patent clichés of romantic plot, unwittingly gets caught in one himself. Furphy's more serious concern attaches to Tom's role as narrator. Tom bases his claim to veracity on the use of his randomly selected diary entries, yet since these entries as quoted at the beginning of each chapter are compressed and cryptic in the extreme, Tom's recreation of events from those brief notes has to be taken on trust; in themselves they do not guarantee realism. What Furphy reveals is Tom Collins turning life into art, by writing it up from his diary.

When at the outset Tom announces his antipathy to the ways of the romancer, he presumes as a corollary

> the more sterling, if less ornamental qualities of the chronicler. This fairly equitable compensation embraces, I have been told, three distinct attributes: an intuition which reads men like sign-boards; a limpid veracity: and a memory which habitually stereotypes all impressions except those relating to personal injuries.[19]

Tom's assumption is tacitly conceded, but events show that romance and chronicle are not in practice mutually exclusive; indeed, the either/or categorization does not hold good. Tom is an unreliable narrator. His limpid veracity is called into question (the name 'Tom Collins', meaning the unverifiable source of rumour, puts us on our guard); he misses the reality in front of him again and again, and most appropriately when his own romantic fantasies lead him on; while the stereotyping memory, limited by its fixity, inspires no confidence in Tom's ability to discern the whole truth of what he chronicles. Additionally, Tom provides a different kind of ornamentation, the ostentatious display of book-learning. But while Furphy does not wish to contradict Tom's position in the on-going argument the realists were conducting with the romance, he does indicate that Tom's literary theories largely determine how he sees life, and what he sees in life. Tom's realism is almost as artificial as the romancer's. His narrative is over-loaded with literary quotation, and his evidence for his several theories of life comes from literature too, rather than from the actual world.

Tom, then, is caught going both ways. His formal procedure—the random selection of diary entries so as to preclude 'plot', or the cause and effect explanations of fiction—is at odds with his many attempts to provide just that explanation of life through theories and hypotheses and conceptions, all based on an appeal to the authority of great literature. He attempts, ambitiously, an accounting *for* life rather than an account *of* life. Life, Tom's relation to the social world, is described, but almost despite him. Tom, 'wisely lapt in philosophic torpor', is very nearly left out of it. The terms in which Furphy first advised the *Bulletin* of his manuscript have become famous: 'just finished a full-sized novel, title, *Such is Life*, scene, Riverina and Northern Vic.; temper, democratic; bias, offensively Australian.' These phrases are carefully chosen to attract the interest of the *Bulletin* in the first instance, for its temper is democratic in a qualified sense, and its bias, though Australian, is comic wherever offensive, and in any case, subordinate to the concern with how best to present a fair picture of Life. Tom Collins's world consists of very finely observed hierarchies, determined by occupation and 'usefulness', and then various more subtle factors. The rigid caste system on the stations is spelled out by Tom, but among the wage-slaves and others is an equally carefully preserved gradation of bullock drivers, station hands, sheep drovers, fencers, boundary riders and so on, to the sorriest specimens of all, the down-and-out sundowners. Tom does not fit easily anywhere into this system. The bullock-drivers are suspicious of his friendliness with the squatters, and they in turn are uncertain which privileges should be extended to him.

But Tom is by temperament separate from his fellows too. Thompson sums him up: 'He calls himself a philosopher ... but his philosophy mostly consists in thinking he knows everything, and other people know nothing.' There is a sting of truth in that. Tom does not have sufficient regard for others' knowledge, or wisdom. He is inattentive to what they can contribute to his understanding of the engaging problem of life. In *Such is Life*, as in *Rigby's Romance* (serialized in the *Barrier Truth* 1905–06, and not published in full until 1946), and *The Buln-Buln and the Brolga* (1948), Furphy allows his narrator to set himself apart from the main body of conversationalists. Tom is exceptional in the steady procession of memorialist narrators in Australian fiction: where their narrative reflects their subsidiary participation in public occasions, Tom is only nominally a chronicler of such events and is, instead, much busier extrapolating some quasi-determinist explanation of why events happen as they do (alternative theories are supplied by other characters). Although he is present at the various campfire conversations and riverside symposiums, meditative musing competes with conversation (often to comic effect); the reflective mode is at odds with the social. Tom is less affable than he thinks, and dangerously close at times to becoming like the anchorite who 'lives to himself; and ... is merely a person who evades his responsibilities.'

The social vision that Tom and the bullockies all apparently subscribe to, a kind of Christian socialism as Tom describes it, is tested in several other ways. The calm fellowship at eventide in *Rigby's Romance* is undercut by the recognition that each of the men gathering by the river is competing against the others to catch a huge (if Shandean) Murray cod, while in *Such is Life*, whenever one of the teamsters leaves the camp-fire, the others immediately fall into a precise and cutting commentary on the unfortunate's character. That does not deny the egalitarianism they all believe in but it does question the pretense of solidarity, just as Tom himself dispels the myth of homogeneity. Part of the compelling truth of Furphy's representation of Riverina life is its exact register of the many tensions and divisions that exist within its fabric, as well as the various speech patterns of the denizens.

In its local reference, Furphy's fiction explores the implications of the bush code, ranging from the political significance of a box of matches to the practical assistance readily given to the distressed. When Tom's account of the bush ethic is examined closely, however, it reduces to a travesty. For example, Tom's assistance to Warrigal Alf stops short of accepting any responsibility for him, and while his avoidance of Murdoch, the swagman, though fatal in its effect is well-intended, Tom's treatment of Andrew Glover is not just morally evasive but reprehensible. Tom is heartless about women; he can reverence Ouida's tawny-haired tigresses, but he is ungenerous about women in life. Indeed, Furphy is so determined to be unsentimental that he goes too far, and Tom's comments on the unfortunate Ida are in distinctly poor taste. And while Tom records many examples of mutual assistance, there is equally a persistent current in the novel of individuals helping themselves to whatever comes to hand—dogs, horses, saddles, bridles, bullocks. This steady trade is initiated by Pup, Tom's kangaroo dog (and he virtually ends it when he carries off the trophy, in *Rigby's Romance*). Everyone is an opportunist—and opportunism differs only in degree from the celebrated procedure of the squatter in taking up his land. Bush morality is simply that 'in the Riverina of that period, it was considered much more disgraceful to be had by a scoundrel than to commit a felony yourself.' But, being had, it is essential not to show any response, especially not surprise or chagrin. It is bush style to maintain a certain heroic impassivity—as the title of the novel suggests.

Rigby's Romance is reconstituted from one of the large sections deleted from the original manuscript of *Such is Life*, and while it must be regarded as operating in its own frame of reference, there is considerable carry-over from one book to the other. Like *Such is Life*, *Rigby's Romance* begins with Tom announcing his stance towards his narrative: 'The fact is that I object to being regarded as a mere romancist, or even as a dead-head spectator, or dilettante reporter of the drama of life.' Rather less is made of the stern veracity of the annalist, however. Tom flatters himself instead on his good fortune in being the 'eyewitness and chronicler of a touching interlude', a little heart history. There is rather more discussion in *Rigby's Romance* of the right way to tell a story, and given the essentially static nature of the occasion, a fairly sustained portrait of bush etiquette. And even more than *Such is Life*, and despite the apparent sociability of the gathering, *Rigby's Romance* is imbued with a sense of solitariness. The effect is more metaphysical than social ('But though Rigby was now fairly started, he still failed to connect . . .') and two factors largely account for it.

Tom Collins is much more subdued as narrator, and Rigby is permitted to dominate the conversation, so much so that the argument seems a monologue rather than a debate, though alternative views do manage to get an airing. Tom is much less inclined to interpose his views here; indeed, his admiration for Rigby's oratory is a little immoderate. (Furphy valued Rigby as voicing his ideas of Christian socialism.) He is somewhat like the memorialist of the occasion, the recording angel of a plenary session of delegates gathered to a symposium on the machinery of the moral universe, but lured actually by word of the thirty-pounder.

Jefferson Rigby is the obsessed philosopher in this novel, and the rest have not his single-minded infatuation with the ideal of State Socialism. Like Tom he is a comic figure, but as he observes, 'comedy is tragedy, plucked unripe,' and his commitment to ideas is all the more forlorn because it is at the expense of love deferred for twenty-five years. Rigby's notions of socialism, built upon a premise of mutual concern, are defeated by events; he forgets to keep his appointment with Kate. As so persistently in Furphy, man inevitably contradicts his own philosophical structures, and theories are most comically and most profoundly inadequate when they become a substitute for life. For all the broad comedy and multiple ironies, the final note is inescapable: 'from that time forth an accession of sadness was observable in [Rigby's] bearing, with an abatement of the cynicism which had lent a kind of fascination to his homilies.'

The Buln-Buln and the Brolga is a simpler work again. In it, Furphy sidesteps the vexed question of providence and fate, and turns once more to the persistent theme of how fiction may best convey a truthful portrait of life. The particular terms of the issue this time are Memory and the Imagination. Tom still holds to 'the impulse of reminiscence, fatally governed by an inveterate truth-fulness' that he had acknowledged in his introduction to *Such is Life*, and refuses to concede that the imagination offers an alternative mode of perceiving reality. Yet Fred Falkland-Pritchard (the buln-buln or lyre-bird of the title) and Barefooted Bob (the native companion, or brolga—the puns are characteristic of Tom Collins), together with the more conventionally romantic Mrs. Pritchard, in the course of an evening's conversation display such virtuosity in their verbal elaborations and imaginative transformations of the truth as to win his admiration. A lie, sufficiently well told, for all its re-structuring of the truth is nevertheless a version of the truth, and the kind of accommodation the three make to each other is seen to take into account a more important awareness of human factors than Tom's commitment to stern veracity recognizes. Tom is more mellow in this novel, more capable of sympathetic understanding of his fellows, yet the very act of understanding indicates a degree of difference, of separation from them. Typically, he fails to understand his own part in this scene, and his closing comment, that this has been merely 'a glimpse ... into the vast and ageless volume of human insignificance', is as much a silent testimony to Tom's philosophical variant of the law of diminishing returns as it is an expression of Furphy's ironic realism.

Furphy is essentially a novelist of strategies. These are concealed within an overly elaborate narrative manner, for apart from the convincingly natural idiom of the bushmen's dialogue, Furphy's—or rather Tom's—style is a pastiche of literary reference, misapplied quotation, strained puns and, in Collins's, reveries, part facetious, part serious rhetorical pomposities. Furphy does not trivialize in this, for he is serious in his concern with the relation between literature and life, and between the attempts to systematize knowledge and the human divagation from that attempt. What we see in Furphy's fiction (or perhaps, in the light of Tom's particular theories, anti-fiction), is that men create their own realities, and while that does not disqualify his scorn for the contrivance of romantic novels, it does raise questions about the exclusive claims of Tom's brand of realism. Behind him, Furphy has constructed his own ingenious arrangements to show what life is like.

Although he appears to evolve from the surging nationalism of the nineties, a wholly indigenous writer, the extensiveness of his reading took him to Shakespeare and the Bible, Darwin and Dickens, Plato, Paine and Carlyle, and beyond to less familiar sources. He was highly literate, even if he did not always know what to do with his learning—a common enough dilemma for the writer in Australia. Furphy stands out from his Australian contemporaries by his awareness and exploitation of the possibilities of fiction. Conrad and James were at the time also experimenting with the use and the effect of multiple narrators, and diminishing the conventional importance of plot.

In terms of Australian literary history Furphy is not progressive. His fiction does not lead towards anything accomplished in the twentieth century, although recent Australian fiction is also inclined to dispense with continuity of plot. Like the *Bulletin* writers, Furphy deals with the immediate past, with the end of the era of opening up the country. The sedentary pace of his narrative, the reflective mode, the attitude to language and especially to the colourful vernacular, and Collins's and Rigby's love of erudition, all confirm the recent past as surely as the diary dates. Even Tom's reactionary criticism of colonial romantic fiction tends to be counter-productive. Furphy's very independence and originality bring him close to eccentricity, and a much less innovative writer, Henry Handel Richardson, whose fiction is derived from the nineteenth-century novel in Europe, is more directly linked to the literature of the turn of the century.

Like Furphy, Henry Handel Richardson was caught up in the struggle for an adequate realism. Unlike Furphy, however, who by the circumstances of his life had to evolve his own theory of fiction as best he could, Richardson had the advantage of living close to seriously entertained discussions of realism and naturalism; she had the advantage of a rich and lively cultural milieu, and additionally she benefited from the scholarly judgment of her husband, J. G. Robertson (later the first Professor of German at London University, and editor of *Modern Language Review*). She had left Australia to take up music studies in Leipzig, and in middle age returned only briefly to confirm some of the background material for *The Fortunes of Richard Mahony*. She is not the first expatriate novelist—the literary careers of Mrs. Praed and 'Tasma' for example belong to their post-colonial life—nor did she leave Australia for reasons of cultural suffocation, as Randolph Stow seems to have done. She claimed to have always considered herself a good Australian, but did not feel it was important to insist on the fact in her novels; and that provoked the hostility of the assertively nationalist writers, such as the much more passionate, and less accomplished, Miles Franklin, who sneered at *The Fortunes of Richard Mahony*—

> here at last was a work by an Australian in which the English-thinking Australians could take pride . . .[20]

Yet Richardson and the other expatriate novelists, such as Martin Boyd and Christina Stead, and even lesser writers like George Johnston, have contributed in a very important way to Australian fiction. Their discovery of Europe and the Mediterranean as sources of spiritual enrichment is proposed in a positive sense. It is not projected as an indictment of Australian cultural insufficiency; rather, it is an alternative to the potential insularity, however exotic, of the quest for the centre, and it frees the novelist from the pressure to 'write Australian'.

In Europe, Richardson read carefully the great novelists, especially Tolstoy and Dostoevsky and Flaubert; and she began her literary career with two translations, Jacobsen's *Niels Lyhne* (which she published as *Siren Voices*) and Björnson's *Fiskerjenten* (*The Fisher Lass*). Jacobsen's book was widely influential among the young generation of European writers, and had its effect on Richardson too: '*Niels Lyhne* . . . stirred me as few books have ever done, either before or since.' From Flaubert she learned how to handle a theme objectively; but Jacobsen, who also admired Flaubert, showed her something else. With him, she realized (in her article on Jacobsen in the international magazine *Cosmopolis*, 1897), that naturalism was only 'an outer garment'; in his novel the inner form follows a different aesthetic. Richardson herself, especially in *Maurice Guest*, her first and arguably her most accomplished novel, finds that naturalism cannot sufficiently display what she discerns of the truth of character. In her fiction, naturalism devolves towards psychological impressionism, so that she may hint at the workings of the inner life.

In both *Maurice Guest* (1908) and *The Getting of Wisdom* (1910), her original plan was 'merely to paint a milieu'—and in both books the main character gradually took over. *Maurice Guest* is set in Leipzig, the Leipzig she had known in the early 1890s as a music student. Like *Niels Lyhne*, which had originally been conceived as 'The Story of a Youthful Generation', it investigates the phase of life in which the individual has still to discover what he is and what he will be, and in which choices rather than decisions are made, and only immediate consequences are apprehended. The student life with which the novel begins, student hopes and ideals and anxieties, provides intensity rather than range of experience, for the student knows very little of life, though he may have large plans for it. Yet *Maurice Guest*, drawing on this most romantic phase of life, heightened by the milieu in which it is set, is in the end anti-romantic.

The opening of the novel, when the crowd disperses to leave Maurice to his thoughts, is somewhat theatrical, and the slightly operatic exaggeration is suitable to Maurice's inexact judgement and his state of elation. He is excited by the beginning of his dream's realization, as well as by the performance of Beethoven's Fifth Symphony he has just heard. His amorphous rapture is carefully presented, but Richardson withholds her irony momentarily, until his day-dream of himself as a brilliant concert-pianist becomes too pretentious:

> And he was overcome by a tremulous compassion with himself at the idea of wielding such power over an unknown multitude, at the latent nobility of mind and aim this power implied.[21]

Shortly after, the sensible Madeleine Wade dismisses the morning performance abruptly: 'an indifferently played symphony that one has heard at least a dozen times'. Richardson does not intend to mock Maurice, however, but through his undiscriminating enthusiasms establishes his provincial ignorance of life and his tendency to romantic reverie. Both help to explain his lack of comprehension, his unawareness of what is about him. In the early stages of the novel these are relatively harmless, but when he abandons his music for his obsession with Louise, the narrow, self-regarding intensity of his feelings brings about his undoing.

Maurice's all too patent failure in love is likewise anti-romantic. He is unable to understand Louise's sensuality, nor does he appreciate that his passion for her, initially idealistic, becomes increasingly sensual. Richardson is critical of romantic notions in *Maurice Guest* on something like Furphy's grounds—they prevent, or at least inhibit, recognition of reality—and so she denies a tragically or poetically fitting end. Maurice's death is not tragic; it is apparent well before his suicide that he has wasted his opportunities and his life. The distance between his early ambitions and aspirations, and what he finally comes to, is ironic, and a pity, but the relentless exhausting of Maurice's last spiritual resources allows little of the pathos that she accomplishes in the last section of *The Fortunes of Richard Mahony*.

The crux of Richardson's anti-romanticism, however, lies in her opposition to romantic notions of art, and in particular to the Petrarchan proposition that art is the product of passion and love (Parts One and Two of the novel carry epigraphs from Petrarch). In *Maurice Guest*, love and art are in conflict, for art is egotistical. And those students who succeed, in their different levels of competence, all make the necessary choice. Madeleine is characteristically sensible, Dove overcomes his absurd disappointment and applies himself well, and the likely genius Schilsky, who seems to fit a romantic stereotype, abandons Louise for a large part of the novel to concentrate on his career. They all are quite realistic in their appraisals of what is necessary, even Louise, for her ready return to Schilsky, which may be counted her success—music is a secondary concern for her—puts in perspective the steadily suffocating affair with Maurice. They all have the necessary egotism.

For Maurice, however, success is elusive. His is not simply the story of an inferior talent who suddenly finds himself attempting a standard of work beyond his capabilities, as Richardson is careful to allow Maurice some accomplishment. Success and failure are to be measured not in the eyes of the world, but in terms of what the experience means for the individual. The old man who inspires Maurice to go to Germany speaks of his own choice of failure:

> Failure! success!—what *was* success, but a clinging fast, unabashed by smile or neglect, to that better part in art, in one's self, that cannot be taken away?—never for a thought's space being untrue to the ideal each one of us bears in his breast; never yielding jot or tittle to the world's opinion. That was what it meant, and he who was proudly conscious of having succeeded thus, could well afford to regard the lives of others as half-finished and imperfect; he alone was at one with himself, his life alone was a harmonious whole.[22]

Maurice is not at all attentive to this; he is more impressed that the old man had seen life. Yet some of the novel's ironies can be traced from this passage. The nature of Maurice's passion for Louise is such that the better part of him gets very little airing, and the ideal he carries is continually modified as the affair progresses, from the original romantic infatuation which Madeleine warned him against to his final despair. Instead of pride, he is full of misgiving and jealousy, and his is the half-finished life. He has learned something of life, perhaps most of all from the enigmatic and unsettling Krafft, who also shows him the way to death; but he has not the ability to learn *from* it, to be enlarged by his experience.

The nature of Maurice's commitment to art (music) is questionable too. His first need had been to get away from his provincial origins: 'to go out into the world and be a musician—that was his longing and his dream'. Richardson forces the point, that Maurice's desire and his dream are interwoven, and that the dream of being a musician is in reality a means by which he may escape into the wide world. His initial resolve then ('What a single-minded devotion to art, he promised himself his should be!') is not merely ironic in view of what is to happen. He deludes himself because he has not honestly faced up to his reasons for coming to Leipzig. The declaration is an expression of his emotional excitement, rather than a statement of fixed intention. And while subsequent events emphasis the dream rather than the desire, both are within his grasp, yet he fails to reach out to them. The dream is never to be realized, while the romantic Bohemian life he had vaguely anticipated in fact confronts him with currents of ideas and behaviour beyond his moral comprehension (Nietzsche is named, Freud is pervasive, and Wagner is as darkly disturbing to him as Krafft's unrecognized homosexual advances). His understanding is at a remove from direct experience—he reviews his own behaviour to the point of exasperation, he responds indirectly to Louise, he is repeatedly discovered looking out at life from a window—whereas Louise displays a strongly felt immediacy of response, whether it is her overwhelming physical attraction to Schilsky, her hostility to Maurice or her hatred of Krafft. Even at his happiest, when Maurice first possesses Louise, we are aware that he has failed to make contact with reality. The satisfaction of the novel is that the ironic design of it does not sit heavily on Maurice Guest. Where Richard Mahony struggles with an overwhelming fate, and the ironic intention of the novelist is everywhere apparent, Maurice is more responsible for his fate, though blind to it. What happens to him emerges from the kind of man he is, a rather ordinary young man, and is not imposed upon him. *Maurice Guest* is, as Richardson said of *Niels Lyhne*, 'a book of unrealized ideals'; here, too, life rather than fate hems in the characters.

The novel suffers from weaknesses Richardson was never to eliminate from her fiction—occasional stilted writing and wooden dialogue (perhaps because of rather than despite the meticulous eleven years' writing and re-writing), surprising clichés, disproportionate emphasis and a too deliberate placing of recurrent images. Yet these deficiencies are more than compensated for by the objectivity of the work, her avoidance of sentimentality, the clear-sightedness of her penetration into the springs of her characters' behaviour and the subtlety of her projection of facets of their inner life, the completeness of her recreation of the milieu and the authority of the novel's imaginative conception. It is, as Hugh Walpole testified in his introduction to the second edition (1922), a remarkable first novel. (According to him it was, along with the work of E. M. Forster and Dorothy Richardson, one of the modern novels most deeply and persistently influential on the younger generation. The evidence for that, however, is difficult to discover.)

The Getting of Wisdom builds much more intimately on Richardson's personal experience, yet the nature of its truth is not autobiographical. Its account of Laura Rambotham's education holds once again to the combination of romanticism and realism that is central to her work—characters with romantic aspirations, placed in a precisely rendered setting, and whose idealism is tempered by the actualities of life. Because of her limitations of experience and opportunity, Laura's imaginative powers initially are exercised in the manifold fantasies of endless tale-telling (as 'Wondrous Fair'), but at school she has to discriminate between confusing, divergent pressures. By the social proprieties, tale-telling is reprehensible, though not the polite lie of social pretence. At the literary society, tale-telling must be probable rather than merely true, while her history lessons insist that however her imagination is excited by events, she must recite only the hard facts. The wisdom Laura slowly and painfully acquires is to distinguish between moral and imaginative truth, to learn discretion (the first Bible verse she memorizes is, appropriately, 'I wisdom dwell with prudence and find out knowledge of witty inventions').

Richardson began The Getting of Wisdom while she was still writing Maurice Guest, 'partly as a relief from that book's growing gloom'. She considered Laura a girl with a difference, carrying already the taint of her calling, like Joe Wilson ill at ease among his mates, and unable to say why. Yet Laura's experiences are not all that unusual, not enough really to determine her as an artist in the making (with perhaps the one exception of her curious, detached but sustained, scrutiny of the girl who is expelled). Laura's oddities, her uncertainty, her misery and her triumphs, and her exaggerated sensitivity, are a common, that is representative experience.

The novel offers two revealing lessons. Part way through her schooling, Laura submits a series of stories to the literary society. The first, a lurid piece of romantic adventure, 'after Scott', is a splendid extravagance just carefully short of burlesque; Laura's seriousness covers Richardson's amusement. That is followed by a mercilessly factual piece, Tom Collins' stern veracity run riot; and then a story comprised of things Laura knows, but re-assembled so that while not one word is true, 'every word of it might have been true'. The truth of fiction derives from a controlled imaginative restructuring of the known; realism means the essential probability of fiction. It had been difficult for Laura to accept this, for her reading of *A Doll's House* had bewildered her, as both true and unreal. This brief sketch of a theory of fiction is matched by events in the novel—the schoolgirls are crass realists yet hungry for romance, and Laura herself is inclined to seek not the truth but the miracle. The most persuasively 'probable' chapter of the novel, describing Laura's vacation at a little weatherboard cottage in the sand-dunes, also re-affirms her persistent evasion of the truth.

The particular miracle Laura seeks is divine assistance with her examinations. Laura's increasing religious fervour owes something to *The Fisher Lass*, though it stops short of the near-swooning ardour of equivalent sections in Björnson. She is given the opportunity to cheat in her history examination; afterwards, she decides that God has failed the test by trapping her into fresh sin, and her disdain for God's deceitful strategies is reminiscent of Olive Schreiner. This crisis of faith poses the question of truth at a much more intimate level for Laura than the problem of narrative realism. Yet Laura's resentment is not quite convincing, partly because her extremism has all along provided most of the novel's irony, and also because she is still too unformed to carry off such a large, independent gesture; right to the end her school friends call her 'child'.

Richardson chooses to represent Laura as a solitary figure, defensive and suspicious, unable to make friends easily, and intensely possessive of the one close friend she makes. Her passionate attachment to that girl friend carries strange echoes of the relationship between Maurice Guest and Louise Dufrayer, whereas her silent and stubborn determination ('she held her head erect, and shut the ears and eyes of her soul') anticipates, though faintly, Richard Mahony's lonely attempt to make his own sense of life. For Laura's brooding upon her unfitness, her 'uncomfortable sense of being a square peg, which fitted into none of the round holes of her world', remains ultimately a slightly comic opposition. Her profound moral outrage, the momentousness of her stand against God, does not result in any lonely existential vigil; the freedom she claims at the end of the novel is not an escape into life but an escape from the strict supervision and inhibiting social grooming of a young ladies' school.

Laura's getting of wisdom is, then, at odds with her nature. This is a wry yet sympathetic version of the book of unrealized ideals, unsentimental about Laura's education, alert to the insistent romanticism as well as the devastating pragmatism of the colonial young, and above all tempering Richardson's objectivity with a quiet irony of perception.

The Fortunes of Richard Mahony (1930: the three parts were published separately, *Australia Felix*, 1917 ; *The Way Home*, 1925; and *Ultima Thule*, 1929) is the book for which Henry Handel Richardson has been best known, a large-scale and remarkably detailed re-creation of the life and society of colonial Australia, ranging from a storekeeper's hut on the Ballarat goldfields to the fashionable houses of Brighton, and accurate in its depiction of setting and character alike. It represents the minutiae of the Ballarat diggings and their breaking up of 'what has been sanctified as final', and captures the very habit of thought, the reticence and rectitude of the mid-Victorian mind. And it is clinically accurate about the stages of Mahony's physical and mental deterioration. (In her incomplete autobiography, *Myself When Young*, 1948—itself as selective as her 'scientific realism'—she acknowledged that Mahony was modelled upon her father.) Yet Australian life remains the external reality, to which the inner life of Richard Mahony responds and against which he reacts; it is that life which hems him in.

Like so many Australian novelists (more recently, Patrick White explaining in 'The Prodigal Son' the need to discover the subtle mystery and poetry of Australia, the extraordinary behind the ordinary; George Johnston re-writing the legendary Australian; or Thomas Keneally declining to write only on Australian subject matter), Henry Handel Richardson was consciously reacting against the superficial romanticism of such Australian fiction as she knew:

> So far, all the novels about Australia that had come my way had been tales of adventure; and successful adventure: monster finds and fortunes made in the gold fields, the hair-raising exploits of bush-rangers, and so on. But there was another and very different side to the picture, and one on which, to my knowledge, no writer had yet dwelt. What of the failures, to whose lot neither fortunes nor stirring adventures fell? The misfits, who were physically and mentally incapable of adapting themselves to this strange hard new world?[23]

It is her concentration on the mental difficulties of the misfit, her study of the misgivings of the individual disconcerted by his failure, that impresses, more than the sustained accumulation of verifiable detail. In accomplishing a full and sustained analysis of character she changes the usual practice of the Australian historical novel; whereas her patient and somewhat relentless scientific realism merely extends it.

The Fortunes of Richard Mahony is in form an inverted chronicle. The first volume projects a commanding sense of the life of the community, and observes impassively the activities of a wide range of characters. These are not quite so individually rounded as in *Maurice Guest*, and show evidence of their origins in literary convention. As the novel proceeds, Mahony's separateness from the life of the community is seen to be more and more fundamental; and with that the narrative concentrates on an increasingly reduced world, a constricting perspective, the function of which is to emphasize the mounting pressures of Mahony's destiny, his misfortunes, upon him. And although there are indications that Mahony's son, Cuffy, will suffer from the same debilitating sensitivity, the chronicle's customary suggestion that the pattern of life is repeated from generation to generation is countermanded by the absolute finality of the closing vision of Mahony's forgotten grave. While in the larger sense life goes on, and the earth abideth forever, the third volume expresses the moving defeat of the individual and records a foreclosure upon life. Mahony's wayward, vagrant spirit has no place here; all human activity ceases, whereas the chronicle affirms its continuity and its value.

Because the narration is variable, Richardson's clumsinesses are more pronounced in the trilogy than in the earlier novels (*The Young Cosima* is uniformly lame). Her style tends to be ponderous at the best of times, and her solemn manner is imposing. She does not do well, then, to ape the cloying literary affectation of how little children speak, and long Ciceronian sentences do not seem the proper vehicle for Mahony's sharp social indignation. Richardson's artistry builds rather upon discerning steadiness of perception, and upon the subtle reverberations within a situation—the irony derived from this supports and to some extent substantiates the novel's relentless vision. The climactic scene in *Australia Felix*, for example, in which Richard collapses from a combination of heat, fatigue and moral distress, characteristically concentrates within itself a number of themes, and is taut with unsprung ironies. It anticipates Richard's eventual, much more severe collapse, and in its details alludes to other aspects of his career. The narrative here duplicates the inner mutterings of a distressed mind, but not Mahony's delirium, for Richardson confines her exploration of his spirit and moral nature to the various levels of consciousness, until the harrowing moment in the final volume when his mind snaps.

The earlier collapse is pivotal in several ways. Mahony breaks with his own past, and his youth; further, he admits to himself the solitariness of his own nature, and prepares the way for his decision to return to England. The real change, however, is in his relationship with his wife. After the crisis in their domestic relations, Mary no longer accepts his views unquestioningly but begins to doubt his wisdom and his commonsense. From this point on, she secretly lives a little against Richard, influences his judgment, and her love for him becomes by barely discernible stages supervisory, maternal. This is the role which circumstances will increasingly require her to take up, just as it is what Mahony reacts against in his last barely rational thoughts.

The continually altering balance in the relationship between Mahony and Mary is one of the novel's major accomplishments. Richard's restlessness, the movement from Australia to England and back again, and from house to house, while expressing in the most obvious and external manner a man never at ease with his environment, is the more dismaying when read in terms of his marriage. Richard is slow to recognize that he and Mary are of quite opposite temperaments, and only indirectly does he understand that the balance between them keeps shifting. Mahony has the ascendancy to begin with, and Mary—Polly as she is then known—is the diminutive, apprehensive and submissive young wife. Richard congratulates himself on his success in developing her, in bringing her to the flowering of womanhood. But as he loses ground, and becomes unequal to life, he begins to surrender some of his status in the novel to her, until by the end he is entirely in Mary's care and keeping. As the boundaries of his physical and mental life are reduced, she becomes a stronger, more commanding figure and more of the novel conveys her perspective upon events. Towards the end of the novel, however, Cuffy also becomes one of the sources of narrative commentary, no doubt in part to modify the potency of Mary.

The conflict between Richard and Mary is a conflict between idealism and pragmatism, between the dream and the real. In Dublin, Mahony's mother and sisters maintain an increasingly shabby dream of gentility, for they are impoverished and everything about them is marked by decay. Richard's scrupulous adherence to a code of behaviour is likewise impractical and in the Australian context a mark of difference, if not oddity, rather than distinction. On the other hand, the materialism of colonial society, with which Mahony identifies the commonsense of Mary and the stern self-sufficiency of her brother John, grates on his sensibilities. John Turnham is a man who makes his fortune, whereas Richard, like the diggers, tries his luck; and the difference in point of orientation is acute. It is in this sense that John Turnham is said to die as he lived, on his own responsibility. Richard's hopes for life are no more rational than the diggers hoping for the lucky strike. His investments are beyond his control, and his only active attempt in speculation is clearly unsuccessful. He has little control over his own fortunes.

Material anxieties sponsor Richard's spiritual anxieties and equally it is at the height of his good fortune that he most comfortably experiments with spiritualism. These experiments are seen as directly counter to Mary's firm grasp of fact, her unsympathetic commitment to the actualities of this life. Mahony alone has a conviction of the spiritual life (with the exception of such a minor figure as Mrs. Marriner). The others are all orthodox but their sense of life is in fact contained by the secular world. But his conviction eventually falters. Spiritualism, first seriously enquired into in reaction to the barren conclusions of science (Darwin's investigations into the origin of species leave untouched the greater questions of life's ultimate goal, and the moral mysteries of the soul of man), is a social fashion by the time of the Mahonys' second trip to England. Later, at Barambogie, Richard's only successful contact with the spirit world, through automatic writing, amounts to the trivial—a proof based on a doll's nose, and a recalcitrant child-ghost who will not leave her fossicking. He can draw no reassurance from this 'experience', other than that the past recedes from us, and in confirming once again the doom of man, that mortals are forever transients, Mahony merely reiterates his earlier proposition: '*Panta rei* is the eternal truth: *semper idem* the lie we long to see confirmed'. There can be no confidence from Mahony's spiritualism that his restless, wayward spirit will persist beyond the perishable body.

The other major accomplishment of the novel for which Richardson has won so much admiration, is her control over our response to Mahony's defeat. If his sufferings were to be accounted for in strictly medical terms, and he were the victim of a physical condition for which he is not in the least answerable (at least as shown in the novel), the final image of Mahony would be less powerfully moving, less far-reaching in its human significance. There is anguish in that as a doctor he knows what his prognosis is, but with no means of control. The depiction of his suffering, his poor life slowly ground out, is dreadful; yet it is not painful in Arnold's sense, in which everything is to be endured and nothing to be done. When John Turnham dies of cancer, his will and his pride sustain him to the end, and Mahony congratulates the dead man on his bravery: 'Well done, John ... well done!' There is a slightly unpleasant presumption in that, but also a latent irony, for although Mahony too dies with 'no whining for pity or pardon', he cannot be said to die well. He dies mindlessly—all the soul has gone out of his eyes, and Mary has no time to regret the past or to grieve for the inevitable—and that compromises both the poetic concept of a relentless and malevolent fate, and any notion of Mahony attaining tragic stature. *Ultima Thule* draws heavily on our compassion; it moves us to pity but not to fear.

The most evident limitation of *The Fortunes of Richard Mahony* is in momentary failure of the imagination. The particularities of the landscape remain authentic, but may not consort with the inner reality of character, the narrative becomes at times merely summary, the prose may lapse in the most highly charged episodes into platitude and cliché. That failure becomes sustained in *The Young Cosima* (1939). Across the span of her literary career, Richardson increasingly relies on verifiable detail, on source material, and distrusts her powers of invention unless they are grounded in fact. *Maurice Guest* has more imaginative freedom and control than her subsequent fiction; *The Young Cosima*, on the other hand, is published with an appendix of 'Sources and Authorities'.

Between the last two novels she issued a volume of short stories, *The End of a Childhood and other stories* (1934), in which she continued the story of Cuffy a little. (At one time she had thought to extend the trilogy.) The four chapters on Cuffy are only faintly interesting, not for themselves but as after-echoes from the novel; the other stories are competent but undistinguished, and carry a slightly stale taste of late nineteenth century European literary modes and manners. With the exception of *Maurice Guest*, Richardson's fiction is reversionary, either specifically or by literary coloration.

In *The Young Cosima*, a laboriously written work, Richardson's faulty judgment of tone is particularly evident. In *The Fortunes of Richard Mahony* she occasionally startles the reader with the most commonplace domestic metaphors—the earth is baked like a pie-crust, the skies are a Reckitt's blue—and that throwaway tendency is aggravated in the last novel by a more disconcerting practice of what one can only see as heavy-handed buffoonery, possibly appropriate to her subject but not to her theme: Wagner blowing his nose with a trumpet-peal, Bulow dropping a letter in the honey-pot. Wagner is venerated as the Master; and Richardson is disinclined, or unable, to establish his human reality. These burlesque touches serve only to turn the characters into grotesques.

The novel is defeated by its own premise. Cosima and Hans Bulow, Liszt and Wagner, all sacrifice their life to Art, and the consequence is that the novel itself loses the sense of life. Richardson needs to show for example that Hans's first love is for Wagner, but she does not reveal the nature of his fascination with the man, only his commitment to the Cause—taking Wagner's music to the people. And because that music is a reality outside the boundaries of her fiction, Richardson assumes and does not demonstrate that Hans's sense of mission is warranted. Similarly the stature of Liszt is imported into the novel; within the novel he is formal, distant, reserved and undeserving of the profound respect, admiration and love of Hans and Cosima.

95

In contrast to Cosima's reaction to *Tristan* ('A dream world, that was yet realer than any reality; that, by the sheer intensity of its dreaming, turned the real into the dream. A world in which ... soul spoke nakedly to soul, stripped of convention's veneer'[24]), the novel is dominated by its list of sources and authorities, and offers neither the dream nor the reality of the naked soul. Several of Richardson's persistent views about art and the artist are embedded in the narrative, especially the Wagnerian notion of the imperiousness of art, art as a curse. But the views and theories, like the facts, remain unassimilated into any unifying imaginative vision. It is a novel which has too evidently been an effort to write.

Richardson's best writing belongs to the earlier period. Although her career spanned nearly fifty years, her imaginative sympathies did not move with the times. In her private life she retired from the world, and wrote from the store of her own early understanding and emotional experience. She gave Australian fiction its first sustained analysis of character, maintaining that the novel's main end was character-drawing, 'the conflict of personalities its drama'. Her themes are romantic, set in a world both convincingly recreated and seriously entertained. Richardson is not only the doyen of realism in Australian fiction, scrupulously objective and impassive, she is also the first substantial Australian novelist to convey a large consistent vision of life. Furphy develops his propositions about life from a theory of fiction; Richardson's profoundly ironic and unsentimental recognition of the stature of man is met by the fiction, not evolved from it.

William Gosse Hay, writing across the same span of years, is an oddity. Like Richardson, he was serious, aloof, intent on the world of his fiction and painstaking in assembling the materials for it. Like her, he was absorbed by the relation of character to fate, and in his last novel approves Balzac's exact equation. Yet his fiction is thoroughly romantic. What he criticised in the Australian novel was its debasing of the proper idealism, its settling into sentimentalism (as in Miles Franklin):

When I began writing, just before the beginning of this century, Australian novels had relapsed entirely into fifth-rate tales of the 'paddock and stockyard variety', in spurious imitation of Rolf Boldrewood's distinguished work. I felt it was necessary to try and raise Australian literature out of that desolate bog, and turned to her ballad-like and tragic history and its proper costumes.[25]

By that he meant the border ballads, rather than the bush ballads; in early Australian history he found the potent mystery, the strongly felt but barely expressed passionate depths, and the imaginative colourfulness of the traditional ballads.

Hay had peculiar gifts. His characteristic manner is to infer, to suggest, to present the barely tangible or the fine nuance in setting, character, or theme. When he cannot avoid an open statement it most often, and disconcertingly, emerges as melodrama. He is meticulous about detail, but towards an end that remains elusive. Characters are described, yet there is no visual statement. They exist more as attitudes than as figures. In the one novel on which Hay's reputation rests, *The Escape of the Notorious Sir William Heans (and the mystery of Mr. Daunt): A Romance of Tasmania* (1919), the Meredithian elaboration of his style sustains a suspension, a stasis, in which mounting pressures gradually assert themselves. But all that potency is directed to an inadequate because insubstantial end— nothing equal to it issues from the buckling tension ('Heans ... with his pale, handsome face tense and unutterably dignified in its withheld anger ...'). Hay has a moral vision, of the compounding of good in evil and evil in good, yet for all the elaborate machinery it is a rather simple comment, as in the fierce rivalry between two brothers, ultimately reconciled by a good woman, in *Captain Quadring* (1912).

The faults in Hay are astounding. There is persistent awkwardness in structure and design, and insufficient narrative control. His plots are caught up in distracting convolutions, the dialogue is wasteful. The writing is sometimes clumsy, often wordy, the images slurred. Explanations break into the narration, either in long clumsy flashbacks, or in advance of the sequences that give rise to them. The narrative of *Sir William Heans*, for example, is curiously presented. Much of it is straightforward omniscient narration, yet from time to time Sir William Heans appears to have supplied a biographer-historian, perhaps memorialist, with subsequent commentaries upon various of his experiences ('Sir William Heans has confessed to us ...', 'From Sir William's account ...'). At others, the narrator is a silent participant in the scene, guessing at Sir William's thoughts or feelings from external evidence and admitting his uncertainty; or an intervening editor, or an author on polite terms with his reader ('Perhaps you and I would have been chary of interfering ...'). A topical story Captain Shaxton tells his wife is consigned to a footnote. Certain epithets and phrases are reiterated with maddening persistence. And Hay can be discovered attempting to elevate his theme by laborious poetic circumlocutions.

Yet *The Escape of the Notorious Sir William Heans* is strangely impressive for its stillness, its projection of emotional strain, and the firm will imposed upon it. Like all Hay's fiction, it deals with the convict situation, though Heans is a special case, a superior Irish gentleman who chafes under the curbs to his liberty even though, as a gentleman, he is allowed certain privileges not extended to the common prisoner. Hay is not particularly interested, as Clarke and Astley are, in the workings or iniquities of the System. It is Heans himself that Hay is attracted to, and more precisely what Heans represents.

Heans's stiffness, his irritating pride, even his pallor, draw attention to the exactness of his social manners. Yet his *amour-propre* is a shade too deliberate, too exclusive. His social accomplishments become his moral failing, his superiority is his weakness, just as in the admittedly operatic *The Mystery of Alfred Doubt* (1937), the hero's goodness of heart is met by disbelief, and brings Alfred to the point of death. The social proprieties observed by Heans and the Shaxtons appear at first to be only part of the period costumery, but in fact they relate directly to the kind of moral idealism Hay proposes in his books. Heans's first attempt at escape is unsuccessful because he offends in that grave area where social and moral conduct fuse—he urges Matilda Shaxton to leave with him. When he surrenders his second chance to escape, by returning to rescue a young girl from being molested, his action is again to be measured in those joint terms. It is not the splendid action of a Jim Marston rescuing Miss Falkland, for example, but a recognition and an acceptance of moral duty. The third book, culminating in his successful escape, is then virtually an epilogue.

Because of Hay's practice of depicting moral values through social behaviour, his characters do not appear to have any substantial core. Their moral conduct is set down with their manners, but not their moral nature. We do not on any occasion penetrate to Heans's inner life. The limitations of Hay's kind of fiction are marked when he is compared with Richardson; and yet in portraying in such a serious and elaborate manner the claims of moral duty, even though within an artificially coloured and romantically remote historical setting, he is not really so very different from the many English writers of the turn of the century who similarly accepted unquestioningly the lofty idealism of the social and moral proprieties. In Hay's fiction only the wicked defy these.

Hay's scorn for the paddock and stockyard school sets him aside from the main currents of Australian fiction, for local taste continued to run to up-country and bush stories. In juvenile, popular and serious literature, in the journals and papers, bush life was proposed as the authentic Australian experience. Yet whether Boldrewood, Paterson, Ethel Turner or Mrs. Aeneas Gunn, all alike endorse a sentimental core as the heart of their image of the real. This residual sentimentalism, the key to character and imaginative vision alike, is also discovered in the emergent literature of the city experience. The bush is exchanged for the push. Lawson's working youth from Jones's Alley, and Edward Dyson's *Fact'ry 'Ands* (1906) begin to identify the type, the sketch of the lout who suppresses all sense of the good and the decent, but whose capacity for sentiment is touched at last. In 1909 C. J. Dennis published the first of his larrikin pieces, 'Doreen', in the *Bulletin*, although *Songs of the Sentimental Bloke* was not published until 1915.

Louis Stone's *Jonah* (1911) is a delightful but mixed study of street life in the inner suburbs of Sydney. He is careful to catch the idiom and the humour of Cardigan Street, the manners and the values of the neighbourhood, the lawlessness of the push. Yet for all his conscientiousness in familiarising himself with this world, the story itself is too patently concocted. Its realism is only superficial. The characters, for example, are presented in clear outline, but not substantially; distinguished only by the exaggerated features of their personality. They are simplified, mere sketches of character, in the manner of the *Bulletin* paragraphs and illustrations. In Stone's second novel, *Betty Wayside* (1915), this characteristic becomes a much more damaging limitation.

In fact Stone's approach to the novel is mainly sentimental. The activities of the push are confined to two or three early episodes, but these serve only as a point of departure. For Jonah, the captain of the push, suddenly develops hidden talents and ambition, and ends up a relentless, enterprising businessman. His change of character is brought about when he admits to his feelings; he is quite overwhelmed by the touch of his infant son, and shows himself to be a sentimental bloke after all. The cliché of this conception is controlled by two modifications—the comic pathos of his wife's dispirited slovenliness, and the ironic outcome of his passion for a music teacher. The gradual process by which Jonah's

99

wife, Ada, becomes an alcoholic is one of the most persuasive of the novel's sequences because in it Stone accomplished continuity between character and environment ('s'elp me Gawd, when I married you I married Cardigan Street', Jonah complains). Ada's sense of her own inadequacy is a sad truth and a dishonest justification for her tippling. Interestingly, the combination of realism and satire anticipates an increasingly common practice in Australian fiction: Ada's drinking companion, Mrs. Herring, is not very different, really, from some of Patrick White's poisonous women.

Jonah's mate Chook, in his courting of Pinky, more closely resembles C. J. Dennis's sentimental bloke. His cheerful love for Pinky is the positive accomplishment in the novel's system of values, as enunciated by Mrs. Yabsley, Cardigan Street's moral commentator and a substantial comic figure: 'I tell yer the best things in life are them yer can't see at all, an' that's the feelin's'. But where the feelings of Chook and Pinky are adequately enough projected, Stone is clumsy with Jonah's. Jonah is self-contained, and his sentiments are summarized and asserted, rather than displayed; and that summary is in a language entirely unsuited to Jonah's order of emotional experience. Stone at such moments becomes novelettish, just as he does in coyly alluding to Ada's pregnancy as her 'disaster'. Although Australian fiction is very often sentimental, the novelists do not deal with sentiment at all comfortably, and Stone's awkwardness is revealed in the unnaturalness of the narrative manner, from the forced writing of passages saturated with similes, to the much too artificially heightened descriptions of setting, and the somewhat pretentious idiom of his narrative commentary.

Henry Handel Richardson and William Gosse Hay wrote with only the faintest recognition of the groundswell of national sentiment that spawned so many would-be poets, balladists and short-story writers through the nineties and the beginning of the twentieth century, and Stone's city landscape likewise pays no attention to the newly accomplished Federation. But Miles Franklin, whose successful first book *My Brilliant Career* (1901) was encouraged by the *Bulletin* and supplied with a brief preface by Henry Lawson, is pre-eminently a novelist of the paddock and stockyard variety, such as Hay condemned. For the next fifty years her novels preached, and sometimes ranted, the same unrelieved passionate nationalism. Like so many of the nationalist school she was muddled in her thinking but fierce in her loyalties, ardently committed to the distinctively Australian (which meant the rural landscape in both its aspects, the idyllic and the defeated; the simple decencies of bushmen, who also supplied her with examples of absurd and occasionally offensive behaviour) and vituperative about anything servile, anything less than manly, anything that revealed the 'cultural cringe'. Like the nationalists she claimed to be a realist, but for all her avowed anti-romanticism her narrative is heavily romantic in theme and in treatment. She shrilly insists on her independence of convention, and on her determination to accomplish something 'on her own hook'; yet her earlier work succeeds where it draws upon and mocks the novelettish conventions, while the later historical sagas and pioneering chronicles are such a morass of cliché and stereotype as to be almost immediately forgettable. Hers is a fiction which, though aggressively opinionated, does not really know its own mind.

The world of Miles Franklin's novels is essentially the world of the pioneers, the veteran land owners, rather than Lawson's straggling bushmen. Although she trumpeted the egalitarianism of the nationalist creed she was, in fact, preoccupied with lineage, with the inter-connections of the leading old families in a district—with, quite frankly, a better class of people. It is not a conscious snobbery, but she gives only scant or comic attention to the selectors, station-hands and townspeople. Her serious characters are esteemed in terms of their attachment to station life, and the moral worth of a family is reflected in its homestead and property. The older generation is invested with the elevated status of ancestor figures. History attaches to them, for they are its creators as well as products of it; and Miles Franklin's pride in the accomplishments of the past, rather than confident anticipation of the future, is the true, if sentimental orientation of her nationalism.

Her values, that is, are curiously external and her characters no more than a set of attitudes—with the exception of the young heroines in her fiction, whose closet uncertainties and anxieties tend to repeat themselves from novel to novel. The emotional confusion of Franklin's writing in this respect is intriguing. Her fiction is essentially adolescent and romantic in its incomplete perceptions of the emotions, and shows little development to emotional maturity, little wisdom about feelings. She is strident, and precocious, about 'the sex question', and early saw through the pretty myth of love to the imposed inferiority of women. Yet with her outbursts against 'the atrocities which appear to be a normal risk of marriage', and so on, she does not face up to the full implications of her fascination with, and revulsion from, sexual encounter.

My Brilliant Career, the fictitious autobiography of Sybylla Melvyn, created a local sensation when it appeared, and is certainly the freshest and most memorable of her many books. Its portrait of the touchy uncertainties of an adolescent country girl carries some conviction. Sybylla is self-conscious, matter-of-fact, egotistical; she is subdued and she is aggravating, brash and apprehensive. There is liveliness and wit in her presentation. Yet she has more than a touch of unpleasantness in her nature, and eventually she ceases to be attractive to the reader, and becomes tiresome. Her changeability makes us impatient with her, while her insistence on fun, no end of fun and merriment, is mere adolescent noisiness. As Havelock Ellis commented in a review article shortly after the novel's publication,

> Something more than emotion is needed to make fine literature; and here we miss any genuine instinct of art or any mature power of thought, and are left at the end only with a painful sense of crudity. Miles Franklin is ardently devoted to Australia, but to a remote ideal Australia ...[26]

More than anything else, her enthusiasms and her tirades seem mindless, her passionate convictions are without a rationally coherent basis, and there is considerable doubt about the book's emotional coherence.

In the introduction, Sybylla announces that her autobiography is neither a romance nor a novel, but 'a *real* yarn', without a plot because life itself has no plot. Her initial literary formulae anticipate Furphy's more elaborate practice. Yet nearly all the propositions of the introduction are defeated by the novel itself, for it is both a romance and a novel (Franklin referred to it in both terms) and it does follow a rudimentary plot. Even the advice that there will be no such trash as descriptions of beautiful sunsets is directly contradicted by the novel's sentimentally self-indulgent final paragraph. The narrator, that is, is unreliable. The problem of what to believe and what not to believe is compounded by *My Career Goes Bung: Purporting to be the Autobiography of Sybylla Penelope Melvyn* (written immediately after *My Brilliant Career*, but not published until 1946), which presents the 'true' autobiography of Sybylla. It acknowledges that Sybylla's book (*My Brilliant Career*) was a new style of autobiography, a spoof autobiography written in deliberate reaction to the orthodox style; the difficulty is to determine how far the second autobiography is also in the new style—that is, how far it too is intended to be a sardonic reply to the literary and social conventions, and how seriously its theory of egotism is to be entertained.

Both books offer an account of Sybylla's experiences and behaviour; with the peculiar flatness of the dialogue and of much of the narrative approach (despite the sparks of exaggeration) they tend to offer a report of events rather than an interpretation of character. Sybylla is too wholly egocentric to be a memorialist, too assertively individual; there is no doubt that she alone is the focus and the *raison d'être* of these memoirs.

After several years as a freelance journalist in Sydney, Miles Franklin went overseas, first to the United States and then with the outbreak of World War I to England, and apart from occasional brief visits remained abroad for nearly thirty years. This expatriate experience had only the most trivial impact on her fiction. It did not widen her mental horizons. The one observable benefit was to provide Brent of Bin Bin with a mailing address in the British Museum. Miles Franklin refused to admit that she was Brent of Bin Bin, though there can be no doubt that the six Brent of Bin Bin novels are hers. These were mostly written in the late twenties, but three were not published until the 1950s. Together with the most acclaimed of her pioneering sagas, *All That Swagger* (1936, published over her own name), these affirm her vision of Australia. They range much more broadly than the early work, and while they commemorate the nationalist sentiments of the nineties, they are at the same time limited by that loyalty to an earlier set of attitudes. Franklin's creative imagination did not respond to later times, and although she attempted to write of the 1930s, the result is stilted and ineffectual. Her chronicles of the Pooles and the Mazeres and the Delacys are more satisfactory when they escape into the sentimental past, and when her romantic enthusiasm can turn itself to the heroic elevation of the ancestors and the celebration of landscape.

Her novels, like most of the historical novels of the thirties and forties—by Barnard Eldershaw, Helen Simpson, Brian Penton and Eleanor Dark, for example, each so different from the others—are to a degree realistic in their external details, but romantic at the core, especially in their identification of the heroic qualities of the

Australian spirit as embodied in the landscape. They are all more responsive to landscape than to character, and to the typical rather than the distinctive. They cater to the insistent hunger for detail that is so prominent a feature of Australian cultural statements, and encourage the assumption that Australia *is* its landscape.

That notion was passionately advanced by writers for the next thirty years, and is still persistent. Yet its eventual sterility, recognised by all the leading Australian novelists, is unwittingly exposed at the end of *All That Swagger*. Despite the aggravation of her occasionally shrill and hectoring language, the suffocation of too many events, or the vagaries of her yarning narrative manner and structure, the most serious check to Miles Franklin's image of Australia is that ultimately it is empty:

> The westering sun . . . retreated to the core of a continent over which as yet man has no dominion. A land of distances, a land dependent upon distances for preservation; a land gorgeously empty and with none of the accumulations of centuries of human occupation; a continent surveyed, fenced, patrolled and policed by the nucleus of a nation analogous to a patriarchal family with unwieldy wealth.[27]

It is not a vision which welcomes man; indeed, man is very nearly excluded from it. Again and again, her lyrical exaltations ignore man. In something like the manner of the colonial poets, she lodges her ideal in a landscape without human evidence or human interest. Spiritual values from such a source are peculiarly detached, either opposite to man as in D. H. Lawrence's astonishingly astute *Kangaroo* (1923), or void, as Patrick White argued in his 1958 article 'The Prodigal Son', in describing the Great Australian Emptiness.

Although Lawrence was in Australia only briefly, *Kangaroo* catches the features and the moods of Australian scenery brilliantly. What he says about Australian life is something of a muddle, half invented, half distorted, yet with glimpses of real discernment; but Lawrence is unrivalled in his response to the landscape, to its brooding mystery and to the suggestion that it partakes of a different order of experience (the 'dark forces'). Where he seems to be observing the details of the bush or the sea-shore, however, or recreating the genial indolence of the Australian worker, and offering a naturalistic statement, his responses are, in fact, all interpretive. Lawrence guesses about Australians—he can hardly claim to know them on the strength of such a brief contact. His true genius shows, instead, in his many intuitions of the landscape, in, for example, his poetically alert response to the bush in the moonlight. Somers, the hero, can find no sign of life among the 'weird, white, dead trees, and . . . the hollow distances of the bush. Nothing!' Yet he perceives that there is nevertheless something, big and aware, and hidden and waiting.

The novel is fractured by that disjunction, between the unapproachable presence which Somers senses from time to time in the 'vast, uninhabited land', and the conviction that in Australia men are hollow, their inside soul withered, their democratic freedoms a terrifying vacancy. Lawrence cannot find a means of mediating between the two. The new social systems which are offered, Kangaroo's fascism and Struthers' communism, both based on an ideal of the bonds of brotherhood, struggle with and defeat each other, while Somers, who maintains the freedom of the uncommitted soul, must leave Australia. Nothing has been changed, nothing accomplished. The *status quo* is preserved. Men without understanding live superficially in a country of still hidden subtleties.

Like Henry Handel Richardson, William Gosse Hay, Miles Franklin and Katharine Susannah Prichard, Norman Lindsay belongs imaginatively to a period, though like them he wrote over a protracted span. An early short story was published in the *Lone Hand* in 1907, and his last novel, *Rooms and Houses*, appeared in 1968 although some of it had been written nearly fifty years earlier. More an artist than a novelist, more an enthusiastic ideas-monger than a thinker, he personally encouraged and directly influenced many of the developing writers of the earlier part of the century. His notions of art and life were rummaged mainly from Rabelais and Nietzsche, and the resulting amalgam is peculiarly his own. In the novels and paintings alike his leading ideas and values are undercut by the rather adolescent attitudes of his characters.

Lindsay's novels delight in scandalizing crimped middle class morality, 'wowserism', and the comic gusto with which that is carried out is still entertaining. But the novels have no enduring substance. The characters are cartoon figures, identified by their eccentricities and idiosyncracies. The world they inhabit is as timeless as the world of P. G. Wodehouse because never set in any time, dated yet without a precise date, comic because arrested. The narrative manner is amusingly over-emphatic, the action exaggerated. As the real world steadily leaves behind the whimsical world of Norman Lindsay, concepts like wowserism have settled into history; his attacks on cheerless moral constraints and hypocrisy now appear less urgent, and more a pleasant but moderate naughtiness with which youth chooses to offend middle age. It may be seen as a comic larrikinism—Lindsay has some touches in common with Stone and C. J. Dennis, as does Miles Franklin in her early fiction. An indication of the nature of Lindsay's artistic temperament is that the one work which has proved to be enduringly appealing is a children's classic, *The Magic Pudding* (1918).

Where Lindsay thought he was interpreting character, he was in fact imposing his Hyperborean ideals upon it. He requires his characters to discover Life; but that amounts to little more than breaking through conservative taboos on sexual behaviour. Provocative and titillating as they might once have been, and however vital to Lindsay, the novels are now only lightweight entertainments. They are mainly fantasies, and have fantasy's freedoms from time and place, although the sensitive burghers of Creswick thought they recognised themselves in *Redheap* (banned as slanderous when published in 1930).

In one thing he may have contributed to Australian fiction. He is free from its obsession with landscape realism and its preoccupation with details of scenery and bush life. *Saturdee* (1934), though set in a country town, is happily independent of the 'authentic Australian' mode. Lindsay was in fiction, as in life, remarkably inattentive to his surroundings. He was driven by ideas about life rather than life itself.

PART THREE: THE TWENTIES AND THIRTIES

Between the wars, Australian fiction for the most part persisted in its obstinately insular ways. While in the twenties and thirties there are signs that some writers were beginning to tire of the nineties ethos, for most of them—the less imaginatively independent—it was a period of consolidating and enhancing the legend of the nineties and imposing the orthodoxy of that version of the Australian experience. This was the era in which Lawson became 'canonized', and Gordon popular again. Mary Gilmore published her *Old Days, Old Ways* in 1934 and *More Recollections* in 1935, and Keith Hancock's formative history, *Australia*, also endorsing the nationalist slant, appeared in 1930. The novels and stories of the period asserted a sentimental reading of the past: the convicts were harshly treated by British justice, and were transported for petty theft, and the old squatters and selectors were resilient, independent men, made of the stuff of heroes but stubbornly anti-heroic in their values. And they unwittingly attempted to straddle competing ideals: the establishment of a family dynasty is allowed to be consistent with the powerful myth of social equality, except in such rare instances as Brian Penton's caustic and aggressive anti-chronicle, *Landtakers* (1934) and its rather indifferent sequel, *Inheritors* (1936). For the most part, the writers of this phase show little response to overseas writing. They had accepted the call for an indigenous literature, but for too many of them the nationalist response was inhibiting because they unquestioningly accepted it—almost as an act of faith—as the main line of an Australian tradition, and failed to work out their own approach. They confused the quite proper determination to be ourselves, with the determination to see ourselves as unique, different. In writing what they assured themselves was the real Australia they, in fact, identified a colourful but limited aspect of the full range of possible Australian experience; and their gauge of literary value had more to do with feelings than with artistry. It is a persistent vein in Australian fiction; Frank Dalby Davison, William Hatfield and the short stories of Katharine Susannah Prichard are early examples, Alan Marshall and Kylie Tennant later, and more recently Xavier Herbert. It is also the popular writer's approach, from Ion Idriess to D'Arcy Niland and, in recent times, Colleen McCullough.

For a few writers, however, the retrospective manner, endemic among the nationalists, proved intolerable as an approach to fiction. Katharine Susannah Prichard and Vance Palmer at their best both avoid the nostalgic drift of their less accomplished contemporaries. If a different kind of sentimentalism is at the heart of their work, political and moral, they at least focus on a life directly in front of them, and begin to assess the psychology of character. Lawrence had shown both in *Kangaroo* and in *The Boy in the Bush* (1924), which he wrote with Molly Skinner (or rather, whose manuscript he revised and altered), that a productive tension could be set up between character and landscape, even though he failed to achieve a usable resolution to it. Havelock Ellis published a brief novel, *Kanga Creek: An Australian Idyll*, in 1922. Written in the mid-eighties in the manner of Olive Schreiner and with much the same half-dreaming passionate fancy, it is meticulous about external detail, but much more centrally directed to mood, impression, awakening emotional (and specifically sexual) consciousness. The setting does not affirm its own independent reality. It exists only to correspond to the anonymous young man's dawning rapturous perceptions of his inner being. The landscape is not idealized, but in its gentle translucence reflects his idealisms. Chester Cobb left Australia as a young man, and wrote only two novels, *Mr. Moffatt* (1925) and *Days of Disillusion* (1926) but he, too, is interested in the inner world, the world of the consciousness of a character. Though his was a much slighter talent, he anticipates Christina Stead in adapting the stream of consciousness technique, and handles the alteration between interior monologue and external observation quite confidently.

Frederic Manning's *Her Privates We* (published in 1929 as *The Middle Parts of Fortune: Somme and Ancre*, by 'Private 19022', and published in an abridged edition in 1930 as *Her Privates We*) is another of the novels which break from the preoccupation with the distinctively Australian. Admired at once by such distinguished writers as Arnold Bennett, Edmund Blunden and T. E. Lawrence, its account of the Somme offensive in World War I is controlled, observant and reflective, and shows an impressive literary intelligence. While it does not avoid describing the fighting, and the horrors of trench warfare, it is more concerned with the common soldier's attitude to it and his response to what he cannot comprehend. The exhaustion of the men, the creeping moral numbness, their persistent loyalty to their fellows (in the unnatural circumstances of war, 'good comradeship takes the place of friendship ... its opportunity is greater'), these are the substance of Private Bourne's perceptions and reflections. He is a thoughtful, not unduly sensitive man, whose internal meditations and annotations deepen to questions of moral philosophy and psychology. The title, and the Shakespearian quotations at the head of each chapter, indicate that Manning proposed to write more than a mere narrative, and aspired to touch the more profound, human significance of the war experience. In a prefatory note, he wrote:

> War is waged by men; not by beasts or by gods. It is a peculiarly human activity. To call it a crime against mankind is to miss at least half its significance; it is also the punishment of a crime. That raises a moral question ...[28]

Manning handles his theme sensitively and seriously. He understands the nature of the men, laconic or gruff, and admires the preservation of fellow-feeling among them; and he judges the war against the cost to the individual. The circumstances of war are so extraordinary, however, that it cannot comment appropriately on the normal life outside itself. Bourne is a common soldier from the ranks, and we know the man only in that context. *Her Privates We* may be an admirable war book, but that eventually limits the range of its human testament.

It is clearly a finer work than Leonard Mann's war novel, *Flesh in Armour* (1932), which suffers from uneven writing and awkward super-impositions of national assertiveness, characteristic of much of the fiction of the period. This novel is constructed somewhat as a series of protracted sketches, discrete sections of narrative linked by the continuing but contrived fiction of the sensitive ex-teacher, Frank Jeffreys. The narration has nice touches of humour, but it is at other moments remarkably stodgy, especially where Mann attempts to say too much at once. In prosy passages of narrative commentary, when, like Mrs. Praed, he seems determined to prove to the British that Australians are not spiritually be-nighted—and proves instead that they are culturally gawky—Mann offers perceptions which the fiction fails to demonstrate. And he is disconcertingly indifferent to the fracturing of his imaginative vision when, in the midst of his account of individual aggravations and miseries, and the dreadful waste of spirit as well as loss of life, he obtrudes a jaunty pride in the A.I.F. ('The Australians—the Australians... They should all be one—one corps, one and indivisible in body as they were in spirit. Were the Tommies afraid of the new nations?').[29] He proposes that the war had shown that the Australians were a people, yet 'the life of this generation was finished', and the novel is effectively about defeat, and wasteful rather than productive sacrifice. The critical problem he poses, then, is not about the strength or the consistency of his sense of national identity, but about narrative tact, and sensitivity to balance and form.

Angela Thirkell's *Trooper to the Southern Cross* (by 'Leslie Parker', 1934) is a much better work, and much more completely than Mann's a novel about being Australian. It is a splendidly sustained satire, accurate and witty both in the manner of its delivery and the values which it exposes. Thirkell's strategy is to rely on a narrator who is a complacent but crashing bore. Major Tom Bowen's account of what happens on a troop-ship returning to Australia is in the meandering, yarning fashion of Furphy's anecdotalists, and with even less immediate point. But Tom, whose conscious pose is as the memorialist of a rather ordinary sequence of events, is unwittingly his own biographer; and with his selfishness and inconsistency, his naivety and bigotry, his ignorance and his assumptions, he provides the means and the occasion for a satirical essay upon the Australian character. For Tom completely and uncritically identifies himself with his countrymen, and submerges his individual self in the commonplace of the collective identity. With him, *aut Australia aut nihil.*

The leading comic device is that Tom has no sense of perspective, indicated in the rhetorical incompetence and the recognizably authentic flat monotone of his narration ('I am quite a religious man myself in my quiet way, having thought very deeply on some subjects ...') and in the kinds of judgment he makes, or is unable to make. But Tom is not entirely a figure of farce. Angela Thirkell allows him a sense of humour that is in keeping with his own concept of himself, and he adheres to his sense of propriety most of the time. It is in the inadequacy of his thinking that he is such a joke. Yet even in this she makes concessions. When he looks at the Suez Canal in the moonlight, and is reminded of some lines of Tennyson he once read and cannot remember, she permits Tom a momentary perception of something more than mundane, even if he is reduced to the mundane in his attempt to express it.

Angela Thirkell's satirical approach is both comic and devastating. She does not adopt the conventional tactic of attacking values and attitudes through personal ridicule. The diggers exist in the mass, and her whole attention is on their attitudes. It is their behaviour which draws her attack, Tom's unshakeable belief in the superiority of the species. The general tendency in the Australian novel, almost without exception in those with the satirical itch, and even among the more gifted satirical writers, such as Patrick White, Thomas Keneally and Thea Astley, is to concentrate the attack on individual figures. The effect is inevitably towards the distortion of caricature; for example, one of Keneally's best satirical figures, that doughty man and pompous bishop-elect, Costello (in *Three Cheers for the Paraclete*) is thoroughly and wholly an object of satire and so, in spite of our enjoyment of Keneally's handling of him, only a fictional contrivance. Satire, like comedy, operates at a distance. Angela Thirkell narrows that distance because it is difficult to decide at any moment in what way attitudes have been distorted, if at all.

The varying accomplishments of Ellis, Manning, Thirkell and the like were scarcely recognized. Their work was extraneous to what had become regarded as the first requirement for an Australian literature—to depict the national life. The mood of the period was strongly conformist; anything extravagant, or experimental, or exceptional, was resisted. It is this purposive local patriotism, as much as any proposition of a cultural cringe, that explains the resistance to innovation in Australian fiction. The sentiments and the fictional forms of the nineties lived on, but with an important change. For where that social and moral ideology had an essentially political cast, the new phase in fiction was, at its core, romantic. It discovered that its subject was not life on the land, but the relation between character and the land. It discovered, as poetry and painting had, that the source of the Australian identity, or national life, was *in* the land itself. In the late twenties and the thirties, the romantic concept of the spirit of place took firm root. It was the whole platform of the Jindyworobak movement; and it is still a potent factor in Australian cultural statement—in the recent resurgence of Australian film, for example.

The two dominant writers of the period, Vance Palmer and Katharine Susannah Prichard, accepted the romantic mystique of place. They were both dedicated writers, more fervent than professional, with strong loyalties to craft and country. Both were directly influenced by the writers of the nineties, both nurtured a sense of mission, and with their protracted literary careers they both tend to loom rather larger in the accomplishment of Australian literature than their talent really warrants. Indeed, Australian literature has been over-freighted with grand old men and dames of literature—apart from Vance and Nettie Palmer and Katharine Susannah Prichard, one recalls Mary Gilmore, Walter Murdoch, Hugh McCrae, Norman Lindsay, Miles Franklin and Frank Dalby Davison—and one wonders whether such a persistent weight of seniority has affected the character as well as the nature of literary development here.

Vance Palmer was the compleat man of letters. Essayist, editor, critic and commentator, novelist, poet, short story writer and playwright, he took as active a part in promoting Australian literature as he did in writing it. With his wife Nettie, he maintained an extensive correspondence with many of the recognized and budding writers of the day, Nettie most often writing the letters and offering precise encouraging criticism, but Vance very much a presence in the background, as proposing the standards by which an authentic Australian literature was to come into its own. Throughout his long career he argued a coherent and carefully reasoned case for nationalism in literature. As early as 1905 he had identified the principles he was to maintain. Art interprets life, and literature in Australia, if it is to become accomplished literature, must express Australia:

> Art is really man's interpretation of the inner life of his surroundings, and until the Australian writer can attune his ear to catch the various undertones of our national life, our art must be false and un-enduring.[30]

In essays and broadcasts as well as in his fiction he attempted to define and refine a new style of national feeling, and to interpret the inner reality of Australian life. But like so many of his generation Palmer had a defective ear. He located the national life in the country—'we are a bush people'—and was unable to free himself from a preconceived notion of what image of itself Australia should project.

For all his literary activity, the measure of his achievement is not unfairly summed up in the remark that he is a representative writer of his time. There is nothing exceptional in his writing; in everything he did is a factor of restraint, even of diffidence A habitual politeness of manner as well as a distrust of rhetoric prevented him from making his most persuasive case. His appeal was to unimpassioned good sense, advanced so steadily as to become in fact aggravating. His novels in particular lack both variety and spontaneity. They move smoothly to their appointed ends, and resolve the characters' moral and spiritual crises in accordance with a clearly predicated set of values. But they lack the sense of life itself. They rehearse ideas about life, and the characters are subordinated to those ideas. Palmer's imposed reading of character inhibits his fiction, for like so many of the novelists of the period, he too patently manoeuvres his figures to demonstrate a theory. He is not entirely doctrinaire. He understands his characters' emotions, and he seems to recognize what feelings are suitable to the occasion. But that is a far cry from the quickening leap of the imagination, or the intuitive recognition of the core of a character's inner life.

Palmer's cautiousness about feelings can be detected in the habitual narrative manner of his novels. Characters circle uneasily about each other, unwilling to commit themselves to the relationships which the story requires. In *The Man Hamilton* (1929), for example, the central situation is a love affair. But Palmer is never comfortable with romantic relationships; his is essentially a world of men, and Hamilton surrenders his chance of happiness to a sterner duty, and does the decent, manly thing. The sentiment is no doubt admirable, but Palmer's approval of the rigid, unrelaxing will is disturbing. It is a novel about solitariness, for all the characters draw attention to their separation from each other—man from wife, parent from son, brother from brother. Even the lovers know very little about one another, and they do not appear to talk much. It is not Palmer's version of 'The Wandering Islands', in which the condition of life is that men and women do not come together, but live in inevitable isolation; rather (and characteristically) it is a novel full of the great unsaid. Even within the individual, the emotional self is only guessed at, and the author, who does the characters' feeling for them, and asserts what he fails to depict, can manage little better than an approximation to their inner life: 'Nina had a feeling that . . .', 'He had the air of a man who . . .', 'the indefinable look of', 'the girl looked intimate and comprehensible'. That mode of expression demonstrates the critical deficiency of Vance Palmer's imagination. In these novels, an emotion or a feeling is something a character *has*, it is not a state he expresses. Nina has a feeling, she does not feel. The effect is of uncertain judgment on the author's part.

Palmer's fiction is limited in another way. In depicting the world of men (the indicative title of his first volume of short stories), he celebrates the masculine virtues—fortitude, strength of will and purposefulness, leadership and restraint, physical dominance, and so on. But that perspective imposes particular restrictions on the range and meaning of the experiences he depicts. Hamilton holds a view that indicates the nature of this limitation: 'he felt a girl was different from a man, not so near the earth'. The terms are revealing. It is man's special privilege to be close to the earth, to live and work in harmony with the natural forces, and to find fulfilment in knowing he belongs to a place; women find their fulfilment in man. 'He gave her a sense of her own permanence, satisfied an instinct deeper than affection', Clem McNair concludes at the end of *The Passage* (1930). The debased Miltonic arrangement of the relationship between the sexes was too commonly approved by novelists between the wars, and inroads against this and other sedimentary cultural notions were made only slowly, with the emergence of novelists of real social intelligence, such as Martin Boyd and Christina Stead. Few local writers managed to depict relationships adequately, especially relationships between men and women, and few were able to offer a balanced portrait of society.

The inadequacies of Palmer's early fiction show that he was not entirely free from popular influence. The stiffness of his characters and the awkwardness with romantic encounter strongly resembles the pulp fiction that was beginning to burden municipal library shelves; and although he wrote carefully his material is mostly conventional fare. And as station life was becoming an increasingly distant experience, and the urban life of Australia pressed for recognition, Palmer found himself increasingly defending the old bush code—both because he was a traditionalist, and wished to preserve continuity with what he had identified as the authentic Australian experience, and because he was unable to establish imaginative contact with the cities. His most fertile years were those at Caloundra, in Queensland, after he and Nettie left Melbourne, and withdrew from the active attempt to form a national literary movement (his work with Louis Esson and the Pioneer Players had not resulted in anything like the Abbey Theatre, for example). Here he wrote the books that established his reputation, and began his planning of the Golconda trilogy.

The Passage, which is set on the Queensland coast, obviously draws on what was immediately in front of Palmer and is probably his most well received novel. It is somewhat idealised in arguing the case for the fulfilment available to man when he lives in close relation to his landscape, close to 'the earth'. But his recreation of a pattern of life is substantial. While Palmer is familiar with the landscape of his other novels, and at ease in evoking it, here his selection of detail is less obviously managed, the description more confident. The brief surf-fishing scene in *Seedtime* (1957) also carries a fuller imaginative conviction than is usual in Palmer, and is so much more completely realized than his inland material, that one suspects the coastal life is his true but unrecognized subject. *The Passage* strives too hard to make its point, though, and characters are simplified to suit that design. It is a novel in which little really happens; the external life is undramatic and the inner life is suppressed, for Palmer's inveterate habit is to summarize reflections as well as conversations, and so to pre-empt the characters' possibilities for animation. Where he is best is in the subsidiary details, the arrangement of recurrent images and the peripheral features of setting or supporting dialogue. Acceptance of the novel's argument has to rest on a sentimental conviction, for its imaginative focus is blurred.

Palmer was always disappointed with the reception of his novels, and despite the effort he put into the Golconda trilogy, his literary career closed with that same sense of expectation not quite realized. It is uneasily a chronicle and an individual history, a study in the shifting political fortunes of Macy Donovan, and a record of the loss of the old nineties idealism. In the first volume, *Golconda* (1948), Palmer not infrequently loses sight of Donovan; secondary plots of varying interest are started here and there, artificial climaxes are engineered, and the book reads almost as though intended for radio serialisation. Donovan is a presumptuous, slightly disagreeable individual, for although he is energetic and well thought of by the workers, he is sullen at the core, a lone wolf (Palmer's over-emphatic image) content to go with the crowd but keeping essentially to himself. He has no mate, and has never wanted one—his social loyalties are patently separate from the old ethos. The animal vigour that Palmer ascribes to him is not readily evident, and one fails to see the seeds of greatness in Donovan, or the makings of a future premier of Queensland. (Nor is Palmer given to satirical structures.)

Donovan follows no plan of life. Rather, opportunity is offered to him, and something like a concept of *mana* appears to operate at times ('Power was flowing back to him'), though at other times Palmer returns more explicitly to his notion of the spiritual resources of place—when, for example, Donovan returns for the election to Golconda, his political and spiritual base. He is not in charge of his destiny, though, and seems too naive a man, and too limited both in temperament and experience to achieve high political office. Equally Donovan is bewildered by his personal life; in neither the public nor the private realm is Palmer able to make him an exceptional character. He has failed to meet his own early requirement, that it is the business of the writer to create interest in the life around him.

The memorable accomplishments of the trilogy once again lie not in the large structure but in the incidentals—in small sequences such as Hugh McCoy fishing, or lesser characters such as old Christy Baughan, survivor of Lane's expedition to Paraguay. He is more at ease with the tangential comment, and the fragments of sub-plot, than with the elaborately planned main action. His instinct for the revealing aside, and the brief character study, as well as a certain staleness that develops from the languishing extent of his novels, all signal that his forte is the short story. Palmer's lyricism, his preference for the revealing significant experience, and the natural reach of his imagination are more happily accommodated in the modest limits of the short story. That form itself, rather than imposed narrative structures, provides the controls he needed. Yet even in the short stories recurrent weaknesses surface—unfortunate switches in point of view, occasional inappropriate idiom, signs of over-emphasis. He is not particularly successful when he adopts the *Bulletin* anecdotal manner ('Travelling') or the staple short story pattern up to the mid-century, the bush story with a serious ending. The best of his stories are those of adolescence or late childhood, where he is sensitive both to the mood that attaches to the child's outlook on experience, and to the apprehensive doubts which follow from an incomplete understanding of the meaning of an experience. In these stories of the edge of innocence Palmer taps the concealed potency of images—the Honey Man in 'The Rainbow Bird' startles just by being named, and the axe in the stump in 'The Foal' sets up troubling, sub-conscious reverberations. The best of his work reduces to a bare handful of stories, for though he was a conscientious writer he had very little freshness or vigour of insight. With his earnest championing of nationalist sentiment he won respect for his essays on Australian literature and culture, but that earnestness was imaginatively blighting in his fiction.

Where Palmer had doggedly to create his career, and start as many other Australian writers did by publishing, however modestly, in England, Katharine Susannah Prichard began much more successfully, with something of the same éclat as Miles Franklin. In 1915, when Palmer brought out his first volume of short stories, and another of poetry, Prichard won the Australian section of a Dominion fiction competition with her first novel, *The Pioneers*. It was yet another historical romance following the usual pattern, and not very distinguished. The flatness of this slackwater phase of Australian fiction was interrupted, apart from D. H. Lawrence's *Kangaroo*, only by Katharine Susannah Prichard's *Working Bullocks* in 1926, followed shortly by *Coonardoo* in 1929.

Prichard's best work belongs to the twenties. Throughout that decade she maintained her vitality and enthusiasm, and her pre-occupation with the spiritual potency of the landscape had not faltered into the imaginatively abrading ideological set pieces of her subsequent fiction. It is the period of her best plays (*Brumby Innes*) and most widely regarded short stories ('The Cooboo', 'The Grey Horse'). Here her passionate intensities were suitably directed into the narrative, her admiration or indignation embodied in the imaginative design of the fiction.

Though different in temperament and manner, she shared Palmer's view of the function of the writer in Australia, and identified her mission in national terms:

> My work has been, chiefly, I think, knowing the Australian people and interpreting them to themselves ... I wanted to bring a realization of the beauty and vigour of our life to Australian literature.[31]

The interpretation was often enough ideological, but the vigour of Australian life was identified as deriving from the earth. That is, Katharine Susannah Prichard draws on two sources, the theoretical and the intuitive. With her commitment to Communism, she made the mistake of pronouncing through her characters a necessary programme of reform. Her admiration for the Australian way of life conflicts with what she saw as the need for political and social correctives. Her writing is more vigorous and colourful when she responds directly to life, and acknowledges the deep bond that can exist between man and his setting. As early as *Black Opal* (1921) she had asserted the need to 'keep close to the earth', and to stay 'in tune with the fundamentals', yet despite her care in presenting a thoroughly detailed study of Australian life, her image of the real, with its celebration of the life force and the mystique of place, is highly romantic.

Working Bullocks is the first memorable Australian novel to offer a strong, simple patterning, with its structure based on poetic rhythms and the fusion of character with symbol. Few novelists have subsequently managed to draw as directly and impressively on the sense of the elemental. Randolph Stow, who was later to adopt much the same procedure, transmutes the real into the symbolic, whereas Prichard asserts the poetic in life. Stow is inclined to be precious, Prichard is closely attached to the real.

In its depiction of the instinctual life, the response of characters to deep forces they barely recognize, and the evocation of setting, *Working Bullocks* has been regarded as imitative of D. H. Lawrence. But Prichard's primitivism is of a different kind, less emphatically sexual in its orientation. It appears to owe more to Thomas Hardy than to Lawrence; its affinities are with Lawrence in expression, Hardy in spirit. Red Burke is 'a man like one of his bullocks, rooted in deep natural instincts, powerful and intent, with a capacity for dumb and obstinate endurance', while Deb's life is governed by a powerful intimation of the natural life around her: the trees 'had that way of making her like themselves when she was among them'. It is unfortunate that Prichard feels the need to explain her effect. The characters plausibly merge with their setting, and know their relation to the life around them. The images of growth and fertility are proper to this setting, and the irresistible laws of life apply to both tree and man. Yet for all the potent poetic texture of Prichard's representation of the world of the timber-workers, her novel rests on a basis of imprecise emotion. The life style of the timber-workers is both admired and criticised, for these are men obedient to the natural forces, yet unaware of or indifferent to the rights due to them. Sentimentally, Prichard is warm to the old ways. Timber felling and carrying is an age-old, sanctioned industry, in harmony with the laws of the forest. But the new age of the mills and machinery is emerging, and with them Prichard's political passions intrude into the novel. Both language and perspective change when she summarizes the 'evangel of the right of the workers'. Her political commentary provides a set of terms to criticize the values of the Karri people, and so to suggest the limitation to the kind of happiness possible to Red and Deb. Their final choice of life however is made in the only terms available to them, and her foreshadowing of inevitable social change offends our sense of the novel's imaginative design.

Coonardoo is also innovative, for it is one of the first extended studies of an aborigine, and its setting was comparatively new to Australian fiction. The harsh, arid lands of the interior had still to be imaginatively discovered. (Minor writers like Ernest Favenc had made some excursions into that territory, and E. L. Grant Watson had attempted to express the spiritual mystery of the desert. In the next decade, most famously with *Capricornia*, writers were freely availing themselves of it.) In *Coonardoo*, Prichard's inclination to simplify limits the possibilities of development in character while it permits a heightening of the structural pattern. The relationship that exists between the individual and the landscape is altered: instead of the individual suffering when he leaves the place, the cattle station Wytaliba is cursed with bad seasons because Coonardoo's spirit is withdrawn from it. The landscape becomes Hugh Watt's waste land once he banishes Coonardoo from his property, but Prichard is unable to define Coonardoo's personal relationship to it because she has been unable to create a clear sense of Coonardoo herself. She assumes, or summarizes, the inner life of her characters; she fails to project it. Coonardoo remains a figure rather than a character, beyond the range of Prichard's knowledge though not beyond her sympathy, and seen most clearly when seen externally.

In both novels Prichard reveals somewhat masculine aspirations. Mrs. Watt is known to the Aboriginals as Mumae, father; while Mrs. Colburn, mother of eighteen, is admired for the youthful virility of her face. Prichard does not handle women's roles easily. Coonardoo is more convincing as a stockman than as the fertility spirit of the local landscape. The female principle moves most comfortably when most amorphously in the world of men. Yet, with one exception, this disposition does not rise to the surface as a particular proposition about the relations between men and women. Katharine Susannah Prichard writes according to the compulsion of her feelings rather than by the clear discoveries of the mind.

The one exception is *Intimate Strangers* (1937), a novel in which Prichard turned her attention to the pressures and frustrations of suburban living. In her only sustained attempt at psychological realism, she candidly expresses the difficulties of married life, and traces the tensions that build towards an inevitable crisis—but then the novel's imaginative design is betrayed, its emotional logic denied by an implausible reconciliation, perhaps because the fiction coincided too narrowly with her own life. She did not write so exacting an analysis of character again, but retreated, as did so many writers of her generation, to the convenient formulae of historical romance and the safe sentiments of bush realism and social idealism.

Intimate Strangers is flawed in its expression as in its structure. Like Palmer, Prichard can never lift herself entirely clear of the manner and matter of popular or magazine fiction. Yet it provides a key to the pattern of Australian fiction in the thirties. This was a decade which took up ideas, and delighted in applying its discovery of theories. The fiction of the period entertains propositions about social and economic reform, or it advances notions of national feeling, or criticizes it; it reconsiders history, worries about politics and investigates what it understands of psychology. The common factor is the regard for source ideas. P. R. Stephensen stressed the point in his essay 'The Foundations of Culture in Australia' (1935), when he wrote:

> Nothing is permanent in a nation except its culture—its ideas of permanence, which are expressed in art, literature, religion, philosophy; ideas which transcend modernism and ephemerality, ideas which survive political, social, and economic changes.[32]

Writers in this period commonly identify their characters by what they stand for; and they earnestly insist that their characters know what they stand for. There is some ingenuousness in that, because the enthusiasm for issues too often displaces the human actualities of experience. It was the age of the novel of ideas, and in various guises that impetus can be recognised in Australia too.

Very little of this fiction impresses, usually because the ideas are not suitably integrated into the fabric of the narrative. Frank Dalby Davison, for example, wrote a number of short stories in the Palmer manner, outwardly relaxed; but the control which ought to have emerged from within the shaping of the experience is, instead, asserted in the narration. Davison is a clumsy stylist, tending to exposition, long wordy sentences and an unnatural level of idiom:

> It is possible that the root of the trouble on these occasions was deeper than either of the participants suspected; that it had less to do with the ostensible cause of dispute than with the inherent capacity of the sexes for disappointing each other.[33]

His irony gets lost in that. The two novels for which he is popularly known, *Man-Shy* (1931), and *Dusty* (1946), are similarly uneasy in their conception. These animal stories operate too much inside a human frame of reference to be read as natural history, and they are too sentimental to be a satisfactory representation of the human will to freedom. *Dusty*, for example, pales as a statement of the conflict between heredity and environment when compared with say Jack London's *Call of the Wild*. In his last, massive novel,

The White Thorntree, published in 1968 but a cenotaph to thirties attitudes, Davison's dogged pursuit of 'sex-complexes and unnatural repressions' is so exhaustive as to allow insight into only the sexual nature of his characters. It is not a psychological novel, but an engrossed documentary. His procedure is to expound, not reveal behaviour; it is all applied theory, and fact, and the sense of life eludes him.

The most stimulating novels of the period have a psychological interest. Katharine Susannah Prichard never wrote so directly of the individual as in the first phase of *Intimate Strangers*, when she attended to the reality of her characters and examined the forces at work in their inner life. When she lost her grip on the novel, she reverted to her more customary allegiance to social realism. Eleanor Dark, in her early novels *Prelude to Christopher* (1934) and *Return to Coolami* (1936), and Kenneth Mackenzie are alike in their sensitive and intelligent portrait of the interplay between emotion and thought, and reach deeper into the core of character than those of their contemporaries committed to the increasing barrenness of social realism. Dark writes best when she narrows her focus, and concentrates on the subtle adjustments of personal response, both internal and manifest, that characters make to one another. The broad sweep of her *The Timeless Land* trilogy, with its romantic contrast of pre-historical and historical origins, suits neither her technique nor her imaginative intelligence. But in her early novels particularly she displays remarkable narrative skills. *Prelude to Christopher*, for example, anticipates the method of composite recollection used in Patrick White's *The Eye of the Storm*. A critically injured central figure recalls fragments of his past at different levels of consciousness, and other characters also contribute their memories. The past is gradually reassembled for the reader, and in the process the nature of the relationship between characters is clarified. The transference of the narrative centre from one character to another is smoothly managed. Like White, though more modestly, she supplies a framework of literary reference. Yet it is also a novel of ideas, with an interest in genetic determination, sexual freedom, madness and morality. Dark does not labour the topical issue of the morality of eugenic experimentation; the novel requires her instead to emphasize the rational scientific mind taken with an idea. The weakness of this otherwise intelligently balanced novel is some slight theatricality of effect. Brief touches of romantic excess recur throughout Dark's fiction. A later novel,

The Little Company (1945) is also a novel of ideas, but as it were self-consciously, for in following the protagonist's increasing involvement with ideas, doctrines and movements, Dark provides a compressed intellectual history of the thirties and the early war years.

In his first novel, *The Young Desire It* (1937), Kenneth Mackenzie—who published his novels over the name Seaforth Mackenzie—showed a lightness of touch and a sensitivity to shades of feeling that he was unable to reproduce in his later work. The strange languorous unreality of his narrative manner, which in the subsequent novels becomes irritating, is here appropriate to the depiction of an adolescent's wakening into self-consciousness. The drifting phases of feeling plausibly express the stages of the boy's discovery of beauty and sexual awareness, his troubled innocence of the schoolmaster's attentions to him, or his recognition of his mother's possessiveness: he is, as his tutor says, a boy who understands more than he knows. The evanescence of this brief season of his life is confirmed in the novel's end; he learns that love's great happiness entails sadness.

Very little happens: even in *Dead Men Rising* (1951), an account of an uprising in a prisoner-of-war camp the sensational possibilities of the prison escape are only briefly indulged. Mackenzie is not a novelist of incident. *The Young Desire It* is an introspective novel, quiet despite the intensity of private feeling, and responsive to changes of mood. The accomplishment of the novel is peculiarly disturbed in one particular however. A school-friend, Mawley, begins to appear in the narrative, and his old notebooks are alluded to from time to time as confirming some detail of Richard's behaviour or appearance. The novel, it seems, has a concealed narrator and a concealed temporal distance. The events appear to take place close to the narrative present, but the references to Mawley indicate that they must belong to the past. The novel is, in fact, almost without a sense of time, not because it imitates the notion of the timeless land, but because the intensities of youthful experience ignore it. Randolph Stow, Christopher Koch, and Joan Lindsay in her popular *Picnic at Hanging Rock* (1967) all develop the same perception.

Mackenzie's last novel, *The Refuge* (1954), is less sensitive. In its determination to account for everything, it loses its sense of perspective. Important and insignificant details are given equal weight. The novel is subtitled 'A Confession', but Mackenzie's self-conscious narrator does not quite focus on the centre of the events he relates. His preoccupation with himself is inhibiting, for he is a tedious, earnest, humourless man, and his confessions become rather strenuous self-justification. The novel's failure is not that the narrator is dull and repetitive; but rather, that it does not make clear just what principles the protagonist really holds. And the heroine also remains elusive. None of Mackenzie's women, with the exception of the mother figures, is sufficiently realized. They are objects rather than subjects, known only in part and from the outside. The particular interest of the novel, apart from its revival of the mood and manner of the thirties novel of ideas, is in the invention and handling of the narrator, a figure whose confessional role sets him in the forefront of events, yet whose temperamental detachment removes him to something like the memorialist's stance.

The concentration on the individual's perception of self rather than of life, and the accumulation of internal detail, are at once the signature and the potential weakness of this alternative mode to the customary realistic novel. Christina Stead's fiction emerges from this stream, as does Patrick White's—his first novels are recognizably a product of their age. Martin Boyd's minor fiction can also be identified in this company. But Xavier Herbert's *Capricornia* (1938) is virtually unaccountable in either set of terms. It is *sui generis*, and requires its own frame of reference. It shows a comparable massing of detail, though of external event, and through it he constructs an unabashedly fictitious world, a world 'realler than reality' pieced together from brief sketches of the violence and the loveliness of the land, and of people 'comical, not so bad as mad, as aren't we all?'[34] Moral judgment is not set aside, for Herbert is a fiercely indignant writer, and denounces all those who are heedless of what he called the Australian Ethos. But that indignation, however warranted in itself, is unconvincing in a context of vigorous farce. Herbert obviously delights in large scale comic anarchy, in the unthinking, irresponsible and extravagant behaviour of men, and the earnestness of his social concerns is denied by his celebration of the vital if directionless energies of Capricornia life. He can hardly object to violence when his humour, like so much Australian humour, carries violence at its core.

In the preface to his volume of short stories, *Larger than Life* (1963), Herbert wrote:

What I mean by 'plot' is a contrivance with what purports to be a portrayal of life so as to give the reader a greater sense of satisfaction than the viewing of real life usually does. Truth may be stranger than fiction, but true life is mostly unexciting in description .... Life is really larger than it appears to be ....[35]

The contrivance and the excitation in Herbert's narrative is everywhere apparent. More lively than life-like, he is closer to caricature than realism. He exaggerates and over-stresses, whether in the careless comic violence of his action or a too evident and therefore suspect anti-sentimentalism. His effects are often bizarre, or melodramatic, his rhetoric clumsy, the pathos crudely handled. It is tempting to accept his own valuation of the novel as 'a botch'. Yet all that indiscriminate assertiveness serves to endorse a vision that is larger than the sum of its parts.

Herbert's representation of the real is extraordinary, a vast sardonic travesty. It is a world of stupidity, mindlessness and riot that generates a sense of cosmic misgovernance rather than of human folly and vice. The behaviour of men enthralls him but men are part of a larger pattern. Although they engagingly follow their inclinations, their actions invariably initiate some unforeseen adverse consequence; Herbert is heavy-handed in his irony. Occasions of decency, or pathos, or of individual tragedy are debased, or made insignificant in the larger scale of Herbert's perspective. The gratuitous proliferation of incident and consequence is only secondarily about life in Capricornia. It is rather an energetic representation of Herbert's view of life itself as anomalous and disorderly.

For the authorial presence dominates *Capricornia*. Whether in the unsubtle (even slightly distasteful) naming of characters, the limitation to the kinds of action he permits them, or the summary comment he makes on them, the omniscient narrator intrudes directly into the novel. Herbert is technically a detached author, but in fact never an impassive one. Everywhere he invades the novel, at the one moment maintaining his separation from the events narrated and at the next over-riding the world of his creation in long expository passages on such issues as exploitation of the land and the people. When one of his more sympathetic figures argues for recognition of the Aboriginal, his lines are taken over by the author. When Norman hears the song of the Golden Beetle, Herbert announces the meaning of the experience; Norman is not allowed to discover it for himself. The inner life of the characters is observed only as it is projected in external actions, or by summary authorial assertion. And this external, annotational procedure of characterization, and the authorial perspective, transforms the representation of experience into a comic mode. Because of Herbert's objective narrative stance, the death of Tim O'Cannon on Christmas morning is neither harrowing nor a sentimental indulgence, but another example of ironic fate. The figures in his world are comically simplified and distanced, for their function is only to demonstrate the separation of character and destiny.

The authorial presence counterbalances the representation of a disordered world. Capricornia's moral anarchy and carelessness of life is met by a set of attitudes and convictions brought to the fiction by the author himself, both in his sardonic explanations of the action ('Ket was delighting himself with an illusion') and in his endorsement of the spiritual authority of the land. Herbert is if anything more passionate in this than Palmer and Prichard, and he is also less constrained by specific locality. While his feeling for the landscape of Capricornia cannot be questioned, a fundamental romantic principle is contained within the anti-romanticism of his comic mode. Man's understanding of himself is determined by his relation to nature, and his recognition of nature's contrariety. The turning point of the novel, when Norman comes to accept his mixed ancestry, is also the point at which he first responds fully to the Spirit of the Land. The characteristic comic reversal which immediately follows, with Norman cursing the universe, reflects the defeat of his mood of philosophic contentment by harsh social reality, but does not disturb the novel's vision of what Herbert later called the Ethos Idea, the spiritual reality of the Australian experience.

The success of *Capricornia* becomes the liability of his subsequent fiction. Herbert was unable to repeat its comic boisterousness, or to generate the same combination of emotional impetus and sardonic distance. His autobiography, *Disturbing Element* (1963), reveals a coarseness and vulgarity that betrayed him in *Soldiers' Women* (1961), and lapses of judgment that told against his most recent work, the mammoth *Poor Fellow My Country* (1975). Herbert sadly misjudges the sustaining interest of his narration in this last novel, for while the set pieces of landscape description, or accounts of the more arcane Aboriginal experiences skilfully include a suitable emotional response to the scene, too much of the narration is flat dialogue or prosy exposition. The social anthropology is explained, not dramatized, the thesis of the white man's denial of the spiritual reality of this ancient land too relentlessly insisted on. The book is a vast jeremiad, dedicated to 'my poor destructed country'; the passion of Herbert's convictions fails to sustain his creative energy, and the narrative proceeds only fitfully. The despondency at its core suggests glowering prophetic vision grounded in the thirties, rather than in the observed reality of contemporary Australia. Herbert, one feels, is writing exhaustively into the past. *Capricornia* offered a fictional world of some difference, and originality. In his subsequent fiction Herbert reveals that imaginatively he is, like Frank Dalby Davison, stranded in attitudes, convictions and prejudices that are increasingly dated.

Herbert's fiction is directly an expression of his long experience of the bush. Soon after *Capricornia*, and without any such extensive acquaintance, Sarah Campion wrote a similarly boisterous, antisentimental novel of the bush. *Mo Burdekin* (1941) curiously resembles Herbert's mode of comic anarchy, though on a reduced scale. The Prologue in particular recalls *Capricornia*, both in its narrative energy and in its off-handed acceptance of the bizarre and the violent as the inevitable condition of life. But Campion has a sharper sense of humour than Herbert; she is witty where he has an ingrained, perverse conviction of irony, and there is more playfulness in her perception of the absurd. The story is set in the ancestral past of the end of the nineteenth century, but precludes any sentimental indulgence. Although Mo and Lucy are mates, their example hardly endorses the great code. They are individualists, and wary of the world. Campion's images of society are unflattering, and her characters are comically subordinate to the mischances of fate, yet an optimism is maintained. The subsequent novels of the Mo Burdekin trilogy, *Bonanza* (1942) and *The Pommy Cow* (1944), are less successful, for they increasingly impose the constraints of history on the vigorous imaginative freedoms of her fiction, fettering her responsiveness to the anomalies of the landscape and disrupting her sardonic perception of the bizarre.

Eve Langley displays an even stronger sense of the ludicrous in *The Pea Pickers* (1942). Her self-conscious narrator, Steve, is a girl dressed as a man but not disguised as one, a thorough romantic, besotted with poetry and the picturesque, and yet with a shrewd eye for the ridiculous. Langley's handling of Steve's double standard is the key to the novel's original humour. There are perceptions of the genuinely absurd in human behaviour, both in the observed and the observer, and there is comedy in Steve's inflated poetic determinations, her playfully rapturous rhetoric, defeated by the laconic language such as men do use in Gippsland. She reveals herself while she observes the world around her; the novel is Steve's frustrated love story as well as her revision of the old bush nostalgias in the face of the new social realities. That is, the direction of the narrative is both inwards and outwards, and Langley in some respects anticipates Hal Porter's later fictional strategies, while her use of the participating, remembering narrator also recalls the half-committed stance of the memorialist. The novel is not all a mocking self-parody, for while the real is both guyed and rendered fantastic, the narrative keeps sight of the basic reality. Nor is the romantic impulse just a freak. Despite Steve's ardent hyperbole, the landscape does have its romantic features, and her growing recognition of love is real, and painful, however comical and eccentric it appears to be. The multiple strands of Langley's humour increase our delight, but they also permit an innovative compacting of realism and romanticism, and that combination locates her close to the centre of the emerging Australian tradition. Her distinction is that she was able to exploit the mixture of modes to considerable comic effect. Further, she is unlike the writers of her generation in locating her realism not in the ordinary circumstances of everyday life, but in an attitude to life. We learn very little about pea-picking from Eve Langley, but we are affected by the serious core to the Emily Kimbrough and Cornelia Otis Skinner gaiety of the two sisters' adventures.

The weakness of *The Pea Pickers* is that the imaginative fusion is incomplete, and that the narrative alternately staggers and surges forwards. Langley's elaboration is not constructive, as Furphy's is; it is a joke which vastly amuses her, but it goes on for too long. Her second novel *White Topee* (1954), makes an effort to recapture the jauntiness of the earlier book, but the effort is noticeable. The narrator, Steve, has become relatively comfortably established, and is no longer so comically vulnerable.

PART FOUR: POST-WAR AND MODERN

Langley is a rare, innovative talent in a period when the fiction is remarkably ordinary. Very little prose of the forties is memorable; flatness of narrative manner, sentimental gestures in lieu of clear thinking, and mistaken assumptions about the sufficiency of subject interest were endemic. It is as though the writers had determined on undistinguished fiction. Whether on ideological grounds, or from individual limitation, they eschewed any sense of style. Yet that mediocrity is avoided in writing of a documentary and popular historical kind—in the war books and documentaries of Alan Moorehead, for example, and the later widely praised war histories of Chester Wilmot and Gavin Long, and travelogues of Colin Simpson. There were impressive accomplishments in biography too.

The forties and the fifties are in fiction emphatically the time of journalistic realism, whose dreary, dun-coloured offspring Patrick White was to complain of. It is a fiction which boasts its radical spirit, and claims to preserve intact what it thought of as the Lawson-Furphy tradition. But that radicalism is in fact no more than an affirmation of working class values, and important as that has been in the formation of Australian social patterns, it has not led to the best Australian writing, just as it is not the central truth about Furphy and Lawson as writers of fiction. It is a limited radicalism, cautious about exploring new formal possibilities. It is careful to set down the conditions men lived in, and by, but it avoids coming to grips with character and fails to arrive at a profound sense of life. That is, its realism tends to be of the periphery. Representation of the superficies of life is confused with recreation of the bare actualities, as the indiscriminate use of the fashionable term of commendation, 'stark realism', indicates. The social conscience of this mode is recognizable, but has lost its urgency with the years, and the woodenness of structure and expression, the banality of the writing, is increasingly apparent.

This is particularly true of the short story, which revived in the forties and recovered much of the widespread popular appeal it had held fifty years earlier. The inception in 1941 of *Coast to Coast*, an annual selection of the year's best stories, ratified the new vogue. (It continued to appear each year until 1949, when it devolved into a biennial; and the series lapsed altogether in 1973.) As Nettie Palmer found in reconsidering the short stories of the nineties, so it can be said of the forties that the accomplishments in the short story of the period are legendary but not realized in fact. The names are quickening, but the short stories above the names are disappointing.

The common fault is that in both serious and comic stories, a particular kind of sympathy is not so much generated as expected. For example, both Gavin Casey (*It's Harder for Girls*, 1942) and Alan Marshall (*Tell Us About the Turkey, Jo*, 1946) draw on aprioristic sentiments. Their fiction does not scrutinize the nature and the meaning of the experiences presented; rather, they confirm values and patterns of behaviour, and their chief interest for us is in historical terms. Even Peter Cowan, a more substantial writer, chooses to register emotional flatness. The area of his interest is in characters who are not in contact with each other, or incompletely recognize each other, but his fiction does not always manage to make contact with them either, and dissipates itself in an over-elaboration of circumstantial detail. In his recent stories (*The Tins and Other Stories*, 1973), where he has simplified his manner or expression, exploiting the possibilities of sentence fragments and attempting to generate from that an increased directness of statement, the emotional temperature of his fiction remains low. The limitation of conventionality of insight is widespread, and the deliberately cultivated difference of perspective, the whimsical irony of Ethel Anderson and the playful exaggerations of Dal Stivens, lie remote from the prevailing manner.

Kylie Tennant, a much more facile novelist than Sarah Campion or Eve Langley, endorses the radical sympathies of the period but, determined to be both independent and carefree, writes a sportive, undisciplined narrative of events, and avoids serious engagement with the social issues her novels raise. She claimed to have reached maturity, with Vance Palmer, in the Depression years and she is recognizably a product of the thirties: 'Many of us have had our outlook coloured by the drab times and have probably never lost the attitudes formed at that time'.[36] But temperamentally she is more closely aligned with the next decade, as is evidenced in the kind of sentimentalism underlying her thinking in *Australia: Her Story* (1953), her version of Australian history. Her first novels rely on a forced liveliness of expression, for their imaginative substance is thin and they operate at the level of caricature rather than character. Her later fiction continues in the unruly manner of documentary, and with a corresponding slightness; more earnest, it loses the relative advantage of her interruptive sardonicism. Early and late, her fiction is less than serious, even as comedy. It has the false realism, the factitiousness, of the popular fiction of the period, affirming the amorphous legendry of a working-class (or unemployed) Australia but failing to formulate a co-ordinating vision of its own.

In writing not of life itself, but of a characteristic or representative version of Australian life, Kylie Tennant anticipated in part the theoretical preoccupations of the social realists of the fifties. For Frank Hardy and his Realist Writers coterie in Melbourne, the literature of the inner life was less important than a view of society, and more particularly of the social struggle which shaped man's destiny. Socialist rather than merely social, Hardy, Jack Beasley and others proposed a doctrine of the typical, as distinct from the ordinary or average, in depicting character; but John Morrison and David Martin, the two talented writers from this group, resisted the propagandist intentions of socialist realism and followed their insights into particular characters and situations. Those situations, however, are devised to make a general social comment.

Frank Hardy is altogether too programmatic, and shows little sensitivity to writing. In some respects he is hardly a novelist at all. *Power Without Glory* (1950) is a long-winded, ambitious documentary study of corruption and extortion, clumsy in structure and style, and only partly salvaged by Hardy's moral fervour. His true ear is for anecdote, the pub yarn. In *But the Dead are Many* (1976) which analyses the disappointments and disillusion of a few tired Australian communists, he has experimented with several different stances, including that of the memorialist, in first person narrative (the blemished and ideal selves of John Morel and his alter ego and biographer Jack, together with an intrusive author who steps between John Morel and the reader from time to time), but forces his novel to imitate the structure of a fugue. The supervising pattern is so tight that the novel appears to exist for the fugue form, rather than to derive advantage from it. The contrapuntal action and the characters' self-preoccupation fail to interest because in the first place the characters are themselves uninteresting. Only towards the end does the pressure of real feeling begin to emerge.

Where Hardy displays residual traces of the novel of ideas, Judah Waten is a less ambitious, simpler writer. His instinct is for the brief unstructured sketch, whether in the short story or the novel. *Alien Son* (1952), a set of linked sketches, displays a pleasant if ponderous sense of humour, but falters into sentimentalism or clumsy over-reaction when Waten becomes earnest. In the novels, he is frequently unsure in his narrative stance, drifting erratically between external detail and inner perception, and unable to define his exact relation to his subject.

Dorothy Hewett's *Bobbin Up* (1959) is also incompletely realized. With her, as with other writers of that generation, and of that persuasion in matters both political and literary, the impulse to create is secondary to the commitment to social protest. But with David Martin and John Morrison, the truth of individual experience is paramount. Martin, who began his literary career before he came to Australia, wrote in *The Young Wife* (1962) a sensitive novel of the lives and behaviour of Greek and Cypriot migrants in Melbourne, allowing the difficulties and misunderstandings of the cultural minority to provide the special terms in which the individual story of happiness and jealousy is worked out. He reconciles in the one sustained perception the truth of observed, external detail with the movement of the inner life. John Morrison also elicits the meaning of his experience for the individual. Although he has written two novels, Morrison is essentially a fine short story writer, meticulous without being fussy, quiet, low-keyed but attentive. Unlike the other social realists, he is content to set his stories against a reduced background, a restricted environment rather than a society, with the effect that the balance of interest lies closer to the situation of the character than to intimations of universal, moral or social design. Morrison is a writer without pretensions. Neither the large ideological assumptions that are built into the aggrieved fiction of the socialist realists, nor the dreary accumulation of detail, intrude upon the quiet integrity of his work. The best of his stories appear in his later volumes: *Black Cargo* (1955) and *Twenty-Three* (1962).

The achievement of the social realist school and the radical tradition which predominates in the immediate post-war era is put in its proper literary perspective, however, by recalling that Christina Stead had by that time completed her most important novels, Martin Boyd was entering his last and most impressive phase, Hal Porter had published his first volume of short stories and Patrick White had written *The Aunt's Story* (1948). The novels and short stories are simple in form and essentially innocent in their image of society; they are sentimental in their appeal, they address themselves to the general, the representative, the collective, and their well-meant account of class struggle frequently reduces to accidental caricature. They fail to come to terms with the particular and the individual. The best Australian fiction has come from writers who are independent of that tradition, though not necessarily opposed to its ideals. Christina Stead, for example, is clearly aligned to its social and political sympathies, but rejects the formal conventions of that kind of novel.

Although, like Henry Handel Richardson, virtually her entire writing life was spent overseas, and although she only drew directly or indirectly on her Australian experience in her earlier work, Christina Stead has maintained that she is an Australian writer, on the grounds that she was formed before she left Australia in 1928. But nationality is not an important issue for her. The turbulent years immediately following her arrival in Europe seem to have had a lasting influence on her, for her fiction is persistently about disrupted and oppressed lives and economic hardship, and the strain of meagre living—or, in *House of All Nations* (1938) the ironic obverse portrait, of the financiers who manipulate and exploit the economy. Her interests are none the less continuous with those expressed in Australian fiction, but the manner in which she investigates them is unmistakably her own.

Her situations are not in themselves very remarkable; most often their terms are domestic, or mundane. From such unprepossessing matter she constructs elaborate studies of character, and charts the intricacies of human relationships. Her revelation of character is skilful, her analysis of motive, feeling and desire is subtle and persuasive. In *The Man Who Loved Children* (1940), her most successful novel, Stead probes the dangers inherent in the restricted family unit; everyday domestic tensions conceal deep-seated antagonisms and damaging emotional pressures. In *Seven Poor Men of Sydney* (1934), the one novel Stead has set entirely in Australia, the ordinary lives of a number of unremarkable men and women are defined against the social conditions of working class Sydney in the twenties. In *For Love Alone* (1944), a young woman takes advantage of the 'chances of distant seas' that Sydney, as a seaport, offers; she rejects home and family and, a wilful solitary, eventually makes her way to London. But the novel is really about the inner voyage to Cytherea, the process of self-discovery through a growing understanding of love. In each case, for all the massive detail of the circumstantial world, the substance of Stead's fiction lies in her detailed presentation of her characters' inner perspectives. The elaboration is inordinate, the aggrandisement disproportionate, and Stead's ambition to account for character in terms of individual inclination and social determination outstrips her capacity to control the imaginative design.

Stead's fiction characteristically expresses loss, exhaustion and defeat. It is genuinely unsentimental, unlike the fake anti-sentimentalism of the realist school of Australian writing. It documents the context of the action as thoroughly as the naturalist novel of the turn of the century, and maintains that neutrality of point of view; but her narrative also expresses, in disconcerting prolixity, the inner life of her characters, and registers the varying intensities of their experience. Her fascination with the individuality of character competes with her interest in social theory, and only rarely (in Sam Pollit, for instance) does she manage to reconcile the two. Perhaps, like Patrick White, Stead seeks the extraordinary within the ordinary. What she discovers though is not poetry but nervous strain, furtive desires and contradictory impulses. Her domain is psychological not spiritual; she is more interested in depicting the quality of experience than in exposing the failure of the world to recognize its own mystery.

The most distinctive feature of Stead's fiction is her style. Combining the excessive and the ordinary, it is designed to convey the whole consciousness of a character—undiscriminated detail and barely recognized emotion are registered together with characteristic tricks of personal expression and habitual trains of thought. The aberrant and the fine co-exist, and express the mixed nature of her characters, but the conglomerate style presents special difficulties. The disposition of her characters to indulge their neurotic anxieties, to coerce rather than to persuade, ceaselessly to talk, the very barrage of words in which they signal their confusion, deceit, fear or anger, proves exhausting. Yet it is also a prose of large energies, restless, unco-ordinated in terms of the usual expectations of fiction, but responsive to the impetus of the novels' events. The vocabulary ranges from the further limits of scientific precision to the romantic extravagance of fantasy; yet for all her exactness of reference, she does not attempt a corresponding exactness of definition, but rather identifies her subject by continuous approximation.

Stead resists the conventional procedures of the novel. She dispenses with plot in its usual sense, and diffuses the action through several characters, allowing for a variety of perspective rather than devising a unifying but artificial structure. The 'story' is essentially an examination of the conflicting demands and hopes her characters have of life, their confused motivations, disappointments and determinations. She rejects the distortions of conventional fictional strategies, just as her view of life precludes the sense of ordained pattern: 'I know life offers all sorts of chances, so it's a question of luck'.[37] Her novels present the range and texture of experience but will not impose a shape upon it.

In this Stead can be seen as taking up, though in different terms, some of the fundamental issues which Furphy has raised. She is sensitive to the seriousness of fiction: 'A novel is philosophic. A person who writes a novel is being philosophical about society, but he needn't have a social line'.[38] She does not furnish a plot, then, because such is not life; she attempts to determine a more appropriate, more inclusive form in fiction for coming to terms with life. But where the paradox of constructing the sense of the unconstructed led Furphy to his comic perceptions of the relation between fiction and reality, for Christina Stead that has usually led to a negative or defensive stance. Her characters resist imposed social definitions, fight free of constricting personal relationships and protest against any determinism, and what positive movement may be allowed in their questing restlessness is towards such large, open-ended goals as freedom and knowledge. Thus her closing images of attainment are contradicted by the imaginative impetus of her work; for example, Louie Pollit, at the end of *The Man Who Loved Children*, crosses a bridge and is escaping into the world, but the misery and emotional bullying of the preceding experiences cannot be left behind on the authority of a mere image.

The inclination to inclusiveness is extravagantly indulged in her earlier fiction. In *Seven Poor Men of Sydney*, description of the setting is not only interesting in itself, but also serves to contain some of the apparent formlessness. Yet more important than her image of the city is her reconstruction of the feel of the period. The circumstances depicted are not unique to Sydney, for everywhere obscure men were trying to come to terms with the large shifts in history. Stead recreates the conflicting idealisms of the time, and the contending social philosophies, when the patriotic fervour of the Great War was countered by emergent socialism. It was a period of labour unrest and economic uncertainty, and of cultural and spiritual doubt. The setting is a climate of ideas and attitudes, a social temper, and the local detail is subsidiary and supportive, except in several unfortunate passages where the description becomes over meticulous. In an extended peroration on the historical meaning of Australia, Stead appears to take up the fashionable nationalist stance; but the mystique of the land she proposes is of bitter genius and the poetic soul is led towards despair rather than a heroic future. The weight of the novel eventually lies on personal, not historical destiny; on the romantic tragedy of Michael, for example, and the more distressing retreat of his exhausted, irritable sister Catherine to madness. The historical component identifies only one set of terms in which explanations might be attempted. What Stead fails to resolve, however, is whether these are to be explanations primarily of character, or of social philosophy.

In this strange, amorphous novel no one particular view is established, although the narrative tends to approve the modesty and unassertive normality of Joseph Baguenault. He is one of the few quietly attractive figures in Stead's fiction, one of the meek who shall inherit the earth. For the other characters, the very restlessness of the style—florid excess of language and rhetorical gesticulation, extravagant incantatory passages and long monoton-ous keening, visionary projections and protracted theorizing—expresses both their immaturity and their near-exhaustion. Though Joseph too has had his dreams he is temperamentally reconciled to his lowly status and does not surrender to the social and metaphysical discontents of his cousins and his friends.

Stead's practice of ranging widely from within a limited world is at once the triumph and the weakness of *The Man Who Loved Children*. It is a thoroughly convincing study of a particular family, drawn in part from her own childhood, but amplified and fully endowed with its own sense of life, and of defeat. Its terms are both unique and universal. Sam Pollit is ambitious for his children to know everything, and personally directs their scientific and moral education. Yet the family is increasingly isolated, especially by poverty, and they have very little direct experience of life. Within the family itself, however, is displayed the whole gamut of emotional behaviour, generated by the conflicting temperaments of the parents. It is a squalid situation, with the behaviour of both Sam and Henny vile in different ways. They ceaselessly goad each other, and the children are vulnerable to their emotional bullying and cajolery. But the children have an instinct for resistance. They are not defenceless, for although they do not always understand exactly what is happening, they are sensitive to it. And they are protected ultimately by their egotism; indeed, Christina Stead's is a world without innocence.

In a context which consists almost entirely of talk and rhetorical display, in which the Pollits drown each other out with their talk, and rarely listen to each other, their real nature is disguised, from themselves as well as from each other; they are incapable of true dialogue. The eldest girl, Louie, in particular remains a puzzle to her parents because of her reticence. Her reactions are not openly expressed, but contained within the uncertainties and building resentment of her inner consciousness. Because of her role as witness to the main strife of the family, she acts a a centre of gravity in the novel, and since her private self develops according to its own rules, her perspective provides a means of discrimination in the shifting allegiances and hostilities of family life. By this means *The Man Who Loved Children* achieves more firmness of shape than is usual in Stead.

The persistent melodramatic tendency of Stead's fiction, to rely at last on the force of gesture rather than perception, is given free play in *For Love Alone*. The first half of the novel, set in Australia, is fixed accurately in an actual environment, social and natural, but that vitality is largely missing from the deadened second part, set in a strangely surreal London. The novel's terms change with the transfer of locale. Teresa Hawkins' need for love becomes a need to escape, through love, into a larger world.

Teresa grows through all the degrees of an understanding of love, from adolescent romantic idealism and erotic fantasies to freedom of sexual expression and confidence, if not maturity, in her emotional life. The carnal intoxication of the early stages of the book is extravagant for in her attempt to express Teresa's state of mind as well as the emotional climate she lives in, Stead veers unevenly between the obsessive and the bizarre. She intersperses brief passages of slightly hard-edged social mockery with long interior monologues, in which Teresa turns aside from the uninteresting real world to the other reality of her secret, interior life; or in which Teresa attempts to explain to herself the meaning of her situation and expresses instead her own stubbornness and naivety. The effect is a disjunction between inner and outer circumstance. Teresa has no past and a severely limited present; she has been a student, and she is a teacher, yet her mind is completely undisciplined, attracted to pre-Raphaelite trimmings, filled with the indiscriminate litter of library books, and swayed only by the compulsion of her desires. Yet she gives the impression that she is as unlettered as Joseph Baguenault. In her interior image she seems one of the obscure poor, the disadvantaged, whereas her circumstances, though restrictive, are not as difficult as Stead would have it. They become oppressive by her determination to resist them.

The final image of Teresa claiming her freedom ('I am thinking I am free') is a gesture only, designed to complete a thesis about moral autonomy. It complicates the balance of the novel. A brief affair after establishing a secure relationship demonstrates her independence, but its effect is also to diminish her 'husband's' authority as a character. As she outgrows him, his asserted sensitivity and intelligence emerge as rather limited, if not trite. Character is sacrificed to idea. Similarly the external and imposed Odyssean allusions, which at first had seemed to offer an imaginative reference for the Australian experience, but are eventually identified with the homeless traveller of the world, serve only as intrusive ornamentations of the real testament of Teresa's story. It is a long, uneven and cumbersome novel, oddly limited in its emotional range yet powerful in its recreation of Teresa's questing consciousness, and especially of her oppressed and exhausted spirit.

Stead's subsequent fiction confirms the accomplishment of her major novels. She ceased publishing for nearly fifteen years, but in the mid sixties, when her earlier novels were also revived, she brought out new work which continued her concentration on 'the drama of the person', expressing the inner convictions and delusions of her characters and recreating the semi-transparent envelope of their life; but the world of her imagination had become increasingly separated from the immediate pressure of real events. In *Cotters' England* (1966), Nellie Cook's remorseless bullying derives in part from her earlier political enthusiasms, which now have no substantial focus. In *The Little Hotel* (1973), a novel muddled in its narrative address, the stories of the various guests depict a decayed mode of life, while *Miss Herbert (The Suburban Wife)* (1976) elaborates the shallowness of a woman, who, through her tiresome self-preoccupation, is blind to the social changes taking place about her. In all these novels Stead's characters take up a stance, and fail to hear or notice anything which opposes them. They are all egotists, and they are rarely attractive. Though they appear to follow their own disposition, what they express is not themselves so much as a life aligned to governing ideas of social and political principle. While ideology may in some sense form the texture of the characters' mental life,[39] the mental life is also determined by innate inclination, and to that extent there is in Stead's fiction an imperfect adjustment between inner and outer realities, an interesting misalliance of the novel of character with the novel of ideas. Stead's recreation of the social circumstances of the thirties and forties is impressive, and equally thorough is her expression of a particular kind of life. But it remains uncertain just how far one accounts for the other.

The distinction of Martin Boyd, a much finer writer, lies precisely in the balance of style and vision, in the just proportion between social comedy and serious moral concern. Like Christina Stead, he was an expatriate writer, and although he had won the first gold medal of the Australian Literature Society for *The Montforts* (1928), he was not much regarded until his finest novel, *Lucinda Brayford* (1946). His fiction was not Australian enough, apparently, in either manner or matter to satisfy the entrenched nationalist determinations, and in spite of the success of the Langton tetralogy in the fifties, ingrained prejudice against the favoured social class he chose to write about prevented his novels from being read sensitively. But his Australian credentials could hardly be faulted, for the Boyds have for generations been pre-eminent in the arts; and while the concentration of his fiction is on a restricted social group these were, after all, the kind of people and the life he knew best. But in any case, Martin Boyd's admitted preoccupation with family history is not an end in itself. His concept of character specifically denies 'virgin birth' (as he puts it); character is determined by factors both innate and external, by heredity as well as by social and cultural circumstance. For Boyd, a man's genealogy identifies not his social pedigree but the essence of his moral nature.

The title of his first book, a volume of poems, *Retrospect* (1920), anticipates Boyd's persistent stance towards his material. With the exception of the rather light and mannered novels of the thirties, his fiction is retrospective, recalling and unobtrusively assessing a past of personal and social conduct. Even in *The Montforts*, which is in temporal range the most extended of his novels, Boyd changes the usual features of the chronicle and the romantic exercise of the historical imagination to a different recognition of the past, the past as contingent upon the present (he proposed for the Langton series the collective title *The Past Within Us*). The limitation of *The Montforts* (Boyd continued to find it distasteful when he revised it in 1963) is that it is too systematic in its design and, compressing too many generations into its programme, tends to undervalue the significance of the individual. The working hypothesis about character is demonstrated at the cost of deep human truths. Certain favourite themes emerge, for example the restlessness of a family divided in its attachment between Australia and England, and Boyd may be seen as experimenting with different ironic narrative perspectives; but this novel does not accomplish the more serious testimony of his later books.

At his best, no Australian novelist rivals Boyd in his narrative control. Suspicious of mere technique, especially when it becomes a substitute for genuine perception ('art for art's sake'), he insisted that the value of a novel lay in its content of humanity. He not only affirmed the uniqueness of the individual, but watched also for the more profound significance of individual actions, for evidence of the spiritual nature of man. Through Guy Langton he acknowledged that one can make exact statements of fact but not of truth, and throughout his fiction he investigated techniques of projecting the truth, through the actions of characters, through the cross-reference of social and cultural attitudes, and through comic and ironic indirection. These are not just strategies for a more convincing realism, however, but the means of reaching to the more abiding truths, those that transcend the individual and speak to all men. Individual actions sometimes acquire the significance of parables, aspects of the Myth, touching the great prototypes of moral behaviour and spiritual truth. And the novels themselves may be regarded in the same way. *Lucinda Brayford* became a parable of his life and times, and the Langtons' story is 'a parable of our civilization'. For Boyd accepted the view that 'imaginative writing only enters the region of creative art when the parable pushes its way in.'[40] It is in these terms, no doubt, that *When Blackbirds Sing* (1962) was so important to him. Where for the reader that is a rather spare narrative, for Boyd it is resonant because it lies close to his personal mythology.

The later novels are admirable for their graceful comprehension not just of the human spirit, but of the spiritual in human affairs. The background of *Lucinda Brayford*, for example, is the decline of England through the two wars and the Depression. Yet civilized conduct is maintained by a few individuals even while civilization in its social and moral aspect is everywhere in disarray. These few are true to the Holy Ghost within them. In brief but moving experiences of illumination, when the individual soul responds fully to the beauty of the moment, the world is redeemed. On lesser and more recognizably Lawrentian occasions, as when Lucinda and Hugo Brayford, making love in the hills, are at one with nature, the epiphanic moment consecrates nothing, for the meaning of the intense experience is set aside, and only the intensity is remembered. It celebrates a pagan pleasure of the senses. However, when Dominic in *A Difficult Young Man* (1955) responds to the beauty of the night and walks naked in the bush, the reconciliation between pagan and Christian myth has quietly taken place, for what the action expresses is Dominic's feeling of spiritual harmony, that there is nothing between himself and God.

Boyd does not concede, then, an inevitable division between the human and the spiritual. Man's chief need is to reconcile himself with God, and in that he fulfils his humanity. The Christian terminology is important to Boyd with his commitment to the world of the spirit, but it does not dictate the pattern of his thinking. He also avails himself of the great classical statements of art—in music, sculpture, painting—as testimony to the capacity man has to recognize the moral law and to express its beauty and its truth, 'the ancient sorrows and passions of humanity.' The special and moving consequence of this is that Boyd is the one Australian novelist with the emotional and spiritual maturity to write, with natural dignity, of the moral beauty of compassion. By a combination of poise and concern, he accomplishes a graceful perspective on the significance of human affairs. His understanding is of humanity. He writes sensitively of the individual and never undervalues a character, not even those most antipathetic to him, such as the socially ambitious Baba or the retired Colonel Rodgers. The one exception would be Straker, the wealthy businessman who recurs in the background of *Lucinda Brayford*, and who has nothing to redeem him. Boyd's real interests are the abiding and universal concerns lodged in the individual: the interweaving of good and evil in our lives, the disjunction between moral law and the law of State and society, reason, truth and justice, and the need to discover and acknowledge the essential self.

Boyd's preoccupations and intentions amount to a framework of ideas, but he was not a systematic thinker, nor did he have a theoretical mind. His wit and liveliness of perception are everywhere apparent; his was an intelligence which responds to life, and finds its pleasure there, and does not impose his will. For him, as for

Mr. Smith in *Nuns in Jeopardy* (1940), the bounding heart takes precedence over the teeming brain. Yet there is in Boyd a determination to make a case, an impulse to explain his position or to justify his convictions, even though he seems to have recognized in himself, and in the various characters who are occasionally his spokesmen, an insufficiency in argument. This impulse is given fullest expression in his privately published essay *Why They Walk Out* (1970), in his 'subjective travel book', *Much Else in Italy* (1958), and in the two versions of his autobiography, *A Single Flame* (1939) and *Day of My Delight: An Anglo-Australian Memoir* (1965).

Inside the novels ideas carry weight, but are rarely expressed systematically, and the spokesmen for various important opinions may have their authority undercut. For example, Paul Brayford's views on art, the aristocracy and the condition of England become extravagant, the arguments become illogical, and Paul himself becomes a comic figure. Yet the notions themselves are not discredited; they are clearly views with which Boyd is sympathetic. Guy Langton, who is another of Boyd's travesties of himself, is disposed to intrude comments on social manners, art and morality that have only an oblique bearing on the narrative itself. These interruptive disquisitions do not distort the fiction, for they are consistent with the kind of characters who are responsible for them. It is very much Paul Brayford's manner, and Arthur Langton's, and Russell Lockwood's, to deliver themselves of their firm opinions (though Russell Lockwood has acquired his, they are not his own). In his novels of the thirties, however, when Boyd was perhaps more directly influenced by the novel of ideas, the airing of his favourite notions is more stilted, and does not consort so well with the imaginative texture of the work.

Those novels are characterized by the freshness of their vision, the lightness of their dialogue, some whimsicality of characterization and the lucidity of their theme. Boyd's own objection to them, that he did not thoroughly know the sort of people he was writing about, and knew only the outward circumstances of their lives, is astute. The absence of inner conviction does not reduce the characters to stereotypes, but converts the novels into elegant social fables, in which the established codes of conduct are challenged by an awakening sensitivity to the emotional bases of life. However, *Scandal of Spring* (1934) has less of the vernal in it than of the ultimate loneliness of the sensitive individual. In *The Lemon*

Farm (1935) two young lovers are unequal in spirit, and the boy's more selfish love leads eventually to tragedy. At work here is a preliminary exploration of Boyd's perception of the interweaving of good and evil in human affairs, the first intimations that 'every perfect moment must be succeeded by some ambushed evil'.

Nuns in Jeopardy (1940) takes the fiction deliberately towards the fable. Heavily allegorical in its general contours, it also delights in description at the natural level, Boyd's intention being to integrate the natural and the spiritual. A group of nuns and sailors is shipwrecked on a tropical island; the sacred and the profane must be redeemed, and this is accomplished in a natural paradise, for the heaven they seek requires them to drop their inhibitions, to reconcile the inner and outer selves, to become completely natural. In choosing a luxuriant tropic setting, Boyd was writing in a long-established vogue, then dominated by W. Somerset Maugham; but a persistent sub-stratum of Australian fiction had looked to the reefs and islands also, from the many popular stories by Louis Becke, first published in the *Bulletin* in the nineties, to the pulp novels Vance Palmer wrote as 'Rann Daley' and Norman Lindsay's *The Cautious Amorist* (1932) and *Age of Consent* (1938), while E. J. Banfield's memoir, *Confessions of a Beachcomber* (1908) early established itself as a local classic. It is a romantic vein which has continued intermittently since then, in novels dealing with war experiences in the Pacific, and more recently novels of the decline of Australia's authority in Papua New Guinea. For Boyd the difficulty is that the island paradise is such a cliché; he cannot resist treating his figures playfully, so that the seriousness of his moral discriminations is called into question.

Lucinda Brayford is admirable for many things, but perhaps chiefly for its content of humanity, Boyd's own measure of a novel's value. It traces the intermingling of Lucinda's modest ambition to achieve happiness through love with her increasing experience of sorrow, and this is set against a background of social change and the erosion of traditional values, a process which Boyd hints had begun several generations earlier. Boyd presents character in search of values, not character for its own sake; character, that is, in the making. Lucinda is initially an uncommitted figure, living only for pleasure. Her Australian youth is a time of innocence, of freedom from anxiety and trouble, and therefore remote from an acquaintance with profound human truth. In this section of the novel Boyd concentrates on her external circumstances, especially her family background. She is an object of admiration, a beautiful shell. After she marries and leaves Melbourne for England, she does not so much slough off her provincialism as join the 'living stream of culture'. Her pleasure in that is tempered by her first experience of unhappiness. Increasingly her inner life, her emotional being, is identified; but Boyd's adjustment of narrative focus is matched by more frequent references to the historical context, especially to the encroaching war with its threat to all that civilization stands for. Lucinda's growing brittleness is seen then as both the outcome of her personal unhappiness, and of her disillusionment with the living stream, which has lost its contact with life. What she seeks is a reconciliation of European cultural awareness with Australian vitality, but that is too narrow an ambition. At the novel's climax, her son Stephen dies, killed by the law of the land for his devotion to humanity and to the good and the beautiful, the moral law. As Lucinda recalls what an ordinary boy Stephen was, she suddenly realizes that his very ordinariness is a promise of the regeneration of humanity; in a scene of considerable emotional intensity and beauty, she perceives that his death has redeemed the world, and she can take new hope in it and in herself.

This redemption ('Eya, Resurrexit!') which follows the agony of Stephen's 'crucifixion' indicates the grounds on which Boyd thought of the novel as a parable of his times. The concentration of the novel has been continually on the refinement of moral perception and the appreciation of beauty and truth. Yet the quality of the narrative impresses as much as the moral significance of it. It is more sensitive in its control of tone than elsewhere in Boyd, with the exception perhaps of some parts of *The Cardboard Crown* (1952); elegant, gentle, evocative, tinged with sadness, and capturing in its own expression echoes of the sorrows and passions of humanity which Boyd constantly identifies with the beauty of classical art.

In 1948 Boyd returned for a few years to Australia; the first of the Langton novels, *The Cardboard Crown*, appeared in 1952, followed by *A Difficult Young Man* (1955), *Outbreak of Love* (1957) and *When Blackbirds Sing* (1962). Again in these novels he writes of a particular period and a particular social class, and his preoccupation with the continuing influence of the past upon the present, with the difficult choice between natural good and social regulation, and with the evil of war, is continued in them. More specifically than in *Lucinda Brayford* he identifies Italy as the source of civilization, where the Greek and Christian myths are reconciled; and halfway through the tetralogy he himself went to Rome and lived there for the rest of his life. The 'divided loyalty' of the Anglo-Australians is not geographical schizophrenia, but a restless search for the abiding city. The loyalty in question is not to the ancestral past but to the essential self, and the truth of humanity.

Unlike *Lucinda Brayford*, these novels more completely encase the quest to discover the essential self in social portraiture, and their foreground presents the manners and the life-style of Melbourne in its colonial and provincial phases. *Outbreak of Love*, set on the eve of the First World War, is a delightful comedy of manners, depicting the social hierarchy that the Langtons generally take for granted, since their position in it is assured. But Guy Langton, who is intermittently the narrator, lacks the confidence in himself that he discovers in his family, and he acts as a particularly entertaining, diffident and ironic commentator on his own part in the social whirl.

The novel has a counter-statement of a much more serious nature, however, investigating once again what civilization consists in, and where one's moral responsibilities lie. Although Guy's aunt Diana prepares to leave her husband and live with Russell Lockwood in Europe, she chooses not to, much as in the more impressive *The Cardboard Crown*, Alice chooses to sacrifice her chance of personal happiness for the sake of her family, who are dependent on her. That is a repeated motif in Boyd: when the opportunity comes, circumstances have so changed as to make the acceptance of it ironical, or impossible. Boyd is not a pessimist. Rather, he wants to show that character is formed by the difficult decisions one has to make. Both Alice and Diana make the right choice; Russell Lockwood shows how little character in its moral sense he has, by transferring his attentions to Miss Rockingham at Government House, and Guy Langton manages to hint at some deviousness in Aubrey Tunstall's attentions to Alice.

Guy Langton's role in these books is all important. He does not appear overtly in *When Blackbirds Sing* but in the others Boyd uses him as a special kind of narrator, the historian of his family and so incorporating features of himself, yet meticulous about drawing attention to the difficulty of preserving complete objectivity and impartiality. He is one of the most substantive of the memorialists, those participating chroniclers who continually reappear throughout the history of Australian fiction. In both *The Cardboard Crown* and *A Difficult Young Man*, Guy meticulously identifies the sources of his evidence (Alice's diaries, Uncle Arthur's anecdotes, his own recollections), and because Boyd does not believe that the truth of a character can be directly stated, he chooses a method of indirect commentary, and conscious speculative interpretation, to allow for the contradictions that exist in character and in the truth. That is, he proposes interpretations of events and theories of character but is scrupulous not to insist on Guy's as the only possible interpretation. While Guy attempts to account for the darkness of his brother's soul, or the goodness of his grandmother's, and reminds us that the narrator's perception is inevitably less than the whole truth, he draws attention away from Boyd's careful arrangement of detail, so that Guy's interpretation can be adjusted by the evidence that he does not always choose to take up. Some of this evidence relates to features of his own personality. For example, he represents his brother Dominic as a tormented romantic, who has inherited the disturbed passions of their ancestor the duque de Teba. That explanation of Dominic seems more satisfying to Guy, himself a romantic though of a much more delicate kind, than to anyone else (unless the sentimental innocent of the family, Aunt Mildy). Certainly Guy's parents do not choose to account for Dominic in such dramatic terms, and Laura in particular, who stands almost without notice close to the centre of most of these experiences, observes that everybody watches Dominic to provide them with shocks for their amusement. By the pressure of their attention upon him, they create the outrageousness of his behaviour. Guy suggests that Laura is driven to defend Dominic because the de Teba strain is transmitted through her. The notion that the Langtons collectively invent the characters of the individual members is not investigated by Guy, but it hovers over all four books as another kind of explanation.

The stories that Guy reveals to us are sensitive, moving, satisfying in themselves; Guy's relation to them increases the subtlety of Boyd's characterization, and makes possible a fuller revelation of the books' values. For example, when Guy relates the incident of Baba appearing to push Dominic into the bull-ring, that expresses as much about Guy's views of Baba as of Baba's attitude to Dominic. Guy detects such hatred in her soul that he accepts that she would be capable of attempting to murder Dominic. Yet nothing else in *A Difficult Young Man* suggests any such thing. This is not capriciousness on Boyd's part, but a carefully planned technique by which character is identified sufficiently to determine its moral boundaries, though the exact definition of character continues to be elusive.

Boyd's concern with the truth of character, and the truth of the spirit, is a clear indication of the change which was gradually taking place in Australian fiction. Where the earlier writing had sought either romance or literal truth, 'realism', subsequent writing came more and more to arrive at its truth in terms of artistry—the book Guy is to write about his grandmother may be true 'either literally or artistically'. To arrive at this more complex truth, Boyd found he needed to devise a narrator with a rather special relation to his narrative; and in *Much Else in Italy* (1958), it may be noted that he again takes up a self-conscious narrative stance as he guides the Irish boy towards a sensitive appreciation of the spiritual meaning of art. Patrick White, whose preoccupations are also generally spiritual, develops a somewhat different alignment to his fiction, though it is no less self-conscious.

Like Boyd and Stead, White too is inclined to draw on a particular and increasingly distant period. Imaginatively, he is captivated by the wasteland years, the years of the rise of modernity which are also the years in which Australian social attitudes were consolidated. His techniques and his themes reflect the eclectic interests of the post-Lawrence, Joyce and Woolf era. His own distinctive narrative manner is forged from characteristic features of their style, and his absorption with the spectrum of interests that includes mysticism, symbolism, psychology and religious philosophy also derives from the intellectual climate of that period. Yet his characters tend to congregate in a special cultural eddy indifferent to the kinds of events that meant so much to Boyd. The war, for example, was a nuisance for White, an interruption to his proper work.

In spite of the fashionable revival of his kinds of interests in the sixties, when White emerged as one of the world's leading novelists, his novels, his short stories and his plays are all somewhat remote and detached from the cultural movements of the time. His fiction elaborates the individual rather than the social, and persistently moves from the external reality of the ordinary world to the inner consciousness of character or the latent concealed implications of speech and behaviour, and to the core of permanence beyond the illusion of permanence. White is careful to define historical circumstances in his novels, yet the transcendental aspirations of his fiction lead him away from a preoccupation with the period sense, to cross other boundaries of art and understanding.

When he does bring the action forward, White examines not the contemporary but the accumulating past as it sanctions the present. In *The Eye of the Storm* (1973), for example, the past flows into and triumphs over the present, while in *The Vivisector* (1970) each of Hurtle Duffield's paintings is in itself a retrospective. On the evidence of the short stories and plays, where White has attempted to make some statement of the contemporary, it is apparent that he is more comfortable with the purposely indistinct twenties and thirties. For White needs some displacement to establish his ironic perspective on human affairs, and in the immediacy of the contemporary context, the peculiar distortions of character and event through which he opens up the possibilities of new orders of experience are liable to become clumsy or distasteful. His experiments with time, with the interfusion of levels of consciousness and memory, by which he enriches the individual's perception of life, appear merely a contrivance under the duress of the immediate. In particular, the idiom by which he expresses his version of the ugly Australian, the immensely entertaining vulgarity and brutally revealing speech of the denizens of Sarsaparilla, is more and more evidently artificial, a language devised for a satirical purpose. Suburban Australia is still vulgar, but its idiom has changed, and the mannered, theatrical dialogue White uses is increasingly recognizable as selective and compacted, created out of the vernacular rather than representative of it.

Patrick White has quite deliberately turned away from the realistic novel, as remote from art. In his view the novel should heighten life, and offer an illuminating experience. His fiction attempts to represent the transcendence that exists above human realities, but while he has his own faith in superhuman realities the critical issue for his fiction is whether that higher order appears imposed by the author, rather than emerging from the contexts of his fictional world. Where Boyd's characters discover spiritual truth in the testament of humanity, White shows spiritual progress as an abnormal pursuit, and his protagonists are harried into pursuing illumination, either to fulfil their character or their destiny ('it was intended'). Because they are not entirely free agents, but act out a role (as visionary, illuminate, divine fool, quester), and because aspects of the main characters are projected into other supporting characters, the fiction is to that extent quasi-allegorical dramatization, and the spiritual truths are peculiarly external realities. There is in Patrick White, just as there is in modern Australian painting, a tendency for the symbolism to verge on spiritual allegory. The construction of significant patterns of experience, the imposition of meaning on detail, and the heightening of consciousness by reverberant incident, all these cumulative narrative effects constitute an astonishingly elaborate and imaginative scaffolding for his prevailing themes of suffering and redemption and the progress toward illumination. But instead of displaying the infinite they draw attention to the boundaries of White's artistry; his intuitions of the subtler mysteries are at some cost to the complete realization of character, for the passionate intensities of felt experience are rarely conveyed in White's novels. The contradiction at the heart of his work is revealed in his remark that what he is interested in is 'the relationship between the blundering human being and God'.[41] Although he means to explore that connection, his terms disclose an essential and inevit-able disjunction. White's novels yearn for and attempt to impose by the authority of his narrative design a final image of harmony, totality, spiritual fulfilment; in fact they depict the movement of the human experience towards fragmentation, and particularly to a recognition of the irresolvable tension between the flesh and the spirit.

The sense of devised patterns of significance, of the construction rather than the discovery of meaning in experience, is most obtrusive in the early work, in the plays (*The Ham Funeral* is stiffly allegorical) as well as in the fiction. His first novel, *Happy Valley* (1939), set in southern New South Wales but imitating something of the manner and the concerns of the English provincial novel, is an uneven and artificial work, contrived to demonstrate the validity of its epigraph, that the law of suffering is the one indispensable condition of human existence. It fails because the sets of relationships are patently arranged to demonstrate his thesis, and do not evolve in response to what appear to be the characters' true natures. The texture of the writing, too, is brittle. It has not enough density of accumulated detail to support the over-riding heightening of reality which has become his later, habitual, manner. The range of experience remains limited; White had not yet discovered the enlarged vision. All his concentration is on the solitariness of man, both social and spiritual. The constricted sense is at odds with the possibilities of release latent in his setting, and which only the patient, intuitive characters appear to sense. The need for spiritual enlargement is more precisely the focus of *The Living and the Dead* (1941), White's portrait of the cultural and intellectual sterility of London in the thirties. The novel does not itself altogether avoid the sterile cleverness of Elyot Standish, who discovers at the last that he has separated himself from life. Once again the patterning is restrictive, the characters cannot escape their role as representative figures, and Elyot's final condition is more an affirmation of the novel's moral design than of his burgeoning commitment to the positive sense of life. In these two novels White has begun not with an idea of a character, but with a theory about moral and spiritual nature.

But with *The Aunt's Story* (1948) White changed his approach considerably. Although once again he offers a heightened perception of life, this emerges directly, and sensitively, from Theodora Goodman's disintegrating world. The fracturing of perception, of imagery and of character is not so patently an authorial design, but may be seen as manifesting the changing nature of Theodora's lucidity. Within the dissolving order of the normal world, the disappearance of provincial Australia and the collapse of the 'gothic shell of Europe', Theodora undergoes not so much a crisis of identity as an eventual release from the constraining sense of self. Her rational intelligence, initially unconventional but acute, is gradually abandoned as she pursues the desirable state of selflessness, and at the end of her spiritual odyssey she achieves a new personal calm that may also be madness. The ambivalence is skilfully controlled. Theodora's situation finally is neither pathetic nor comic. She is a modest figure, and her aspirations are entirely free of the more extreme ambitions of White's subsequent visionaries and luminaries. It is perhaps the most compassionate and good humoured of White's novels, sensitive to the individual's own terms of life, and relatively free of intrusive authorial direction. But in demonstrating Theodora's eventual acceptance of the irreconcilable dualities, of life and death, illusion and reality, the self and the other, White announces the paradox that troubles his subsequent fiction. The quest for a transcendent harmony, the reaching towards a vision of totality, competes with his sensitive understanding of character. White's novels reproduce a tension between the ideal, articulated through the imaginative assertion of symbolism, and the real, the more direct and imaginatively convincing response to experience. Character as archetype conflicts with character as individual and real. Theodora, truly humbled (in White's idiom, one of the necessary conditions for knowledge of the real), accepts life and the simple honesties of common objects such as tables and chairs; but having achieved this acceptance, which is also a measure of life and fulfilment, she is both rejected by the world and withdraws from it. Although the design of the novel is to concentrate wholly on Theodora, and to express her altering mode of consciousness, her spiritual quest is ultimately less moving than the simple kindnesses of people and the warm compassion with which her character is presented. Compassion, rather than understanding, is the end achieved.

In terms of the history of Australian fiction, White's next two novels are his most influential. Despite the sensitivity to character and to language in *The Aunt's Story*, and perhaps in part because of its experimental manner (though it was not particularly innovative in technique), White did not win serious attention until the fifties when with *The Tree of Man* (1955) he virtually closed off one of the persistent strands of Australian fiction, and with *Voss* (1957) he initiated another. *The Tree of Man* corrected the superficialities of the novel of the land, by disclosing the possibilities for metaphysical speculation in the traditional features of earlier fiction: the sequence of hardships (flood, fire, storm and drought), experience tested against an extended scale of time, the large rhythmic basis of structural arrangement, the intimate attachment to the spirit of place. His close attention to the common details of the natural or literal world revealed intimations of the non-literal, the extraordinary behind the ordinary. *Voss*, on the other hand, established the mythic potentialities of Australian history, set a fashion for heavily symbolic and image-ridden writing, and localized the journey of exploration as spiritual metaphor.

Where Theodora Goodman achieved a lucidity beyond reason, Stan Parker in *The Tree of Man* is an ordinary though solitary and uncommunicative individual, searching for such answers as are available to a naturally humble man. But White expands the significance of Stan's modest life and experiences to represent not just the old pioneering way of life, but the way of Life itself. Stan Parker is in the classical sense, as well as the local sense, a countryman; he is even at times a type of Adam, and the allegorical mode of White's fiction is very much in evidence in this aggrandisement of the narrative's frame of reference. The tension between the natural and the spiritual is especially marked here. The routine activities of Stan and Amy, their attachment to their land and the slowly adjusting terms of their relationship as well as the limits of their understanding of each other are movingly presented, for White's depiction of the simple events of their life, the release of the spirit in a rain-storm or Stan's uneasiness on a rare visit to church, is sensitive to the emotion of the experience. But when he ceases to follow the premise of the ordinary, and disrupts the common texture of their experience (as in Stan's reactions to a performance of *Hamlet*), White becomes less convincing. His determination to invest the Parkers' lives with significance is too often an imposition upon the imaginative fabric of the narrative; despite the highly charged writing, the climactic scene of Stan's death in the garden, for example, is not entirely satisfactory because the moment of illumination reduces to an unnecessarily dramatic re-affirmation of Stan's affinity with the natural world. Yet even with such manipulations of design, and those occasions in the narrative when White must announce for his taciturn hero the meanings of experiences, his intimations of the spirit remain most movingly attached to the world of ordinary men. Stan's efforts to comprehend, his uncertain pursuit of illumination and understanding, the procedure of his life and not the end of it, these are where the real artistry and the accomplishment of *The Tree of Man* lie.

Voss is the most florid of White's novels, and perhaps the most triumphant because of the rhetorical excess. Here, experience is depicted at a different, heightened register, in keeping with the exalted sense of self and the overweening ambition of the man who is determined to discover the infinite, and by an act of will to prove that he may become God. Voss's commission—to explore the interior of Australia—merely serves his transcendent purpose. Though White draws on the explorers Leichhardt and Eyre for the external circumstances, the expedition is to a different interior, to map the contours of the spirit and to achieve illumination through suffering.

What saves Voss is the very humanity which he seeks to slough off as rendering him vulnerable. As he proceeds by stages through a land of great subtlety, he defends himself against the humility of Palfreyman, the endurance of the ex-convict Judd, the poetic intuition of Le Mesurier, and the love of Laura Trevelyan. But his pride proclaims him man, and Laura is, after all, able to comprehend him; his legend is written down, and his spirit survives in myth.

The apotheosis of Voss is essentially an effect of language, however, and the enigmatic communication between Voss and Laura is not so much telepathic as literally symbolic. White's narrative dispenses with the normal continuities. His characters do not develop by an evolving relationship but by a series of encounters; scenes are juxtaposed for ironic possibilities, not smooth narrative progression. It is essentially a dramatic technique, and consistent with his fragmenting of character into projected types but, most important, it provides White with a means of expressing his characters' moment of illumination. For the many resonances of the language allow for the interplay by which the real and the spiritual are fused. In *Voss*, however, once the climactic event itself is over, the long coda in which the external world attempts to absorb what it can of the mythic significance of Voss shows that the fusion of the two levels, the real and the surreal, is incomplete. The connection remains metaphorical.

Voss is eventually a novel about the spiritual and mythical potential of language. *Riders in the Chariot* (1961), which makes much the same elevated demands of language and proposes a visionary experience no less ambitious, appears much more contrived in its structure (and *The Solid Mandala*, 1961, is more mechanically schematic again) for it is less independent of the context of limited reality, and its importation of literary, Biblical and mythic reference is patently supplementary to the narrative. Specifically, the religious allusions are integrated into the imaginative texture of *Voss*, whereas they are imported in what remains an awkwardly allegorical manner in *Riders*. Voss in his presumption rivals Christ, but the mock crucifixion of Himmelfarb, the immigrant Jew, is a structural device, not an integral feature of his character nor of his destiny as one of the elect. *Riders in the Chariot* is also the one novel in which White presents an elaborate portrait of evil, of potent malignancy and self-consuming spitefulness depicted however in caricature terms, so that with the counter-vailing principle of love a somewhat medieval sense of moral allegory is reinforced.

The four visionaries who became the riders in the chariot are all social outcasts, 'burnt ones' whose experience of suffering prepares them for the ultimate redemption. Although White's design is for the riders to merge their divergent understanding, Mrs. Godbold the washerwoman's experiences do not match the personal history of Himmelfarb the Jew who, in Germany and in Australia, has suffered all the wrongs of his race, or the instinctive life of Mary Hare who has merged with the natural world, or the corruption of Alf Dubbo, the half-caste aboriginal painter. These separate lives are brought together in the midst of Sarsaparilla, and while the archetypal structure of the novel leads towards a grand apocalyptic resolution, the novel's most telling scenes belong to its secular vision, to the occasions of mutual help and the observed gestures of compassion.

White's first collection of short stories, *The Burnt Ones* (1964) elaborated several of his key themes, but in particular it offered further studies of the Sarsaparilla ethos, and so complements the plays (*A Cheery Soul* was adapted from a story of the same title); these are comic, satirical, scathing and compassionate by turn. The best of the stories, however, are a loosely related group of Greek stories, all alluding obliquely to the Turkish sack of Smyrna as providing a serious undertone to the shallow chatter and un-important social distinctions, and all with more subtlety of characterization and social interplay than the Sarsaparilla stories, which tend to rely on stereotypes.

With *The Vivisector* (1970) and *The Eye of the Storm* (1973), White appears to have entered a new phase, confirmed by the second volume of stories, *The Cockatoos: Shorter Novels and Stories* (1974) and *A Fringe of Leaves* (1976). The word consciousness is still a dominant feature, the dialogue stylized and the narrative deliberately literary. His fiction continues to call attention to itself as a richly textured construct, to insist on itself as self-conscious art, patterned meaning. Particularly in *The Vivisector*, where words must act as a substitute for paint, the heavily symbolic and allusive language is seen (though with some warrant in the circumstances) as inventing rather than invoking the vision. In describing the pictures the text indicates rather the imaginative energy which has gone into the making of them, and which may be derived from them; but in describing Hurtle Duffield's intimations of the mystery, White fails to persuade us that the vision is more than a product of words. Elizabeth Hunter's central experience is also, but less successfully, a mysticism of words. For all the religious overtones, it is not possible to determine precisely what the experience itself was.

The change is in his handling of character. Although character continues to dominate his fiction, the central figure becomes the catalyst for the various relationships which are examined, and precipitates the painful truth about themselves the various supporting characters have failed to recognize. They contribute to Duffield's life studies, or the slow dance of life about the dying Elizabeth Hunter. That is, the role of the visionary has changed, and with it the nature of the illumination. Ellen Roxburgh in *A Fringe of Leaves* comes closest of all White's protagonists to reconciling the flesh and the spirit, the human and the divine, because her experience of suffering leads her to a recognition of the persistence of the human spirit, and particularly as it is expressed in love and compassion; and this novel, partly in response to the period sense which White is careful to reproduce (it is based on the survival of Eliza Fraser among the aborigines early in the nineteenth century), but also because humanity appears to have been accepted without any reservation, is free of the restless convolutions of his other work. The fiction is much less forced; yet as all his work does, it presents itself as fable. It is illumination enough to discover the terms by which the spirit survives.

The award of the 1973 Nobel Prize for Literature inevitably drew the attention of the world to White's fiction. His later novels, however, have had surprisingly little direct impact on Australian writing. The observable influence is from his middle career, and particularly from *Voss*, the first of a number of novels to reveal the prophetic and mystical qualities of the Australian landscape, and locate the Australian experience in the solitariness of the individual psyche. Randolph Stow's *To the Islands* (1958) was one of the first novels to repeat *Voss*'s excursion into the realm of the spirit, the strange country of the soul—but without drawing on the mythical possibilities of history, which was another of the leads *Voss* opened up. Before this Stow had published a volume of poetry, and two unremarkable novels, *A Haunted Land* (1956) and *The Bystander* (1957). These were novels of the land in the 1930s, lending-library manner, eloquent in their response to a rather stark landscape, but imaginatively inhibited in their examination of character and the complications of family relationships, and stilted in dialogue. While all Stow's fiction favours eccentricity, in these two early novels the eccentric figures are merely melodramatic; in *A Haunted Land*, for example, he traces the effects of Andrew Maguire's cynical love and distorting will on his children, but is much too cursory in providing the grounds for Maguire's behaviour. The result is an empty gothicism, though set in a landscape which was already beginning to reveal for Stow a special meaning, a landscape characterized by decay yet beyond change, and containing within itself the country's spiritual heritage.

To the Islands is by abrupt contrast much more a spiritual fable, in which an old missionary Heriot, who has lost his faith, makes a long journey of self-discovery through a precisely envisaged wilderness landscape, at once real and surreal. While a comparison with Lear is too patently courted, Heriot is credibly a type of deracinated modern man, who discovers the insufficiency and the vanity of the ego. But like White in his mid-career, Stow transposes his concerns from the personal to the metaphysical; and he takes up something like White's expressionist mode. The narrative rides the boundaries between inner consciousness and external reality. Initially, Heriot is opposed to the land about him, because he is out of sympathy with it. By the novel's end he has actually merged with it. His aimless wandering in the wilderness is a carefully patterned ritual of initiation into the spiritual realities of the land as the aborigines know them. Heriot is guided to the sacred places until he comes to his final destination, his apotheosis (again *Voss* affords a comparison) into one of the ancestral spirits, and inner consciousness and external reality become, at the last, fused. Yet the novel is imaginatively unstable. Though it seeks to delineate the contours of Heriot's abraded spirit, it in fact presents what he perceives, not what he is; though the narrative increasingly functions on a plane of heightened significance, and though Stow affirms in a prefatory note that this is not a realistic novel, he nevertheless hesitates to relinquish his hold on external reality. Like Conrad (whom he studied formally, and whose influence on Stow is oblique but persistent), he is intent on discovering the spiritual core, but he is unable to commit himself wholly to the destructive element, and without a Marlow to provide the common perspective of reality, he resorts to the clumsy, interruptive device of returning the narrative from time to time to the outside world of the mission.

Stow's style is so uncomplicated as to make the imaginative perception of his narrative seem slender, and the inflating of simple incident to universal significance precious. In *Tourmaline* (1963), however, the narrative is more consistent, because the point of view is wholly determined by a participating narrator; the Law, who sets down his testament of the parched town and its temporary revival by a charismatic diviner who promises water, and finds only gold. The landscape here is not so much a desert wilderness, as a wasteland, and the narrative insists on its symbolic import, hinting heavily at systems of meaning derived variously from Christian mythology, *The Golden Bough* and the *Tao Teh Ching*. None of these accounts for the novel's meaning, and the allusive symbolism is inconclusive; only the Law, memory and conscience of Tourmaline, provides a co-ordinating frame of reference. He is the law as historian rather than the law as authority, and takes seriously his role as memorialist, linking the town's past with the present ('I say we have a bitter heritage') which is also, by a preliminary authorial note, to be imagined as taking place in the future. As Stow adapts this persistently recurring figure in Australian fiction, the memorialist is part supervisory narrator, and part chorus, though a chorus somewhat nearer the centre of the action than is customary. *Tourmaline* is hauntingly enigmatic, not just because Stow has reduced the texture of experience to its bare bones, but because of the special narrative stance. The gentle rhetoric of the Law conveys a meditative sadness that is strangely separate from both his own involvement in the town's revived hopes, and from the various philosophical systems that are insinuated into the main action.

With *The Merry-go-round in the Sea* (1965) and *Midnite: The Story of a Wild Colonial Boy* (1967), Stow returns to rather more conventional fictional forms. *Midnite* is a relaxed and entertaining fantasy, an amusing *omnium gatherum* of clichés and conventions from both colonial history and colonial literature, and can be seen as a comic embroidery of Rob Coram's more categorical loyalty to his cultural traditions. *The Merry-go-round in the Sea* continues to pay homage to the notion of heritage, and is somewhat insistent on a set of values which belongs to an older conception of Australia. It recalls the attitudes of an earlier generation in its celebration of the timeless land and the mystique of place, and Stow's persevering search for permanence can be seen as an extension of those older preoccupations. Yet it is a novel in which constructed meaning conflicts with discovered meaning, and the imposed patterning of images of permanence is inevitably defeated by the pressing fact of time itself. The novel records an important transition, not just in a young boy's growth to early adolescence, but in general cultural attitudes for, like George Johnston's *My Brother Jack* (1964), it confronts the old order with the new. The Maplestead clan, fifth generation Australian, produces its apostate and the conventional social patterns are exposed as maintaining a legend, if not a ritual, that is increasingly remote from the actuality of Australia. Yet the novel is nostalgic for that past, and touched by the beauty of the ancient landscape; it is a sentimental novel in its inception, loosely and naturally structured in its affectionate reminiscences, though preposterously over-ridden by its too emphatic patterning. *Tourmaline* is Stow's best and most satisfactory novel because the temperate humanity of the narrator manages to compensate for the allegorical dimensions of the narrative, and checks Stow's disposition to immoderate poetic determinations in his fiction.

Although he has continued to publish an occasional poem, Stow has to date produced no further substantial fiction.[42] In that brief span of active publishing, he was regarded as an exciting young writer, the natural successor to Patrick White. Yet his last two works show him turning away from White's enriched rhetorical manner and insistent symbolism, to his own more delicate (though still poetic) impressionism. Another writer who, until his recently published novel, *The Year of Living Dangerously* (1978), seemed to have lacked the imaginative substance to build upon his early promise, is Christopher Koch. Koch, together with Stow, was seen as the most likely new talent in the late fifties, and his *The Boys in the Island* (1958; revised 1974) was widely praised. Somewhat uneven and dislocated, it nevertheless depicts sensitively and perceptively the double consciousness of a young boy who, growing up in Tasmania, preserves the idealized world of his private imaginings from the disappointments of his ordinary, outward life. The novel does not completely disguise its basis as a series of poetic intervals, and like Stow's fiction it occasionally falters into preciousness. Koch is prone to exploit what he knows he can do well.

The rather insistent pressing of the narrative's moral import, the occasional startling lurid touches, and the slight detachment of the hero from the order of the experiences he is caught up in, are features which reappear in Koch, particularly in his virtually unnoticed second novel, *Across the Sea Wall* (1965). It is not necessarily a limitation that Koch has elected to examine motive and sensibility but not character, and has preferred the examination of secondary characteristics to primary understanding. The altered focus is refreshing in providing new perspectives on behaviour, and allowing new insights into social structures. *Across the Sea Wall* is conceptually a stronger novel than *The Boys in the Island*, and not so determined upon lyric evocation. Like Stow, Koch is a conscious stylist; but he leaves nothing to chance, and in his early impressionist phase he has not Stow's ease of movement.

The disappointingly slender accomplishment of Stow and Koch (at that time) is emphasized by contrast with the overwhelming diversity and activity of Hal Porter, the most idiosyncratic stylist among those authors who rejected the pedestrian manner and unappealing though serviceable prose of the realist writers. Although Porter belongs to the preceding generation, and had published a few short stories as early as the thirties, and a privately printed volume of short stories in 1942, he was hardly heard from for the next decade—because editors then found his style and his stories unsuitable, according to his 'Author's Note' in *A Bachelor's Children* (1962). When the literary climate gradually changed in the fifties and sixties, Porter came into prominence, publishing volumes of short stories as well as poetry, novels, plays, autobiographies and documentary works. Some of this had been written earlier; but the later work too, and certainly the best of it, his short stories and his autobiographies, remembers the twenties and carries the impress of the thirties. Even more than his contemporaries Christina Stead and Patrick White, Porter manifests a period sensibility, and much of the pleasure in reading his fiction is in sharing his seemingly inexhaustible fascination with the exact and detailed recovery of time and place.

Though he has written of various worlds (London, Venice, Rome; Occupied Japan and nineteenth-century Hobart), he is thoroughly local in attachment, a regional writer, choosing to depict especially the cultural and geographical territory he knows intimately (southern, provincial Victoria). But it is also, for him, a matter of compulsion. He has repeatedly insisted that he has not the imagination to invent, and takes his characters and stories directly from life. The challenge of mastering detail as well as effect, particularly within the formal confines of the short story and the restraint of fact in autobiography, constantly absorbs him. It is consistent with this determination to hold true to life that the best of his novels, *The Tilted Cross* (1961), is also controlled by fact:

all the thoughts and actions of his central character are from Wainewright, his historical model.

So extraordinary is the range of his vocabulary, so elaborate his familiarity with ornamental detail, and so precise his eye (and ear) for the bizarre, the extravagant, the vulgar and the exotic, the comic and the malicious, the *outré*, that the material substance of his work is largely overwhelmed, and the manner rather than the matter of his writing fixes itself as the centre of attention. His relish for paradox, his verbal wit, the wrought irony of his style all serve to identify attitudes to experience; they are devised to announce a manner, to determine and express an attitude, however obliquely it might emerge, in order to reveal the core of reality that lies behind the facade, the presented image. Porter's narrative stance is usually ambiguous, both detached and personal, ironically self-aware yet obedient to what is actually perceived. The poetry—*The Hexagon* (1956), *Elijah's Ravens* (1968), *In an Australian Country Graveyard and other poems* (1974)—suffers from being too mannered. It has the hectic word play of Edith Sitwell at her most relentless, and when the surface display is penetrated the sponsoring concept is most often found to be rather slight, and certainly unequal to the verbal elaboration. However, the word-consciousness and the emphatic mannerisms lend themselves well to drama, and his plays, conventional in their structure and somewhat melodramatic in inclination, are memorable for their arch and lively repartee, especially *Eden House* (1969).

In his fiction, Hal Porter writes against the pressure of time, of time past and passing, and of the interaction of the past upon the present, the past being remembered. What he writes, then, also determines the rememberer, the narrator as both agent and object, while in the autobiographies he investigates his stance as a watcher, watching himself as a young boy watching (in *his* mind's eye) himself at play, or observing the world he inhabits. The narrator in these books is Porter himself, in various roles and stances. According to the mood of the moment he is at times on the writer's mission of prying into others' lives, at times discovering in himself offensive actions, nostalgias, amusement, disdain, and the melancholy, half-suppressed admission of life's ultimate instability. To remember the past, whether personal or public, is both to preserve it and to concede that it is, after all, the past. Man's defence against his unacknowledged knowledge of both the transience and the absurdity of life, is to construct saving illusions; yet the business of a writer, and particularly one of Hal Porter's rigorous and fearless truth-seeking, is to strip away illusion. There is a genuine complexity of perception in Porter's fiction, then, as well as a disconcerting clarity, and not, as Vance Palmer would have it, the 'affectation of a jocose and sophisticated view of the world'.[43] Porter has made a triumph out of his mastery of the self-conscious mode, and through that arrives at increasingly subtle perceptions of the layers of sensibility and deceit in man.

For forty years he has maintained a high standard of accomplishment, in stories ranging from the relatively straightforward, a simple plot with a twist at the end, to the increasingly complicated and, recently, more experimental manner. In the early stories he is inclined to look for the whiff of scandal, the bizarre, the eccentric, the neurotic, the melodramatic, the gothic. To anticipate these is in some measure to invent them; his later view is that the freakish and the exaggerated do not have to be sought out, and the special effect does not have to be arranged. Though Porter may take his copy from 'life', he is more than disposed to manufacture a mood, and he consciously sets the tone, heightens certain details, chooses an approach to best suit his disclosure of the truth of the experience. Typically, this is to establish an elaborate surface by the massing of detail, the observable or remembered features of an actual world—household paraphernalia and domestic lore, the itemizing of public taste, films, plays, songs and books of the period—and then to reveal, or suggest, the presence of something furtive, if not evil, just below the surface, the social or individual truths that are kept out of sight, the secrets of character. It is a technique he admired in Katherine Mansfield, the representation of 'the breathtaking surface texture and, simultaneously, what the x-ray showed'.[44]

A Bachelor's Children includes revised versions of all but two of the stories in *Short Stories* (1942). *The Cats of Venice* (1965) collects stories from a briefer period, the early sixties, and while these display a wide range of interests they tend to identify a common attitude that ranges in expression from broad humour to satirical wit; the tendency of the earlier stories to sentiment and melodrama has been arrested. *Mr. Butterfry and other Tales of New Japan* (1970) reveals a re-alignment in Porter's view of Japan since his earlier experience of it in the Occupation, a revision presented in a more substantially documented account, *The Actors: An Image of the New Japan* (1968). *Fredo Fuss Love Life* (1974) shows Porter changing his strategy, particularly by reducing the governing detail in his stories: the 'whole' story is not provided. The result is too frequently that the stories become exclusive. Where 'The Cats of Venice', for example, supplies whatever is necessary of the locale, and makes no assumptions, in these later stories the expressed attitude suffers from an awkward self-consciousness, the narrative becomes self-indulgent or unfortunately dismissive (instead of challengingly so), while the title story reveals Porter engaging in suppositional narration.

In his novels, Porter shows some difficulty in achieving and maintaining narrative focus. The continuity of his first novel, *A Handful of Pennies* (1958), derives not from a sustained theme, but from a dominant attitude emerging from the narration itself, a satirical disdain which is expressed more than revealed. Structurally, the novel resembles a somewhat contrived arrangement of interweaving short stories, of which the most moving is the destructive affair of a country girl, Imiko, with an Australian officer. It is the least central of the various stories, but most tellingly expresses the effect of the Occupation on Japanese life. *The Tilted Cross* develops its themes and preoccupations more firmly, though the characters are more grotesque and the style more elaborately mannered. Porter superbly reconstructs colonial Hobart, with its opposing codes of behaviour, the barbarity underlying the veneer of civility and good breeding and the fulsome vitality of the under-world, the icy lovelessness of genteel manners and the personal concern and affection of the socially outcast. The contrast is both colourfully comic, and frankly appalling. At the centre of the narrative Vaneleigh, Porter's reconstruction of Thomas Griffiths Wainewright, is contrasted with Queely Sheill, a handsome and good-hearted Cockney. But there is an imbalance between the two, for Queely is too strongly a type of the 'hero', and Vaneleigh's persistent withdrawal from the world about him to the internal world of his own remembered past separates him from the rest of the novel's activities. He is the book's central figure, yet he is overshadowed by a subordinate figure and he is withdrawn from the main course of action.

Porter's third novel, *The Right Thing* (1971) is a fragmented narrative, with too many commentators, and as if to compensate for the proliferation of point of view, he dwells on both the phrase and the notion of 'the right thing' to well past the point of distraction. Gavin Ogilvie, the most enigmatic of the characters in the book, is the most interesting of the several commentators. Parts of the novel are entries from his journal, and this device allows Gavin to reflect upon the experiences he records so that, unlike the others, he is permitted a measure of detachment from the events in which he participates. In spite of the brittle repartee at the Ogilvie dinner-table and the domineering character of old Mrs. Ogilvie, *The Right Thing* suffers from longeurs. The resolution relies on what appears an imposed and certainly melodramatic action, and Porter seems to have drifted unhappily into the fictionally discursive, away from his proper mode, the imaginatively concentrated.

His most accomplished work is in non-fictional prose, the first particularly of the three autobiographical volumes, *The Watcher on the Cast-Iron Balcony* (1963). All his characteristic tricks of style, the long catalogues of detail, the interplay of past and present, the switch of personal pronoun to adjust the narrative point of view, the elaborate metaphorical and recitative manner, the clever play on words and startling reversals of expected meaning, are on display here, together with his distinctive angle of perception and his preferred themes (the loss of innocence, the re-definition of the present that is achieved through the act of remembering, the barely admitted intimation of death). It is memorable for the exactness of its recollection, as well as its discrimination and understanding; it evokes suburban Melbourne and provincial Bairnsdale in the early decades of the century but, more impressively, it clearly delineates a way of life, unexceptional in itself yet made exceptional by the very clarity with which Porter recalls it, and appraises it. *The Watcher* differs from the novels and stories in the kind of control he establishes over his narrative, for while he details his own autobiography he is simultaneously writing the biography of his mother, and the interplay between the two imposes the strict control of fact, while allowing the freedom of enlightened elaboration. In this work, he carefully investigates his own role as both narrator and subject, and since in his childhood experiences he was rarely the dominant active participant, and his habitual manner is rather the watcher's, what emerges is yet another intriguing version of the self-conscious, half-committed narrator. In *The Paper Chase* (1966), a book somewhat uncoordinated though lively enough in its details, Porter is even more elusive, developing the concept of the writer's necessary many selves, and so his absence of self. In *The Extra* (1975), Porter identifies his sense of his role as writer by the title; here, the anecdotes of prominent literary figures in Australia are developed at a more leisurely rate. They are given narrative shape, again within the over-riding necessity of writing only according to what has actually happened, and what actually is. In Hal Porter, the relation of fact to fiction is a persistent concern. It is the premise of his art, not an issue for debate; and one consequence of incorporating so much of life, his life, into literature, is that he has infinitely refined the technique, and the uses, of first person narration.

In 1964 George Johnston, a free-lance journalist who had written a number of nondescript books (documentaries, popular histories, novels of shallow attainment), sometimes in collaboration with his wife Charmian Clift, published his one major success, *My Brother Jack*. Capitalizing on the public interest in Alan Seymour's play *The One Day of the Year* (1960), Johnston popularized a change in attitude which had been slowly taking place in the fifties and early sixties, the de-mythologizing of the Australian type. (Hal Porter's ambition to write of Australians as they really are, and not how they seem to be, is consistent with this moving spirit.) More like Ray Lawler than Seymour, what Johnston devised was not so directly an attack on social and cultural cliché as a story in which he could depict the process of the gradual replacement of the cult figure, the traditional male hero, by the more plausible, less heroic, successful but treacherous narrator, Davy. Indeed, Davy's success comes directly at the expense of his brother Jack.

Davy presents himself with that peculiar detachment which is recognizably the preferred narrative stance in Australian fiction, and in so far as the story is his, the novel is candid, honest, true to the realities rather than the myths of Australian life. It falters towards a different kind of artifice though in its determination to make just that point. In its reminiscences of Melbourne from one world war to the next it served, together with *The Watcher on the Cast-Iron Balcony*, to prompt a minor vogue for local memoirs and autobiographies, for example Graham McInnes' series of books beginning with *The Road to Gundagai* (1965), chiefly memorable for its account of his mother, Angela Thirkell; or Donald Horne's *The Education of Young Donald* (1967). But in its account of the replacement of the stereotype by the real, *My Brother Jack* confirmed the end of the golden age of nationalist sentiment.

In Elizabeth Harrower's fiction, the characters happen to be Australian, but that is not important in determining the kind of people they are. She does pay some attention to local setting, of course, and like all Australian satirists she delights in exploiting the vulgarity of the ordinary man. Her novels, increasingly serious yet always with a sharp ironic wit, are careful studies of beseiged characters, characters caught in a trap which leads to emotional and sometimes physical violence. In some respects she bears comparison with Christina Stead, though Harrower is a much more firmly disciplined writer. She preserves a fine line between a schematic fiction, in which moral values are shown as assailed and resisting, and a fiction which is above all else true to the determining characteristics of her heroines. Her first novel, *Down in the City* (1957), is somewhat contrived in its opening premise and remains rather thin fare, but by the end it has become emotionally and spiritually flattening, for the abuse of the heroine's innocence is both morally outrageous and powerfully affecting. *The Watch Tower* (1966) is a much stronger study of the same theme, for where in the first case the victim is defeated by the coarseness of the man she married, the second rests on a factor of malice; it is a novel of considerable psychological astuteness, rather than of moral principle. In *The Catherine Wheel* (1960), the psychology is closer to an intellectual game, not a particular kind of explanation of character, and the altered perspective is determined precisely by Harrower's narrative method. Clem, in *The Catherine Wheel*, is curiously separate from the experiences she recounts, and can hardly believe they are happening to her. Only a part of her is involved, a part remote from the cool, observant eye. Clare's role in *The Watch Tower* is less fully controlled, for she is not as much a captive as her sister is, yet she is strangely reluctant to take her freedom. Hers is the same, objective understanding of what is happening, but she seems unable to act upon her perception.

Elizabeth Harrower's special strength is her understanding of character, and her perception of the ambiguity of relationships, and she has a correspondingly quick satirical eye for the stereotype and the comic possibilities of the unthinkingly conventional. After a series of character sketches in his first novel, *Young Man of Talent* (1959), George Turner too has steadily developed a particular interest in depicting characters under various kinds of mental and social pressure. The 'Treelake' chronicles—*A Stranger and Afraid* (1961), *The Cupboard Under the Stairs* (1962), *A Waste of Shame* (1965) and *The Lame Dog Man* (1967)—are especially arresting for their perception of motivation, and for the surprising degree of self-awareness and self-perception that he recognizes in his characters. Turner's approach is to analyse and estimate character, rather than depict it, and since his tactic is not to reveal too early the hidden explanation for behaviour, his novels are in fact like well-plotted detective novels. The tendency is for his fiction to become drama-tized case-history, in which cause and motive is revealed rather than discovered. In *Transit of Cassidy* (1978) he begins to experi-ment with changes in point of view and alternation of present and past, but the effect is to make this a rather ordinary book, for it distracts Turner from concentrating on character. *Beloved Son* (1978) carries the experimentation into science fiction, where his interest in systematizing behaviour, and in establishing cause and effect on precise, logical grounds, is turned to advantage.

As in Elizabeth Harrower's fiction, Sumner Locke Elliott's social portraiture is both accurate and witty. His novels are not con-trolled by a strongly determining plot, though the sense of fabrica-tion is strong in *Edens Lost* (1969); rather, they may be seen as proceeding by a continued re-grouping of characters. Locke Elliott writes entertaining social comedy—especially in *Water Under the Bridge* (1977)—and portrays sensitively and accurately the remembered middle ground of Australian society, not the demotic and not the exclusive. Both his plays and his novels enact the drama of the ordinary, and his occasional surrender to more exaggerated effects is, in the fiction, a false sense of the theatrical.

Like Sumner Locke Elliott, Shirley Hazzard is an expatriate writer. She began as a regular contributor of short stories to *The New Yorker*, and published them as a collected volume, *The Cliffs of Fall* (1963). These, together with her novels *The Evening of the Holiday* (1966) and *The Bay of Noon* (1970), are stories about love, but more of the regrets of love than of its pleasures. She is the most precise and most elegant of this group of writers. Her fiction is delicately but firmly controlled, her phrasing perfectly modulated. Irony and poignancy counterbalance each other, both in narrative technique and in her understanding of character; her candour about the emotions prevents the fine-tuned comic perspective from becoming brittle. Her preferred strategy is to establish in her characters an appraising inner consciousness that is brought to an ironic recognition of the self's detachment from experience. Her characters are strangely divorced from emotion and feeling, and faintly surprised at finding they are so indifferent. In her satirical collage, *People in Glass Houses* (1967), the exactness of her own style condemns the 'realms of nonsense' being institutionalized in the United Nations Organization, where the misuse of language endorses, and imitates, the misuse of reason. Her attack on the system is not only that it is irrational, but also that it is impersonal, which terms indicate the classic disposition of her temperament. Shirley Hazzard is not anti-romantic, but she is clear-eyed and unsentimental. Underlying everything she writes is a concealed compassion which is no less moving for being understated.

Much the same kind of discerning intelligence, refracted through comic and ironic wit, is discovered in Thea Astley; and also, much the same condensation of experience. They both write of individual anxieties and private truths, or vanities, and neither attempts large subjects. But where the exacting slenderness of Hazzard's fiction is enveloped in a mantle of cosmopolitanism, Astley is specifically a writer of local attitudes and values, and Elizabeth Harrower's *The Long Prospect* is closer to her imaginative territory. In style, however, Astley displays a tendency to arch mannerisms and even on occasions to the 'Gothic splendours' of Patrick White ('Certain captive objects were practising their own form of insubordination'). The curious result is first that the substance of her fiction tends to be diminished by the playful intelligence of the narration; and more critically, that the liveliness is separate from the imaginative centre of the narrative. Her scrutiny of the moral nature of her characters appears only half-serious, and though their failure to rise to the testing situation in which she places each of them is both a saddening spectacle and confirms the limitations of their moral nature, it is also disturbed by the inherent comic direction of the narration.

Astley is at her most assured in portraying the unimpressive life. Since she chooses not to pursue character at any great depth, what emerges as the truth of a character is ultimately less penetrating than is anticipated, and the perception of life itself, however witty and intelligent, confirms the known without revealing new insights. The earlier novels are at a disadvantage by their deliberately reduced range; they fail to develop an imaginative impetus. Only in *The Well-Dressed Explorer* (1962), where the absurdly self-infatuate protagonist is permitted to betray himself throughout, does ironic vision sufficiently harmonize with the irony of narrative comment. In *The Acolyte* (1972) the irony is transmuted into parody and mimicry, and the novel's concerns are called into doubt. Particularly, the genius of the central figure is beyond ready belief. *A Kindness Cup* (1974) concentrates on its theme of the ungenerous spirit to the point of excluding substantial detail. Description is minimal, and the care with historical reconstruction seems then oddly irrelevant, while the characters tend to become figures in a fable, rather than in a reconstituted world.

Thea Astley has remained committed, in her fiction, to the real world. Thomas Keneally, David Ireland and the more recent novelists have increasingly dispensed with the literally observed, and show the extent to which Australian fiction has freed itself not only from local compunctions, but also from conventional fictional forms. But none of them is a daringly innovative or experimental writer. For both Keneally and Ireland, as for Morris Lurie and Peter Mathers, as well as the short story writers, the experimentation carries a touch of self-consciousness, as though it were a predetermined gesture rather than the most appropriate artistic response to the demands of the subject matter. Even the comic anarchy of Peter Mathers, in the formal literary sense the most independent and radical of these writers ('To write, to put something down, is an act of subversion'),[45] derives much of its impetus from its recognition of contemporary fashions and attitudes. In his flair for fantasy—but not in the disturbing underside of that comic extravagance—Mathers resembles the more conformable comic riot of Barry Oakley. But his imaginative restlessness is finally inhibiting: although the political subversions of *Trap* (1966) are effectively mirrored in the narrative manner, *The Wort Papers* (1972) lacks direction. He wants the sardonic watchfulness of Murray Bail, whose short stories *Contemporary Portraits and Other Stories* (1975) accommodate Mathers' iconoclasm and absurdity without relinquishing, as he appears to do, narrative control. In Oakley's novels and short stories—*A Wild Ass of a Man* (1967), *A Salute to the Great McCarthy* (1970), *Let's Hear it for Prendergast* (1970) and *Walking Through Tigerland* (1977)—the absurdity is matter of farce. His narratives are boisterous and hectic, and segmental in structure, and do not so much develop a unifying comic vision as assume it. The vigorous antics of his characters belong to the stage rather than to fiction, where they seem patent inventions, and Oakley's subsequent commitment to drama acknowledges his true talent.

Where Harrower, Hazzard and Astley are distinguished by the wit and intelligence of their moral discriminations, and by the constancy of attitude that informs their narrative stance—all are ironic, none is uncharitable about man—the fiction of Keneally and Ireland, of Mathers, Oakley and Lurie, seeks to make a larger comment on human affairs, and to identify the individual against some intimation (nihilist, comic, ironic, melodramatic) of the scheme of things. Keneally, the most widely acclaimed of modern Australian novelists, persistently writes of conscience and choice, and more particularly his fiction investigates the difficulty of maintaining one's vision of life. His novels explore conflicts of principle, and find their resolution in the affirmation of the basic human decencies: compassion, generosity, integrity. His earlier fiction was too ambitious in the terms in which it required the moral choice to be made, and the resolution was in each case heavily melodramatic, just as the style was unduly self-conscious. Yet that tendency to over-emphatic effect indicates one aspect of his success as a novelist, for Keneally has combined the advantages of the popular forms of fiction, especially immediacy of effect, with seriousness of theme and thoroughness of imaginative design.

Keneally is unconstrained by subject matter. He finds his stories everywhere—in medieval France, the Yugoslav resistance, Australian history, Antarctica, in a womb (*Passenger*, 1978). He attends meticulously to style and cadence, particularly from *Blood Red, Sister Rose* (1974) on, though his characteristic rhythms and turns of language were in evidence as early as his first successful novel, *Bring Larks and Heroes* (1967). (Curiously, these accomplishments of style did not translate very well to the stage in the dramatized version of that novel, *Halloran's Little Boat*. What in his fiction seems lyrical and eloquent, in each of his plays is heard as stylized and artificial. Patrick White shows much the same failure in *Big Toys*.) Keneally's heroes are mostly rather ordinary people who have to deal with their destiny in whatever terms they can. Their perception of themselves is alternately comic and rueful, yet their perseverance towards the good as they see it does not waver, however that might bring them into conflict with an institutional orthodoxy they have always accepted. They are frequently reluctant heroes, preferring quietness yet forced by their private convictions to act in ways which ironically bring about their defeat. Maurice Erzberger, who negotiates the Armistice terms on behalf of Germany in *Gossip from the Forest* (1975), is the most sensitive of

Keneally's studies of a character forced unwillingly into a public role.

Keneally's depiction of character, however, is held to a particular focus. Character itself is not really his concern; his characters are not full portraits. What he shows instead is the manner of their response to circumstance, and the way they sense the meaning of events, or discover that there is a design to life, a rational destiny. Halloran, the sacrificial hero of *Bring Larks and Heroes*, accepts the confident assertion that there is a plan, and with it the corollary that the plan exists without regard for the individual. In *The Chant of Jimmie Blacksmith* (1972), Jimmie is lost part way between tribal and Christian systems of belief, and fails in his attempt to construct his own meaning. Keneally's comment here is, in the most immediate sense, social indignation. In *A Victim of the Aurora*, where by the very nature of the landscape man has to impose his own meaning, the perception is sadder. Though in many ways it is a slight work, and appears a superficial novel of sensation (Keneally has never avoided the sensational), it is more seriously a tableau of the modern century's loss of innocent vision. The notion of a comprehensible design is itself over-ruled as a too innocent certainty, and history similarly rolls over Joan of Arc, Maurice Erzberger and Jimmie Blacksmith. The particular character of Keneally's fiction derives from a perception that man is not secure, and that despite the honest heart and the other human decencies, man's fate is of very little significance against what he can detect of the meaning of life. Though Keneally is not a pessimist—there is much comic verve, and much generosity of spirit in his fiction— his novels are more chastened in mood than one immediately recognizes, and convey with some feeling the irony of human limitation. Repeatedly he depicts men unable to meet the compromises forced upon them, yet against that he does assert the necessity of holding to as much of the truth as man can discover for himself. From the rather elementary fables of goodness and violence in his early 'Australian' novels, Keneally has come to a more complex and more universal view of man.

Like Keneally, David Ireland poses questions about the kind of sense man can make of his experience. Ireland's range of reference is much more precisely local, but he is also a much more disturbing novelist. His fiction ranges from the chaotic violence of *The Chantic Bird* (1968) to the satirical constructions and absurdist extravagance of *The Unknown Industrial Prisoner* (1971), *The*

Flesheaters (1972) and *The Glass Canoe* (1976), and the moral sardonicism of *Burn* (1974). In each novel, his protagonists devise an attack on life itself, for behind each of them lies the despairing cry of *The Chantic Bird*: 'If there is no other life, why is this one so lousy?'. But that attack is, in fact, a violent response to a more deeply exhausting apprehensiveness that life is meaningless. They are driven by an urgent need to discover purpose and meaning in life, and that anxiety itself makes sense of the apparent absurdity the aimlessness of life in the modern city. Australian fiction continues to be governed by the need to meet reality, but in its recent manifestation the realism is conceptual, not actual.

Though in their range of satirical reference Ireland's novels reflect a real enough Australia, his narrative is elusive, a fiction in which the usual moral, social and spiritual perspectives are altered to recreate the sadness and the cruelty of the meaningless world. It remains the world, however, not the void; it is all the slender chance of life we have. Despite its bleakness, Ireland's steady integrity of reflection is impressive, as is the care with which he integrates it with the imaginative texture of his fiction.

In contemporary Australian fiction very few new writers have established their presence. Only in the short story does anything comparable to the activity in drama and poetry occur. At the end of the sixties and in the early seventies, a group of writers in Sydney, dominated by Frank Moorhouse and Michael Wilding, became a local force, asserting in their stories the 'alternative lifestyle' of the inner-city suburbs, and startling the conventionality of middle-class social values. They were also quick to recognize the absurdity and pretentiousness of those who affected the new freedoms; yet in the process, they developed their own conventions, which again they have recognized and taken advantage of, Wilding for comic effect and Moorhouse for irony. It is an extravagantly self-conscious mode, a neo-romanticism which affects a pose of realism. Moorhouse's stories are loosely coordinated, and form a discontinuous narrative of what he calls the urban tribe. Although his characters proclaim the necessity of personal integrity and aggressive honesty about the self, they exist in their collective identity. They are not allowed to develop fully and they fail to recognize the nature of their defects and deficiencies. The pattern of experience for them is predominantly negative; the folly and the vice of the tribe, the drop-outs and the radicals, are echoes of the folly and the vice located in the larger background from which the tribe has dissociated itself. It is characteristic of these stories that the new human and social ideals are inferred, without anyone being credited with the capacity to achieve those ideals—particularly the first-person narrator Moorhouse has so frequently used, who, like the traditional figure of the narrator as memorialist, both records his increasingly receding times and reveals his half-commitment, half-resistance to those values and attitudes. Like Murray Bail and Peter Carey (*The Fat Man in History*, 1974), Moorhouse and Wilding are more concerned with situation and meaning than with character. The common feature of this new writing is its characteristic narrative approach: to watch events happen, to watch, at a distance or with some inevitable degree of detachment, how people behave. The narrative manner is almost the true subject of the story itself.

The 'new writing' is confined, in prose fiction, almost entirely to the short story. The return of Christopher Koch to print with *The Year of Living Dangerously* (1978) and David Malouf's two novels, *Johnno* (1975) and *An Imaginary Life* (1978), indicate a mood quite directly opposed to those radical tendencies, a fiction characterized by cool deliberation and meticulous craftsmanship. Malouf's *Johnno* pits the first person narrator, Dante, against the friend he remembers; that is, increasingly he assesses himself against his memoirs of Johnno. But the style is overly studied. The narrative appears to attend to the arranged manner of expression rather than to the perceptions recollected: it is self-indulgent to a fault, and surprisingly leisurely. A more substantial criticism of the novel is that Malouf fails, finally, to identify his interest in Johnno. The contrast with Dante is too abrupt, and appears to have been contrived to make a point, much as George Johnston arranged in *My Brother Jack*. His second novel, *An Imaginary Life*, is also a first-person narrative, about the transforming powers of the sympathetic imagination, about the possibility of the negative capability of being, finally, what one perceives. Its concerns are poetic, not moral, and while it is a book of considerable intelligence and skill, the studied elegance of its style betrays it, for the precious writing becomes brittle rather than refreshing.

Koch's novel is set in Indonesia, and its structure is derived from the symbolic patterning of the *wayang kulit*, the classical Javanese shadow-puppet plays. Its mode is an intriguing combination of allegory, symbol and documentary realism, for the narrative concerns a number of foreign journalists (one of whom is the first-person narrator) observing Indonesia's political and public affairs in Sukarno's year of Confrontation. Narrative technique and perception are more evenly balanced than in his two previous novels; although Koch again surrenders to touches of melodrama, these are partly defensible by virtue of the emblematic values of the shadow-show legends, the ancient dreams of the Ramayana and the Mahabharata.

It is a novel full of observers, each of them both a participant in and a recorder of the momentous events of that year—a novel with a receding series of memorialists. The persistence in Australian fiction of the participating chronicler as the narrator indicates the extent to which attention has been given to the mode of narration itself. From the responses of the early memoirists to the fact of their new experience, to the studied laconicism of the bush anecdotalists, the considered decencies of Astley and Keneally, or Porter's irony or White's address to the 'unprofessed factor', Australian fiction has been especially concerned to identify its narrative stance. Indeed, the stance itself becomes the subject of some of the fiction: it is clearly of great importance to the bush school and the nationalist writers, and it is thoroughly investigated in Furphy's *Rigby's Romance*. Similar narrative self-consciousness dictates the terms and effects of writers as different as Frank Moorhouse, Christina Stead and Patrick White. Tom Collins' remarks on the right way to tell a story, however insufficiently he heeded his own advice, were not gratuitous but seriously intended instructions. Interest in the procedure by which the narrative is presented is just as important a feature of Australian fiction as the concern with reality, in its different guises. The choice of the participating chronicler provides the writer with the means to develop his fiction as close to or as far from the controls of fact as he wishes. But above all, it is a device which has shown that the chief consideration of Australian fiction has persistently been man's suspended disbelief in the world of his experience.

DRAMA

TERRY STURM

PART ONE: 1788–1900

F. C. Brewer, author of the first substantial survey of nineteenth century developments in Australian drama *The Drama and Music of New South Wales*, 1892, concludes his account with a characteristic appeal to Australia's British origins, as confirmation of the quality of its taste for theatre:

> The record given in these pages will show that the Colony has not stood still in two matters that form such a large share in the education and legitimate amusements of the people ... sufficient is given to prove that the progress of Australia, the youngest daughter of the British Colonial Empire, has kept pace with the rest of the world in the development of a taste for the Drama and Music.[1]

In voicing sentiments like these, and in seeking to provide a social rationale for the history of names, dates and events he chronicles so enthusiastically throughout his book, Brewer was an eloquent spokesman for the dominant theatre-consciousness of nineteenth century colonial society. The colonial *idea* of theatre, in Australia, included an intense degree of self-consciousness about the relationship between theatre and society. It can be traced, as a developing history, in the plays themselves: from the 'literary' drama of David Burn, early in the century, in which highly stylized forms embody a belief in theatre as a powerful cultural force in a new society, through to the popular Anglo-Australian melodramas of George Darrell, later in the century, in which audiences are invited to recognize, and celebrate, an emergent colonial identity. It can be traced, also, in discussion and debate about theatre from the beginning of the colony; in the official utterances of those who sanctioned and patronized early amateur and convict productions, and who subsequently legislated and licensed theatres into existence; and, especially, in newspaper journalism—a rich source of commentary, criticism, advertisements and anecdotes through which colonial society expressed its understanding of the workings of theatre.

The decisive influence shaping Australian theatre in its earliest years, before the establishment of permanent institutions in the early 1830s, was the fact of penal settlement itself. It gave a special urgency to the question repeatedly asked in this period, which was *not* 'What sort of theatre should we have?' but 'Should we have theatre at all?' It was a question which would hardly have been asked in England itself, where a long history of theatre had made the institution seem part of the natural order of things. In Australia it was as if, in a quite elementary way, the very need for theatre was open to doubt, forcing into the foreground debate about fundamental social aims and needs.

Until 1800 convicts were involved in all dramatic ventures of which there is any record. The first performance in Australia was a convict production of George Farquhar's *The Recruiting Officer*, played before an audience of sixty, including Governor Phillip and the officers of the garrison, at Port Jackson, on 4 June 1789. At Norfolk Island, between May 1793 and January 1794, Lieutenant-Governor King sanctioned convict theatricals 'in hopes of its being a means of making every person contented in their situation and pleased with each other'.[2] Sydney's first (short-lived) theatre was built by convicts and opened in January 1796, under the management of Robert Sidaway, an ex-convict turned merchant. The acting company of this theatre, according to David Collins, was made up of 'some of the more decent class of prisoners, male and female', who had been informed, as a condition of performance, that 'the slightest impropriety would be noticed, and a repetition punished by the banishment of their company to the other settlements'.[3]

Behind the chequered history of early convict performances—the abortive experiment at Norfolk Island, and Governor Hunter's on-again, off-again policies at Sydney between 1796 and 1800—the central social issues which determined the shape of nineteenth century Australian theatre were being formulated. From an Enlightenment point of view, drama was one of the noblest and most civilized of human pursuits, the most rational and intellectual of all amusements. Hence in a new society, and especially in a convict society, it was an instrument for reforming vicious tendencies and maintaining social stability. Captain Watkin Tench's early account of the first convict performance in Sydney said little, in detail, about the production, but stressed the social utility which the theatricality of the occasion served.[4] However limited its actual resources, theatre was visible evidence of civilization in the making, providing an opportunity for ritual reaffirmation of British ideals and customs. Its significance lay less in what was performed on stage, than in the wider sense of social identity, and sociableness, which performance was thought to make possible.

This consciousness gave colonial theatre its characteristic shape throughout the nineteenth century, promoting conventionality itself as the norm by which local dramatic success might be measured and affirmed as a social value in circumstances which threatened the growth and stability of a new society. For Tench, the ability to produce conventional effects out of the most unpromising materials ('three or four yards of stained paper, and a dozen farthing candles stuck around the mud walls of a convict-hut') was the most creative achievement of Australia's first dramatic performance. Colonial fascination with the makeshift ingenuity of actors in contriving conventional theatrical illusions is wittily illustrated, also, in James Tucker's fictionalized account of a brief meeting between official dignitaries and convict performers after a production at the Emu Plains convict theatre in the late 1820s.[5]

Convict theatre was sanctioned on the ground that it served the useful social function of reinforcing authority and boosting morale. It neutralized potential conflict by absorbing it into an action whose essence was the celebration of convention. There are fragmentary early records of other kinds of dramatic performance, in which issues of authority and morale were also raised: performances by soldiers in military barracks, and by the naval personnel of visiting ships. Throughout this period, in fact, theatrical activity needs to be seen as extending well beyond what was occasionally presented on improvised stages. It gave a distinctive character to the public acts of the colonial authorities, which were marked by a highly theatrical feeling for ceremonial occasion, pageantry and spectacle. It played a significant role in the social habits of polite society, where it became the fashion to stage elaborately formal balls, dinner parties and concerts, which were written up at length by the newspapers of Sydney and Hobart as if they were theatrical events. Theatre also exercized a powerful influence on the dominant literary forms of the period (such as loyal odes), which were by their nature public poems. Self-conscious formality of style in early travel narratives and reminiscences might also be seen as a representation of Culture's triumph over what was often felt to be a barbarous, inhospitable environment.

Display, ostentation and flamboyance were thus to become distinctive values in nineteenth century colonial theatre. Novelty, originality, and individuality, for their own sake, were rejected, though they provided a particularly powerful image for colonial audiences if they could be seen to be directed towards, and yet contained within, what was recognizably conventional. To be the first to introduce in Australia the most recent theatrical success (play or player) on the English stage; to make ingenious or inventive use of limited local resources in contriving effects which 'would not disgrace the boards at Covent Garden or Drury Lane', to show unusual enterprise, under difficult conditions, in building a theatre modelled on a known British example, or in writing a play on a local theme whose style and conventions were instantly recognizable from British models—these were all theatrical values because they were also social values. They illustrated Australia's ability to participate in the progress of British civilization.

This sense of the special cultural importance of drama in a new society is particularly clear in the work of Australia's first playwright of significance, David Burn, an educated man of letters who had migrated in 1826 from Scotland to Tasmania (then Van Diemen's Land) as a free settler-farmer. Burn wrote eight plays over the next two decades. Five of them were included in a two-volume edition of plays, poems and prose which he published in Hobart in 1842—the first collection of plays to be published in Australia. He was also a journalist and polemicist on political, military and literary matters, and the author of a number of works of a historical and descriptive character including the three narratives, *An Excursion to Port Arthur in 1842*, *Vindication of Van Diemen's Land*, and *Narrative of an Overland Journey . . . to Macquarie Harbour*.

Burn's critics have usually confined discussion of his work to two of his plays with local settings, *The Bushrangers* (1829) and *Sydney Delivered* (1845), endorsing the judgment of a contemporary English reviewer in *The Athenaeum*, 1843 that his other plays were 'curiously wrought in fustian', and written in a 'high-toned and heroic' mode 'wonderfully in the Crummles vein'. These other plays included a romantic melodrama set in Sicily, *Loreda*, and a nautical farce, *Our First Lieutenant* (both written at the same time as

The Bushrangers), and a later series of blank verse tragedies on historical themes: *De Rullecourt, or Jersey Invaded*; *The Queen's Love* (set in seventeenth century Scotland); *Regulus*; and an unpublished play, *Mary Stuart*. Selective emphasis on Burn's Australian plays, however—dismissing the others as literary or derivative—produces curious distortions. Such a distinction would have made little sense to Burn himself, who saw his historical tragedies as the main plays on which his reputation as a founder of Australian drama rested. From his perspective, the most locally significant, since most clearly demonstrative, of his plays were those, like *The Queen's Love* and *Regulus*, modelled on the highest forms of British drama.

The Australian performance history of Burn's work is particularly revealing in this respect. Neither of the two plays with local subjects and settings, *The Bushrangers* and *Sydney Delivered*, ever received a local production, although the former was performed twice in Edinburgh in 1829. *Sydney Delivered* was published in 1845, with a revealing explanatory note:

> a fear that the lavish seasoning of French pepper might prove too pungent to obtain the Dramatic Licencer's permission for Stage representation prevented the attempt being made.

Burn also omitted *The Bushrangers* from his 1842 volume, perhaps because he felt that its themes of convictism and bushranging, and its emphasis on factional conflict between Tasmanian officialdom and free settlers, would undermine the book's patriotic aims. In any case, like *Sydney Delivered*, it would almost certainly have been refused official permission for performance in the climate of the 1840s, because of its locally objectionable subject matter. For both these plays, official licensing practice, with the direct political aim of keeping contentious local themes off the stage, coincided with acts of self-censorship on Burn's part, motivated by a conception of himself as a dramatist who spoke for the nation as a whole, and not for any merely sectional interest. In the course of a long review of the Sydney production of *The Queen's Love* in 1845, 'one of the best and most inartificial tragedies we had ever witnessed' the *Australian*[6] called for an appropriate recognition of its patriotic significance, which it saw as transcending local political and sectarian rivalries.

The other play of Burn's to be performed in the 1840s was *Our First Lieutenant*. As with *The Queen's Love*, it is in the circumstances

of performance, rather than in a 'literary' search for local references in the play's text, that the drama's local significance can be
most clearly seen. Nautical drama, the British genre to which
Burn's farce belonged, had a special significance and popularity in
the colony not only because visiting sailors made up an unusually
large proportion of the audience for drama in places like Sydney,
but also because colonial audiences in general were acutely aware
that their very existence depended on the lifeline with 'Home'
maintained by British merchant ships and defended by its naval
power. The conventional elements of such plays emphasized
spectacular deeds of heroism and the true-blue loyalty, initiative
and romantic appeal of Jack Tar, the common British sailor, and
drew strongly on imperial 'Rule Britannia' sentiment, in a
language heavily interlaced with naval slang and puns. Such qualities boosted colonial morale, encouraging audiences to identify
with those special qualities exemplified in Britain's strength as a
maritime power.

In Burn's mind the performance of *Our First Lieutenant* in
Sydney (in November, 1844) had an even more immediate
purpose. In the later months of 1844 he had been alarmed by
reports of French naval power, and anxiously scanned naval
magazines for information about the relative sizes of the British
and French fleets, which he published with gloomy prognostica-
tions in the local press. He also wrote several longish prophetic
poems under the name 'Agamemnon' which were published in
the colonial press and sent to naval magazines in the United States
and England. Another poem on the same theme was incorporated
in the performance of *Our First Lieutenant*. The play *Sydney
Delivered*, a lively satirical burlesque in which the French fleet
suddenly steamed up Sydney Harbour out of nowhere and surprised the City Council in the act of voting itself increased salaries,
was the final outcome of this sudden burst of activity. Based on a
news report of the capture of the fort of Tahiti and Queen Pomare
by French pirates, *Sydney Delivered* develops as a parable of French
naval ambitions in the Pacific region. Its farcical humour is
conveyed through comic parodies of popular sentimental and
patriotic songs, grotesque costuming and absurd sound effects, and
by a running burlesque of the Revenge theme in Shakespearean
tragedy. Burn's underlying point, however, is quite serious. The
play is a double-edged satire on colonial indifference to the threat

of foreign domination, and on British complacency about its imperial mission.

Performance of *Our First Lieutenant* in 1844 was thus one element in an active campaign Burn was conducting at the time, both in the theatre and through poetry and journalism. His blank verse historical tragedies were local propaganda for Britishness in a larger sense. Their characteristic themes are patriotism and heroism, the nature of statesmanship in the faction-ridden world of high politics, and the conflict between public responsibility and personal or domestic ties. Although it is tempting to read such plays as parables of specific events in Australia, their aim is more general—to create through the immediacy of theatre a sense of history and high culture, which was felt to be especially under threat in a colonial society isolated from the centre of civilization. Burn shows considerable dramatic skill in manipulating conventional tragic elements (passionate blank verse utterance and vigorous melodramatic action, with emphasis on spectacle and pageantry) in order to involve audiences in the recognition of the British traditions they had inherited. The deliberate display of formal tragic models (Addison, Alexander Home and, beyond these eighteenth century figures, Shakespeare) was an essential aspect of such plays' social function. Although Burn's historical plays, with the exception of *The Queen's Love*, remained unperformed, costume plays on historical themes, with the more entertaining nineteenth century ingredients of romance, sensation and spectacle, were exceptionally popular on the Australian stage throughout the century, for reasons which Burn's self-conscious historicism helps us to understand. In such plays, Australian audiences could see the melodrama of their own history writ large, part of the universal pageantry of human history.

Burn's astuteness as a dramatist is particularly apparent in *The Bushrangers*, a play loosely based on the exploits of Matthew Brady, the leader of a gang of convicts who escaped from the penal settlement at Macquarie Harbour in 1824 and remained at large in Van Diemen's Land until 1826. Burn's romanticizing of Brady's career has often been noticed, though its actual purpose in the play has been less clearly understood, and in some accounts interpreted as an early expression of a distinctively Australian anti-authoritarian ethos in which the 'noble bushranger' figures as a radical stereotype. Burn's purpose, however, is essentially to defend the interests of the free settlers in Tasmania against government policies which treat them as if they were convicts, denying them British rights and privileges. In the words of the Governor (a thinly disguised caricature of Governor Arthur):

> This, sir, is a *penal* colony. Such *free* settlers as choose to emigrate hither, I regard as the mere instruments of prison discipline—nothing more than jailers to the convicts they employ. The Military I consider as necessary to keep the ridiculous notion of *civil* rights entertained by those *free* gentlemen under wholesome restraint. As a body, sir, the settlers are a vile, troublesome set, and have done all in their power to embarrass my government.

The play's romanticizing of Brady is not so much an attack on the penal system, as an enlistment of Brady in the cause of those British values which Burn identified with the interests and aspirations of the free settlers. Burn makes this connection through clever manipulation of melodramatic conventions in a loose sequence of episodes which carefully distinguish Brady, as hero, from other convict villains, like the cruel overseer, Rex, the treacherous Cohen, and the escaped murderer and seducer, Jefferies. Brady also speaks throughout in an educated poetic prose, an indication of the superior moral and social status which he sees as justifying his escape. By isolating Brady in this way, and making him the object of an uncomprehending personal vendetta by the Governor, Burn's satire gains a double force: if colonial official-dom in the person of the Governor cannot recognize Brady's superior moral qualities within the penal system whose admini-stration serves as a pretext for authoritarian policies, what hope is there of its recognizing the legitimate rights of free settlers outside it?

In *The Bushrangers*, Burn is essentially rationalizing Australian history, making Brady the spokesman for values on which he believed Tasmania's development as a civilized British colony depended. The play's inclusion of an Aboriginal scene is of par-ticular interest, since it provides the first example of what was to become, throughout the nineteenth century, a stereotypical stage image of Aboriginal life and character. Since the play was written for performance in Edinburgh, the scene was partly designed to exploit British curiosity about exotic Aboriginal customs. But it was also concerned to demonstrate that Aboriginals were hope-lessly incapable of understanding or profiting from the benefits of white man's culture, and the scene's climax in fact rationalizes their murder. Burn makes his point throughout in very theatrical terms, emphasizing visual elements, a vigorous stage action, and dramatic musical effects. Comic dialogue underscores the mental inferiority of the Aboriginals, their inability to understand white morality ('Black fello no want onor—him want rom') or white political concepts. The fact that all the white characters in the scene are stereotypes drawn from inferior groups in white Australian society emphasizes the inferiority of the Aboriginals. If there is such a mental and moral gulf between blacks and whites at this level, Burn implies, then what must be the predicament of the educated and respectable colonial gentry in Tasmania, of which he was himself a member? The effect is also underscored by scene painting. The Tasmanian setting in which the action takes place is described, in the scene's opening stage directions, as 'park-like', made to look like a traditional English romantic landscape, with one or two homely details added.

(The Shannon. A beautiful plain presents a park-like appearance. Large ornamental trees are studded here and there. The background is filled with lofty mountains. A fine, broad, but in many places, shallow river, crosses the scene. On one side is a hut, formed of upright logs and at the door MRS BROADHEAD is seen knitting and DOLLY sewing. Music as the curtain rises.)

Such a scene effectively rationalizes European occupation of Tasmania by turning the historical process inside out. In the action which follows it is the Aboriginals who appear as strange, unnatural interlopers on the natural setting, not the Europeans.

Burn's plays were written in the period when professional theatre was beginning to establish itself permanently in Australia's main cities. That he held so passionately to a belief in theatre as a rational pleasure with a cohesive and stabilizing social effect is partly explained by the nature of the debates which accompanied agitation for permanent theatre in the late 1820s. The key issue in these debates, as with convict theatre earlier, was whether the tendency of theatre was social or anti-social. At their centre, in Sydney, was the colourful figure of Barnett Levey, a brother of one of Sydney's wealthiest merchants. He had conceived an ambitious plan to provide Sydney's rapidly expanding population with bread and circuses on a lavish scale in the form of a multi-purpose building complex containing a large flour-milling operation and warehouses (with a windmill on top), a hotel with shops, bars and a saloon-cum-ballroom, and a theatre in the Georgian style capable of seating up to 1,600 people.

Governor Darling was an implacable opponent of public theatre, warning Levey that he was 'fully determined to resort to every means within his power, to put a stop to your unauthorized proceedings in this and other respects'.[7] In adopting this policy Darling had the support of the exclusivists in colonial society, of many of the established clergy (whose spokesman, Archdeacon Thomas Hobbes Scott, argued that theatre would be the resort of the vile, the vicious and the debauched),[8] and, with reservations, the *Sydney Gazette*:

> We very much question the policy of such a species of amusement being as yet introduced amongst us. However laudable and spirited it may be in individuals to contemplate and enter upon such a subject, yet we are decidedly of opinion—not that we are in any way desirous of affecting the interests of any party who may have embarked in such an undertaking—that the state of colonial society is as yet unfitted, and wholly unprepared, for the establishment of a Theatre.[9]

Darling's actions continually reveal that emergent class interests were strongly involved in the renewed debate about theatre's social or anti-social tendencies. He did not immediately act to suppress the flourishing convict theatre at Emu Plains (which had been established under Macquarie's successor, Governor Brisbane, in 1824–5), even though newpaper reports had drawn invidious comparisons with Sydney. An image of stability could be carefully nurtured in the controlled convict environment of Emu Plains. Sydney, on the other hand, in the mind of Darling and those who supported his stance, was a very different matter.

What Darling failed to see, in taking a hard line against public theatre—and what newspapers like the *Gazette* half recognized, in their ambiguous attitudes to Levey (praising his initiative, while deprecating the possible effects of a popular theatre)—was that Levey's commercial enterprise represented a harnessing of the earlier colonial belief in theatre's social and moral utility to the aspirations of an upwardly mobile and increasingly affluent middle class, seeking to extend its beneficial influence over a much broader mass audience. The emancipist element in this new consciousness reinforced the general drive to express a colonial identity, in the theatre, by means of the most thorough-going demonstrations of conformity to British forms and conventions, and to British social norms and ideals.

Governor Bourke's reversal of Darling's ban on popular theatre in effect legitimized these aspirations. The *Sydney Monitor*, reviewing a production which the Governor himself attended within a month of the opening of Levey's Theatre Royal, saw commercial theatre as an alliance of 'the middle and higher orders' for the moral and intellectual improvement of the 'lower orders'. In doing so it provided a characteristic social rationale for what became, from this point on, the dominant theatre consciousness of colonial society.

It was no accident that commercial theatre in Australia had its beginnings at a time when the transition from penal colony to an active frontier of British enterprise had been effectively achieved. Commercial theatre catered for the expanded popular audiences which this transition made available, in economic forms which were essentially capitalist in character. The cultural connections which this alliance of arts and commerce affirmed were represented, in symbolic terms, in the façade which Levey originally planned for his theatre. An early painting of the building, according to Eric Irvin's description

> ... showed a grand colonnade of the Corinthian order on the front of the building. On two wings were figures representing Comedy and Tragedy. Over the front was Apollo surrounded by the Muses, and surmounting the whole on a pedestal was the Genius of Australia supported on the right by the Genius of the Arts and on the left by Commerce.[10]

So grandiose a conception of theatre, harnessed to images of patriotism and commerce, in forms and figures which evoked the presiding muses of classical British tradition, did not, of course, exclude the idea of entertainment, since it was precisely in the opportunities which public theatre offered for controlling and satisfying the need for entertainment that its social usefulness could be most clearly demonstrated. As the *Australian* wrote in 1844, echoing Cunningham's justification of the 'manifest utility' of 'some such innocent recreation as theatricals' two decades earlier,[11] such a need was especially urgent in a colonial society, which was 'destitute of those social circles which characterize every grade of the community at home'.[12]

The need to promote an image of theatre's social utility is seen particularly clearly in the history of licensing legislation. Throughout the nineteenth century a justifying rhetoric of freedom—the idea of 'free institutions' which in the early agitation for permanent theatre was felt to be a peculiarly British birthright and privilege—was accompanied in practice by unusually rigorous legislative control. In the 1840s the condition which had restricted Levey to plays licensed for performance in England was relaxed to allow for the performance of plays written by colonial play-wrights. But it was accompanied, in practice, by a more rigorous form of official censorship, such plays requiring the prior written approval of the Chief Secretary, and the lodgement of a copy in his office, for permanent record. Again, such a practice worked to the advantage of both the civil authorities *and* theatre managements, since the former retained strict control over what was performed, while the latter were able to capitalize on the advertising potential, and the novelty, of plays which had 'the express sanction and permission of the Colonial Secretary'. In the mid-1840s a further restriction was introduced, giving the Colonial Secretary power to prohibit the performance in Australia of plays which had in fact been licensed in England. It was a characteristically colonial extension of 'freedom', designed to ensure practical control of that image of British culture which commercial theatre in Australia had originally set out to promote: a defence of British standards, in Australia, which British theatre itself might fail to maintain.

Levey's Theatre Royal opened in Sydney in 1833, and performed some four hundred British plays, drawn primarily from the range of nineteenth century British drama but including a sprinkling of eighteenth century plays and Shakespearean productions. It closed in 1838, the year in which Joseph Wyatt opened the Royal Victoria Theatre. Despite a number of attempts to set up rival theatres, the Royal Victoria dominated Sydney theatre for the next decade and a half. In Tasmania dramatic activity was equally vigorous. Regular professional theatre was presented in Hobart, in temporary premises, between 1833 and 1837, the year in which the Theatre Royal (subsequently re-named the Royal Victoria) began its long life as Hobart's main theatre. Adelaide and Melbourne followed a similar pattern in the late 1830s and early 1840s, and by the mid-1840s had established, remarkably quickly, their own equivalents of the major theatres in Sydney and Hobart—the Queen's Theatre Royal in Melbourne, and the Queen's Theatre in Adelaide. Smaller towns like Launceston, Port Adelaide and Geelong also developed professional theatre; and significant amateur activity occurred, in the 1840s, at Perth, West Maitland, and Port Macquarie.

Since none of the cities or towns had populations large enough to support more than a single permanent commercial theatre during this period, competition for control of such theatres was intense, and often bitter. The most dynamic of the mid-century entrepreneurs was George Coppin, an actor-manager who emigrated to Sydney from England in 1843, and became the driving force behind theatre in Adelaide and Melbourne from the mid-1840s on, eventually building a Melbourne-based theatrical and entertainment empire which lasted into the 1880s. Competitive pressures also meant insecurity for performers struggling to make a professional career in the theatre. Actors and actresses like Conrad Knowles, Eliza Winstanley, George Meredith, Joseph Simmons and John Lazar, all of whom learnt their craft in Levey's Theatre Royal in the 1830s, survived to become influential managers and performers in the 1840s, when they were joined by competing immigrant-actors like Francis Nesbitt and Morton King, and by groups of actors and actresses recruited from England by Mrs. Clarke (the manager of Hobart's Royal Victoria) and Wyatt. A characteristic feature of the period, however, was the mobility of managers and performers, a constant flow from one theatre, and one city, to another. It was primarily a result of competitive pressures, and had the immediate effect of varying the dramatic fare offered at particular theatres. It also ensured, on a longer term that basically the same kinds of drama were offered in theatres throughout Australia. The tendency of commercial enterprise in the theatre—in a country where the main centres of population were distant from each other, and often torn by inter-colonial rivalries—was a unifying one. History, in this instance, vividly confirmed David Burn's belief that in a colonial society theatre had a powerful cultural role to play in building a sense of nationhood.

The relative smallness of the populations which these early Australian theatres served, and the limited stage and acting resources, placed severe demands, not only on the ingenuity of managers in producing sufficiently varied programmes and novelties, but also on the versatility and endurance of performers themselves. Apart from the popular Christmas pantomimes, which by the mid-1840s in Sydney could run for up to two weeks, plays could rarely be expected to achieve more than two or three consecutive performances, with occasional revivals of the more successful productions. At least two, and usually three programme changes were needed each week. Moreover, the entertainment formula consisted of at least two plays each evening (normally, a full-length main feature, followed by a shorter after-piece), interspersed with musical items and variety acts. In a not unusual instance cited by Brewer, Conrad Knowles on one occasion

> sustained the character of Shylock in the *Merchant of Venice* and afterwards sang in the duet 'Pretty Polly Hopkins' ... following with a comic recitation in broken English, and winding up with the part of Mazzaroni in the drama of *The Italian Brigand*.[13]

The hit-or-miss character of many of the productions, resulting from hasty rehearsal and faulty memorizing of lines, can be traced as anecdote in many of the amused or censorious newspaper reviews of the period; but so, too, can the versatility, and the genuinely theatrical improvisatory skills, which the best performers, mechanists, scene-painters and musicians developed, making a virtue out of necessity. One of the liveliest Australian plays of the 1840s, Edward Geoghegan's *The Currency Lass*, built its plot on precisely this theme—the superior versatility of the locally-born performer—and was in fact written for a local actress, to enable her to demonstrate such skills.

With the establishment of permanent theatre, locally-written plays began to appear in increasing numbers, especially in Sydney in the 1840s. In the 1830s, the main impetus had come from Tasmania, where Burn was writing his later plays. Henry Melville's *The Bushrangers* (1834) and Evan Henry Thomas's *The Bandit of the Rhine* (1835) were both performed in Hobart and Launceston, the first locally-written plays to achieve Australian production. Sydney's only play of the 1830s was Charles Harpur's *The Tragedy of Donohoe*. Harpur had tried, unsuccessfully, to become an actor in Levey's company at the Theatre Royal, and the *Sydney Monitor* published excerpts from his play in 1835, recommending performance. However, it remained unperformed, despite successive revisions (including a change of title, to *The Bushrangers*) over the next twenty-five years, and Harpur went on to make his name primarily as a poet.

The most significant Australian playwright in this period was Edward Geoghegan, a convict whose identity and role as unofficial 'playwright-in-residence' at Sydney's Royal Victoria Theatre in the years 1843–46 have only relatively recently been uncovered.[14] Because he was a convict, Geoghegan's authorship of plays could never be publicly acknowledged. They were submitted to the public either anonymously, or under the names of the actors or managers (like Francis Nesbitt, Patrick Riley, and John Lazar) whose Benefits they were written for. Geoghegan was the author of a least nine or ten plays, which formed the nucleus of more than a score of local plays performed at the Royal Victoria in the 1840s.

The interest of these plays, modelled on a wide range of conventional Victorian genres (musical drama, melodrama, blank verse tragedy, comedy, and farce) lies in the closeness of the relationship between their writing and performance. Geoghegan's work, always written with particular actors and actresses in mind, is especially revealing in this respect; but of the other half dozen or so authors whose plays were produced at the Royal Victoria (Charles Nagel, Charles Dibdin, Conrad Knowles, H. C. O'Flaherty, J. L. Montefiore, Thomas Wilson, Joseph Simmons) Knowles and Simmons were leading actors, Dibdin a prompter, and O'Flaherty an actor and musician married to the leading lady, Eliza O'Flaherty (who was subsequently to establish a reputation in England, as the actress and popular Victorian novelist Eliza Winstanley). These playwrights, together with David Burn, achieved a total of close to seventy performances of their plays at the Royal Victoria in the period 1842–46.

Geoghegan's plays provide a remarkable insight into the workings of colonial theatre at this time, partly because of their range, and partly because of the theatrical self-consciousness they reveal—an awareness of the resources of the theatre he was writing for, and of the expectations of local audiences. *The Currency Lass* demonstrates the versatility of its heroine's dramatic talents through an ingenious (and highly improbable) plot device which makes acting talent a condition of her gaining the consent of her lover's eccentric English uncle ('an elderly gentleman much devoted to dramatic composition'), to their marriage—a marriage which he has forbidden under the mistaken impression that as a 'native girl' she is an Aboriginal:

> I'm positively determined that not a penny of my property shall go for the purpose of perpetuating the family features in bronze.

The Currency Lass is a slight play, an entertainment piece, but it nevertheless contains a sophisticated social consciousness of theatre which a more ambitious playwright like David Burn would have recognized and approved. The contrivance of a comic counterplot, which functions as a play-within-the-play, is the central device through which Geoghegan invites his audience to recognize theatricality as a norm by which the values of colonial society, concentrated in the figure of the Currency Lass herself, can be tested and affirmed. By deliberately playing with the established British conventions of the romantic comedy of intrigue and of operetta, and appropriating them to a local setting and action, he enables his audience to enjoy them for their own sake, and in the process celebrate convention itself as a sign of colonial vitality and identity. Colonial sentiment in the play is not so much anti-British, as an intensified and more inclusive awareness of what it is to be British. The deception of the 'new chum', the English uncle, carries the implication that colonial theatre (and hence colonial society) is far more robustly British than the degenerate contemporary stage he represents.

The effect of the play as a whole, then, is to concentrate and display established British conventions, in the interests of affirming a colonial identity. The Currency Lass's ability to perform a number of stereotypical roles convincingly is one such demonstration. Sentimental and patriotic songs interspersed throughout the play function in a similar way, with Geoghegan's original words set to popular traditional airs like 'Cherry Ripe', 'Malbrook' and 'The Lincolnshire Poacher'. The careful selection of representative English, Scottish and Irish musical items is designed not only to evoke sentimental associations for different groups in Geoghegan's audience, but, beyond this, to contain and absorb these separate nationalities within a unified consciousness of colonial identity. The emphasis given to Irish song and comic characterization in the play (making Irishness, effectively, a constructive rather than an alien element in the expression of colonial identity) is of special local significance, since it both defines the positive 'British' components of colonial culture, and enables others to be rejected. The plot of the play hinges on a racist pun, and a demonstration that 'native girls' in Australia are not necessarily afflicted with 'ebony visage, flat nose, sausage lips and woolly hair', but combine the separate beauties of English, Scottish and Irish women in a composite colonial image: 'one who unites the charms of all concentrated in herself—a Currency Lass!'.

Apart from this careful patterning of romantic, comic and operatic elements, much of the incidental dialogue is also designed to appeal to a theatrical self-consciousness in the audience. Lanty

O'Liffey's account of his visit to the Royal Victoria (the theatre in which the play itself was performed) is a typical example:

> Didn't you sind me to take places for you in the theayter? And whin they directed me to the next door, d'ye think I could lave the place with the curse ov the fair upon me, as we say in Donnybrook, and it with the Queen's name over it? No, in troth! So I left them Her Majesty's picture (bless her!) and got a dhrop ov the right stuff in exchange and staid listenin' to them divils of play actors gosterin' and jokin' at the bar. Be me sowl, thim's the quare boys. We don't meet the likes ov thim in the bush anyhow.

The speech associates conventional qualities in the comic Irish-man with genially patriotic British sentiment, and through its joking allusion to the actors as 'quare boys', 'gosterin' and jokin' at the bar'—with real lives, that is, outside their stage roles—heightens the audience's consciousness of theatrical conventions. For Geoghegan and his audience this serves an essentially social end: if the play's theme is the nature of colonial society, its mode of putting conventions on display invites audiences to recognize the role theatre itself plays in forging such an identity.

Geoghegan also wrote (or adapted) a witty local farce—*True Love, or The Interlude Interrupted*—with the similar aim of making an entertaining appeal to the theatrical self-consciousness of his audience at the Royal Victoria. The play's subject is theatre, its setting the Royal Victoria itself, and its satirical theme a light-hearted attack on those who confuse dramatic performance with real life. A humourless contemporary reviewer of one of the four performances the farce received, grudgingly conceded its popu-larity with the Royal Victoria audience:

> The fossil remains of the few old jokes that are introduced, have been carefully preserved, and we trust the author will take care to do the same with a copy of the entire farce. However, if the merit of a piece be determined according to the amount of merriment and applause produced among the audience, our Sydney dramatist has every reason to be satisfied with the success of his lucubrations.[15]

The source of the audience's enjoyment was clearly Geoghegan's ability to involve them in humorously familiar recognitions of their own theatrical environment, confirming the pleasure of theatre as a value in colonial life. The play is, in effect, propaganda for theatre as a 'rational pleasure' and a force for social harmony, engaging the audience's sympathies on the side of management and performers against the intrusions of moralists and utilitarians.

Geoghegan did not always make so direct a thematic connection between the values of theatre and the needs of colonial society. In his most popular play, *The Hibernian Father*, melodramatic elements of suspense and tragic sensationalism are focused on the anguished conflict within a man whose public duty as Warden and Chief Justice of Galway forces him to condemn his son to death for murder, and in a grim final scene carry out the execution himself. The play's climax, with its almost exclusive concentration on visual and spectacular elements (spelt out in detailed stage directions) is typical of the theatricalism of all Geoghegan's melodramas. Despite the remoteness of its setting from the Australian scene, however, and its seemingly innocent use of the entertainment conventions of melodrama, the play's local political implications are striking, as an Irish tale of crime and punishment performed when a large proportion of Geoghegan's audience were either ex-convicts or the sons and daughters of convicts. The Colonial Secretary's licence for *The Hibernian Father* included the cryptic phrase 'as now altered',[16] a comment implying that Geoghegan had been required to make changes to the play before permission to perform it could be given. Its sympathetic focus on the stubborn tragic conflict between justice and parental love in the Warden is in fact complicated by other elements less readily assimilable to the conventional moral pattern of such plays: the execution of an innocent man, the suggestion of a citizens' revolt on behalf of the accused, and the prolonged action and graphic detail of the execution scene itself.

It is difficult to gauge how conscious Geoghegan was of such elements in his plays, though he would clearly have been aware of the rigour with which official censorship was exercized at the time. H. C. O'Flaherty's *Life in Sydney; or The Ran Dan Club* (1843), a picaresque sequence of boisterous comic episodes modelled on the popular English play *Tom and Jerry; or Life in London* and introducing an English 'new chum' to Sydney's low life, was refused a licence on the ground that it contained 'matter of a libellous character independently of other objections'.[17] James Tucker's *Jemmy Green in Australia* (probably written at Port Macquarie in 1845)[18] was modelled on the same English play, and introduced a cockney new chum to a host of local hucksters and rogues, shady lawyers and dealers in real estate, all intent on stripping him of his money and possessions. The result is a comprehensive satirical portrayal of greed and materialism in colonial life, in the bush as well as the city. A Melbourne play, J. R. McLachlan's *Jackey Jackey, or The Australian Bushranger* (1845)—an adaptation of an article in *Tait's Magazine* by Thomas McCombie—was refused a licence on the grounds that the principle which rendered 'dramas of analogous character, such for instance as *Jack Shepherd*' objectionable in the United Kingdom, 'should apply even with greater force here'.[19]

Although Geoghegan appears to have deliberately avoided using such locally objectionable characters and settings, a play like *The Hibernian Father* illustrates in much the same way as Burn's plays, that local content in Australian drama throughout the nineteenth century cannot, without distortion, be confined to the literary evidence of the written text. All the elements of performance—including the activities of scene-painters and mechanists, the familiar presence of known local acting personalities, and the participation of local audiences, whose expectations and sense of dramatic occasion Geoghegan was so conscious of—shaped the colonial character of Australian drama. These elements were present in all productions, not merely in those with such typically Australian subjects and settings as bushranging, convictism, and gold discovery. Geoghegan's melodramas, distanced in subject and setting from the local scene, are characterized by a vigorously dramatic sense of visual and spectacular effect. Sumptuous or elaborate formal interiors (drawing rooms, state rooms or ball rooms) are often sharply juxtaposed with wild romantic landscapes, expressing Geoghegan's sense of conflict between social order and lawless passions, between realism and romance. In his adaptation of *The Last Days of Pompeii* (1844) the anarchic natural forces of earthquake and volcanic eruption, associated throughout the play with the mysteriously diabolical powers of an Egyptian necromancer, invade and destroy an elaborate formal setting of columns, temples and pedestals, in a sequence of spectacular stage effects: 'the most gorgeous spectacle ever produced at this theatre',[20] according to John Lazar, the Royal Victoria's master of such effects, for whom Geoghegan wrote the play. Such plays catered in a special way for the colonial audience's love of colourful display and spectacle for their own sake, its desire for a drama which was larger than life, in which imagination and fantasy might be given a freer reign than circumscribed colonial reality allowed.

After 1846, with Geoghegan's disappearance from the scene, the number of locally-written plays performed in Sydney fell sharply. Productions elsewhere in the 1840s were sporadic. Burn was produced briefly in Hobart and Melbourne. A locally-written play, *Negro Vengeance, A Tale of the Barbadoes*, was written and performed in Maitland. In the later 1840s and early 1850s a Melbourne actor, Francis Belfield, following Sydney practice, wrote three plays for performance by the Queen's Theatre Company: *Retribution; or, The Drunkard's Curse*; *Rebel Chief*; and *Zisca the Avenger*. There is evidence, however, that from the earliest period of the establishment of permanent theatre, local content found its way into a much greater range of forms than is generally realized. The shorter variety acts interspersed throughout performances in the 1830s and 1840s provided opportunities for introducing brief local items—songs, ballads, recitations, comic or satirical skits—which were not, apparently, subject to the censorship procedures required for plays.

The popular Victorian form of pantomime also offered a great deal of scope (in its second part, after the transformation scene at the end of the first part) for local or topical allusions. Pantomime offered precisely that mixture of romance and realism, in a conventionally fixed relationship to each other, which Geoghegan's very different plays had appealed to. A surviving manuscript of the comic scenes of John Lazar's Grand Easter Pantomime at the Royal Victoria in Sydney in 1846—*St. George and the Dragon; or, Harlequin and the Seven Champions of Christendom*—reveals how detailed these local Sydney scenes were, inviting audiences to recognize local landmarks, business premises and settings in George Street, Brickfields, Parramatta, and Crows Nest. The Christmas Pantomime for 1844 at the same theatre—*Harlequin Jack Spratt; or, The Fire Fiend, and the Fairy of the Evening Star*—advertized 'a new panorama 253 feet long, a short way of showing the various points of a voyage from Greenwich to N.S.W.'[21] The panorama, according to one reviewer, 'excited much wonder and admiration'.[22] So much so, that when repeat performances were given at Easter, 1845, advertisements apologized that 'In consequence of the numerous novelties produced on the benefit nights, the Panorama has been unavoidably painted out; but two new scenes will be substituted'.[23] The 1845 Christmas Pantomime—*Jack and the Beanstalk; or, Harlequin Ogre*—produced a house 'crowded to excess':

'The pantomime was received with shouts of laughter, especially the local scenes'.[24]

Throughout the nineteenth century, the essential action of locally-written drama might be described as a containment of reality within convention. The process occurs in higher as well as lower forms. The conventions of Australian melodrama, in the many subsequent plays modelled on this form, rationalized what was experienced as new and unpredictable, challenging and threatening in colonial life, conferring on it the logic and predictability, and the moral validations carried by the conventions themselves. The conventions of comedy, fantasy and magic in pantomime, and of Shakespeareanism and blank verse in a play like Harpur's *The Bushrangers*, performed a similar function, making the local scene an imaginative setting for universal impulses. This relationship between derived and local elements gives locally-written drama its characteristic shape throughout the century. It is neither a purely derivative nor a purely Australian tradition, but a special colonial transformation and use of received conventions in response to specific local pressures. Australian drama made up only a fraction of the total output of professional theatre, which was then (as in the twentieth century) primarily devoted to the production of overseas plays.[25]

The discovery of gold in New South Wales and Victoria in the early 1850s gave new impetus and direction to Australian drama. The initial effect of the sudden growth in population was a spectacular expansion of theatre construction, not only in goldfield townships like Ballarat, Bendigo and Bathurst, but in the main cities themselves, especially Melbourne and Sydney. By the mid-1850s Melbourne and Sydney each had three major theatres and two of these, Melbourne's Theatre Royal and Sydney's Prince of Wales Theatre, were capable of seating audiences of three thousand. Australia's new prosperity and optimism also brought with it, as Brewer rhapsodized in 1892, the first waves of overseas touring companies and visiting stars:

The sudden development of the auriferous wealth ... immediately brought Australia most prominently before the whole world, and communication was at once opened up by steam between London, San Francisco (via Panama), and Sydney and Melbourne. From 1853 to the present time there has been a constant influx of professionals into the colonies ... With very few exceptions the colonists have witnessed the performances of the monarchs of the stage ... in every branch of dramatic art; so that in this respect we stand upon the same platform as the rest of the English-speaking races.[26]

A new element in this overseas enterprise in Australian theatre was the size and scope of American involvement. Along with English and European celebrities like G. V. Brooke, Charles and Ellen Kean, Montgomery, Charles Matthews, Madame Ristori, Mrs. Scott-Siddons and Sara Bernhardt, a host of American performers and troupes continued to pass through from 1853 onwards. The arrival of J. C. and Maggie Williamson with a spectacularly successful American play, *Struck Oil*, in 1874—the first step in what was rapidly to become Australia's largest and most enduring theatrical empire 'The Firm' of J. C. Williamson—was not an isolated event, but the culmination of a twenty year history of American influence, which had included earlier tours by such key figures of American theatre as Marie Provost and Joseph Jefferson. From the 1850s on it thus becomes less and less possible to see colonial theatre simply as an offshoot of British theatre. Its development has to be seen (in the twentieth century as well as in the second half of the nineteenth century) as a distinctively colonial variant of Anglo-American theatre, in which American and British impulses continued to interact in ways which were never possible in America or England themselves.

One effect of the influx of overseas companies and stars into Australia was to intensify competitiveness between managements. The cost of such ventures demanded, and in turn generated, capital investment on a very large scale, and this eventually led, in the latter part of the century, to a concentration of economic power in the hands of a relatively small number of entertainment empires, as smaller entrepreneurs either fell by the wayside or were absorbed into the larger enterprises. A second effect was a rise in professional standards of acting and staging. The professionalism of visiting actors and actresses who had spent a lifetime perfecting a relatively small number of roles, and of productions which could draw on more specialized resources and expertise at every level of presentation, made the earlier period of versatile colonial enterprise seem makeshift by comparison.

The underlying trend, however, was an increasing specialization in every aspect of theatre—a trend which is often missed, or misinterpreted, in what seems on the surface to be a natural expansion of theatre to meet the needs of a natural expansion of audiences. It is most clearly seen in the specialization of repertoire which was an essential competitive element in the operations of touring companies and celebrities. By the end of the century theatre in Australia had largely become organized in these terms, with companies specializing in light opera and musical comedy, in melodrama and spectacle, in comedy about fashionable society, in Shakespeare, and in vaudeville. The growth of the star system was another manifestation of this trend. It involved a specialization of starring roles, the subordination of other roles, and the gearing of all the elements of performance to a dramatic action whose effect is the audience's identification, in fantasy, with the larger-than-life personality of the star. In theatre management also there was an increasing specialization of role and a growing isolation of management from performance, especially as control of theatre became more and more concentrated into large entertainment empires.

This latter development, in particular, can easily be missed, since the older actor-manager system, which at its best had achieved a relatively close working relationship between employer and employee, initially underwent an expansion in the more competitive conditions that prevailed from the 1850s onwards. The activities of George Darrell and Alfred Dampier as actor-managers of their own Australian companies, for which they often wrote or adapted their own plays and encouraged others to write, represented a high point in this expansion, from the late 1870s into the 1890s. This period is often seen as a golden era of Australian theatre, a time of vigorous local melodrama, home-produced stars, (especially in the fields of light opera and comedy) and spectacular Shakespearean production.

Ironically, however, it was the fact of specialization itself that contributed most to the rapid decline, after 1900, of the kinds of Australian and Anglo-Australian melodrama popularized by Dampier and Darrell. It was not only that the visual elements on which such drama strongly depended—sensational action, spectacle, fantasy—could be more lavishly catered for by the resources of bigger companies, but also that because of their dependence on visual effect the plays were particularly vulnerable to competition from silent films. Melodrama and spectacle were the theatrical forms which translated themselves most readily into the purely visual terms which film depended on in the pre-sound era. Bland Holt, producer of the most spectacular and meretricious of realistic illusions in plays like *The Breaking of the Drought* (1902) which belong to the dying stages of Australian stage melodrama, pointed unwittingly to the superior technology of film in an interview in the *Lone Hand* magazine of May, 1908: 'I want the drama of action, one that a deaf man can be interested in'.

Australian melodrama was ultimately the victim of its concentration on a relatively narrow range of themes (convictism, bushranging, and gold-discovery) in its effort to compete with other kinds of imported drama. As the events on which such plays were based faded into the past, their immediate imaginative appeal was lost. The decline of Australian melodrama, the dominance of large-scale overseas theatrical interests and the rise of the film industry provided the background against which, early in the twentieth century, non-commercial theatre began under the guiding theoretical and practical inspiration of Louis Esson.

A form which rivalled melodrama in importance, in the process of specialization which took place from the 1850s on, was pantomime, whose most prolific authors were W. M. Akhurst, in Melbourne in the 1850s and 1860s, and Garnet Walch, in the 1870s and 1880s. Like Australian melodrama, pantomime depended for much of its effect on the liveliness of its topical allusions, its burlesquing of local events and personalities, improvised within a containing framework of fantasy through which, conventionally, tensions were always happily resolved. The titles of such plays, which usually emphasized whimsical or fantastic elements, rarely indicate the scope and detail of the local allusions they contained.

Walch was also one of the local writers whom Dampier encouraged to collaborate with him, an association which produced the adaptation of *Robbery under Arms* and two American-modelled action dramas, *The Scout* and *The Trapper*. Another was Thomas Somers, who was associated with two of Dampier's most popular Australian productions, the adaptation of *His Natural Life* (1886) and the original spectacular melodrama, *Marvellous Melbourne* (1889). The local writer most closely associated with Dampier in his earlier years was Francis R. C. Hopkins, whose first play *All for Gold* (1877) established Dampier's reputation, and initiated his own writing career as a specialist adaptor of French and English melodramatic novels along conventional British lines. Of the other local writers from the 1850s on the most important were George Darrell, Walter Cooper, and a group of Melbourne-based playwrights (of the 1860s and 1870s) who were loosely associated by virtue of their fringe-Bohemian activities as journalists, litterateurs, and authors. These playwrights included—in addition to Akhurst and Walch—the journalists James Smith and R. P. Whitworth, the actor George Fawcett, the doctor and influential drama critic, J. E. Neild, and the writer best known as a novelist, Marcus Clarke.

Clarke's activities as a playwright in the late 1860s and the 1870s provide a particularly revealing illustration of the difficulties a potentially talented playwright faced in a period of increasing specialization. Clarke's novel *His Natural Life* was itself the work of an author with a highly theatrical imagination, drawing on the methods of melodrama for its disposition of scenes, its dialogue, its portrayal of character, its plotting, and its creation of effects of spectacle and tableau. Yet none of the numerous plays he wrote achieved the spectacular success of the stage versions of his novel (especially Dampier's) which appeared after his death. Clarke was an extremely versatile writer. The twenty-odd plays and fragments which he wrote (of which more than a dozen were performed) read like an inventory of the specialized forms of later nineteenth century theatre: pantomimes, farces, melodramas adapted from works by Reade, Dumas, Wilkie Collins and Sardou, light vaudeville (including sketches for Harry Rickards, who was later to establish Australian vaudeville), operettas and musical comedies, and an Australian comedy of manners (*Reverses*), one of several plays written in collaboration with R. P. Whitworth. He is also thought to have collaborated in a satirical operetta, *The Happy Land*, which achieved notoriety in 1880 when an attempt to censor it was made by the Victorian premier, Graham Berry. But whereas this kind of versatility had been a strength in Geoghegan's work for the Royal Victoria in the 1840s, in the changed theatrical conditions of the 1870s it represented a dissipation of energies. Unlike his contemporaries, who were able to specialize in particular kinds of play, and who found actor-managers willing to encourage them, Marcus Clarke's dramatic writing gives the impression of restless and hasty experimentation across the range of available forms, and a sense of frustration at his inability to make theatre a vehicle of the larger statement he had achieved in his major novel.

The playwright whose work effectively initiated the tradition of spectacular melodrama with an Australian content continued by Darrell, Dampier, and Bland Holt, was Walter Cooper, a Sydney journalist, barrister and politician. His earlier plays, performed in the late 1860s, were an operatic burlesque (*Kodadad and his Brothers*), a comedy (*Colonial Experience*), and a farce (*A New Crime; or 'Andsome 'Enery's Mare's Nest*). These were followed, in the early 1870s, by three extremely successful sensational melodramas in the manner of Dion Boucicault (*Foiled, or Australia Twenty Years Ago, Sun and Shadow,* and *Hazard*), and in 1880 by a local comedy, *Fuss.*[27] No text of Cooper's influential sensation dramas has been discovered. The most substantial of the earlier plays, *Colonial Experience*, was a Sydney-based domestic comedy of intrigue, drawing on staple elements of the genre. Its melodramatic plot is centred on the theme of the rightful heiress, and farcical complications are introduced through the machinations of a quick-witted Sheridanesque gentleman-rogue, an imposter attempting to pursue a life of leisured gentility through his parasitic manipulation of the fortunes of the main characters. The victims of the play's multiple villainies are a pair of lovers—an orphaned Australian heroine and her English cousin, a new chum—whose estrangement and eventual reconciliation, as beneficiaries of a concealed will, conform to the typical romantic conventions of so many nineteenth century plays.

The play's lively local satire, directed at lives motivated by greed and self-interest, is contained within this general pattern, through which deceptions are exposed, villains unmasked, and the predictable moral drawn (in the heroine's concluding words) that 'from day to day the world's experience ever teaches us that in the great game of life HONEST HEARTS are always trumps'. A usurer, standing for parliament as 'the people's friend', offers an image of colonial politics as self-interest:

> I'm anxious to serve my country (aside) for a consideration. (Aloud) I am a thorough liberal (aside) as long as it pays.

The would-be aristocrat, unmasked as an ex-army tailor, is ironically identified with the money-conscious Sydney shop-keepers he affects to despise. A young would-be bushman voices a city-bred contempt for bush life at the same time as he romanticizes its hardships as a schooling in the colonial virtues of self-reliance and endurance. Cooper's most interesting adaptation of stereotype, however, is the new chum himself, whose arrival in Australia precipitates the play's conflicts. As in earlier plays like Tucker's *Jemmy Green*, he is a device for exposing colonial hypocrisy and self-interest, and for revealing the underlying identity of British and colonial goals. The play's local tensions—its suggestion of a conflict between urban and rural life, and its portrayal of colonial materialism and double-dealing—are resolved through a quite conventional appeal to the goodness of heart shared by the Australian heroine and the English new chum, which triumphs under the benevolent agency of a type figure of the faithful servant fulfilling a sacred trust to his dead master.

A similar pattern, in which the reconciliation of lovers is linked with the restitution of property and the acquisition of wealth, occurs in George Darrell's *The Sunny South*. Darrell's 'Dramatic Company for the Production of Australian Plays' presented his first play *Transported for Life* in 1877, the year in which Dampier presented Hopkins's first play, *All for Gold*. Darrell's career, over the next decade and a half especially, matched Dampier's, reaching a high point with his sixth play *The Sunny South* (1883), an Anglo-Australian drama which according to some estimates achieved as many as fifteen hundred performances, with seasons in Sydney and Melbourne in 1883, 1885 and 1891, in London and America, and touring productions throughout Australia and New Zealand. It is the only play of Darrell's for which a text has survived,[28] and provides a remarkable insight into the practised skill with which he adapted the novel elements of colonial life—goldfields excitement, bushranging, colonial stereotypes and colonial vernacular speech—to the conventional formulas of melodrama.

In Cooper's play *Colonial Experience* is defined as the triumph of loyalty and goodness of heart over city-bred acquisitiveness. In Darrell's *The Sunny South* it provides a bush schooling in the British virtues of patriotism, physical courage, and independence of spirit, celebrated as the vigorous energies of a young colonial society in the making. Few nineteenth century Australian melodramas offer quite so concentrated and exuberant a display of sensational conventions, or illustrate quite so clearly the nature of the relationship between stereotypical British and Australian elements in all such plays. The initial complications of its plot—a decline in the fortunes of an aristocratic English family through wilful extravagance and the machinations of an unscrupulous Jew—occur in England, in the opening two acts. Its resolution—the recovery of wealth, the unmasking of Grup, and the marriage of the English heroine—occurs in Australia in the subsequent three acts, through the agency of an Australian hero, whose return to England as the rightful owner of the English estate completes a pattern (typically improbable and fantastic in its manipulation of coincidences) in which English and Australian destinies have been carefully interwoven.

The effect of Anglo-Australian counterpointing both in the larger structuring of the play and in its incidental details is to make 'Australianness' a vital, demonstrative expression of colonial identity. The sophisticated 'Morning Room' interior of the English country house in the first two acts forms an obvious contrast with the open-air bush images of Australian life (a gold-mining camp, a bushranger's lair, a spectacular zig-zag railway) which provide settings for such sequences as a bank hold-up, an abduction, and violent shoot-outs. Life in the colonies is shown as having a vigour and clarity of moral outline, lacking in England. The devious villainy of English stereotypes is contrasted with the overt villainy of the bushranger Dick Duggan (based on Ned Kelly), yet the fortunes of both are interwoven, so that the defeat of the one coincides with the unmasking of the other. Similar contrasts are developed in the play's language, between various kinds of refined or formal English utterance, and informal or slangy Australian vernacular speech. There is also a counter-pointing of the main English and Australian characters: the English lovers (a refined romantic heroine and a foppish new chum) and the Australian lovers (the frank, manly and impeccably chivalrous colonial hero, and 'Bubs Berkley', bred to a new kind of self-reliant femininity in the bush); the comically class- and status-conscious English servants, and such local egalitarian stereotypes as a loyal and generous digger and an amiable colonial larrikin. Darrell brings his effete English characters to Australia as a kind of outward-bound education in the virtues of self-reliance and patriotism, to witness, and recover, dimensions of Britishness more truly present in colonial life than in their own. It was precisely this sense of the robust superiority of the Australian characters to their English counterparts, within a demonstrated identity of social goals and values, which explained the immense popular appeal of Darrell's plays, and of Australian melodrama itself as a form.

Alfred Dampier's reputation as an author, co-author, adaptor, producer and actor of Australian melodrama was largely based on his energetic activities in the decade following his highly successful stage adaptation of *His Natural Life* in 1886. During this period he produced more than a dozen such plays, in addition to the more conventional melodramas he had been associated with since the later 1870s. These later plays included contemporary urban melodramas like Thomas Somers's *Voices of the Night* (1886), set in Sydney, which provided a model for the popular Melbourne-based melodramas *Marvellous Melbourne* (1889) and *This Great City* (1891), outback melodramas such as adaptations of Boldrewood's *Robbery Under Arms* (1891) and *The Miner's Right* (1891), and American-modelled action dramas like *The Scout*, *The Trapper* (both set in America), and *To the West* (set in Western Australia). Other plays capitalized on popular local topics such as hypnotism (*For Love and Life*, 1890) and a contemporary murder case (*Wilful Murder*), and on historical themes—*The Wreck of the Dunbar* (1887) and John Perry's centennial play, *The Life and Death of Captain Cook* (1888).[29]

Dampier's productions deal with similar subjects to Darrell's, and in the same general form, but without the simplification and stylization of elements apparent in a play like *The Sunny South*, and with a much more vigorous concentration on local colour and spectacle for its own sake. The American influence on Australian melodrama, apparent in some of the plays of both Cooper and Darrell, is particularly strong in Dampier's work. *Marvellous Melbourne*, by comparison with *The Sunny South*, is a much more fragmented and violent play. Its contrivances and coincidences of plot, and the desperate acts of its larrikin-villain are even more fantastic than Darrell's. So, too, are the piling-up of sensational effects of horror and suspense, and the continued nick-of-time foiling of the villain by a range of characters who turn out to be assumed roles of a master of disguise engaged in a relentless pursuit of the seducer of his daughter. The hero's multiple-identities (as an honourable English gentleman, an American-style super sleuth, a new chum, a Jewish money lender and a 'Murrumbidgee whaler') offered Dampier the same opportunity to demonstrate versatility as a quality of the colonial actor, as Geoghegan had offered the Currency Lass earlier in the century.

Alongside the unalloyed sensationalism of its effects, however, and the transparent contrivance of the plot, the play contains a realism of setting and—amongst its minor characters especially—of local characterization and dialogue, which is quite different from anything in *The Sunny South*. This is especially true of the play's low life scenes in central Melbourne—at the Railway Station, in Bourke Street, in a Chinese opium den, at the Falls' Bridge and wharves, and in a brothel. The rendering of the cosmopolitan energies of city life, with its larrikin pushes and its ghettos, of anti-Chinese feeling (which is both comically exploited, and questioned, in the play), and of an incipient working class consciousness, give aspects of the play an authenticity and immediacy quite at odds with the fantastic qualities of its plotting. The energy, and the originality, of Dampier's work were an expression of tensions in a form on the point of collapse. His realism anticipated the work of Louis Esson. His sensationalism and his interest in purely visual spectacle anticipated stage melodrama's transformation into one of the most popular forms of early twentieth century Australian film.

PART TWO: 1900–1960

The period 1900–1960 saw the fitful and uneven development, under difficult tensions and pressures, of a variety of new dramatic practices, often in an uneasy relationship to each other and to mainstream commercial theatre. The temptation to over-simplify developments in this period—in particular to seal it off from what went before and what has happened since—has been particularly strong. The new drama's own most articulate publicists tended from the beginning to emphasize its evident aspects of opposition to established theatrical practice.[30] Furthermore, under the impetus of new kinds of local drama from the mid-1960s on, an earlier 'post-colonial' or 'nationalist' phase in Australian drama seemed to have been naturally defined: beginning with Louis Esson's prophetic appeal, early in the century, for a national theatre, and ending on a note of major achievement and promise with Ray Lawler's *Summer of the Seventeenth Doll* (1955) and its immediate successors in the late 1950s.

Interpreters of the period encompassed by these two major figures have seen the notion of an emergent national identity as the distinctive aim and preoccupation of the most significant locally-written drama. According to this nationalist model, colonialism is essentially an outmoded phenomenon of Australia's nineteenth century past, an infant phase of dependence on the parent culture (England), marked in literary and dramatic practice by a sterile derivativeness. The period of the 1890s, then, came to be seen as a crucial stage of transition, in which scattered and rudimentary elements of a truly indigenous culture (shaped fitfully in earlier years by convicts, bushrangers, and the creative effects on the human spirit of a pioneering, outback environment) underwent a remarkable consolidation and expansion. Nationalism, it was argued, in this period replaced colonialism as the dominant consciousness, and a new, authentically Australian culture, a uniquely Australian national character, was felt to have emerged.

A major difficulty in this nationalist model, however, is its monistic and reductivist account of actual conflict and tension in Australian society. Australian drama as an 'alternative' movement, or series of movements, this century, seems repeatedly to have drawn its strength from an awareness of such tensions. To see a play like *Summer of the Seventeenth Doll*, for example, as primarily an expression of, or contribution to the formation of a national consciousness, a uniquely Australian cultural identity, is to suppress the meaning of the play's central tensions, which are worked through, in its powerful action, to a point where the very notions of national character and stereotypically Australian behaviour are exploded, and re-interpreted in terms of an underlying tragic pattern: illusions inevitably destroyed, relationships inevitably broken, by processes of time and change beyond the control of individuals. Lawler's own description of the play's central theme reveals how clearly the play's social particularities are absorbed into this more general tragic pattern, recognizable (from the examples of Chekhov, O'Neill and others) as one of the major forms of twentieth century bourgeois tragedy:

> there is a central theme to hold the pieces together, that of the unbearable nostalgia and bewilderment felt by a group of people when an enchanted private world, built almost entirely on a physical basis, crumbles away under the stress of years and changing circumstances. It is meant to be the tragedy of the inarticulate who feel far more than they rationalize or express.[31]

Perceived tensions in Australian life: the betrayal of a code of mateship, the collapse of masculine self-images built on rugged individualism and sexual dominance, and the irreconcilable conflict between a middle class goal of respectability and domesticity and a working class claim to a fuller and freer personal life, are thus made to seem part of a universal and permanent tragic pattern in human relationships. What is often spoken of as the realism of Lawler's play is precisely this skilful manipulation of particular tragic conventions. In a well-made three-act framework relationships are traced through a pattern of increasingly intense confrontations and precarious recoveries and compromises to a point of inevitable and overwhelming breakdown, beyond the control or understanding of the protagonists. In a significant minor irony the play's later scenes suggest that the pattern will be repeated by a younger generation, confirming the presence of an inescapable cycle in human relationships.

What is new, however, in a play like *Summer of the Seventeenth Doll*, is the evident difficulty of resolving the local social tensions inherent in the various relationships. In nineteenth century Australian drama, melodramatic conventions resolved these simply and easily, bringing villains to book and estranged lovers to a happy marriage, uniting families, and disposing of wealth and property, according to what was assumed to be a fixed social and moral code, vigorously displayed and celebrated in the theatre. In Lawler's play social tensions are not so much resolved as displaced onto a universal plane: what is true of these particular relationships, the play implies, is true of all relationships. Such a perspective, however, readily lends itself to inversion in a way which makes social relations themselves disturbingly problematic. If all relationships are subject to such tragically destructive pressures, no form of social relations has special validity. Lawler's play continually challenged audiences by questioning Australian myths and social practices—mateship, male and female stereotyping, class conflict, and urban/rural tensions.

As this analysis suggests, *Summer of the Seventeenth Doll* is problematic at precisely those points which nationalist approaches to Australian drama assume to be essentially unproblematic: in its use of derived conventions of characterization, dialogue, dramatic structure and tragic action, and in its implicit rejection of the idea of a dominant national character in favour of an emphasis on conflicting (and apparently irreconcilable) social relations. The new emphasis on tragedy, in twentieth century Australian drama, is of quite exceptional significance. Yet its presence appears hardly to have been noticed, other than incidentally, in the urge to identify and promote, in optimistic and romantic terms continually belied by the plays themselves, the burgeoning of a national culture and identity.

In the period between 1900 and 1960 in particular, tragic conflict is a recurrent element in almost every significant Australian play: in much of the work of Louis Esson, in the best plays of newly important women writers like Katharine Susannah Prichard

(*Brumby Innes*) and Betty Roland (*The Touch of Silk*), in the intensely sombre plays of Sydney Tomholt (especially in examples like *Bleak Dawn* and *Anoli: the Blind*), in the 1940s verse drama of Douglas Stewart, and (in addition to Lawler in the 1950s) in plays like Richard Beynon's *The Shifting Heart*, Peter Kenna's *The Slaughter of St. Teresa's Day* and Alan Seymour's *The One Day of the Year*.

The derivative elements in Lawler's play also reveal the continuing significance of overseas influences on the development of Australian drama in the twentieth century. A list of the main new impulses between 1900 and 1960 would include the growth of a national dramatic movement early in the century, accompanied by an emphasis on the importance of realism and naturalism as new conventions, the rise of the Repertory movement and of Little Theatres (including Authors' Theatres and Art Theatres), the establishment of a proletarian New Theatre movement in the 1930s, the brief vogue of verse drama in the 1940s, and the institutional achievement of government subsidy for professional theatre in the 1950s. All these developments, however, which often supported very different kinds of drama and ideas about drama, and very different audiences, followed a similar pattern to developments in British and American drama, and for this reason cannot be assimilated to a naively Australianist interpretation. The audiences for even the most popular of the plays which came out of these impulses were always, as elsewhere, minority audiences.

The most popular mainstream tradition of Australian drama this century has remained, as in the nineteenth century, that of the commercial establishment. Nationalist ideology, with its emphasis on colonialism as a faded or rapidly fading relic of the past, and its scapegoating of commercial theatre as unAustralian, as a conspiracy practised on an unsuspecting public by foreign interests, continually under-estimated the strength of commercial theatre and the fact that it was sustained from within Australian society itself. Commercial enterprise in drama has expanded with the same energy as in the nineteenth century, and in the same pattern of intense competition and specialization. The new elements in this expansion were provided, successively, by cinema, radio and television, in which major commercial institutions and empires were created.

Commercial theatre this century—as distinct from the dramatic forms and professional methods of commercialism, which were carried over into the new media and reproduced in new ways—declined relative to cinema, radio and television. But it also showed a remarkable resilience. While a fledgling theatrical tradition of Australian melodrama was virtually wiped out by the impact of silent film, the bigger managements were able to specialize in areas where silent film could not compete.

The musical spectacular, for example—the long-running show from London or New York—achieved a new prominence in the 1890s and early decades of the century. So, too, did the forms of vaudeville, variety and revue, which exploited the intimate appeal of live performers, and produced one of Australia's most popular vaudeville stars, Roy ('Mo') Rene. With the advent of film, there was also the possibility, for larger managements, of operating in both media. 'The Firm' of J. C. Williamson expanded into film production, but was eventually taken over by the management of J. and N. Tait, who had pioneered the production of Australian feature-length films early in the century, and expanded (in an opposite direction) from film into theatre. The Australian film industry itself initially made an original contribution to world film production. Its most famous early director, Raymond Longford, continued the pioneering tradition associated with figures like Alfred Dampier in the theatre. It eventually succumbed, in the 1920s, to massive American capital investment in the Australian industry, in a process which reproduced earlier developments in commercial theatre and intensified pressure on it.

By the 1930s the fortunes of commercial theatre had reached a nadir. The advent of radio and sound films (which made possible the development of such Hollywood specialities as musical comedy, taking over a field which commercial theatre had made peculiarly its own), and a combination of local economic factors which included the Depression and a government Entertainment Tax which the cinemas, but not the theatres, could afford, hastened the decline. For a brief period, perhaps the only period in Australia's history, it could be argued that the strengths of commercial and non-commercial theatre were about the same: ironic companions in different misfortunes. Commercial theatre never recovered its dominance as a medium of popular entertainment after the 1930s, but it has moved into new fields such as the popular 'clubland' entertainment industry. It has also exploited the live stage appeal of actors and actresses whose popularity was initially established in television or film.

There is an essential continuity between nineteenth century commercial enterprise in the theatre, and its expansion, in the twentieth century, into the new forms of entertainment. The history of dramatic conventions makes this continuity apparent. There has been a tendency on the one hand to see commercial theatre as steadily declining after its later nineteenth century 'Golden Age', and on the other to see the history of each dramatic medium as essentially separate and self-contained. In fact all the major popular forms of film, radio, and television drama are transformations of earlier dramatic forms as they existed within nineteenth century commercial theatre.

The popular early Victorian 'musical drama', and its related forms of operetta and musical burlesque, are the direct ancestors of light opera, the musical extravaganza, musical comedy and rock opera. The equally popular Victorian 'historical drama'—the costume play with an emphasis on spectacle, heroic action, and romantic intrigue—developed into the twentieth century film and television forms of the historical epic and the lavishly-costumed period drama (often, in fact, duplicating the nineteenth century habit of adapting historical novels and romances). The twentieth century equivalent of nineteenth century nautical drama is Armed Services drama: heroic drama, comedy or action drama, featuring the army, navy or air force, which continue to provide staple entertainment. The earlier forms of farce, domestic comedy and domestic tragedy have also undergone a spectacular transformation into radio and television situation comedies and the long-running soap opera. One of the most successful Australian commercial plays of the earlier part of the century, Bert Bailey's production of the 'Dad and Dave' play *On Our Selection* (1912)—a bucolic comedy, set in rural Australia, offering a mixture of farce and domestic comedy and tragedy—reveals how readily such a form could be adapted. Originally dramatized from the fictional sketches of 'Steele Rudd' (Arthur Hoey Davis), it enjoyed extraordinary popularity on the stage, in a series of films, and eventually as a long-running radio serial of several thousand episodes. For several generations of Australians it created a set of stereotyped images of the national character, and of its formation under the vicissitudes of an outback environment.

These continuities need to be stressed because a false picture of the operation of the commercial system, and the proportions of overseas to locally-made dramas can be given by concentrating on one or other of the media in isolation from the rest. Australian melodrama declined in the theatre in the late nineteenth century, but provided the basis of an extremely vigorous Australian film tradition (from 1900 into the 1920s) within the same commercial system, and continues in the form of Australian-made commercial radio and television drama. If the history of the commercial media is considered as a whole, the proportion of locally-made to over-seas products, in all the forms mentioned above, has remained much more static than various partial accounts of one or other of the media might suggest. These local products, as in the nineteenth century, continue to define the 'Australian way of life' in terms of the norms and values of the products of American and British commercial enterprise.

The history of non-commercial theatre from 1900–1960 records a continued and often heroic struggle for survival in competition with the immensely superior professional, technical and economic resources of commercial theatre. A crucial development in twentieth century commercial theatre was the phenomenon of the long run, successful productions sometimes running for several years. It ensured both polished professional competence in performance, and relative continuity and security of employment for performers (even if only in minor roles), which struggling little theatres could not hope to match. William Moore's annual 'Australian Drama Nights' (the first serious attempt to introduce new kinds of Australian drama to Australian audiences, on a single night each year between 1909 and 1912 in Melbourne), Louis Esson's Pioneer Players (which lasted effectively, on a semi-regular basis, for only two years, 1922–3), Carrie Tennant's short-lived Community Playhouse in Sydney (1929–30), and the various main city Repertory movements (beginning in Adelaide, but more influentially associated with Gregan McMahon's vigorous spon-sorship and direction, in Melbourne and later in Sydney, from 1910 into the 1930s) are the main examples of independent initiative in the theatre in the early decades of the century.

The problems each had to face were a compound of indifferent local scripts, minimal time and scope for adequate rehearsal, dependence on amateur resources, and small coterie audiences: a vicious cycle, in effect, of economic insecurity and comparatively makeshift production resources and facilities, which meant that promising local authors and plays could rarely be given the stable environment needed for the development of skills and talent. 'No single factor', Margaret Williams has written, 'has influenced the drama's development so profoundly as this alienation from the professional stage and its wider conglomerate audience.'[32] With rare exceptions like Louis Esson, many of the authors of significant Australian plays between 1900 and the mid-1960s are better known in fields other than drama: Vance Palmer, Katharine Susannah Prichard, Douglas Stewart, Patrick White and Hal Porter. Others, like Sumner Locke-Elliott, Ray Lawler and Alan Seymour, became expatriates. In the 1930s and 1940s the problem of limited resources recurred, and new theatres sprang up to replace those which had collapsed. A potentially talented playwright like Sydney Tomholt received little stimulus from performance. Others like Betty Roland, George Landen Dann, and Sumner Locke-Elliott were supported by occasional Repertory productions, or by production in theatres like Doris Fitton's semi-professional, repertory-style Independent Theatre in Sydney. Roland and Dann also received productions in the New Theatre movement, along with other politically committed playwrights like Katharine Susannah Prichard, and from the 1940s on, Oriel Gray, Mona Brand and George Farwell.

The chequered history of the Repertory Movement in Australia offers a revealing insight into the pressures under which Australian drama was written and performed in the first half of the century. Australian Repertory began in reaction to the kind of theatre offered by commercial managements (melodrama, spectacle, and trivialized entertainment). Funding itself on a subscription basis, it remained theoretically committed to the twin principles of offering Australian audiences the best overseas plays and encouraging local playwrights, recognizing also that there was a need to encourage new kinds of production techniques and acting styles, if new and significant drama was to be effectively staged and the neglect of commercial theatre in all these areas challenged.

In actual practice, however, the record was much more ambiguous: a mixture of innovation and compromise which from the start aroused the suspicion of playwrights who, like Esson, were committed to more radical change. The best overseas plays which Repertory valuably introduced to Australian audiences— work by Ibsen, Shaw and Chekhov in particular—also carried with them a great deal of inferior overseas drama: conventional West End society dramas and fashionable comedies often barely distinguishable from the offerings of commercial managements. The ratio of Australian plays to overseas plays also varied considerably. The Adelaide Repertory Theatre, which began in 1908, aimed to produce one Australian play each year. Between 1911 and 1917, the Melbourne Repertory Theatre, under McMahon's direction, produced 13 Australian plays out of a total number of productions of at least 65. Between 1921 and 1924 Sydney Repertory—also under McMahon's direction, in association with the commercial management of J. and N. Tait—produced three Australian plays in 24 productions.[33] The most promising Australian plays also carried with them a great deal of inferior work of a crudely imitative kind. Australian Repertory was ultimately the victim of its concentration on the vogue of 'Ib-Shaw' realism, social comedy, and the conventionally well-made play— on the styles which had provided its original impetus. Courageous individual ventures, like Doris Fitton's Independent Theatre, which performed eighty Australian plays between 1930 and 1972, supplemented the activities of the main Repertory groups, and occasionally sought to provide alternative directions, or to support different kinds of drama.

The most innovative Little theatre groups in the 1930s and 1940s were those which made up the New Theatre movement in Australia's main cities. A committed theatre of the communist and socialist Left, the movement evolved a style and a policy which anticipated some of the work of later experimental theatre groups, like the Australian Performing Group associated with the La Mama and Pram Factory theatres in Melbourne in the late 1960s and 1970s. The New Theatre movement introduced contemporary work from overseas (*Waiting for Lefty*, agit-prop plays, and—in the later 1930s—Brecht). It tried to make contact with working class audiences, performing plays in the streets, at factory gates, and at political meetings and rallies. It encouraged the writing of local plays on issues of immediate concern to the working class movement (like *Penalty Clause*, written by Katharine Susannah Prichard and performed at Perth in 1940), as well as performing Australian plays of broader political interest, like Esson's Eureka play *The Southern Cross*, Roland's *The Touch of Silk* and Dann's *Fountains Beyond*. In the organization of its acting groups it attempted a more democratic, less director-oriented style than had been the case with many of the Repertory and Little theatre groups, whose driving force was often provided, as in the old actor-manager system, by a single personality. It also encouraged authors to collaborate in workshop activities, the most successful result being the 1890s-based folk-musical play *Reedy River* (1953), 'a striking example of a repertory show being literally built up from idea to production inside a theatre',[34] which was performed all over Australia and by 1959, according to one estimate, had been seen by 130,000 people. Again, in this example, the adaptation of popular elements from older traditions, in the interest of serious political statement, anticipated one of the most significant emphases in recent Australian theatre.

Louis Esson (1879–1943) was the most creative and original of a handful of playwrights who attempted, in the early decades of the century, to establish an alternative Australian drama. Between 1910 and the late 1920s he wrote some fourteen plays (half of them full-length and half of them short one-act plays). Only nine of these plays (including five full-length plays) were performed during his lifetime, most of them in two concentrated pre- and post-war periods. His first three plays (*The Woman Tamer, Dead Timber* and *The Sacred Place*—all one-acters) were performed at William Moore's Annual Drama Nights for Australian plays, in Melbourne, between 1910 and 1912. A full-length political comedy, *The Time Is Not Yet Ripe*, was also performed in 1912 by McMahon's Melbourne Repertory Theatre, which had been associated with the Drama Night production of *Dead Timber* the previous year. This was to be the last of Esson's plays performed in the established Repertory theatre. He went overseas (to the United States and England) in 1917, returning to Melbourne in 1921 to help found the Pioneer Players with Stewart Macky and Vance Palmer. Strongly influenced by W. B. Yeats, whom he had met and who had admired his work, Esson saw the Pioneer Players as an attempt to 'substitute a national Australian movement' for the Repertory movement, modelling it on the nationalist aims of the Irish Abbey Theatre:

> I would like to get a new movement started, with no connection with any repertory society. We can't do everything; and personally I'd have nothing but local and original works, however inadequate they were, a kind of Folk-Theatre ... I can see the plays clearly; they should be lively, simple, with plenty of colour, non-intellectual, without 'middle-class' sentiment and drawing room ethics.[35]

The first production of the Pioneer Players, in 1922, was a new full-length play by Esson, *The Battlers*. This was followed, in a series of seasons in 1922–23, by another sixteen Australian plays, four of them full-length plays (including Esson's *Mother and Son*), and the rest one-act plays (including a new play by Esson, *The Drovers*, and a revival of *The Woman Tamer*). Although Esson revived the Pioneer Players briefly in 1926 for a production of his new play, *The Bride of Gospel Place*, its life was effectively over by 1923—a combined result of inadequate production resources, poor audiences, and a shortage of the kinds of plays and playwrights whom Esson had hoped the venture would attract. Apart from his own contribution of five plays, the main contributors had been Palmer (four plays), and Stewart Macky and Katharine Susannah Prichard, with two plays each. Esson continued writing plays for a few more years. One of these, a historical play about the Eureka Stockade, *The Southern Cross*, was performed by the Workers' Art Guild at Perth in the 1930s, under its vigorous director, Keith George. But by the end of the 1920s his energies had been sapped and his practical involvement in Australian theatre came to an end.

Although the body of plays which Esson wrote is small, it was profoundly original in its time, introducing new subject matter, themes and attitudes into Australian drama, and opening up formal possibilities which have remained influential ever since. His first full-length play, *The Time Is Not Yet Ripe*, was a lively satirical political comedy, a Shavian parody of the melodramatic conventions of a typical drawing room comedy of manners, with an underlying Ibsenite realist thrust against the ways in which Australian political hypocrisy, egotism and power-seeking disguise themselves in platitudes and moral idealism. It was clearly a play written for, and suited to the tastes of the new Repertory audiences, and far superior to other Australian examples (like Arthur H. Adams's *The Wasters* and *Mrs. Pretty and the Premier*) drawing on similar conventions and also presented in the Repertory theatres. Esson's play is deliberately and self-consciously theatrical in a way which challenges and undermines the conventions of melodrama and society comedy in late nineteenth century colonial theatre. By insisting, through comically exaggerated emphases at the level of plot, characterization and dialogue, on the artifice and contrivance of such conventions, Esson exposes their illusory character and their failure to represent truth-to-life. He then proceeds to make these new valuations, in the play's main critical thrust, a measure of the corruption of the world of Australian parliamentary and party politics which provides the play's immediate subject. The conventions of melodrama and society comedy provide the play's comic images of what that world is like: politics as melodrama (in which it is possible for an authoritarian Prime Minister's vivacious and intelligent daughter to fall in love with his deadliest political enemy, a socialist, and for the two lovers to find themselves political opponents for the same parliamentary seat); and politics as mere style and talk—sophisticated and witty drawing room talk sometimes, election platform talk at other times, platitude and empty moralizing most of the time. In *The Time Is Not Yet Ripe* the melodrama of parliamentary politics is judged as corrupt and absurd in terms of an implicit appeal to a valued real world beyond the theatre, and beyond the theatricalism of its characters. In one sense, for Esson, that other world is a vision of what Australia might *really* become; in another sense, it is a different Australia which *actually* exists, beyond the drawing rooms and committee rooms, and beyond the consciousness of those who inhabit them.

Esson's realistic plays, which established a much more immediately influential tradition, were an attempt to make the nature of this other 'real world' explicit, by getting it onto the stage, in necessarily different conventions. What is immediately noticeable about them is their studied anti-theatricalism, their deliberate attempt to avoid melodramatic contrivance or sensational effect. The brevity of many of the plays, which itself established a pattern for local writing in the early decades of the century, was one aspect of this rejection of established theatre. It implied new conventions of performance, new styles of acting, and a new 'literary' sense of the importance of the playwright in the theatre, as an initiator of change. It also gave an impressionistic flavour to the plays themselves, which was crucial to their effect of realism, and of registering new aspects of rural and working class urban life in casually suggestive ways, without pressing them into pre-determined moulds. As his comment on a proposed production of *The Drovers* suggests, Esson saw them as being most effective when performed in an understated way:

> my intentions about the play [are] to avoid American 'suppressed emotion', 'strong silent men' atmosphere, false stresses, etc. It needs to be played simply to make any effect.[36]

The Drovers is Esson's best, and his main contribution to the imaginative literature of the Outback represented by the bush ballads and the fiction of Lawson and Furphy. As in a Lawson story, the quality of understatement is present in every aspect of the play—in its plotlessness, its economy of dialogue, and the simplicity and poetic suggestiveness of its stage effects. The play's setting is early morning in a remote outback droving camp, against a background of 'plains, unbroken by timber, stretching to the horizon'. The event which triggers its action (a cattle stampede in which a drover is fatally injured) occurs offstage in its opening moments, a typical example of Esson's displacement of what would have provided a spectacularly central event in a sensational melodrama in the Bland Holt tradition. The actions which follow are of the simplest kind. Esson's focus is not the event itself, as in an action drama, but its aftermath: how a dying man and other members of a droving gang cope with the sudden intrusion of human tragedy, in an environment in which human life itself seems reduced to a precarious, elemental struggle for survival. The language of the play is laconic, factual, and unemotive, the language of men who refuse to sentimentalize their situation. Yet the apparent matter-of-factness with which death can be so casually rationalized and accepted, as 'hard luck', by the youthful drovers is ultimately questioned in the play, in a way which amounts to a probing of the sufficiency of the Australianist values embodied in the legend of the Outback. This questioning achieves its fullest force in the final exchange between the dying man and his boss, as Esson allows these two longtime mates a more self-conscious assessment of their relationship, and of the ultimate meaning of their lives, centred on the question 'Why should it end like this?' The sense of loss is clearly more acutely realized at this point, and its realization and acceptance much harder.

Despite the power of the final scene, as it elevates the cruder insistence of the others on 'hard luck' into a more classical sense of fate, the play's final perspective is not simply an endorsement of stoic acceptance and endurance. These attitudes are placed within a larger, much more ambiguously tragic sense of human life as intrinsically absurd and pointless, a significance carried, especially, by the most obviously theatrical elements in the play's structure. Its brevity is one such element, suggesting the essentially temporary, contingent nature of the human drama momentarily enacted on stage. The visual focus on the dying man, which is enforced throughout the play—as the others come and go around him, and finally go—is another, ensuring that the image of death finally dominates, whatever provisional accommodations have been made to relate it to some significant human pattern. The scene of the camp itself, with its packs and saddles strewn about, its visible signs of the makeshift and temporary, is part of this larger design, an image of the human reduced to the absurd and transitory. And finally there is the vivid impressionism of the surrounding scene—the vast plains stretching into the distance, the violently destructive impinging energies represented in the sound of the stampeding cattle, the silence which descends as drovers and cattle depart into the wilderness. Like *Summer of the Seventeenth Doll*, Esson's play is not a conventional social problem play at all, but its particular form of tragic deadlock anticipates Lawler's as a questioning of Australian values and myths.

Esson's other short plays lack the concentrated poetic suggestiveness of *The Drovers*, but their general aim and method is the same. *Dead Timber* is a play about rural poverty, the struggle of the small farmer and his family on the land, offering an image of the Australian petit-bourgeois dream of material prosperity and domestic fulfilment turned sour. The play's atmosphere is permeated with a sense of hopelessness and bitterness, its 'realistic' elements intended to challenge the more conventional sentimentally cheerful or comic stereotypes of the man on the land (the kind of stereotypes popularized by Steele Rudd), and also the stereotype of the 'Aussie battler', the man whose moral fibre is moulded through persistent struggle and vicissitude. *The Woman Tamer* turns to urban life, the life of Melbourne's inner-city working class poor, unemployed, and fringe-criminal underworld. The play's picturesque realism, its lavish use of Australian vernacular speech and prison slang, its small gallery of colourfully nick-named characters, and its pattern of apparently casual interactions within a framework of a brief 'slice of time' creates what Vance Palmer called a 'smouldering underworld life'.[37]

The Bride of Gospel Place (1926) is a full-length play which develops the elements of black comedy in *The Woman Tamer* into a larger tragic vision. Against a more fully characterized background of fringe-working class Melbourne life, evoked in an opening act set after midnight in an all-night cafe, the play develops primarily as the story of a single relationship. Although it is marred by its blurring of realistic and melodramatic elements— especially in its third and fourth acts, which attempt to impose a redemptive pattern on suffering and death—the socal deprivations which precipitate the tragedy are powerfully evoked, in terms which often suggest Olive's aspirations for a fuller life in *Summer of the Seventeenth Doll*.

It is typical of Esson's plays, however, that a felt sense of dissatis-faction expresses itself less as political consciousness, than as romantic aspiration. The connection between the realistic plays and *The Time Is Not Yet Ripe* (with its rejection of the politics of the right *and* the left) is clear at this level. Its origins, as David Walker has argued,[38] stem from the formative influence on Esson's think-ing of his involvement in the intellectual and literary currents of Melbourne's Bohemian élite at the turn of the century. It gave his radicalism a strongly nationalist and literary flavour—a belief that art could accomplish social change more effectively than politics. In *The Bride of Gospel Place* tragic conventions in effect displace social tensions into art, of a characteristically *fin de siècle* kind. Esson himself described the character of the play's heroine as a 'difficult and artificial part',[39] and her actual functioning as a tragic symbol carries a number of typically Decadent religious associations. She is a figure of frail beauty surrounded by squalor and brutality, of perpetually suffering innocence and purity. Finally, through her suffering, she is a redemptive force. Lily's name, her address (Gospel Place), her nickname (The Bride), and her white dress all associate her with the Virgin Mary, in this Aesthete's vision of Melbourne's underground life. Katie, the ruthlessly manipulative man-tamer of *The Woman Tamer*, and Lily, an image of self-sacrifice and unattainable beauty, are the twin aspects of Esson's *femme fatale*.

A similar image of the *femme fatale* is of central significance in *Mother and Son*. Esson described this play, set in the Wimmera district of Victoria, as a primitive tragedy. Its theme, as Vance Palmer put it, is

> a study of the half-artist, the young man with a touch of poetry in him he is unable to express except occasionally with his violin or in flickering rebellion against the life around him.[40]

The tragic conventions of the play—despite the shift to a rural setting—are again characteristically Decadent. Harry Lind, the young 'half-artist', is a strangely dissatisfied character driven by self-destructive impulses, and frustrated in his attempts to achieve the fuller and richer life he longs for. His alienation takes a typically Aesthetic form, suggested initially by his obsessive attach-ment to his violin. He enjoys the spurious excitement of committing petty crimes. He is unusually sensitive to Nature, to the idyllic natural landscape of the surrounding countryside. He is often aloof, and given to bouts of depression. These self-destructive tensions in his personality are brought to a crisis by a hopeless infatuation.

Mother and Son is Esson's most delicately-toned play, Chekhovian in its use of unemphatic natural symbolism to create an atmosphere expressing the tensions within and between the main characters. The dramatic force of the sense of tragic deadlock depends strongly (as in all such plays) on Esson's ability to create convincing images of *both* the bourgeois environment of the mother, and—more problematically—the unconventional, more vital and passionate life through which the son seeks to express a real, though buried, self. The individual's struggle to express a true sense of self, to break free of what are felt as the restricting conventions of a bourgeois environment is one of the major themes of the Australian realistic tradition in the theatre, recurring in the work of Esson and Palmer, of Prichard, Roland and Stewart, of Lawler and Seymour, and more recently of playwrights like Peter Kenna. The values of the bourgeois world are most fully and sympathetically portrayed, in *Mother and Son*, in the mother, a figure with immense reserves of courage and determination and generosity. Yet these qualities operate, ultimately blindly and destructively, within a narrowly conventional and domestic range. Those who espouse or seek other ways of life are finally beyond the range of her understanding. Her personal tragedy, at the end of the play, maintains the sense of deadlock: she is not simply a victim of events, but quite uncomprehending of the meaning of her son's death, maintaining her self-image as his 'saviour'.

Esson's contribution to the Australian theatre was to make possible a continuing re-appraisal of the dominant images of Australian life popularized and sustained by established theatre, in terms which themselves challenged its conventional practices. Taken as a whole his work has a strongly critical edge, suggesting a tragic dimension in the history of European occupation in Australia, offering new images of urban and outback life, of the petit-bourgeois values sustained by the man on the land, of Aboriginal life, of relations between the sexes, and (in the Eureka play, *The Southern Cross*) of the nineteenth century colonial past. Almost every significant Australian play, in the period up to 1960, is a re-working or extension of one or other of these issues, in terms which drew, with varying degrees of success, on the possibilities of realism as Esson had conceived them.

Spenser Brodney's *Rebel Smith* (1925), for example, was a play which attempted to harness realism to the politically controversial subject of union militancy. Its language, despite the injection of Australian vernacular elements, never quite loses its literary flavour, its effect of being formally written rather than spoken language. Its action is also heavily reliant, at crucial points, on the contrivances of melodrama. These weaknesses recur in the work of a number of talented playwrights attempting to extend the possibilities of an Australian realistic tradition, and provide a telling indication of deficiencies in practical theatrical knowledge and experience.

Vance Palmer and Sydney Tomholt, contemporaries of Esson, remain essentially minor talents for these reasons. Like Esson, Palmer, in the small number of plays he wrote during a life devoted to many different kinds of writing, gives the impression of consciously cultivating understatement as a theatrical method. His short plays characteristically offer a brief, close-up focus on immediate relationships, introducing a single element of tension and playing ironically on conventional expectations of how it will be resolved. But the effect is often more banal, more unsurprising than intended, partly as the result of an insufficiently energized dialogue, and partly because Palmer's insistent deflection of potential tensions into anticlimactic irony often seems, in the end, an evasion of the full implications of the issues the plays raise. These issues are centred, in different ways, on the imaginative idea of an emergent 'Australia of the spirit', a distinctive democratic-humanist national ethos, rooted in rural life and behaviour, whose development Palmer was later to theorize and celebrate in his most influential work, *The Legend of the Nineties* (1954). With its idealist emphasis on the nation-building character of Art (including folk-art, legend and myth) and on the special imaginative achievements of writers like Lawson and Furphy, who took the Bush as their main subject, *The Legend of the Nineties* was an eloquent reaffirmation of Esson's Yeatsian formulation of the Artist's spiritual mission in Australia.

Slight though they appear to be in substance, Palmer's plays, with their exclusively rural, homestead or shanty, settings, are expressions of this impulse to define an emergent national spirit. Their low-keyed ironic strategies generally function to defuse the social tensions which provide their initial dramatic impulse, in the interests of this larger purpose. His best play is *The Black Horse* (1923), a tragic vignette of country life recalling aspects of Esson's *Mother and Son*, in which the delicate, temperamentally sensitive son of a physically tough, strong-willed cattle boss is accidentally killed after being bullied by his father into attempting to break in a wild horse—in effect, a sacrifice to his father's desire to 'make a man' of him, according to a bush code placing its highest value on the masculine virtues of physical strength and endurance. The strongest conflict in the play, which this incident brings to potential crisis, is between the father and mother. The latter's hatred of the harsh outback station life has been channelled into romantic dreams of her son's escape from it, through education, into the civilized life of a professional position in the city. The play ends, tantalizingly, with the parents facing each other over the lifeless body of their son, through whom each has projected an opposed vision of the future. It is as close as Palmer comes, in his early plays, to a questioning of the sufficiency of the myth that the conditions of bush life were inevitably fostering a new, creative spirit of national identity, although this more sombre note is also present in Palmer's much later play *Hail Tomorrow* (written 1943–5 and published in 1947), a historical play whose subject is the Queensland Shearers' Strike of 1891–2.

Sydney Tomholt, most of whose plays appeared in a single volume (*Bleak Dawn and Other Plays*) in 1936, had a much more vigorous sense of dramatic action and visual effect than Palmer, whose tendency to rely too exclusively on discussion and debate in *Hail Tomorrow* is also apparent in other examples of social realism like George Landen Dann's *Fountains Beyond* (performed by the New Theatre movement in 1942), an otherwise workmanlike, unpretentious play aimed at exposing the plight of Aboriginals dwelling on the fringes of white townships, cut off from their traditional way of life and deprived of access to white society. Tomholt's *Bleak Dawn*, a longish one-acter, was one of the first plays to attempt to deal sympathetically with the plight of the divorced woman in Australia. Set in 'one of the poorer suburbs', the play's realism evokes with unusual subtlety the internal conflict in the feelings of the woman herself, and the pressure to conform in a society in which marriage functions, for a woman, as a moral imperative. Tomholt's other plays, all short one-acters, offer a kind of theatre very different from the realism of *Bleak Dawn*, though hardly less intense or anguished. He appears to have been one of the few Australian dramatists before Patrick White to have been aware of movements in European theatre, like expressionism and symbolism, outside mainstream realism. One of his earliest plays, *Anoli: the Blind* (originally intended for production in London, in a bill of four short Australian plays arranged by William Moore and Esson in 1919)[41] hinted at this interest in expressionism, associating luridly melodramatic effects, exotic passions and intense animosities with an outback North Queensland setting which itself suggested a reduction of the human to a barbarous and primitive struggle for survival. In later plays Tomholt experiments with dream states, psychodrama, and the possibilities of dramatic fable, in starkly reduced, symbolic settings. Images of death, disfigurement and violence recur, but they never quite lose their air of melodramatic contrivance, of overstated emotionalism.

One of the most powerful, authentically realistic plays to be written in Australia prior to the 1950s was Katharine Susannah Prichard's *Brumby Innes*, an outback play which won a playwrights' competition run by *The Triad* magazine in 1927. It remained unperformed until 1972—an indication of the timidity of Australian theatre in coping with a play which dealt so directly and controversially with the subjects of sexual relations and racism in Australia.[42] Although Prichard made her name primarily as a novelist, her connections with Australian theatre went back to the origins of alternative drama earlier in the century. She had contributed a short play to William Moore's Australian Drama Night in Melbourne in 1909, and in a six-year period spent after this in London as a journalist, during which she involved herself in the Women's Movement, she had had two short plays on feminist themes produced by the Actresses' Franchise League. Two further plays (*The Pioneers* and *The Great Man*) were produced by the Pioneer Players. In the 1930s her political commitment (as a founding member of the Australian Communist Party in 1919) led her to write several plays for the newly formed workers' theatre movement (The Workers' Art Guild) in Perth. Prichard's relations with the theatre, occasional as they might seem in comparison with her writing of fiction, epitomize several important elements in the rise of alternative theatre activity: the significant, if not decisive, contribution of women (from the time of Janet Achurch's first Australian production of Ibsen in 1890) in introducing the new feminist-oriented drama of Ibsen and Shaw into Literary and

Drama societies, and eventually into the Repertory movement (with later figures like Carrie Tennant, Doris Fitton and May Hollinworth carrying on this tradition of women's initiative in the sponsorship of new drama); the increasing importance of women as playwrights, from the 1930s on—especially (but not exclusively) as politically conscious writers; and the new importance, from the 1930s on, of Perth as a centre of continuing creative activity in alternative theatre.

Brumby Innes is set in the remote north west (Pilbara) region of Western Australia, and gains much of its strength from its evocation of a specific place and people, visited and observed from first-hand experience.[43] Remoteness functions as a powerful, authenticating device for the play's realism, making the kinds of social breakdown which it documents in such vivid and violent detail (the destruction of Aboriginal culture, the reduction of personal and sexual relations to brute force) seem natural and plausible. Ultimately, however, it is the romantic image of the outback as a realm of the natural and primitive which the play undermines, in a pattern of highly theatrical Brechtian ironies designed to exhibit the political and cultural content of even the most instinctive, natural behaviour. The effect is a total absence of moralizing or sentimentality in the play, of the sort so often associated with the 'social problem' play or with conventional social realism. The authenticity of Brumby Innes's character is primarily an effect of stripping his behaviour of any *conscious* motivation, and of allowing its 'naturalness' to be expressed in immediately theatrical terms, as a commanding physical presence on stage, evoked primarily through violent action and gesture. Brumby never questions his own motives, never moralizes, never feels the slightest guilt about even the most brutal of his actions, and never considers their consequences; his 'instinctive' reaction, his 'natural' response to events is physical force—the gun, the fist, the manhandling of women, like cattle; his speech shares this quality of physical immediacy, its colloquialism and slang, its natural imagery, its violence always directed unconsciously towards the satisfaction of immediate needs. No play, at the time *Brumby Innes* was written, had offered quite so uncompromising an image of the effects of white civilization in the outback.

In contrast with *Brumby Innes*, Betty Roland's *The Touch of Silk* (1928) became one of the few plays of the period to establish something of a history of regular performance—not on the commercial stage, but in Repertory and Little Theatres, and especially, from the late 1930s into the 1950s, in numerous radio productions.[44] *The Touch of Silk* was Roland's first major play, and became her most well-known, in a writing career which included, in the 1930s (during a period spent in the Communist Party) a number of agitprop pieces and a full-length political play, *Are You Ready, Comrade?* (1938), performed by the New Theatre movement. In the 1940s she wrote a substantial number of plays, adaptations, and popular serials for the A.B.C. and commercial radio, and since the 1950s she has devoted herself mainly to prose writing—children's books, travel books, and novels.

The Touch of Silk is primarily a study of bourgeois manners and morality in a small provincial Australian rural township (a 'small town in north-west Victoria' with a population of five thousand), drawing on the conventions of melodrama and the three-act *pièce bien faite* in a manner which recalls the methods of Ibsen's similar provincial studies in his middle period 'social problem' plays. This Ibsenesque combination of a complicated melodramatic plot made over to serious social comment about middle class morality and sentiment might explain why it was so ideally suited to the knowledge and resources of Repertory theatre, and to the tastes of its audiences. The play's central dramatic device is the introduction of an Outsider (an impulsive, intelligent young Frenchwoman, Jeanne) into the small, tightly-knit rural community. Her presence generates conflict, and in the intensifying and unravelling of this conflict (through a conventional three-act structure of exposition, crisis and dénouement), Roland explores the underlying rationale of the community's attitudes and values. Her control of these conventional elements, despite occasional creakiness in the machinery of the play, is the main source of its strength.

There is a major difference, in critical emphasis, between Roland's use of an Outsider stereotype,[45] and its use in earlier colonial melodrama. The commonest form of Outsider in the earlier drama was the New Chum, a specifically British stereotype, whose ignorances and prejudices about life in Australia generated humour and conflict, but whose eventual acceptance into the community generally involved a mutual recognition by both of their essential identity. The difference between the New Chum and the 'dinkum Aussie' in such plays turns out to be merely superficial: in learning to become an Australian, the New Chum recovers a lost dimension of *real* Britishness, patriotism, manliness, self-reliance and resourcefulness, which is only truly present in colonial life itself. In *The Touch of Silk* (as in other major twentieth century Australian plays using the same Outsider device—the middle-class figure of Pearl, for example, in the working class environment of *Summer of the Seventeenth Doll*) there is no such sentimental rapprochement between Outsider and In-group. The play's tragic dénouement forces Jeanne to live out a lie which will brand her perpetually to stereotype, as an insidious foreign influence whose different values place the community at risk. Much of the play's incidental detail is comic, especially in its opening expository act, set in the township's general store, which introduces a range of characters and lightly sketches in their small-scale social snobberies, mannerisms, and gossip. But its more serious focus emerges as the psychology of a closed community.

The advent of radio in the later 1930s played an important role in encouraging and sustaining dramatists like Betty Roland—especially the National network (the Australian Broadcasting Commission), whose Federal Drama Editor, Leslie Rees, and Federal Controller of Productions, Frank Clewlow, were actively committed to the sponsorship of Australian plays.[46] The most original work it sponsored was the verse drama of the poet Douglas Stewart, who in a burst of activity between 1939 and 1947 wrote five plays—three radio plays (*The Fire on the Snow*, *The Golden Lover* and *The Earthquake Shakes the Land*) and two stage plays (*Ned Kelly* and *Shipwreck*). Stewart's work was the most distinguished expression, in Australia, of the impulse which had produced a distinctly modernist tradition of poetic drama in the work of Yeats, Auden and Isherwood, MacNeice, Eliot and others. But it also had a distinct Australian history behind it. It was a reassertion of the tradition of High Cultural dramatic enterprise which had motivated early verse dramatists like Burn and Harpur, but which had become increasingly attenuated in the later decades of the nineteenth century, surviving (in the twentieth century) in the closet drama, often purely literary in form, of figures like Norman and Jack Lindsay, and Hugh McCrae.

It was possibly the stimulus of writing initially for radio (*The Fire on the Snow*), i.e., for a non-literary medium which of its nature could exploit possibilities of speech and sound other than those demanded by stage realism, which enabled Stewart to revive this older tradition of Australian verse drama in terms which challenged realism as the dominant alternative style in contemporary Australian drama. None of Stewart's plays completely solves the central problem of the modern verse dramatist as T. S. Eliot saw it, the creation of a poetic speech which is dramatically convincing to a modern audience. But they at least opened up possibilities for a different kind of dramatic speech and action in the theatre. Patrick White's use of a stylized 'natural' speech (which is not verse, but draws heavily on such verse conventions as patterned imagery, vivid metaphors, and heightened rhythms), and Dorothy Hewett's poetic sense of theatrical texture in a play like *The Chapel Perilous*, are recognizable products of the same impulse.

Stewart's occasional writings about drama, and about his own purposes as a dramatist, continually emphasize Greek and Shakespearean poetic tragedy as examples of drama's importance in the creation of national identity:

> The playwright, I think, creates the myths by which the people live: the heroic, gigantic, legendary figures, fathers of the race, ancestors spiritual or actual, to which the living man can point and say, 'That is what I am made of; that is what makes us different from other people; that is what I believe in; those are my gods and my devils.' If you were a Greek you needed to know about the valour of Achilles and the crimes of Oedipus; if you are English, you must know the dreadful folly of Macbeth, the darkness and splendour of the kings, the enormous substantiality of Falstaff, gross, rich, and stable as the earth itself. In Australia—[47]

Although the emphasis here on the playwright as creator of 'the myths by which the people live' looks similar to the formulations of nationalists like Esson and Palmer, its basic direction is very different from, indeed, opposed to, their democratic-humanist sympathies. Stewart found his central image of the human spirit not in collective myths and ideals celebrating the virtues of the common man, but in the spectacle of heroic aspiration defeated: man pitted against the elements in a hostile environment; individualism pitting itself against the restraining conventions of society; and the Nietzschean drama of man pitted against himself, striving to attain some form of self-transcendence. Through such themes, the truly metaphysical dimensions of human experience might be grasped: the paradoxical sense of human nobility and creative effort, and of human limitation and evil, which he saw as the central experience of Greek and Shakespearean tragedy, the source of its myth-making, nation-moulding power.

Stewart's poetic drama was an attempt to create a 'tragic mythology' in these terms for Australia, drawing on history and legend for its subject matter in a revealing shift away from the contemporary subjects and settings of Australian realism: Scott's expedition to the South Pole, in *The Fire on the Snow*; the legend of Ned Kelly; Maori fable, in *The Golden Lover*; and Pelsart's expedition in the Pacific (1629), in *Shipwreck*. The plays affirmed Harpur's and Burn's historical consciousness of Australia's European roots, but with a much more ambiguous awareness of the achievements and failures of European culture. They also implicitly questioned the sufficiency of the creed of democratic humanism in Australia, with its emphasis (in Stewart's view) on a primarily social account of man, its neglect of individuality and rejection of religious or metaphysical explanations. In developing such ideas, with their strongly idealist and romantic slant, their displacement of social concerns, ultimately, into metaphysics, Stewart was strongly influenced, in Sydney, by the dominant intellectual and literary tradition established through writers and poets like Brennan, Norman Lindsay, Slessor and FitzGerald. The dominant dramatic influences, however, were Eliot and Yeats. As in their plays, Stewart introduces poetic speech as a device of stylization, aiming to create a more flexible dramatic language than is possible in naturalistic plays.

This kind of flexibility is particularly apparent in *Ned Kelly* (1943), Stewart's most successful stage play,[48] which offers a searching evaluation of the legend of the Kelly gang as a quintessentially Australian legend, and, beyond this, of the tragic metaphysical implications of this particular example of heroically individualist aspiration defeated in its confrontation with an alien environment, with the social conventions of law and order, and, especially, with its own destructive and self-destructive impulses. The play's structure is essentially a manipulation of opposed points of view, a selective organization of events in the life of the Kelly gang in order to emphasize a sequence of major verbal confrontations between Ned Kelly and Joe Byrne on the one hand (spokesmen, respectively, for the heroic and individualist aspects of the legend), and a number of representative spokesmen for the forces of law and order. A large cast of minor characters complicates this central opposition of points of view, expressing attitudes to Kelly ranging from near idolatry to outright contempt. The effect, finally, is of tragic paradox. It is the coexistence of vital, freedom-loving impulses alongside morally atrocious deeds which fascinates Stewart, providing the play's central symbol of inexplicable meta-physical dimensions in human behaviour.

Ned Kelly employs a variety of different kinds of speech, rang-ing from the ordinary language of realism to heightened poetic utterance, to convey these multiple perspectives. Ordinary speech, primarily the language of the minor characters, offers a mundane perspective on events, occasionally suggesting a sense of the social comedy of ordinary Australian life, especially in the play's two longest scenes set in the pubs at Jerilderie and Glenrowan. But it can also function as an ironically deflating device, under-cutting the rhetoric of the major characters, as well as representing shifts of mood in the main characters themselves—the larrikin element in the Kelly gang, for example, or the tough-guy element in Kelly himself, conveyed in a language that suggests deliberate parody of the conventions of American Westerns:

> Come here, Living; look at the barrel of a gun. It's black down there. It talks out of that blackness. And it's ready to talk. You won't like what it says.

Stylized poetic speech, by contrast, intensifies the sense of a dimen-sion beyond the realistic in the events of the play, a sense of the characters as in the grip of forces and ideas much larger than them-selves. It is the speech of mythic self-consciousness in Ned Kelly himself, presenting his heroic self-conception as the living embodiment of a new spirit of Australian freedom inherited from the great bushranging heroes of the country's past. In Joe Byrne it is the voice of this consciousness in a more purely romantic, spontaneous form: celebrating the values of action for its own sake, for its immediate pleasures, without the need for Ned's justifying rationalizations. Gribble is the most passionate opposing voice, committed to established traditions of law, order, morality, and social conformity, as a precondition for Australia to develop as a society at all. Poetic speech is finally, as in all Stewart's plays, the ambiguous voice of an important non-human protagonist: the elemental natural environment itself. Two of the most carefully developed images in the play are the Bush (a deceptive realm of freedom and vitality, beyond civilization and the cities, which increasingly reveals itself as a realm of solitude, emptiness and silence); and the heat-drenched rock and desert landscape of the interior, which initially promises a heroic intensity of experience but is associated increasingly, in the course of the play, with violent and self-destructive impulses.

The main weakness of the play lies in what might be called its low-intensity, middle-range verse, a speech which is written as poetry but sounds like prose, and is in fact neither, a kind of hybrid, artificial prose serving primarily as a bridging language between the scenes of realism, comedy and farce, and the scenes of high poetic intensity. Eliot faced the same problem in his later plays, settling on a variable three-stressed line which was so flexible that the distinction between poetry and prose crucial to the theatrical effect of poetic drama was often lost. In *Ned Kelly* the effect of this low-keyed poetic speech is to over-verbalize the play, dissipating its strongly theatrical central tensions. Yeats' more effective solution to the problem of making poetic speech theatrical was to simplify the action, heighten the effect of stylization, and generate tension, and dramatic interest, by exploiting the possibility of an ironic relationship between visual elements and speech: in effect, an expressionist solution. The most effective theatrical moments in *Ned Kelly* are usually of this sort: Ned's nobility of utterance undercut by larrikin or bullying behaviour; Living's servile philosophy set beside an actually exhibited personal courage; the scene of Aaron Sherritt's murder by Joe Byrne, in which an atmosphere of suspense culminating in violent action offers its own unspoken comment on Joe Byrne's rhetorically-invoked ideal of mateship. Perhaps most powerful of all is the visual image of Ned Kelly in the play's short final scene. Grotesquely attired in makeshift armour, isolated on stage, defiantly rhetorical to the last as he advances towards the unseen troopers, staggering and falling, quite simply, as a shot rings out, he provides a heroic image qualified by the suggestions of absurdity, of obsessiveness and madness, and finally, of simple human fallibility.

Despite the originality of Stewart's efforts, his plays did not produce any significant shift of direction in Australian drama, partly because of their own theatrical weaknesses (of construction, and language), and partly because poetic drama was itself too narrowly-based a form to sustain more than a coterie audience. *Ned Kelly*'s questioning of bush legend, however, in terms which suggested more strongly than earlier drama that Australia's dominant values were the product of city and suburban living, did signal a shift of focus, in the remarkable resurgence of naturalistic drama in the mid and late 1950s. This shift was confirmed in

Sumner Locke-Elliott's *Rusty Bugles*, an anti-war play which enjoyed immense success, amidst public controversy and official efforts to ban it on the grounds of objectionable language, when it was produced by Doris Fitton at the Independent Theatre in 1948. Despite its obvious theme—an unheroic image of war, focusing on the boredom, frustrations and nostalgias of a group of soldiers manning a remote Ordnance Depot in the Northern Territory—*Rusty Bugles* might also be seen as the last significant play in the tradition of Outback realism. Its image of the Outback is totally negative: a suffocating environment of intolerable climatic extremes, squalid and makeshift living conditions, and repetitive work, from which the soldiers' single, obsessive desire is to escape. Life, for all the characters in the play, is quite simply what happens in the cities and suburbs they have been forced to leave, the glamour and freedom of the 'Big Smoke', the domestic comforts of 'home'.

Locke-Elliott had had numerous plays performed at the Independent Theatre during the decade before *Rusty Bugles*. His comments on the play, which stress its unusual closeness to personal experience, suggest one reason for its immediate success:

> This is a documentary. It is not strictly a play. It has no plot in the accepted sense. Its characters are drawn from life—they all existed and I knew and loved them well ... The events of their lives whilst they were cut off from home, family, and normal life, and which have been reproduced here, are authentic, and no one event in the play is fictional.[49]

Yet it is ultimately the craftsmanship of the play, transforming these raw, documentary details, which enables him to capitalize on the controversial aspects of subject and theme so essential to the impact of a realistic play. Its loosely episodic structure (a series of ten scenes arranged chronologically over a six month span) enables him to achieve effects impossible in a conventionally plotted work. In this anti-heroic play, no single character dominates. The effect is a gradual definition of individual personalities, each with its own separate history, motivations, and idiosyncrasies, against a background of enforced, ritual routine. Despite its vivid documentary surface, the realism of setting and situation, the acutely accurate registering of vigorously colloquial and earthy Australian male speech, the main method of the play is ironic understatement. Long before David Williamson's drama, *Rusty Bugles* made considerable comic play out of the tendency of

Australian men to express affection and group solidarity through extravagant rituals of derogatory or abusive language. Deeply felt frustrations or aggressions, by contrast, are masked in silence, or expressed through impulsive and apparently irrational actions. Both the theme of the play—of apathy and fatalism—and its ritual presentation, were to receive new emphasis in much of the 'new wave' Australian drama of the late 1960s and 1970s.

The upsurge of naturalistic drama in the wake of *Summer of the Seventeenth Doll* represented a tracing of the displaced lives of Locke-Elliott's play back to their roots, in the domestic, working-class living rooms and backyards of Australia's inner-city suburbs. It was a rediscovered awareness, after Esson, of the *existence* of such lives; and more especially, a new and often controversial awareness of stresses and tensions within them. Lawler's play itself set the pattern, with its inner-urban Carlton setting, its awareness of conflicting outback and urban lifestyles and of class divisions within urban life, and its unself-conscious acceptance of a situation in which valued and permanent sexual relationships exist outside marriage. In Alan Seymour's *The One Day of the Year* (1961) class consciousness provides an even stronger source of tension. At a domestic level, the play is a study of conflict between the generations in Australian life (a bitter clash of attitudes between a working class father and his university-educated son, complicated by the pressure of long established emotional ties and loyalties which neither really wishes to break). At a more directly (and controversially) political and social level,[50] it probes the significance of the institution of Anzac Day as the embodiment of a quintessentially Australian myth of national identity. No play up to this time had explored so powerfully, and from so sympathetic a stance, the psychology of working class identification with myths of nationality: both its sources, in an actual social and economic alienation and deeply-felt class inferiority; and its effects, in an intensified hostility towards foreigners, and an intensified commitment to such demonstrative, public rituals as those of Anzac Day. The myth of national identity, as it is presented in Seymour's play, contains and rationalizes an actual class tension, sustaining the central character in the illusion that he belongs, in a society which has in fact relegated him to the bottom of the existing social order.

The action of the play is a testing of this illusion, and a gradual revelation of the psychological compulsions behind it, through a particularly skilful adaptation of the conventions of domestic melodrama. Although it has sometimes been argued otherwise (on occasion by the author himself), the social theme of the Anzac myth of national identity is more than simply incidental to the 'primary' theme of personal confrontation between father and son. The play's delicately balanced conclusion, with both characters half-recognizing and half-evading the implications of its action, leaves the possibility of change or compromise unresolved. As in Lawler's play, this sense of deadlock thrusts the audience back into the central tensions in the play, reinforcing the characteristically 'realistic' effect of depth and complexity of presentation.

A similar adaptation of conventional melodramatic, comic and farcical elements from domestic drama occurs in Richard Beynon's *The Shifting Heart*, the most successful Trust-sponsored Australian play to appear after *Summer of the Seventeenth Doll*. First performed under May Hollinworth's direction at Sydney's Elizabethan Theatre in 1957, the play is set in the backyard of a terrace house occupied by an Italian migrant family in Melbourne's inner-city suburb of Collingwood, dealing with the theme of racial tension in Australian society in the aftermath of the post-war boom in government-sponsored immigration from the countries of Southern Europe. As in Seymour's play, the location of social conflict within a domestic situation serves as a central device of intensification, involving the main characters (and the audience) in a directly personal and emotional experiencing of racial prejudice and its effects. This mode of involvement, the particular form, as in Seymour's play, of its realism, gives the play its strength as a study of the psychology of racism and of its victims. It is precisely because of its invasion of family and marital bonds that prejudice is seen as a deep-rooted, unconsciously motivating force in the behaviour of Australians, affecting migrants as a destruction of personal identity.

The late 1950s also saw the emergence of the Sydney-born playwright, Peter Kenna, whose first substantial play, *The Slaughter of St. Teresa's Day*, was performed in 1959. Like Kenna's later plays, it is a most unusual variation within (or on the edge of) the tradition of Australian realism revitalized by Lawler. Its subject, a 'St. Valentine's Day Massacre' in the Paddington house, in Sydney, of the play's colourful heroine, a thriving S. P. bookmaker, recalled the criminal and the fringe-criminal underworld of Esson's plays earlier in the century. Its main theme, the destructive effects of the heroine's sentimental attachment to the past, recalled *Summer of the*

Seventeenth Doll. Unlike Lawler's play, however, which depended on the economy and concentration of its handling of the conventions of the well-made play, Kenna's play employs these conventions much more loosely, retaining a skeletal well-made framework with a spectacularly violent climax (a knifing, followed by a shoot-out) at the end of the Second Act, but fleshing it out with elements deriving from much more self-consciously theatrical styles of presentation. The end result is a quite unusual blend of realism and theatricalism. But it is as an exploration, at once critical and sympathetic, of the Irish-Catholic sensibility in Australia that the play achieves much of its social significance. Kenna's plays have continued to explore this sensibility, in terms which challenge the conventional Irish stereotypes (comic, sentimental or heroic) familiarized in the established theatre from the earliest years of the colony.

One of the most significant elements in the revival of Australian realism in the 1950s, immediately distinguishing it from earlier examples, is that its main authors (Locke-Elliott in the late 1940s, Lawler, Beynon, Kenna and Seymour) were all, like their new-wave counterparts in England in the 1950s, associated with the theatre themselves, as writers, actors, or actor-directors. This fact, together with the advent of the Elizabethan Theatre Trust, the appearance of talented new directors like John Sumner, Robin Lovejoy and Wal Cherry, and the emergence of a generation of actors and actresses acquiring fuller professional experience of the stage than had previously been possible, indicated that a period of protracted amateurism in non-commercial Australian theatre was slowly coming to an end. The naturalistic impulse expressed in these plays was itself to come under challenge, repeatedly, in the early 1960s and afterwards. Yet, however tenuous and uncertain developments in the 1950s were, the plays themselves reflected something of the confidence and the sense of craftsmanship of dramatists conscious of writing for an actual stage.[51]

The plays are more than simply period pieces, though they are sometimes, now, presented that way. For the first time in any sustained way, major characters had been created (Roo and Barney, Olive and Pearl in *The Doll*, Clarry and Maria Fowler in *The Shifting Heart*, Oola Maguire in *The Slaughter of St. Teresa's Day*, and Alf Cook in *The One Day of the Year*) whose complexity offered a real challenge to the interpretative skills of performers and directors: characters whose lives on stage enacted a movement (and demanded a performance) beyond stereotype. From the perspective of subsequent developments in Australian theatre, in which new and more obviously *theatrical* impulses asserted them-selves, often in reaction to these earlier plays, it is possible to under-estimate the sheer technical skill in manipulating older conventions which they reveal at their best: Beynon's and Seymour's inventive use of comic and farcical situations, and their skill in creating a sense of stereotypically accurate Australian vernacular speech; Lawler's unerring sense of timing in *The Doll*, his motivation of events and interactions in ways which con-tinually fulfil expectations and generate new ones; Kenna's innovative use of the yarn, and his continually surprising mixture of the comic, the sentimental and the grotesque.

Repeatedly, however, the most moving moments in these plays, as in the best of the earlier plays from Esson onwards, occur outside such conventions. At crucial points, given conventions of language, behaviour and belief lose their explanatory power, leaving the central characters exposed and vulnerable, and in the process involving audiences in the same experience of exposure and loss. Australian realism, from the time of Esson onwards, achieved its most authentic insights in these critical moments beyond words, which evoke Australian life in tragic images of inarticulate bafflement, frustration, and deeply-felt alienation.

PART THREE: DRAMA SINCE 1960

In the period after 1960 it becomes possible for the first time to describe Australian drama as achieving a creative significance comparable with that of fiction, poetry and the other arts. The energies released by new playwrights, directors and performers were sustained by an unprecedented growth in audiences responsive to new and often critical contemporary emphases. The most striking quality of this work—linking playwrights whose aims and styles are often diverse—is its new emphasis on theatrical values, on the need to discover modes of drama, beyond literature and naive representationalism, through which theatre could develop its own, distinct, imaginative vision in Australia.

Jack Hibberd's *A Stretch of the Imagination* (1972), one of the major achievements of the 'new wave' of Australian drama originating in small alternative and experimental theatres in the later 1960s and early 1970s, typifies this impulse, offering an image of Australian life as literally theatrical. The play's single character,

Monk O'Neill, is a compound of Australian stereotypes: bush philosopher and yarn-spinner, epic lover and mate, heroic battler and individualist, sardonic iconoclast, sportsman, cultured man-of-letters and bon-vivant. Compulsively *performing* these roles, as he acts out memories and fantasies, he invites audiences to 'stretch their imaginations' and recognize, through their involvement in his virtuoso performance, the ways in which their own lives conform to stereotype. Like many other recent Australian plays, Hibberd's draws on a number of popular entertainment conventions of nineteenth and twentieth century theatre to emphasize this effect (the one-man show, vaudeville and variety, mime and popular songs), as well as parodying, episode by episode, the conventions of melodrama and domestic drama, romantic and drawing room comedy, classical tragedy and contemporary realism.

The recognitions which this display of parodied conventions offers, however, are disturbingly ambiguous, a long way from Geoghegan's or Darrell's 'innocent' use of similar devices in order to celebrate and confirm the emergence of a valued colonial culture and identity. The image of imaginative life as theatrical play is continually subverted by the play's consciousness of a 'real world', a sheerly physical environment, whose properties of time, change and death undermine the imagination's desire to believe in the permanence of its own fictions. An irony in the play's title implies that the mind is imprisoned by the workings of the imagination. From such a perspective, cultural conventions, like theatrical conventions, are seen as problematic and provisional, temporary forms of imaginative dominance over one's environment. Arbitrariness and transience are reflected in the episodic, improvisatory character of the play's action, the seeming randomness with which it shifts from one set of parodied conventions to another, as its protagonist attempts to give dramatic shape to his impressions, memories, and fantasies. The play's movement suggests a gradual contraction and physical degeneration of Monk's life, and prophesies the extinction of European culture in Australia ('the predatory upstart albino ... the small pink tribe of mistletoe men').

Hibberd's play is deliberately theatrical in a way which challenges the methods and assumptions of established Australian theatre. By using a rough style of presentation in an intimate acting space, and directing attention to a single performer whose improvisations and ritual behaviour are outrageously bizarre and manic, he forces audiences into critical recognitions—at once comic and tragic—of their own stereo-typical expectations.

In the development of Australian drama since the early 1960s, the importance of this new consciousness of theatre, and of its imaginative possibilities for comment on life in Australia, could hardly be underestimated. It represents a belated discovery of trends in European theatre, reaching back to the turn of the century, which had steadily eroded the representational impulse of naturalism—the style which had become entrenched, over half a century, in serious Australian drama primarily because of its identification with Australian nationalism. Apart from isolated examples (Esson's political satire *The Time Is Not Yet Ripe*, some of the work of the New Theatre movement in the 1930s, and Stewart's verse drama) there was little sustained work outside the conventions of the well-made play and the naturalistic criteria of representational set and costuming, plausible speech, gesture and action. The possibilities of expressionism and symbolism, of stylized action or episodic structure, of Brechtian political theatre or Absurdist theatre, had all remained virtually unexplored in Australian drama up to the early 1960s. The impulse to explore them first appeared in the drama of Patrick White and was strengthened in the subsequent work of playwrights like Jack Hibberd, David Williamson, Alexander Buzo, John Romeril, Barry Oakley, Dorothy Hewett, Michael Boddy, Robert Ellis, Ron Blair, and Bill Reed.

It would be possible to write the history of this new drama simply as a record of overseas influences on specific playwrights, theatres, acting and production styles: the American model of Betty Burstall's influential coffee-house theatre (the Café La Mama) established in Melbourne in 1967, the influence of Pinter and Albee on aspects of the work of Williamson, Buzo and others, of Beckett on Hibberd, or of Brecht and expressionism on much of the work of Romeril, Hewett, Blair and Louis Nowra. However, the impulse was never simply derivative. As had happened throughout the history of nineteenth and twentieth century Australian drama, the borrowed conventions were actively transformed, given new emphases and set in new relationships to each other.

The dominance of naturalism in new Australian drama, for something like half a century after Esson's initial impetus, was itself an example of the transformation of a particular overseas form in response to local pressures. In the 1950s, the influence of American playwrights like Arthur Miller and Tennessee Williams (whose plays were regularly produced, professionally, by such companies as John Sumner's Union Repertory Theatre Company in Melbourne) was noticeable in Australian naturalism. This American influence, with its unusually intense focus on tragic personal conflicts, is repeatedly found alongside the more purely British conventions of the well-made play. As in the history of other dramatic forms—like Australian melodrama in the later nineteenth century—it might be argued that it was the interaction of Anglo-American impulses within Australian naturalism which gave it its distinctive character, as a variant within a more general form.

Australian drama since 1960—and especially since the later 1960s—has also actively transformed the styles and conventions it has borrowed. The most immediate local pressure came from the prolonged dominance of naturalism itself, a fact which lent a peculiar intensity to its rejection (or its transformation) in plays which often retained some of its elements but developed them in ways which were not, finally, naturalistic at all. It also accounts for the unusual energy, and diversity of approach in the search for alternative styles. It was repeatedly argued that Australian naturalism dealt only with the surfaces of life, that its criteria of plausible action, characterization and dialogue, within the distanced illusion of the two-dimensional proscenium frame, produced a merely photographic representation of behaviour, with insufficient explanatory power, and—in the wake of Brecht's denunciations—insufficient recognition of theatre's capacity to confront and transform the consciousness of audiences. Moreover, because of its links with nationalism, it became critically implicated in arguments about the repeated failure of Australian drama in the previous fifty years to establish strong roots: that it had become a parochial and provincial drama, cutting itself off from new overseas ideas and influences; that by limiting itself to the possibilities of one particular dramatic method, among many others, it was itself responsible for the drama's failure to attract or sustain large audiences.

In recent Australian drama, however, naturalism has retained its strength in ways which suggest that this kind of criticism is inadequate, or incomplete, as an account of the possibilities of its methods. It is a major element, for example, in the work of two of the most substantial playwrights of the 1960s and 1970s, David Williamson and Peter Kenna. Its power to confront and shock, to expose social issues and conflicts, through its creation of characters whose personal lives and backgrounds are plausibly motivated and realistically presented, has not diminished. Williamson's *The Removalists*, a play about the psychology of violence in Australian life, and Kenna's *The Cassidy Album*, a trilogy which (among other themes) contains a sympathetic account of the personal dilemmas of the homosexual in Australian society, provide clear indications of the undiminished strength in what is now an established local tradition.

Rejection of the methods of naturalism, and their transformation in the work of playwrights like Williamson and Kenna need to be seen, also, as the expression of new kinds of social consciousness in Australian theatre. A shift in conventions was necessary in order to accommodate these on the stage, beyond the domestic sitting rooms and backyards on which realism had depended so heavily. Recent dramatists have concerned themselves with social mobility in Australian life, with work patterns and life-styles growing out of increasing post-war affluence, and with changing patterns of sexual and social behaviour in younger generations of Australians. A recurrent theme is the power of bureaucracy in Australian life, and of political, legal, economic, educational and mass media establishments. Violence and racism within Australia, and in its post-war international relations, have also been seen as significant by politically conscious playwrights. Conventional realism's focus on family relationships in domestic settings, which could accommodate such themes only as an impinging background, seem increasingly obsolete.

A major development within this social consciousness is a new preoccupation with Australian history. Realism's limitations were particularly evident in confronting the problems of getting Australian history onto the stage. They had been clearly revealed in earlier plays like Esson's *The Southern Cross* and Palmer's *Hail Tomorrow*, with their static emphasis on 'committee room' conversations and debates, and their image of history simply as a product of the personalities and moral dilemmas of its leading protagonists. The two most impressive examples of historical realism in Australian drama are much more recent works in the form of trilogies, using special structural effects that belong to the episodic play. The impression of historical depth and definition in Kenna's *The Cassidy Album* (*A Hard God*, *Furtive Love*, and *An Eager Hope*) derives, as its title suggests, from its imaginative exploration of three 'snapshot' images, cross-sections of the personal lives he deals with in depth over a time span of twenty years (1946, 1955, 1966). Lawler's *The Doll Trilogy*, with its two much later companion pieces to *Summer of the Seventeenth Doll*, *Kid Stakes* and *Other Times*, uses a similar technique, over a time span of sixteen years (1937, 1945, 1953), to create its realistic effect of individual lives enacting the representative history of a particular generation of Australians. In both instances, the effect is a special transformation of realism, drawing on methods which had been vividly exploited in deliberately non-realistic plays like Hewett's *The Chapel Perilous*, and Buzo's historical play *Macquarie*. The former traces the growth of a rebellious and highly individualistic feminine sensibility against a background of formative social and political events in Australia in the 1940s and 1950s; and the latter uses a similarly swift-moving episodic structure to convey a sense of multiple social and political forces during the period (1810–1821) of Macquarie's Governorship of New South Wales.

Underlying these formal rejections and transformations of realism, however, and the allied thematic impulse to explore new areas of Australian social, political and historical experience, the discovery of new overseas methods of drama (especially the stylized and ritualistic elements in expressionism, and the parodic, farcical and anti-theatre elements in absurdism) enabled a new consciousness of theatre's relevance to Australian life to be expressed. As in Hibberd's play, the presiding muse of Australian drama since 1960 is the spirit of comedy. It has led to a resurgence of the older entertainment conventions of 'low comedy' (slapstick, farce, vaudeville, music hall and revue) as well as of the more sophisticated conventions of intellectual comedy (wit, parody, irony and satire), and of modern black comedy and tragi-comedy. Esson resolutely suppressed the comic impulse underlying his political satire, *The Time Is Not Yet Ripe*, in his realistic plays. Recent Australian drama, rediscovering that impulse and applying it to Australian life as a whole, has produced an unusually comprehensive critique of some common Australian attitudes. The power of convention itself, and the compulsion to demonstrate conformity to given conventions and demand it of others, are major social themes in recent Australian plays, repeatedly emphasized

239

through self-consciously theatrical effects of stylization, ritual and farce, in which Australian stereotypes are seen to be compulsively acting out social roles. The comic spirit, in the best of the plays, has thus confronted Australian audiences with a disturbing image of themselves.

This new comic impulse was first released into Australian theatre in a sustained way in the work of Barry Humphries, who began his acting career in John Sumner's Union Theatre Repertory Company. He introduced what was to become his most famous comic creation, Edna Everage, in a satirical sketch for the company's annual Christmas Revue in 1955, and subsequently went on, in the later 1950s and after, to establish a career as the author and performer of regular one-man comedy shows in England and Australia—including *A Nice Night's Entertainment* (1962), *Excuse I* (1965), *Just a Show* (1968), *At Least You Can Say You've Seen It* (1976) and *Isn't It Pathetic at His Age* (1978). Each show is a loose sequence of satirical sketches and songs, requiring a capacity for extraordinarily versatile mimicry of the idiosyncratic manner-isms, gestures, and speech habits of Australian stereotypes, and relying in increasingly sophisticated ways on ambiguously edged rituals and game-playing between Humphries as performer, and audiences who are at once being entertained and sent up. The originality of Humphries's work lies both in its recovery of a highly self-conscious mode of theatrical artifice for the Australian stage and in its exploitation of this theatricality for the purposes of a mocking, satirical vision of Australian society. This vision has grown in substance over the years, primarily through the continu-ing development of his main character, Edna Everage, who has taken on something of a mythic status as a latter-day picaresque, globetrotting heroine of Australian affluence, the eccentric embodiment of the robust energies of middle class manners, morals and tastes. Humphries has also developed a range of equally grotesque supporting stereotypes, in a process which has at once mirrored, and provided an edged commentary on, the main social and cultural trends of Australian life from the 1950s into the 1970s.

Humphries's main initial target was the closed society of an increasingly affluent post-war Australian suburbia. His subsequent work, however, left few of Australia's most cherished illusions and myths untouched. It is precisely through the eccentricity and extravagance of Edna Everage's stage presence—reinforced by the fact that she is a woman impersonated by a man—that she has achieved her representative significance, offering an image of Australian behaviour as obsession with role play and with style, taste and fashionable opinion. The world in which Edna Everage ostentatiously parades fashionable opinions, (in much the same way as she parades the latest fashion in dress design, hairstyle, or household gadgetry) is defined, and judges itself, solely by appearances and surfaces. Humphries's gallery of grotesques satirizes a world in which politics has been reduced to image, culture to cult and fashionable trend, and ideas to packaged commodities marketed through the mass media. His comic characters are the innocent, unconscious automata of such a world, at once its victims and its most vociferous defenders. Humphries's example has been especially influential for its inventive use of theatre. The one-man play has had a quite unusual significance in recent Australian drama, not only in plays like Hibberd's *A Stretch of the Imagination*, but in the work of Blair (*The Christian Brothers* and *Mad Bad and Dangerous to Know*), of Steve J. Spears (*The Elocution of Benjamin Franklin*), and of one-man performers like Reg Livermore. Even more influential was his foreshadowing of the serious possibilities of techniques associated with popular stage humour: the satirical sketch, the comic devices of mimicry, impersonation and ritual game-playing.

The playwright who most immediately extended these possibilities was Patrick White, four of whose plays were produced between 1961 and 1964. The first of these plays, *The Ham Funeral*, had been written much earlier in England, just before White returned to settle permanently in Australia in 1948.[52] It was certainly, in the context of Australian theatre in the early 1960s, a most unusual play. It deliberately flouted the conventions of realism, demanding an imaginative use of stage and acting resources, and an engagement on the part of audiences, of a kind never previously attempted in Australian drama. Its opening Prologue, a mixture of diffident soliloquizing and direct address to the audience by the main character, an unnamed Young Man whose interior life and fumbling quest for identity provide the play's central subject, rejects the conventions of naturalistic illusionism, and invokes the expressionist aim of triggering introspective processes in the audience itself. The dominant image the play offers, especially through its symbolic use of stage space and its emphasis on ritual action, is of fantasy and illusion as compelling, motivating forces in human behaviour. White's focus is ulti-

241

mately—as it is in *The Aunt's Story*, the novel closest in time, and in theme, to *The Ham Funeral*—the moral implications which flow from a recognition of 'the reality of illusion' in human life, from the knowledge that individuals exist as shadowy fictions in the inner lives of others.

The Ham Funeral, in its deliberate avoidance of the naturalistic emphasis on specific place, time and social milieu, and its probing of what is envisaged as universal and recurrent in human behaviour, was concerned with Australian life only by implication. The implication was nevertheless striking in a play which offered a compassionate study of characters wrestling with defeat and frustration, yet challenged—as a delusion of the ego—the notion of a world ordered by moral absolutes, asserting that what might be real in human life was the interior drama of individual psychic experience. The three plays which followed the production of *The Ham Funeral* turned directly and explicitly to Australian society, as if exploring the local significance of the ideas broached in the earlier play.

In *The Season at Sarsaparilla* (sub-titled 'A Charade of Suburbia'), satire is the dominant mode, defining a society in which moral absolutes reign supreme, demanding conformity to fixed conventions of behaviour, condemning and destroying those who fail to meet that demand. No character, in this play of many characters, remains unscarred by his or her experience of Sarsaparilla. Its conventions are invoked through a barbed and witty satirical language, and also, as in *The Ham Funeral*, through a highly inventive use of stage space. The permanent set consists of three identical raised platforms, with skeletal structures 'representing the three kitchens of three houses'. Domestic actions within each frame, often expressed through mime, are at times juxtaposed against each other, or ritually synchronized to suggest routine monotony. An ingenious interweaving of conversations within and between each frame, provides the audience with a composite image in which, again, effects of repetition or of contrast can be emphasized. Shifts of lighting momentarily isolate separate actions in each house, or accomplish rapid time shifts, enabling repetitiveness to be enacted in time, as well as through the spatial arrangement of the set. The effect, overall, is of a containment of individual differences within an essential sameness, defined by the work routines of husbands, the domestic routines of wives, and most importantly of all, by the identity of bourgeois goals—

material security, domesticity, and social status—to which each family is committed. Sarsaparillan morality ultimately triumphs over all the underground energies (a birth, an adultery, and a suicide) which threaten its stability.

A Cheery Soul, which White re-worked for the stage from one of the main short stories in his collection *The Burnt Ones*, advances a stage further the exploration of Sarsaparillan society. The presentation of a society-in-action in the earlier play, with its farce-like complications of plot and multiplicity of interacting characters, is replaced here by a concentrated focus on a single figure of larger-than-life dimensions. Its central character, Miss Docker, represents, in its purest and most absolute form, the ethic to which Sarsaparillan society subscribes—cheerfulness and optimism, charitable good works, and evangelical Christian piety. In the drama of Sarsaparillan life she might be described as a natural actress, one who knows her lines by heart and is word perfect. This image of theatre is central in White's method in the play and the source of Miss Docker's richly idiosyncratic stage presence among characters unable to perfect and sustain their roles. A gradual fragmentation of dramatic conventions provides the play's strongest image of what Sarsaparillan society *really* is, beneath the social comedy of its surface. It also traces a pattern of increasing isolation for Miss Docker herself, as the victims of her goodness turn increasingly against her. If she is the scourge of Sarsaparilla, reminding it of its failures to live up to its professed norms, she is also, ultimately, its victim, a scapegoat through whom it rationalizes those failures and resists any impulse to change.

After the production of his fourth play of this period, *Night on Bald Mountain*—a tragedy of epic proportions set in the mountains beyond Sydney, in which all the major themes of the earlier plays found concentrated expression, in an abstract, almost apocalyptic vision of a social world on the point of collapse—White lapsed into silence as a playwright until the later 1970s. The appearance of *Big Toys* (1977), along with imaginative new productions of *The Season at Sarsaparilla* (1976) and *A Cheery Soul* (1979), itself pointed to the remarkably changed theatrical climate which his experimentalism in the early 1960s had helped to initiate. *Big Toys* is White's most overtly political play, written in the aftermath of political upheavals in Australian society in the mid-1970s and taking the form of a barbed parody of the sophisticated romantic comedy of manners. Manners, in this play, assert the shallow style of wealthy behind-the-scenes power brokers in Australian society—the world of foreign-derived corporate power and its local political, financial and legal entrepreneurs. Its plot (a version of the conventional triangle of husband, wife and lover) provides a pointed comment on the dangerous games they play with each other, using society and, in an era of the mass exploitation of natural resources, the planet itself, as their toys.

Big Toys was only one of a number of similar recent Australian plays, written with an awareness of the increasingly sophisticated and affluent audiences attracted to Australian drama in the 1970s. Elements of this kind of parody were present in David Williamson's work as early as *Don's Party* and they were developed further in subsequent plays like *What If You Died Tomorrow* (1973) and *A Handful of Friends* (1976). Oakley's serious bedroom comedy *Bedfellows* (1975), and Buzo's later romantic comedies, *Coralie Lansdowne Says No* (1974), *Martello Towers* (1976), and *Makassar Reef* (1978) contained similar transformations of conventions belonging, traditionally, to high comedy, with the aim of exploring and commenting on new aspects of Australian social life.

Hal Porter's elegantly fashioned plays of the 1960s are a variation on the same dramatic mode. *The Tower*, in particular, is a most unusual historical play set in Tasmania in 1850, using a deliberately stagey, melodramatic plot, mannered behaviour, and class- and status-conscious stereotypes to project an image of a rigidly stratified society obsessed with its inheritance of the 'convict strain', and of lives motivated and destroyed by predatory, power-seeking impulses. The more perfectly the characters behave, the more egotistic and shallow they show themselves to be, revealing themselves ultimately (in what amounts to an ironic inversion of the theme of convictism) as prisoners of the conventions they worship.

The production of White's new drama in the first half of the 1960s was a relatively isolated event, although the Union Theatre Repertory Company in Melbourne, in addition to mounting new productions of Lawler, Seymour and Beynon, and resurrecting older plays by Palmer and Esson, performed new plays by Alan Hopgood and others, including Hopgood's play about Australian Rules football, *And the Big Men Fly*. The first sign of a substantial breakthrough into new styles of drama occurred in 1966, with the mounting of a season of six Australian plays at the newly-established experimental Jane Street Theatre in Sydney. This was a joint project of the Old Tote Theatre and the National Institute of Dramatic Art (NIDA), which was attached to the University of New South Wales in 1959 as a professional training school for performers, directors, designers and technicians. The Old Tote Theatre had itself been established in 1963 under the auspices of NIDA and of the Elizabethan Theatre Trust, and was eventually, in the late 1960s, to become the New South Wales link in a chain of professional State companies instituted under new government subsidization policies.

The Jane Street season introduced new plays by Thomas Keneally and James Searle, whose *The Lucky Streak* was one of the first Australian plays to register the influence of Harold Pinter's style, offering a comic but compassionate image of the fears and fantasies of a landlady, and of a rootless group of younger generation urban Australians lodging in a nondescript boarding house. The most theatrically innovative play, however, was Rodney Milgate's *A Refined Look at Existence*, an erudite and witty farce offering a comic pastiche of Greek myths, including an up-dated parody of Euripides' *The Bacchae*. In this play an Australian pop singer features as a modern Dionysus, and the pop cult synthetically generated around him, with its mass hysteria and hero-worship, functions as a contemporary version of the Bacchic orgies, demanding ritual sacrifice of a latter-day Pentheus who refuses to go along with the mob. The play is both a philosophical disquisition on the nature of reality and a satirical attack on the consumerist values of mass Australian society, projecting these themes on stage in the fragmented form and trappings of an absurdly tragic farce, by means of a full-scale attack on the notion of reality underpinning the illusionist theatre of naturalism. At times, the play suggests something of the Goon Show zaniness, flippancy, and intellectual wit of Tom Stoppard's drama. However, in its adaptation of popular conventions—popular songs, mime, farce and vaudeville—the play was also the earliest example of what became, over the next few years, a recognizable style associated with Jane Street and the early productions of the Nimrod Street Theatre.

The Jane Street programme established a pattern for much subsequent Australian drama. It introduced the work of younger playwrights interested in contemporary themes, experimented with new styles of drama, and also revealed a new historical consciousness (Keneally's tragic play, *Halloran's Little Boat*, was based on his novel of penal times, *Bring Larks and Heroes*, and Geoghegan's *The Currency Lass*, recently discovered, was given its first performance since the 1840s). In Melbourne, in 1967, similar impulses took shape in the small fifty-seat Café La Mama Theatre established by Betty Burstall in Carlton, on the model of Ellen Stewart's off-off Broadway La Mama theatre in New York. Within a year, numerous short plays by Jack Hibberd, Barry Oakley and others had been performed, and the nucleus of a regular La Mama company formed, with a committed workshop orientation.

La Mama acted as a magnet for a younger generation of performers, writers and audiences (many of them nurtured in the university milieu of political dissent and counter-cultural disaffection of the later 1960s) united in their dissatisfaction with the stuffiness of what was currently offered in the professional theatre, and especially with what was felt to be its failure to give sufficient encouragement to Australian drama. The La Mama company committed itself to the idea of an Australian drama with an energy and dedication unmatched in earlier theatre history. By 1969 it was sufficiently established to perform thirty plays over a period of ten days at the National University Arts Festival. In addition to its work inside La Mama it engaged in Street Theatre activities, providing open air performances of an agit-prop character (using masks, puppets, slogans, simplified gestures and utterance) at anti-Vietnam War demonstrations and rock festivals.[53]

By 1969 and 1970 there were clear indications of substantial talent emerging from the many playwrights whose work was performed at La Mama. Jack Hibberd's *Who?*, *One of Nature's Gentlemen*, *Dimboola*, and *White With Wire Wheels*, and John Romeril's *The Man From Chicago* and *I Don't Know Who To Feel Sorry For* were all promising early plays. Early plays by Alexander Buzo (*Norm and Ahmed* and *The Front Room Boys*) had also been performed. In 1970 David Williamson's first full-length play, *The Coming of Stork*, was performed, followed in 1971 by a La Mama production of *The Removalists* and an Australian Performing Group production of *Don's Party* at the Pram Factory Theatre.

The Australian Performing Group had developed in 1969 out of the earlier La Mama company, establishing La Mama's reputation, outside Melbourne, in productions of *White With Wire Wheels*, *The Front Room Boys*, and *The Man From Chicago* at the Perth Festival in

1970. The formation of the Australian Performing Group was essentially an effort to provide a structure and direction—especially a radical social and political direction—for what had previously been random and makeshift in La Mama activities, within a 'laboratory' environment allowing for an open testing of theatrical ideas and practices, and a questioning of received orthodoxies about Australian theatre and culture. A satirical and historical pageant play, based on and taking its title from Dampier's *Marvellous Melbourne* (1889), scripted by Hibberd and Romeril, and directed by Graeme Blundell and Max Gillies, was the first product of the co-operative workshop environment established at the Pram Factory in 1971. In the following years it sponsored work by Hibberd (*A Stretch of the Imagination, Peggy Sue, A Toast to Melba*), Romeril (*The Floating World*) and Oakley (*The Feet of Daniel Mannix, Beware of Imitations* and *Bedfellows*). A 1972 production (*Betty Can Jump*) by the Women's Group within the Australian Performing Group was the first expression of the new feminist consciousness in Australian theatre.

Comparable activity in Sydney in the 1970s, after the beginning made at Jane Street in the later 1960s, occurred in the small Nimrod Street Theatre (a converted stables in Kings Cross seating an audience of a hundred and fifty) established by Ken and Lilian Horler, John Bell and Richard Wherrett in 1970. Like La Mama and the Australian Performing Group it was interested in a rough, unpretentious style of theatre, exploiting the possibilities of a closer relationship between actors and audiences than was possible on the conventional stage. It was interested also in the popular, improvisatory, knockabout techniques which had contributed so strongly to the success of Michael Boddy and Robert Ellis's *The Legend of King O'Malley* at Jane Street and the Old Tote in 1970. Above all, it was committed to the production of new Australian plays. But there were also significant differences of emphasis: a less programmatic concern with political and counter-cultural aims, a greater respect (especially after its shift to new premises in Surry Hills in 1974) for professionalism and for the literary dimensions of the text, and a strong commitment to contemporary productions of classical drama. The Nimrod Street Theatre's influence on Australian theatre in general has been as strong, through its fresh interpretation of classical plays, as it has through its sponsorship of Australian plays, although these have always constituted the main proportion of its work. It provided Sydney audiences with continuing access to the work of Williamson, Buzo, Ron Blair, Michael Boddy, and later on to newer playwrights like Jim McNeil, Alma de Groen, Michael Cove, Jennifer Compton, Steve Spears and Louis Nowra, as well as to the main Australian Performing Group writers.

The energies generated by the activities of these small alternative theatres in Melbourne and Sydney had a profound impact on the shape of Australian drama, not only inspiring a resurgence of little theatre activity throughout Australia, but also influencing a re-thinking of aims, and often of practice, in the established State professional theatres, which since the formation of the Australian Council for the Arts (as a successor to the Elizabethan Theatre Trust) in 1968, had been the prime beneficiaries of greatly increased government subsidies. In the wake of the antagonisms which arguments about subsidizing practices often generated, it is possible to over-simplify the problematic relations which existed (and still exist) between alternative little theatres, the subsidized professional 'establishment', and commercial theatre. In many instances there has been considerable mobility—of actors and actresses, directors, and writers themselves—across all three kinds of theatre, as well as into television and film. Although in Melbourne it could certainly be argued that the new impulses were a direct challenge to professional theatre, in Sydney the subsidized professional network of NIDA, Jane Street and the Old Tote itself initiated the changes in theatrical climate subsequently developed in the little theatres, and nurtured many of the most talented performers and directors of the new drama.

The Legend of King O'Malley, more than any other play constituted a turning point for Australian drama in Sydney, making large audiences aware that quite new things were happening in the theatre. It offers a comic strip image of scenes and events in the colourful life of a little-known American-born Australian politician of the Federation and First World War period, drawing in its first act on the entertaining pantomimic theatricalism of a revivalist meeting, sentimental romantic melodrama, and a patriotic pageant. In a series of swift-moving episodes it evokes O'Malley's life before his entry into Australian politics, inspired by the liberal-nationalist dream of a new society purged of the corruptions of the old world. The second act turns to the techniques of vaudeville and music hall—song and dance routines, clown and specialty acts, sight gags and patter, satirical sketches and lampoons—evoking the political world of Federation and the First World War, and O'Malley's increasing disillusion with its imperialist allegiances and the Labour Party's betrayal, under Hughes, of its democratic principles.

It is entertaining, involving theatre, with satirical topical allusions woven into its historical action, especially its extended second act parallel between O'Malley's opposition to Hughes's conscription campaign and the Vietnam War anti-conscription campaign of the late 1960s. Its social significance lies not so much in its relatively conventional themes, as in its general style, its image of Australian politics as vaudeville. Its uninhibited, knockabout style debunks *theatrical* pretensions—the theatre of Good Taste and moral earnestness—at the same time as it debunks Australian politics.

Romeril's and Hibberd's *Marvellous Melbourne*, (the inaugural production at the Pram Factory in 1970–71) drew on similar conventions, but revealed the much rougher and more confrontational style of the Australian Performing Group in Melbourne. Whereas *King O'Malley* has a single figure (and in a sense a single issue—conscription) as its central focus, *Marvellous Melbourne* offers a composite satirical portrayal of Melbourne society from 1888 (the year of the Centenary Exhibition) to the opening of the first Federal parliament at the turn of the century. Its montage of scenes is designed not only to provide a colourful evocation of Melbourne's past, but also to demonstrate in a more systematic way the main social and political forces at work, and their direct connection with contemporary Australian society. The satire is more biting, and its targets more comprehensive. The caricatures, especially of political hucksters and financial swindlers, are grotesque and savage, in the manner of Hogarth or Gillray. The performing area, Hibberd commented:

> seemed populated by a menagerie of grotesques and buffoons, seedy varlets and middle-class innocents, political thugs and puritanical hypocrites. The exhilarating group-gargoyle style of performance owed an enormous amount to the early improvisational and non-verbal workshops.[54]

Documentary and narrative elements, and songs and pageantry, are incorporated into the play in a Brechtian fashion, spelling out significances and establishing vivid contrasts between one scene and the next. As in *King O'Malley*, the play's deliberate theatricalism unifies its disparate scenes and characters: its pompous and corrupt dignitaries, its larrikins, new chums and wharfies, its artists, its cosmopolitan mixture of Chinese, Arabs, kanakas, and Aborigines, its prostitutes, suffragettes, and its melodramatic heroine, Lily Dampier (who might have been acting one of the many such roles she had performed in her father's plays). The play's technique of montage carries the strong implication that the presentation of history is not simply a matter of assembling facts and dates, but also a mode of imaginative reconstruction rooted in the present. The dramatic image of Australian history which the Australian Performing Group offered, enacted 'live' in an essentially improvisatory mode making full use of the physical immediacy of the Pram Factory performing area, and with an emphasis on characters playing grotesque political, social and cultural *roles*, challenged audiences to re-think contemporary Australian history not in terms of personalities, but in terms of ideological forces still operative in Australian society.

Marvellous Melbourne, like *King O'Malley* in Sydney, sparked a number of plays which turned theatricality itself to imaginative account in exploring aspects of Australia's past. Jack Hibberd's own later plays exploring the lives of Australian popular legendary figures (*The Les Darcy Show* and *A Toast to Melba*) are expressions of this consciousness. Its more immediate effects, however, were seen in Australian Performing Group productions of plays which established Barry Oakley as a substantial playwright. *The Feet of Daniel Mannix* (1972) and *Beware of Imitations* (1973) are both iconoclastic portraits of politically influential figures in twentieth century Australian history; Dr. Mannix, Archbishop of Melbourne, satirized as the legendary embodiment of the militant spirit of Irish-Catholic anti-Britishness, sectarianism and anti-communism, and Sir Robert Menzies, lampooned as 'Sir William McLuckie'.

In two short earlier plays performed at La Mama— *Witzenhausen, Where Are You?* (1967) and *A Lesson in English* (1968)—as well as in his novels, Oakley had already demonstrated an unusually inventive comic imagination, a flair for creating farcical situations and comic dialogue combining sophisticated wit and broad slapstick humour. *The Feet of Daniel Mannix* probes the key events in which Mannix had been involved over a period of fifty years. Oakley presents these events episodically, introducing pointed Brechtian popular and comic songs (some of them parodies of traditional airs, others written by Williamson and Romeril as well as by Oakley), and creating a comic-strip effect through his simplification and exaggeration of the characters of the main historical protagonists. Grotesque and farcical visual effects provide a literal stage rendering of the clichéd political metaphor, 'the machinations of power', and produce biting political satire. 'Humour, vaudeville, farce', Oakley has commented

> are a kind of fish-eye lens that give events and characters a new perspective, an ironic distance ... The comedy lies in the disproportion between the power wielded and the ordinariness, frailty, fallibility of the person wielding it; and this disproportion is both comic and grotesque.[55]

The Feet of Daniel Mannix conveys this comedy and grotesqueness primarily through its ingenious use of simple stage contrivances which function as extended sight gags, evoking an image of Australian politics as an absurdly complicated mechanism. This image of Mannix and others as the operators and fixers of a political machine (ultimately, its robot-like victims) is very close to the political cartoons of Bruce Petty.

John Romeril, author of twenty-five plays in the period 1968–78 (ten of which were, like *Marvellous Melbourne*, collaborations with other Australian Performing Group writers or actors), is the most directly political of the writers associated with the Group. Because of the nature of his commitment both to the group's collective style (with its uncomprising rejection of the tyranny of the text), and to the idea of theatre directly involved with its immediate community, many of his plays are concerned with local projects and issues, set in a very specific environment and deliberately ephemeral. For this reason his wider significance resides less in the substance than in the style of what he has achieved.

Nevertheless, a small number of his plays—*I Don't Know Who To Feel Sorry For* (1969), *Chicago, Chicago* (1969–70) and *The Floating World* (1974)—have travelled beyond their immediate environment. Their main theme might be described as the politics of an Australian paranoia: the kind of paranoia which the Ghost of Peter Lalor, in *Marvellous Melbourne*, had invoked as the psychic malady of a society yet to outgrow its colonial insecurities, transferring its neo-colonial allegiances, in the 1970s, 'from capitalism of Australians, by Australians, for Britons, to capitalism of Australians, by Australians, for Americans'.[56] *I Don't Know Who To Feel Sorry For* was a typical example of what was often dubbed, in the early La Mama-Australian Performing Group productions, a style of 'quasi-naturalism with absurdist overtones'[57]—a description which applies equally to the early work of Hibberd, Buzo and Williamson. It offers a bleaker, more sharply defined image of the alienated contemporary lives evoked in Searle's *The Lucky Streak*. The naturalistic surface is continually disrupted by moments of direct interaction between performers and audience, and by farcical elements and ritual games which continually suggest (like the plays of Pinter and Albee, whose influence can be traced in many of the early plays of the late 1960s) personal obsession and group paranoia. The play's conclusion, a bitter confession-cum-diatribe by an ageing mother, as she realizes the emptiness of the values bequeathed by her own generation to a younger generation lacking any sense of purpose other than the pursuit of self-interest, also reveals something of the moralism of Romeril's work—the kind of moralism which underlies his description of the comic and ritual elements in the play as '*concessions* to the need to entertain'.[58]

In *Chicago, Chicago*, the farcical and absurdist elements in the earlier play are transformed into a thorough-going expressionist psychodrama in the manner of Van Itallie's *American Hurrah*. Romeril's play offers a collage of twenty fragmented scenes set in Chicago at the time of the turbulent Democratic Presidential Convention of 1968, expressing the paranoid fantasies of a delegate (the Man) too terrified to leave his hotel room because of the violence in the streets. The play's American theme and subject were designed not only to offer a counter-image of American society during a period (at the height of the Vietnam War) when Australia appeared to have embraced a dependent, neo-colonial role of unqualified support for the American war effort, but also to suggest a more universal contemporary image of 'the soul of urban man under capitalism'. Its surrealistic methods, in which nightmarish images of violence and insanity recur, along with bewildering transformations of identity, are designed to make audiences experience alienation quite directly, as a disorientation of their own capacity to distinguish between illusion and reality on stage.

In *The Floating World*—one of the best plays to come out of the new wave theatre in the 1970s—the relationship between night-marish surrealist elements, an expressive vaudevillean humour, and a gradually disintegrating naturalistic surface is much more carefully controlled, creating a complex, unusually sympathetic portrait of the personality of a single character (an ex-prisoner of war in a Japanese prison camp) whose trip to Japan on the '1974 Women's Weekly Cherry Blossom Cruise' turns into a nightmare reliving of the past. Haunted by the guilt that he is scabbing on mates who had died or been tortured, his fantasies become paranoid and murderous, culminating—as the boat reaches Japan—in his running berserk with a knife. Like Seymour's *The One Day of the Year*, *The Floating World* is a study of the psychology of racism and of its relation to the nationalist mythology of ordinary Australians, intensified for Les Harding by his humiliation at the hands of the Japanese, and by the sense of betrayal and bewilderment which post-war global power shifts, and the Japanese cultural and economic penetration of Australian society, have created in him. The social comedy and vaudevillean antics of shipboard life are gradually undercut as the action becomes increasingly internalized in the hallucinatory visions of the main character. The effect, finally, is of tragedy and compassion, especially in the play's concluding monologue, an imaginative *tour de force* reminiscent of the ending of *I Don't Know Who To Feel Sorry For*, in which all Les Harding's suppressed hatreds, fears and fixated loyalties come to the surface.

Jack Hibberd's plays represent a different strand and emphasis within the general idea of theatre explored by the APG—in particular, its uncompromising rejection of the performance conventions of the commercial and professional stage. Hibberd's vision of a 'rough, relevant and ribald'[59] new Australian drama is less narrowly political in conception and less moralistic than Romeril's, and more closely related to the ideal of a national folk culture which Esson had sought to celebrate earlier in the century:

Popular Theatre in general suggests for me a theatre of accessibility that is above all Australian in theme and substance, a theatre for the populace that deals with legendary figures and events, perennial and idiosyncratic rituals, mythically implanted in the nation's consciousness. It is a form of folk theatre without being folksy. It is a theatre of gum without being gumnut, as in the more jejune and sentimental outback literature. It can usefully intermingle celebration with satire, fun with gravity, fiction with information, ignorance with politics, slang with poetry.[60]

In his earlier Melbourne University and La Mama plays of the late 1960s (plays like *Who?*, *One of Nature's Gentlemen*, *White With Wire Wheels* and *Dimboola*), the dominant mode is satire, a critical dissection of stereo-typical Australian behaviour and of its underlying myths and values. The popular elements in these plays include a remarkably earthy imaginative rendering of Australian vernacular speech (especially its obscenity, its scatological obsessiveness, and its violence) and an inventive, simplified use of stage resources and stage space, which implies a clear rejection of the sophisticated sets of the proscenium stage and exploits the physical closeness of performers and audience.

White With Wire Wheels was one of the first of the new wave plays to explore the lifestyles of young newly-affluent urban males—executives-in-the-making—whose obsessive preoccupations are status, fast and expensive cars, beer, and sex. The play's main quality, as in Hibberd's work as a whole, is its economy of structure, its streamlined, ironic patterning of episodes to suggest repetitive rituals, stereo-typical social behaviour and speech. This concentration on social surface and role provides the play's main image of de-personalized lives in a consumerist society, outwardly conformist, but beneath this engaged in a fiercely competitive, anxious struggle to achieve status and accumulate admired possessions. Throughout the play, there is a key association of cars and women: both identified, in the minds of the males, in terms of performance, style and image; both ego-boosting commodities for conspicuous male consumption. The most inventive of the play's theatrical effects is the performance of its four female roles by a single actress, an indication of the degree of attention paid to the women by the men (for whom 'all women are the same'). In a later play, *Peggy Sue* (1974)—a more positive expression of the feminist commitment which developed from the formation of a Women's Group within the Australian Performing Group—Hibberd reverses this device, giving the female characters separate personalities and making the varied male roles, performed by a single actor, define a single dominant male identity.

Hibberd's rich and often weirdly imaginative language, and his feel for the physical possibilities of an intimate acting space, find their most creative expression in *A Stretch of the Imagination*. The play creates a complete imaginative world out of the most ordinary objects (a hut, a table, a chair and beach umbrella, a clock, a pumpkin, a four gallon drum for 'nitrogenous waste'), and through its use of one of the oldest popular forms of theatre—the one-man show. It is physical theatre in the fullest sense of the term (more than half the play's printed text consists, in fact, of acting directions), a literal presentation—through gesture and mime, and a densely physical texture of sound and speech—of the parody-credo which Monk O'Neill enunciates towards the end of the play:

I contrive to walk. I breathe. I cerebrate. I have no soul. What more could a man desire?

Against the gross physical dimensions of the world in which Monk moves Hibberd opposes the imaginative dimensions of his 'cerebrations and desires', the provisional identities and meanings he creates (or recreates) through the fantasy of mime and the fictions of speech, in a process which interprets Australian life as a mythic history, a tragi-comic enterprise of the human spirit. Hibberd's medical and Irish-Catholic background appears to have strongly influenced the sceptical comic vision offered in *A Stretch of the Imagination*, which has recognizable connections with the vision of Yeats's later plays, and with Joyce and Beckett.

Hibberd's plays since *A Stretch of the Imagination* explore more fully the mythic dimensions of Australian life, shifting from the primarily satirical mode of the earlier work to a more positive affirmation of Australian popular culture, in the past as well as the present. In *The Les Darcy Show* (1974) and *A Toast to Melba* (1976), he celebrates the energy and determination, amidst contradictory social and cultural pressures, which motivated the achievements of the boxer Les Darcy and the singer Nellie Melba. These plays combine a particularly fluid form of stage action and lively reportage, with an emblematic focus on selected incidents, swiftly, simply and economically presented. Such techniques enable him to give a vigorous shape and outline to documentary material requiring rapid transitions in time and place, as the characters pursue (or are trapped by) their colonial dreams of fame: Melba in England and Europe, Darcy in America. Above all, these plays—like *Dimboola*, the early wedding reception play which enjoyed remarkable popularity in a range of different venues after its revival in a professional production by the Australian Performing Group in 1973—reveal the persistence with which Hibberd has explored modes of drama which are not dependent on the 'remote two-dimensionality'[61] of the proscenium stage of conventional

255

commercial and professional theatre. No other Australian play-wright has explored these possibilities as thoroughly or effectively.

In comparison with Romeril and Hibberd, David Williamson is, in dramatic terms, a much more conservative playwright. Although his plays draw on some of the innovatory techniques associated with the Australian Performing Group movement (in which his early plays, *The Coming of Stork*, *The Removalists* and *Don's Party* were first performed in 1970 and 1971), their main preoccupations reflect a psychological interest in the nature of role-playing and the mechanisms of power, in small-scale, specifically defined and closely analysed social situations. In effect, his plays offer a drama of transformed naturalism, whose primary subject is the cause and nature of stereotypical behaviour. Williamson has himself described his style as 'a sort of naturalistic comedy of manners'[62] and as 'heightened naturalism ... some-where around the border between satire and naturalism'.[63]

Williamson's first full-length play, *The Coming of Stork*, was his most unconventional, using a loose revue-style structure, with farcical situations and gags, to emphasize the clownish antics of an eccentric university drop-out with anarchist tendencies, who is used as a device to expose the underlying competitiveness and insecurity of others. Much of this insecurity has its source, as in Hibberd's *White With Wire Wheels*, in male sexual rivalries and anxieties. While the play appears to exploit the new stage freedom of the late 1960s, which allowed audiences to enjoy an uninhibited language full of inventive obscenities, sexual puns and gags, and an unconventional frankness of sexual behaviour, its underlying movement implies a questioning both of the effects of sexual liberation amongst a younger generation of Australians, in a competitive, status-conscious society, and of the attitude towards home and marriage of older generations.

Williamson's next two plays, *The Removalists* and *Don's Party*, established his reputation outside Melbourne in 1971 and 1972, in major productions (of *The Removalists*) by John Bell at the Nimrod Street Theatre and on the commercial stage, and (of *Don's Party*) by John Clarke at Jane Street and subsequently on the professional stage at the Old Tote's Parade Theatre. In both these plays, the characteristic qualities of Williamson's dramatic style appear in a remarkably mature form. He concentrates on character inter-action within (or close to) the conventions of a 'slice of time' play, captured through a richly expressive version of Australian vernacular speech, often comic or violent, but always plausibly motivated. He has a strong, psychological grasp of ironic sub-textual nuances in speech and gesture, especially of human relations as power games and rituals, in which aggression and extroversion often mask deep-seated insecurities, and civility and introversion an unspoken hostility or contempt. Dramatic structure in his plays is neither randomly episodic nor neatly and conventionally plotted as in well-made naturalism, but contains residual elements of both in a deceptively casual relationship to each other. The complicated interaction of shifting groups and pairs of characters in *Don's Party*, for example, suggests residual elements of farce. *The Removalists'* well-made framework is complicated by a quite unconventional double dénouement, which intensifies the audience's shocked response to the spectacle of irrational violence.

The characteristic action of Williamson's plays, however, is not so much—as in conventional realism—an undercutting or challenging of the idea of stereo-typical behaviour, as a probing of the psychological compulsions motivating it. His characters rarely change or develop in significant ways in the course of his plays, remaining locked in stereo-typical roles, prisoners of particular conventions, hardened stances, even when they are forced into critical recognitions of their conformity. This quality gives the plays their most noticeably Chekhovian flavour: the sceptical detachment with which comedy and absurdity are blended with an underlying pathos and bleakness, providing a double-edged sense of the predictability of human behaviour. It is also a major source of the plays' continuing accessibility to wide audiences. *The Removalists* draws on police force and working class stereotypes in its probing of the link between authoritarianism, sexuality and violence, using these stereotypes, rather unsubtly, as an authenticating device for the play's spectacularly brutal display of violence. But Williamson's later plays draw their stereotypes primarily from the kinds of audience which plays like *Don's Party* initially helped to attract to Australian theatres—educated, increasingly affluent, professional or semi-professional groups, in whom liberal-progressive and permissive attitudes co-existed with an actual conservatism of life style.

Don's Party draws much of its strength from the kinds of recognition it offered such audiences. It deftly parallels the political hopes and frustrations of its characters (as the 1969 election night

257

results provide increasingly gloomy confirmation of the defeat of the Labour Party), with their personal and sexual hopes and frustrations. These are reflected initially in the sparkling comic surface of the party's apparently liberated sexual games and rituals, and eventually in the gradual revelation of marital tensions, sexual inhibitions, and the failure of career ambitions. The dream of political liberation, like the dream of personal liberation, is seen ultimately as a rationalization by characters whose actual lives are an unsatisfying compromise with the conservative values they affect to despise.

What If You Died Tomorrow portrays a particular segment of Australian society in greater depth and complexity. It also depicts the creative writer struggling to resist its competitive pressures, and to reconcile conflicting drives and responsibilities in his personal life and art. These pressures are casually plotted in a pattern which suggests the movement to personal crisis in well-made naturalism. Its opening situation establishes the terms in which an unusually complicated marital relationship have been provisionally worked out. Its subsequent action, premissed on generation clashes, sexual rivalries, parent-son conflict, economic competitiveness and culture shock, creates the play's effect of social depth while intensifying the writer's feelings of disorientation. The play's seeming fragmentation is quite deliberate, controlled by its probing of the implications of its title, with its posing of questions about personal and social and artistic responsibility in a world of pressing temporary sexual, marital and family needs, and high pressure salesmanship. The play's strongest visual image of this tension is a visual one. At various points of personal crisis and bafflement in the play, the writer returns to a 'structure' he is building with children's blocks. Initially assuming a 'clincial correctness', its shape, at the end of the play it 'is chaotic, but not randomly so ... It is quite aesthetically pleasing'. The multiple significances of this image—its linking of art with a child's intuitive gameplaying, its suggestion that such play offers an escape from, or defence against, the tensions of real life while giving them a significant, if provisional, shape and form—provide an illuminating insight into the shape and motivation of this particular play, and indeed of Williamson's work as a whole.

The Department (1974) and *The Club* (1977) are both more tightly structured plays in the manner of *The Removalists*, moving away from the up-dated lounge-room settings and leisure-time activities of plays like *Don's Party*, *What If You Died Tomorrow* and *A Handful of Friends*, to more exclusively male realms of work and play: the power relations within the Engineering Department of a tertiary college, in *The Department*, and behind the scenes of the highly commercialized professional world of an Australian Rules football club, in *The Club*. Both plays are comedies. *The Club* draws more uninhibitedly on the conventions of farce and on the possibilities of boisterously obscene masculine dialogue than any of his plays since *Don's Party*, and both plays create an acutely observed range of academic and sporting stereotypes. The effect of social and political parable is much stronger than in the other plays because of the self-containment of the worlds each play portrays. *The Department* provides a model of bureaucracy in action, for which the setting itself, a thermodynamics laboratory, is a witty metaphor, revealing characters whose personal motivations and conflicts function, thoughout, to perpetuate the grotesque workings of an impersonal mechanism. *The Club* suggests, in a similar way, the systematic workings of corporate, commercial greed, breeding a new generation of administrative technocrats whose impersonal concerns with profit margins claim a confused older generation as their victims, as well as constituting a threat to the needs and interests of the young. The play's underlying image of Australian society is of a new ball game, with changed Australian Rules, operating—under the pressures of commercialism—in more devious and covert ways. Both plays add significant social and political depth to the vision of a playwright whose work has always remained closely tied to the contemporary Australian scene, observing and analyzing its emergent subcultures and lifestyles.

Alexander Buzo attracted attention as a playwright of unusual talent and imagination remarkably quickly, with a series of plays (*Norm and Ahmed*, *Rooted* and *The Front Room Boys*) performed mainly in smaller experimental venues and programmes in the period 1968–70. Like David Williamson, he went on to produce a substantial body of mature plays on the established professional stage during the 1970s. Although aspects of his plays continually invite comparison with trends in the work of other contemporary Australian playwrights, his work as a whole represents a quite distinct, personal variation of them.

Buzo's sense of theatre is strongly premised on a rejection of well-made naturalism, and of the nationalist demand that plays

259

work at a single level of social expressiveness (their 'Australian-ness'), providing a mere transcript or documentation of local realities:

> I would like to think that in modern theatre we are moving away from the well-plotted, well-made exposition-climax-denouement kind of form into a new and freer style where the structure of a play is dictated by the energies of what is being expressed.[64]

Imagist and surrealist effects imaginatively transform the local detail of his plays, giving them their most striking effects of comic surprise and shock. They provide a constant element, despite the shifts of mode which have characterized his development as a dramatist, from early absurdist and expressionist phases to his more recent satirically tinged romantic comedies. And they are present not only as unusual visual effects in the action and settings of the plays, but also in the vivid textures of imagery built into their dialogue.

Norm and Ahmed, for example, contains oddly suggestive, surrealistic images in its setting and lighting. Details which seem, at first sight, innocent and natural—a building site with scaffolding and a white protective fence, and the play of light and shadow against a dark background—gradually assume sinister proportions during the encounter between the Australian and the foreigner, cutting across what seems to be a process of rapprochement between them. The violence which ends the play is primarily a product of this visual environment, offering a disturbing image of racism as a compulsive, irrational force in Norm's behaviour, and suggesting a larger symbolic dimension in the play. The building site and its white protective fence function as a symbol of white Australian society in the making, and Norm, prowling suspiciously in front of it, is its self-appointed guardian, on the lookout for those, like Ahmed, whom he fears might be trying to get in.

The action of *Rooted* is framed within the two poles of social success, power and affluence on the one hand, and defeat and humiliation on the other, represented in absurdist fashion by two characters who never actually appear on stage but are evoked through the awestruck and contemptuous allusions of others. The main character's history, revealed in a structure of episodes which suggests a mediaeval wheel of fortune, traces an inevitable downward curve, a gradual loss of self-esteem. Other characters are in varying degrees of ascendancy. All are engaged, despite superficial mateyness, in a fiercely egotistic, competitive struggle. The language of the play also suggests absurdism. Long monologues convey obsessions and fears which are half-recognized, half-rationalized. There are comic confusions and uncertainties of communication in the dialogue. And the main character oscillates between pompous bureaucratic jargon (associated with his Civil Service job and ambitions) and the in-group clichés and slang of his mates. However, as in *Norm and Ahmed*, the play's dominant image of alienated characters driven by obsessions and illusions is conveyed only partly in verbal terms. Surrealist effects—the main character's wife mechanically abusing him through a tape recorder, choric parodies in which his friends ritually engulf him in clichés, scenes without words in which apparently mundane details take on a strange quality of tableau—all reveal aspects of his humiliation and defeat which he is pathetically unable to see or acknowledge.

The Front Room Boys is one of the few plays to present an image of contemporary Australians at work, focussing on the day-to-day routines of white collar office employees in a large inner-city business corporation. Buzo's method in this play is comic ritual. An episodic twelve-part structure (one scene for each month of the year) offers a variety of farcical and grotesque images of stereotypical behaviour, mindless conformism, and subservience to the mechanistic functioning of a bureaucratic system. The central dramatic metaphor of alienation is provided by a parody of mediaeval cycle drama and popular tribal festivals, with their celebration of creative seasonal rhythms and harmonies.

The tendency to diffuseness in this play, despite the comic gusto of the dialogue and the sheer inventiveness of much of the parody, was replaced, in *Macquarie*, by a firm, central focus on the historical figure of Governor Macquarie himself (1810–21). The play traces a pattern of rise and fall in his fortunes in a manner which again suggests an interest in a mediaevalist patterning of action, and a continuing interest in exploring techniques different from the 'well-plotted, well-made exposition-climax-denouement kind of form'. The dramatic method of *Macquarie* deliberately asserts itself as a selective contemporary interpretation of historical events, exploring the 'Classic Liberal Dilemma' of being 'stranded midway between the forces of conservatism and revolution'.[65] A connection between past and present is built into the play by presenting two actions—historical and contemporary—in counterpoint, with a narrator involved in both, and with actors playing double roles in order to suggest continuity. The actual style of the play is cinematic, creating striking visual images, fast-moving changes of scene and action, static moments of tableau, and simultaneous actions in counterpoint. These effects continually collapse disparities of time and place and provide powerful Brechtian ironies, establishing visual connections between events, situations and characters superficially different, and giving the exemplary force of a parable to the play's historical image of liberalism's defeat by reactionary forces.

The play's interest in the personality of Macquarie, amidst characters who are primarily depicted in representative social and political roles, marks a shift in Buzo's method of characterization which was to become increasingly significant in his work. Three later plays (*Coralie Lansdowne Says No*, *Martello Towers* and *Makassar Reef*) are Australian variations on the form of the romantic comedy of manners, retaining the verbal richness, the farcical elements and imagist perspectives of the early plays, but integrating them much more subtly with the inward dimensions of his characters' lives. These plays are all partial parodies of the forms they adopt, manipulating the conventions of romantic comedy of manners and exploiting its possibilities for trenchant, witty and topical dialogue, in order to satirize contemporary social attitudes.

Coralie Lansdowne, like *Macquarie*, concentrates on a single character, who is faced with the problem of reconciling different aspects of herself brought into play by her relations with three contemporary suitors and her sister, and of tailoring her romantic energies and idealism to a real world in which none of the available options is perfect. A suicide, early in the play, establishes a tragic undercurrent to the comic surface, and the same kind of undermining of conventions occurs at the end of the play, in which the comic-romantic resolution—the device of a happy marriage—becomes a source of uncertainty and ambiguity. Imagist effects in the play include a large tree which 'grows up through the ceiling in centre stage', an image of Coralie's energies bound by, yet struggling against convention. Exotic images of decadence and physical deformity also suggest, throughout, the destructive pressures against which Coralie's robust vitality is pitted. In *Martello Towers* the conventional romantic ending of a reconciliation between husband and wife is similarly made to carry both a satirical weight (as a witty comment on a society in which marital breakdown has become a fashionable affectation of pseudo-characters who 'dress up their boring neuroses with ideological refinery'), and a tragic undercurrent, emphasizing the isolation of the husband's younger sister amongst a new breed of smooth-talking commercial predators and cultural middlemen in Australian life.

Buzo's manipulation of the conventions of sophisticated farce in the action of this play is particularly skilful. It carries an implicit general questioning of various contemporary rhetorics of social and sexual liberation, and of the new kinds of mobility which allow the peculiarly deracinated characters in the play the apparent freedom to drift, collide, assume new life-styles, and exploit each other. Farce is the appropriate form for the coincidental encounters and sudden shifts of direction in the characters' lives. It also allows Buzo to introduce a series of deftly-paralleled comic confrontations, whose eventual resolution reveals underlying personal motivations, and provides a sympathetic insight into the dilemmas of first-generation migrants in Australia. *Makassar Reef* works in a similar way to counterpoint the personal histories and casual relationships of a small, ill-assorted group of Australian expatriates, tourists and adventurers, local Indonesian types, and a shabby Dutch 'hippy thief', who are briefly thrust together in the microcosmic world of the decaying Indonesian seaport-capital of the Celebes Islands. It is Buzo's bleakest play, effectively dismantling conventional images of South-East Asia as the exotic locale for 'tales of romance, mystery and adventure'. In its parody of such conventions, revealing morally bankrupt, purposeless and maimed personal lives, the play offers a parable of the destructiveness of the Western (and Australian) presence in South-East Asia.

Like Buzo, Dorothy Hewett is an idiosyncratic presence in contemporary Australian drama. Her plays clearly reflect the wider contemporary interest in expressionist methods and in popular styles like music hall and variety, but adapt these styles to an intensely personal romantic vision which is at once more extravagantly (and demandingly) theatrical, and more poetic, than that of any Australian playwright since Patrick White. Three themes in particular unify her work: an exploration of women's experience in Australian society, and especially of rebellious feminine individualism (an interest which overlaps, but is ultimately very different from, that of the feminist movement); a fascination with large-scale mythic and legendary perspectives on human life; and an ironically tinged celebration of the psychic realities of dream, nostalgia and illusion as compelling motivations in human behaviour. Dorothy Hewett's theatre creates its larger-than-life effects through spectacular visual and musical devices, through an unusually expressive use of popular or sentimental songs and poetry and of stylized or ritual action, and through a sensuous and emotively charged language. Such effects are designed to display the inward dimensions of her characters' lives, relating them to larger mythic rhythms in human existence.

Dorothy Hewett's first play, *This Old Man Comes Rolling Home* (1966) is a domestic play set in the working class environment of Redfern in Sydney, where the author had worked at a variety of jobs in the 1950s before moving to Perth. The play is primarily naturalistic in the manner of *Summer of the Seventeenth Doll*. However, in its use of a Greek chorus of three old women and its inclusion of a derelict character described as a 'myth character— Old Father Time perhaps', and especially in its celebration of energies continually reasserting themselves against the crippling deprivations of environment, the play looks forward to the more lavish expressionism of the later plays. This expressionist impulse, which links her work with John Romeril's, appears uninhibitedly in *The Chapel Perilous* (1971), a vividly theatrical portrayal of a woman's quest for identity and personal fulfilment, in the face of parental, social and institutional pressures to conform. In the half dozen plays she has written since then, Dorothy Hewett's portrayal of quest-figures—characters whose lives are envisaged and presented as an enactment of mythic and legendary patterns in Australian life—has developed in range and depth. *Bon Bons and Roses for Dolly* (1972) is a musical fable of lost innocence. The 'Crystal Palace' dreams of three generations of Australians from the 1890s into the 1940s are evoked through images of the glamorous American showbiz and film idols with whom they identified, dreaming futilely of escape from the family and work routines of Australian life. *The Tatty Hollow Story* (1974) builds up a fragmented image of the play's central character through a series of re-enactments of her relations with various lovers, dissolving her identity into their obsessions, memories and dreams, and offering an ambiguous comment on the cliché that a woman is all things to all men. *Pandora's Cross*, Dorothy Hewett's most recent play, reverts to the theme of lost innocence, in a wry celebration of the legend of King's Cross in Sydney, embodied in its bohemians, writers, black magicians, strippers, prostitutes and drag-artists. Their lively, vulgar and nostalgic self-dramatizations reveal a world in decline, turning into legend, as it is displaced by commercial developers.

More recent voices in Australian drama suggest a continuing development of patterns initially established in the late 1960s. Alma de Groen's early plays, *The Sweatproof Boy* and *The Joss Adams Show*, were in fact written in the late 1960s, though their Australian performance history, together with that of her later plays (including *The Afterlife of Arthur Cravan*, *Going Home* and *Chidley*) belongs to the period from 1972 onwards. *The Joss Adams Show*, a macabre and shocking play about a woman who kills her baby, uses a fluid stage technique (of sharply etched scenes dissolving one into another) to reveal the parental and marital pressures, and the mental deprivations and ignorances, which leave the woman defenceless to cope with the experience of childbirth and child-rearing. *Going Home* (1976), a play about four Australian expatriates—artists and their wives—struggling to cope with domestic, career, and creative pressures in Canada, reveals the author's skill in depicting complexly motivated characters in close interaction and collision with each other, creating a densely textured comedy of manners on the theme of spiritual alienation and exile—its theme and its method similar to Anne Brooksbank and Robert Ellis's locally-based play *Down Under* (1975). Alma de Groen's main subject might be described as the psychology of deprivation and eccentricity, depicted in ordinary domestic worlds, as in *Going Home*, or in the fantastic worlds of the late nineteenth century Australian sex reformer William Chidley or of the eccentric Dadaist nephew of Oscar Wilde, Arthur Cravan. These worlds are explored with a particularly sharp critical consciousness of the social and cultural pressures which define the limits of normality.

Jim McNeil's prison plays also question conventional distinctions between the normal and the abnormal, the social and the anti-social, in human behaviour, in ways which challenge stereotypical conceptions of prison life. McNeil creates mirror-images of prison behaviour in terms which both reflect the values of the outside world—domestic rituals, power games, self-protective role-playing—and provide an ironic comment on that world's real power games, in which the prisoners are, in the fullest and most literal of senses, victims and losers. The effect is both a humanization of the image of the prisoner, and a questioning of the larger social norms which require the existence of prisons. McNeil's development of this vision—initially in two shortish plays, *The Chocolate Frog* (1971) and *The Old Familiar Juice* (1972), and subsequently in two major works, *How Does Your Garden Grow* (1974) and *Jack* (1977)—has shown an increasing subtlety and sureness. In its naturalness of dialogue, its presentation of convincing interactions amongst characters, and especially in its creation of a claustrophobic atmosphere, and of lives seeking escape from regimentation through simple games and pleasures, *How Does Your Garden Grow* is one of the main achievements of post-1960s naturalism in Australian drama. *Jack* is McNeil's bleakest and most directly political play, an angry protest at the dehumanization of a prisoner through the denial of even the most elementary claims to dignity. As an exploration of violence, it possesses the same disturbing power as Williamson's *The Removalists* and John Powers's play set in a contemporary outback iron-ore mining camp, *The Last of the Knucklemen* (1973).

The playwrights whose work has been discussed in this section can hardly be reduced to a single tradition (*the* Australian tradition), but they are linked in their consciousness of drama as both a literary and theatrical medium, whose particular conventions are not simply those of the written word, but of performance. The development of this consciousness in the 1960s and 1970s, and the remarkable creative energy it released, were made possible by—and in turn generated—new styles of production by directors and designers, new kinds of performance skills and of theatrical institutions. The significance of these developments is misunderstood, however, if they are seen simply as comprising an autonomous history. Like any other conventions, dramatic and performance conventions are value-laden, expressions of particular social assumptions, perceptions and attitudes. The critical character of the new drama, as a response to life in Australia, is unmistakable, even in those writers, like Williamson, whose method is definition and analysis rather than social protest and moral judgment.

This note of disenchantment and challenge, fitfully present in Australia drama during the first half of the century, but vigorously and widely explored since, in satire and celebration, comedy and tragedy, has enabled recent drama to achieve for the first time a creative significance comparable with the other arts in Australia. In forging its individual style, it has produced imaginative insights into the nature of past and contemporary Australian life, with an often disturbing force. The kind of history written here—a history of the significance of changing forms and conventions—owes its focus and its method to the critical self-consciousness of recent Australian drama.

POETRY

VIVIAN SMITH

Great poets are few and usually far between; and the history of Australian poetry is, broadly speaking, the history of accomplished minor poets, with a few outstanding figures. It seems important to begin any discussion of the whole of Australian poetry with some such large saving statement because it is a history which many find especially engrossing and rewarding and it has much to offer the scholar and the cultural historian. Nevertheless it is important to keep perspective. Any account of Australian poetry up to the present must begin with an obvious point: no Australian poet has so far had any major impact on world literature. There have been no equivalents to the influence that Poe or Whitman exerted on French literature for instance. There have been no recent figures like Vallejo or Robert Lowell. This is partly due to obvious historical reasons and circumstances but it is also partly in the nature of poetry itself. Christina Stead and Patrick White in the novel, and the work of some modern dramatists have had an impact on world audiences that no poet can claim. As Auden said poetry is an

> ... unpopular art which cannot be turned into
> > background noise for study
> or hung as a status trophy by rising executives,
> > cannot be 'done' like Venice
> or abridged like Tolstoy, but stubbornly still insists upon
> > being read or ignored.[1]

Apart from the nature of the art there are other reasons. Australian poetry has always been traditional and deeply derivative. No Australian poet has been responsible for any formal innovations or revolutions in technique; and it is probably true to say that until recently the main struggle of Australian poets has been on the level of content: to accommodate their visions of Australia, its landscape, flora and fauna and the experience of Australian living, to the poetic moulds and patterns inherited from Europe and America. To say that Australian poetic culture is derivative is not to deny the signs of individuality and personal life in the work of the poets. Australian poetry has its own distinctive preoccupations and character, and its tendencies and movements have not always been neat analogues of those elsewhere.

The derivativeness of Australian culture is a fact to take for granted from the beginning and not a conclusion to work towards. It is as obvious in the rigid pindarics of Michael Massey Robinson, the first Australian poet, as in the present cult of specialized American influences in some of the most recent Australian poets. But somewhere between the pressures of inherited forms which need to be individually mastered and not simply imitated, and the burdens of a culture in perpetual difficulties, individual work of considerable value and impressiveness has been created.

The development of Australian poetry from its beginning to the present shows a clear pattern of continuity in two broad streams. One is popular, based on songs and ballads and simple and fairly crude narratives related to the main facts of Australia's development. It is vernacular poetry, idiomatic, colloquial. The other is learned and literary, drawing on the whole European heritage, civilized and cultured in aspiration, using language in consciously heightened ways.

I want to suggest, while still giving an outline of the main phases of Australian poetic development, that Australian poetry has been at its most forceful when it has moved in the middle ground towards the mature use of the vernacular and that it has been at its weakest when it has identified too closely with either the extremely popular or the remotely highbrow. Paterson and the balladists are rightly remembered, even revered in some quarters, as national monuments, but they had in them elements which led to C. J. Dennis and an abased use of an inauthentic vernacular. On the other hand poets who claimed to function on the level of prophecy—the tendency is there already in Harpur—end up in the cul-de-sac of William Baylebridge or even, at times, R. D. FitzGerald or James McAuley, by losing contact with the living language and merely creating verbal artifacts with little idiomatic life of their own. Poets who identify too easily or too exclusively with what they interpret to be the stream of high culture often run the risk, or yield to the temptation, of the literary, the mannered, the poetical or the rhetorical; while the popular poets sometimes give the impression of machines churning out reams of poetical jingle. Each poet has to solve his problems and get his poems written in his own way. But it is probably true to say that a poet needs to keep his distance between extremes, and just as the language of a poem partakes of the qualities of speech and song, and may be either wholly one or the other, so the poet has to find his way between too close an identification with an easy and complacent audience, or between too stifling a sense of remoteness from any audience at all. Australian poets have often suffered irreparable damage from both sides, though perhaps the greatest damage was done to those exceptional flawed figures who had little, if any, sense of an audience at all.

PART ONE: THE COLONIAL PHASE

Australian poetry begins with amateurs, and one might risk an incautious generalization and say that the tradition of Australian culture has been such that the amateur has always been warmly encouraged, while the dedicated, would-be professional has had to contend with extremely unpropitious conditions of a kind that has often distorted or thwarted creativity. One might risk another generalization and say that Australian poetry is essentially the poetry of gifted minor poets with major ambitions, and that this is one of the problems for the historian of Australian literature. It is hard to classify and order the merely minor without becoming either myopic or impatient and losing perspective in one way or another. It is also true that past histories, in their generosity and inclusiveness, as well as in their desire to show that Australia had a literature with a history, have included a number of figures who have now fallen by the wayside. Their proper place is in the bibliographies or period anthologies, or the kind of recovery and excavation work often carried out by literary scholars. No one likes to be considered unjust or aridly dismissive, but an account of this scope cannot hope to be fair to every writer and must work in large blocks and wide overall arrangements. In a critical outline of this kind a rigorous principle of selection applies, and only what is considered of central importance in a writer's work will be touched on.

The complete history of their own poetry is not something Australian poets or readers take for granted and the lack of a sense of dialogue with the past has until recently been an impoverishing factor in Australian literary culture. Most readers are familiar with a few contemporary figures; but it is probably true to say that to the modern reader Australian colonial poetry remains almost an unknown world. There is still no complete authoritative edition of the works of Harpur, Tompson, Wentworth, or Daley, for instance. Editions and selections of Gordon and Kendall were frequent enough up to the First World War, but the colonial poets diminished in importance as the past receded and for the generations between the two world wars they tended to remain neglected, largely unknown and unread or else violently rejected. In recent years, due mainly to the critical work of Judith Wright and others, there has been a renewal of interest, and as more texts become available and more individual and period studies appear this can only gather momentum. The renewed interest in colonial art and colonial painters over the last twenty years is finding its equivalent in the field of literature. The most important development in Australian literary culture over the last forty years has been the recovery of a new sense and understanding of the colonial heritage. Writers of the generation of Vance Palmer and Kenneth Slessor felt obliged to attack or dismiss writers like Marcus Clarke, Kendall and Gordon: they wanted to get rid of the colonial influence. But writers of a later generation, like Judith Wright, James McAuley, A. D. Hope and others, were able to initiate a personal dialogue with the past which proved beneficial to their own work. There is much to reward leisurely reading and browsing in the poetry of this area but, as with most minor poetry, the interests are largely historical, cultural, and sociological. There is much to engross the eighteenth century specialist in the work of the first verse writers, much to engage the reader of Victorian poetry and the student of Victorian and colonial attitudes in the work of Harpur, Kendall and Gordon; who represent particular phases of colonial and Victorian feeling. But such concerns should not let us overlook the real aesthetic returns that can be found in colonial poetry. Fossikers are often rewarded with real gold:

> ... A stray gust of wind
> Pent in and wasting up the narrow lanes,
> Shall breathe insinuations to our age
> Of youth's fresh promise. Even a bird, though caged,
> Shall represent past freedom, and its notes
> Be spirited with memories that call
> Around us the fresh fumes of bubbling brooks
> And far wild woods. Nay, even a scanty vine,
> Trailing along some backyard wall, shall speak

Love's first green language; and (so cheap is truth)
A bucket of clear water from the well
Be in its homely brightness beautiful.

The poetry written and published in Australia between 1789 and 1845 bears the imprint of the eighteenth century from which it springs. The tones and modes, the cult of genres, the formalities of diction and, the sense of decorum (not always fully observed) bear an eighteenth century cast and stamp. This may be why these poets have until recently been treated with scant respect and concern and had little influence on the poets that followed them. They have been the subject of antiquarian curiosity and in recent years they have provided literary scholars and academics with something of a field day. Tracing influences and sources, recognizing overtones and allusions can be a particular pleasure for eighteenth century specialists let loose in this area. None of these elements can keep poetry alive; but it would be a mistake to underestimate or dismiss these early figures. They are as interesting in their own way as the first Australian painters.

Australian poetry starts with the indelible stamp of the cultivated amateur. It is fitting, given the country's history, that the first Australian poet should have been a convict. Michael Massey Robinson (1747–1826) is remembered now for his odes, written to be recited at royal celebrations and to celebrate military occasions. Barron Field (1786–1846), a friend of Wordsworth and Lamb, and a Judge of the Supreme Court of New South Wales for eight years, published a tiny volume *First Fruits of Australian Poetry* (Sydney, 1819) but is best remembered for his poem 'The Kangaroo'.

Kangaroo, Kangaroo!
Thou Spirit of Australia
That redeems from utter failure,
From perfect desolation,
And warrants the creation
Of this fifth part of the Earth.

His other poems are worth looking at, notably his sonnets, and his curious 'On reading the controversy between Lord Byron and Mr. Bowles', with its strange foreshadowings of words and ideas like those in A. D. Hope's poem 'Australia' (1940). Early colonial poetry derives from the eighteenth century kind of thinking that judges a poem by the genre to which it belongs. There were no major colonial attempts at the epic, though epistles, odes and satires are

found, and the descriptive, meditative poem derived from
Thomson's *The Seasons* and Cowper's *The Task* was the most
frequent, as in the work of Charles Tompson (1806–1883) who
remains one of the most attractive of the early versifiers. As with
all eighteenth century poets, his work aims at the typical and
towards moral generalization; but there is a real delicacy of feeling
and individuality of observation and response beneath the period
mannerisms, as in his poem 'Black Town', with its reference to an
early attempt to educate a group of Aboriginals:

> Ill-fated hamlet! from each tott'ring shed,
> Thy sable inmates perhaps forever fled,
> (Poor restless wand'rers of the woody plain!
> The skies their covert—nature their domain)
> Seek, with the birds, the casual dole of heav'n,
> Pleas'd with their lot—content with what is given.
> Time was, and recent memr'y speaks it true,
> When round each little cot a garden grew,
> A field whose culture serv'd a two-fold part,
> Food and instruction in the rural art.
> The lordling tenant and his sable wife
> Were taught to prize the sweets of social life,
> And send their offspring, in the dawn of youth,
> To schools of learning and the paths of truth.

William Charles Wentworth's (1790–1872) *Australasia*, published in
London in 1823, remains one of the most authoritative of the early
Australian poems. Constructed of rough-hewn couplets, the poem
is an ode celebrating the development of a new Britannia in
another world and is marked throughout by a rugged individuality of touch. The descriptions of an aboriginal corroboree, of the
fate of La Pérouse and his expedition, as well as of Sydney and its
surroundings, are among its most admirable sections, and there are
parts which, as an evocation of the Australian past and history, are
comparable with more recent attempts to celebrate Australia, like
The 'Last Vision' section of James McAuley's *Captain Quiros*. The
poem has never been widely published in its totality and much
more scholarly work in this area is still needed but, like much early
Australian poetry, it is due for reassessment and a more positive
estimate of its value as a whole than previous histories of
Australian literature have accorded it.

The earliest Australian poets were gentlemen for whom
accomplishment in verse writing was part of their cultural back-

ground. In this, too, they were true to their eighteenth century inheritance. But, civilized as their devotion to verse craft may have been, none was an author to whom poetry, and being a poet, was of central shaping importance in life. The change came with Harpur and Kendall.

Charles Harpur (1813–68) was the most underestimated of Australian nineteenth century poets until the restoration work begun in the 1960s by Judith Wright and Normington-Rawling. An unpopular poet, his work was never properly or adequately published in volume form during his lifetime, and even now there is no complete edition of his work. The son of convicts, his life is representative of the sad lack of fulfilment that marked so many Australian nineteenth century writers. He was considered arrogant and abrasively self-assertive, and his radical republicanism, his fierce spirit of independence and his rationalism were not designed to ingratiate him with the local conservative establishment. His life is moving for its examples of endurance, loyalty and integrity to his art and his convictions, and his poetry deserves to be much more widely known and more highly estimated.

In 1845 he published *Thoughts: a Series of Sonnets*, the first sonnet sequence to appear in Australia; addressed to Rosa, they trace the course of his love for the woman he finally married. In 1853 he published *The Bushrangers and Other Poems*. This included some of Harpur's most important pieces, 'The Creek of the Four Graves', 'The Bush Fire', 'To the Comet of 1843' and 'The Dream by The Fountain'. Harpur was naturally influenced by the verse fashions of his day. He greatly admired Milton, Wordsworth, Coleridge and Emerson, whose presence can be felt in parts of his work, but some of his most attractive poems show his sense of affinity with Marvell and Shelley, which had a beneficial effect on his work, turning it away from orotund profundities towards a poetry of precise observation and sensuous and airy enjoyment, as in the delightful 'A Midsummer Noon in the Australian Forest'

> Not a sound disturbs the air,
> There is quiet everywhere;
> Over plains and over woods
> What a mighty stillness broods.
> Even the grasshoppers keep
> Where the coolest shadows sleep;
> Even the busy ants are found
> Resting in their pebbled mound;

> Even the locust clingeth now
> In silence to the barky bough:
> And over hills and over plains
> Quiet, vast and slumbrous, reigns.

Nothing that Harpur wrote is faultless, but apart from its literary associations and affinities, a poem like 'A Basket of Summer Fruit' reminds one of the work of William Gould (1804–1853) in still-lives like 'Flowers and Fruit' which he was painting at about the same time as Harpur was writing such poems. They have the same slightly primitive naiveté and charm which comes from their imperfect attempt to imitate works which belong to a long, sophisticated tradition, and they are among the most pleasant products of colonial art.

> First see these ample melons! brinded o'er
> With a green mingled brown, is all the rind;
> For they are ripe and mealy at the core,
> And saturate with the nectar of their kind.
>
> And here their fellows of the marsh are set
> Covering their sweetness with a crumpled skin;
> And here pomegranates, dull without, and yet
> With vegetable crystals stored within.

Harpur was, however, nothing if not ambitious, and he was not content to be merely a miniaturist. In this he sets a pattern that many subsequent poets were to follow. He strove throughout his career to be an intellectual and philosophical poet. He said himself of his own poetry

it has never been a mere art with me but always the vehicle of earnest purpose. Nay, rather might I say, that it has always been the audible expression of the inmost impulses of my moral being, the very breath of my spiritual life.

And in one of his earliest poems, 'The Dream by the Fountain' he records how the Muse of the forest enjoined on him:

> Be then the Bard of thy country. O rather
> Should such be thy choice than a monarchy wide,
> Lo, 'tis the land of the grave of thy father!
> 'Tis the cradle of liberty!—Think, and decide.

Something of his range and strenuous scope can be discerned in 'The World and the Soul' (original title 'Geologia') (1847), a daring speculative poem about the soul and its place in the natural scheme

278

of things. One has to wait for Brennan before a similar note is again struck in Australian poetry, and then for Judith Wright with her poems on the evolutionary cycle. In his poem, Harpur reflects on evolution and the development of man, with the growth of art, music, poetry, religion and virtue; and celebrates the indestructible power of the soul to progress towards 'Perfection', through 'Creation and advancement' up to 'the unfailing consciousness of God'. It is a strangely moving and impressive poem, asserting his belief in spiritual evolution and the power of knowledge to lead man to final enlightment. Some of its religious and philosophical views are now embedded in the currents of belief and thought of his time, but the poem has a note of affirmation and conviction that lifts it well above the level of the speculative versification of the period.

Harpur's sense of personal dedication and election is apparent in all he wrote. This is expressed either directly, as in poems like 'The Dream by the Fountain', or indirectly, as in his narrative and land-scape poems, which communicate a sense of the grandeur and glory of God to the awed spectator. Harpur's range is quite wide. He is to be taken seriously as a political poet and satirist. Poems like 'The Temple of Infamy', in which he attacks his political enemies, and the short poems on literary themes, where he attacks rival styles and approaches, his literary enemies and disparagers, and attempts to demolish restricting ideas, have edge and relevance even today. But his landscape and narrative poems, in which he tries to come to terms with the Australian environment are still his most impressive. If later writers have concentrated on the arid monotonies of the Australian landscape, merging their sense of its social and cultural limitations with the sense of the repetitive sameness of the land, Harpur emphasised its picturesque, dramatic and more violent qualities, again rather in the manner of the early colonial landscape painters. Harpur had behind him the late eighteenth century and early Romantic tradition of descriptive and landscape poems, but it is worth noting how frequently his titles and subjects, 'The Bush Fire', 'The Creek of the Four Graves', 'Dawn and Sunrise in the Snowy Mountains', 'A Coast View', 'A Storm in the Mountains', 'The Kangaroo Hunt', are also found as the titles and subjects of some of the most important colonial paintings—from Glover, Roper, Martens and Buvelot, to von Guérard and Chevalier. There is in the poetry, as in the painting, the same sense of vastness, with the emphasis on vision and views, a

279

sense of the sublime. A detailed study of landscape in Australian poetry would, I believe, show a gradual development away from the dramatic panoramas and the large view of the first colonial artists to a microscopic focus on things in the landscape, to the tiniest insects, plants and animal life—so that now a mere boulder or pebble or a bird can be invested with the sense of the sublime and mysterious once found only in an enormous coastal view or mountain sweep. But both tendencies are already present from the beginning in Harpur, who can give as much attention to a vine growing on a fence, or a summer beetle, as to some grander vision of the awe-inspiring or the violent.

Harpur believed in the use of verse as a political instrument. Historians of colonial culture have already paid attention to the part he played as a reformer in his society. He took his role as a public poet very seriously, and his scope and ambition are remarkable in his time and place. His dramatic monologue, 'The Sorrows of Chatterton, or Genius Lost' (1836–37) is contemporaneous with Alfred de Vigny's play *Chatterton* (1835) and both are concerned with the trials of poetic genius in its attempt to remain undefeated by the world's neglect and disregard.

Two of Harpur's larger and more ambitious poems are *The Tower of the Dream*, published in pamphlet form in 1865, and *The Witch of Hebron*, his blank verse epic, which he boasted to Kendall was 'as magnificent as an oriental palace and terrible as a thunder storm'. *The Tower of the Dream*, a blank verse narrative with song interludes, recalls the atmosphere and trappings of a Gothic novel with touches of Edgar Allan Poe fantasy, but it is curiously effective as an early Romantic exploration of the world of dream.

It is open to various allegorical interpretations. It can be seen, through its images of night and darkness, as showing the forces of tyranny which prevent the dreamer's union with love and liberty, the evil that makes it impossible to achieve perfection, or the poet's longing to be reunited with his anima. It can lend itself to Freudian and Jungian schematizations. But it is part of the age-old power of the Eden theme in literature, the search for primal unity, to be able to provoke a whole range of resonances.

The Witch of Hebron was Harpur's last major achievement, his attempt to round off his career with a poem of epic proportions. It is a powerful narrative of some 200 lines of blank verse, drawing on the Oriental moral tales so popular in the eighteenth century. Divided into seven sections, the narrative begins with Rabbi

Joseph, a traditionally wise doctor, summoned to the deathbed of a mysterious, beautiful woman. He gradually realises that this woman is possessed of an evil spirit which, when he has exorcised it, proceeds to tell the story of the various transmigrations and transmogrifications it has undergone in the course of its life. It has been the centre of a conflict of good and evil and has passed from one body to another in its search for salvation. Originally the spirit has the soul of a high ranking courtier of the Pharaoh Ptolemy Philadelphus. He is corrupted by power and wealth and forced to flee the court after murdering a would-be assassin. Faustian overtones enter the poem as the central spirit figure is given further life in return for his soul; he comes under the influence of the evil spirit Sammael, but is rescued by God's angels; he then becomes a lion and an eagle. Once more won back by Sammael, the spirit inhabits the bodies of women and is reborn as the daughter of Bin Baghal, the friend of the Rabbi Joseph. At the end the woman dies, begging the Rabbi to pray for her.

Classical and biblical subjects were as important to colonial as to European Romantics, and they gave Harpur the same opportunity to display his preoccupation with the sublime and the visionary and the inner world as did his larger landscape poems. Australian readers have probably rated the landscape poems more highly than Harpur's other imaginative endeavours, because through them we can study a poet at work and see the beginnings of the process by which the landscape was named, and to that extent tamed, as it entered the world of art. But no understanding of Harpur or Kendall—or of the Colonial imagination—is complete without some knowledge of their poems based on classical, biblical and oriental themes, which relate them directly to similar kinds of poetry that were being written in England and Europe at the same time.

Henry Kendall (1839–1882), like most of the other Australian colonial writers, fell into partial eclipse from the 1920s until the 1950s when the revival of interest in the colonial phase started. But like Harpur he can now be seen quite clearly as an important and impressive poet in his own right. There is still perhaps a slight tendency to underestimate his work and its value, but there can be no doubt that *Leaves from Australian Forests* (1869) and *Songs from the Mountains* (1880) are two of the most important books of Australian colonial poetry, books which whatever the merits of individual poems have a total impact greater than their parts.

Kendall was the most prolific of the colonial poets: his facility and undisciplined ease of production go with the lyrical impulse that was behind most of his work. It is significant that two of his titles contain the word 'songs': an effortless warbling seems to be the source of a great deal of his work. Compared with Harpur's craggy, hard and austere will, Kendall seems at times to be glibly fluent and over-mellifluous but, for all his superficiality and sentimentality, his lyrics can be forceful and touching, and he remains a considerable and sometimes powerful poet.

His first volume *Poems and Songs* (1862) was published when he was twenty-three. Kendall's great ambition was to be a 'Native Australian Poet', and from the first his poetry shows a deliberate and conscious attempt to reflect his Australian environment, especially the landscapes of the South Coast, with its creeks and waterfalls, ferns and moss, its lyre-birds and forest flowers. Kendall was as patriotic as Harpur and gave added voice to the aspirations towards nationhood of his time. His narratives record some of the significant happenings in the development of the country, but from the first, his idealizing tendencies are present. In his personal poems he expresses a longing for Aidenn (Eden)—the possibility of a perfect life—and a yearning for an ideal personal love relationship. From the first, too, a pervasive melancholy can be felt as the basic emotional tone of his personal lyrics. He seems to have been of a depressive temperament, given to self doubts and deep inner uncertainties. His lack of self-confidence made him over-prolific, and a sense of his own shortcomings was often the subject matter or inspiration of some of his most poignant lyrics, while his sense of the ideal was so acute that it was probably unattainable by any mortal. Kendall was haunted by a vision of a world beyond this world, a virgin world of 'unknown shores', 'undiscovered skies' and of 'cliffs and coast by man untrodden', 'the land where man hath never been, the country where etherial glory shines', where the ideal might be realized, discovered or recovered. In his early poems we see him—

> Yearning for a bliss unwordly, yearning for a brighter change,
> Yearning for the mystic Aidenn, built beyond this mountain range.

The longing is often incarnate in a lost love.

Kendall's attempts to present the life of the Aboriginals, even to incorporate some of their words, is one important aspect of his early poetry, comparable with similar undertakings on the part of the colonial painters to render their environment and the new world in which they found themselves. Harpur's 'An Aboriginal Mother's Lament' may have influenced Kendall here, as elsewhere in his work, though Kendall's pieces, notably 'Koroora', 'Urara', and 'Ulmarra' have their own unique interest. These laments and death songs have a certain dignity and force, which is more than can be said for some of Kendall's later, rather tasteless grotesqueries such as 'Black Kate', with its insensitive patronising tone and mockery. Perhaps nothing that Kendall wrote about the Aboriginals now reads quite as offensively as some of J. B. Stephens' pieces, but they are, as cultural and social documents, troubling pointers to the decay of standards and values among the colonials in their attitude to the natives. A. Patchett Martin declared in 1898: 'you cannot write epics on the Australian blacks: you might as well compose a sonata on a monkey'.

Leaves from Australian Forests (1869) shows Kendall coming into his full range and power as a poet, though the years between his first book and this one were a time of personal difficulties and hardship. In spite of the warm support and approval of a small circle of friends, Kendall's books did not sell as well as he had hoped. He had family and money troubles and in 1869, six months before his book was published, he moved to Melbourne, where he thought his literary opportunities would be greater, to start a new life. It proved an unwise decision.

Leaves from Australian Forests contains nature and landscape poems of the kind found in his first volume, love poems and commemorative verses, and narratives with Australian subject matter or based on biblical or classical themes. Just as the colonial painter Robert Dowling saw no discrepancy between painting one large canvas of a 'Group of Natives of Tasmania' and another of a 'Sheikh and his son entering Cairo on their return from a pilgrimage to Mecca', so Kendall, like Harpur before him, was equally prepared to turn his attention to subjects like 'A Death in the Bush' or 'The Voyage of *Telegonus*', without any sense of cultural conflict. Tennyson, Browning, Arnold, Rossetti and Swinburne—all of whose work was known to Kendall—had tried such themes and it was natural to Kendall to try them as well. These narratives are due for general reconsideration and are now coming to be recognized as being among Kendall's highest achievements.

Leaves from Australian Forests contains the two lyrics by which Kendall is best known, 'Bell Birds' and 'September in Australia'. Both poems are musicalized idealizations of real things and places, but because Kendall did not have a flawless touch and they are not quite perfect, these two poems have been at the centre of many critical quarrels between those who think they succeed in their own way and in their own terms and those who think they do not. It is as well to remember that Kendall was an almost exact contemporary of Paul Verlaine, whose poetry and personality in many ways resemble his, and in his imperfect, colonial way Kendall may have been moving towards some instinctive discoveries of the possibilities of the extreme musicalization of verse. We can never really know, because in art a failed experiment, an incomplete success, looks like incompetence; but I confess that in reading Kendall's lyrics I am frequently inclined to give him the benefit of the doubt. He so often very nearly gets there.

> October, the maiden of bright yellow tresses,
> Loiters for love in these cool wildernesses;
> Loiters, knee deep, in the grasses, to listen,
> Where dripping rocks gleam and the leafy pools glisten:
> Then is the time when the water-moons splendid
> Break with their gold, and are scattered or blended
> Over the creeks, till the woodlands have warning
> Of songs of the bell-bird and wings of the Morning.

'Bell Birds' cannot be diminished or dismissed for a few lapses. This surely catches a magical moment of waiting and tender expectation. It has to be admitted, however, that the dividing line in Kendall between magic and moonshine can be very thin. The emphasis is often not on the thing seen or thought, but on the mood or feeling provoked, and Kendall lacks the accuracy of observation which can capture an intangible state. An example is the curious line in 'September in Australia': 'wild wings with the halo of hyaline hours' where the alliteration seems to be intended to express some sense of a halcyon moment, but fails to do so because no field of reference for the sound pattern is set up in the lines.

Nearly all Kendall's nature lyrics are flawed by small verbal excesses; some of these are mere hair cracks, others go deeper and are more damaging. There is a pervasive uncertainty of touch, with the dispersal rather than the concentration of emotion and feeling, and a consequent dilution of impact. Nevertheless *Leaves from Australian Forests* contains some of Kendall's most achieved lyrics—'Moss on a Wall', 'Araluen', 'Bell Birds' and 'Arakoon'. The opening stanza of 'Rose Lorraine', with its characteristic imagery of moving and merging lights, could have been written by Kenneth Slessor:

> Sweet water-moons, blown into lights
> Of flying gold on pool and creek,
> And many sounds, and many sights,
> Of younger days are back this week.
> I cannot say I sought to face,
> Or greatly cared to cross again,
> The subtle spirit of the place
> Whose life is mixed with Rose Lorraine.

In his best lyrics, Kendall is the poet of dreams, nostalgia, loss, and of moments of recovered peace and wholeness in a landscape where the setting heals and restores:

> And when by sudden fits and starts
> The sunset on the moss doth burn,
> He often dreams, and lo, the marts
> And streets are changed to dells of fern!

> For, let me say, the wilding placed
> By hands, unseen amongst these stones,
> Restores a Past by Time effaced,
> Lost loves and long-forgotten tones!

> As sometimes songs and scenes of old
> Come faintly unto you and me,
> When winds are wailing in the cold,
> And rains are sobbing on the sea.

Although Kendall's general reputation has rested on his lyrics, the four main narrative poems in *Leaves from Australian Forests* show the range and variety of his talent. 'The Voyage of *Telegonus*', 'King Saul at Gilboa', 'A Death in the Bush' and 'The Glen of Arrawatta' have not, over the years, received the attention and admiration they deserve, though T. Inglis Moore and A. D. Hope have written enthusiastically of their form and power and have led a new generation to look more closely at these previously neglected or dismissed works. A. D. Hope's 1973 essay on Kendall, which introduces the most recent selection of the poet's work, contains an authoritative reassessment of 'King Saul at Gilboa'.

285

Hope writes 'what is astonishing about the poem is the tragic force of its language, and the tense, driving energy of its verse.'

It is written in heroic couplets and this gives it a charge and energy that perhaps make it superior to the other pieces mentioned. Kendall is able to suggest the rise and fall, the ebb and flow of the energies involved in battle, and the whole has a controlled emotional logic that makes it one of Kendall's most satisfying achievements. The need to reinterpret an old story, yet to keep close to fact, seems to have had a salutary, disciplinary effect on Kendall's art. The narratives all have a crispness of line that makes them structurally more complete than the personal lyrics, with their often self-indulgent, unpruned and unfocussed exuberance. All show connections with and influences from other poets and poems. 'Saul at Gilboa' is influenced by Tennyson's 'The Passing of Arthur', 'The Voyage of *Telegonus*' by Matthew Arnold's 'Sohrab and Rustum', *Ogyges*, Kendall himself said, was 'after the manner of Tennyson's "Tithonus" and Horne's "Orion"', while a strong pervasive influence of Wordsworth—essentially the Wordsworth of 'Michael'—can be sensed in 'The Glen of Arrawatta' and 'A Death in the Bush'. But these influences are on the whole assimilated, and if the strengths of these narratives are sometimes borrowed, they are nevertheless strengths, and the poems have an assurance and a confidence often lacking in the personal lyrics. Kendall's Australian narratives were doubtless influenced by Harpur's poems on the early days, particularly 'The Creek of the Four Graves'. Effective enough, they are not as poetically powerful as 'King Saul at Gilboa', but they have historical importance for the way they reveal aspects of colonial experience and feeling, and as part of the continuing attempt writers were making to express the pioneering days in works of art.

Songs from the Mountains (1880), the last book Kendall published during his lifetime, does not make the same substantial impression as his preceding volume, but it contains some of his very best poems, and several new points of departure. Kendall had a high sense of the poet's vocation and pursued throughout his writing life his idea of poetry as a cultured art, but in a handful of his later poems, in some of his satires, and in poems like 'Jim the Splitter' and 'Bill the Bullock Driver', he made enterprising use of the vernacular in a way that foreshadows the more openly sardonic vernacular and popular poetry of the 1890s. The poems written in 'The Shadow of 1872', 'The Voice in the Wild Oak', 'Narrara

Creek', 'Mooni', as well as 'Araluen' and 'On a Street', are all plangent with self-pity. Kendall is still too close to the unresolved problems, conflicts and tragedies of his own life to succeed in giving them an ultimately impersonal resonance, but all have curious touches of pathos and a poignant distinction. It is characteristic of Kendall that in 'After Many Years' he is able to turn his rather wistful sense of defeat and failed aspirations into a poem which paradoxically achieves what he claims he has failed to do:

> But, in the night, and when the rain
> The troubled torrent fills,
> I often think I see again
> The river in the hills.
> And when the day is very near,
> And birds are on the wing,
> My spirit fancies it can hear
> The song I cannot sing.

The two most important poems in the book are 'To a Mountain' and 'The Sydney International Exhibition', originally entitled 'Australia', and among the first of a whole line of Australian poems to bear that title. 'The Sydney International Exhibition', celebrates, in mostly sustained and forceful couplets, Australia's past, her natural beauty, Sydney itself 'the shining city of a hundred spires', and the future of the nation. If the poem recalls Wentworth, it also anticipates later writers like FitzGerald and McAuley with its admiration for the discovery and settlement of the land, from the first explorer to Captain Cook's arrival in 'the bay of flowers', making way for the later appearance of Phillip and the First Fleet.

The poem asks a question that Australian poets have been asking ever since:

> Where are the woods that, ninety summers back,
> Stood hoar with ages by the water-track?
> Where are the valleys of the flashing wing,
> The dim green margins, and the glimmering spring?
> Where now the warrior of the forest race,
> His glaring war-paint, and his fearless face?
> The banks of April, and the groves of bird,
> The glades of silence, and the pools unstirred?

Kendall celebrates the benefits and advantages of white civilization—the carving of a city out of the wilderness—and

287

proudly proclaims the qualities that have gone into the development of the nation:

> The human hands of strong, heroic men
> Broke down the mountain, filled the gaping glen,
> Ran streets through swamp, built banks against the foam
> And bent the arch and raised the lordly dome.

Like Wentworth's *Australasia*, it is cast in the mould of Augustan public poetry, enlivened by Kendall's genuine patriotic feeling, which at times almost lifts it to the level of a celebrant hymn.

Kendall was a divided man and the styles found throughout his poetry reflect his divided cultural situation. A colonial poet, he celebrated his developing nation in authoritative impersonal tones and sang his own weaknesses in songs of pitiful regret. He is a minor Victorian Romantic, but part of his poetry drew on the Augustan tradition, its modes and tones, which survived in Australia long after they had fallen out of fashion in England. This can be seen also in his formal satires such as 'The Gagging Bill' and 'The Bronze Trumpet'.

It seems appropriate to end with reference to one of his most powerful poems 'To a Mountain', which can be read as a reckoning of his whole poetic career. Kendall himself believed that he was best as a descriptive poet. He wrote to J. Brunton Stephens, 5 June 1880, 'I was born in the forests and the mountains were my sponsors. Hence I am saturated with the peculiar spirit of Australian scenery ...' The poem celebrates the mountain landscape, the rivers, the green and gold (two of his favourite words) of foliage and light; it is full of a sense of dedication and aspiration to an ideal—a dream of poetry, of commitment to the powers that can transform the frail self. Kendall believed in a transcendent spiritual force. His invocation to the mountain recognizes it as a source of stability and strength, beyond change because united with God. Religious feeling is pervasive throughout Kendall's work (holy is one of his most frequent adjectives) but here the feeling is for once fully embodied in the poem as the poet sees it embodied in the mountain. As A. D. Hope has written:

> It is a beautiful and elevated invocation, in plain and moving language, Kendall's profession of faith and his central vision of the world he celebrates. ... It is a noble and sustained music, which whatever it may owe to Wordsworth and Tennyson, is Kendall's own

voice. Had he been an English poet writing in England it would have won him ... recognition ...[2]

Kendall frequently lamented 'the lot austere/that waits upon the writer here', and it is possible that his talent was thwarted in some way by the difficulties he found in the culture around him. But the development of his poetry in its strengths and limitations gives a very strong sense of a context and of having its roots in the life and society of his time. This is not something one could safely say of some of the poets who came after him.

Looking back on Australia's colonial poetry one can say that the earliest aspirations of both Harpur and Kendall were fulfilled: history made Harpur 'the founder of the country's poetic heritage', Kendall was recognized as a 'native Australian poet'.

Adam Lindsay Gordon (1833–1870) is the most difficult of the colonial poets for the modern reader to sympathize with. Harpur and Kendall have both continued to rise in reputation, but Gordon, the most adulated and popular poet of his time and the only Australian to be given a place in Poets' Corner in Westminster Abbey, has not survived nearly as well.

Harpur and Kendall never wrote as badly as Gordon sometimes wrote, but they lacked the recognition he received because of his Anglo-Australian background and because his posthumous friends like Douglas Sladen had friends and influence in the right place at the right time. A. Patchett Martin wrote in *The Beginnings of an Australian Literature* (London 1898):

> Gordon's poems, which were of so little use to him in the battle of life, have indeed now become almost household words in the land of his adoption; and he appeals, as I have said, to a certain class of adventurous men all over the world, as few, if any, of our greater poets do.

> A short time ago, when one of our unending little wars had broken out in Africa, it was reported that the officers of a regiment carried with them into the desert the poems of Gordon. High Indian authorities, such as Sir Mountstuart Grant Duff and Sir Alfred Lyall, bear testimony to Gordon's wide popularity in the remote military stations of Hindustan. It could hardly be otherwise; for the light of battle is in his verse, and Gordon is, indeed, the laureate of the soldier's true friend—the horse.

There is little sensibility in Gordon's work, and not much sense of poetic personality. Gordon is facile, a poet of action, and though brooding melancholy and a constant sense of the inevitability of death underlay much of his poetry, it is a body of verse almost entirely without resonance. Yet up to the time of the Second World War Gordon was the poet who was considered to epitomize the colonial spirit. Both as a person and as a poet he gave the colonial experience the stamp that it seemed to need. His most devoted champion, Douglas Sladen, expressed the situation as he saw it in his Westminster Memorial Volume of 1935: 'Gordon did not absorb into his poetry the country's characteristic flora and fauna, or the distinctive features of its landscape and its seaboard. Gordon's poetry was "a poetry of Exiles" '. Subject matter and intention were important, but it was Gordon's uncomplicated directness and the sense of purposeful energy that emanates from his verse that accounted most for his appeal. His preoccupation with horses springs from personal predilections, but unlike Gericault's, Delacroix's or Degas's where great, almost primeval energies, or a fascination with social attitudes and life styles are involved, Gordon's seem merely to reflect the commonplaces of his background and character—the English gentleman with a tradition of hunting and riding behind him, in the colonies where horses and horsemanship were fully appreciated. Gordon legends of sensational and reckless feats of horse-riding abound in his biographies and his tragic suicide set a romantic seal on his life. But whatever the complexities of Gordon's life and character, his verse leans on the simplest emotions and poetic forms.

Much of Gordon can be dismissed as doggerel. *Ashtaroth* (1867)—his attempt to revive the Faust theme—survives only as a literary curiosity, showing the extent of the influence of the Gothic novel in Australia. However, his first published book *The Feud*, written to match a set of engravings by Noel Paton, an eminent Scottish artist, to illustrate *The Dowie Dews of Yarrow*, has a continuously strong narrative line and several of Gordon's finest lyrical moments.

Gordon's first volume shows the influence of English and Scottish ballad poetry—Macauley, Scott, Southey and Campbell are familiar presences—as well as a range of Latin and Greek influences; like Kendall he fell under the sway of Poe. Gordon was very fond of Latin tags—for all his love of action there was a bookish side to him and all that he wrote. So that as well as appealing to a wide audience he was also able to give the impression of high culture and learning to the many who admired his verse.

There is much in Gordon that anticipates Paterson, but there is a note of melancholy, self-reproach and pessimism in poems like 'Wormwood and Nightshade' and *Quare Fatisgasti* that are quite beyond Paterson's scope and temperament. Gordon is a continually literary and derivative poet, despite his simplicities of attitude. Scott is a palpable presence in 'Fauconshawe' and 'The Romance of Britomarte'; Swinburne's influence is noticeable in 'Bellona' and 'The Swimmer', 'Delilah' and 'The Song of the Surf'; Browning's influence is apparent everywhere—particularly the Browning of 'Childe Roland' and 'How we Brought the Good News from Ghent to Aix'; 'The Roll of the Kettledrum' shows the influence of Tennyson's 'The Charge of the Light Brigade'; 'Bellona' and 'Borrowed Plumes' owe much to Edgar Allan Poe. There are no local influences. Gordon called his poems 'Rhymes and Ballads', suggesting verse that is more direct and down to earth than songs or sonnets; but the literary element dominates the poetry, with all its romance and adventure and simplified rhymes.

Sea Spray and Smoke Drift (1867) contains 'Ye Wearie Wayfarer: This Ballad in eight Fyttes', one of Gordon's most characteristic groups, first published in the sporting paper *Bell's Life in Victoria*: the opening lines help to explain why Gordon's verse attained such heights of popularity:

> Lightly the breath of the spring wind blows,
> Though laden with faint perfume.
> 'Tis the fragrance rare that the bushman knows,
> The scent of the wattle bloom.

This easy evocation of a familiar scene, with the rider resting under a tree and the horse rolling on the ground, nonchalantly evokes a time, a place and a mood that all his readers could recognize. But the sequence is devoted to thoughts of England, and to link the two countries together in a relaxed conversational tone was no negligible achievement on Gordon's part.

Gordon's facile proverbial moralizing is now well known, through frequent quotation in the 'In Memoriam' columns of newspapers:

> Life is mostly froth and bubble,
> Two things stand like stone,
> Kindness in another's trouble,
> Courage in your own

291

It can descend to this:

> All hurry is worse than useless. Think
> On the adage, 'Tis pace that kills':
> Shun bad tobacco, avoid strong drink,
> Abstain from Holloway's pills.

But there are throughout moments of grace and relaxation. Gordon is exceptionally uneven, more uneven than Kendall or Harpur. His cultural references are often extremely learned and wide; like many colonial writers he liked to show his width of knowledge, but he kept his feet on the ground, he celebrated common sense and the basic truths of ordinary existence. We cannot hope to understand the colonial experience as a whole without his poetry, and it is no surprise that later poets like Barcroft Boake and Paterson were able to learn from him how to speak naturally about their environment and experiences in simple rhythms that had an irresistible appeal for the general public. All art works through various degrees of simplification and intensification. Gordon, in adapting the English ballad and popular poetic forms to his situation, enabled a whole line of later poets and reciters and readers to find significance and sense in their way of life. He paved the way for the writers of the bush ballad. The beginnings of one Australian tradition are found in his work. The ballad form gains in simplicity and directness what it loses in subtlety and complexity, and the pioneers needed Gordon's expressions of basic, practical wisdom. Gordon expressed the few kinds of simple truth that enabled them to keep going; the emphasis on fortitude spoke to their needs. The modern reader is still likely to value Gordon for the way he responds sensitively to the Australian landscape—

> Hark the bells on distant cattle
> Waft across the range,
> Through the gold-tufted wattle
> Music low and strange.

—or for his exile's memories, when Australian bells remind him of the bells of home—

> Like the marriage peal of fairies
> Comes the tinkling sound,
> Or like chimes of sweet St. Mary's
> On far English ground.

Bush Ballads and Galloping Rhymes (1870) was published the day before Gordon shot himself. It contains the poems by which he is still best known, 'The Sick Stockrider', 'How we Beat the Favourite', 'A Dedication', 'From the Wreck', 'The Romance of Britomarte', 'Wolf and Hound', and 'The Rhyme of Joyous Garde', and of all these 'The Sick Stockrider' is still the most impressive. Marcus Clarke, in his preface to Gordon's poems claimed '(the student) will find in them something very like the beginnings of a national school of Australian poetry', and though he was referring to Gordon's poetry as a whole, it is 'The Sick Stockrider' and its subsequent influence that gives force to his statement. 'The Sick Stockrider' is not only an elegy for a representative figure of the pioneering days in the bush, it is also an elegy for a whole way of life that was passing and, in and through its language, for the whole Anglo-Australian phase. Gordon almost certainly based his poem on another poem: the subject had already appeared in verse from the 1840s; but in the poem itself the 'dying fall' is everything; the reminiscent, meditative note and the celebration of a shared past are what account best for its popularity and its unmistakeable appeal. Its language is often literary and mannered—Gordon does not handle the colloquial mode easily: 'Twas merry in the glowing morn' does not suggest the speech of an Australian bushman so much as that of an Anglo-Australian like Gordon himself: and the chase after the bushrangers is merely another version of the English fox hunt. But nothing dates more quickly than the vernacular, and Gordon has succeeded in turning what was doubtlessly complex into the simple, in the manner of the pastoral elegy. Gordon, in fact, has captured in a representative image the sense of a passing world, or an image of a world that is about to pass, and the theme and mood ('And where are now Jem Roper and Jack Hall?') recall the tone and emphasis of Villon's 'Où sont les neiges d'antan?' The poem, through its roll call of names—Hughes, Sullivan, Mostyn and Carisbrooke, suggests briefly in outline the lives and the limitations and the possibilities found in the old colonial school. Harry Heseltine has pointed out that a dramatized personality does not exist in the poem; but the poem is less about a person than a way of life, and its rhythms suggest less the presence of a dying man than acceptance of, and resignation to the inevitable. The poem could never have achieved its popularity without touching the great commonplaces of human thought and feeling. Elizabeth Perkins has written that Gordon was convinced that

> he belonged to a transitional generation existing in the no man's land between the end of one era and the beginning of the next. Australia herself at this period, the mid-sixties to the nineties, was feeling the transition from an early pastoral ascendency to the beginnings of trade unionism, commercial and industrial power. Gordon's sense of exile and loss was a personal one, but it was also a national one, to which many factors contributed, political, economic and social.[3]

It seems to me likely that 'The Sick Stockrider' owed its appeal to the way it captured this mood in a popular image and rhythms, suggesting a way of coping with life, touched with sentimentality:

> I've had my share of pastime, and I've done my share of toil,
> And life is short—the longest life a span—
> I care not now to tarry for the corn or for the oil,
> Or for the wine that maketh glad the heart of man;
>
> For good undone and gifts misspent and resolutions vain,
> 'Tis somewhat late to trouble. This I know,
> I should live the same life over, if I had to live again;
> And the chances are I go where most men go.
>
> The deep blue skies wax dusky and the tall green trees grow dim
> The sward beneath me seems to heave and fall,
> And sickly, smoky shadows through the sleepy sunlight swim
> And on the very sun's face weave their pall.
>
> Let me slumber in the hollow where the wattle blossoms wave,
> With never stone or rail to fence my bed;
> Should the sturdy station children pull the bush flowers on my grave
> I may chance to hear them romping overhead.

Barcroft Boake wrote to his father in 1889

> . . . there is not a bushman or a drover who does not know a verse or two of 'How we Beat the Favourite' or 'The Sick Stockrider' . . . Gordon is the favourite—I may say the only—poet of the back blocker . . .[4]

His work was highly praised by A. Sutherland and Francis Adams, though by 1913 A. G. Stephens, with his usual sharpness and independence, was pointing out that Gordon was popular with Australians because of his life and personality rather than because of intrinsic poetic qualities.

Any comment on Gordon should mention 'The Rhyme of Joyous Garde' one of his most successful and achieved pieces. In this poem Lancelot, a Knight of the Round Table and the lover of Queen Guinevere, repents for his sin of faithlessness to the King; the whole has a range and an unmistakeable energy that carries the theme along and brought out Gordon's best qualities. It is also interesting to see Gordon participating in the medieval idealizing that is one of the important elements in Victorian writing.

If the adulation Gordon received as 'National Poet of Australia' now seems misguided and excessive, it is not difficult to understand why it occurred, and on what grounds his poetic ability was assessed. Gordon, an immigrant, was able to speak to the sense of the exile in the Australian adapting to a new country, loaded with nostalgia for England and the Old World. His melancholy attitudes and statements suggested depths of feeling which are not embodied in his verse, while that part of his work which draws on Arthurian legends, border ballads, Spanish bullfighting and the war in the Crimea suggests a wider range of learning and emotional experience than he in fact possesses. 'The Sick Stockrider' remains his best known and most memorable poem, and his own best epitaph. Gordon's work, for all its limitations, can be seen as representing the divided situation of the poet in exile: much of his poetry is imitative romantic verse looking backward to medieval times, while the poems he is best remembered by, especially 'The Sick Stockrider' show his attempt to respond to and record the colonial experience he knew. Kendall, although locally born and with no outlets in the world of action, also reflects the same sense of division and conflict. Harpur and Kendall, with whom the process of the transformation of the landscape became more complete, had a deeper and more lasting effect on Australian poetry. We can now read them in a way that we cannot quite read Gordon, and find their work enriched by that of the poets who have come after them. They belong to their times, but they belong to the present too, and they inaugurated that tendency of 'naming' the country, of turning it into poetry, and thus transforming it, that still continues to the present day.

Brian Elliott in his essay 'The Colonial Poets' has commented on the pervading melancholy of the lyric mood which appears in colonial Australian poetry. He accounts for it first as an historical survival—a continuation in the colonies of literary modes which were already out-dated in England. Secondly, he sees it as a means of coping with the discrepancies between inherited styles and expectations and the actual realities that surrounded the writers:

295

In the third place, the element of melancholy does truly represent a certain mood of the landscape, especially the vaster, more open aspects of it, where the imagination is aware of a pathetic contrast between the limitless magnitude of nature and the powerlessness of the isolated human spirit ... there was, in fact, no cure for this disease, as long as the Colonial mood of mind prevailed. But the rising temper of Nationalism (already alert in Brunton Stephens's 'The Dominion of Australia' 1877) began to turn the substance of the complaint to a more aggressive account as the Colonial spirit faded. Hence the disappearance of the abject note of apology and the substitution of a new tone of proud defiance:

I love a sunburnt country ...[5]

Kendall's death in 1882 marked the end of a phase. Local critics were soon complaining of what they saw to be the deficiencies of colonial poetry. George Knox, writing in The *Sydney University Review*, July 1883, commented on the failure of local poets to engage with the minute particulars of the nature that surrounded them. He pointed to the general nature of poets' descriptions, their emphasis on the sublime and the ideal rather than the specific and the precise. Similarly, R. Kyndon Ellis, writing in *Light*, July 1888, on 'The Characteristics of Australian Poetry', was critical of what he considered the deficiencies of colonial verse. Such contemporary documents are always of interest, whether or not they are accurate and justified. They show that the critical tide was already turning; new modes and new approaches were being demanded.

A number of themes dominates colonial poetry, but something like a pattern emerges. The early expression of a nostalgia for England is often coupled with a baffled sense of being in unfamiliar, even uncongenial surroundings. There is some sense of divided loyalties and affections—of wanting to be in England and yet aware of and involved in new-found surrounding realities. Even Kendall, who was born in Australia and never knew England, has nostalgic English references in his work, which shows how widespread such expectations and reflections were in the writing of the time.

As the century develops the sense of metropolitan culture and civilized values being associated with London, where the reputations are made and the rewards and honours are found, rather than with the Australian cities or towns where the hard work is done, takes on new tones and contours. But however it is expressed London and England remain significant reference points until the Second World War, and the need for overseas recognition was an important element in the development and shaping of all Australian writers.

During this whole period the endless process of assimilating the landscape, of describing it and naming new places, animals and plants and capturing them in verse is begun, as is the recording of local historical events. One can trace the appearance in colonial poetry of the first branch of wattle, the first kangaroo, and the first lyrebird. This fact alone is a comment on the nature and quality of colonial poetry as a whole—whether in volume form or as published in newspapers. The poetry, whether lyrics, squibs and satires or extended narratives is on the whole the product of cultivated aspiring minds drawing on the European cultural heritage yet trying to assimilate local experience and knowledge. The Aboriginals make an early appearance in colonial poetry, and scholars have shown how many of the themes of later writers and those considered typical of the nineties were already present in the writers of the 1830s and 1840s. The returns from reading colonial poetry in general are larger than one might think when one casts one's eye over the field. As Brian Elliott points out in *The Landscape of Australian Poetry* there is much Victorian moralizing sentiment throughout; the metal is larger than the tiny jewel it holds, but the jewels are there none the less. The conflicts, often in the same writer, between colonial and immigrant tendencies highlight one of the central divisions in Australian writing, between the local and the universal. It is only when the universal is expressed through the local, or the abstract through the concrete, that a fully mature poem is conceived. In colonial poetry in general the language still does not reveal the object, or does not quite focus on it. The writers interpret Australian reality through the English, American and European authors of their time whom they attempt to acclimatise to Australian conditions.

Cecil Hadgraft has commented in *The Patterns of Australian Culture* that the failure of colonial poets compared with the colonial novelists is due to language: 'Their diction draws a thin veil between reader and reality.' But this is part of their permanent interest and something similar is found in the colonial painters. One has to wait for the so-called nationalists of the 1890s before the unmistakeable Australian note emerges in writers like Lawson and Furphy, who remain unique landmarks of Australian literature because they combine the two characteristics that T. S. Eliot

297

maintained all such landmarks should possess: 'The strong local flavour combined with unconscious universality.'

PART TWO: THE 1880s TO 1920

The nineties have at times been over-simplified, because this was the period when nationalist and obvious Australianist tendencies were most stridently articulated. It is now clear that the period from 1880 to the end of the First World War has as much to offer in the way of variety as that of unity, and that the period's range of work is larger than is usually assumed. It was the time when Australia was starting to achieve self-consciousness as a nation; the popular nationalist note is often the most insistent, but it is not the most artistically enduring. The conventional literary groupings of the period can still serve as a starting point, as they indicate the main pressures and tensions that were present in Australian poetry until the 1930s, and in Australian literary culture up to the 1950s. There is, however, much more overlapping and interweaving than such a schematization allows for, and a writer may be found to participate in more than one group.

The most popular group, with the largest following, was that of the bush balladists. A more isolated and loosely linked group of poets drew in various ways on European models and the aesthetic stream in post-symbolist development, poets like Daley and McCrae, who would be called colonial aesthetes. There were Utopian socialists like O'Dowd and Jephcott, who used erudition as a weapon, and a number of public poets like George Essex Evans, John Farrell, William Gay and James Brunton Stephens who voiced some of the aspirations, hopes and tensions of the time. The two outstanding poets of the period, Brennan and Shaw Neilson, belong with the poets of the aesthetic stream and owe much more to the English writers of the nineties than scholarship has even yet revealed; but by sheer force of individuality they transcend the tendencies they, too, can be seen to represent.

The bush balladists were the most popular poets in their day and are still taken by some to represent the essential spirit of the nineties. More than any other group they seemed to give the authentic Australia a voice, and because their appeal was wide, cutting across barriers of education and class, they seemed to chime in with the democratic, egalitarian tendencies of the time. Before the bush balladists appeared, Australia had already built up a

298

repertoire of old bush songs, and there is a whole complex history of popular verse dating from the beginnings of the country. These old bush songs, mostly anonymous modifications and adaptations of songs and tunes that had previously existed, need to be distinguished from the work of the bush balladists who were more literary in formation.

On the whole the old bush songs were intended to make life bearable—and to fill people with a sense of courage and good cheer, or else to fix the facts of Australia in a verbal shape. Intended to be sung by Australian bushmen and shearers, gold diggers and fossickers, drovers on the cattle track and shearers in the sheds, they were in a sense the pop songs of the period, and like modern pop songs many were American in origin. Most of them were anonymous, and in the processes of transmission they were often subtly changed. Some bush songs started as convict songs and as conditions changed in Australia so the words changed to suit the new situation. Others are protest songs—songs invented in anger or a sense of outrage against particular social anomalies or injustices—like the shearers' and strikers' songs of the 1890s. Historians have shown that most of the early ballads are adaptions from a variety of sources: London street ballads, Irish songs, songs from English music halls and American stage songs, brought to Australia at the time of the gold rushes or earlier.

As H. M. Green shows in his *History of Australian Literature*, the old bush song is democratic in the extreme—it is against the government, law and order, the squatter and the boss; sometimes it is against the whole nature of things. It reflects the widespread revulsion in the Australia of the early days against autocratic government, the convict system and the land monopoly of the squatters. They are rebel songs, and the rebellious note is particularly strong in the bushranging ballads, where the bushrangers rob the rich to help the poor and the police are stupid and cowardly. Some of the most famous of these folk songs are poems like 'The Wild Colonial Boy', 'Brave Donohue', 'Botany Bay', 'The Overlanders'. 'The Wild Colonial Boy', most accessible through the various collections edited by Stewart and Keesing, takes up the historical situation of a young man who becomes a bushranger and is finally outnumbered and shot by the troopers. It is a celebration of stoic courage and is crisp, economical and effective. The laconic tone and unfaltering rhythm make the hero's fate a foregone conclusion, but, without pathos, there is still poignancy about his death, coming as it does at a moment of innocent delight in the beauty of nature. On the other hand, 'The Dying Stockman', which begins:

> A strapping young stockman lay dying,
> His saddle supporting his head;
> His two mates around him were crying
> As he rose on his elbow and said—
>
> (Chorus) Wrap me up with my stockwhip and blanket,
> And bury me deep down below,
> Where the dingoes and crows can't molest me,
> In the shade where the coolibahs grow.

is much more sentimental, with a nostalgia for the simplicities of childhood and the dignity of a well lived life. I suspect it is based on some American melody or folk song. Typical pieces like 'Bullocky Bill', 'The Sandy Maranoa' and 'Click go the Shears, Boys', deal with cattle drovers and shearers. What features do they have in common? First, a resolute cheerfulness in front of the inescapable facts of life; they do not hide these facts—physical hurt and discomfort of all kinds—but they are not cowed by them. Singing in the face of trouble and difficulties is one way of coping with them, both a way of showing courage and keeping up one's courage—and this is typical of nearly all the old bush songs. Australia has always been plagued by natural hazards and disasters—(one notices the frequent mention in these poems of dust and drought, flood and fire)—and the odds against the pioneers were very great.

'Click go the Shears, Boys' is more light-hearted in subject matter—a song about a simple pattern of masculine hard work and hard drinking, with its devil-may-care attitudes. These are not poems of any great depth, but they do give us a glimpse into unfamiliar ways of life and they give us some idea of what the people who lived such lives felt and feared. These ballads, while mostly about one person, tend to fall into two groups—those, like 'The Wild Colonial Boy', 'Mooneenee', 'The Death of Morgan', 'Brave Ben Hall', which celebrate unique rebels fighting against odds much in the manner of ancient European heroic sagas; and those where the individual is the focus of a group image—like 'The Sandy Maranoa', 'Click Go the Shears' and 'The Numerella Shore', 'On the Road to Gundagai', 'The Diggins-oh'—where the trivialities and discomforts of everyday life are given a sense of purpose by the dimensions of a more monumental outline of the shared and necessary existence.

One of the most famous of all bush songs is 'Waltzing Matilda' which was collected and published by Banjo Paterson. Originally anonymous, it is a haunting song now hallowed by tradition, even having been considered as Australia's national anthem. Apart from its catchy refrain, it is popular because it captures two important aspects of the Australian experience—that of the battler, the tramp carrying his swag in the outback, and the need for the poor man to escape from the injustice of the rich man, from the law. It encapsulates, in a series of scenes sparsely and sharply outlined as woodcuts, the experience of the haves and the have-nots which is fundamental not only to Australia, but to nearly all societies. Like 'The Wild Colonial Boy', 'Waltzing Matilda' gives one a strong sense of nature; of the outdoor life with its vigours and rigours. It should be repeated however that 'Waltzing Matilda' is not a product of the people, but a clever pastiche of folk idiom by a sophisticated town dweller who had been raised in the outback and had developed a love of the country and keen understanding of its people.

It is noteworthy that the Australian bush songs, unlike the medieval ballads of Europe, are never love ballads. They are about a particular way of life and they do not attempt to go beyond this. They rarely touch the depths of human passion; they have no religious overtones and rarely the mysterious dimension or haunting ghostly presences that one finds in the older European ballads. There is no foreboding here. This is because they aim to cope with reality, with a specific situation—and usually the situation is so difficult and so typical that coping with it is an end in itself.

These early poems are anonymous, chips off the old folk-lore block. But as they developed and became more and more popular, so more trained and educated writers became interested in them and tried consciously to write ballad poems dealing with the same themes and subject matter, i.e., man against nature, man against the law, mateship. These are known to historians as the literary balladists—the two most famous being Henry Lawson and A. B. 'Banjo' Paterson, whose work was most popular in the 1890s and the years before the First World War. Both can be seen as developing from Gordon's 'The Sick Stockrider'.

301

For many years the Australian bush ballad of the nineties was considered to represent authentic Australian poetry. It showed something of what Australia was like during the period of settlement and exploration. Filled with stockmen, cattle, settlers, gold diggers, battlers and squatters, it gave a popular-level currency to a genuine image of Australia. The bush ballads are not great poems, some are not even good verse, but they are significant human documents and part of the whole Australian literary experience.

Lawson and Paterson are the two outstanding and the best remembered writers of popular verse in their era. Their work is still worth exploring, for its own sake, for what it tells us about the time in which it was written and because it has had continuing influence across the decades: in the verse of a host of minor versifiers like Vance Palmer and D. H. Souter; on more considerable poets like Douglas Stewart, David Campbell and John Manifold in the forties, who were all involved at one stage in the search for a popular Australian tradition; and more recently on the work of A. D. Hope, of all people.

Lawson's outstanding achievement was in his prose, though it was his poetry that gained most popularity in his lifetime. He is often soppy with self pity, salted and vinegary with resentments and hostilities, but there is an energy and a sense of personality and feeling in everything he wrote:

> And still the rough work shines
> Because the blood was on the pen—
> The soul within the lines.

Paterson on the other hand was content to declare:

> There's nothing here sublime
> But just a roving rhyme
> Run off to pass the time . . .

Paterson's poetry gives the impression of having been written by a tradition rather than a person. He does not deal with individuals, but types and often types created by a situation or an atmosphere. His world is the womanless world of outback action. Paterson is closer to the polished anonymity of folk ballads, Lawson to the lachrymose sentiment of parlour songs. There may not be on the whole a great deal to choose between Paterson's depersonalized heroics and Lawson's tear-jerking lamentations. But both at their best are undeniably accomplished versifiers and both should be read together if only because the images of Australia which they project in their rhymes complement each other. Harry Heseltine has summed up the difference with emblematic neatness: 'Paterson had something of the cavalier view of the man on horseback, while Lawson employed the harsher perspectives of the traveller humping his swag'.

Lawson's verse has more variety of subject matter, tones and modes than Paterson's, although he has only three main preoccupations—protest, patriotism, personal failure. He first achieved fame through such passionate protest poems of 1888 as 'The Army of the Rear' and 'Faces in the Street', poems of courage and force which gave voice to the sense of social injustice which Lawson felt so keenly throughout his life. Lawson is not in the true sense of the word a balladist, though he uses the verse shapes and forms associated with the ballad writers, many of whom adopted them from Kipling. He rarely allows an incident to speak for itself and to exist as a self-contained and self-explanatory narrative: he uses it as a vehicle for moral reflection, often of emotional regret. Lawson is a sad, often depressing versifier. He shows the grim realities of the down-and-out, the meaning of failure, those who have destroyed themselves through inner weakness, encouraged by circumstance. His great theme is what might have been, or 'the man I might have been', in all senses. The phrase 'the man I might have been' crops up throughout Lawson's verse, whether in a small piece of 1914 'On Looking Through the Old Punishment Book at Eurunderee School, 20 April, 1914' or 'Written Out' (1904). There is even a poem of 1897 called 'The Men We Might Have Been'. When it is not used directly it is often implicit in the story a poem tells. It is seen at its best in poems like 'Sweeney'. Lawson knew the depths of human misery and failure.

Everything about Lawson is interesting. He was a writer for whom verse was an engaging social activity; thus the abundance of his work and his use of verse to pay tributes to fellow writers, like Daley, Hugh McCrae, Louis Becke and others. He took a craftsman's delight in experimenting with different verse forms and patterns. His three volumes of collected verse, amounting almost to 1000 pages, always provide new or unusual insights into his personality or the times in which he lived. He had a penetrating awareness of the self-induced sufferings of failure, but his resentments at his critics, rooted in insecurity, often gave his pen a special

303

sharpness; and he was clear-eyed about literary hostilities, jealousies and the lower levels of human motive.

If Lawson has more scope and range of felt experience than Paterson, he never wrote any verse that had the popularity and currency of 'The Man From Snowy River', 'Clancy of the Overflow' or 'Waltzing Matilda', which is always associated with Paterson's name, and which have become national monuments. Nor did he write anything as humorous as the comic narratives 'The Geebung Polo Club', 'Saltbush Bill' or 'The Man from Ironbark'. Yet Paterson never wrote any poem as skilfully turned or as succinctly penetrating as 'Middleton's Rouseabout'—or even 'Second Class Wait Here', and much of his work merely consists of verses of a cheerful externality to which their characteristically rollicking and often merely mechanical rhythms happily correspond. Lawson gave voice to urban and rural miseries. Paterson high-lighted for city dwellers outback heroics seen through a haze of humour, and asserted that the man from the outback and the life he lived were superior to the city man and his life. Paterson had panache, the patrician touch. He knew how to grip his audience. He was untouched by uncertainty or self-doubt. His patriotism was direct, simple-minded and fervent. He presented with all the power of radical simplification, and the swagger and conviction of the coiner and juggler of clichés, the heroic conception of outback Australia. With the unfailing skill and flair for the typical that even today makes it possible for a commercial artist to stamp the image of a product on a decade, Paterson projected a view of the Australian male from the outback—independent, anti-authoritarian, courageous, sardonic—which served the nation's need for a self-image and which fed into some of the self-feelings of the Australian now enshrined in the images of Anzac. Such images as Paterson projected often gain their greatest power and representativeness when the world they reflect is vanishing—and that Paterson was drawn to enshrine a passing world is clear from his collection of *Old Bush Songs* (1905)—which is still the closest that Australia can come to a body of folk lore. Paterson was the most popular poet of the time (*The Man From Snowy River* (1895) has probably sold more copies than any other Australian book of poetry) offering the public a set of images it could admire and respond to. The images he made popular are also the images most frequently found in Australian popular fiction of the time—the drover and the bushman, the jackeroo, the station owner, the trooper, the horseman, the shearer and the swagman; man in action, man with animals. Paterson, unlike Lawson, was also able to project images untouched by class feeling or the resentments and hostilities they engender and to appeal to many different groups of people from all social levels. The sheer lack of inwardness of his work was part of its attraction, as was his lack of concern for or belief in his country's shortcomings. His undeniable and continuing popularity comes from the way he celebrates masculine bravado in verse charged with the energy of obeyed constraints. His appeal comes also through the way he was able to capture certain effects of light and heat—the astringent dryness of the Australian landscape—as effectively as Tom Roberts or Arthur Streeton. This, together with the characteristic masculine tone of his verse, gives his best poems their strong local flavour and that unconscious universality referred to before.

There were, of course, many other balladists and popular poets at the time, like W. H. Ogilvie (1869–1963), E. J. Brady (1879–1952), Edward Dyson (1865–1931), and Barcroft Boake (1866–1892) probably the most remarkable of them all as a poet and prose writer (to judge by his letters) whose early suicide deprived Australian writing of a promising talent. Together they presented a collective picture of active, working Australia that readers seemed to need, perhaps fully aware that the picture was dramatically over-simplified. They fed the conviction—so strong in writers of the time from Francis Adams to C. E. W. Bean and to Vance Palmer and the members of his generation, that the authentic Australia, the true spirit of the country, was to be found in the outback. But what arose from the genuine needs of the time gradually became a stereotype, and set its own fashions with its own rigid artificialities. What originally created and reflected a reality, and offered stereotypes and images important in their time and place, ended by imposing blunted and over-worked shapes on the whole of life and helped to create a constricting tradition that later poets had to demolish so that they could find the truth of their own experiences and new formal ways of expressing them.

The balladists presented an easily transmittable and easily assimilated image of Australia, unlike O'Dowd, for instance, whose appeal was limited to the intellectuals of the time; other poets of the period voiced the nationalist note explicitly in more formal poems devoted to public themes and issues. Poets like Brunton Stephens ('Fulfilment') and George Essex Evans ('Federal Song') celebrated in rather facile public poems Federation as a longed-for and worked-for achievement. They proclaimed without questioning it the fulfilment of the British connection. Others were less optimistic. Poets like Daley, Lawson and O'Dowd, who believed that Australia should become a republic, asserted that even Federation would not cure the old persisting ills of social and economic inequalities. There are clear distinctions and various separate threads to observe between the poets and poems of the time, but all were united in a general belief first expressed by Oscar Wilde during his American tour in 1882: 'There can be no great art, no great sculpture, no great drama without a noble national life'. Some of the poets would not have accepted Wilde's definition in its wording, but the spirit behind it was one which they too felt.

O'Dowd has suffered the fate of those who put prophecy before poetry: he has been relegated to the purgatory of the cultural historian, and is now largely unread, judged for having created cultural exhibits rather than living poems. This fate would have amazed him, as it would have surprised his younger contemporaries, intellectuals like Nettie and Vance Palmer, Katharine Susannah Prichard and Frederick Macartney—all of whom have eloquently testified to the impact O'Dowd had on their generation and the writers of their era. Still, historical interest is interest of a kind, and O'Dowd is not negligible. He was all bard, believing that poetry should teach and inspire; but though he wrote no completely perfect poem, he is the author of many memorable lines and stanzas of poetry that strike deep into the national consciousness. His sense of form is limited to couplets and quatrains, which tend to be rigid and gnarled in conception and execution. Like Gilmore and Neilson he was deeply impressed by the simple hymn shapes he first encountered as a child, and although he corresponded with Walt Whitman and admired him so much that he used to wear a leaf of grass in his buttonhole, his own sense of poetic form was of the conventional kind.

O'Dowd, an internationalist in outlook who never left home, was part of the radical ferment in Melbourne as a young man. His main beliefs and convictions are outlined in 'Poetry Militant', first delivered as an address to the Literature Society of Melbourne in 1909. Like Tolstoy's 'What is Art', first published in English in 1904, which may well have influenced it, 'Poetry Militant' is basically an attack on 'Art for Art's sake' or 'Poetry for Poetry's sake'—an attack on that nineties conception of poetry exemplified in Australia by the work of McCrae and Victor Daley, who were nevertheless personally excluded by O'Dowd from his strictures. 'Poetry Militant' is subtitled 'An Australian Plea for the Poetry of Purpose,' and in spite of its period flavour, some arid patches and naive excesses, it is a sound and serious document, well worth reading for its own sake. O'Dowd wants serious content, earnest moral purpose:

> the worthy subjects of great poetry—politics, religion, sex, science and social reform ... The high seriousness rightly demanded of the true poet is hardly possible in making beautiful poems that say nothing.

Unlike Brennan, O'Dowd would not have known what to make of Mallarmé's 'L'Aprés Midi d'un Faune'. He was too much concerned with 'subordinating the call of the verbal music to the more important call of the thought-motif and spiritual theme.' That O'Dowd considered himself as a prophet—or that the poet should be a poet-prophet—is clear in all he wrote. In 'Poetry Militant' he asserts:

> At no time in the history of the world was the need for the Permeator poet, the projector of ideals, the Poet Militant, greater than in the present reconstruction of all things beneath the wand of Evolution theories, and in no place greater than in this virgin and unhandicapped land of social experiments, embryonic democracy, and the Coming Race, Australia! ... The fact of evolution and the fact of Australia make Australian Poets, if they will, essentially poets of the dawn— poets whose function is to chart the day and make it habitable— marching poets, poets for use, poets militant.

There is a touch of Nietzsche and Whitman as well as of Carlyle, in this manifesto, and like everything O'Dowd wrote, it is full of hammering conviction and genuine passion and it is moving as an indication of his faith in the power of poetry as a moral force. He declares: 'To the silent influence of good poetry for permanent good there are absolutely no bounds' 'Poetry Militant' is a justification and explication of the kind of poetry O'Dowd himself wrote, and while his later poems are less doctrinaire than his earlier pieces, they do not mark any great break with the main arguments and attitudes of 'Poetry Militant'. Indeed, one central statement: 'The poets' function is to create gods, and in every age of human progress the poet has been the most authentic and effective creator

307

of gods and of the mythologies that give them bone and blood and power', could serve as an epigraph for 'The Bush'.

For all his stridency and assertiveness, however, O'Dowd's poetry is more probing and at times more uncertain and insecure than some of his bardic utterances might suggest. His first book *Dawnward?* (1903) expresses his radical discontent with the materialism and commercialism of his society and his hopes and aspirations for a better future, but the question mark incorporated in the title indicates his worried uncertainty, his puzzlement. He bluntly attacks the forces that threaten the Utopian future he envisages: 'Proletaria,' 'The City,' 'The Press':— are battle cries of a kind and assert the need to change society and create a new world. His message is clear in 'Young Democracy':

> That each shall share what all men sow:
> That Colour, caste's a lie:
> That man is God, however low—
> Is man, however high.

Dawnward? was preceded by his most famous poem, the sonnet 'Australia' in which the balance of opposites, hopes and expectation which O'Dowd delighted in is fully exploited. A poem which celebrates Federation and the beginning of a new century, it is built around a series of questions and images suggesting the unfolding scroll of the future. Will Australia simply repeat the mistakes and injustices of the old world or does she augur a new future for humanity? The sonnet skilfully combines images of the sheer age of Australia—'last sea-thing,' 'cenotaphs of species dead elsewhere'—with images and thoughts about its newness, its position and its potentialities for a fresh start. It is highly wrought and mannered, rather in keeping with some of the scrolls that adorned late Victorian public buildings and which it might well have served to embellish.

Like Furphy and Jephcott and other related figures of the 1890s, O'Dowd was largely a self-educated man, although he at least received university training. Unable to identify completely with the over-simplified popular ballad tradition of the time and rejecting the purely aesthetic line, these writers tended to use erudition for display, though Furphy of course was aware of what he was doing. Products of their society and time (the Age of Evolutionism), they perhaps over-rated knowledge for its own sake: wide as their learning was, impressive and admirable in itself and to their contemporaries, it was neither lightly won nor lightly worn and it now adds a slightly provincial or dated touch to their work: intended to lift them aloft, it now weighs them down. O'Dowd was extremely proud of his erudition and the range of reference in his work is remarkably wide, probably as wide as Brennan's, with whom in his exploration of myth he is comparable. (And while Brennan's and O'Dowd's myth-making may be seen as an attempt to compensate for Australia's lack of history, there are passages in both poets where they seem to anticipate aspects of Wallace Stevens' 'supreme fiction').

O'Dowd's next two books, although they are like the first in form and structure, show some change in preoccupation. *The Silent Land* (1906) is concerned with a spiritual other world which exists beyond this world, yet is influenced by it and brings its influence to bear on it; while in *Dominions of the Boundary* (1907) he explores the nature and purpose of the ancient gods, showing their significance in the contemporary world. *The Seven Deadly Sins* (1909) marks another change, and in this sonnet sequence he rids himself of the self-imposed restrictions of the fourteener, thus freeing himself for the later longer works in couplets, *The Bush* and *Alma Venus*. The interest in the sequence resides in the fact that each sin is discussed in two sonnets, one of which attacks the sin, while the other defends it. O'Dowd was progressively freeing himself from the dogmatic constraints of 'Poetry Militant' and thereby achieving, perhaps unwittingly, more examples of Poetry Triumphant in his work. The sonnets contain some of his best single lines:

> Into the ape I breathed, and you were men (Pride)
> I wait with ancient stars until they set (Sloth)

The Bush (1912) shows O'Dowd's devotion to technical constraints and tight formal shapes. In the original edition each stanza of ten pentameter lines is printed on a page by itself, made up of two quatrains separated by a couplet. O'Dowd may have invented the stanza himself, though it bears some resemblance to the dizain so beloved by the 16th century French poet Maurice Scève. O'Dowd's interest in technical questions is attested throughout his work; and he may well have met the original in translation. It certainly contributes greatly to the overall sense of shape and design and formal coherence of *The Bush* which is to my mind his most impressive poem. It belongs to a long stream in

Australian writing, beginning with Wentworth's *Australasia* and Kendall's Sydney Exhibition poem and continuing through later poets, like R. D. FitzGerald's *Essay on Memory*, Rex Ingamells's *The Great South Land* and McAuley's *Captain Quiros*, but it is also O'Dowd's most directly autobiographical piece.

The Bush is a poem of vision by a poet with a mission—a vision of the future where Australia is seen to hold a place akin to the classic civilisations of old. O'Dowd sought a mythology for a land that did not have one of its own, and the argument of *The Bush*, persuasive and simple enough in itself, reveals his strange mixture of naivety and sophistication. Everything Australians are doing, and all that has been done here, is material for the great poem of Australia that will be written in the future. What has happened in the course of time in great civilizations in other parts of the world—Greece, Egypt, Italy and India—will happen in Australia in time to come. O'Dowd insists with the emphasis of his early poetry that Australia must become Eden or Utopia or Hi-Brasil, and free from the social mistakes of the Old World. She is 'the whole world's legatee'. *The Bush* as a whole is imbued with an intense sense of piety and adoration—the sense that man can draw some superhuman support and strength from the Bush itself: Australia will be born of the Bush, ushering in the new dawn and fulfilling man's millenarian hopes.

The importance of *The Bush* for Australians in its time can be attested by Nettie Palmer's reaction. She wrote about O'Dowd and his influence throughout her literary life, from 1907 until her book on O'Dowd in 1954. In a letter to her younger brother, Esmond, 10 March 1915 she commented '... read *The Bush* a good deal ... I mean the last half chiefly. Some of the stanzas are pure poetry ...' and in her influential essay *Modern Australian Literature* (1924) she wrote '*The Bush* is O'Dowd's most important contribution to Australian literature itself. It is the book a young nation needs, a meditation, a prophetic book and a seed-bed of poetry.' To Nettie Palmer and her generation O'Dowd was a major figure, voicing the nationalist aspirations of the Australia of his time, and proclaiming the mystique of the bush that was of paramount importance to the writers of that era. A new generation, setting out to explore the past of Australian poetry, is likely to find fresh interest in several aspects of O'Dowd's work and thought. Much of it has now receded irrevocably into the past, but it touches on areas and perceptions that are still active and alive in the national consciousness.

The same is true of Mary Gilmore (1862–1962), a figure who is likely to prove of special concern to historiographers, biographers and cultural historians if only because of her apparent contradictions. She was a socialist, a royalist, a D.B.E. yet during her last years a contributor to the Communist *Tribune*. Like O'Dowd and Neilson she has her poetic origins in the popular ballad and hymn shapes of her time (she once said that 'the ballad and the hymn, being closest to the roots of human effort and aspiration, are the forms that most endure'), but one is struck by the oddly eclectic and casual occurrences of different forms and genres throughout her work: she can move from the ballad or the song to attempts at free verse and the formal ode, from the Georgian nature lyric to the crisp, epigrammatic use of quatrains. As a reflection of the attitudes and tensions of her time, she is particularly interesting: in her work colonial, nationalist and imperial themes combine. Russel Ward has pointed out that to most Australians up to the Second World War

> positive and unquestioning loyalty to Throne and Empire was in no way inconsistent with an equally fervent loyalty to Australia: rather, it was a condition of it. For most, but not all people, national and imperial patriotism were complimentary, not contradictory.

And there can be no doubting that in her later volumes Gilmore clearly intended to project herself as the poet of the Commonwealth, the Empire and the Nation.

Thematically Mary Gilmore is important for the way she brought Aboriginal subject matter, Aboriginal words and usage into her poetry. ('The Lament of the Lubra', 'At Lost Field', 'Primeval Australia', 'The First Footers'); and in poems like 'The Birds' and 'I saw the beauty go', she foreshadows some of the major preoccupations later explored by Judith Wright, many of whose concerns are close to hers—conservationist issues, the encroachment of the cities on natural life, the desecration of the land, and the convict past ('Old Botany Bay'), the impact of war on personal feelings, and the various manifestations of love felt by a woman and a mother. Like so many Australian writers of her time she was restless in searching for the Australian tradition that her poetry celebrates and tries to take for granted. 'The Ringer' (El Campeador) and 'El Campo Santo' are the best illustrations of this trend; but there are throughout her work references to important historical events—Eureka, Gallipoli—and to significant Australians of the past and of her time—not only its explorers, but also Monash, Kingsford Smith, William Lane, Henry Parkes, Kendall, Daley, Lawson and others. The naming of things and places constitutes a long line in Australian poetry from John Dunmore Lang's 'Colonial Nomenclature' onwards, and Mary Gilmore belongs to it. The few brief poems by which she is best known in anthologies, 'Nurse no long grief', 'The Tenancy', 'Nationality', and 'Never Admit the Pain', with their charge of feeling and their aphoristic wisdom, do not quite do justice to her variety.

Frank Wilmot ('Furnley Maurice') (1881–1942) remains one of the most interesting and appealing of the poets to emerge between the end of the nineties and the First World War. An over-productive poet, he wrote far too much for his talent and seems to have lacked the capacity for astringent self-criticism. He began to write in a vein of soft-centred lyricism that fed at the genteel stream of poeticizing that trickled throughout Australian poetry from the 1880s to the 1960s. Much of his work is irreparably damaged by such influences, but the best of it was nourished by other stronger and more urgent impulses. Wilmot was born into a Melbourne socialist family and was a pacifist with reformist zeal. He was no aesthete, as Vance Palmer makes clear in the commemorative tribute he published in honour of Wilmot in 1942 and one might well compare him with his contemporary McCrae. McCrae's poetry is impoverished because it lacks a sense of the pressures and necessities of every day living; one cannot live in a doll's house for long, or on a diet of fastidiously wrapped bon-bons. Wilmot is almost too aware of life's pressures and his poetry suffers because he is insufficiently devoted to the full aesthetic demands of poetry as an art. This may seem an odd judgment, because, with Slessor, Wilmot was the technically most aware and informed poet in Australia between the wars. He knew about Pound and Eliot (and Carl Sandburg and Vachel Lindsay) probably earlier than anyone else in Australia; he knew the work of Stevens, Williams, and Marianne Moore, who wrote to him about one of his poems; he makes consistent attempts throughout his poetry at modernity: he experiments with free verse, liberated lines and unpredictable patterns that break with the easy mechanisms of verse. He had a surface technical range greater than that of any other poet of his generation, he felt the pressure of indignation, the drives of radical protest and condemnation, he had something to say. What went wrong? Why did these different elements not cohere more forcefully into achieved wholes? The answer lies in his sense of language and rhythm. His diction is not as modern or as aware as his technique. He was unable 'to make it new'. He remains a poet caught uneasily between the old and the new: interested in the use of colloquial speech rhythms and cadences, yet not fully committed to a living vernacular; interested in and influenced by high culture, but too self-doubting, too self-defeatingly modest to aim for the heights.

Nevertheless Wilmot remains a consistently interesting and worthwhile poet. No other Australian poet of the time would have entertained the notion of writing a poem with the idiosyncratic title 'To a Telegraph Pole' or a piece 'Upon a Row of Old Boots and Shoes in a Pawnbroker's Window'. If the former represents a good idea marred by out-moded poetic diction, it is nevertheless characteristic of Wilmot's sense of novelty, his eye for the unexpected. And in 'Plunder' he achieves verbal and musical effects comparable with some of Slessor's best stanzas.

> Spill out your netted hoard, your toll of scales,
> The snared amazement that your gullery pulls
> From the drowned gardens where slow water-gales
> Wash unknown jungles and world-weary hulls!
>
> Fishes moustached, spotted and spikey-finned,
> Flash terror-struck and burst upon the sands!
> Now, from your slippery mass, toll of the wind,
> Sort the slim pike with eager, calloused hands!

Wilmot is best remembered for three main groups of poems: poems inspired by the First World War, the poems in *The Gully and Other Verses* (1929) and *Melbourne Odes* (1934). Wilmot did not participate personally in the First World War and while his poems on war themes are full of decent protest and indignation, they are based on the rhetoric of humane attitudes, not on the particularities of personal experience. 'To God, From the Weary Nations', first appeared in *The Book Lover* in December 1916, and was later included in his volume *Eyes of Vigilance* (1920)—where 'weary' was changed to 'warring'. It is a poem which belongs very much to its period; but it is powerful in its way, and its fifteen short sections hold together as a unity. The poem is full of a sense of the horror of war and questions the idea that war should be accepted as an inevitable part of life. Wilmot insists that the enemy, too, are human beings. The poem aroused considerable controversy at the time and was followed within a month by 'Headsman to the Light', a poem which celebrates and praises the armies of his country. There is much bewildered pity and irony in this poem. The two pieces coming so close together reflect something of the confusions of attitude surrounding Australia's involvement in the First World War. But Wilmot's anti-war stand is clear in poems like 'The Supreme Sacrifice', 'For Valor', 'Nursery Ryme' and the still-impressive 'Echoes', which gives voice through a returning soldier to a deep sense of post-war disillusionment.

Wilmot was very much a man of the metropolis, but his sequence 'The Gully' (1925) is a poem about the bush (more precisely the foothills of the Dandenongs, near Melbourne) and its profound spiritual impact on him. It belongs to a particular tradition in Australian poetry—a tradition proclaimed in O'Dowd's *The Bush* and more recently and more subtly in the poetry of Les Murray, particularly 'Evening alone at Bunyah' and 'The Gum Forest'. The last stanza sums up the theme very well:

> Now I have touched your soil I will go back
> Chastened and cleansed; the plover calls his mate;
> I'm bright with ardour, faithful till the wrack
> Of hurtling Time is piled at Heaven's gate.
>
> You are sufficient, bird and stone and fern:
> From you I have gained fortitude and drawn
> Serenity to suffer those who spurn;
> I move through the dullness, visioning the dawn.

'The Gully' is a poem about the need for a national poetry; it meditates on the processes by which a great Australian poet will emerge, for whom poets like Wilmot and others will 'prepare the passage'. Like many of the writers of his generation—Palmer, Miles Franklin, Frank Dalby Davison—Wilmot had a sharp awareness of the limitations of his own abilities and achievements. Vance Palmer, who knew him well, commented 'He saw his work as a contribution poured into the common pool—the end being the creation of a culture that would water the dry soil of this country and give it a richer life'. It is the realization of this personal situation—the sense of contributing and preparing, the awareness of inadequacy—that gives 'The Gully' its particular historical interest, apart from the fact that it contains some of the best lines Wilmot wrote.

Like Brennan and Slessor, Wilmot was most at home in the city, and his seven 'Melbourne Odes' are among the first, if not the first, attempts by a local poet to depict life in a specific major Australian city. Wilmot has often been praised for sounding the note of 'modernism' in Australia but it has to be said that the modernism of *Melbourne Odes* is now faded, and even in its time had more in common with the 'modernism' of Hilaire Belloc or Osbert Sitwell than with that of Pound or Eliot, though it is possible that there is some influence of Eliot's 'Rhapsody on a Windy Night' in 'To the North Wind'. Wilmot's purpose was to show how:

> Loving new things newly,
> Loving old things in an old measure!
> Time alters deeply, truly,
> The hues of deathless treasure.

He wants to find the sense of romance (the period word betrays) in the everyday, to bring the city's past and its present together, and to combine the satirical and the sardonic with the romantic and the fantastic. It is quite an ambitious attempt, pleasant and good humoured in tone, with some completely successful passages, but it moves uneasily between light verse and journalism. It depicts 'The Towers at Evening', remembers cobblestones and horse-drawn cabs, the Victoria Markets, pawnshop windows, concerts in the Town Hall, and the Agricultural Show with its side-shows and the return home for the city visitors who have had their annual glimpse of another life.

Wilmot deliberately set out to capture aspects of Melbourne, rather in the way Douglas Stewart later set out to explore the spirit of out-back Australia in his sequence 'The Birdsville Track'. But there is something rather external in the approach. *Melbourne Odes* has the attractiveness of capable commercial art—say an accomplished early modernist mural in an avant-garde cafe of the Melbourne of the thirties. One has only to think of Sydney and its more naturally felt and intimate presence in Slessor's work, or Melbourne as it is presented in Vincent Buckley's 'Golden Builders', to be aware of Wilmot's limitations as a poet. But his achievement, minor and flawed as it is, has sincerity and purpose and among the mass of mediocre verse produced at the time, Wilmot's emerges with freshness and individuality.

The same cannot be said of William Baylebridge (1883–1942) whose main work also belongs to this historical phase. Baylebridge had considerable impact in his time on various readers and critics. He was the subject of a significant revaluation in T. Inglis Moore's *Six Australian Poets* (1942)—a book which omitted Wilmot and Slessor—and he has recently been studied in close detail by Noel Macainsh in his important book *Nietzsche in Australia* (1975). Macainsh's book however, makes clear where Baylebridge belongs: to the history of ideas, rather than to the history of poetry. Compared with his contemporaries—O'Dowd or Neilson or Frank Wilmot, all of whom have been the subject of remarkable memoirs—Baylebridge does not emerge as an appealing personality. The elements of deliberate secrecy and mystification in his life and literary activities seem part of a strategy of self-aggrandisement, his expensively and privately published and carefully re-issued books part of a programme of conscious self-promotion. This would of course be irrelevant if his poetry were better, but these facts are related closely to various aspects of his writing, to its weaknesses and vices. The harsh truth seems to be that Baylebridge was a rich man who wanted to be a poet and that most of his poetry was an elaborate and in some senses scandalous pastiche of other writers, that hardly ever comes to terms with any kind of immmediate experience; what experience there is behind it is so muffled and oblique (an evasive eroticism) that one cannot but wonder what the real object of it was. Reading the Australian poets of the early twentieth century, who wrote so much that one's mind bounces off, I am sometimes inclined to think that most of them (apart from O'Dowd, Brennan and Neilson) will be best remembered for their prose: McCrae for his letters and memoirs, Mary Gilmore for her books of reminiscence, and Baylebridge for *National Notes* and *An Anzac Muster.*

Although Baylebridge spent the years 1908–1919 in England and Europe, where he published several collections of verse at his own expense, the only literary impact he ever made was in Australia. Renouncing all elements of a popular style, he aimed at the high literary approach, earnestly studying the Elizabethan poets, the Metaphysicals, as well as Petrarch in the ninteenth century translations, and various German writers

His mind displays no great subtlety. Even his most sympathetic recent critic and editor, Noel Macainsh, who has unique knowledge of Baylebridge and his work, has commented, 'The whole mode of Baylebridge's expression was adapted to laying down the law, not searching for it.' Baylebridge seems to have absorbed a certain amount of the Nietzscheanism that was in the air at the time (and his idea of the superman and his emphasis on the will draw on the vulgarized versions of the ideas that often conglomerate around and crudify the more delicately articulated ideas of a great mind) and he was almost certainly influenced—as Judith Wright has suggested—by Bergson's idea of the *élan vital*: 'the evolutionary life-force unrolling in time'. Baylebridge develops the concept of man ascending to superman; and he merges man into an evolving humanity, the individual self making its contribution to a larger self or 'The Greater Me'. 'There is no creation and no death; all that is left to man is his will. Out of will comes energy, out of energy everything.'

Confusion and pretension is visible throughout Baylebridge's thought. His views on eugenics and birth control express at best the detached and inexperienced theorizing of the eternal intellectual bachelor; at worst they touch on the theories of Nazism and the polemicists of the totalitarian state. However one looks at them, whether expressed in aphorism, prose or verse, they are marked by a rather chilling inhumanity. Particularly suspect is Baylebridge's failure anywhere in his writing to acknowledge directly any of the sources of his writing or thought. It is not only a question of a lack of generosity: he states of *National Notes* ... 'it is the synthesis, the emergent idea, that most give the book whatever value it has finally, and this synthesis was, without qualification of any kind, my own.' Baylebridge was simply able to get away with it all in the Australia of his time. The inflation of his reputation in the 1940s is a cultural fact as significant as the Ern Malley affair.

Baylebridge's poetic reputation rests on the poetry he published between 1910 and 1920. *Moreton Miles*—very much influenced by the style of lad's love lyrics so frequent in England from the nineties to the First World War—is close to *Love Redeemed* as a sequence; both have a similar framework of events. The moods of love is their real subject matter. *Moreton Miles* shows an interesting use of the Eden theme, so pervasive in Australian poetry up to the nineteen thirties, and in places some Australian names are given and there is some genuine attempt to render landscape and the Australian background. But throughout Baylebridge's work there is the nagging sense of insincerity and pretension—the feeling that inevitably rises when there is such a discrepancy between the writer's intention and his actual achievement. The attention given to Baylebridge in previous histories and surveys of Australian literature is indicative of the basic weaknesses in the culture of the time. Too many people of goodwill seem to have been over-impressed by his sense of solemn self-dedication. His poetry is essentially poetry bred of poetry. It had no influence at the time it was written and has had none since. It is hard to believe that the future will continue to take it seriously.

Although there were quite specific local factors at work at the time, the Australian writers of the nineties owe much more to their English counterparts and their precursors than has hitherto been recognized. Literary historians have pointed out that the English nineties were characterized by a taste for the brief concentrated lyric, and in prose, for the short story: writers tended to eschew rhetoric and moralising and distrusted theory and system. The same tendencies prevailed in Australia. The influence of France was as strongly felt by Australian writers as by the English: Brennan, Boake, the Lindsays and A. G. Stephens are obvious examples, and the Australian writers in Sydney and Melbourne had the same kind of Bohemian literary clubs as those that flourished in London. Many of their thematic preoccupations were the same—the cult of the city (Daley, Brennan and Adams), preoccupations with love, death and beauty. There was even a cult of the ballad tradition among the English poets: Kipling was of course a major influence on the Australian balladists but as R. K. R. Thornton points out in his annotated anthology *Poetry of the Nineties*, 'The ballad tends to imply traditional subject matter, the heroic event, the national myth', and some of the English ballad writers of the time were just as jingoistic as their Australian counterparts. Thornton notes, too, among the English writers 'the rising interest in the rights of the ordinary man, as exemplified by the socialist movement.' The interest perhaps found stronger outlet among Australian versifiers, where the aesthetic awareness was not so strong a disciplining factor, though both factors came together for instance in the work of Victor Daley, (1858–1905). And though the Australian poets of the nineties did not produce any religious poetry of the calibre or kind produced by Coventry Patmore, Lionel Johnson, Alice Meynell and Francis Thompson in England, there is a religious note in some of Daley and George Essex Evans that adds to our sense of the scope of the verse of the period. Brennan is not a religious poet in any obvious sense, but his poetry can only be understood in the context of the religious, spiritual, and philosophical thought of his time, while Shaw Neilson needs to be taken more seriously as a religious poet than he has been. Thornton also observes that 'the dying fall, the gentle, somewhat pallid languor, the exquisite boredom, are rightly thought of as characteristic of a good deal of nineties poetry'. They can certainly be found in Daley, and it is likely that if he had not migrated to Australia at nineteen, he would have found a place for himself in the English poetic circles of the period. All the Australian colonial poets had disastrous, unhappy or failed lives: Harpur, Kendall, Gordon, Boake, Daley. It is a sad roll call of alcoholism, suicide, slow self-destruction or tragic illness. And the pervasive sense of death in Daley's *At Dawn and Dusk* (1898) certainly springs from personal factors associated with his health, as the sense of the dying fall in his work springs from personal experience and a characteristic emotional tone. It is not a mere aping of period mannerisms.

Daley is one of the most attractive poets of the nineties in Australia. He once told A. G. Stephens that he had tried 'to make a pleasant little garden of dreams'. This sounds wanly ninetyish, but it probably contains a direct reference to his poem 'Dreams' which is still one of his most remarkable pieces, very much of its period, and yet strongly individual:

> I have been dreaming all a summer day
> Of rare and dainty poems I would write;
> Love-lyrics delicate as lilac scent,
> Soft idylls woven of wind, and flower, and stream,
> And songs and sonnets carven in fine gold.
>
> The day is fading and the dusk is cold;
> Out of the skies has gone the opal gleam,
> Out of my heart has passed the high intent
> Into the shadow of the falling night—
> Must all my dreams in darkness pass away?
>
> I have been dreaming all a summer day:
> Shall I go dreaming so until Life's light
> Fades in Death's dusk, and all my days are spent?
> Ah, what am I the dreamer but a dream!
> The day is fading and the dusk is cold . . .

This poem both registers a state of mind and evaluates it. There is enough self-knowledge here and elsewhere in Daley to recognise the sense of opportunities lost, but also the nourishment and imaginative renewal afforded by dreams. 'In dreams begins responsibility', Yeats was to state in 1914. What makes the poem appealing is the way Daley is able to bring together the world of nature and the world of art. He dreams of songs and sonnets (one notices the nineties preference for the slightest lyric forms) 'carven in fine gold'—a Théophile Gautier-like conception of the survival value of art—but nature is present everywhere: the love-lyrics are delicate as lilac-scent, and the soft idylls are 'woven of wind, and flower, and stream'. And the sense of heightened awareness is related to the day and even includes the intense awareness of sunset, dusk and coming dark. Daley was tubercular, and poignantly aware of death and the passing of time, as the frequent references in his poems show.

The titles of both Daley's major books are significant: *At Dawn and Dusk* suggests his preoccupations with two images basic to his work and period. The image of dawn was central to other Australian poets too—Brennan, O'Dowd, Baylebridge and others—as well as to English poets of the time. And one remembers Joseph Furphy's significant statement at the end of his celebration of 'the monotonous variety of this interminable scrub' that its potentiality can only be 'deciphered aright by those willing to discern through the crudeness of dawn a majestic day.' The title *Wine and Roses* catches another important aspect of Daley's work—his Bohemian drinking songs—while the image of the rose was part of the verbal iconography of the period, as Brennan also shows. An interesting literary study could well be written on the imagery of dawn and sunrise in Australian poetry and prose from 1880–1920, relating it to *fin de siècle* images and preoccupations in England and the sense of a new century beginning and showing that they have been grafted on to Australian conditions to become part of a unique development in the Australian context.

While Daley fits easily into the picture of Art Nouveau in Australia there is another side to his talent much sharper, more probing, realistic and clearly focused—the side that consists of his satires, squibs and epigrams.

Daley had more poetic sense than many of his Australian contemporaries: his sense of language and rhythm is quite precise within his limits, and this can perhaps be more readily appreciated in his social pieces than in his consciously 'pretty' poems. By Daley's time the division between high and low poetry was fairly complete: the ballad writers and the general versifiers certainly had a wider public than the more serious poets. But to keep the different strands of his talent separate—so that the readers of his left-hand productions would not know of his right-hand work—Daley produced much topical verse under the nom-de-plume Creeve Roe. The aphoristic side of Daley's talent is already apparent in his first volume *At Dawn and Dusk*, in pieces like 'The Ascetic' and 'The Serpent's Legacy', and in the posthumously published *Wine and Roses* with pieces like 'Philosophy', 'St. Francis' and 'Faith'.

> Faith shut her eyes
> —Poor self-deceiver!
> The last God dies
> With the last believer.

This volume also contains the strikingly good piece 'When London Calls'—something of a companion to Henry Lawson's more taunting and bitter 'A Song of Southern Writers', but where Lawson rails at a situation, Daley allegorises a whole way of life by giving London the attributes of the *femme fatale* of romantic and post-symbolist iconography. She has some of the features of one of Gustave Moreau's Circe—sphinx-like harlot queens:

> Crowned Ogress—old, and sad, and wise—
> She sits with haunted face
> And hard, imperious, cruel eyes
> In her high place.
>
> To him who for her pleasure lives,
> And makes her wish his goal
> A rich Tarpeian gift she gives—
> That slays his soul . . .
>
> And when the Poet's lays grow bland,
> And urbanised, and prim—
> She stretches forth a jewelled hand
> And strangles him.

The inevitable lure and appeal that London had for many writers and artists, from Lawson ('The Rush to London') through to Palmer, Prichard and W. J. Turner, not to mention more recent figures, as well as the effect of London's tastes and needs on painters like Roberts, Streeton and Lambert, is one of the major facts of Australian culture and helps to give the poem its enduring edge. Daley was aware of the needs and temptations of expatriation for many of his contemporaries; he was equally aware of the deficiencies and limitations of Australian culture in his day. In 'Corregio Jones' he mocks the painter who derides local subject matter in favour of derivative shapes and traditions. 'His body dwells on Gander flat,/His soul's in Italy'. Daley is not here condemning a great tradition but the attitude of many Australians of the time, for whom culture was elsewhere and art not to be found in the things around them. Daley returned to cultural themes in two other poems of note: 'An Australian Mummy' (well worth comparing with A. D. Hope in the same vein) and 'Narcissus and some Tadpoles', a penetrating skit on A. G. Stephens, the editor of the Red Page of the *Bulletin*, and his rather mechanical tampering with other writers' work. It catches in its tone that sense of brusque well-intentioned conceit that one senses elsewhere as one of Stephens' characteristics. Although Daley writes with some personal sharpness, his position as an 'outsider' may have given him more critical detachment than his Australian-born contemporaries were able to achieve when it came to seeing the cultural climate of the time. His more politically motivated verse needs to be taken into account to get a true idea of his range. His poem 'The Model Journalist' is pointedly effective and cuts close to an enduring truth and is comparable with similar pieces by modern poets like Bruce Dawe and David Malouf; and even in his lightest verse—such as 'Tall Hat' he is able to use effective word play:

> He keeps the Hoi Polloi in place
> With opiates of Kingdom Come.
> His is the Glory that is Grease
> The Grandeur that is Rum.

There are some interesting contradictions in Daley: the religious feeling in some of his serious lyrics needs to be balanced against his attacks on institutionalized religion in some of his squibs and satirical verses, his pretty 'dream' poems against his sharper pieces on contemporary society and its values. Daley belongs very much to his place and time, but there is genuine individuality of touch in his best work.

Hugh McCrae (1876-1958), like Neilson and Mary Gilmore, Frank Wilmot and O'Dowd who all lived well on into the twentieth century, had his beginnings and formation in the 1890s. His work is part of the whole picture of what the nineties in

Australia meant, but where O'Dowd, Gilmore and Wilmot belong to the stream of radical left-leaning writers and political idealists to whom poetry was not so much an end in itself as a means of conveying a message, a protest, a series of ideas or attitudes, McCrae belongs to that group of *fin de siècle* writers which includes Victor Daley and Shaw Neilson in some aspects of their work, who were more devoted to a concept of Beauty—Art as Beauty—which derives from the poets of the Celtic Twilight and the English poets associated with *The Yellow Book* and *The Savoy*.

Beauty is a perishable product and the poets who dedicated themselves entirely to this stream of highly aesthetic minor poetry rather than the ragged vitality of life have not worn particularly well. McCrae's first poem 'Owner Going West' was published in the *Bulletin* in 1896; his first and perhaps most significant book *Satyrs and Sunlight* in 1909. Throughout his life McCrae stood aside from every public ferment—especially the nationalist ferment of the nineties, devoting himself to confecting his own rococo stucco world. Strangely enough he was for over thirty years one of the most influential of Australian poets, especially in Sydney and most importantly, of course, on Slessor, who addressed a fine poem to him and acknowledged his direct influence. But Douglas Stewart, Kenneth MacKenzie, A. D. Hope, Ronald McCuaig, Rosemary Dobson and a cluster of lesser figures also show traces of his influence. McCrae, as Slessor has so eloquently testified, in some witty and penetrating pages in *Bread and Wine* (1970) stood for two things for his generation: he broke with—or rather simply ignored—the bush-ballad and radical tradition of the nineties, and he stood for the autonomy of art 'art for art's sake'—imaginative independence, artistic integrity and enterprise, Poetry Triumphant rather than O'Dowd's idea of poetry militant. It is amusing but also perhaps illuminating to juxtapose two passages set in a similar landscape:

> Then, lo, in the pool of the valley,
> Cries centaur to centaur,
> As, plashing, they leap the white moonbuds
> The goddess had leant o'er.

> They climb the steep sides of the chasm
> With hollowy thunder—

> Whole cliffs at the stroke of their hoof-beats
> Split tumbling asunder!

323

> They climb the steep sides of the chasm,
> And rush through the thicket ...

and

> Then fast the centaur followed, where the gorges deep and black
> Resounded to the thunder of their tread,
> And the stockwhips woke the echoes, and they fiercely answered back
> From cliffs and crags that beetled overhead.
> And upward, ever upward, the wild horses held their way,
> Where mountain ash and kurrajong grew wide ...

The first is from McCrae's 'Fantasy', the second from Paterson's 'The Man from Snowy River'. The comparison makes clear that McCrae made no attempt to shape or transform the world in art—he simply replaced it with another world of artifice. McCrae seemed to his admirers to stand like a peak above the tepid swamps of the provincial versifying of the day, and to do this quite effortlessly, without any revolution or resistance, simply by not caring and going his own way. McCrae is a cultural fact of some significance in the history of Australian poetry. Norman Lindsay (who always over-praised his friends and disciples) wrote in *Bohemians of the Bulletin* (1965) that 'the poetry of Hugh McCrae (was) some of the greatest lyrical poetry written in the English language'.

To the modern reader it looks much simpler. McCrae who came from an artistic, cultivated Bohemian family, was indifferent to the Australian ethos of his time and in being so seemed to stand for the values of the free spirit: but it was as a transmitter of European culture in the local scene that he seemed to have most to offer. It is always attractive in a provincial or colonial culture when this can be done by an intermediary on the spot. But McCrae did not spring freshly born from the head of Athena: Daley was ahead of him; some of Brennan's work had been published, and there were other local 'cosmopolitan' versifiers who were drawing on the English writers of the nineties, with their cultural eclecticism and rifling of the cultures of the ages. 'The movement was not ... a conscious reaction against the naturalistic Australian school represented in the bush ballads ... but simply a parallel movement of the period.' One of the attractions of McCrae for the young of the time was that where others participated in both traditions, McCrae opted simply for the one.

Eclecticism of subject matter is McCrae's striking characteristic. His poetic world, like that of Art Nouveau, is full of satyrs, centaurs, unicorns, fauns and nymphs. He draws on the world of Greek myth, the medieval past, particularly through the Scottish border ballad and the French middle ages; he appropriates a Watteau-like vision of the eighteenth century, full of columbines and pierrots, filtered through the English poets who adopted them from Verlaine—particularly Ernest Dowson, to whom McCrae owes so much. He also dabbles in Asiatic themes with his own kind of chinoiserie or japonaiserie. There is some unity in fantasy in the sources of his subjects and imagery: they are nearly all set in the past or in some imagined world. One can understand why McCrae seemed to bring a wholly new note into Australian poetry. His airy-fairy confections are at the opposite extreme from O'Dowd's dogmatic assertiveness and cult of myth. Technically the poems are rhythmically simple and formally unadventurous: McCrae tends to focus on a moment of sensation and nothing more. There is no sense of involvement with the outside world at all and not much sense of a private, individual life: all the important historical events of his time are ignored, with the possible exception of one later and jocular reference to Hitler. McCrae creates an imaginative world outside of time, in a cultural void, and the language he uses contributes much to this effect as in 'The Watchers':

> We sat beside the water
> And we saw the ringdoves fly
> Against the cloudy castles
> Of the Genie in the sky ...
>
> They went into the distance,
> Through faded flower and tree,
> Like thin transparent phantoms,
> On an ancient tapestry.

His consistent artificiality can lead him to use pastiche Scottish dialects or Elizabethan English, and this pervasive, ingrained habit affects his language sense in other poems. His ear was never as good as his friends claimed; his language sense is limited. He was simply not in touch with the spoken language of his day. There is no sense of the living vernacular in his work, only of artificial constructs, as in 'Spring':

Now doth the devil, laughing, prance,
To feel his bride, the spring,
Become, with many a sidelong glance,
Again his own sweet thing.

And, even man beyond his prime,
A day's march off the grave,
Walks backward in this joyous time . . .
To look, and laugh, and wave.

His poetry as a whole shows no development and is often incomplete and fragmentary, relying on suggestions and a surfeit of suspension points. In the Australia of his time he was able to go a long way on very little. Discerning anthologists will be able to find an unexpected poem among his works to represent him by, such as 'Down the Dim Years', 'Fragment', or 'Evening', but he is well represented by the songs for which he is best known: 'Columbine', 'Fantasy', 'I blow my pipes', 'Song for Pierrot', the vivid image of the centaurs in 'Ambuscade' or the technically clever and almost parodic 'The Mimshi Maiden',

His delicate artifice has its appeal; but even Judith Wright, who has written so appreciatively of McCrae's charms and delights, observes that his poetry 'has not the weight of meaning to attach itself to life'. McCrae's three main themes are nature, time and love; and it is only in the treatment of sensual love that the resonance of an individual voice is sometimes discernible under all the decorative arabesques which make up the surface of McCrae's poetry. This is noticeable not only in direct statements of the love theme, 'The End of Desire', 'Old Satyr', 'Lament', and 'Sensual Love', but also in the nature poems, where an erotic treatment of the theme produces more original and unified imagery than the rendering of nature into tapestry which is often typical of McCrae:

How tenderly the evening creeps between
The fading curtain of this apple-bough,
A ghost of rose and grey, mid foliage green
Jewelled with stripes of rain.

Ah, look where now,
Trembling, but joyous, like a challenged bride,
The moon, along a bed of daffodil,
Opens a cloud against her golden side . . .
As one expectant of her Lord's sweet will.

Since his death, Brennan has been the subject of more books and tributes than any other twentieth century Australian poet. His work has inspired some of the best examples of criticism and exegesis devoted to an Australian, and he has continued to exert a long-range influence and fascination on continuing generations of scholars, intellectuals and writers. The man whose life ended in a sense of tragic waste and failure has since had a building named after him in the University from which he was dismissed; scholars have re-assembled the books he owned; scattered poems and fugitive pieces of prose have been gathered together. He has become a cultural hero. His posthumous reputation is still continuing to grow.

Brennan looms large in the Australian literary landscape. His impact came through his formidable scholarship and learning, his intellectual capacity: he knew French, German, Italian, Greek and Latin in their literatures and languages: he made significant contributions to Greek textual scholarship, and to philosophical thinking: his papers on symbolism and romanticism are still among the most important contributions on these topics. For all his apparent isolation in the Australia of his time, he seemed to put the country on the intellectual map of the world, and at one stage to represent the European tradition in Australia, to stand for intellectual maturity and power, and cosmopolitan values against the more naive outpourings of the literary nationalists, the bush bards and the genteel jinglers. Like most Australian writers Brennan has been both over-rated and under-rated. The claims for him as a poet and scholar have been pitched rather high at times: the reasons for this would require a more detailed analysis and critique of Australian literary culture than can be undertaken here; suffice it to say that Brennan compares favourably with other literary scholars of his time, like A. E. Housman, Arthur Symons and John Addington Symonds, whose careers bore in part some resemblance to his and all of whom, like Brennan, lived under special social and psychological tensions.

The reaction among some younger writers and critics has been correspondingly severe and intemperate. We can probably only start to get Brennan into some kind of perspective if we begin from the fact that he was an Australian poet writing in English from the 1890s to the First World War and that he belongs ineluctably to the English poetry of the nineties, which had a considerable impact on a number of other Australian writers of his generation. Brennan, like Daley, would fit quite easily into a collection like R. K. R. Thornton's *Poetry of the Nineties*, and his work, with some minor adjustments for the colonial Australian background, could take its place perfectly well under the headings Thornton provides: 'All the Arts', 'The Hound of Heaven', 'Love and Death', 'Fire from France', 'The Roses Fall'. Brennan's work is saturated in period diction and iconography: all the stock *fin de siècle* words occur: roses, stars, pale and dim, old, grey and weary, dream, sorrow and passion: and various period influences can be felt, beginning with Rossetti and Pater through to Yeats and the heavy influence of Arthur Symons on 'The Wanderer' and the 'Epilogues'. Like most of the other poets of the era of Art Nouveau, he was greatly influenced by French poets, especially Baudelaire and Mallarmé, but also by Nerval and several other figures from Hérédia and Kahn to Henri de Régnier. He is, to my knowledge, the only poet of his epoch to have been genuinely and extensively influenced in the texture of his verse and his sense of syntax by Mallarmé's poetry—which says much for his considerable assimilative and appropriative powers, though Brennan lacks Mallarmé's exquisite musical ear and his delicate, tactful wit. Brennan was much influenced by all aspects of the Symbolist movement, but like the other poets of his epoch he stands on the threshold of modernism rather than fully participating in it. At times he seems to anticipate Pound and Eliot in his use of myth and literary allusion. His poetic diction was not as outmoded in his day as some critics have claimed: many of the archaisms he uses can be found in the early work of Pound, for instance. But in the last resort, he must be judged to be more backward looking than forward looking. His work is inextricably embedded in a past tradition rather than opening towards future developments. The date in the title of his major work *Poems (1913)* (not published until December 1914) thus seems curiously and significantly emblematic. It is generally agreed that the Great War changed Europe and the modern mind profoundly, and while poets like Pound, Eliot, Yeats and Rilke went on to develop and renew their poetry in unprecedented ways after 1914, Brennan's work as a poet was virtually finished before the War began. Even the few poems he wrote later are shaped in the diction and style he had formed before the turn of the century, and show no new developments or change.

Two main points need to be kept in mind about Brennan's *Poems (1913)*: they are the work of a young man (the bulk of his poetry had been written by the age of 33) and they are still one of the most ambitious and original undertakings in the history of Australian poetry. That Brennan is an imperfect writer seems to me to be clear; there is some gap between his intention, as we can discern it, and his achievement. And this is borne out, paradoxically enough, by those critics who take the intention for the deed. That he did not have a sure knowledge of his own powers is one of the themes he explores and embodies, particularly in 'The Twilight of Disquietude'. It has been said that what we call genius in art is an inner consistency, an extreme fidelity to impressions, which comes instinctively to reject all that has not been truly observed and felt: and that the lack of this consistency results in a spoiled and flawed talent. Most readers, I think, have this sense of something flawed in Brennan's work, though the reasons given vary from critic to critic. Several recent studies have demonstrated that Brennan is much more conscious and consistent than many have realised. But such writings, often flawless performances themselves, remind one of a master pianist interpreting perfectly a piece of music: at the end of the performance one says yes, perfectly played—it couldn't be better, but it is Rachmaninoff, not Mozart or Beethoven, who has provided the score. Recent examples of French structuralist criticism have shown that it is possible to demonstrate the perfect unity and interior consistency of a novel by Balzac which everyone agrees is one of his minor, less impressive works. The attempts to prove the structuralist perfection of certain sections of *Poems (1913)* may not be a service to Brennan in the long run; they give the impression, and scholarship proves, that *Poems (1913)* were built up slowly like an overworked and highly wrought mosaic. (There seem to be similarities between Brennan's sense of style and Henry Handel Richardson's —and the many features and qualities these two writers have in common could well be pursued further.) A greater service is done to Brennan by admitting his imperfections, by stressing his incompleteness, and by trying to account for his undeniable force, which continues and endures in spite of these limitations.

Brennan has a persisting power. There is the sense that the whole of *Poems (1913)* is greater than the sum of its parts, even that its flaws may be inextricably bound up with its enduring strengths. Writing of *Poems (1913)* when Brennan's *Verse* was first published,

329

in 1960, I said that it seemed to me like a magnificent ruin, with the whole plan visible but only a few sections still intact. I would add now that some ruins can be more significant to us, can possess a greater power over the mind and imagination than some more complete and perfect achievements.

What is the source of Brennan's impressiveness? First, it stems from his attempt to unite the various elements of *Poems (1913)* into a concerted whole. Brennan states clearly that he aimed to arrange *Poems (1913)* into a unity and it is to be read as a single work. The whole has a clearly delineated architecture with a firm external structure, divided into five main parts, 'Towards the Source' (1894–1897) 'The Forest of Night' (1898–1902) 'The Wanderer' (1902–   ) and 'Pauca Mea' and the 'Epilogues'. Each is bound together by the sense of a quest, of a search for self-fulfilment and transcendence, a search to recover an Eden vision, a lost perfection, or to regain what A. E. Housman, another nineties poet, called the land of lost content. Brennan is a more ambitious poet than Housman: aware of the imperative dominance of subjective moods in the individual life, Brennan nevertheless restlessly strove to move beyond the vagaries of experience into an exploration and explanation of their cause and reason, and so wrote a myth poem centred on Lilith who both reflects and explains man's frustrations and aspirations. But the structure of *Poems (1913)*, as well as being firmly external, is also intimate and internal, and in the symbolist sense, musical. Brennan wrote to Brereton in February 1898, '... I try to catch the harmonies of things, so that if you lift a thread you shake the whole veil.'

Poems (1913) is written as a *livre composé* in an ordered sequence, and like *Les Fleurs du Mal* has its own 'unity and secret architecture' embracing 'a whole imaginative life and experience'. Like other symbolists, Brennan knew how the physical and visual presentation of a work can contribute to its structure. G. A. Wilkes points out that:

> As Brennan conceived the art of the *livre composé*, there was a significance in the typography employed, in the placing of the poems on the page, and even in a page left blank ... Two different type-faces are employed, to distinguish levels in the action: the verses in bold face either have the function of commentary ... or else serve as 'interludes' and 'epigraphs' linking one phase to the next.[6]

In his awareness of the importance of the visual presentation of his poems Brennan again shows how much he learnt from Baudelaire and Mallarmé about the total impact of a work of art.

There are recurring motifs, phrases, tones, tunes almost, which echo and re-echo each other; there are important recurrent images—images of dawn and dusk (*fin de siècle* in mode and origin, but given a peculiar individuality in the cycle), images of night and the stars, the wind and the sea; keys and gates; the desert and the forest; jewels and roses; gold and darkness; seasons and historical epochs, and throughout, images of separation and loss, often experienced at moments suggesting intimacy and wholeness, and played off against images of conscious rejection and refusal. A line of Mallarmé's—'nuit, désespoir et pierrerie'—might well serve as an epigraph for the central sections. *Poems (1913)* is not only one of the most considerable of night poems, it is also a poem about rejection, loss and suffering. The myth of Lilith is an attempt to explain the Fall from a state of primal unity, but the experience of *Poems (1913)* is a personal one of alienation, isolation and separation, and the attempt to overcome and transcend them through understanding.

There are contrasting rhythms of moods throughout and a progression from one state to another, sometimes in the same poem. The unity of *Poems (1913)* is intellectual—a matter of arrangement and sequence—but it is experienced aesthetically and organically rather than schematically, so that repeated readings always yield up a new image or motif whose full appeal one had not noticed before. G. A. Wilkes wrote: '*Poems (1913)* has not two themes or three or four; it has one theme only—the quest for Eden.' Brennan was familiar with Neo-Platonic, Hermetic and alchemical writing and pressed this learning into service in his poem to show all the ramifications, the turnings and returnings involved in the pursuit of self-knowledge. The loss of his religious faith in early manhood and during the period when his poems were written was probably the most significant intellectual event in his life, and the whole of *Poems (1913)* may be seen as a desperate attempt to explain his loss of faith and to fill the void it created. Brennan himself said that he could not 'conceive of poetry otherwise than as an expression of the religious instinct' and that art, poetry included, is necessarily an expression of the religious instinct since it is 'a mediator between us and our perfection ... a prefiguration of the final harmony ...'

331

Brennan's ambition is visible in the structure of the whole poem which shows how uneasily he moved between the old and the new in late nineteenth century poetry. He clearly had an epic ambition as his use of the Lilith myth, and the verse mould into which he cast it indicates; but he knew that he was writing at a time when, in his own words, 'the necessity for, or the possibility of, epic or poetic drama ... seem(ed) to have exhausted themselves,' and when the tendencies of the time were pointing towards the *livre composé*, 'a new ideal of the concerted poem in many movements.' He knew that the long poem was disappearing and that a full scale modern work would have to be composed of sequences of short poems. But Brennan needed the support of sustained structures and a conceptual scheme and was not prepared to abandon them entirely. The Lilith poems with their harsh, acrid power, and their taut couplets extended over drawn-out and complex verse paragraphs, are the centre of *Poems (1913)*, the vertebral column of the whole work, and they give it its enduring, impressive force. Lilith is not an allegorical figure, she is a dramatic presence in the poem, the cause of man's longing for certitude and a symbol of his incertitude. From another point of view Lilith can be seen as the Muse of symbolism itself, both a brooding presence and a haunting absence. 'We use poetry', Brennan wrote, 'to express not the perfect beauty, but our want of it, our aspiration towards it.'

Brennan's *Poems (1913)* is the record of an hermetic search for

> ... the word
> that shall become the deed of might
> whereby the sullen gulfs are stirr'd
> and stars begotten on their night.

—a search for the knowledge and power by which fallen man will recover his original Eden state: 'The voyage through oneself toward self'. In 'Towards the Source' Brennan records how man longs for his original unfallen state. His 'paradisal instinct' is frustrated in the modern city. 'Ah, who will give us back our long-lost innocence/and tremulous blue within the garden?' he asks. 'Then rise and seek for aye the garden that we knew.' In this section images of constriction and confinement and a sense of being sullied and soiled, are balanced against images suggesting freedom, spaciousness and an apocalyptic cleansing. He declares that everything is in the seeking:

Psyche! our feet are set towards the eastern star,
our eyes upon the spaces of the morning air;
what tho' the garden goal shine o'er sad seas afar,
tho' young hope guide us not, our soul shall not despair.

Enough, we shall have dream'd that solitary emprise,
enough, we shall have been true to our austere thought,
that, if we ne'er behold with longing human eyes
our paradise of yore, sister, we shall have sought.

All man's achievements are part of the attempt to recover Eden. Art, science, power, religion, the works of civilization—these are Eden substitutes; and only the enlightened few know that Eden is the real goal that man is seeking. Similarly, sexual love is our attempt to recover paradise. Many of the poems in 'Towards the Source' are on the theme of nuptial expectation, longing and disillusionment, and are open to the biographical interpretations often given to them by commentators; but already in this section there are intimations of the presence of Lilith. Not all the poems are of equal artistic success, whatever their place in the larger structure. In some there are occasions where the language lapses, where form and content are out of step, as in the rather ponderous 'Prelude'. Frank Kermode once commented:

> Too often in these poems one sees the metal of a distinguished imagination run off into banal moulds, and always, of course, with a reduction of that very complexity of effect for which Brennan was trying.[7]

But even in these relatively youthful pieces there are signs of the qualities of the true poet, uncertain, tremulous, grappling with an enormous theme which often remains the subject that the language is talking about, rather than being embodied in it.

The power of the poem is in its core 'The Forest of Night'. None of the main sections of Brennan's work opens well, and 'The Forest of Night' is no exception, although the opening sonnets and 'Liminary' have an important place in the structure. But 'The Twilight of Disquietude', which immediately follows, is extraordinarily impressive in its time and the whole section has a cumulative strength as Brennan presses more closely on his main theme, the restoration of Eden, the desire to penetrate and explore the unknown.

Lilith is a complex and powerful symbol, a figure of man's fallen state, associated with night (the Lady of Night), who keeps man out of Paradise, but reunited to him could restore him to his original state. In Jewish legend she was Adam's first mate, and the original fall of man occurred when Adam forsook her and took Eve as his wife. Lilith is a monumental, ambivalent figure, cast in the form of the *femme fatale* of the Romantic Agony: La Belle Dame Sans Merci, Keats' Lamia and Moneta, she almost certainly derives directly from Rossetti's sonnet 'Lilith', and 'Eden Bower', where Rossetti associates her with roses and poppies, two of the guiding motif images throughout Brennan's cycle. To fallen man, Lilith is a forceful source of attraction and fear. Lilith seeks reunion with man, who longs to be reunited with her, but this is the tragic impasse that the poem presents, for Adam still loves Eve. Lilith is a magnificent obsession, and there is justification in these sections for judging *Poems (1913)* to be a profoundly frustrating poem about frustration.

Lilith is not a simple allegorical figure, but she has the magnetic power to draw to herself clusters of meanings. In one sense she is so inclusive a symbol that she almost loses any precise meaning; she suggests almost everything from the Absolute to aspects of the divided self. Professor Chisholm has said that 'Lilith is a symbol for a faith that Brennan lacks, a faith that he is desperately trying to forge for himself so that it can make up for the loss of his Edens.' However we look at her, the power of this section stems from the way Lilith resists allegorical formulation, and the way she suggests the impasse of the modern mind; union with her would represent the regaining of the paradisal state, but Brennan presents the numbing reality of the Lilith experience: she is a memory of a state of perfection once known and now lost, a vision of the fulfilment that might yet be achieved. Man's agony arises from this sense of being locked in an impasse.

'The Wanderer' marks a change of mood through its more relaxed rhythms, which are greatly indebted to the poetry of Arthur Symons. 'The Wanderer' represents the unconquered impulses of man, who realises that his search may have no immediate goal or success but who is determined to seek and not to yield. The restless surging movement of the verse, the forceful imagery of sea and wind suggest the spirit of unsatisfied striving amidst conflict, the resistance to the impasse and stasis met in the Lilith sequence. It is a unified section of its own, and if the Wanderer does not quite have the dimension of Lilith as a mythical figure, this is because it is too easily associated with

334

fin-de-siècle moods and modes and because the Wanderer takes on perhaps a little too readily, romantic notions of the alienated or frustrated artist—or the *poète maudit*—and his place—or failure to find a place—in society. If Lilith represents the Absolute, the Wanderer is forced to recognize, in the progression of the series that bears his name, that there are no absolutes, that attitudes are often assumed and discarded, and that relative negatives play a profound role in life. The gradual realization of this brings the Wanderer to his sense of self-knowledge and feedom, his recognition of his own humanity, and gives 'Pauca Mea' and the 'Epilogues' their calculated place in the harmony of the whole. The Wanderer is initially caught in the same impasse as Adam with Lilith: there seems to be no way back and no way forward. He can either hold on to the past, the familiar and the routine, or escape into the perilous freedom of the wind and the sea or succumb to a drifting mood of helpless defeatism. He has to realise and accept that there is 'no ending of the way, no home, no goal'. The Wanderer compares himself with the folk: he pities them and insists on the isolated superiority of his own self-knowledge; he admonishes them for their servility.

The Wanderer in his mood of wondering desolation reflects on the nature of heroic quest and achievement. Using images from *The Twilight of the Gods* and *The Song of Roland*, he sees his past life as a battle with absolute forces, the eternal foe, and hopes, if not for final victory ('in some last fight'), then at least 'that last hope of a glory won in defeat'. The Wanderer can hope for no fixed certainties in a world of absolutes, only 'the courage to front the way', the peace that comes from accepting the knowledge that there can be 'no ending of the way, no home, no goal':

> I am the wanderer of many years
> who cannot tell if ever he were king
> or if ever kingdoms were: I know I am
> the wanderer of the ways of all the worlds,
> to whom the sunshine and the rain are one
> and one to stay or hasten, because he knows
> no ending of the way, no home, no goal,
> and phantom night and the grey day alike
> withhold the heart where all my dreams and days
> might faint in soft fire and delicious death:
> and saying this to myself as a simple thing
> I feel a peace fall in the heart of the winds
> and a clear dusk settle, somewhere, far in me.

There can be no permanent home, no resting in absolutes, in myth or history. It is when the Wanderer finally realises his own humanity that the pretences of his heroic pride and vanity and ambition fall aside. The precarious peace realized in the last lines of the poem is felt by the Wanderer in a moment of rare self-knowledge and understanding, and gives a note of poignant resignation to the whole. It represents a moment of achieved integrity, when all the aspirations and conflicts of the Wanderer's divided self are brought into union and a sense of balance and harmony is achieved, if only momentarily.

'Pauca Mea' and the 'Epilogues' are not mere summings-up, but integral parts of the whole, further stages on the way. 'Pauca Mea', a group of four poems, expresses disillusion, self-pity, and inner misery only to reject them as insufficient in a mood of self-admonishment. The two Epilogues, dated 1897 and 1908, review the whole of *Poems (1913)*. 1897 was the year of Brennan's marriage and of the appearance of *XXI Poems: Towards the Source*, and in the first Epilogue he reconsiders his early ambitions and aspirations, his sense of isolation and proud difference from the crowd or folk. The Epilogue of 1908 reviews his position at the end of the whole undertaking that *Poems (1913)* records. In 1908 Brennan was appointed to the University of Sydney and the poem is set in a precise cityscape, the spire of St. Benedict's Church and the tower of the University in the distance, both images of the two institutions that had marked and formed him most. He sees the crowd ('the folk' of the earlier poems) and now feels some sense of identification with them. In looking back over his past, his lapse from the Church, his intellectual development, he states that Eden was once his but the experience was momentary, a promise more than a possession, a state of being rather than of having. While the poem records a sense of diminished pretensions and a recognition that in spite of his greater awareness he is a 'fellow pilgrim' with the 'listless captives of the street', it nevertheless ends on a paradoxical note of election and pride, of being above 'the shoal of shiftless lives'. Self-dedication is the theme: and there is a note of subdued defiance and refusal to be merely one of the crowd:

> and many an evening hour shall bring
> the dark crowd's dreary loitering
> to me who pass and see the tale
> of all my striving, bliss or bale,

dated from either spire that strives
clear of the shoal of shiftless lives,
and promise, in all years' despite,
fidelity to old delight.

Brennan has not been an easy poet for Australians to come to terms with. It has been said that he belongs to European rather than Australian poetry, but he is very much a poet of his time, and reflects many of its cultural conditions and tensions. His background was metropolitan rather than rural or urban like Neilson's; his learning drew on cosmopolitan sources. Part of Brennan's fascination for Australians springs from his metropolitanism, and he is in fact the first significant metropolitan poet Australia produced. In the sense in which one critic can say that 'Lawson's bush stories capture the sparse dryness of Australia in summer' it is true to say that Brennan's *Poems (1913)* capture the experience of metropolitan life in a major Australian city at the turn of the century. Many poets of Brennan's time wrote about the differences between the city and the bush; only Brennan embodied metropolitan and cosmopolitan experience in his poems.

There is much in Brennan's work, which has been the subject of unprecedented study for an Australian poet, to stimulate and encourage the scholarly mind. But when the limitations of exegesis are admitted, as well as the justice of the most trenchant criticisms that have been made against him—his pedantry, unevenness and obscurity—the impressiveness remains. *Poems (1913)* is a powerful period piece which transcends the limits of its period. It has a desperate seriousness and honesty, and it is (with Neilson's best lyrics) the only poem written in Australia at the time that has the qualities of an aesthetic creation and therefore a continuing life of its own. But what is strange about Brennan— and it is one of the many reasons why he continues to fascinate critics (he will not go away and he cannot be tamed into perfection)—is that for all his myth making and use of impersonal modes, the evocation of literary tradition and the deployment of artifice in the attempt to distance his poems from immediate experience, it is the agonising personal element, the passion and frustration, the spiritual restlessness and aspiration in *Poems (1913)* which account for their power more than their success as intellectual constructs and patterns.

337

Noel Macainsh, himself a poet and a Brennan scholar, has summed up the present position in regard to Brennan in Australia:

Brennan's *Poems (1913)* may appear to some critics to be a gloomy, late-Victorian monument, a great, dark, deserted hall, a *fin de siècle* ruin verbally stuccoed in part with faded diction and absurd syntax, but it is also showing itself to be a kind of labyrinthine, self-renewing palace of mirrors where repeated visitors find their own humanity multiply reflected down shifting perspectives on Western culture, unsettling these visitors and prompting them to seek for the firm ground that lies beyond the questions, Who are we? Where have we been? In an age of television, this great House-of-Analogy is a paradox and lives by it. But, to quote Brennan himself: 'as I have said before, paradox is the most natural thing going.'[8]

Shaw Neilson is the most surprising of all Australian poets and in some ways his life and poetry are still the most moving. What most strikes is the contrast between the circumstances of his life and the quality and qualities of his poetry. This singer of delicate songs, one of the most sensitive of Australian poets, had one of the most difficult and unpropitious lives. It is the contrast between the nature of his life and the quality of his work that makes him in his own unemphatic way 'one of the masters of the human spirit'— though how inappropriate Hope's assertive and commanding phrase seems when applied to Neilson. It is no accident that recent Australian poets like Judith Wright and James McAuley in their search for simplicity have drawn inspiration from Neilson and that recent Australian painters like Charles Blackman have been moved to re-create aspects of his poetry. Neilson is not just an historical figure, he is also a presence and a part of a living tradition.

Neilson had a hard life and came of a line of battlers. He was born at Penola in South Australia, 22 February 1872; his parents were of Scottish descent. His father, a small farmer and contractor, also wrote poetry and encouraged his son to become a poet. In contrast to his contemporary Christopher Brennan, Neilson had little formal education. But he was one of those on whom nothing is lost and he seemed to know instinctively what could nourish and enrich his art. His knowledge of poetry was probably much wider than is realized. He had an inborn gift for poetry and an imaginative power that transfigured and transcended the circumstances of his life. Seen from the outside, Minimay may have been an arid and discouraging place for his family to farm a selection, but Neilson recalled later in 'The Poor, Poor Country':

My riches all went into dreams that never yet came
    home,
They touched upon the wild cherries and the slabs
    of honey-comb,
They were not of the desolate brood that men can sell
    or buy,
Down in that poor country no pauper was I.

Not only did Neilson's family struggle hopelessly against eroding poverty for years on a selection in the Mallee, but their life was marked by ill health, early deaths and finally defeats as the family was gradually driven off the land. Neilson's sight began to fail in 1905, and from then on he had to dictate his poems for others to write down. Neilson spent most of the rest of his life as a casual manual labourer, working on the roads, in railways and quarries; he worked for a time fruit-picking (grape picking he liked 'The mass of green foliage ... seemed to benefit (his) eyes very much', he told James Devaney later). In the early twenties Neilson met some of the literary figures of the period who had already become interested in his work; he met A. G. Stephens for the first time in 1926—though Stephens had been handling his work for many years before this. Through the influence of literary friends he became a messenger (he was already over fifty) in the main office of the Country Roads Board in Melbourne but the conditions of city life were oppressive to him. His *Collected Poems*, edited by R. H. Croll, was published in 1934. By 1941 his heart was obviously failing; he spent four months in Brisbane at the home of James Devaney, who wrote an important and moving memoir of him, but finally returned to Melbourne, where he died on 12 May 1942. Since his death and the wider publication of his poetry, his reputation has continued to grow. He now stands with his contemporary Brennan, who also started writing in the nineties, as the foremost poet of his generation.

In spite of his limited schooling, Neilson came of a literate family, and though he was not as widely read as Brennan he knew some of the work of Shelley, Coleridge, Scott, Burns, Thomas Hood, Tennyson and Kipling. He knew some old Irish and Scottish songs, as well as the popular drawing-room songs and ballads of his day. The names of Blake and Traherne are frequently used in connection with Neilson; he reminds one at times of Clare, Davies and Verlaine. But Neilson's greatest influences and affinities were the more popular sources of inspiration. The beautiful poem 'The Sweetening of the Year' has always seemed to me to owe something to the nursery rhyme 'There was a man of double deed,' and one can find a gnomic touch in parts of Neilson, reminiscent of nursery rhymes, riddles and proverbs. He also frequently reminds one of the Victorian writers of album verses or the composers of Victorian parlor songs, as for instance in 'Inland Born'. There is always more direct sentiment in Neilson than in traditional rhymes and songs; it is significant that he has a poem addressed to Stephen Foster. There were local as well as imported and inherited influences. Neilson and his father read *The Bulletin* and knew and admired the work of Banjo Paterson, Lawson and Ogilvie, whom he accused of conceit. His remarks about other writers were always perceptibly individual, and given the nature of those which he made to Devaney about Wilmot and T. S. Eliot, for instance, he was obviously in touch with what was going on around him. One cannot help feeling that Neilson had a way of picking up information which he made intuitively his own and it is not unlikely that he absorbed some information about Rimbaud and Verlaine in his own unique way. Neilson was confidently aware of himself as a poet, of his poetic calling: apart from the jobs which he undertook to support himself, the whole of his life was dedicated to the writing of poetry. Anyone who looks at some of his variants, fragments, rejections and rewritings, will become aware of how conscious and conscientious a craftsman he was. But his work needs sifting.

Some of his weaknesses are obvious. And it is as well to mention these limitations first, because the source of a poet's strengths is often intimately related to the source of his weaknesses. The bulk of Neilson's work consists of songs and lyrics and his real variety lies in the differences of tone between poems rather than in variety of forms. With this rather restricted formal range goes an over-reliance on repetitions and repeated stanzas. At their best, these repetitions can give the poem a sense of rounded, self-contained completion, a moment of perception held in a rhythmic trance. At their weakest they tend not to reinforce but to dissipate the total impact of individual poems. Cecil Hadgraft once declared that 'no worse service could be done to Neilson than to read his poems at one sitting; for the lack of substance then becomes evident.' One might want to express this rather differently, but it is a salutary warning because the less achieved poems can suffuse the work at times with a certain muffled languor.

No one will question Neilson's delicacy of ear at his finest; his poems do not jar, they only rarely fail in tone when he is sentimental, or imprecise in phrasing. His weakness is rather a certain visual smudging, a melodious melting and merging. In his less successful poems his images neither focus nor fuse; we are left with a mellifluous blur. Neilson lacked a sound constructive technique: where his vision fails him he has hardly any external strengths to fall back on. But one makes these criticisms with considerable hesitation because Neilson is not the kind of poet who should be boiled down to his best pieces. Even poems which do not cohere as wholes often contain impressive images, stanza fragments, or a combination of words of a strange unexpectedness or profundity. But plush and pathos of the *fin-de-siècle* kind do not wear well, and both can be found occasionally in Neilson.

Several critics have commented on the circularity of Neilson's poems. Judith Wright has stated that the form of his poems was largely dictated by his necessity to keep them in his head until they could be written down. She writes 'often Neilson begins with a statement of the theme in the first verse, followed by variations and repetitions, with the last verse possibly repeating the first, or at least recurring to it, so that the poem is circular in its motion'. 'Tis the White Plum Tree' is a clear illustration of this, though the same movement can be found in 'Love's Coming', 'Song be Delicate', 'The Girl with the Black Hair', 'Schoolgirls Hastening', 'You, and Yellow Air', 'The Crane is my Neighbour' and many others.

Sometimes the sense of circularity arises from the situation of the poem, where a human figure like the girl in 'The Orange Tree' or the bird in 'The Crane is My Neighbour' is concentrated in a centre of awareness or thought, drawing intimations to itself. The circularity is then less a question of the structure than of the image associations of the poem. Such poems are like the ripples on the surface of a pool, suggesting hidden depths. 'The Hour of the Parting', one of Neilson's best poems, will serve to illustrate this point:

> Shall we assault the pain?
> It is the time to part:
> Let us of Love again
> Eat the impatient heart.
>
> There is a gulf behind
> Dull voice and fallen lip,

The blue smoke of the mind,
The gray light on the ship.

Parting is of the cold
That stills the loving breath,
Dimly we taste the old
The pitiless meal of Death.

Neilson's poetry is grounded in the great commonplaces of the lyric. His principal subjects are spring, love, life, time, birth and death. Often a poem rises out of the traditional ideas associated with proverbs or everyday sayings, picking up by a process of suggestion related images or accruing impressions. Behind the poem 'The Hour of the Parting' is the old saying that to part is to die a little, *'partir c'est un peu mourir'*, that to experience separation is to have a foretaste, an awareness of death. There are two main groups of images in this poem: one associated with eating, the other with a voyage, the sense of going into the unknown. In the first stanza there is the pain of departure, the determination to snatch what one can from the moment. In the second stanza the emphasis is on the shared but unspoken sense of desolation and separation:

There is a gulf behind
Dull voice and fallen lip,
The blue smoke of the mind,
The gray light on the ship.

In the last stanza ('dimly' is often associated with death in Neilson's poetry) parting is a foretaste of death, which is the final word that the poem comes to rest on. It is not unreasonable, I think, to find in this poem submerged references to, or rather overtones suggesting, the Last Supper. There is the feeling of a meal being sacramentally shared, ending in inevitable separation and death, the sense that this meal together may be the last. It is part of the strange power of this small poem, and characteristic of Neilson's work at its best, that it is able to generate such associative images in the reader's mind without making them fully explicit. The religious overtones, and the sense of piety and reverence ('Beauty imposes reverence in the spring') in many of Neilson's poems would seem to justify this reading.

Neilson is certainly in an important sense a religious poet. He reacted against the strict Presbyterianism of his childhood 'it was a hard, hard religion. I know now that those old ideas of God and man that we had were all wrong.' But he never lost his belief in 'a Creator of the Universe' whatever he thought of organized religion, and he seems to have been critical of the Salvation Army's effect on his mother and sister. His was an undogmatic mind; and though he remained tentative in his beliefs ('I'd like to believe in a future life, but I don't know'), the religious note, and metaphysical and philosophical implications are present in all that he wrote.

One of the basic situations in his poetry is the moment of communion, intimacy or rapt contemplation often leading to a revelation of some kind—whether the girl with 'the orange tree' or a 'courtly crane' in 'The Gentle Water Bird'—or to a sense of the sacramental as in 'The Poor Can Feed the Birds'.

> But 'tis the poor who make the loving words.
> Slowly they stoop; it is a Sacrament:
> The poor can feed the birds.
>
> Old, it is old, this scattering of the bread,
> Deep as forgiveness, or the tears that go
> Out somewhere to the dead.
>
> The feast of love, the love that is the cure
> For all indignities—it reigns, it calls,
> It chains us to the pure ...
>
> Still will the poor go out with loving words;
> In the long need, the need for happiness
> The poor can feed the birds.

The sense of sharing may be fragmentary and partial; even if it is complete Neilson never forgets life's negatives. 'Along a River', a poem so completely true to its mood of a filled and shared moment, ends:

> Across the stream, slowly and with much shrinking
> Softly a full-eyed wallaby descends
> To the blue water's edge ... I see him drinking ...
> And he and I and all his folk are friends.

But the stanza is preceded by another which registers the sense of threat, and latent hostility in nature. The sense of distances overcome, of differences observed and transcended, is what gives the poem its final unity. Nothing is violated, there is no trespassing, but 'across the stream' something is truly shared.

Neilson's poetry touches on the enigmas and mysteries of life, not on problems that can be solved. It is a gently questioning art of

343

invocation and evocation. Questions and question-marks are frequent, his tone is never assertive but it conveys a constant sense of the unity of all life and inter-relationship of things. But while his art is evocative rather than descriptive, his evocation is always grounded in the particulars of emotionally heightened observation. Images of light and innocence recur (threatened innocence is one of his major themes); the words 'holy' and 'divine' are frequently used; there is a pervasive sense that all things in the created world reflect the existence of God. But Neilson's is not a naively celebrant art. His poetry was disciplined, and he was an alert and conscientious craftsman. He was fully aware of the enigmas of life, that light and darkness are in perpetual dialogue, that life and death, good and evil are inseparable. His sense of the central puzzle of life is reflected in various poems, such as 'The Bloom and the Fall' ('O, riddle of the bloom and fall'), 'The Walker on the Sand' ('They all have feared the Riddler, he who planned/The reptiles/and the fishes hungry from the sea') and perhaps more completely in 'You Cannot Go Down to the Spring'.

'The green is the nest of all riddles: you cannot go down to the Spring', suggests not only the perpetual miracle of the season, but also the inexplicable sense that life is to be constantly experienced and participated in; it cannot be held or possessed. There is something appropriately riddling about the poem itself which like a number of Neilson poems sets up a network of metaphysical suggestions and is not reducible to any single one. Neilson's religious sense is pervasive, but is best examined in poems like 'Schoolgirls Hastening' in 'Heart of Spring' with its sense of resurrection and 'The Dream is Deep'. 'He Was the Christ' is one of the most explicit of Neilson's religious poems, but the poem 'The Lover Sings' might well serve as an epigraph for this aspect of Neilson's work, indeed of his work as a whole:

> Mourners move onwards from the gloom—
> Not for himself the lover sings:
> Give us, they cry, the buds, the bloom,
> The long light on our journeyings.
> Star follows star in the dull grey,
> Deep is the dark, it drinks the day:
> For very love of God he sings.

It might be true to say that love is Neilson's abiding pre-occupation. The word itself occurs in many of his poems. In

'Love's Coming' and 'Song Be Delicate', love is associated with a tender sense of love's gentleness and quietness, its unbidden presence; but in both there is a profound sense of the forces that constantly threaten love or can stifle and diminish it. Love is a spiritual value, associated with quietness and a wise passivity. Neilson perhaps more than any other Australian poet possesses 'negative capability' as Keats defined it. He is capable of 'being in uncertainties, mysteries, doubts, without any irritable reaching after fact and reason.' Love for Neilson is the still centre in his sense of the permanent, unrepetitious renewal of life, the sense that through love all is made new. Neilson's sense of love used to be compared with Hugh McCrae's to show how McCrae was the more maturely erotic of the two poets; but McCrae is rather deficient in sensitive feeling compared with Neilson, and Neilson's poems are often much more delicately erotic and sexually aware than has been allowed. In 'The Fire Unquenched' he writes:

> Love, envious Love did every conquest find:
> It burned between our eyes and we were blind . . .
>
> But Love it resteth not nor ever will:
> It hath no end, and who shall call it sire
> From out whose womb came Love that is a fire?

A poem like 'The Hen in the Bushes' balances the force of imperious instinctual maternal love against the forces of destruction, cruelty and death. 'At a Lowan's Nest', an exquisite, almost perfect poem (worth comparing from the point of view of subject matter and tone with Hope's 'Pyramis') also associates the power of maternity and love with creativity. One notices how often in Neilson love is positively defined against the forces of pride and harm to others; love is not a product of the will.

Love in Neilson's world tends to be feminine; passion tends to be male. One of his finest poems can serve to illustrate this. 'The Orange Tree' is a poem that Neilson worked on for a considerable time. It has given rise to conflicting critical interpretations and opinions, but it is a poem that is largely concerned with adolescent sexuality. It is a complex structure, a delicate balance of forces, and too much emphasis on any one element of the poem could damage its delicate fabric through over-simplification, but the poem is certainly threaded with clear sexual overtones and suggestions. It has the quality of a painting, where the girl receives something like an annunciation from the tree itself. Throughout,

345

the poem is concerned with defining a mystery, by asking questions about things known in an attempt to find out about something unknown, unknowable, or unsayable. But in every stanza the emphasis falls on some aspect of sexual love associated, as so often in Neilson with the awakening of spring: 'faltering flute', 'love in the blossoming', 'white sap', 'compulsion of the dew', 'a waste of love', 'a fluttering heart that gave/Too willingly': the implications are delicate and without emphasis, but unmistakable in their freshness and their sense of burgeoning natural impulses. In the stanzas in which she speaks the girl rejects the questions as irrelevant to her state or to her illumination. She has clearly gone beyond the questions or experiences mentioned in each stanza to another, perhaps higher, more concentrated stage as she herself becomes transfigured like the orange tree itself. There can be no key to this poem other than the work itself; but the poem continues to move the mind deeply.

There are often touches in Neilson which remind one of Shakespeare. In 'The Sweetening of the Year' this association is more direct than in many other poems. Neilson told James Devaney that in this poem, which he thought 'pretty good', he was concerned with 'the old glamour of spring over again. I think I got started on this piece after seeing a song of William Shakespeare about the spring, but I didn't know that till after'. Neilson's statement is interesting because it confirms what one senses in much of his poetry that his art while always individual has its roots in the great traditions of the lyric and that his sources combine the intensities of experience with the conscious elaborations of art. His authoritative simplicity is something he worked to achieve; it is of the art which transcends art:

> When old birds strangely-hearted strive to sing
> and young birds face the Great Adventuring:
> When manna from the Heaven-appointed trees
> bids us to banquet on divinities:
> When water-birds, half-fearing each blue thing,
> trace the blue heavens for the roving Spring:
> When school-girls listening hope and listening fear:
> They call that time the sweetening of the year.
>
> When schoolboys build great navies in the skies
> and a rebellion burns the butterflies:

Sunlight has strange conspiracies above
and the whole Earth is leaning out to Love:

When joys long dead climb out upon a tear:
They call that time the sweetening of the year.

This poem further illustrates the circularity or encompassing inclusiveness of Neilson at his best. The poem enfolds the whole of nature, beginning with the birds and finishing with the human realm. Again it is a poem about the impulses released and renewed by the coming of spring. Its couplets fall into two self-contained halves, two sentences each. 'The Sweetening of the Year' celebrates the processes of the sweetening of life, but the poem conveys the sense that it is all happening for the first time. The old birds, even though they have experienced spring before, are 'strangely-hearted'—as if this is happening for the first time for them as for the young birds who face the 'Great Adventuring'; it is like a blessing from above, associated with heavenly gifts and graces; the birds who are participating in the rite of spring seem to be searching for the very impulse which propels them; the school-girls who 'listening hope and listening fear' are aware of the new life ahead of them; schoolboys dream of adventures, and the butterflies are stirred by a self-consuming violence of life. Spring has enchanting effects of light and the whole Earth is moved by the vernal impulses towards love; those who have been full of sorrow or grief feel a new sense of joy and change. The couplets are rich and suggestive, bringing together and relating a sense of the old and the unexpected, the new and the familiar, what is above with what is below, what is inward with what is outward in a sense of inseparable unity or inter-relationship. Even the language gives a sense of linking the old with the new: Biblical images and literary allusions are combined with straightforward statements.

Neilson's ballads are important, both for their own sake and because they add another dimension to the enchanting world of the lyrics, and because they are so different from the Australian ballads which were popular at the time Neilson started to write. Neilson believed that 'The Moon Was Seven Days Down' was the best of his work in this field. It is without the moralizing of the local ballad of the time and it has a genuine ballad impersonality: the situation and the story speak for themselves and are not depersonalized. It will remind readers of Lawson's story 'The

347

Drover's Wife' and is remarkable for the way it captures and holds an element of Australian life and conveys it through a simple dramatic moment. Neilson said of the poem

> Women are superstitious about the moon. The woman I had in mind was a farmer's wife where I was working once. She was very nice, but she had a very hard life of it, and very little in life. The rest was my invention. Women do often suffer a great deal in the bush. This woman's husband was not as fine or sensitive as she was, and wouldn't notice things.[9]

Neilson frequently uses a contrast between a woman's need for another kind of life, and male indifference to any needs but those of activity and work and being absorbed in the moment. The sense of incompatible temperaments and needs is finely balanced in the poem, which communicates with rich resonance a sense of the cost in suffering and thwarted hopes which marked the lives of those who first settled the land. The grim realism is touched with a strange beauty that heightens what might well have been a fairly common event of the past into a sense of a recurrent, almost timeless tragedy. 'The Ballad of Remembrance' is about Australia's convict past; it, too, works through the effective use of dialogue and like 'The Moon Was Seven Days Down' it has some of the quality of the border ballads. In this case a local event is lifted on to a level that suggests man's inhumanity to man, and the sense of a justice that is higher than man's concept of mere law and order.

Neilson and Brennan are both remarkable for the sheer inwardness of their art and their unswerving devotion to the values of inner life at a time when most of the verse written in Australia was robustly external in its concerns or else loudly rhetorical in approach. Much in their work is period in flavour and tone, but through their individuality and their unshaken commitment to the values of art they rise above their time like islands in the stream—or perhaps more accurately like oases in the desert.

PART THREE: 1920–1960

By the end of the First World War it was clear that the ballad tradition of the nineties had exhausted itself and that it could provide no real starting point for the new generation of creative writers. The war which claimed 60,000 Australian dead produced little poetry of consequence apart from Vance Palmer's *The Camp* and Leon Gellert's *Songs of a Campaign*. The best writing of the time has been collected in J. T. Laird's excellent anthology *Other*

Banners (1971), but apart from poems by non-combatants like Nettie Palmer, J. le Gay Brereton and Shaw Neilson, the poetic response was frail and meagre. Australia produced no crop of war poets of the quality of those in England. The most impressive work was done in prose.

The nationalist aspirations of the nineties continued in the post-war novel, in the attempts of writers like Vance Palmer and Katharine Susannah Prichard and others to show that contemporary realistic fiction written about Australia could hold its own with fiction being written in England and America; but nationalism finally came to represent a constricting tradition that also needed to be demolished by the newer generation of emerging poets. The magazine *Vision* seemed to offer a new beginning to a new generation. Although only four issues appeared in 1923, it was a focal point for all the new major developments in Australian poetry until the middle of the next decade. *Vision* gave voice to Norman Lindsay's ideas as expounded in *Creative Effort* (1920), and reacted against European post-war disillusionment and defeat. But while it helped to filter some aspects of modernism into Australian poetry, Norman Lindsay himself was essentially anti-modernist and reactionary, rejecting Joyce, Lawrence, the Sitwells, Picasso and others; he called for allegiance to the great tradition of his own eclectic pantheon: Marlowe, Rubens, Catullus. The young poets associated with *Vision* all went their own different ways later, but one sentence in the 'foreword' to one of the numbers of *Vision* is significant. 'We prefer to find truth by responding to the image of beauty, to vitality of emotion'. In other words *Vision*, far from marking a really new beginning merely showed the continuation of *fin de siècle* aestheticism into the 1920s. It is no accident that Hugh McCrae should have been one of their revered figures.

Vision and Norman Lindsay were a liberating influence on the young writers associated with them, and though Lindsay's weaknesses are now apparent, especially his opinionated arrogance, in the Australia of his time he offered these young writers a high conception of art and showed that it could be a vocation to follow for its own sake. Although Norman Lindsay either did not understand or else rejected so much that was creative and valuable in his epoch, he was in search of a tradition. He opposed puritanism, colonialism, nationalism and killing conformity. It was partly through Lindsay's influence and his cultural eclecticism (which may in origin merely reflect a colonial provincial nostalgia for a high European cultural heritage or the longing for the security of hallowed values) that Slessor was gradually able to link Australia, in a handful of poems, to an existing tradition, to relate the old to the new, the local to the universal and to bridge the gap between the past and the present with form, elegance and refinement. Although Slessor's output is small yet he is the outstanding Australian poet to emerge between the two world wars, and the only one to make modern Australian poetry truly modern.

Modernism starts to enter Australian poetry by the end of the First World War. Frank Wilmot, who as a poet stood so awkwardly between the traditional and the new in his own poetic practice, was lecturing about Ezra Pound to the Melbourne Literary Club in 1918, and the pages of *The Bookfellow* and other literary magazines of the time show that the newer American poets, Wallace Stevens, Carl Sandburg, Conrad Aiken and others, were quickly known here. Melbourne writers like Frank Wilmot and Nettie Palmer were just as critical in their attacks on stultifying traditions as the *Vision* writers. In an essay on 'National Poetry' published in *Romance* (1922) Wilmot declared

> There is something baffling about modern American poetry, but there is no mystery about the poetry that is printed in Australia today. It is the last word in conventional English verse production. It is done to worn-out patterns discarded in the land of their origin. It is more conventional in form and matter than any verse now published in England by English poets.

It is a complaint that will be voiced in every decade up to the present though the wording will change to suit the times. A study of Australian literary culture shows that there has never been any lack of cultural information at any time; rather the problem has been knowing how to assimilate it and use it in an individual way. Kenneth Slessor is the first Australian poet to do this and his poetry, besides revealing some debts to Pound and Eliot and Wilfred Owen, is also full of echoes of many lesser modern writers from Amy Lowell and the Imagists to Osbert Sitwell.

Slessor stands at the head of most major developments in modern Australian verse: its thematic preoccupations with time, memory and history, its humanizing of the landscape, or using it symbolically to embody states of mind; its sardonic use of humour to question and puncture illusions. He was one of the first of modern Australian poets to write of the city, to celebrate the modern metropolis, and see in it a subject as fit for poetry as any other. He also continues that stream in Australian writing which draws on the European cultural heritage to write poems based on paintings, music and other works of art to give the imagination horizons wider than those defined by nature and landscape. But if Slessor has been able to stand through the last forty years as the poet who gave modernism its voice in Australia, this has been both through the content of his work and through his remarkable gifts for language, through the scoured cleanliness of his diction, his acute and fastidious sense of the concrete and the particular. Slessor was aware from the beginning of the fragility and fragmentation of modern life. For him there were no absolutes and poetry could not be a forum for the expression of moral certitudes or national pieties. This sense of the absurd present in the early poems of the 1920s, relates him in some ways to post-1940 French writers— especially Camus, with whom he shares a delighted sense of the beauty of the surfaces and images of life as well as a tragic aware- ness of its futility and despair. In his best poems, from the late twenties to the end of the thirties, he gives the sense of speaking from within a representative modern experience—fastidious, urban—like Eliot with touches of fatigued elegance and alerted languor—and expressing moods, feelings and states of mind which are recognizably contemporary, particularly through his awareness of patterns without overall or final design or meaning. But for all his modernism, Slessor remained in many ways a traditional and conservative poet. He brought a new expressiveness and flexibility into Australian poetry, but like Brennan, who rejected the extremes of Rimbaud, Slessor did not accept the more radical and way-out aspects of modernistic innovations. He rejected the disruption of normal syntax and punctuation, and the elimination of poetic logic which only entered Australian poetry en masse in the late sixties. A vivid sense of contemporary images expressed in the present-day idiom of a man living in a godless universe and a highly individual music and rhythm were more than sufficient for Slessor's needs.

Much has been written about Slessor; nearly every aspect of his work has been the subject of responsible and detailed investiga- tion, from the cult of the grotesque in his early work under the influence of Norman Lindsay, to his so-called nihilism in the later speculative poems—the assumed nihilism to which some earlier critics attributed his silence; the exquisite use of sound in Slessor's poetry—sound inseparable from meaning—has been studied in

351

considerable detail, while other commentators have catalogued the cultural exhibits and the period furniture to be found in Slessor's imaginary museum or listed his use of images to reveal a uniquely personal work. One thing has been overlooked: the sense of ambivalence suggesting and arising from complexity of response which gives unity and expressiveness to Slessor's work in its various aspects and phases. It is this ambivalence which accounts for the verbal liveliness and the emotional fluidity of his minuscule world. A play of opposites, a balancing of tensions—an attempt to hold the contradictory aspects of experience together—these are found throughout his work. His poetic world conveys less a spectacle or sense of the abyss as some critics have claimed (though his sense of desolation and despair should not be understated), than a sense of poised suspensions, the oscillations and dynamism of consciousness itself. 'Tentacles, not wings, are Apollo's natural members' Nabokov has claimed. The best of Slessor's poems convey something of this sense of tentacular movement, of restless groping to reconcile conflicting alternatives, tendencies and impulses.

The early poetry written under the influence of Norman Lindsay has worn better than might have been expected. Some of the subjects taken from German art and literature reflect Slessor's interest in his German background, but all are geared to reflect his Lindsayan aspiration to a fuller creative awareness of life. Small, doctrinal poems, their explicit emphasis is towards spontaneity and vitality. 'Thieves' Kitchen', 'A Surrender', 'Marco Polo' can all be read as illustrations of the Lindsay aesthetic, even of Lindsay paintings and etchings; all are attempts to escape from commonplace existence into a vision of the finer, fuller life. But through Slessor's acute awareness of paradox and ambivalence all these poems are fraught with a sense that such an escape is impossible. So 'Thieves' Kitchen', for instance, ends with a clear if feverish sense of the inevitability of death; while 'Marco Polo' registers through its tone the defeat of the aspiration it ostensibly records.

The pictorial, visual side of Slessor's poetry has been long and justly admired. What is less frequently remarked is that in these early poems sound values are even stronger than the images. Sometimes the images may be basically old and worn, even literary in origin, but the sound pattern is new. The static picture starts to shimmer.

352

The important early poem 'Winter Dawn' introduces the focussing theme of Sydney Harbour into Slessor's work:

> At five I wake, rise, rub on the smoking pane
> A port to see—water breathing in the air,
> Boughs broken. The sun comes up in a golden stain,
> Floats like a glassy sea-fruit. There is a mist everywhere,
> White and humid, and the Harbour is like plated stone,
> Dull flakes of ice. One light drips out alone,
> One bead of winter-red, smouldering in the stream,
> Quietly over the roof-tops—another window
> Touched with a crystal fire in the sun's gullies,
> One lonely star of the morning, where no stars gleam.
>
> Far away on the rim of this great misty cup,
> The sun gilds the dead suburbs as he rises up,
> Diamonds the wind-cocks, makes glitter the crusted spikes
> On moss-drowned gables. Now the tiles drip scarlet-wet,
> Swim like birds' paving-stones, and sunlight strikes
> Their watery mirrors with a moister rivulet,
> Acid and cold. Here lie those mummied Kings,
> Men sleeping in houses, embalmed in stony coffins,
> Till the Last Trumpet calls their galleries up,
> And the suburbs rise with distant murmurings.

Visually this is reminiscent of a Turner painting, with its combined sense of richness and sparseness, lavishness and economy. As in much of his work Slessor concentrates on the movement of light (itself an emblem of consciousness), pictorially presenting the shift from the first misty light of dawn to the emerging brightness and colour as the sun appears. The first stanza is tuned to words like 'glassy', 'mist', 'humid', 'dull flakes of ice' and 'the one red light', with the emphasis predominantly on muted 'f', 'm' and 'l' sounds. In the second stanza colour begins to flood the scene: 'the sun gilds the dead suburbs', 'the tiles drip scarlet wet', 'sunlight strikes/Their watery mirrors with a moister rivulet'. The sounds become sharper with 'k''s predominating (already prepared for in the muted 'touched with crystal fire' in stanza I), the sharper sound corresponding to, even enacting, the sense of a more precisely focussed scene. Such extremely subtle effects are clearly unconscious (and should be distinguished from Slessor's more deliberate and explicit experiments, as in 'Music'), coming from some deep level of the mind where sound and meaning are initially perceived as one. But their presence can be detected and analyzed; and in the present, incomplete state of our knowledge of the workings of such things, they nevertheless remain as guarantees of the imaginative integrity of the experience of the poem.

It was perhaps inevitable that a poet as acutely sensitive as Slessor to the sights, sounds and surfaces of things should have been so aware of their transience. Some of his less successful early poems, such as 'The Ghost', 'Mangroves', and 'City Nightfall' are rather flatly insistent, in their moody emphasis, on the underlying vanity of things. In conveying little of any corresponding sense of the value of what is to be lost, they provide too easy evidence for those who wish to accuse Slessor of nihilism on the basis of content alone.

The themes and preoccupations that emerge in *Trio* (1931) and *Cuckooz Contrey* (1932) are already foreshadowed in *Thief of the Moon* (1924) and *Earth Visitors* (1926). There was no abrupt transition in Slessor's development, though these two new books mark a new level of achievement in his work. His interest in the imaginary and the exotic (old books, maps and charts) is brought to focus on the sea and sea captains, while explorers rather than artists come to embody his concern with creative effort and achievement in the lives of men who struggle to fulfil themselves against extreme odds.

Changes and shifts of imaginative focus in a writer's development are inseparable from technical changes, and the transition from the early work to the later (largely prefigured in 'Music') is a transition from conventional verse forms to more open forms and a more flexible use of speech rhythms.

The change is usually attributed to the combined influences of Eliot and Pound; given *Vision*'s immature initial resistance to these figures it might be as accurate to attribute it to Amy Lowell. Developing poets are often able to learn more quickly from minor figures than from the major authors of their time. At any rate, the young Slessor would seem to have found something corresponding to his own needs in her 'An Aquarium' from *Men, Women, and Ghosts* (1916)

> Streaks of green and yellow iridescence,
> Silver shiftings,
> Rings veering out of rings,
> Silver—gold—

> Grey-green opaqueness sliding down,
> With sharp white bubbles
> Shooting and dancing...

The emphasis here on liquidity, bubbles and iridescence, the attempt to fix movement and shifting colour in an image correspond to some of Slessor's own developments at this period. It was as much from the Amy Lowell of 'Violin Sonata by Vincent d'Indy' and 'Chopin', both from *Pictures of the Floating World* (1919), that Slessor was directed towards his own experiments in 'Music' as from Hilaire Belloc, and the Edith Sitwell of *Façade* (1922). Like Sitwell's poems Slessor's are 'patterns in sound', but his experimentations in language do not verge on artifice, unreality. His images, like Amy Lowell's, remain concrete; his language rarely becomes a mere word game.

Both his poems and his rare critical comments make clear how closely Slessor remained in touch with significant overseas developments during the formative time of his writing career; he 'made it new' by being modern and to be modern in that sense is to run the risk of becoming old fashioned, and historically encrusted in the course of time. There is decorative emptiness in the early and middle Slessor, as there is in much poetry of the 1890s and of the 1920s. And even the sustained use of imagism which certainly served the poet's individuality does not provide sufficient stiffening and bracing to lift some of the poems beyond the level of accomplished period pieces. In the less impressive poems aestheticism in one form or another constantly threatens to swamp the real feelings and the real sensations that are trying to find expression.

'Captain Dobbin' and 'Five Visions of Captain Cook' are rightly seen as important advances in Slessor's career; both are 'character' poems, both have a loosely sequential unity; both are marked by a relaxed, conversational ease of rhythm and diction; both contain exceptionally fine dramatic and lyrical moments, particularly in their eloquent final sections, which are among the most moving lines Slessor has written. A structuralist view of 'Five Visions of Captain Cook' can be used to relate each part to the whole, showing the different aspects of Cook's personality—his humanity, his exceptional gifts, his impact on others while he was alive, the importance of his actions for the future after his death. The danger of the structuralist view is that it may too readily lead us to assume that the poem is using what we sense as flatness, weakness or uncertain shifts of tone in some 'higher' way. However we look at them, sections II, III and IV of 'Five Visions of Captain Cook' are written out of impulses which are too simple to engage the reader's responses in the way that the superbly evocative V section does. 'Five Visions' as a whole is impressive and effective, but it is perhaps not quite as coherent or as dramatic a series of perspectives on the meaning of Cook as Slessor intended it to be.

Slessor's finest poems are those where a complex ambivalence comes into play, not as an end in itself, but as a way of expressing something beyond itself. It is necessary to make such a distinction because ambivalence as a state of mind is often the explicit subject matter of his lyrics. So in 'Burying Friends' a sense of loss is flatly played off against a sense of being unfeelingly deprived of a part of oneself; in 'Gulliver' the sense of being painfully oppressed by neurotic feelings is exacerbated by the awareness of their triviality, 'William Street' and 'Polarities' contrast like and dislike as possible reactions to the same thing or person: but there is no sense of powerful emotional control or mastery in these two poems, only the desire to point to the obvious contraries of life.

What, on the other hand, impresses one about a poem like 'Elegy in a Botanic Gardens' is the way it reconciles contrasting, even opposed moods at a deeper imaginative level than that of mere statement or juxtaposition or contrast:

> The smell of birds' nests faintly burning
> Is autumn. In the autumn I came
> Where spring had used me better,
> To the clear red pebbles and the men of stone
> And foundered beetles, to the broken Meleager
> And thousands of white circles drifting past,
> Cold suns in water; even to the dead grove
> Where we had kissed, to the Tristania tree
> Where we had kissed so awkwardly,
> Noted by swans with damp, accusing eyes,
> All gone to-day; only the leaves remain,
> Gaunt paddles ribbed with herringbones,
> Of watermelon-pink.

This lyric works through contrasts; now it is autumn; then it was spring; then it was the more evocative personalized Tristania tree; there was no time for Botany then, but now it is the Latin name.

Now there is the bare autumnal feeling (the herringbones of leaves, the beetles, broken stones and statues suggest dryness, an acceptance of reduction,) whereas previously there was the illusion of spring, with everything imaginatively transfigured, then it was Headlong Hall, now it is the Herbarium. The poem is contrasting and relating two different ages or stages of development:

> Never before
> Had I assented to the hateful name
> *Meryta Macrophylla*, on a tin tag.
> That was no time for botany. But now the schools.
> The horticulturists, come forth
> Triumphantly with Latin. So be it now,
> *Meryta Macrophylla*, and the old house,
> Ringed with black stone, no Georgian Headlong Hall
> With glass-eye windows winking candles forth,
> Stuffed with French horns, globes, air-pumps, telescopes
> And Cupid in a wig, playing the flute,
> But truly, and without escape,
> THE NATIONAL HERBARIUM,
> Repeated dryly in Roman capitals
> THE NATIONAL HERBARIUM.

The poem is an elegy for a dead self or for a dead part of the self, with contrary feelings still surreptitiously tugging at each other. A state of heightened awareness is contrasted with flat perception, regret for the past is played off against the frank clear acceptance of the present. One might say that spelling it out becomes the meaning of the poem as a whole and that this central ambivalence accounts for the paradoxical strength of the poem, the strength of patient disenchantment or the vitality of acceptance.

Slessor's best lyrics give that satisfying sense of an experience that shapes and fills the whole poem. Among his landscape poems, 'South Country' is the most remarkable for its fusion of mood and style. This too is a highly ambivalent piece—the initial solution of the plain landscape gives way to an oppressive sense of vastness and overwhelming clarity, the sense of understanding gives way to the sense of being obliterated. It expresses mingled distaste and fear:

> And over the flat earth of empty farms
> The monstrous continent of air floats back
> Coloured with rotting sunlight and the black,
> Bruised flesh of thunderstorms:

357

> Air arched, enormous, pounding the bony ridge,
> Ditches and hutches, with a drench of light,
> So huge, from such infinities of height,
> You walk on the sky's beach
>
> While even the dwindled hills are small and bare,
> As if, rebellious, buried, pitiful,
> Something below pushed up a knob of skull,
> Feeling its way to air.

The combining and relating of images of decay with phenomena like sunlight and thunderstorms, usually associated with vitality and renewal ('the monstrous continent of air'; 'coloured with rotting sunlight and the black/Bruised flesh of thunderstorms') contributes powerfully to the ambivalent feeling of the whole. So does the sense of deadening immensity further reinforced by the image of the hills, so far away that they are dwarfed by the enormous sky and yet asserting themselves against the emptiness: they are buried by air. The poem's balance comes from this dynamic fusion of the dead and the living, the human and the inhuman, the growing and the diminishing. Here one feels that landscape is not being used to convey a mood or a state of mind but that both inseparably illustrate each other.

A similarly tightly-layered poem, framed as a prolonged question and reply, is 'Sleep'. The poem is about 'sleep' as an image of Nirvana and oblivion, of the unconscious beckoning to and wooing consciousness, of the movement from being to non-existence:

> Do you give yourself to me utterly,
> Body and no-body, flesh and no-flesh,
> Not as a fugitive, blindly or bitterly,
> But as a child might, with no other wish?
> *Yes, utterly.*

There is throughout this lyric an oscillation between the need for abandonment and resignation, and the forces that drive out into the wilderness, that thrust one out into the world of division and separate identity. The dynamic unity of the lyric is in the way opposites meet and are related. The sound and meaning—the resignation and total surrender of '*utterly*' is played off against the significantly half-rhymed 'bitterly' (the bitter inescapable knowledge of the riving and the driving forth), while the realities of *flesh* ('pangs and betrayals of harsh birth') are related to 'wish'—the wish to escape the tensions of consciousness, into the oblivion of death. A further aspect of the poem's controlled ambivalence comes from the fact that it is very firmly and logically articulated, in a way that sets up a resistance to the suggestiveness of some of the dream-like images but which yet highlights this suggestiveness. There is throughout responsiveness and yet opposition to the sense of being 'dissolved and bedded'. More detailed analysis of this and other Slessor poems would provide additional evidence of that auditory imagination which T. S. Eliot defined as 'the feeling for syllable and rhythm ... sinking to the most primitive and forgotten, returning to the origin and bringing something back'.

Slessor's sense of ambivalence may be approached in different ways, thematically, or through his characteristic use of imagery. It can be seen in his use of the image of the sea, for instance, the destructive element which is also the area of achievement and creation; or in his more personal use of the image of bubbles— from the decorative 'cold stars ... bubbling', 'bubbling silk', 'bubbling drums', and 'bubble of flowers' of the early poems to the highly expressive 'bubble's ghostly camera' of 'Out of Time' where it is used with deepened insight to suggest the power of consciousness, the sweet miniscus that can hold a whole scene together and create, if only momentarily, the sense of a coherent world. Such moments of pure consciousness are tokens of meaning and stability in a world given over to the flux of time. It is perhaps not always fully appreciated how the sense of transience and flux was a stimulus to Slessor's imagination, showing how the artist can fix and transfigure what floats and disappears. Thus his obsession with oxymoron and with contrasting images: Time as wave and knife blade; ropes of water; the harbour bony with mist. And so, too, his preoccupation with works of art that outlast time, his concern with the strength of remembered moments.

These various themes are all brought together in 'Five Bells', rightly considered Slessor's most sustained achievement. The poem is both an elegy for a dead friend and a meditation on the meaning of memory and existence—the power of memory to hold out images of significance against the destructive force of oblivion. The progress of the poem is, so to speak, musical, consisting of balanced questions and negative replies, moving around the paradox of 'the flood that does not flow', the two kinds of time that we live by, and the struggle between a sense of nothingness and the equally strong sense of a remembered presence. The poem faces the fact that little can be salvaged from death but that life is full of significant experience. It is characteristic of Slessor's ambivalence that the poem should say at one and the same time that aspects of life are both profoundly significant and totally incomprehensible, and that the sense of no reply should be embodied in a poem whose beauty and resonance are themselves a protest against and a challenge to any annihilating sense of insignificance.

> I felt the wet push its black thumb-balls in,
> The night you died, I felt your eardrums crack,
> And the short agony, the longer dream,
> The Nothing that was neither long nor short;
> But I was bound, and could not go that way,
> But I was blind, and could not feel your hand.
> If I could find an answer, could only find
> Your meaning, or could say why you were here
> Who now are gone, what purpose gave you breath
> Or seized it back, might I not hear your voice?
>
> I looked out of my window in the dark
> At waves with diamond quills and combs of light
> That arched their mackerel-backs and smacked the sand
> In the moon's drench, that straight enormous glaze,
> And ships far off asleep, and Harbour-buoys
> Tossing their fireballs wearily each to each,
> And tried to hear your voice, but all I heard
> Was a boat's whistle, and the scraping squeal
> Of seabirds' voices far away, and bells,
> Five bells. Five bells coldly ringing out.
>
> *Five bells.*

Like 'Captain Dobbin' and 'Five Visions of Captain Cook', 'Five Bells' is in a sense a 'character' poem, focussing on aspects of the life of an individual, a poem searching for the meaning of lost significances. It is interesting to note that all Slessor's characters seem to live for, or in or through memories. But there is a special relationship between 'Five Visions' and 'Five Bells' which has not been noted by anyone before, through the use of the word 'Five', which may have had some special private significance for Slessor himself. 'Five Bells' is, to schematize crudely, the other side of 'Five Visions', and taken together they can be seen to present the two sides of Slessor's view of the world: the one a vision of fulfilment, achievement and enduring success in the face of death, the other an image of gradual dissolution. Cook shows what creative effort means—the enlargement of life afforded by exceptional minds—men who change the face of the world and who unforgettably influence all the people they come into contact with. Joe Lynch suggests the power of self-destruction and defeat and the insidious allurements of the will to failure. If this is so, then it is likely that Slessor ceased to write because his poetry had embodied all that he had to say, and that his vision of the human condition came to rest somewhere between these two extremes.

R. D. FitzGerald was, with Slessor, one of the two most important Australian poets to emerge in the 1920s, but though Slessor's poetic career was finished by 1944, FitzGerald has gone on working to the present in a craggy individual style which has hardly changed in the course of a long career. He remains a poet of the twenties in the way that Vance Palmer remained a novelist of the twenties, and his work has been virtually untouched by modernist techniques. Although his verse stands like a monolith in the poetic landscape of the time, his handling of language has never been assured: his point of departure is not the spoken language, with its natural idioms and rhythms, but rather a 'thought' language, reflecting the convolutions of his highly idiosyncratic ruminations. While Slessor was absorbing Eliot and Pound and ridding himself of the influence of Flecker, FitzGerald was imitating the poetic modes and diction of Robert Bridges, John Masefield and Christopher Brennan, and while his poetry has its successes and its strengths, he has only rarely succeeded in relating his lyrical vision to a natural use of expressive speech rhythms. He is an awkward poet, and an awkward poet to come to terms with.

Like Slessor, FitzGerald began as a member of the *Vision* group: he is a romantic vitalist and as such an important and interesting transitional figure, who certainly influenced Douglas Stewart and Judith Wright in some phases of their work, and more recently Thomas Shapcott ('Portrait of Captain Logan') and Bruce Beaver. Although the *Vision* group was ostensibly opposed to any limiting ideas of nationalism, FitzGerald's poetry in many of its aspects is close to the nationalism it is often assumed to be rejecting. The convictions expressed in 'Essay on Memory' and 'Heemskerck Shoals' are not so far from those of the Bernard O'Dowd of 'The Bush' and the sonnet 'Australia' as is sometimes supposed, and a strong Australianist element is subtly present in Slessor:

361

'So Cook made choice ..., So men write poems in Australia'. But even though the two poets had similar beginnings, they are very different as writers. Slessor remains a uniquely gifted verbal artist; his poetry is always concrete. FitzGerald is more explicitly philosophically minded; his language tends to be abstract and remote. Both Slessor and FitzGerald are poets fascinated by the phenomena of moonlight, but one has only to compare FitzGerald's description of moonlight on Sydney Harbour in 'Traditional Tune', with the quicksilver Feininger-like description at the opening of 'Five Bells', or FitzGerald's poem 'In Personal Vein' with 'Beach Burial' to see that with FitzGerald the idea predominates over the image, clear statement and indignation over paradox and pity. But whatever the limitations of his poetry from the point of view of sensuous immediacy or vitality and flexibility of language, FitzGerald is a humanly appealing poet, and one can only warm to a writer who is so resolutely optimistic, so prepared to celebrate the world of human action and endeavour— whether in the past or in imagining the interplanetary explorations of the future; a poet who in old age can regret that he 'will not be around to stand on Mars'. FitzGerald is the most positive and in some ways, the most reassuring of Australian poets. He has a deep, optimistic belief in the power of the life force, of some central energy in existence which keeps life moving. He believes, above all, in the value of action, of doing things: 'All good is effort and all truth encounter and overcoming'. One of his couplets could be used to sum up much of his work and belief:

'To be up and about and moving and ever upon quest
Of new desires of the spirit, not sunk in soft rest.'

This positive note, with its emphasis on progress, action and endeavour, FitzGerald partly inherited from Norman Lindsay and his idea of creative effort and partly—like O'Dowd—from various evolutionist thinkers from the late nineteenth century on. Some of it is purely temperamental in origin.

FitzGerald's first important book, *The Greater Apollo: Seven Metaphysical Songs* (1927), shows, like some of Slessor's early poems, a predilection for Romantic images and phrasing. The title poem explores two impulses of the mind. On the one hand there is an aspiration to the ideal, called in this sequel 'The Greater Apollo'. This ideal is in tension with a more sceptical impulse which accepts the world simply as it is, things as they are being the only reality.

The poem tries to establish and convey the sense of an underlying unity in the universe and yet the sense of endless diversity as the mind experiences it. In Section II, for instance, FitzGerald talks about the importance of the tangible and the real, of 'colours and shapes'—but he talks about them, he does not show them; and a sense of colour will not be found in the poems themselves. Nearly all FitzGerald's poems are declarations of faith:

> The valley path is calm and cool
> as I walk here between green walls—
> and those are diamond waterfalls;
> this is a bird; and that's a pool.
> I heard their far insistent calls
> and gladly have returned to these.
> What is revealed to me and known
> beyond material things alone?
> It is enough that trees are trees,
> that earth is earth and stone is stone.

This is simple and direct enough. But it should be said that FitzGerald's poems can be difficult, and their difficulty arises not only from his constant concern with metaphysical speculations and questions, but because they do not immediately communicate their arguments through the image, though they consistently use images to illustrate their arguments. There are frequent occasions in FitzGerald when the abstract and the particular, which should be inseparable in poetry, tend to drift apart rather than fuse and illuminate each other.

FitzGerald is best known for his two long speculative poems *The Hidden Bole* (1934) and *Essay on Memory* (1937), the most obviously ambitious Australian poems of the 1930s: both are attempts to express the inexpressible and a sense of the fundamental, indestructible unity of being. A stanza from Yeats' 'Among Schoolchildren' sums up the whole endeavour of *The Hidden Bole*:

> Labour is blossoming or dancing where
> The body is not bruised to pleasure soul
> Nor beauty born out of its own despair,
> Nor blear-eyed wisdom out of midnight oil.
> O chestnut tree, great rooted blossomer,
> Are you the leaf, the blossom or the bole?
> O body swayed to music, O brightening glance,
> How can we know the dancer from the dance?

363

Like Yeats, FitzGerald uses the two images of the tree and the dancer to express the sense of the invisible unity of being. Both *The Hidden Bole* and *Essay on Memory* are wisdom poems, looking for an attitude, a meaning, an answer. *The Hidden Bole* explores the way in which our sense of beauty is involved with our sense of decay and death, our sense of the unchanging with our sense of permanent change. Wisdom lies in the acceptance of growth, the fragility of things; permanence is death. *Essay on Memory*, a poem twice as long as *The Hidden Bole*, but written in the same style and form, deploys central images in the same way and uses aspects of the lyrical to assist and advance its speculations. The unifying images here are rain and memory—and memory in this poem means the life force itself, which FitzGerald equates with rain, without which life could not exist. Much of the poem asserts and celebrates the values of Lindsayan 'creative effort', though it would be interesting to know just how much it owes to Samuel Butler's (1835–1902) ideas. We depend on the dead, the present lives on the past achievements of the great (the Nelsons, the Newtons and the Phillips who helped to make Australia). The poem ends with rhetorical conviction and assertion: the urge of creative effort made us human and we must be loyal to this central energy and impulse of the race. The controlling image of the rain has not the sense of full appropriateness or complete inevitability that one finds in the images of the banyan and the dancer in *The Hidden Bole*, but despite its clogged and awkward lines, it is an interesting work, particularly for its optimistic vision of man's future in Australia.

FitzGerald's position in Australian literature is still uncertain and can probably never again be quite as high as it once was. His poetry does not give the sense of width of experience or of feeling; and there is a certain homogeneity of theme and preoccupation—a limitation of range—which his complex rhyme schemes and structures cannot disguise. One is often struck in FitzGerald by the discrepancy between the complicated and involved verse forms he uses and the simplicity of his content; or the patterned indirectness of his approaches to his subject: one could sometimes wish that the poetry were more lyrically direct, and as charged with rich and immediate metaphor as it is with intellectual life. It is likely for example that his reputation as a poet of the twenties and thirties will rest more securely on such moving and graceful lyrics as 'Long Since ...' and 'Rebirth'; and that the hitherto underrated aphoristic side of his art (as in 'Glad World') will come to be more admired than the longer discursive and reflective essays. Most of his finest poetry has been written since the 1940s, and his great contribution to Australian poetry is in poems like 'The Face of the Waters', and his various historical pieces. 'The Face of the Waters' shows a free-wheeling expansiveness unusual in FitzGerald's work, and is probably the most unexpected of his poems. It is characteristic of his dauntless ambition that the poem should be about the creation ('And the earth was without form and void; and darkness was upon the face of the waters') and attempt to explain or suggest the way life and thought originally emerged from nothingness. It is one of the most remarkable of FitzGerald's ruminative poems, enacting the sense of a struggle, communicating almost desperately through images something that cannot be expressed in any other way. This gives the whole poem its sense of necessity.

In the early 1940s, perhaps under the influence of Slessor's 'Five Visions of Captain Cook', perhaps merely in response to other developing pressures and awarenesses in his own and in his country's development, FitzGerald started to find in Australian history, and the history of his family, the subject matter of some of his best poems. Like Slessor's discovery of the image of the sea, FitzGerald's discovery of some of the possibilities of historical subject-matter gave a new focus to his work, historical events now providing occasion for his speculations. The short historical poems have a stripped economy of phrasing and utterance and are among FitzGerald's most impressive pieces and are likely to prove his most enduring work. Beginning with *Heemskerck Shoals* (1944), one sees that these poems, while preoccupied with the meaning of historical events and past actions, nevertheless continue to develop the reflective, quasi-philosophical note of poems like *The Hidden Bole* and *Essay on Memory*—the effect of the past on the present and the future, the relation between determinism and heroic action. *Heemskerck Shoals* is flatly ruminative,—the tone of calm reflectiveness is appropriate to Tasman's deliberations, functional in projecting the image of a character. The note of prophecy is characteristic of all semi-epic or historical poems but whatever tension of a speaking voice might be present at the beginning of the poem falters and wavers out, so that Tasman becomes spokesman for FitzGerald's own ideas about causation and the White Australia Policy. Slessor is able to dramatize Captain Dobbin and

365

Cook so that they objectively exist as characters; Slessor's very language conveys the vigour and excitement of the drama and discovery. FitzGerald talks about a quest: he does not show it in action. *Heemskerck Shoals* is about the significance and meaning of Tasman's quest—its outcome—it does not embody the quest itself. Slessor, of course, in 'Five Visions of Captain Cook' writes about success, FitzGerald about a kind of failure; but the distinction between the two poets serves to show how FitzGerald is a discursive, reflective poet, Slessor more immediate and dramatic.

Between Two Tides—the long poem FitzGerald wrote between 1944–1952—suffers like McAuley's *Captain Quiros* and Ingamells's *The Great South Land* from its too meticulous fidelity to historical sources, and from its deliberately plotted lack of dramatic immediacy. But all good writers make virtues out of their limitations and FitzGerald has turned necessities into advantages in his handling of a complex and difficult narrative. *Between Two Tides* is a study of the meaning of political power and, like nearly everything FitzGerald has written, of the relationship of the past to the present. It lacks the broadly based simplicity of narrative line that such a poem must have if it is to become popular, and while its Conradian indirections can be justified there are complications and difficulties which arise from the shifting points of view and the interweaving of narrative incidents and philosophical reflections. Nevertheless it is an impressive work.

In the fine, shorter historical poems, 'Fifth Day', 'Transaction', 'The Wind at Your Door' and 'The Road North', FitzGerald is more content to let events speak for themselves, though again they serve to illustrate his worried preoccupation with the connections between the past and the present, the need to grasp life and a sense of meaning through action; his admiration for dogged persistence and the sheer capacity to endure, his sense that every thing and person is significant and must have a place in the scheme of things. His imagery is largely drawn from the world of tides and currents, rocks and stones, pylons, metal towers, concrete and steel-images of things that both endure, change and flow, or else represent spiritual and mental creations. FitzGerald first won acclaim for his handling of the long poem: he seemed to work better at the long stretch than any other poet of his generation. Now we are likely to admire more his shorter poems—those just mentioned above, a cluster of lyrics dealing with moments of frustration, uncertainty, ageing and fragility, and poems like 'The Stair', 'Beginnings' and 'Proceedings of an Historical Society'.

While FitzGerald could be called a philosophical poet in a way that would be inappropriate if applied to Slessor or A. D. Hope, his poetry does not express a series of easily formulated ideas, and cannot be reduced to the few schematic preoccupations that underpin it. He has no neat solutions to offer to the problems of life—though he believes that attitude and bearing matter.

If Slessor appeals to our sense of the flux and unpredictability of life, of transience and mortality, FitzGerald explores our need to explain, justify and state, to understand (if only in broadly acceptable ways) meanings and motives, the connections between the past and the present, and our sense that there must be relationships of some kind somewhere.

The Jindyworobak movement was one of the few significant literary movements in Australia. Together with the Pioneer Players and *Vision* (1923–4) it exercised a decisive influence upon the course of Australian writing between the two world wars. Jindyworobak means in the Aboriginal language 'to annex' or 'to join'. Rex Ingamells (1912–55), the founder of the movement, seems to have used the word originally in the sense of joining Australians more closely with their environment. He was intent, not on taking up a position away from our European cultural inheritance, but on

> ... clearing away from Australian thought ... such evidences of it as have prohibited the liberal appreciation of qualities indigenous to Australia.[10]

He also stated

> The Jindyworobaks, whose whole campaign has rested upon the uniqueness of the Australian continent among the lands of the world, believe that this uniqueness is properly explained only by understanding of Australia's primeval story, as revealed by scientists.[11]

Ingamells wanted to bring Australian art 'into proper contact with its material' i.e., with primal Australia.

In its neo-nationalist way, the Jindyworobak movement continued and developed some tendencies already present in Australian culture. The ideas of Bernard O'Dowd in 'The Bush' were not so very remote from theirs, and Kenneth Gifford (another Jindyworobak spokesman) was quick to touch on the old 'city versus the bush' theme in statements which read like paraphrases of articles Vance Palmer was writing twenty or thirty years before.

'The Australian poet', Gifford wrote in *Jindyworobak, Towards an Australian Culture* (1944)

> almost invariably writes in the town and of the bush. There is an inescapable sense of contrast between two cultures, and the poet in choosing that of the bush has chosen that which alone is capable of developing into the true national culture we must have before we may lay claims to nationhood. The conflict between the city and the bush is a conflict between an alien and an Australian culture.

He added

> If we are to achieve an Australian culture we must sacrifice much to which we have been accustomed in the past, and in its place we must find an even older past, a past that is truly Australian ... Australia has suffered too much for her foreign ties. Europeanism chokes our minds from birth.

It was inevitable that the pro-European, cosmopolitan group, Angry Penguins should develop in reaction. At the time it seemed to some that it was all a battle of young midgets wielding giant themes; but in retrospect it can be seen that for all its limitations the Jindyworobak movement had a positive influence on the development of Australian poetry. Most new literary movements and impulses arise out of a stock-taking situation and this is essentially what the Jindyworobak movement was in its time.

> The stage has been reached when, after a vigorous era of colonization, Australians should take stock of past and present and so give effective thought to the future,

Ingamells stated in *Conditional Culture* (1938):

> From Aboriginal art and song we must learn much of our new technique; from Aboriginal legend, sublimated through our thought, we must achieve something of a pristine outlook on life.

Ingamells overstated his case, and in reacting against the pressures that imported culture were exerting on Australian art, oversimplified the real problems that faced Australian writers at the time. In their emphasis on the mystique of the land, they ignored what had already been done in this area by writers like Vance Palmer in *The Passage* for instance, and they overlooked the attempts made by other writers to overcome the feeling which many Australians experience of being alien in their landscape. But they were probably the first to emphasize the pre-European, Aboriginal qualities of the land itself.

The positive effect of the Jindyworobak programme was to help cleanse Australian poetry of dead poeticisms and to try to find a new range of words for local sights, sounds and things. It helped to enlarge the whole sense of landscape in Australian poetry. It is worth noting, however, that Ingamells himself in his first book *Gum Tops* (1935) wrote a poem 'Sea-Things' which is reminiscent of Rupert Brooke; elsewhere in the volume de la Mare peeps through the diction, while in the poem 'In The Bush' he writes:

> I see yon aged royal gum
> Lift his tremendous limbs with grace;
> But there is sadness on his brow;
> Forlorn appears each shaggy bough.

There is not much sense of primeval Australia there!

Much of Ingamells' early verse consists of variations on the old 'city versus the bush' theme, with the bush becoming the primeval centre as the poetry develops. His main preoccupation is the contrast between trivial humanity and the inhuman grandeur of nature itself. Ingamells is not an outstanding poet: his verse is often slap-dash and journalistic, but already in a number of early pieces like 'Forgotten People' and 'History', one finds a foreshadowing of themes that will reappear in *The Great South Land* (1951). Indeed there is a sense in which all his early verse is a mere preparation for the later long poem which deserves something better than the oblivion it enjoys at present (McAuley and FitzGerald were able to learn a great deal from it), and which despite its indiscipline and lack of economy compares quite well with other Australian poems of its kind. The truth seems to be that Ingamells had an epic vision of Australia which was the guiding thread of all his actions and writing but was, like Vance Palmer, who also pursued certain ideals of national identity, unable consistently to embody his ideas and feelings in fully achieved works of creative art.

The Jindyworobak movement had a stimulating effect on Australian writing through its publishing programmes and antho-logies; it elicited sympathetic interest in its aims from senior writers like the Palmers, Walter Murdoch, James Devaney and Leonard Mann; it printed books by Max Harris, William Hart-Smith, Gina Ballantyne, Roland Robinson, Colin Thiele, Victor Williams and Peter Miles. Poets like Ian Mudie and Flexmore

Hudson were associated with its aims. But of the Jindyworobaks only Robinson and Hart-Smith went on to write significant poetry, and it is interesting that neither of those poets was born in Australia.

It often happens that literary movements have more positive effects on those who do not belong to them than on those who do. The rich flowering of nature poetry in the 1940s with writers like Stewart, Campbell, and Wright and the continuing development of the 'voyager poem' tradition with writers like Webb, Stewart and Hart-Smith using all the resources of European poetry at their disposal, owed much to the Jindyworobak stimulus and its sense of 'environmental values', while other developments in the fields of neo-classicism, cosmopolitanism and surrealism arose in positive opposition to all that Jindyworobak stood for.

Although Max Harris was originally interested in the Jindyworobak movement, his Angry Penguins group rose to oppose Jindyworobak insularity; it tried to adopt internationalism instead of nationalism, surrealism instead of social realism, and modernism in all its various manifestations instead of cultural primitivism. Like the Jindyworobaks, the Angry Penguins produced no major poets; their real and lasting influence was in the realm of painting. Just how much artists like Sidney Nolan, Percival and the Boyds owe to the Angry Penguins still remains to be determined, but their cosmopolitan journal (1940–46) performed a useful function during the war years by stirring up stagnant local waters and keeping channels open to overseas writers.

The Angry Penguins who gathered round Max Harris lacked judgment and discrimination, and there was a great deal of pretension and pose in their way of expounding and embracing European modes of thought and art. Their youthful brashness and arrogance were devastatingly exposed by the notorious Ern Malley hoax. The Ern Malley poems were written by two traditional and conservative poets, James McAuley and Harold Stewart who sent them to Max Harris as editor of *Angry Penguins*. Harris accepted them and asserted they had genuine qualities. McAuley and Stewart then revealed that the poems were deliberate concoctions, intended not to humiliate Harris personally, but to show how meretricious much contemporary poetry is, and particularly the kind of poetry associated with The White Horsemen and the New Apocalyptic verse in England of the early forties. A few more points need to be made about that *cause célèbre*. If poetry is related to a sense of the truth of human experience and imaginative wholeness, then these poems are clear fakes. Half a dozen suggestive lines do not make a significant, coherent work of art, whatever fertilizing effect they may have on individual imaginations. The Ern Malley poems have provided artists like Sidney Nolan with stimulus for paintings and sketches, and several recent writers, critics and poets, with titles for their books and articles. The poems are brilliant concoctions—at their best, satiric parodies. So far no one has commented on the inspired quality of the Ethel Malley letters which seem to me as good as anything similar in White, Porter or Humphries. It has been asserted that the hoax killed genuine experimentalism in Australia: if this is so then it is a comment on the thinness of Australian poetic culture, and the lack of nerve in the poets themselves or else self-delusion on the part of later writers and critics. It seems best to remember that the Ern Malley hoax came towards the end of the war, which would have altered poets' writing habits and practice in any case; but it also came at the fag-end of the first phase of surrealism, when the movement was for a time played out and not to be internationally revived and reinvigorated for another twenty years.

The Ern Malley hoax has been a focal point for modern Australian culture. In its tiny way it touches on fundamental artistic issues of conscience, honesty, responsibility and artistic integrity. It is the kind of case that will always provoke interest as showing up conflicts between the conservatives and the radicals, the ancients and the moderns, the traditionalists and the experimentalists. But for anyone to think now that the poems add up to achieved artistic wholes is to lose all sense of standards and perspective.

Although his first fully fledged collection *The Wandering Islands* did not appear until 1955, A. D. Hope started publishing in the late thirties, when he began to establish a reputation as a critic and satirist. In the Australia of the Jindyworobaks and the Angry Penguins he was considered an academic conservative. An arch anti-modernist, he did not hesitate to attack Eliot and Pound. He relied on strict traditional verse forms, conventional syntax and logical imagery at a time of general experimentation. Unimpressible in his critical attitudes, he stood aside from the immediate impulses and pressures of his time, convinced that none of his contemporaries had solved the problems they had created. Hope created his distinctive poetry using all the resources of past tradition. While his contemporaries were preoccupied with the Australian present, its environment and history, he engaged in a dialogue with the European past.

Hope is an extremely gifted and complex poet, and it has taken a long time for his work to fall into perspective. He first appeared as a challenging and deliberately provocative poet—self-assertive and disdainful in his attitudes and determined to excoriate the narrowness and mediocrity of his society. He was isolated from the pervading literary tendencies both in Australia and overseas, and his isolation led to an attitude of hostility in much of his work, particularly his criticism. His uncompromising sense of integrity made no attempt to win the reader's sympathy or approval. Hope first became known as a satirist, for poems like 'Standardization', 'The Explorers', 'The Return from the Freudian Islands'. It is characteristic that at roughly the same time as Auden was writing his poem in honour of Sigmund Freud, Hope should attempt his mockery of debased Freudian ideas.

Hope's early poems spring from highly critical states of mind and reveal in different ways a certain division in the author himself. Aggressive in intention, aiming at the revaluation of a situation, poems like 'Australia' and 'Standardization', written in 1938 and 1939 respectively, are full of that gritty mixture of tones and textures that put early critics' teeth on edge, but which can now be seen as an essential element in the creation of his pearls.

Hope's approach, in his satirical pieces, is militant; he reduces and deflates in order to show things in their proper perspective. His point of departure in 'Standardization', for instance, is the attitude of those who are constantly complaining about industrialism, the modern age, the loss of individuality. In his attack on this attitude he subtly uses four predictable stereotypes of pseudo-intellectuals—themselves standardized figures—who might be expected to reject the modern world: 'The journalist with his marketable woes', the green aesthete, the theosophist, and the maudlin nature poet. What Hope attacks is their lack of tough-mindedness, of resilience—their inability to see the truth about the Nature in whose name they claim to speak. Whenever he hears them protesting about progress and industrialism, he sees

> ... stooping among her orchard trees,
> The old, sound Earth, gathering her windfalls in,
> Broad in the hams and stiffening at the knees ...

> For there is no manufacturer competes
> With her in the mass production of shapes and things,
> Over and over she gathers and repeats
> The cast of a face, a million butterfly wings.

In these stanzas the awareness of nature, its miraculous patterns of repetition, takes on a plenitude of feeling, a sense of celebration, that expand the dimension of the poem beyond that of satire. Nature is not sentimentalized here; she is heavy and homespun and business-like. Hope is showing the indestructible richness and sameness of nature, its untroubled intactness, (one of his major preoccupations) that puts the opinions and beliefs of little men into perspective. The last stanza is more sardonic and it clinches the argument for Hope. Even beauty which seems an exception to any kind of conformity and standardization is itself part of a natural pattern.

The intellectual pleasure of such a poem comes from the way it suddenly reverses our expectations and ideas. It is a challenging and aggressive poem, assured and even contemptuous. In fact, however, the aim is not as accurate as the tone would have us believe, and Hope is obscuring the target rather than hitting it. The aesthete's objection is not to natural conformity but to a mechanical stereotype. The potter, like nature, is constantly producing the same shape, but each jug has its own evolution and variation within this uniformity, unlike a mass-production plastic jug. Hope's poem is effective, but it works like much of his poetry through broad distinctions and large analogies, rather than fine discriminations; and it makes its point at the expense of the whole truth it claims to be.

'Australia' is just as barbed and imaginatively aggressive, but to a different end. The title is significant. Eliot would not have written a poem called 'America', Baudelaire one called 'France' or Rilke one called 'Austria'. Behind Hope's poem is a particular cultural phase, a different intellectual milieu and a completely different historical situation. In poems like Brunton Stephens' 'Australia' or Bernard O'Dowd's 'Australia', there is the sense of Australia's future and destiny, and the country tends to be viewed through the colours of fervent patriotism rather than dispassionately observed. 'I love a sunburnt country', Dorothea Mackellar wrote in a well known piece, 'My Country', that nostalgically and vigorously compares Australian landscape with English landscape.

373

Hope sweeps all this sort of thing aside. His poem is a 'Wanderer's Return'—a traditional 'homecoming' poem—so that the point of view presented in the beginning is that of someone returning but seeing his country from the outside and as if for the first time after a long absence. It is necessary to keep this in mind to understand the apparent change in the last two stanzas. The poem begins in a tone of disenchanted, sardonic but completely accurate observation: 'a nation of trees, drab green and desolate grey'—'her hills, those endless, out-stretched paws of sphinx demolished or stone lion worn away'. He evokes the monotonous colour, the flatness, the sense of age and attrition.

So much that Hope felt about Australia in the 1930s—its aridity, its stupidity, its colonial timidity—is suggested in these lines, and all the more forcefully for being expressed from within by an Australian who love-hates his country. It is interesting that at a time when so many Australian writers and painters were expatriates, Hope practised a kind of inner expatriation in an attempt to transcend the insularity of Australian culture. If Hope's 'Australia' consisted of nothing but its five opening stanzas, it would have an impressive conciseness, a directness of statement that would impose its own emotional tone and conviction. But the last two stanzas are the important ones for the feeling of the whole; and they change what would be a disillusioned comment into a paradoxical affirmation of the place. Whatever its defects, Australia to Hope is home. He in fact returns somewhat like the prophets of old to the desert. Not only is Australia 'placed' in relation to the rest of the world as in the opening stanzas, the rest of the world is 'placed' in relation to Australia. Here quiet work is possible, undistracted concentration, and hope for the future; above all, contact with something ancient and elemental and profound, as opposed to the superficial and the glitter of the modish which is too often considered to be civilization. (These questions are taken up and developed again twenty years later in 'A Letter From Rome'.) 'Australia' is a tough-minded poem, intent on facing the facts without subsiding into despair or ascending into empty optimism.

It is significant that Hope's satire usually attacks particular issues and concerns rather than individuals, and that the attack is usually made in poems that employ multiple levels of imagery. One of the staples of satire is to evoke the image of a Golden Age with which to measure the modern world. Many of Hope's satirical pieces are about the mediocrity of modern man and the banality of modern life. So in 'Sportsfield', for instance, he shows how the great ages of sport and love have gone—people are now only 'existing' and not 'living'; and he does this through clever puns and humorous, mock heroic situations.

Hope often works in devious, metaphoric ways in his satirical poems, using layers of images drawn from one area of experience to illuminate, explore or interpret other aspects of experience. While this is common to all metaphor, Hope is unusual in making it a structural principle of whole poems. In an early poem like 'The Explorers', imagery drawn from jungle exploration is used to illustrate the nature of adolescent female sexuality, while 'The Brides' takes the image of an assembly line of cars to highlight one of Hope's main preoccupations: that nature is a factory. These poems are clever, but cleverly crude. A much more brilliant use of this device is found in 'Parabola', a late poem about the poet's own destiny or place as a poet, the relationship between determinism and chance, drawing its imagery from the world of fairy tale and the science of genetics.

Hope's satirical vision is inseparable from his use of the macabre and the grotesque. 'Conquistador', (1944) which may owe something to Auden's ballads like 'Victor' and 'Miss Gee' as well as to the novels of Evelyn Waugh and Aldous Huxley, uses images from conventional adventure films and cartoons to highlight suburban fantasies of erotic exploits; but here its vision is embodied in an anti-hero and a narrative situation used to show that modern man is incapable of any great exploits, whether of passion or adventure. 'The Kings' likewise takes as its point of departure the heroic standard. Compared with the past, which had its emblems of greatness and power in the lion, the eagle, the leviathan, its kings and heroes, the emblem of the modern age is the tape worm, which Hope describes in all its solitary, sexual splendour. Here the tone is formal, lofty, hieratic, applied to a repulsive object; in 'The Martyrdom of St. Theresa', the contrast is between a colloquial tone applied to a sacred or taboo subject; in both cases, the tension set up by the deliberate discrepancy between subject and tone is part of the strategy of the poem. 'The Martyrdom of St. Theresa' is a violent attack on human credulity through the cult of relics, showing how close to the surface are primitive greed and butchery; a corresponding savagery in the poem is used to attack

375

the cruelty it exposes, and the rhyme of 'brisket' with 'basket' rasps like a saw on bone.

Hope's satire is very varied: a plangent yearning tone in 'The Lingam and the Yoni' is effectively employed to suggest the disconsolate separation of lovers, while the deliberate trivialization of imagery in 'The House of God' is employed to expose the pettiness of the motives of the congregation. Hope ranges through a whole spectrum of colours and tones from harsh rejection, brutality and disgust, to light-hearted or struggling acceptance, all to focus on fundamental contradictions and absurdities of attitude or belief. The satires or sardonic poems are generally impersonal, directed at the nature of things rather than social ills, as in 'Phallus', which shows the ineluctable power of impulse and instinct over individual decision and will. The paradoxical result of all satire, with its challenge and ridicule, is to inculcate some sense of humility and human acceptance of limitations. Varied as Hope's satires are, this is their ultimate effect.

Hope's satires give expression to conscious intellectual superiority, and aim to warn, challenge, provoke, horrify and amuse. But indignation at human folly can blind a writer to other aspects of life and experience as a whole. The grotesque and macabre side of Hope's talent has to be considered if one is to see his work steadily and whole; but it is only one side of his work, and it is not the side where his achievement is found at its most impressive.

Although Hope is an intellectual poet, it is the way that his poetry is rooted in the physical, in the life—the terrors and joys—of the body, that accounts for his undeniable power. Yeats has been a considerable influence on Hope and at the heart of Hope's poetry is the refusal to let the 'body be bruised to pleasure soul'. Some of his more negative poems like 'The Martyrdom of St. Theresa' and 'The Lingam and the Yoni', touch on this, while later pieces like 'Crossing the Frontier' and 'Advice for Young Ladies' express his sense of the injustice and inequality of the human conflict. But Hope's finest poems are those that celebrate the plenitude of being, the sensual miracle when the 'whole animal breathes and knows its place, In the great web of being and its right'. One thinks here of poems like 'The Gateway', parts of 'Chorale', 'The Young Girl at the Ball', 'Soledades', 'An Epistle: Edward Sackville to Venetia Digby' and above all, 'The Double Looking Glass'. Hope's best poems are firmly grounded in what Baudelaire called *'l'horreur de la vie et l'extase de la vie'* and it is the failure of critics to notice this—while emphasizing his ideas or his philosophy of poetry—that results in the serious lack of balance one notices in comments on his work. While many of his poems stray into the flatlands of the didactic and the over-explicit, the best express real sensations and leave the reader to draw his own conclusions.

It has been pointed out that the opposite of the satirist's butt is the heroic individual, who in tragedy or epic is pictured as standing alone in his moment of triumph or defeat. Several of Hope's poems are directly concerned with aspects of this heroic vision. One of the best known is 'Pyramis'. Hope's view of the heroic energy of the creative artist expressed in this poem needs to be balanced against his vision of the isolation of the individual, expressed for instance in a poem like 'The Wandering Islands'. Both ideas are closely linked in the early poems. Creative achievement, effort of will, is seen as one of the ways out of the dilemma of human isolation in a world without religious belief. In 'Pyramis' Hope celebrates the demonic will which rises above the general mediocrity of life. It is a Nietzschean vision of man or poet as superman who overcomes the circumstances of life through supreme effort and will power.

It is interesting to note that in many of his poems Hope uses a persona or a mask through which to speak, or else a figure or a symbol as a means of objectifying his emotions and feelings. This can be seen in 'The Death of the Bird' (1948), one of the most perfect of his poems. In this poem he returns to his preoccupation with the theme of isolation, with the sense of being alone in an indifferent universe. Although it is, so to speak, an objective poem about the last migration-flight of a bird, it is a poem in which the rhythm and tone, as well as the central images, point to the great antitheses of life felt by every individual. The inevitability of death is balanced against the sense of the persistence of life; the sense of being at home is played off against the sense of being in exile; the feeling of being supported and part of a community is related to the equally strong sense of being completely abandoned. Through patterns of relationship and contrast the bird becomes an image of the human soul in its journey through life—its sense of the unavoidable and predictable, its bewildered helplessness and frailty in front of the question of death. It is a measure of the poem's power that it reverberates with not one but many related meanings.

Hope is a poet of many contradictions as well as of consistent preoccupations. There is a conflict in the centre of his poetry between the world of nature and the world of intellect. Some poems can be harsh and grudging; others finely disciplined and tender. Reading his poetry as a whole one often has the impression that the writer himself finds the cure for his own excesses: One poem acts as an antidote to another; a later poem like 'Parabola' for instance can be seen as a deepened consideration of some of the issues touched on in 'Standardization'.

Certain themes have dominated Hope's work at different phases of his development. If at times he has viewed man in his absurdity and triviality, he has at other times shown him in his splendid, almost tragic isolation, or in the guise of energetic genius or Nietzschean hero. The idea of man standing alone in victory or defeat occurs in various ways—in poems like 'The Trophy' or 'Man Friday'—but it is as well to recall that Hope called his first book *The Wandering Islands*—a title drawn from Book II, Canto XII of *The Faerie Queene*, but used with sardonic reference to rebut John Donne's 'no man is an island ... I am involved in mankind'. The poem of the same title flatly outlines a map of the human condition where the emphasis falls on isolation and solitude, with the burden of separation relieved by 'the sudden ravages of love' which draws people 'closer and close apart'. The tone is rather that of 'this is your captain speaking', and the diagrammatic detachment of this depiction of the human condition is designed to create ambiguities and also to give the sense of dealing with established and unalterable facts. That the poem works through a sleight of hand does nothing to diminish its bleak mood, its blunt reporting that this is 'all that one mind ever knows of another' in a godless universe. But the authoritative tone cannot disguise the fact that it reports a state of mind, not the whole truth about life.

Hope's treatment of this existentialist theme differs in tone and approach from poem to poem in the early work, but in 'The Ascent Into Hell', one of his finest earlier poems, he confronts the theme directly in his own name, so to speak. The title of this poem of self-questioning in search of self-knowledge refers to the old belief that the hero or individual who wished to achieve anything had first to descend into the underworld to face the negatives of life so that he could ascend, reinvigorated and fortified in purpose, but Hope plays on this idea by suggesting that our growth in knowledge leads to our awareness of suffering and self-division. Hope has recorded that as a child he was worried about questions of predestination and hell-fire and such fundamental religious intensities have obviously been absorbed into the fabric of the whole poem. The image of islands—so central to Hope's early work—is here an organizing principle in the poem, starting realistically with Hope's memories of his childhood in Tasmania ('my receding childish island'), isolated islands of experience ('from island to island of despairing dream') and islands of imagination, where Tasmania and its stony ridges becomes transformed into an Easter Island of the mind. The image conveys the idea of a map of experience, a map of the mind with its sense of fragmentation and isolation, but also its sense of unity and underlying pattern. 'The Ascent into Hell' is one of the few poems where Hope gives the impression of speaking in his own voice, though other poems like 'The Death of the Bird' or 'Meditation on a Bone' where he uses some distancing or generalizing device, have a personal accent, a voice that is unmistakably Hope's own. (It is interesting to note that Hope in 1943/44 was touching on aspects of autobiography long before such forms were to become more frequent in the 1960s under the general rubric of 'confessional verse', though he is not a confessional poet in the current modern sense: it would be almost impossible to adduce a biography from his poetry except for one of his obsessive themes of a lost or a frustrated love.)

Hope's vision of man—moving from the world of Henry Clay to that of the Pharoahs, Milton and Blake—can seem extreme. It tends either to aggrandise or diminish its subjects, to concentrate on the transforming power of passion and art or man's absurdity and futility when left to his own devices. There is not much exploration in his poetry of the middle area, and one will not get from his *oeuvre* that sense of the details of a whole personal life that one finds in Judith Wright, for instance. But his extraordinary fictions give him an Archimedean point of view on modern western civilization quite without equal in modern Australian poetry.

In 'Pyramis', one of his best known poems, Hope presents an image of heroic energy defying time and defying the too easily accepted limits of the human condition. The central image is drawn from one of the seven wonders of the ancient world; the basic idea is the Renaissance notion of the work of art that outlives time. The whole emphasis of the poem is on demonic energy and

379

will, the ruthless drive of genius in its super-human effort to leave its artistic monuments behind—and the cost is nothing less than a whole life. In his later poetry the emphasis falls much less on Yeatsian 'monuments of unageing intellect' and more on a Shakespearean sense of 'great creating nature', less on the sense of rebellion against the human condition than on acceptance of being part of a process, though this is expressed not in any formal changes but merely in the contents of his poems, which retain the same metrical patterns and the unusual combination of monumentality and intensity which is one of the most striking features of his work.

The theme of art, intimately related to the theme of self-knowledge and self-transcendence through love, occurs in many of the late major poems: 'The Double Looking Glass', 'Vivaldi, Bird and Angel', the Digby Sackville epistle, and 'Conversation with Calliope' and is inseparable from his speculations and explorations in the same poems on the relationship between nature and art and the meaning of the poetic imagination. Hope has never been afraid of the heights, or of large subjects ('No lion-soul acquires its habit/From close acquaintance with the rabbit') and he has shown a capacity for dealing with them unequalled by any other Australian poet. Perhaps only White among his contemporaries has shown the same scope.

More than any other Australian poet, Hope has shown a continued interest in the themes of the European tradition, the myths and legends of Rome and Greece as well as those of the Bible and other areas of European mythology. Like other modern poets—Yeats, Rilke and Valéry, he has drawn on a handful of well known myths and stories in which the chief figures are Circe, Odysseus and Penelope, Judith and Holofernes, Lot and his daughters, Adam and Eve, Pasiphae and Persephone, Prometheus and Fafnir, Faust and Susannah and the Elders. Hope once complained that he found Australia a country 'without songs, architecture, history', without the reassurance of a tradition, and he was not, like some of his contemporaries, drawn to the poem of Australian historical narrative or event or to creating a local mythology from scratch. He is (with Brennan and O'Dowd) one of the most allusive of Australian poets, with a large body of knowledge at his disposal. But he does not merely aim to recreate historically or atmospherically the history of the legends of the past, centred on a single striking figure or group. The myths provide him with convenient familiar fictions. To use a myth situation and characters, however much they are reinterpreted or reversed, provides the poet with a ready-made foundation; the poem does not have to start below ground level to establish its basic reference, and the poet can rely on the reader to supply a set of attitudes. Whether he develops or reverses them, he has not had to create them within the poem: they have been as it were previously authorised:

> We should have certainty to conjure with,
> Acting the saving ritual of our myth—
> Yet myth has other uses: it confirms
> The heart's conjectures and approves its terms.

'An Epistle from Holofernes' expounds Hope's use of myth. Often in his myth poems he traces lovingly (and sometimes lushly) over the outlines of stock mythical figures

> Stared with his ravenous eyes to see her shake
> The midnight drifting from her loosened hair
> > 'The Return of Persephone'
>
> The ruddy fire-glow, like her sister's eyes
> Flickered on her bare breasts and licked along
> The ripeness of her savage flanks . . .
> > 'Lot and his daughters'
>
> When straight her fierce, frail body crouched inside . . .
> > 'Pasiphae'

and then charts a new inner map of feelings and realizations that are contained in this figure

> Yet the myths will not fit us ready made,
> It is the meaning of the poet's trade
> To recreate the fables . . .

Hope's mythical poems almost all give the impression of being based on a painting—some of course explicitly are—or at least on a 'still' from the action of the myths, where every line and detail of a situation can be dwelt on and then presented within a changed perspective. Sometimes we have a profound and beautiful exploration of a human state, where the traditional character is no more than a point of departure—as in 'The Double Looking Glass'; sometimes simply a neat reversal of expectations as in 'Faustus' or 'Circe'. Hope has always enjoyed mixed reactions, and the myth poems indulge this as much as, though perhaps more subtly than, his sardonic poems. He has always dealt with big themes and issues, but on the whole his inventiveness is not a question of subject matter or form but of approach, language, and angle of vision.

Hope as a critic and commentator has often projected himself as a classicist, prescribing an Augustan conception of the different *kinds* or functions of poetry. He has advocated and practised the use of genres and the cultivation of a variety of poetic forms: the epistle, the ode, the discursive poem and so on, down to the ballad and the clerihew. But there is often a struggle in his poems between his rigid conception of form and the romantic range and intensities of feeling and passional conflicts they contain. In this he has more in common with poets of romantic individualism, pain, erotic melancholy and savage pleasure like Baudelaire and Leconte de Lisle and Hérédia than with Pope and Dryden.

One of the most remarkable features of Hope's work is its structural complexity, seen particularly in the three-fold patterning of his poems—whether in the long Byronic 'A Letter from Rome', a witty and penetrating epistle about the relationship between culture and knowledge, which is not a consumer product but an inward acquisition, a state of being rather than having—or in the exquisite short 'Moschus Moschiferus', with 'The Death of the Bird' one of Hope's most perfect and maturely serene pieces. This poem is a prayer or a report to Saint Cecilia about the way the power of music is being misused. It would not be completely wrong to call it a protest poem, or even a conservationist's plea to save from extinction the musk deer which are killed for the perfume industry, except that the whole is delivered with all the resources of art and is such a delicate tissue of language and sound. The hunters, like Orpheus, entrance the animals with music and the narrative celebrates music's power and refinement at the same time that it recounts the killing of the deer and the continuing depletion of their numbers. Many have praised the power of music, few have spoken of the uses and abuses it can be put to. There is no need to allegorize the poem; it is a comment on the price to be paid for certain exquisite refinements and pleasures— the final elimination of the very source of their production; but it is a poem that also says something about the misuse and abuse of works of art. Poems like these with their range of humane concerns add a whole new dimension to Hope's work, and may be more effective in the long run than the more macabre and ambiguous poems.

Hope's most recent poems like those gathered in *A Late Picking* do not add anything particularly new to the outline of his work, except where they express the processes of age, change and memory, but they explore their themes with the added urbanity of technical and intellectual virtuosity and range, and there is a notable increase in the warmth of his humour.

Apart from his commitment to traditional verse forms, Hope is altogether less systematic, less doctrinaire and less inhibited than McAuley, with whom early commentators often linked his name. But no other Australian poet gives quite the sense of solidity, weight and achievement that one finds in the whole Hope *oeuvre*.

James McAuley first achieved public attention as one of the perpetrators of the Ern Malley hoax, an act which labelled him clearly as an arch anti-experimentalist, opposed to surrealism, free verse and the dislocation of syntax which the Angry Penguins found so liberating. But if he opposed the modernists, he also opposed the neo-nationalism of the Jindyworobaks. He came to public notice on a wave of controversy, and remained a figure of controversy until his death in 1976. During the bleak decade of the Cold War he lectured at the Australian School of Pacific Administration, with anthropological and field studies in New Guinea that led, through his contacts with some of the French missionaries there, to his conversion to Catholicism in 1952. He always knew what he did not want—the breakdown of traditional standards and values, whether in society or the art of verse. But he was not as singly committed to the art of poetry as A. D. Hope, Judith Wright or Douglas Stewart. He was a public activist, whose role as intellectual, editor, commentator and academic drew on his central energies, and his poetry which fed at widely differing sources was always subservient to his religious beliefs and convictions. In a rough grouping among Australian writers he would stand with figures like Brennan and FitzGerald, and Judith Wright in some phases—poets in whose work intellect and vision predominate over concrete experience, the idea over the observation. His art is often more contradictory than one might suppose from his critical pronouncements, but his contradictions are what make his most poignant pieces memorable. McAuley was obsessed, in his early as in his late lyrics, by the enigmas of the self—by the self as flux, as an ungraspable entity with all its contradictions and conflicting tendencies that can never be reconciled, stabilized or simply accepted. There is a strong but simple conflict in his work between feeling and emotion, intellect and will, issuing occasionally in sentimentality, occasionally in cynicism. This conflict is the subject of many of his poems; sometimes it involves the problems and contradictions found in the longer works *Captain Quiros* and 'The Hero and the Hydra'— where what is said or implied may not be quite the author's intention, and the real interest is in the conflict between the poet and the poem; sometimes as in 'Celebration of Love', which begins with a tone of such firmly-held serenity, there is a progressive dispersal of emotion and mood as intellectual ingenuity takes over. Judith Wright commented on McAuley's early work: 'Sometimes the pressures behind his poems seemed too rigidly held under control: sometimes they seemed falsified by intellectual elaboration and too recondite allusion'. McAuley often tends to substitute in devious ways the will's intentions for the imagination's deeds. This tendency can be found not only in the longer poems, where an intermittent slackening of the generating poetic impulse can be expected, but also in his short lyrics, where elaboration and artifice sometimes distort and flaw otherwise impressive and finely formed poems.

McAuley's first book *Under Aldebaran* (1946) was one of the most brilliant books to appear in Australia in the forties. It contains thirty-three poems of different range, force and interest, the most impressive being 'Envoi', 'Gnostic Prelude', 'Henry the Navigator', the sharp satirical 'The True Discovery of Australia', 'Terra Australis' and 'Philoctetes'. The poems fall into two broad thematic groups which span the full range of McAuley's poetic interests: those on the creative imagination and its relation to its culture; and personal lyrics on themes of inadequacy and inner dissatisfaction. All McAuley's future development and lines of direction are already indicated in this volume. His later cultivation of the short lyric relating observation to personal emotion is already pre-figured in 'At Bungendore', in a mould that lyrics written thirty years later repeat, while the early stoicism that his conversion seemed to transcend or assuage returns in later poems which stoically accept the attrition of many of his aspirations and hopes. McAuley was never greatly interested in the popular stream of Australian poetry—indeed much of his early poetry, with its studied diction and multiple cultural references, can be read as a rejection of that stream—and from the first he aimed at a 'timeless' diction that would not be clouded by merely contemporary or local or transient features. At its best his language is crisply clear and immediate, capable of the sensitive directness of 'Envoi', of probing into the psychological complexities of 'Gnostic Prelude', or of relating autobiographical moments as in the later series 'On the Western Line'; but the danger of McAuley's search for a timeless language is that it often led to dead patches in his work, where the mannered words lack a sense of vitality. McAuley once told me that he thought the word 'cupreous' one of the most beautiful in the English language and that he regretted never having been able to use it in a poem. A cultivated awareness of the subjective force of single words rather than their living relationships as language accounts for the inert passages one finds at times in his work. There are no such faults in the fine 'Envoi', a landscape of the mind, in which he relates his sense of his own limitations to his awareness of the deficiencies of his country and his people

> And there in the soil, in the season, in the shifting airs,
> Comes the faint sterility that disheartens and derides...
> And I am fitted to that land as the soul is to the body,
> I know its contractions, waste, and sprawling indolence;
> They are in me and its triumphs are my own,
> Hard won in the thin and bitter years without pretence.

'Envoi' is worth comparing with Hope's 'Australia' written at the same time. Both poems follow the same lines of structural development and in both there is the same sense of emptiness and sterility, with the emphasis on 'the battler' quality of the people seen from a distance and with a touch of hauteur that changes to the sense of identification and recognition. Hope uses the image of the flowering desert and the prophet to suggest the possibilities of future creative development; McAuley uses the image of artesian bore water to suggest the impulses of the heart and the uneasy relationship between the people and the land they inhabit. His voice is more direct and personal, suggesting the poet's attitude to his own gifts and talents. Hope's poem is sharper, more violent and critical, McAuley's more wistful and resigned. The sense of inner defeat, emptiness and despair—the terms change from poem to poem—is there in McAuley's poetry from the beginning, and while his conversion to Catholicism seemed to give him the explanation for the feeling and for a time to fill the emptiness with a sense of joy, his poetry never completely exorcised the state.

The poems which form 'The Hero and the Hydra' (1947–9) provide the link between *Under Aldebaran* and *A Vision of Ceremony* and *Captain Quiros*. 'Prometheus' is an oblique meditation on our civilisation and its future after the war and after the explosion of the first atom bomb. These myth poems McAuley wrote after

> an increasingly critical reaction to the myth of revolution ... as a means of encountering the agony of civilization which seemed to have lost its principle of coherence, unable to bring together the twin themes of order and justice in the *polis* and order and justice in the soul.[12]

All the poems are about human weakness, the fatal flaw or wound that makes any kind of perfection impossible; but all assert the presence of an intellectual order which must be defended if the values of civilization are to remain. The tension of 'Prometheus' and 'The Death of Chiron' (the best poems in the group) arises from the stoic assertion of order in the face of emptiness.

The slightly earlier poem 'Henry the Navigator'—which fore-shadows *Captain Quiros*—also belongs with this group of poems. Henry is taken as the image of the defender of spiritual values in a frightening world. The poem affirm's that Henry's heroic energy and moral courage are needed in our times if we, too, are to be fully aware of what is happening in our world—and, indirectly, that the world will be saved by like-minded men

> Our age is early too, and must prepare
> Its new projections, or great-circle routes
> Into an unknown world. Thus our despair
> Is put to the Straits again, although in air;
> And the old terrors take new attributes.

'The Hero and the Hydra' marked McAuley's interest in the extended poem or poetic sequence which he pursued up to *Captain Quiros* before abandoning it completely. His attempt to revive traditional verse forms led him in 1953 to write a short narrative poem 'A Leaf of Sage' and a verse epistle 'A Letter to John Dryden'. 'A Leaf of Sage' is one of McAuley's best poems. Based on a story from Boccaccio the narrative recounts how Simona told her lover Pasquino to rub a sage leaf against his teeth to gain eternal life. He does so and shortly after dies; she is accused of murdering him and dies too when she rubs the leaf against her teeth to show that she is innocent. When the sage tree is dug up, underneath it is found a toad, 'the Satan of the bower'. The story is one of innocence and redemption, but above all it is about the mysterious working of providence. McAuley refers to the poem itself as a hieroglyph, with a personal meaning for his own past and development. What it says should be conveyed as a reverberation of the presented facts, but there is some discrepancy between the narrative and the meaning of the final stanza which sends long connecting threads back into McAuley's own early work. McAuley seems in so many poems to have tried to lay the ghost of what he feels to have been a particularly confused and unhappy youth but which the reader senses as the poet's unhappy relationship between his feelings and 'mind unfulfilled'. Most poetry aims at achieving coherence and harmony out of spiritual confusion and disorder, but McAuley's poetry as a whole seems to rest on too simple, too sharp a division between these elements—harmony being associated with intellectual vision and realization, confusion and disorder with the facts of everyday life and the burdens of emotional tensions. Much of his poetry gives the sense of patterns and meanings imposed rather than discovered.

But 'A Leaf of Sage' is a remarkable and impressive poem, notable for its poise, the controlled delight in structure, the swift and clear movement of its narrative line. The same cannot be said of 'A Letter to John Dryden', an argumentative epistle of nearly 500 lines written soon after McAuley's conversion to Catholicism, presenting a potted history of the growth of modern secularism. The poem is uncertain in tone, moving from the serious to the trivial, and is neither sustained as burlesque nor invective, though there are clusters of good lines throughout. Indignation is no substitute for moral passion, and the arguments against rational humanism and the benefits it has brought to the modern world are not impressive.

Captain Quiros (1958–60) marked an important stage in McAuley's career and brought his experiment with the long poem to a close. The narrative, based on the accounts of the voyages of Alvaro de Mendana to the Solomons and on Quiros' expedition to find the great south land to set up a religious community, is divided into three main sections or panels. The first voyage ends in murder, chaos and rebellion, but it is through this voyage that Quiros finds purpose and his own calling. On the second voyage Quiros, who wishes 'to bring the light of Christ to the southland' sets up his religious community on the island of Espiritu Santo, but with ill success. His millenarian hopes are frustrated and he fails to find any kind of this-worldly fulfilment for his ideals. The third section is his prophetic vision of his death bed in Panama—and includes his vision of the history of Australia and its future development, extending to an apocalyptic vision of the end of Time.

Captain Quiros is a story of failure and human incompetence, interwoven with the sense of the continuing possible fulfilment of an ideal. It is a story that contains elements of pathos, self-deception and illusion, but McAuley does not focus on these elements, choosing to see in Quiros the failures inherent in the human condition and the inevitable limitations and frustrations to human aspiration and endeavour. If the poem finally has to be judged as less than a complete success, this should not let us overlook the fact that it contains sections and passages—the crossing of the Pacific, the Malope sections—which are among the best that McAuley ever wrote. The main danger with *Captain Quiros* is that in the attempt to hold so many different levels together, the spiritual and reflective levels will tear adrift from the narrative basis which provides the realistic substance of the whole. McAuley went to great lengths to unify his poem in different ways—primarily through patterns of imagery, especially those of the stars, the sea, the labyrinth and the maze and the natives of the Pacific and the effect of their contacts with white civilization, as well as establishing points of contact and comparison between the two voyages. Parts of the poem are barely transmuted versification of the historical journal of the voyages. There is a notable ease and fluency where the poem is most deeply personal and lyrical and again and again in some of the finest moments it is not the character's but the author's own voice, or divided voices, we hear, either ecstatic or truculent:

> My life's concerns have seemed like ships dispersed
> On different coasts without a rendezvous;
> A set of unrelated roles rehearsed
> Without a play; jig-shapes belonging to
> No single puzzle. Now the parts combine
> And I begin by unforeseen design
> To do the work that I was born to do.
>
> Therefore I have less care who shall approve;
> For poems of this kind are out of fashion,

Together with the faith, the will, the love,
The energy of intellectual passion
That built the greatness which we have resigned.
I play a match against the age's mind:
The board is set; the living pieces move.

Captain Quiros is an important statement of McAuley's belief
that any kind of this-worldly fulfilment is impossible, but it also
has a significant place in the tradition of voyager poems that have
been such a feature of contemporary Australian poetry; as well as
in the tradition of the mystical and patriotic poem of ideas to
which O'Dowd's 'The Bush' and 'Alma Venus' belong.

Apart from his longer poems, McAuley's work consists almost
exclusively of lyrical sequences and sets. Those gathered in *A
Vision of Ceremony* under the title 'Black Swans', written under the
impulse of his conversion to Catholicism aim to reawaken his
readers to the life of the spirit and the sense of recovered spiritual
gains. Individual poems benefit from being read as a group. All use
the simplest traditional lyrical modes: some are didactic in
intention, aiming to demonstrate the belief articulated in 'The Art
of Poetry' that 'universal meanings spring/ From what the proud
pass by'; others are carefully modulated contrasts between images
of light and darkness—a stylizing device to show out of what
struggles and conflict the sense of serenity and light have been
won. McAuley paid a very high price in his search for clarity. The
main danger of such clarity is that it can degenerate into mere
neatness—but the best of these poems, 'Invocation', 'To the Holy
Spirit', 'Nativity', and 'The Inception of the Poem' have a mellow
richness and fullness, or a fine delicacy, which bear witness to the
serenity and gains that he achieved.

Among this group 'To the Holy Spirit' is a particularly interesting experiment, demonstrating how McAuley was trying to bring
out the relationship between the natural and the supernatural at
this stage of his work. The poem (not unlike the pre-conversion
'Chorale' in some aspects) takes an image dear to George Herbert,
and invokes the Holy Spirit in the figure of a bird of paradise.
McAuley's was a highly conceptualizing rather than visualizing
mind, but one notices in 'To the Holy Spirit' the reference to the
bird's feathers 'plumed with glowing iris along each curving wire'.
In 'New Guinea', a more willed and discursive poem, relying on
statement and assertion, the sense of place is evoked through small

389

details such as 'secretive bird voices' and 'forest odours.' In both poems the details are suggestive enough for us to accept the symbolic patterning or interpretation that McAuley places on them. The need to make statements remains; but in some of the later poems like 'St. John's Park' and 'Parish Church' the weight falls on the emotional tone, colour and balancing and interrelation of a succession of images. These later poems, particularly in their use of colour, owe a great deal to the example of Georg Trakl whose work McAuley translated and wrote about a few years before he died and they are more obviously pictorial and emotive than any of his earlier lyrics.

Like his contemporaries, McAuley's development shows that he finally abandoned the ambitions that went into the making of poems like *Captain Quiros* for a poetry of reduced pretensions that aimed to be less stylized, more immediate and human. He seems to have abandoned any belief in the transcendental nature of poetry. The autobiographical poems first published in *Surprises of the Sun*, 'On the Western Line' (which were certainly influenced by the poems Vincent Buckley was writing at his time, such as 'Stroke' and by the autobiographical poems of John Betjeman) show one direction this development took. This is an uneven sequence, moving from the austere honesty of 'Because', the most widely admired of McAuley's later lyrics, to the sad revelations of 'Father, Mother, Son'. In this sequence McAuley focuses on significant remembered moments of his childhood and adolescence in the Western suburbs of Sydney, and in a language spare and reduced to flatness, attempts to render the experience without in any way inflating or heightening it. His technique is diametrically opposed to that of say, Dylan Thomas, in 'Fern Hill'. The poems do not remember with recreated sensuous immediacy; the imagery is one-dimensional, so to speak. They are a series of negatives of the past, rather than fully developed photographs, working through a deliberately charged, emotive reticence. McAuley tries to combine remembered moments and present interpretation, aspirations and frustrations. 'Catherine Hill Bay', however, reveals the dangers of the method, with its repetitions of 'small' and 'little', and its assertions of present opinion superimposed on past experience. To over-insist in such frail lyrics is to become trite—a danger not always avoided. In poetry it is not enough to state what brought about feelings; in the texture and movement of the verse and in the very quality of the imagery, the feelings must be released again and recreated as McAuley himself demonstrates in poems like 'Envoi,' and 'Invocation'.

McAuley achieved this more frequently in the final nature lyrics, like 'In the Huon Valley' and in 'The Hazard and the Gift', *Time Given* and the posthumous verse-journal *A World of Its Own*, which attempt to reflect and articulate his responses to the Tasmanian environment since his move to Hobart. In these later poems, written in the shadow of his fatal illness, there is a sense of diminished energy and a deliberately reduced scope, but also a painful and exceptional honesty. The poems in *Time Given* renounce the celebrant tone, the sacramental patina of the lyrics of the middle period for a humble attentiveness to the observed object, a refusal to see it transfigured by anything not contained within it:

> The world spread open through the window frame
> Offers a language only known by sight . . .
> And all this seems to make a kind of claim,
> As if it had been given that one might
> Decipher it: if there were such a skill
> Which one could learn by looking—

The poems name and state, with a strong sense of the separate observer rather than the resolution of a merging of self and nature. The frequently used abba rhyme scheme closes off the stanzas and returns them to their starting point, and flat, wry statements hold down the tone. The poems have a much stronger visual impact than in earlier periods, with sparse, firmer outlines and a new use of colour. As in 'Black Swans', images of light, darkness, growth and decay are balanced against each other in a consciously pictorial way, but each poem has the mood of its own time and season, not a resolution beyond these. With their frail, austere lucidity, some of the poems, like 'Plein Air', 'Pastoral' and 'Watercolour' are reminiscent of Lionel Johnson, Arthur Symons and other *fin de siècle* poets. If many of the later lyrics are slight the best are by no means superficial, and in the finest like 'At Rushy Lagoon' and 'In Northern Tasmania' the valedictory mood—the sense of a fading life—comes together with the sense of a vanishing way of life to achieve a poignant music:

> Soft sodden fields. The new lambs cry,
> And shorn ewes huddle from the cold.
> Wattles are faintly tinged with gold.
> A raven flies off silently.

Bare hawthorn thickets pearled with rain
Attract the thornbill and the wren.
Timber-trucks pass now and then,
And cows are moving in the lane.

At dusk I look out through old elms
Where mud-pools at the gatepost shine.
A way of life is in decline,

And only those who lived it know
What it is time overwhelms,
Which they must gradually let go.

Judith Wright has been too varied a poet to be summed up in a neat phrase, but one of her main preoccupations, one that she has shared with a great number of Australian writers, has been the transformation of the environment, the imaginative possession of the country. Where her contemporaries have participated in and contributed to this process, she has consciously defined it. She seems, with Vance and Nettie Palmer, to have understood the active, serious local writers' situation better than any other author of her time. In all her work—poetry, prose, criticism—she has been concerned with the relationship between an inherited European vision and the facts of Australia. Indeed, if the writers who followed Judith Wright need no longer concern themselves with some of the questions that engaged her, it is largely because she has solved them—or at least fully articulated them.

Judith Wright's first book, *The Moving Image* (1946) was a major event in modern Australian poetry: it won immediate recognition and is probably the most often reprinted single volume of Australian poems in the last thirty years. It had the same kind of impact that the paintings of Nolan, Boyd and others had in the art world. It presented the facts of Australia—its past, convict and Aboriginal, its war time and post war present, and thoughts about its future—in an immediately recognisable way. Wright had clearly read and assimilated influences from Eliot, Pound, Edith Sitwell and Dylan Thomas. She was able to bring fairly modern techniques to bear on her Australian subject matter in the same way that the painters were able to assimilate various overseas techniques and influences and apply them for their own purposes. She also had the advantage, in writing about Australia, its landscape and its past, of being able to write at one and the same time about her own pioneering family which had such a close relationship with and a sense of responsibility for the land.

The Moving Image contained twenty-two short poems and a fairly long philosophical meditation, the title poem. The titles of the individual lyrics, which could almost be read as the titles of a catalogue from an art exhibition of the day, are indicative of her major concerns: landscape and history, the Aboriginals, trapped animals, figures from the past like the remittance man or the soldier farmer, figures of alienation and solitude, the old country town recluse, the drover, the surfer, the bullocky. She took some uniquely Australian subjects which through a situation or an image sum up a whole phase of the Australian past, and by new vision, lifted them to a higher level. In this mythologizing, transforming process she was doing exactly what Nolan and Boyd were doing in art.

'The Bullocky', perhaps her most famous poem, is an excellent illustration of this. The bullocky is one of the stock, clichéd images of Australian writing. Apart from Kendall and Furphy, he has been the subject of poems by writers as different as Will Lawson, Louis Esson, Mary Gilmore, Rex Ingamells to mention only a few. Wright's poem is not a simple piece of realism or affectionately comic observation like its predecessors; it is a highly-wrought ikon, elevating its subject matter through its range of references and its deliberately mannered choice of words and images. But it bears the same kind of relationship to its predecessors that Hope's 'Australia' bears to the patriotic nationalistic poems which preceded it. The poem relates two backgrounds, that of the bullock driver of pioneering days and that of the shepherd of the Bible, relating his life and the meaning of his existence to that of the Old Testament prophet. The poem is an intricate pattern of symbols. The bullocky is part of the past, lives in the past and finally goes mad in his life of isolation. The sense of strain and isolation and the religious overtones are carefully built up: fiends, angels, the apocalyptic dream. Moses led the Israelites towards the Promised Land and the bullocky too opens up the way for the Promised Land, the future of Australia. Throughout the poem, for all the heightened realism of its detail, a sense of religious awe is built up for the man and his work:

>   beneath
> the half-light pillar of the trees
> he filled the steepled cone of night
> with shouted prayers and prophecies.

393

The bullocky's bones feed the land he helped to open up and the intimacy of the relationship is suggested by the word hand—the vine holds the land closely as in the sealing of a pact or a pledge, with its sense of interrelationship and continuity:

> O vine, grow close upon that bone
> and hold it with your rooted hand.
> The prophet Moses feeds the grape
> and fruitful is the Promised Land.

The poem is shaped towards a sense of affirmation and the celebration of achievement and is an extraordinarily effective and compact tribute to a pioneer. Biblical parallels of the kind used in 'Bullocky' often occur in Wright's work: another example is found in 'Bora Ring', a brief lyric that deftly suggests the tragic relationship between the colonial pioneers and the Aboriginals—and man's inhumanity to man, in its recognition of 'the fear as old as Cain'.

The Moving Image is a volume dominated by the sense of time. Its epigraph from Plato 'Time is a moving image of eternity' explains its central preoccupation, while the title poem itself is a meditation on the theme of time and its place in our lives. The poem owes something to FitzGerald in its sense of striving ambition, while the concept of two times—clock time and time in depth—inevitably recalls the Slessor of 'Five Bells'. Other images show the influence of Eliot ('We inherit a handful of dust and a fragment of stone') and there are cadences which owe much to Yeats, or Yeats filtered through Dylan Thomas ('the first birth and the first cry and the first death') and the neo-Romantic English poets of the 1940s. The poem is impressive in intention and achievement, but it is marred by rhetorical assertions of the kind that occur throughout her work. Judith Wright is an ambitious poet and she has always risked her arm at large undertakings, never settling for the neat accomplishment of the safely tried and known. But, even allowing for this, it is true that her most achieved poems are often her shortest and most modest, or those lyrics like 'Bullocky', 'Brothers and Sisters', 'Remittance Man', 'South of My Days', in which the central figure is associated with an historical phase, or some aspect of the past. Here the poem comes to rest in a concrete image or a sense of a human visage, rather than pressing outwards into some large abstraction where instead of presenting an experience she tends to talk about it, or instead of letting the meaning emerge implicitly she goes on to embroider and explicate it. All Judith Wright's future work, its style, tone, possibilities and future directions, is implicit in her first volume, though she does not focus on the New England tablelands—the home of her pioneering family—in quite the same way again.

'Thought tends to gather in pools', Wallace Stevens once observed, and throughout her career Judith Wright's books seem to have grown out of this poetic process, with one volume seeming to develop from, or even to reply to another. This is especially the impression from the first four volumes which made such deliberate use of their carefully chosen epigraphs. *The Moving Image* was haunted by a sense of the past, of the ravages of time. In *Woman to Man* (1949) Wright explores the meaning of love, the creative effects of time which bring renewal and regeneration. 'Love was the most ancient of all the gods, and existed before everything else, except chaos, which is held coeval therewith.' The first three poems, 'Woman to Man', 'Woman's Song' and 'Woman to Child', poems of conception and gestation, form a kind of tryptych, and while they were unique in poetry as the expression of woman's feeling for man and unborn child, for the sense of created and creating life, the poems are in no obvious way personal or confessional. They are, on the contrary, remarkably formal in tone and construction, with a strong external shape, using traditional, even sometimes conventional emblematic images such as the hunter, the chase, the arc, the crystal and the folded rose, contrasts between strength and weakness, between the unknown and unrepeatable, the cyclic and continuous, the cosmic and the personal; marked only by the change of tone and voice in the last line of 'Woman to Man': 'O hold me, for I am afraid'. In these poems images of seed and plant, dark and light, flower and tree are deployed without any one image dominating to suggest all the related natural processes of birth and growth.

Woman to Man is one of Wright's richest books, containing a variety of her best poems, 'The Bull', 'The Cycads', 'The Old Prison', 'Wonga Vine', 'Stars' and the opening poems just mentioned. Character poems of the kind she made familiar in her first book recur—'The Sisters', 'Metho Drinker', 'The Twins'; poems of night and symbolic landscape and the historical past continue. as well as Blake-like poems like 'The Killer' where she dramatizes the presence of destructive inner forces in the human psyche.

395

Much of Judith Wright's poetry is concerned with origins and ends, with a search for significances; and central to one aspect of her poetry is the preoccupation with beginnings, whether in the cluster of poems that could be called poems of biological vision or the poems on the evolutionary cycle, where she tries to press back to an awareness of the origin of time and consciousness itself. Two of her finest poems, 'The Cycads' and 'Ancestors' illustrate these enduring preoccupations extremely well. The first is a meditation on the paradoxical life of the Cycads, a living fossil which endures and lives like a work of art ('they seem a generation carved in stone'). It has not changed through millennia while the rest of life has evolved around it. Immune from the pressures of birth and death, from change and evolution, untouched and unbroken by life, the Cycads sterile endurance is compared with that of the evolving and therefore 'complicated' birds and flowers whose fragile, delicate lives are so transient. The tension of the poem comes from the finely-held contrast between the timeless perfection of the Cycads and the world of change and transience which is our own, and which the poet invites us to pursue to that point where consciousness reflects on its own non-existence. Similarly in 'The Ancestors' in a moment of vision in a Queensland rain forest, the poet experiences the sense of being at the source of life; the trunks of the tree-ferns suggest shaggy apes, the fern centres foetuses, and the whole sense of being at the heart of an experience fully understood for the first time—our connection with prehistory and the evolutionary cycle (one recalls too the second stanza of 'Woman to Child') is beautifully enacted as consciousness in a timeless moment reflects on its own origins and roots in time:

> That sad, pre-history, unexpectant face—
> I hear the answering sound of my blood. I know
> these primitive fathers waiting for rebirth,
> these children not yet born—the womb holds so
> the moss-grown patience of the skull,
> the old ape-knowledge of the embryo.
>
> Their silent sleep is gathered round the spring
> that feeds the living, thousand lighted stream
> up which we toiled into this timeless dream.

In other poems—'Birds' for instance—the relationship between the human and the non-human is explored in more direct ways as the poet longs to escape from the burdens of the human world into the world of natural harmony and simplicity. But this poem, like several others on the search for singleness and silence, is more interesting for the wider conflict it depicts than for the solution it proposes.

Although there are thematic overlappings, cross references and comparison pieces throughout all the books, *The Gateway* (1953) marks a further step in Judith Wright's progress and search for the self that must be lost to be found. As the epigraph from Blake's *Milton* indicates, her preoccupation is now less with time and timelessness than with time and the enigmas of eternity; but a change in method is apparent in the way poems become more explicitly symbolic and allegorical: meanings and messages are imposed rather than revealed or discovered, and the same applies to the less successful poems in *The Two Fires* (1955) which deals with the creative and destructive forces that govern the world, particularly under the threat of the hydrogen bomb. Across these books moves her concern with various dualities—the search for renewal and regeneration against inner and outer destructive forces. Both of these books led critics to comment on her un-evenness and uncertainty of direction. Her tone can move from the masterly simplicity of 'Our Love is So Natural' to the grandiloquence of 'The Two Fires', and it may have been the author's own awareness of the slips and slides and imprecisions which some of her poems manifested that led her to write another cluster of poems all centred on the sense of the limitations and inadequacies of language itself. 'For Precision', 'Five Senses', 'Nameless Flower', 'Camping at Spur Rock', to name only a few, contain in different ways critiques of the deficiencies of language, revealing a felt conflict between the mind's needs to impose patterns and structures and the heart's need to discover them; and an acute awareness of the imagination's inability to capture and hold the external world as it really is. Judith Wright is the most philosophically explorative of all Australian poets, including FitzGerald, and it is a sign of her acutely self-conscious modernity that her awareness leads her to explore the very tools which are the instruments of her exploration.

The *Gateway* and *The Two Fires* contain some of her finest poems, but also declamatory and unconvincing poems like 'Two Songs for the World's End' with its long string of abstractions which lack any sense of imaginative impact. Both these books

397

mark, too, her explicit concentration on the idea of a spiritual journey—not this time into pre-history, but a journey, often allegorized, into the country of the self. 'The Traveller and the Angel' allegorizes the stages of man's journey through life, finding his identity and purpose first through the assertion of his own strength and power against the first angel, but now waiting for another angel and a deeper spiritual conflict ahead. The poem expresses the fear of what is ahead and a sense of discouragement and anxiety, and seems to be partly answered by the poem, 'The Gateway', which followed it. Here the meaning seems to be that it is only through the acceptance of inner nothingness and the loss of self, and being absorbed in the processes of the dissolution and the flow and change of the world that spiritual strength or renewal can be found.

The use of various kinds of religious imagery in these poems, in 'The Lost Man' and 'Sandy Swamp'—poems which enact a sense of suffering and redemption—obviously express some of the author's own search for meanings at the time, and go hand in hand with her attempt to find significance and spiritual fulfilment out-side the confines of the orthodox or the merely rationalistic. While McAuley was finding his answers in orthodox religion, Hope in asserting the power of the will, Wright like Patrick White was using the figure of the inspired fool or simpleton to express her search for a higher consciousness. In *The Moving Image* Tom of Bedlam served this purpose. Jimmy Delaney, the blind singer in *Woman to Man*, was held to have the special kind of insight reserved for the mad and the inspired. The idea that children, fools and simpletons have access to a richer knowledge than the intellectual or the ordinary articulate person has a long history, but it is especially associated with various aspects of the development of neo-primitivism among modern writers. The assumption behind it is that simple, uncomplicated beings have direct access to the truth in a way denied to more complex and sophisticated mortals, in whom the intellect intrudes.

The basic outlook behind this approach is an irrational one—the belief that reason, intellect, civilization and culture all lead away from the truth instead of closer to it. The poems that belong to this group, like 'Legend' and 'The Man Beneath the Tree' are not Wright's most successful pieces, though the effort and search behind them need to be taken into account to gain some idea of her scope, and it may well be that these poems and the ideas inspiring them prepared the ground for the more successful poems of the time, poems in which the sense of self-consciousness, alienation and division is overcome or transcended.

It was, however, seven years before Judith Wright produced another book *Birds* (1962), and this—one of her finest separate volumes—was marked by an extraordinarily modest approach, a poetry of reduced pretensions and quietly probing, unasserted tones. It is true that at all times Judith Wright had written different kinds of poems, some in a high, slightly mannered diction, others spare and sparse. Humour too has played its role, as in the fine poem 'Request to a Year'. But *Birds* is her most concentrated volume. It marks a considerable, though in no ways abrupt, change in her development. The bardic excesses of the early volumes are discarded, the verse seems to become more relaxed and flexible, less highly wrought and closer to the rhythms of the speaking voice, perhaps partly in response to the general change in this direction that came over poetry in the English speaking world in the sixties, but just as much as an organic development of tendencies already there in previous volumes. The technical assurance, the adroitness of pieces like 'Night Herons' and 'Lyrebirds' is too easily overlooked. Judith Wright's poetry has always been suffused with the values of natural piety and *Birds* is a search for a finer understanding of what is involved in 'the reverence of the heart', which some of her half-extinct, dying or fabulous creatures inhabit.

Over the last ten years two main notes tend to dominate in her work. Her diction has become more astringent and dry, flatter and unemphatic as in 'Habitat', the sequence in *Alive* where she fare-wells her home in Queensland, before moving to Braidwood in New South Wales, while her poems of social protest have become more frequent, more emphatic and sharp in their condemnation of the various ills that torment the country. She is an ardent conservationist and has always condemned unthinking exploita-tion of the land; her own inevitable involvement in these processes of destruction is clear in 'At Cooloola' and in 'A Document'—but where these poems present the inescapable tragedy of the involve-ment, later poems have become more insistently strident and direct—whether about the Vietnam war, the situation of the Aborigines, the problems of pollution, or the gradual extermina-tion of flora and fauna.

Judith Wright is the most varied and exploratory poet of her generation, and her whole *oeuvre*, more than that of any of her contemporaries, gives one a vivid sense of the chaotic modern world with all its personal, social and historical conflicts. Her work is at once global and local in its awareness. Henry James once remarked to Robert Louis Stevenson about Hérédia's *Les Trophées*: 'Yes, it is impressive, but is it a life's work?' Read in its entirety Judith Wright's poetry gives us the sense of being a life's work in the sense that James intended, and the work of a whole life.

Douglas Stewart has been a versatile writer, dramatist, critic, short story writer, literary editor and probably the most important man of letters in modern Australian literary history since Vance Palmer. But while his formative years were the 1930s and the 1940s, it is only in the last twenty years that the full range and scope of his lyric talent has started to come into perspective. Like Hope, Wright, and David Campbell, some of his finest poems have been the product of advancing age.

Stewart's abundant productivity is closely related to his attitude to words. Poets can probably be divided into those who are poets of speech—poets who want to say something in as direct and immediate a way as possible—and poets of language—those who are always working along the grain of language itself so that it is language which finally leads them to the thing said. Stewart does not belong comfortably to either category. For him poetry is not the vehicle for a message or for some important personal 'word', as it often is for McAuley and Les Murray, nor is his use of language notably exploratory or novel like Francis Webb's. His interests range between the two limits, using the vernacular and the colloquial rather than the highly wrought or the intellectual, and while this is part of his unevenness, it is also part of his variety.

Stewart's interest is pre-eminently in verse patterns of a basic range—the ballad, the song, the narrative—and the total effect, more than the fondled details of its saying. The force of his best poems seems to lie in their rhythmic drive ('Terra Australis') or their rhythmic rise and fall ('The Silkworms'), though his finest poems reveal an admirably lucid control of the master-image. Subtle language effects occur: the use of alliteration in 'A Flock of Gang-Gangs', which is part of the whole texture of the poem and not detachable for illustrative purposes, or the effective play of sounds in poems like 'Lyrebird' and 'Kookaburras' ('Like waterfalls exulting down the gullies') show a sensitive awareness of purely poetic values:

> They gobble the night in their throats like purple berries,
> They plunge their beaks in the tide of darkness and dew
> And fish up the long rays of light; no wonder they howl
> In such a triumph of trumpets . . .

It is typical of Stewart that these effects should be used in a poem which conveys a sense of joy and amusement in the happiness of life. Stewart has written narratives, fantasies, humorous and satirical poems, love poems and tall-story ballads, as well as a cluster of exquisite nature lyrics; but it seems to me that the strength of his best poems resides in their evasive scepticism—his ability to see both sides of the question and not commit himself to anything beyond the making of the poem itself—a habit of mind which perhaps comes from Stewart's work as a dramatist. This is strikingly the case in 'Terra Australis' with its zestful, energetic tone. The particular success of this poem—and it is among his outstanding pieces—lies in the way the potentially negative energy of mockery is turned into the good-natured refusal to be defeated: the illusions are mocked, but not the persistency of effort. It is, in fact, notable that Stewart is never savage or dismissive; and a tone of easy acceptance, even of modest mildness and indulgence, characterizes much of his poetry.

One notices how in poems like 'Terra Australis' or 'Mungo Park', whether Stewart is developing an idea, or exploring contrasting points of view, or merely observing an animal or a plant, his imagination seems to work through a series of poised suspensions, hoverings, oscillations. In 'Terra Australis' Stewart brings Lane and de Quiros together, posits a similarity in their situations, suggests a relationship (both have searched in vain for the earthly paradise, both go their separate ways). Similarly in 'Mungo Park' the explorer of Africa meets Sir Walter Scott, the sessile littérateur. Both realise that both are explorers in their different ways. Stewart exploits a sense of contending voices to celebrate good-naturedly the continuity of human effort, a sense of the unceasing quest. The poems simultaneously celebrate and question the meaning of the quest.

Stewart's evasive scepticism can be seen, too, in his most delicate lyrics, many of which tend to pivot on an expressed or implied 'as if' or 'as though':

> Leave it alone! For white like the egg of a snake
> In its shell beside it another begins to break,
> And under those crimson tentacles, down that throat,
> Secret and black still gurgles the oldest ocean
> Where, evil and beautiful, sluggish and blind and dumb,
> Life breathes again, stretches its flesh and moves
> Now like a deep-sea octopus, now like a flower,
> And does not know itself which to become.

Most of his later images, like the fungus itself, 'do not know themselves which to become': 'Moth or flower, flower or moth,/ Neither moth nor flower but both', as he says of the tongue orchid; and through the juxtaposition and deliberately uncertain interplay of these images the object itself emerges with real precision and clarity.

Stewart's most sustained poem in this vein is 'Spider-gums' (in *The Birdsville Track*, 1955), a beautiful virtuoso piece which shows that he can also be a poet of unexpected literary artifice and sophistication. Stewart wants to suggest in this poem the frailty and delicacy of the trees (they are like sketches, lace, visible and invisible) and to celebrate the way they survive and endure 'the killing blast': it is the frail persistence and the tenacity of life and beauty that he delights in.

Stewart's world of nature is often a fantasy world—the dryad in the lemon trees, the water lily as an angel—and while he has written lyrics of fine perceptiveness like 'Helmet Orchid', 'Nodding Greenhood', 'The Gully' and 'Brindabella', where the imaginative grasp is deeper, one can say that the strength of the fantasy world resides in the fact that the author himself does not fully believe in it. He is a very different nature poet from, for example, Roland Robinson. Robinson believes in his visions with a religious intensity; Stewart entertains the idea, or an image—and sometimes adds a wry piece of moralizing to it. It is this which makes him one of the most completely aesthetic of modern Australian poets.

Stewart's development towards his personal style has been slowly made and there are signs in his first book that a very different type of poet might have emerged. *Green Lions* (1936), *The White Cry* (1939), *Elegy for an Airman* (1940) and *Sonnets to the Unknown Soldier* (1941) retain their interest for those concerned with tracing the main lines of his development, but it is hardly too peremptory a judgment to link them all together as apprentice books in which we see a young poet doing what he can with a not unlimited range of emotional and imaginative experience. *Green Lions*, occasionally reminiscent of Roy Campbell and firmly set in Stewart's New Zealand background, contains thirty-four poems in different shapes, from the vigorous free verse of the title poem to the classically cool restraint of 'The Imperishable Image' which begins with a characteristic and, in view of his later development, extremely touching image: 'As soft as candlelight on snow . . .'

The White Cry, with *Green Lions* the best of the early books, shows an almost symbolist awareness of colour and its peculiar power to evoke emotion—especially rose, blue, and above all white and silver, which are perhaps related to Stewart's pre-occupation with snow and ice. But while many of the poems in this volume, as well as those in the book that immediately followed, *Elegy for an Airman*, fail to focus or fuse into achieved wholes, several, including 'The White Rider' and 'Heritage', are moving, and the rich if confused subjectivity of a poem like 'Furnished Room' touches a level of apprehension that was—perhaps regrettably—to disappear from his later work.

Between *The White Cry*, *Sonnets to the Unknown Soldier*, and *The Dosser in Springtime* lie, of course, Stewart's plays—the popular *The Fire on the Snow* (1941), *Ned Kelly* (1943) and *The Golden Lover* (1943); and the influence of these early plays on the final direction of his lyric talent can hardly be overestimated. Free and direct speech is essential in a radio play, and the natural speech rhythms which predominate in Stewart's verse after the writing of these plays is one of its most striking and persistent features. To move from *Sonnets to the Unknown Soldier* to *The Fire on the Snow* is to move in two different worlds of language. Both works celebrate endurance and the values of heroic fortitude, but in *The Fire on the Snow* Stewart has found the concrete situation that suits his ideal, and his words work together to create a world. His most distinctive and best-known work in the lyric has been done since this time.

The Dosser in Springtime marks a decisive development in Stewart's poetry, from the suggestiveness of his early work towards ballad-like statements of a robust cheerfulness. It announces, too, the beginnings of a vein of fantasy and whimsy in his work, which could not have been foreseen from his earlier volumes—fantasy, and quaintness as well, of the kind found in some of the poems of Hugh McCrae, Harold Monro and Walter de la Mare. Both H. M. Green and Robert D. FitzGerald have

403

written enthusiastically of the use of the ballad in *The Dosser in Springtime*, and Stewart has clearly made a significant contribution to the adoption of this form in modern Australian poetry. But his most distinctive contribution lies in his meditative and nature lyrics.

It is notable that many of Stewart's finest nature poems, and especially those in *Sun Orchids* (1952) and *The Birdsville Track* (1955), are devoted to the slightest of bush creatures and bush plants. There seems little doubt that this preoccupation springs both from an observation of the actual natural scene in Australia as well as temperamentally from the lyric's preference for the slight and delicate, and its belief in the persistence of the frail in whatever shape or form.

There are no nature poems in *The Dosser in Springtime* of the kind *Sun Orchids*, *The Birdsville Track* and *Rutherford* (1962) were later to make us familiar with; and this addition to Stewart's work reflects an important phase in Australian poetry. The late forties and the early fifties saw the brief development of a 'school' of nature poets whose most distinguished representatives were Judith Wright (in some aspects), Roland Robinson, David Campbell and of course Stewart himself, who published those poets in the *Bulletin* at this time. This is the kind of interaction frequent in literary history, and it was clearly an important stage in the ecology of Australian poetry. Perhaps no finer proof of the individuality of these writers is needed than to compare their very different poems—for whatever their similarity of subject matter, they differ considerably in vision, texture and technique. Stewart's nature poems, in particular, differ from Robinson's, Campbell's and Wright's both in their sparseness of emotion, their drier, more etched tone, and in the way they tactfully accept the play of image as an end in itself.

Stewart has commented that many of his nature poems are

> essentially an exploration of the mysteries of creation and evolution, especially of the duality of the universe (or God); good and evil, or apparent good and evil, like the flower and the centipede, both coming from the same Hand.[13]

It might perhaps be truer to say that they are illustrations rather than explorations, both because of the visual nature of their appeal—they are almost photographically accurate—and because they attempt to state a moment of vision. A poem like 'The

Goldfish Pool' (with the contrasting images of the water scorpion and the goldfish representing good and evil) makes Stewart's theme explicit, with the image of comets and suns and scaly moons gently and unobtrusively suggesting the creation and the necessary balance between the forces of good and evil in the world. 'The Green Centipede', 'Kindred' and several other poems develop this theme. Less obvious and less commented on are the metaphysical implications of poems like 'Spider-Gums', 'The Last of Snow' and 'Flowering Bloodwoods', poems which suggest thought and feeling trembling on the edge of consciousness, and the intimate unity of all things in nature. Stewart is interested in the dynamic processes of nature and the relationship between being and becoming. Through his use of images he suggests certain metaphysical truths and awarenesses. Stewart rarely states or declares these truths, his poems suggest them. In 'The Spider-Gums' he is suggesting how 'the frail and delicate persist'—like Pascal's thinking reed—and behind many of these poems is the metaphysical paradox: 'Except a corn of wheat fall into the ground and die, it abideth alone; but if it dies, it bringeth forth much fruit.'

The nature poems in *Sun Orchids* and *The Birdsville Track* are frequently short pieces of one sentence each, articulated on an image of varying fancifulness: a mignonette orchid 'like little green bats on a steeple,/Beetle, beetle and beetle'; or Christmas Bells 'dance all day in the heat/Like little bushfires themselves'. The frequent use of the word 'little' in these pieces, the microscopic, miniaturistic view of the world they imply, points to a deliberate restriction of sensibility and imagination. Some pieces in spite of their finely felt fragments of detail fail as wholes through a final lack of imaginative daring; but others like 'Flowering Bloodwoods', 'Spider-Gums', 'The Snow-Gum', 'A Robin', 'A Flock of Gang-Gangs' and 'Brindabella' are marked by a joyful reticence and a controlled flow of feeling, without dryness and untouched by preciosity.

In 'The Snow Gum' Stewart is concerned with an entranced moment of perfection, describing a snow gum with its shadow falling on the snow. The snow gum is one of the basic clichés of Australian iconography, its photograph frequently appearing in grocers' and butchers' calendars and it is typical of Stewart to take up such a worn subject and to invest it with new life and meaning. A poem like 'The Snow Gum' can defy the analytic critic: but one can see in it an example of that perfect congruence between an

405

outer landscape and an inner state—where mood and landscape merge in the exquisite sense of a moment of perfection. The tree is reflected in the snow in the perfect shape of its own shadow. Words like 'miracle', 'eternity' and 'ecstacy' occur, while the word 'perfect' is repeated in each stanza in a way that suggests something of breathless surprise, but also something of an almost mathematical accuracy and precision, while the verbs, 'flowering', 'performing', 'doing', 'flowing' and 'curving' suggest movement and living action. The poem conveys a sense of held movement that is not static, with opposing tensions momentarily but completely reconciled.

It is particularly striking that Stewart's finest and most graceful lyrics, with their characteristic delicacy and flexibility of rhythm and tone, are often concerned with snow and the snow country. Many of his early poems in *Green Lions* celebrate the southern landscape of New Zealand, and images of ice and snow naturally predominate in 'Worsley Enchanted' and *The Fire on the Snow*. Stewart has written of the Australian outback, especially in *The Birdsville Track*, but there is something of a postcard, extroverted quality in these poems, and for all their effective images they do not achieve the precarious tender delicacy and the firmly held poise of the snow poems, with their entranced sense of the 'slow miracle' of nature. Stewart has come more and more to favour the use of half-rhyme, and his use of ghost rhymes in these poems serves to suggest both the precise delineation and heightened clarity of *things* and the enclosing sense of muffling—or momentarily pierced—silence.

Rutherford remains Stewart's most substantial single book up to the present time, and is among the finest works of recent Australian poetry. It contains all the kinds of poems, in the variety of tones, which Stewart has mastered, and it shows a new development in his use of the discursive mode in pieces like 'Fence', the rhetorical 'Easter Island' and in the title poem of the collection. 'Rutherford', written in the long loping casual line that Stewart has frequently favoured, is a meditative discourse on the nature of responsibility and power, developed around the schematic images of the wheel and the hand. One feels at moments that the whole is a little relaxed rhythmically for a poem of its length, and that the point of view—speaking both from inside and outside 'Rutherford'—is not quite dramatically maintained. But the poem is thematically interesting for its connections with the shorter nature lyrics, since like them it asserts the presence of some creative force or power at the heart of life that can be used for good or ill, and like them it tends to declare its truths rather than to explore them.

The strength of Stewart's line can be felt at its finest in 'The Silkworms' and 'The Garden of Ships'—both deeply moving meditations on freedom and action and the limitations of the human world. 'The Silkworms' in particular—outstanding for its ingenious use of ghost rhymes and half-rhymes to reinforce its atmosphere of muted movement and gentle frustration—is marked by a delicate gravity of tone and an unassertive acceptance of the limits of human existence. It is certainly one of Stewart's masterpieces—completely and imaginatively inward with itself, and one of the outstanding poems written in Australia. It can be read in a variety of ways and given political and metaphysical interpretations, though any reading which narrows the suggestive power of the whole does damage to its artistic truth. Some read 'The Silkworms' as a comment on Australian suburbia, or Australian conservatism, some give it a political interpretation, but it is a meditation on the whole of the human condition ('We are born into a created world' D. H. Lawrence once remarked), the way life is fashioned and shaped, ordered and restricted by inhibitions and conventions, protected and made stable and secure by limitations and frustrations. It is a poem about the continuities and the continuing processes of life.

It sometimes happens that a poet writes a poem at some stage of his career which is a summing up of much of his life's work and all that it stands for. Such a poem is Stewart's 'B Flat'. Stewart has commented that he wrote this poem on the day that India and Pakistan went to war. This information does not get into the poem of course, which is in itself a celebration of innocence, of eccentric, civilized values—civilization being that which values the small, the frail, the useless. Stewart commemorates his hero for being 'in the world's enormousness, enormity, so interested in music and in owls', for being gentle and harmless. I see this poem as something of a summation and a critique of Stewart's work—the poem where his interest in the ballad, narrative and the lyric vision that so preoccupied him in his earlier work merge and fuse with his vision of the significance of the tiniest and frailest things in nature. In much of his early work there is a preoccupation with violence and a chest-beating concept of heroism which is subtly and unobtrusively 'placed' in a later poem like 'B Flat'. Stewart is an ambitious poet who has experimented in a variety of modes, but his seemingly unambitious poems, like his nature poems and his meditative lyrics are his finest achievement.

David Campbell, who also emerged in the 1940s, belongs with John Manifold and Douglas Stewart in his concern to continue a popular, vernacular tradition, without losing contact with the highest resources of art, but he has been a more restlessly experimental and consistently productive poet than either of his contemporaries. His first books belong to the ethos of Australian poetry of the forties and mid-fifties. Later volumes are much more exploratory and more uneven, and belong with the new developments of the 1960s and 1970s, in particular the rediscovery of the personal past and the recovery of irrational techniques, much influenced by the neo-Surrealist movement. A characteristic Campbell poem, whether early or late, is marked by its crispness of phrasing, its oddly unexpected yet appropriate imagery, its economy of approach. He works through concentration and intensity, rather than through expansiveness and width. Like Stewart he is one of the poets who has exploited the nature poem most profitably for his own personal ends, and if one sometimes thinks after reading much of the nature poetry of the 1940s and the 1950s that 'slight is trite', one also often has occasion to understand that 'small is beautiful'. Campbell is among the few modern Australian poets who have drawn unselfconsciously and successfully on both the European and the local Australian tradition to make from them something personal and new.

Like Stewart he tried to write lyrics that combine the popular and the sophisticated; like Shaw Neilson he uses only two or three forms—the song, the ballad, the meditative lyric. His first poems, like many of his later ones, are concerned with one theme: continuity through time and change, transformation and metamorphosis. *Speak with the Sun* is preoccupied with presences and absences in a known and loved landscape; the ballads are populated by bullock drivers, swagmen, explorers, drovers, soldiers, barmaids—all the figures of popular Australian folk-lore. Like Judith Wright in 'Bullocky', and Nolan in his paintings, Campbell in poems like 'Harry Pearce' and 'The Stockman', was trying to mythologize and elevate an Australian tradition, emphasizing its continuity and its haunting power (Judith Wright's title *The Generations of Men* could serve as a neat summary of what most

Australian writing was about in the 1940s). Campbell's sense of continuity is not merely a question of the content of his poems: it is demonstrated in his sense of form and technique—in his use of the old bush song and ballad shapes for a new purpose, in the way he consciously uses Australian colloquialisms, terms and references.

Campbell's finest poems have a certain complexity and density of texture; many are half-songs, half meditative lyrics, like 'Night Sowing', 'Words and Lovers', 'Who Points the Swallow', (which develops between song and meditation its theme of the virtues of passivity and its celebration of love as the power which guides and orders life). Then there are sequences like 'Cockys' Calendar', which gathers together emblematic images of the countryside through the cycle of the year: 'Bindweed and Yellowtail' from the series reveals Campbell's art at its best:

> November, sweet with secret birds
> And thin-voiced weeds that cheat the sun,
> For half the season wastes its words,
> But when my silent mood comes on
>
> The little blushing flowers that part
> The grasses where the sheep-tracks meet
> Go deeper than the morning thought
> Of waking lovers or the great;
>
> And these small singers made of light
> That stream like stars between the trees,
> Sum in an inch the long delight
> Of suns and thoughtful centuries.

This is a beautifully concentrated lyric, beginning with a specific month, November, and moving through to centuries, the time span covered serving to show the link between the small and the vast, the one and the many. The theme of the poem is the eternity of now, the sense of timelessness through time. It is the strength of Campbell's art (as of the lyric in general) to affirm the paradoxical resistance of the small and frail in front of the great and over-whelming, in a poem that avoids both sentimentality and preciosity; to demonstrate how a sustaining truth may be perceived through the apparently insignificant.

Campbell's poems always suggest a detached yet involved contemplation of the world around him, a mind that responds to the otherness of nature but always finds human equivalents in it as in 'Prayer for Rain' where man's simple and humble dependence on other powers is evoked with a fine economy of line, or as in the sonnet 'When Out of Love' where the self sufficiency of things in nature imposes a calm on the mind. This sonnet traces the movement from restless self-preoccupation to creative contemplation in a poem which illustrates its own processes.

Campbell's development reveals a growth in depth and sophistication, from the merging of the local bush songs and ballads and the higher Elizabethan tradition of pastoral elegance and ease, to the neo-surrealism of his most recent work. His later landscapes are no longer inhabited by the creatures of Australian tradition and tale; they are landscapes of the mind, places of solitude for communion and awareness. His poems have become smoother and rounder but more deliberately random. He no longer writes with the plucked stacatto tension of *Speak with the Sun*, but his poems have retained one quality throughout: the capacity for looking at the commonplaces of nature and life with a fresh eye. His imagery is always clear and alertly observed in the manner of folk songs.

David Campbell is one of the most considerable poets who had his formative beginnings in the 1940s and he exemplifies the best qualities of the verse of that period. A less retricted history of Australian poetry and of the 1940s would have to find more space for two Sydney poets who came under the spell of Lindsay-inspired aestheticism: Rosemary Dobson and Kenneth Mackenzie: Dobson for her exquisite poems based on works of art and for a handful of poignant personal poems on the loss of a child, Mackenzie for a group of late disciplined hospital and family poems, rather than the brashly erotic early verses. Another poet, much published by *The Bulletin* in the 1940s, which remained for some time under Douglas Stewart's editorship the most fruitful avenue for poetry publishing in this country, was W. Hart-Smith, still perhaps the best experimental poet in modern Australian writing, whose fine series of imagistic observations deserve a much wider currency than they have received. Idiosyncratic, quirky, like John Blight in his remarkable sea sonnets, Hart-Smith has a piercing eye for unusual and revealing correspondences. Both these poets have done more to demonstrate the abundance and variousness of things in nature than any of their contemporaries, and while they have their beginnings in the nature lyrics of the 1940s, they have more fully exploited than any of their contemporaries what David Campbell has called the surrealism of Australian landscape and nature.

Francis Webb, another Australian poet who first emerged through the pages of *The Bulletin* in the 1940s, has continued to exert influence on succeeding younger generations. Webb has in recent years through the tragic relationship between his art and his life become something of a cult figure and he may well exert for succeeding generations the kind of influence that Hart Crane exerted in America or even Gordon in Australia at an earlier stage. One fact is certain: to read Webb in the context of the Australian poetry of the period is to move on a totally new level of language, with a linguistic potency and charge without parallel in this country. Other poets have force, fineness or clarity; Webb has an astonishing richness and diversity of language, encompassing a whole range of tones from the colloquial to the highly learned and mannered, to the prophetic and apocalyptic. Only Hope and perhaps Judith Wright among Australian poets had something of the same command, but Hope decanted his tones into separately shaped and conceived poems, whereas Webb's tones often come together in one piece. Webb was greatly influenced by the early Lowell, more than has yet been assessed. A poem like 'For My Grandfather' is shaped in the language, images and cadences of the last section of Lowell's 'The Quaker Graveyard at Nantucket', in a way which must be judged to be derivative and therefore diminishing, rather than allusive and enriching. In the Australian context he was influenced by Slessor and FitzGerald in particular. He continued to experiment with the theme of exploration and with exceptional figures from the historical past, and is best known for his historical sequences *A Drum For Ben Boyd* (1948) *Leichhardt in Theatre* (1957) and 'Eyre All Alone' (1961). But where Slessor and FitzGerald chose figures like Cook and Tasman to show their influence on others both in the past and in the future, Webb concentrates on doomed heroes who are remembered less for what they achieved than for the riddles and enigmas they reveal. Not for Webb the direct simplicities of ... 'so Cook made choice ... /So men write poems in Australia', but an obsession with 'unexpected angles', the awareness that 'truth is a mass of stops and gaps', and will not be pinned down. Like Slessor with Cook, Webb is concerned to show the effect Boyd had on others, but where for Slessor meaning accrues and gathers, for Webb it tends to dissipate and fragment; Boyd's exceptional energy and power show up the inadequacies of others rather than enlarging their lives. 'Leichhardt in Theatre' (interestingly enough based on some of the same material as *Voss*) is a more dramatically shaped and rivetted work than 'Ben Boyd'. Webb focuses here on a figure seen as quixotic ('playing with windmills in the Never-Never'), idealist and clown, weak and self-dramatizing. Again as in 'A Drum for Ben Boyd' his search is for the truth:

> This is a land where man becomes a myth;
> Naked, his feet tread embers from the truth.

A number of poets from the thirties and forties struggled with the question of the meaning of myth and heroic action. While they brought their searchlights to bear on Australian conditions and Australian experience, it is worth recalling that English poets like Auden and MacNeice, and the English writers of radio plays like MacNiece, Laurie Lee and Henry Reed were much concerned with similar questions. Their influence on Webb and Stewart seems fairly clear. 'Leichhardt in Theatre' is not a mere portrait of the doomed explorer: like many other Webb poems which relate their subjects to works of art and artistic processes as well as to religious suffering and experience, 'Leichhardt in Theatre' is a poem about the processes of writing poetry, or being driven to map or capture in words the violent flux of life as Leichhardt is driven to explore 'time after time the death's-head continent.'

It is significant that Webb's central figures—Boyd, Leichhardt, Eyre, and St. Francis—are not dramatic presences. They are not *there* in the poems built around them in the way that Browning's Duke of Ferrara is present in 'My Last Duchess'. This is because Webb is less concerned with defining characters through word and deed than with showing what they have become—'myths', 'legends', 'monsters', 'clowns'. Webb's sense of the quest, his exploration in search of meaning, is ultimately metaphysical. As Judith Wright has said, 'Webb has . . . always been searching for the same thing—the truth about man and his relationships, to himself, to other men, and in the end, to God.' He moves from creatures of great willpower and assertion with touches of megalomania, like Boyd and Leichhardt, to more selfless figures like Eyre and St. Francis, in poems that explore and assert the sacramental.

Webb is the most difficult of all Australian poets to comment on. There is no doubt about his authority of language, the

command and depth of spiritual experience in his work as well as
its amplitude and the sheer force of his metaphysical range. But all
his longer works leave a residue of dissatisfaction and frustration,
the sense that they have not been fully delivered as a whole. In
many pieces there is a sense that

> ... Words strain
> Crack and sometimes break, under the burden,
> Under the tension ... will not stay in place,
> Will not stay still.

and the multi-layers of meaning in his language often remain
solvable puzzles rather than providing imaginative resolutions or
illuminations.

Webb's larger scale ambitious sequences need to be balanced
against a group of short works which focus on 'the tiny, the
pitiable, meaningless and rare' moments of experience, those
where we realise that: 'The tiny, not the immense, will teach our
groping eyes.' The most perfect of these, and one of the most
transparently direct of all Webb's poems is 'Five Days Old'. Webb's
poetry became more directly religious as he developed, deeply
concerned with showing the immediate relevance of his beliefs to
the facts and events of everyday life, and his strong sense of the
sacramental emerges whether he is imagining the first meeting of
Cook with Aboriginal Australia, watching a flight of crows and
cockatoos, or holding a child, five days old. This lyric achieves a
miraculous sense of balance between tenderness and fragility and a
sense of the weight and significance of the religious dimension of
life, bringing together the simple and the profound, the mundane
and the spiritual, innocence and experience:

> Christmas is in the air
> You are given into my hands
> Out of quietest, loneliest lands.
> My trembling is all my prayer.
> To blown straw was given
> All the fullness of Heaven.

In poems like this and a handful of others—'Morgan's Country',
elegies like 'A Death at Winson Green', the sequence 'Ward Two'
and the poems based in works of art and music—Webb has
written some of the finest poems in the history of Australian
literature.

Recent articles and surveys have had the tendency to catalogue Australian poets according to decades: the formalist ironic-rational late fifties and early sixties give way to the confessional auto-biographical sequences of the following decade, which in turn give way to the new Romanticism, the heightened subjectivity and irrational pursuits of the drug culture of the seventies. One might approach the whole question in a different way and say that every decade in Australian poetry has had its dominating influence: the nineties, Rudyard Kipling; the twenties and thirties, Eliot, the Sitwells, and Walter de la Mare; the forties, Yeats, whose impact was felt by Hope, Wright, Stewart, Campbell and McAuley and a host of lesser writers; the fifties, W. H. Auden; the sixties, Robert Lowell; and the seventies—the decade of diversification—a variety of American poets from Robert Duncan to George Oppen.

The main difficulty with such schemas is that the best poets are not contained by their patterns and that a decade is not a very long time in literary history, though some decades have been out-standing. The dominant tendencies of the last few years have been ably outlined and documented by James McAuley in *A Map of Australian Verse*. But beneath the tendencies and waves, one current survives: the quiet continuity of talent.

A. D. Hope remarked in a survey published in 1963

> The growth of literature in Australia has been a continuous one with few marked or sudden changes of direction or character.

though he went on to add that there are

> ... considerable differences from its condition twenty or thirty years ago.[14]

He was thinking particularly of the important influence university education was having on Australian writing revealed in the work of such poets as Evan Jones, Wallace-Crabbe, Vivian Smith, Alex Craig and Noel Macainsh. In 1961 Chris Wallace-Crabbe published an essay 'The Habit of Irony: Australian Poets of the Fifties' which was the first article to indicate new directions in Australian writing and the emergence of a new generation of poets. It proved to be an influential essay, recommending 'a neutral tone', concern for decent craftsmanship, a plain urbane style. The essay successfully captured a trend and pinned it down just as it was about to escape in a different direction. Sometimes an article which claims to capture a trend merely succeeds in imposing a tendency; but Wallace-Crabbe's essay served several useful purposes. At the time it seemed designed to correct and supplement the image of Australian poetry associated with the rather maligned first edition of *The Penguin Book of Modern Australian Verse*; but it pointed to some of the names which were to dominate in Australian poetry in the following decades—Bruce Dawe, Vincent Buckley, Francis Webb, Gwen Harwood, as well as Evan Jones and Wallace-Crabbe himself. The article failed, I think, to emphasize how much 'The Habit of Irony' was influenced by the English 'Movement' poets of the fifties who had their roots in the poetry of the thirties. Indeed an epigraph from Auden's *Look, Stranger* (1936) might well serve to sum up Wallace-Crabbe's whole argument:

> Since the external disorder, and extravagant lies,
> The baroque frontiers, the surrealist police;
> What can truth treasure, or heart bless,
> But a narrow strictness.

The article also failed to stress important local influences. Evan Jones' 'Noah's Song', which the essay featured, reads like an accomplished imitation of A. D. Hope, while Wallace-Crabbe's own early work had learnt quite a lot about at least one habit of irony from John Manifold. While a new note or new emerging tones surfaced in the late fifties and early sixties the fact remains that in many of the most important poets of the time, not only Webb, Harwood and Buckley but also Stow, Beaver, Dawe and Jones, one often finds a mixed diction, not a neutral tone, with different levels of language, from the flat and colloquial to a higher register of emotions to encompass splendour and tragedy. The general openness of these writers to influences from overseas is attested by the fact that all went on to employ a richer spectrum of colours. Perhaps it is a simple question of development—they started by knowing what they did not want—strength through elimination, and then, as they gained confidence, were able to allow their poetry to admit an increasing variety of tones and techniques to reflect the increasing variety of their experience. The unfortunate effect of all short term views, especially when applied to young and developing writers, is that they often involve a diminution of what has been done in favour of what is fashion-

415

able, so that a well made poem of the fifties or early sixties which may be extremely effective of its kind (Evan Jones' 'Noah's Song' is a good illustration of this point) now tends to be downgraded in favour of current critical demands. In the survey mentioned before, A. D. Hope also observed

> Present day Australian poets write as individuals and express an individual vision and outlook. What they have in common is a return to traditional forms and techniques of verse and a retreat from experimental methods, free verse, surrealist logomania, fragmentary imagism, dislocated syntax and symbolist allusiveness.[15]

All of these were in fact quickly to become the catch-cries and programmes of young writers of the late sixties and seventies and are still with us. Many have had a considerable influence on writers like Vincent Buckley, R. A. Simpson and Gwen Harwood. The older writers who first emerged in the sixties, and one must add Bruce Beaver to the list, have shown a determined capacity to experiment and change forms in ways that would never have occurred to writers like Stewart, Hope, McAuley or even Judith Wright. These forties writers have been attacked for their restrictive conservatism by following generations; a hostile critic might say that later poets have shown considerable facility for swimming with the tide and wooing every current of fashion. It seems more likely that this rapidity of change and willingness to experiment is part of the historical changes that are occurring in Australia's relations to the rest of the world.

The sixties and seventies have opened up new fields of experiment under the influence of American poets, while the example of imaginative freedom and authoritative daring found in Patrick White's novels has had considerable if indirect influence on some of the poets, giving a new breadth and freedom to their work.

Over the last three decades the concept of the poet has changed. Hope and Wright initially projected a view of the poet as seer; this gave way to the fifties-sixties notion of the poet as teacher and entertainer; some of the new poets of the drug culture have recovered the idea of the poet as seer and visionary. But the best mainstream poetry written in Australia over the last few years gives the impression less of striking attitudes than of voicing basic human experiences and feelings. It is significant that the theme of the relationship with 'the folk' that poets like Brennan and Wilmot found it impossible to establish in their art, now comes quite naturally to writers like Dawe and Les Murray and even, after an arduous struggle, to Vincent Buckley. Les Murray, who has spoken so much about the vernacular republic and who is able to project himself quite unselfconsciously in the role of peasant mandarin, song-king and spiritual leader to an extent unparalleled in Australian poetry has never, for all his sophistication, lost touch with the folk element in his art.

Eugenio Montale once stated that the poet searches for 'a precise truth, not for the general truth,' and this statement might well stand as an epigraph for what has occurred in Australian poetry over the last fifteen or twenty years. The fondness for generalizing, or for the encompassing statement that one finds in FitzGerald or McAuley has given way to a poetry of precise notation with more and more emphasis on concrete particulars and concrete observation. Attitudinizing, even playing a role, have given way to the attempt simply and fully to be oneself. One could trace this through the work of any of the more capable poets who emerged in the fifties and sixties, but no one illustrates it better than Vincent Buckley.

Buckley has been an important figure in Australian writing for the last twenty-five years, as critic, poet, editor and teacher, and has probably wielded more influence in these combined areas than any other writer. His three books of criticism *Essays in Poetry, Mainly Australian* (1957), *Poetry and Morality* (1959) and *Poetry and the Sacred* (1968) are essentially collections of separate essays yoked together under a few guiding themes and preoccupations, written in a characteristically rich mixture of passionate persuasiveness and slightly off-hand colloquialism. Buckley was the most important young critic of his time, but he took longer to mature as a poet, to find the authority of language and rhythm. He started off on an ambitious high note and it was some time before he could fully sustain it. *The World's Flesh* (1954) begins with a charming religious lyric 'Poem of Ritual' but the whole book is marked by mannerisms and influences from American poets, particularly Hart Crane and Allen Tate, with a touch of early Lowell. One has only to compare Buckley's poem 'Australia' with Hope's to see how far Buckley has yet to go in the direction of precision and concrete force—or to compare it with 'Borrowing of Trees' in *Masters in Israel* (1961) to see how strain and derivativeness give way to closer observation and truth of feeling. *Arcady and Other Places* (1966), published when Buckley was forty, showed the beginnings of his authentic mature style, and furthered his concern with 'the built and the growing', which together with his religious pre-occupations is the centre of his work. *Arcady and Other Places* contains his sequence 'Stroke', a meditation on the father-son relationship, and probably his most perfectly unified poem, 'Parents'. Here one could not point to a striking line or phrase (as one can in so many of his other pieces) or a remarkable language effect or even an especially skilfully used word. But the whole of 'Parents' is a triumph of poise and tone. Nothing draws attention to itself, but fully communicated are the finely felt subtleties of a relationship. The whole poem 'lives along the line'.

The title sequence of *Golden Builders and Other Poems* (1976) is probably the most widely discussed and written about poem in Australia at present. The long poem or long poetic sequence haunts contemporary Australian poets as the trilogy haunted the novelists of the thirties, and most of the best-known writers, like Beaver, Harwood, Murray, Lehmann, Shapcott and Hall have experimented with various forms of the 'long' poem—not narratives like their predecessors, but sequences related to a theme or character in the modern manner.

'Golden Builders', divided into twenty-seven sections, is a modern sequence poem, centred on Melbourne, the poet's home town, which is presented as a city of the heart and of the spirit. As a long poem it is more comparable in technique with Brennan than with Hope or McAuley. In his longer poems Hope displays an admirable ability to govern the ordering of a mass of details into a unified whole, as in 'A Letter from Rome'. His sense of a con-struction of the poem, planned and shaped as a whole into which the parts fit to achieve a fully adjusted balance is dependent on a unified verse form with modulations of tone in an unchanging metrical pattern. Buckley's method is more obviously modern and disparate: the use of a variety of verse forms, from tight little quatrains to extended lines, to large open spaced phrases, relying on a variety of purely rhetorical devices—repetition, invocation, balanced variations—that accommodate a range of tones and concerns. He is able to include meditation, character sketches, declamatory and lyrical effects, and to assimilate prose rhythms and colloquialisms, while the diction, grounded in daily speech and including catch-cries and slogans, encompasses a register of emotions from compassion to self-mockery. The achievement of the poem is in the way it recreates aspects of the experience of inner city living, particularly through its human inhabitants. It is interesting to note that the poem has so far had a richer response from those who live in Melbourne and who know it well than from those who live outside it. The street names which are repeated, for instance, may appear as mere counters to those who have never walked them or heard of them. But the gallery of human portraits—particularly the whole group of post-war immigrants—Italian, Ukrainian, Lithuanian and Greek—all finely particularized, give the whole a power and a resonance which serve to suggest something of the possibilities and limitations of human destiny. 'Golden Builders' evokes the sense of poverty and deprivation in a great modern city, touched with moments of grace and harmony, though the sense of suffering and confusion is stronger than any sense of joy and order. As a city poem ('Melbourne Made Me') with its theme of the modern metropolis and change, and the images of the gains and losses of a life, it inevitably recalls Blake, Eliot and Lowell, but in its concentration on specific and particularized human visages, it is worth comparing with the almost unpeopled city of Brennan's *Poems (1913)*, where the focus falls on the isolated ego of the protagonist. Buckley's poem interweaves a sense of being at home with a sense of strangeness, of being associated yet alienated, embedded and detached, of being public yet profoundly intimate and private, of existing entirely in the present with long roots in the past; in fact it conveys the sense of a representative modern consciousness. Images and sounds of machines are played off against images of nature and snatches of city music, experiences of love and self-sacrifice against violence and destruction; and the quest for faith seems answered in the poetry by the sincerity and insistence of its questioning processes, not its statements. Buckley as a religious poet has always aspired to universality. In the 'Golden Builders' and a handful of his family poems where he is most completely personal and human, he comes closest to achieving it.

Bruce Dawe is the most popular poet to have emerged fully since the 1960s. *No Fixed Address* (1962), still probably his strongest book, opened a whole new field in Australian writing especially in the way it so convincingly and forcefully presented a sense of the Australian speaking voice. Dawe is a natural; unself-conscious in his Australianness, he has no need to resort to any kind of in-authentic vernacular. He has a sharp sense of the topical, reflected not only in the subject matter of individual poems, but also in the titles of his books (surely, with some of Les Murray's, the cleverest contemporary titles). He has a flair for probing word play, pastiche and parody. Many of his poems appeared in the newspapers in the early sixties, based on the local, national or international events one was reading about in the columns next to the poems, and they had an uncanny immediacy and force in that context. They were verse journalism at its best, commenting on a whole range of events from police court news to international happenings, quick off the mark, pointed, and usually written in an engagingly colloquial way, so different from the measured tones of Hope or Wright or the clotted rhetoric of Buckley.

Many of Dawe's poems are effective poems of comment; they score a point in a variety of tones as they focus on contemporary affairs and trends. Dawe not only brought the immediately recognizable Australian voice into the forefront of our poetry, he also brought the poetry of the suburbs into the suburbs, and his poetry has had its effect on other poets like Chris Wallace-Crabbe and Les Murray. Dawe has commented:

> The themes I deal with are the common ones of modern civilisation, loneliness, old age, death, dictatorship, love. I like the dramatic monologue form, and use it in free, blank and rhymed verse forms, attempting at the same time to capture something of the evanescence of contemporary idiom, which is far richer and more allusive than the stereotyped stone-the-crows popular concept of Australian speech would have people believe.[16]

Dawe's comment shows his awareness of the problems involved, and while many of his poems make effective use of the language of commercials, or the situations from popular Western fiction, to create a dramatic point others, like 'Happiness is the Art of Being Broken', use a richly mannered diction; while poems like 'The Hill Children' echo the language and something of the voice of Larkin and Wain and other English fifties poets. Prosaic colloquial words and more obviously poetic and elevated words jostle each other in a single poem, and if in some poems he uses a dramatic voice which is as Australian as a meat pie, in others like 'The City: Midnight' and 'Public Library, Melbourne' the voice is more deliberately heightened. Dawe must know as well as any informed critic that great poetry, while it is related to the spoken word, is much more than the spoken word, and he has paid the price for his popularity as an entertainer and commentator through the occasional neglect of the aesthetic side of his work. Indeed compared with Les Murray, Dawe often shows an impatience with the whole process of art.

There *are* strong generalizing pressures and tendencies at work in Dawe's poetry; his poems attempt to encompass general truths. Like Hope he deliberately uses provocation, shock tactics, extended metaphors, to drive home a satirical point; and he can move from popular song sentimentality to rhythmical and syntactical complexities of considerable sophistication, as in the serpentine sentences of 'Happiness is the Art of Being Broken'. He has a remarkable range (comic and serious) of subject matter, encompassing poems of decent indignation and a humane awareness of life's fragilities and absurdities—the decay of relationships, the pathos of aspirations and longings, the sadness and transience of existence. Dawe, like Murray, enjoys the multiplicity of life, but he has an alert awareness of the limitations of his society. He probably reveals more clearly than any other poet the real nature of the changes that have entered Australian poetry since the 1960s. His poetry is firmly set in the contemporary world in a way that the work of preceding poets like Hope, McAuley and Campbell is not, but it is not autobiographical or personal in the manner of Harwood, Beaver or Buckley. While it is always topical and up to date, his best poems, like 'Drifters' and 'Homecoming', move out into the area where human sensitivity and responsiveness become the qualities of the art that embodies them. 'Drifters' is a poem to compare with Hardy and Larkin. Dawe, again like Murray in 'Immigrant Voyage', has a remarkable sense of the dignity and pathos of human loves and longings. In 'Drifters' we find his acute sympathy with the no-hopers (the 'battlers' of an earlier generation). Where in many poems he is concerned to make a point, here it is human feelings that he so finely registers. The remarkable achievement of the poem is in its dynamic movement; it moves forward and upward rather than drifting down, to show how in a life of drifting, the elation of hope and happiness and surprise are sustaining elements. This capturing of a sense of unquenchable hope in an otherwise hopeless situation adds to the poignancy of the poem. Something of the same quality is found in 'Homecoming', his elegy for the dead of the Vietnam War. But fine as these poems are and free from the gratuitous touches that indicate failures of sympathy in less successful portrait poems they should not be stressed at the expense of the large number of poems where he is able to extract a wealth of comedy from a variety of tones and characters and situations, like 'The Rock-Thrower', 'Easy Does It', 'Woodeye' and 'Weapons Training'.

It is obvious that no study of a living literature can close on a note of finality; and there is little to be gained from a list of names of poets of promise inscribed with the impartiality of a stamp catalogue. I have tried in this survey to maintain the same distance and perspective in dealing with each stage of Australian poetry including the present. This means that I shall not single out for detailed discussion many writers who at the moment may be in the foreground of the literary scene but who have not yet established themselves by a sustained body of work. Only two poets—Bruce Dawe and Les Murray—have won a wide popularity, and there can be no doubt that they are already among the best poets the country has produced. Their eminence should not overshadow the work of a number of their contemporaries, many of whom are now approaching mid-career. A further, more detailed history would need to find space to concentrate on the work of Chris Wallace-Crabbe, especially the fine group of recent poems that explore the nature and the play of physical and mental energies; Gwen Harwood for her poems of poignant psychological experience and philosophical reflection, as well as some sharp-clawed satires; Bruce Beaver for his series of discursive, confessional poems and his experiments with the *livre composé* and structured sequences; Geoffrey Lehmann and David Malouf, working from different premises and areas, bringing a new cosmopolitanism into Australian poetry while writing prolifically about their family backgrounds and Australian origins.

Lehmann's *Ross's Poems*, a series of 75 poems spoken by Ross, is one of the striking volumes to have appeared in recent years. It is perhaps overlong in its ruminative explorations of the folk voice of Ross, but as an evocation of a vanishing world and a vanishing type, with its sense of haunted presences and intimations of continuities, it is unique in contemporary poetry. Peter Porter—an expatriate who has lived in London for nearly thirty years—has become one of the most important of contemporary English poets. Whether he will have any impact on younger Australian poets remains to be seen, but while he stands a little outside the purposes of this survey, future historians will certainly be happy to reclaim him as they have been to reclaim Christina Stead. It should perhaps be said that Australia has so far produced no important expatriate poets (W. J. Turner would be the only contender) and expatriation has not been essential to the poets in the way it has been to most of our major novelists.

The sheer quantity, variety and diversification of poetry being written in Australia make any generalizations about trends and tendencies particularly hazardous. The last decade or more has been a particularly exciting period, sociologically and critically, with a strong intermingling of the generations at various stages of their careers. Some important facts stand out. The amount of poetry being published in book form has never been so high, nor public readings so widespread. Poets are now taped, photographed, filmed and interviewed to a degree without parallel in the history of the country. The hyperactivity of the mid-seventies, associated with various economic and sociological factors, and a publishing boom, cannot be expected to last. Some of this activity helped to mark the emergence of a new generation of writers—Michael Dransfield, Robert Adamson and others. Summary views of the late sixties and the seventies, as they appear to those participating in them, are available in a variety of anthologies, more of which have been published in the last decade than ever before. At no other time have journals and publishers competed so avidly for up-to-the-minute surveys and selections and articles about the work being done by the young. In a culture where in the past serious writers have suffered real neglect and disadvantage such a change in attitude can only be welcomed, though as the sources of art are intimate and personal, only the future will be able to tell whether the excessive publicity and exploitation may not have damaged some promising young figures.

A new sense of internationalism is one of the main features of contemporary poetry, and this is also associated with the increase in the number and range of translations being undertaken by Australian poets, which can be expected to increase as new writers emerge from the various ethnic groups now well established in the country. There is no modern overseas movement or tendency that is not reflected in the work of some Australian, from experiments with concrete poetry to those of free form—though as often happens it is usually the more gifted and experienced poet who is able to make the most individual use of such experiments, as can be seen in the work of Buckley, Wallace-Crabbe, Bruce Beaver, Gwen Harwood and Andrew Taylor.

For all its increasing internationalism, modern Australian poetry is showing an acute awareness of the forces of regionalism, although this is not, of course, a completely new development. A detailed study of the work of some of the best newer poets—Roger McDonald, Geoff Page, Les Murray to name a few—will show how much of their work develops out of the tendencies of the preceding decades in Australian poetry. The interest in the First World War and its meaning for Australians evinced by these writers and others, shows that they are as preoccupied with questions of national identity and national self-image as many of their predecessors.

One can see this in the work of an interesting poet like Geoff Page, who has been much influenced by William Carlos Williams among others, and has translated Apollinaire, but many of whose preoccupations are strongly regional and even at times national-istic. A rich response to various contending voices is found in all the best of the young writers. Robert Gray, like Harold Stewart before him, has found the kind of enrichment in Chinese and Japanese culture that some recent composers like Sculthorpe and Meale have found in Asian music. Cultural cross-fertilization has always been a feature of Australian writing, but it is being re-asserted with a new vigour and individuality.

The changes that started to be felt in Australian poetry since the late 1960s were changes in both content and form. The dominant political and social concerns—the Vietnam War, conservation and pollution, women's rights, the rights of sexual and other minorities, have all had their impact on the subject matter of Australian poetry, where the 1930s Depression, for instance, had none at all, or else left poets helpless to deal with the issues raised. Changed censorship laws have also meant the release into poetry of words and subjects previously considered taboo. But protest poems, verse journalism and the heady excitements of new liberties rarely wear well on their own account. It is only where these issues are felt or touched on indirectly, or recreated in the immediate experience of a poem, as in Buckley's 'Golden Builders' or some of the poems of Bruce Dawe and Les Murray, that they acquire more enduring forms and artistic validity.

The relationship between adopted and adapted overseas styles and influences brought to bear on local experience and subject matter is one of the most interesting features of present day Australian poetry. Contemporary journals and anthologies show the mixture of subjects and models that are characteristic of contemporary writers. Only a later generation will be able to decide whether they are in fact appropriate ways for dealing with the times and whether they contain real growing points for their authors. We can now see with the benefit of hindsight that Frank Wilmot, for instance, remains a muffled minor poet because he failed to discard the imperfectly assimilated metrics and idioms of the 1900s. The same may well apply in the future to the young writers now embedded in the coils of immediate modes and fashions, and more limited by their culture than liberated by it. On the other hand a poet like Les Murray shows already how the whole Australian past—from the bush to the city—the historical, the ballad tradition, and the Aboriginal past can become alive and active in poetry which is vividly contemporary; and for all its sense of the sacramental and the power of ritual in life, engagingly human and sociable. Here is a poet fully at home in his own country yet cosmopolitan to the core. In his work, more richly, more symphonically than in any other contemporary poet, inter-national voices mingle with mainstream local tendencies to produce poetry of the highest quality.

The changes in form, technique and idiom have not been quite as striking as the new notes of fantasy, humour and surrealism that have entered modern Australian poetry, not only in writers like Michael Dransfield, but in middle-generation poets like David Malouf, Randolph Stow, R. A. Simpson and Wallace-Crabbe, and poets of an older generation like David Campbell and even to some extent the late James McAuley, so often considered an arch-conservative, whose renewed interest in Trakl and negative, highly-charged states of mind seemed to be leading to new directions in his work. The Vietnam War produced one outstand-ing poem, Bruce Dawe's 'Homecoming', but no other poetry of importance. More profound has been the renewed interest in the situation and plight of the Aboriginals, with the emergence of a number of Aboriginal poets, of whom Kath Walker and Kevin Gilbert are the best known. The new awareness of the forces of oral poetry, and Les Murray's superb use of Aboriginal forms and approaches, suggest rich possibilities for future development. Murray was fortunate enough to be born into a vigorous 'folk' community which he has continued to value and celebrate not merely as an expression of a vanishing way of life. He has been able to see that the archaic values it inculcated offer potential for rebirth.

The single most important development in Australian poetry in

425

the last two decades has been the poet's new sense of the past, his new found assurance in his relationship to his predecessors. This has not been entirely lacking before, but it has been subject to breaks, upheavals and uncertainties. The fact that it is now wide-spread must be related to specific historical developments: Australia is approaching its bi-centenary and Australians now have that sense of a usable past that many previous writers felt to be a serious lack in their culture. There is more sense now of being at home in their own world, less emphasis on the sense of exile and alienation. One aspect of this is the number of autobiographical poems that have appeared in this period from poets as varied and from such different generations as McAuley, Campbell, Dobson, Harwood, Buckley, Beaver, Lehmann, Murray and Malouf; another is the sense of a continuing dialogue with the historical past which one finds in the same writers, as well as in older figures like Slessor and Hope. Where many earlier writers were involved in the process of naming the country, a new stage of cultivation has been reached and more and more writers are turning to and establishing intimate inward connections with their predecessors and their local cultural heritage. This is manifested in a new tone of matter-of-fact identity; an unself-conscious notation of the sharply particular rather than the typical; and also in specific literary legacies: McAuley's use of Kendall (the title '*Surprises of the Sun*' is taken from one of Kendall's favourite lines) and Shaw Neilson; Judith Wright's poems about Harpur; Hope's use of Paterson and Brennan and Les Murray's use of Aboriginal songs and oral struc-tures, to mention some obvious examples. It is new and exciting to find so many poets with this sense of a local inherited past, or, like Murray and Lehmann, going a step further and creating a personal mythology from family tradition.

The Australian literary tradition no longer has to be rejected in favour of other traditions, or over-simplified for crudely national-istic purposes. It can be built on and is now as vital a part of the writer's experience and development as his experience of the literature and traditions of other countries. Nettie Palmer main-tained that Australian literature could only develop through a recognition of its own past, through attention to its own inner problems and resources, and by constant accessibility to the enriching influences from without. The new awareness of the continuities within Australian poetry itself is one of the best guarantees for positive future developments.

BIBLIOGRAPHY

JOY HOOTON

LIST OF CONTENTS

I   BIBLIOGRAPHICAL AND REFERENCE AIDS
    1   Major reference tools
    2   Guides and location aids
    3   Manuscripts and theses
    4   Special bibliographies
    5   Dictionaries, encyclopaedias, and biographical dictionaries

II GENERAL STUDIES
    1   General histories, social and cultural studies
    2   Literary history and criticism
    3   Periodicals and newspapers

III INDIVIDUAL AUTHORS
    John Feltham Archibald
    Thea Astley
    Bruce Beaver
    'Rolf Boldrewood'
    Martin Boyd
    David Burn
    Christopher John Brennan
    Vincent Buckley
    Alexander Buzo
    David Campbell
    Marcus Clarke
    Victor Daley
    Eleanor Dark
    Frank Dalby Davison
    Bruce Dawe
    Clarence (Michael) James Dennis
    Rosemary Dobson
    Louis Esson
    Robert David FitzGerald
    Stella Miles Franklin
    Joseph Furphy
    Mary Gilmore
    Adam Lindsay Gordon
    Rodney Hall
    Frank Hardy
    Charles Harpur
    Elizabeth Harrower
    Gwen Harwood
    William Gosse Hay
    Shirley Hazzard
    Xavier Herbert

Dorothy Hewett
Jack Hibberd
Alec Derwent Hope
David Ireland
George Johnston
Henry Kendall
Thomas Keneally
Peter Kenna
Henry Kingsley
Eve Langley
Ray Lawler
Henry Lawson
Norman Lindsay
James McAuley
Hugh McCrae
Kenneth Mackenzie
Frederic Manning
David Martin
Peter Mathers
Frank Moorhouse
Les Murray
John Shaw Neilson
Barry Oakley
Bernard O'Dowd
Vance Palmer
Andrew Barton Paterson
Hal Porter
Peter Porter
Rose Campbell Praed
Katharine Susannah Prichard
'Henry Handel Richardson'
John Romeril
'Steele Rudd'
Kenneth Slessor
Catherine Helen Spence
Christina Stead
Alfred George Stephens
Douglas Stewart
Louis Stone
Randolph Stow
Kylie Tennant
Chris Wallace-Crabbe
Judah Waten
Francis Webb
Patrick White
Michael Wilding
David Williamson
Frank Wilmot
Judith Wright

ABBREVIATIONS

PERIODICALS

ADHSJP	*Armidale and District Historical Society Journal and Proceedings*
ALS	*Australian Literary Studies*
JCL	*Journal of Commonwealth Literature*
JRAHS	*Royal Australian Historical Society Journal*
JRHSQ	*Royal Historical Society of Queensland Journal*
MUM	*Melbourne University Magazine*
Meanjin	*Meanjin Quarterly*
SMH	*Sydney Morning Herald*
THRA	*Tasmanian Historical Research Association, Papers and Proceedings*
WLWE	*World Literature Written in English*

BOOKS

ACE	John Docker. *Australian Cultural Elites.* Sydney, 1974.
ADB	*Australian Dictionary of Biography.* Melbourne, 1966–.
AE	W. S. Ramson. ed. *The Australian Experience.* Canberra, 1974.
ALE	F. T. Macartney. *Australian Literary Essays.* Sydney, 1957.
ALC	G. K. W. Johnston. ed. *Australian Literary Criticism.* Melbourne, 1962.
AN	Chris Wallace-Crabbe. ed. *The Australian Nationalists.* Melbourne, 1971.
AOM	S. Murray-Smith. ed. *An Overland Muster.* Brisbane, 1965.
AT	A. A. Phillips. *The Australian Tradition.* Melbourne, 1958. 2nd edn, 1966.
BBB	Leon Cantrell. ed. *Bards, Bohemians and Bookmen.* St. Lucia, 1976.
DOAF	D. R. Burns. *The Directions of Australian Fiction 1920–1974.* Melbourne, 1975.
IAN	Barry Argyle. *An Introduction to the Australian Novel 1830–1930.* Oxford, 1972.
ISN	Brian Kiernan. *Images of Society and Nature.* Melbourne, 1971.
LC&N	C. D. Narasimhaiah. ed. *An Introduction to Australian Literature.* Brisbane, 1965. Reprinted from *Literary Criterion*, vol. 6 (1964).
Lit. Aust.	Clement Semmler and Derek Whitelock. eds. *Literary Australia.* Melbourne, 1966.
L of A	Geoffrey Dutton, ed. *The Literature of Australia.* Ringwood, Vic., 1964. Revised edn. 1976.
MOB	Chris Wallace-Crabbe. *Melbourne or the Bush.* Sydney, 1974.
NC	A. D. Hope. *Native Companions.* Sydney, 1974.
ONG	C. B. Christesen. ed. *On Native Grounds.* Sydney, 1967.

431

PEAP	James McAuley. *The Personal Element in Australian Poetry*. Sydney, 1970.
PIAP	Judith Wright. *Preoccupations in Australian Poetry*. Melbourne, 1965.
RCL	William Walsh. ed. *Readings in Commonwealth Literature*. Oxford, 1973.
TCALC	Clement Semmler. ed. *Twentieth Century Australian Literary Criticism*. Melbourne, 1967.
WIA	John Barnes. ed. *The Writer in Australia*. Melbourne, 1969.

SERIES

AB	Australian Bibliographies
AC	Australian Classics
AP	Australian Poets
AWW	Australian Writers and Their Work
GA	Great Australians
PAA	Portable Australian Authors
SAB	Studies in Australian Bibliography
SAC	Seal Australian Classics
TWAS	Twayne's World Authors Series

OTHER ABBREVIATIONS

ANU	Australian National University
assoc.	association
CLF	Commonwealth Literary Fund
ed.	edited by
edn	edition
introd.	introduced/introduction
Mass.	Massachusetts
N.J.	New Jersey
NSW	New South Wales
publ.	published
Q.	Queensland
RSSS	Research School of Social Sciences
SA	South Australia
sel.	selected
Tas.	Tasmania
transl.	translated
Univ.	University
Vic.	Victoria
W.A.	Western Australia

432

I BIBLIOGRAPHICAL AND REFERENCE AIDS

1. MAJOR REFERENCE TOOLS. E. Morris Miller's *Australian Literature From Its Beginnings to 1935: A Descriptive and Bibliographical Survey of Books by Australian Authors in Poetry, Drama, Fiction, Criticism and Anthology with Subsidiary Entries to 1938*, 2 vols, Melbourne, 1940, is still the most comprehensive survey of Australian literature before the Second World War, although handicapped by inconvenient organisation. A facsimile edition with an addendum of corrections and additions was produced by Sydney University Press in 1975. Frederick T. Macartney updated, re-arranged and condensed Miller's work, greatly enhancing its convenience, in his *Australian Literature: A Bibliography to 1938 by E. Morris Miller, Extended to 1950 with an Historical Outline and Descriptive Commentaries*, Sydney, 1956. Another useful guide is Grahame Johnston's *Annals of Australian Literature*, Melbourne, 1970, a chronological survey of Australian literature, listing the main publications and literary events for each year (1789–1968), and including a convenient index. A more recent bibliographical aid is L. T. Hergenhan's 'Appendix' in *The Literature of Australia*, ed. Geoffrey Dutton, Ringwood, Vic., Penguin Books, revised edn 1976, an extensively revised version of his 'Bibliographical Appendix' in the first edition of *The Literature of Australia*, 1964. In addition, there are two serial bibliographies of recent publications: the 'Annual Bibliography of Studies in Australian Literature', which has been published in the May issue of *ALS* since 1964, and lists books, articles, and reviews of the preceding year, is the most comprehensive and reliable guide to recent critical and scholarly writing in Australia. A useful supplement is the section on 'Australia' in the 'Annual Bibliography of Commonwealth Literature' published in the December issue of the *Journal of Commonwealth Literature* since 1965. The *MLA International Bibliography* has also contained a limited Australian section since 1957.

2. GUIDES AND LOCATION AIDS. The basic tool for locating books in Australia is *The National Union Catalogue of Monographs, 'NUCOM'*, a union catalogue maintained in card form in the National Library, and now available on microfilm in most large Australian libraries. Another important catalogue is that of the monograph collection of the Mitchell Library, Sydney, *Dictionary Catalog of Printed Books*, 38 vols, Boston, 1968, *First Supplement*, 1970. The Mitchell Library has the largest holdings of

Australiana in the world. J. A. Ferguson *Bibliography of Australia*, 7 vols, Sydney, 1941–69, is the standard bibliography of material relating to Australia, published both within Australia and overseas to 1900. It comprises two parts: a chronological list of Australiana, 1785–1900 (4 vols), and a more restricted, alphabetical list, 1851–1900 (3 vols). Literary works are excluded after 1850. A facsimile reprint was begun in 1975, and is to be followed by 3 volumes of addenda. For more recent publications the *Australian National Bibliography, 'ANB'*, Canberra, 1961–, is the standard guide and lists books published in Australia, as well as overseas books of Australian interest. *ANB* was preceded by the *Annual Catalogue of Australian Publications*, 1936–60, a more restricted listing, especially in the years before 1950. To complement Ferguson and the *Annual Catalogue*, the National Library is compiling an *Australian National Bibliography 1901–1950*. Two guides to Australian bibliography are: *Australian Bibliography and Bibliographical Services*, Canberra, 1960, and D. H. Borchardt's *Australian Bibliography: A Guide to Printed Sources of Information*, 3rd edn, Rushcutter's Bay, 1976, 1st edn, 1963. More recently, Fred Lock and Alan Lawson have produced in *Australian Literature—a reference guide*, Melbourne, 1977, a particularly comprehensive and discriminating aid. An indispensable guide to Australian serials and their location is *Serials in Australian Libraries: Social Sciences and Humanities*, revised edn, 4 vols, Canberra, 1968–74, updated by the monthly *Newly Reported Titles*. In addition, the National Library's *Current Australian Serials*, 9th edn, Canberra, 1975, first published in 1963, is a comprehensive subject and title guide. The locations of both Australian and overseas newspapers are listed in *Newspapers in Australian Libraries: A Union List*, 3rd edn, Canberra, 1973–75, 1st edn, 1959–60, and there are various periodical and newspaper indexes, the most notable being the National Library's *Australian Public Affairs Information Service: A Subject Index to Current Literature, 'APAIS'*, 1945–, and the *Index to Australian Book Reviews*, published quarterly by the Libraries Board of South Australia since 1965. A useful guide to periodical articles in a period that is sparsely indexed is the *Index to Periodicals*, published by the Mitchell Library, 5 vols, 1950–66, covering the years 1944–63. Another index is Marjorie Tipping's *Meanjin Quarterly Index 1940–1965*, Melbourne, 1969. Indexes to Australian newspapers have appeared only at intervals, the most noteworthy being the *Index to the Sydney Morning Herald and Sydney Mail*, 1927–61, and *The Argus Index*, 1910–49. Some attempts have also been made to index *The Bulletin*: microfilms of an incomplete index compiled in *The Bulletin* office 1880–1962 are held by some libraries, and an annual index of limited value was published 1963–65. Two special indexes are: C. H. Hannaford, *Index to 'The Lone Hand': May 1907–November 1913*, Adelaide, 1967, and Margaret Woodhouse, *An Index to 'The Stockwhip' 1875–1877, with a life of John Edward Kelly, 1840–1896*, Sydney, 1969.

3. MANUSCRIPTS AND THESES. Although the main depositaries of manuscripts relating to Australia are the National Library and the Mitchell Library, other State and university libraries have significant holdings. The National Library's *Guide to Collections of Manuscripts Relating to*

Australia, 1965–, describes manuscript collections held in Australian libraries, although so far the series has covered only a fraction of the collections. Some of the National Library's own collections have been described by C. A. Burmester in *National Library of Australia. Guide to the Collections*, Canberra, vol. 1, 1974, vol. 2, 1977, and an *Acquisitions Newsletter*, 1970–, lists important accessions to the library's holdings of manuscripts and rare books. The Mitchell Library has published a *Catalogue of Manuscripts of Australasia and the Pacific in the Mitchell Library, Sydney*, 2 vols, Series A manuscripts catalogued 1945–63 (1967), Series B 1963–67 (1969), and from 1954 a quarterly list of the library's recent accessions has appeared. The State Library of Victoria has published *A Catalogue of the Manuscripts, Letters, Documents, etc., in the Private Collection of the State Library of Victoria*, Melbourne, 1961, and the *La Trobe Library Journal*, 1968–, frequently lists recent acquisitions. Another valuable guide is the *Catalogue of Manuscripts from the Hayes Collection in the University of Queensland Library*, ed., Margaret Brenan, Marianne Ehrhardt and Carol Hetherington, St. Lucia, 1976. Theses on Australian literature are listed in the *Union List of Higher Degree Theses in Australian University Libraries: Cumulative Edition to 1965*, Hobart, 1967, which is regularly updated by supplements, the latest being *Supplement, 1974*, 1976. International indexes frequently contain information about foreign theses and dissertations on Australian literature.

4. SPECIAL BIBLIOGRAPHIES. Two important early bibliographies are: George Burnett Barton, *Literature in New South Wales*, Sydney, 1866, and E. A. Petherick, *Bibliograhia Poetica Australasica. Contribution to the Bibliography of Australasia and Polynesia. Poetry and Drama*, London, 1896. Petherick's bibliography is in manuscript form in the National Library. Percival Serle's *Bibliography of Australasian Poetry and Verse, Australia and New Zealand*, Melbourne, 1925, extensively used by Miller, continues to be a standard reference work. Useful guides to Australian poetry include: Hugh Anderson, *A Guide to Ten Australian Poets*, Melbourne, 1953, J. H. Hornibrook, *Bibliography of Queensland Verse, with Biographical Notes*, Brisbane, 1953, E. I. Cuthbert, *Index of Australian and New Zealand Poetry*, New York, 1963, and *Contemporary Poets*, ed. James Vinson, London, 2nd edn 1975. Guides to Australian fiction include: G. V. Hubble, *Modern Australian Fiction: A Bibliography 1940–1965*, Perth, 1968, and *Contemporary Novelists*, ed. James Vinson, London, 2nd edn 1976. Hubble's bibliography is marred by serious errors and omissions and his subsequent listing, *The Australian Novel: A Title Checklist 1900–1970*, Perth, 1970, is of limited value. As much Australian drama remains unpublished the following guides are particularly valuable: S. M. Apted, *Australian Plays in Manuscript: A Check List of the Campbell Howard Collection Held in the University of New England Library*, Armidale, 1968, and the Fryer Library's *Hanger Collection: Bibliography of Play Scripts*, St. Lucia, 1975. E. F. Ho has also produced an author checklist of about 200 plays in *Australian Drama, 1946–1973: A Bibliography of Published Works*, Adelaide, 1974. Another guide is *Contemporary Dramatists*, ed. James Vinson, London, 1972. Some attempts have been made to document Australia's literary magazines,

many of them short-lived. John Tregenza's *Australian Little Magazines, 1923–1954*, Adelaide, 1964, and the National Library's unpublished preliminary draft, *Australian Literary Periodicals: A Bibliography*, Canberra, 1971, are valuable though incomplete. The history and bibliography of publishing in Australia are dealt with by: F. S. Greenop, *History of Magazine Publishing in Australia*, Sydney, 1947, Henry Mayer, *Bibliographical Notes on the Press in Australia and Related Subjects*, Sydney, 1963, and Geoffrey Farmer, *Private Presses and Australia, with a Check-List*, Melbourne, 1972. Bibliographies of Australian English include: David Blair, 'A Bibliography of Australian English', *English Transported: Essays on Australasian English*, ed. W. S. Ramson, Canberra, 1970, and R. D. Eagleson, *Bibliography of Writings on Australian English*, Sydney, 1967.

5. DICTIONARIES, ENCYCLOPAEDIAS, AND BIOGRAPHICAL DICTIONARIES. E. E. Morris's *Austral English: A Dictionary of Australasian Words, Phrases, and Usages*, London, 1898 is an authoritative guide to nineteenth century Australian English. There have been several facsimile reprints. Two recent dictionaries of Australian English are: the *Heinemann Australian Dictionary*, South Yarra, 1976, and *The Australian Pocket Oxford Dictionary*, ed. Grahame Johnston, Melbourne, 1976. Eric Partridge's *A Dictionary of Slang and Unconventional English*, 7th edn, 2 vols, London, 1970, first published 1937, is a guide to Australian slang, and G. A. Wilkes's *A Dictionary of Australian Colloquialisms*, Sydney, 1978, is invaluable. The major Australian encyclopaedia is *The Australian Encyclopaedia*, ed. Bruce C. Pratt, 6 vols, Grolier Society of Australia, Sydney, 1977. Arthur Jose edited the first edition (2 vols) 1925–26, and A. H. Chisholm the revised editions of 1958 and 1965. *The Australian Dictionary of Biography*, Melbourne, 1966–, is still in the process of production. Six volumes (1788–1890) have been published to date. Meanwhile, Percival Serle's *Dictionary of Australian Biography*, 2 vols, Sydney, 1949 is still a useful reference tool. *Who's Who in Australia*, Melbourne, 1927–, and its predecessors: *Johns's Notable Australians* (1906–08), *Fred Johns's Annual* (1912–14), *Who's Who in the Commonwealth of Australia* (1922) frequently provide information not available elsewhere. Another valuable guide is the *Biographical Register Short List*, produced by the Department of History, RSSS, ANU, new edn, 2 vols, 1963.

II GENERAL STUDIES

1. GENERAL HISTORIES, SOCIAL AND CULTURAL STUDIES. The first history to isolate dominant trends in Australian life was W. K. Hancock's seminal *Australia*, London, 1930. Other short histories include: Brian Fitzpatrick, *The Australian People 1788–1945*, Melbourne, 1946, A. G. L. Shaw, *The Story of Australia*, London, 1955, 4th edn 1972, R. M. Crawford, *Australia*, London, 1952, 3rd revised edn 1970, Douglas Pike, *Australia, The Quiet Continent*, Cambridge, 1962, 2nd edn 1970, Russel Ward, *Australia*, Englewood-Cliffs, N. J., 1965, and his *A Nation for a Continent*, Richmond, Vic., 1977, Fred Alexander, *Australia Since Federation*, Melbourne, 1967, 3rd revised edn 1976, and C. M. H. Clark, *A Short History of Australia*, New York, 1963, 2nd revised edn 1969. The major historical study is C. M. H. Clark's *A History of Australia*, Melbourne, 1962–, of which four volumes have been published so far. Also important is his two volume edition of *Select Documents in Australian History, 1788–1850*, and *1851–1900*, Sydney, 1950 and 1955. Geoffrey Blainey's studies: *The Tyranny of Distance*, Melbourne, 1966, and *The Rush That Never Ended*, Melbourne, 1963, 3rd edn 1978, are invaluable for an understanding of the shaping forces in   Australian history and Humphrey McQueen's *A New Britannia*, Ringwood, Vic., 1970, is an original 'new left' interpretation of Australian history. Collections of essays include: *Australia. A Social and Political History*, ed. Gordon Greenwood, Sydney, 1955, and *A New History of Australia*, ed. F. K. Crowley, Melbourne, 1974. The following are valuable studies of a more social or cultural nature: *Australia*, ed. C. H. Grattan, Berkeley, Calif., 1947, J. D. Pringle, *Australian Accent*, London, 1958, *The Pattern of Australian Culture*, ed. A. L. McLeod, New York, 1963, Donald Horne, *The Lucky Country*, Melbourne, 1964, 2nd revised edn 1968, and *The Australian People*, Sydney, 1972, *Australian Society*, ed. A. F. Davies and S. Encel, Melbourne, 1965, 2nd revised edn 1970, and Craig McGregor, *Profile of Australia*, Sydney, 1966. Important social studies of Australia in the nineteenth century include: John Ritchie, *Australia as Once We Were*, Melbourne, 1975, Michael Cannon, *Australia in the Victorian Age*, 3 vols, Melbourne, 1971–75, K. S. Inglis, *The Australian Colonist*, Melbourne, 1974, and George Nadel, *Australia's Colonial Culture*, Melbourne, 1957. Recent studies of the historical position of women in Australian society include: Beverley Kingston, *My Wife, My Daughter and Poor Mary Ann*, Melbourne, 1975, Miriam Dixson, *The Real Matilda*, Melbourne, 1976, Anne Summers, *Damned Whores and*

God's Police, Ringwood, Vic., 1975 and Helen Heney, *Australia's Founding Mothers*, Melbourne, 1978. An extensive and varied collection of essays, *Racism*, ed. F. S. Stevens, 3 vols, Sydney, 1971–72, deals with the history of racism in Australia. More lighthearted accounts of Australian attitudes include Keith Dunstan's *Wowsers*, Melbourne, 1968, *Knockers*, Melbourne, 1972, and *Sports*, Melbourne, 1973.

Studies that attempt to define Australian myths and traditions include: Vance Palmer, *The Legend of the Nineties*, Melbourne, 1954, A. A. Phillips, *The Australian Tradition*, Melbourne, 1958, 2nd revised edn 1966, and Russel Ward, *The Australian Legend*, Melbourne, 1958, 2nd revised edn, 1966. David Walker's *Dream and Disillusion*, Canberra, 1976, re-examines the Australian literary nationalism of Vance Palmer, Louis Esson and others, Ian Turner's compilation, *The Australian Dream*, Melbourne, 1968, illustrates past and recent expectations of Australia's future and W. F. Mandle's *Going it Alone*, Ringwood, Vic., 1978, considers Australia's national identity in the twentieth century. Surveys of Australian cultural history include: Geoffrey Serle, *From Deserts the Prophets Come*, Melbourne, 1973, and John Docker, *Australian Cultural Elites*, Sydney, 1974. P. R. Stephensen's *The Foundations of Culture in Australia*, Gordon, NSW, 1936, first published *Australian Mercury*, July 1935, and reprinted *WIA*, is an important early document. *Australian Civilization*, ed. Peter Coleman, Melbourne, 1962, is a contemporary conspectus, and Craig McGregor's *In the Making*, Melbourne, 1969, based mainly on interviews, surveys the work and attitudes of many Australian artists and writers. Studies of Australian art include Bernard Smith's major survey, *Australian Painting 1788–1970*, revised edn, Melbourne, 1971, and his earlier *Place, Taste and Tradition. A Study of Australian Art Since 1788*, Sydney 1945. Also valuable are his recent works: *Documents on Art and Taste in Australia*, and *The Antipodean Manifesto*, both Melbourne, 1975. Robert Hughes's *The Art of Australia*, Harmondsworth, revised edn, 1970, is a controversial but stimulating interpretation. Also useful are Alan McCulloch's comprehensive *Encyclopaedia of Australian Art*, Richmond, Vic., 1968, and John Hetherington's collection of profiles, *Australian Painters*, Melbourne, 1963. Works on Australian architecture include: J. M. Freeland, *Architecture in Australia*, Melbourne, 1968, Morton Herman, *The Early Australian Architects and Their Work*, Sydney, 1954, and Robin Boyd's especially illuminating studies, *Australia's Home*, Melbourne, 1952, revised edn, 1968, and *The Australian Ugliness*, Melbourne, 1960, revised edn, 1968. Roger Covell's *Australia's Music*, Melbourne, 1967, and *Australian Composition in the Twentieth Century*, ed. Frank Callaway and David Tunley, Melbourne, 1978 illuminate the history of music in Australia.

2. LITERARY HISTORY AND CRITICISM. The first extended criticism of Australian writing is Frederick Sinnett's 'The Fiction Fields of Australia', *Journal of Australasia* (1856), reprinted with introd. by Cecil Hadgraft, St. Lucia, 1966, and in *WIA*. Other early studies include: G. B. Barton's appreciations *The Poets and Prose Writers of New South Wales*, Sydney, 1866, which supplement his bibliography *supra*, Desmond Byrne's *Australian*

Writers, London, 1896, A. P. Martin's brief account, *The Beginnings of an Australian Literature*, London, 1898, and the survey by H. G. Turner and A. Sutherland, *The Development of Australian Literature*, London, 1898. A. G. Stephens *q.v.,* sub-editor of *The Bulletin*, 1896–1902, ranks in most histories as the prophet of Australian letters, although his writing is too fugitive to be regarded as a consistent body of criticism. The stimulating effect of his forthright approach can be gauged, however, by comparing Vance Palmer's selection of his essays, Melbourne, 1941, with the negative tone of T. G. Tucker's contemporary lecture, *The Cultivation of Literature in Australia*, Melbourne, 1902. The twenties and thirties, before the founding of *Southerly* and *Meanjin*, and notwithstanding the efforts of energetic critics such as Vance Palmer *q.v.,* and his wife Nettie, were relatively stagnant. Most criticism of these years, although issued in book or booklet form is somewhat sketchy, and includes: Zora Cross, *An Introduction to the Study of Australian Literature*, Sydney, 1922, Nettie Palmer, *Modern Australian Literature 1900–1923*, Melbourne, 1924, C. H. Grattan, *Australian Literature*, Seattle, 1929, H. A. Kellow, *Queensland Poets*, London, 1930, H. M. Green, *An Outline of Australian Literature*, Sydney, 1930, A. J. Coombes, *Some Australian Poets*, Sydney, 1938, and 'M. Barnard Eldershaw', *Essays in Australian Fiction*, Melbourne, 1938. In 1939 the journal *Southerly* began publication, followed in 1940 by *Meanjin Papers*, and in the same year E. Morris Miller's *Australian Literature supra* appeared. Most of the seminal critical work thereafter appeared in the new quarterlies, later joined by *Overland*, 1954–, *Quadrant*, 1956–, and *Australian Literary Studies*, 1963–. *An Overland Muster*, ed. S. Murray-Smith, Brisbane, 1965, and *On Native Grounds*, ed. C. B. Christesen, Sydney, 1967, reprint some of the more important essays from *Overland* and *Meanjin* respectively. In addition, independent studies continued to appear, the most important being Vance Palmer's and A. A. Phillips's socio-literary studies, *The Legend of the Nineties*, and *The Australian Tradition, supra*. Other studies include: T. Inglis Moore's *Six Australian Poets*, Melbourne, 1942, H. M. Green's *Fourteen Minutes*, Sydney, 1944, revised edn by Dorothy Green, Sydney, 1950, J. K. Ewers's *Creative Writing in Australia*, Melbourne, 1945, 4th revised edn 1966, Brian Elliott's *Singing to the Cattle*, Melbourne, 1947, Douglas Stewart's reviews, *The Flesh and the Spirit*, Sydney, 1948, Nettie Palmer's informative journal extracts for the years 1925–1939, *Fourteen Years*, Melbourne, 1948, A. P. Murphy's *Contemporary Australian Poets*, Mildura, Vic., 1950, H. M. Green's brief survey, *Australian Literature 1900–1950*, Melbourne, 1951, Miles Franklin's *Laughter, Not for a Cage*, Sydney, 1956, A. D. Hope's 'Standards in Australian Literature', *Current Affairs Bulletin* (1956), reprinted *ALC*, F. T. Macartney's *Australian Literary Essays*, Sydney, 1957, Vincent Buckley's *Essays in Poetry, Mainly Australian*, Melbourne, 1957, Cecil Hadgraft's regional survey, *Queensland and Its Writers*, Brisbane, 1959, and his more extensive account, *Australian Literature*, London, 1960. In 1961 H. M. Green's two volume *A History of Australian Literature* appeared, still an invaluable reference guide to Australian literature and its standard history. Another important, though less ambitious work of the 1960s is the collection of essays, *The Literature of Australia*, ed.

Geoffrey Dutton, Ringwood, Vic., 1964, revised edn 1976. Other studies include: John Hetherington's profiles of Australian writers, *Forty-Two Faces*, Melbourne, 1962, A. D. Hope's brief survey, *Australian Literature 1950–1962*, Melbourne, 1963, Norman Lindsay's reminiscences, *Bohemians of the Bulletin*, Sydney, 1965, Judith Wright's *Preoccupations in Australian Poetry*, Melbourne, 1965, George Mackaness's book-collecting essays, *Bibliomania*, Sydney, 1965, Brian Elliott's *The Landscape of Australian Poetry*, Melbourne, 1967, L. J. Blake's *Australian Writers*, Adelaide, 1968, Vance Palmer's appreciations, *Intimate Portraits*, sel. by H. P. Heseltine, Melbourne, 1969, and G. A. Wilkes's *Australian Literature: A Conspectus*, Sydney, 1969. More recent critical studies include *Authors and Areas of Australia* by Joseph and Johanna Jones, Austin, Texas, 1970, Coral Lansbury's investigation of English, nineteenth-century images of Australia, *Arcady in Australia*, Carlton, Vic., 1970, Kenneth Slessor's collection, *Bread and Wine*, Sydney, 1970, William Walsh's essays on Commonwealth literature, *A Manifold Voice*, London and New York, 1970, T. Inglis Moore's *Social Patterns in Australian Literature*, Sydney, 1971, Clement Semmler's essays, *The Art of Brian James*, St. Lucia, 1972, G. A. Wilkes's *An Alternative View of Australian Literary History*, Sydney, 1975 and Graeme Kinross Smith's major study *Australia's Writers*, Melbourne, 1980. James McAuley has made three contributions: *The Personal Element in Australian Poetry*, Sydney, 1970, *A Map of Australian Verse*, and *The Grammar of the Real*, both Melbourne, 1975. Other collections include: Chris Wallace-Crabbe, *Melbourne or The Bush*, Sydney, 1974, A. D. Hope, *Native Companions*, Sydney, 1974, Douglas Stewart, *The Broad Stream*, Sydney, 1975, and Judith Wright, *Because I Was Invited*, Melbourne, 1975. Of the multiplicityof more specific studies, Brian Kiernan surveys the history of Australian literary criticism in *Criticism*, AWW, Melbourne, 1974, Noel Macainsh explores the influence of Nietzsche on certain Australian writers in *Nietzsche in Australia*, Munich, 1975, Joseph Jones discusses the influence of radical American writers in *Radical Cousins*, St. Lucia, 1976, J. P. Matthews studies the comparative development of nineteenth century Australian and Canadian poetry in *Tradition in Exile*, Melbourne, 1962, W. P. Friederich explores mainly early images of Australia in *Australia in Western Imaginative Prose Writings 1600–1960*, Chapel Hill, 1967, and Joachim Schulz interprets Australian literature from a German point of view in *Geschichte der Australischen Literatur*, Muenchen, 1960. Studies of the novel include: Brian Kiernan, *Images of Society and Nature*, Melbourne, 1971, Barry Argyle, *An Introduction to the Australian Novel 1830–1930*, Oxford, 1972, R. G. Geering, *Recent Fiction*, AWW, Melbourne, 1974, *The Australian Experience*, ed. W. S. Ramson, Canberra, 1974, D. R. Burns, *The Directions of Australian Fiction 1920–1974*, Melbourne, 1975, *Australian Postwar Novelists*, ed. Nancy Keesing, Milton, Q., 1975, and *Studies in the Recent Australian Novel*, ed. K. G. Hamilton, St. Lucia, 1978. Leslie Rees has made an important contribution to study of the drama with his surveys, *Towards an Australian Drama*, Sydney, 1953, the more extensive *The Making of Australian Drama*, Sydney, 1973 and its continuation, *Australian Drama in the 1970s*, Sydney, 1978. Earlier still useful studies include *The Australian Theatre* by Paul and F. M. McGuire and Betty Arnott, Melbourne, 1948, and *A Brief History of the Australian Theatre* by John Kardoss, Sydney, 1955. More recent studies include Hal Porter's *Stars of Australian Stage and Screen*, Adelaide, 1965, Alec Bagot's *Coppin the Great*, Melbourne, 1965, Margaret Williams's *Drama*, AWW, Melbourne, 1977, and Eric Irvin's *Theatre Comes to Australia*, St. Lucia, 1971. Apart from *An Overland Muster* and *On Native Grounds supra* there are numerous collections of critical essays including: a reprint of a special number of *Texas Quarterly*, vol. 5 (1962), *Image of Australia*, ed. Joseph Jones, Austin, Texas, 1962, *Australian Literary Criticism*, ed. Grahame Johnston, Melbourne, 1962, a collection reprinted from the Indian journal *Literary Criterion*, vol. 6 (1964), and titled *An Introduction to Australian Literature*, ed. C. D. Narasimhaiah, Brisbane, 1965, a collection on different cultural aspects, *Literary Australia*, ed. Clement Semmler and Derek Whitelock, Melbourne, 1966, an anthology of reprints, *Twentieth Century Australian Literary Criticism*, ed. Clement Semmler, Melbourne, 1967, and a collection of some of the best writing from *Australian Letters, The Vital Decade*, ed. Geoffrey Dutton and Max Harris, Melbourne, 1968. Particularly useful are: John Barnes's historical collection of literary documents, *The Writer in Australia*, Melbourne, 1969, a collection of essays on literature of the nationalist period, *The Australian Nationalists*, ed. Chris Wallace-Crabbe, Melbourne, 1971, and an important *festschrift*, *Bards, Bohemians and Bookmen*, ed. Leon Cantrell, St. Lucia, 1976. *Considerations*, ed. Brian Kiernan, Sydney, 1977, is a collection of essays, some original, on three Australian poets.

3. PERIODICALS. The following journals and newspapers of the nineteenth century are among the most noteworthy: the *Argus*, 1846–1957, the *Atlas*, 1844–48, the *Australasian*, 1864–1946, the *Australasian Critic*, 1890–91, the *Australian*, 1824–48, the *Australian Journal*, 1865–1958, the *Australian Town and Country Journal*, 1870–1919, the *Centennial Magazine*, 1888–90, the *Empire*, 1850–75, the *Melbourne Punch*, 1855–1925, the *Melbourne Review*, 1876–85, the *Month*, 1857–58, the *Port Phillip Gazette*, 1838–51, the *Review of Reviews*, 1892–1934, the *Sydney Gazette and New South Wales Advertiser*, 1803–42, the *Sydney Mail*, 1860–1938, the *Sydney University Review*, 1881–83, and the *Victorian Review*, 1879–86. Important newspapers, founded in the nineteenth century and still current include: the *Age*, 1854– and the *Sydney Herald/Sydney Morning Herald*, 1831–. The most famous magazine particularly influential from the 1890s to the late 1920s, *The Bulletin*, 1880–, was founded by J. F. Archibald and John Haynes, edited by W. H. Traill 1881–86, and by Archibald, 1886–1902. Other important magazines of the period include the *Lone Hand*, 1907–21, the *Bookfellow*, 1899–1925, the *Triad*, 1915–27, and *Art in Australia*, 1916–42. The twenties and thirties were characterized by diverse magazines such as the journal, *Vision*, 1923–24, and its London-based successor *The London Aphrodite*, 1928–29, *Venture*, 1937–40, and *Jindyworobak Anthology* 1938–53, the main organ of the Jindyworobak movement, the *avant-garde* protest magazine, *Pandemonium*, 1934–35, and the more intellectual journals *Manuscripts*, 1931–35, and *Stream*, 1931. In 1939, *Southerly*, one of Australia's major literary magazines, was founded, and the following year saw the inception of the

equally important *Meanjin Papers*, later *Meanjin*, and then *Meanjin Quarterly*. Both these journals publish creative as well as critical writing, *Meanjin* having a more political and internationalist range than *Southerly*. Other magazines of the forties included *Poetry, A Quarterly of Australian and New Zealand Verse*, 1941–47, which published mainly creative work, *Barjai*, 1943–47, an organ for younger writers, and the social realist magazine, *Australian New Writing*, 1943–46. The modernist magazines *Angry Penguins*, 1940–46, and *Angry Penguins Broadsheet*, 1946, both edited by Max Harris with others, were important organs for the *avant-garde*, a tendency that Harris continued in the later *Ern Malley's Journal*, 1952–55. Interesting magazines of the fifties that failed to outlive the decade include: *Austrovert*, 1950–53, *Direction*, 1952–55, and the *Port Phillip Gazette*, 1952–56. The social realist magazine, *The Realist Writer*, 1952–54, was incorporated in the more interesting and versatile *Overland*, 1954–. *Australian Letters*, an attractively produced South Australian journal, which published both creative and critical writing, ran for just over a decade, 1957–68. Magazines with right-wing affiliations include *Quadrant*, 1956–, recently expanded into a monthly, and *Twentieth Century*, 1946–. The West Australian, *Westerly*, 1956–, is the most regional of the literary journals. Other current literary journals include: *Australian Literary Studies*, 1963–, the academic journals *Critical Review*, 1958–, and *Southern Review*, 1963–, the poetry magazines, *Poetry Magazine/New Poetry*, 1954–, and *Poetry Australia*, 1964–, the North Queensland journal, *LiNQ*, 1971–, and the organ of the Australian Society of Authors, *The Australian Author*, 1969–. The files of the news journals, *Prospect*, 1958–64, the *Observer*, 1958–61, and *Nation*, 1958–72, also contain literary material. *Makar*, 1960–, originally an irregular, roneoed magazine, published in Brisbane, has recently become more established, and another journal, the monthly *Australian Book Review*, 1961–74, was revived in 1978 under new editorship. An indispensable research tool, *Biblionews*, now *Biblionews and Australian Notes & Queries*, the organ of the Book Collectors' Society of Australia, has appeared irregularly from 1947–64, 2nd series 1966–72, 3rd series 1976–. Student magazines have also played an important role, especially *Hermes*, 1895–, and *Arna*, 1918–, both of the University of Sydney, and *Melbourne University Magazine*, 1907–. Others include: *Farrago* (Melbourne), *Lot's Wife* (Monash), *Tharunka* (New South Wales), *Woroni* and *Prometheus* (Australian National University), and *Honi Soit* (Sydney). In recent years numerous titles of underground magazines have emerged including: *Free Poetry, Our Glass, Crosscurrents, Canberra Poetry, Etymspheres, Fitzrot, The Ear in the Wheatfield,* and *Contempa*. Journals which deal with the theatre in Australia include *Masque*, 1967–71, *Komos*, 1967–73, and *Theatre Australia*, 1976–.

III INDIVIDUAL AUTHORS

JOHN FELTHAM (JULES FRANCOIS) ARCHIBALD 1856–1919. Editor. He is best remembered for his co-founding and editing of the *Bulletin* (1886–1902). In a series of articles, 'The Genesis of "The Bulletin"', *Lone Hand*, May-December 1907, he recounts his association with the newspaper. Other accounts of the role of the *Bulletin* and Archibald's significance are: John Haynes's, 'My Early *Bulletin* Memories', *Newsletter*, April-December 1905, S. E. Lee's two articles in *Drylight*, (1961), and in *L of A* (1964 and 1976), and Ailsa G. Thomson's 'The Early History of *The Bulletin*', *Historical Studies*, vol. 6 (1954). Studies dealing more specifically with Archibald include: Norman Lindsay's reminiscences in *Bohemians of The Bulletin*, Sydney, 1965, and Sylvia Lawson's monograph *J.F. Archibald*, GA, Melbourne, 1971.

THEA ASTLEY, b. 1925. Novelist. Her novels include: *Girl With A Monkey*, Sydney, 1958, *A Descant for Gossips*, Sydney, 1960, *The Well Dressed Explorer*, Sydney, 1962, *The Slow Natives*, Sydney, 1965, *A Boat Load of Home Folk*, Sydney, 1968, *The Acolyte*, Sydney, 1972, and *A Kindness Cup*, Melbourne, 1974. In 'The Idiot Question', *Southerly*, vol. 30 (1970), she humorously surveys her reasons for writing. *Walkabout*, vol. 35, 6 (1969) includes a profile by Clifford Tolchard. There are two full length critical essays: J.M. Couper in *Meanjin*, vol. 26 (1967), and Brian Matthews in *Southern Review*, Adelaide, vol. 6 (1973).

BRUCE BEAVER, b. 1928. Poet. His verse collections include: *Under the Bridge*, Sydney, 1961, *Seawall and Shoreline*, Sydney, 1964, *Open at Random*, Sydney, 1967, *Letters to Live Poets*, Sydney, 1969, *Bruce Beaver Reads From His Own Work*, St. Lucia, 1972, *Lauds and Plaints: Poems 1968–1972*, Sydney, 1974, *Odes and Days*, Sydney, 1975, and *Death's Directives*, Sydney, 1978. He has also written a novel, *You Can't Come Back*, Adelaide, 1966. There are the following interviews: (with John B. Beston) *WLWE*, vol. 14 (1975), and (with Thomas Shapcott) *Quadrant*, vol. 20, 4 (1976). There are three substantial critical essays: John B. and Rose Marie Beston's study of his 1969 and 1974 collections, *WLWE*, vol. 14 (1975), and the general appreciations by R. D. FitzGerald, *Meanjin*, vol. 28 (1969), and Craig Powell, *Quadrant*, vol. 12, 5 (1968).

'ROLF BOLDREWOOD' (THOMAS ALEXANDER BROWNE), 1826–1915. Novelist. Although Boldrewood is known mainly for one book, *Robbery Under Arms*, he was a prolific writer. His most notable novels, all published in London, include: *Ups and Downs*, 1878 (serialized 1875, and reprinted 1890, with title, *The Squatter's Dream*), *Robbery Under Arms*, 1888, (serialized 1882–3), *The Miner's Right*, 1890, *A Colonial Reformer*, 1890, *A Sydney-Side Saxon*, 1891, *Nevermore*, 1892, *The Sealskin Cloak*, 1896, *Plain Living*, 1898, and *Babes in the Bush*, 1900. Also valuable are his collection of essays and reminiscences, *Old Melbourne Memories*, Melbourne, 1884, reprinted with editorial commentary by C. E. Sayers, Melbourne, 1969, and his short stories: *A Romance of Canvas Town and Other Stories*, London, 1898. Alan Brissenden's edition, *Rolf Boldrewood*, PAA, St. Lucia, 1979, reprints *Robbery Under Arms* as well as several of his essays and short stories. Criticism of his fiction has centred mainly on *Robbery Under Arms*, and various new editions of the novel contain useful introductions, particularly Alan Brissenden's in the Discovery Press edn, 1968, and R. B. Walker's in the Macmillan edn, 1967. Alan Brissenden's study, *Rolf Boldrewood*, AWW, Melbourne, 1972, is the most substantial critical account to date, and his essay in *AE* provides supplementary material. Other significant essays on *Robbery Under Arms* include: R. B. Walker in *ALS*, vol. 2 (1965), Barry Argyle in *IAN*, and J. H. Rosenberg in *ALS*, vol. 6 (1973). More general studies include: F. H. Mares in *L of A* (1964), and T. Inglis Moore, *Rolf Boldrewood*, GA, Melbourne, 1968. R. B. Walker discusses the background of *The Miner's Right*, ALS, vol. 3 (1967), and R. G. Geering has written an introduction to the novel in a 1973 reprint, published in Sydney. Keast Burke's annotated bibliography, SAB, Cremorne, 1956, is comprehensive though now outdated, and lists some manuscripts.

MARTIN BOYD, 1893–1972. Novelist. He published three novels in London under the pseudonym 'Martin Mills': *Love Gods*, 1925, *Brangane*, 1926, and *The Montforts*, 1928, revised edn under Martin Boyd, Adelaide, 1963. His remaining novels, all published in London, include: *Scandal of Spring*, 1934, *The Lemon Farm*, 1935, *The Painted Princess*, 1936, *The Picnic*, 1937, *Night of the Party*, 1938, *Nuns in Jeopardy*, 1940, *Lucinda Brayford*, 1946, revised edn Harmondsworth, 1954, *Such Pleasure*, 1949, *The Cardboard Crown*, 1952, revised edn Harmondsworth, 1964, *A Difficult Young Man*, 1955, *Outbreak of Love*, 1957, *When Blackbirds Sing*, 1962, and *The Tea-Time of Love*, 1969. He also wrote two autobiographical works: *A Single Flame*, London, 1939, and *Day of My Delight*, Melbourne, 1965, a 'subjective' travel book, *Much Else in Italy*, London, 1958, and a collection of poetry, *Retrospect*, Melbourne, 1920. Statements by Boyd about his life and work include: 'Why I am an Expatriate', *Bulletin*, 10 May 1961, a response to an essay by Brenda Niall in *Twentieth Century*, vol. 17 (1963), *ibid.* vol. 18 (1963), 'Dubious Cartography', *Meanjin*, vol. 23 (1964), reprinted *ONG*, 'Preoccupations and Intentions', *Southerly*, vol. 28 (1968), and 'De Gustibus', *Overland*, no. 50/51 (1972). The most substantial study to date is Brenda Niall's *Martin Boyd*, AWW, Melbourne, 1974, and she has also compiled the most comprehensive bibliography, AB, Melbourne, 1977.

444

Kathleen Fitzpatrick's earlier CLF lecture, Canberra, 1954, and her 1963 monograph on Boyd in the AWW series are still useful. Brian Elliot in one of the first serious essays, *Meanjin*, vol. 16 (1957) praises Boyd's sensitive, discriminating quality, an interpretation extended by G. A. Wilkes in *Southerly*, vol. 19 (1958), reprinted *ALC*. A. L. French, on the other hand, disputes these claims in *Southerly*, vol. 26 (1966), an adverse criticism that is in turn disputed by Leonie Kramer and Thelma Herring in separate essays in *Southerly*'s Martin Boyd number, vol. 28, 2 (1968). Boyd's Langton tetralogy has received the most intensive critical attention. There are studies by: Leonie Kramer in *Australian Quarterly*, vol. 35, 2 (1963), Chris Wallace-Crabbe in *Melbourne Critical Review*, no. 3 (1960) reprinted *MOB*, Dorothy Green in *Southerly*, vol. 28 (1968), John McLaren in *ALS*, vol. 5 (1972), Adrian Mitchell in *Issue*, vol. 3, 10 (1973), Pamela Nase and W. S. Ramson in separate essays in *AE*, Warwick Gould and Brenda Niall in separate essays in *ALS*, vol. 7 (1976), and Brian McFarlane in *Southerly*, vol. 35 (1975). Anthony Bradley presents an analysis of Boyd's persistent themes in *Meanjin*, vol. 28 (1969), as does Dorothy Green, in *Meanjin*, vol. 31 (1972). A. D. Hope has included two essays in *NC*, and there is a profile by Graeme Kinross Smith in *Westerly*, no. 2 (1975).

CHRISTOPHER JOHN BRENNAN, 1870–1932. Poet and critic. Collections of poetry published in his lifetime include: *XVIII Poems*, Sydney, 1897, *XXI Poems. Towards the Source*, Sydney, 1897, *Poems*, dated 1913, published Sydney, 1914 (his major collection, usually referred to as *Poems* (1913), reprinted as a facsimile edn, ed. G. A. Wilkes, Sydney, 1972), and *A Chant of Doom and Other Verses*, Sydney, 1918. A selection from *Poems* (1913), with three previously uncollected poems, appeared as *XXIII Poems*, ed. J. J. Quinn, Sydney, 1938, and fifteen previously unpublished poems were published by Harry F. Chaplin, titled *The Burden of Tyre*, Sydney, 1953. Brennan's work could not be thoroughly appreciated, however, until the scholarly editions of his verse and prose, ed. A. R. Chisholm and J. J. Quinn appeared, the verse in 1960, and the prose in 1962. G. A. Wilkes extensively reviews these collections in *Meanjin*, vol. 19 (1960), and vol. 22 (1963), and also edits verse that was omitted in *Southerly*, vol. 23 (1963). Other verse selections include those by A. R. Chisholm, AP, Sydney, 1966, and G. A. Wilkes, Sydney, 1973. There are various bibliographical studies, the most extensive being: the check-list by G. A. Wilkes, *Meanjin*, vol. 15 (1956), Walter W. Stone and Hugh Anderson, *Christopher John Brennan*, SAB, Cremorne, 1959, and Harry F. Chaplin, *A Brennan Collection*, SAB, Sydney, 1966. Although Brennan's autobiography, 'Curriculum Vitae', in the Quinn papers, Mitchell Library, is unpublished, biographical information is scattered through editions of his work and in critical studies. A. R. Chisholm has also written various accounts, including a chapter in his *Men Were My Milestones*, Melbourne, 1958, essays in *Meanjin*, vol. 29 (1970) and vol. 31 (1972), and reminiscences in *Quadrant*, vol. 1, 3 (1957). Richard Pennington's *Christopher Brennan. Some Recollections*, Sydney, 1970, throws light on his later years. Of the multiplicity of critical studies, the most distinguished are those by A. R.

Chisholm, G. A. Wilkes and James McAuley. Early studies which now have more historical than critical value include: A. G. Stephens, *Chris: Brennan*, Sydney, 1933, Randolph Hughes, *C. J. Brennan. An Essay in Values*, Sydney, 1934, and H. M. Green, *Christopher Brennan*, Sydney, 1939. A. R. Chisholm's *Christopher Brennan: The Man and His Poetry*, Sydney, 1946, is an incisive study, and one of the first in Chisholm's series of essays. His interest in Mallarmé's influence on Brennan is most fully explored in *Southerly*, vols. 21 (1961) and 22 (1962), and in his *A Study of Christopher Brennan's 'The Forest of Night'*, Melbourne, 1970, reviewed at length by Alan Frost, *Meanjin*, vol. 29 (1970). Chisholm has also written general essays in *Meanjin*, vols. 25 (1966), 26 (1967) and 29 (1970). G. A. Wilkes is an important critic of Brennan. His *New Perspectives on Brennan's Poetry*, Sydney, 1953, first published in *Southerly*, vols. 13 (1952) and 14 (1953), analyses a unified sequence in *Poems* (1913), an interpretation that also underlies his essay in *L of A* (1964 and 1976). More specific studies by Wilkes include essays on his literary affinities, *Australian Quarterly*, vol. 31, 2 (1959), reprinted *ALC*, on *Towards the Source*, *Southerly*, vol. 21, 2 (1961), on *The Burden of Tyre*, *Meanjin*, vol. 19 (1960), on the 'Wisdom' sequence, *AUMLA*, no. 14 (1960), and on 'The Wanderer', *Southerly*, vol. 30 (1970). Wilkes's interpretation of Brennan's verse is modified by A. D. Hope in *NC*, and by Vivian Smith in *Quadrant*, vol. 5, 2 (1961), and challenged most extensively by Annette Stewart in *Meanjin*, vol. 29 (1970), and, in a particularly adverse criticism, by A. L. French in *Southerly*, vol. 24 (1964), reprinted *AN*. James McAuley analyses his work and theory in *Christopher Brennan*, AWW, Melbourne, 1963, revised edn 1973. Other important essays by McAuley are: 'Homage to Chris Brennan', *Southerly*, vol. 18 (1957), reprinted *TCALC*, 'The Erotic Theme in Brennan', *Quadrant*, vol. 12, 6 (1968), reprinted *PEAP*, and his chapter in *A Map of Australian Verse*, Melbourne, 1975. Judith Wright has made some notable studies including an essay in *PIAP*, reprinted *AN*, and a lecture printed in *Southerly*, vol. 30 (1970). There are various studies of Brennan's European affiliations: Wallace Kirsop explores his reading of Mallarmé, *Meanjin*, vol. 29 (1970), and of Baudelaire, *Australian Journal of French Studies*, vol. 6 (1969), Margaret Clarke compares his symbolism with that of Mallarmé, *Southerly*, vol. 10 (1949), and L. J. Austin throws further light on the relationship between the two poets, *Australian Journal of French Studies*, vol. 6 (1969). Dennis Douglas in *Meanjin*, vol. 35 (1976) examines the influence of various nineteenth century philosophers, and Vivian Smith traces that of Arthur Symons in *Southerly*, vol. 27 (1967). N. L. Macainsh examines the influence of German literature in *Southerly*, vol. 23 (1963), and of Nietzsche in *Southerly*, vol. 26 (1966). T. L. Sturm, in *Southerly*, vol. 28 (1968), explores his response to the Australian environment. There are also several explicatory essays on Brennan's themes and poetic motifs: Anne Bavinton discusses the meaning of the Lilith symbol in *Meanjin*, vol. 23 (1964), T. L. Sturm in *BBB*, and N. L. Macainsh in *LiNQ*, vol. 3, 3/4 (1974) discuss the structure of 'The Wanderer', Mary A. Merewether in *Southerly*, vol. 30 (1970) links the motifs of *The Burden of Tyre* with those of *Poems* (1913), and R. I. Scott presents a general analysis of *Poems* (1913) in *Southerly*, vol. 18 (1957). Other noteworthy essays include Alec King's criticism of his symbolist practice in *Westerly*, no. 3 (1961), John Docker's interpretation of his romanticism in *ACE* and R. D. FitzGerald's appraisal of the place of *The Burden of Tyre* in his development, *Southerly*, vol. 16 (1955). Studies of Brennan's prose include: Noni Braham in *Twentieth Century*, vol. 17 (1963), Sybille Smith in *Quadrant*, vol. 7, 1 (1963) and Wallace Kirsop in *Southerly*, vol. 23 (1963). Additional recent studies include the essays by Dorothy Green, Mary A. Merewether, Axel Clark, and G. A. Wilkes in *Southerly*, vol. 37 (1977).

VINCENT BUCKLEY, b. 1927. Poet and critic. His collections of poetry include: *The World's Flesh*, Melbourne, 1954, *Masters in Israel*, Sydney, 1961, *Arcady and Other Places*, Melbourne, 1966, and *Golden Builders and Other Poems*, London, 1976. Besides numerous articles, some reprinted in *ALC*, and *TCALC*, various critical works have appeared: *Essays in Poetry, Mainly Australian*, Melbourne, 1957, *Poetry and Morality*, London, 1959, and *Poetry and the Sacred*, London, 1968. He has also written a study of Henry Handel Richardson, *q.v.* An essay in *Quadrant*, vol. 12, 5 (1968), 'Remembering What You Have To', is a summary of his political attitudes which also contains much biographical information. Two informative and searching interviews have been published: (with Henry Rosenbloom) *MUM*, (1968), reprinted *Meanjin*, vol. 28 (1969), and (with Elizabeth Booth) *Quadrant*, vol. 20, 8 (1976). Numerous reviews of his poetry have appeared but few lengthy essays. Of the latter, the studies by Penelope Curtis, *Quadrant*, vol. 6, 4 (1962), and A. K. Thomson, *Meanjin*, vol. 28 (1969) are the most substantial. Peter Steele considers his achievement as a critic in *Meanjin*, vol. 28 (1969), and two essays in *Westerly* (1973) by Veronica Brady and John M. Wright study his latest collection.

DAVID BURN, 1799?–1875. Playwright. His two-volume collection, *Plays and Fugitive Pieces*, Hobart Town, 1842, omitted his one play with an Australian setting, *The Bushrangers*, first performed in 1829, and first published in 1971, edited by W. and J. E. Hiener. His other published play is *Sydney Delivered; or, The Princely Buccaneer*, Sydney, 1845. E. Morris Miller gives an extended account of his life and achievements in *Pressmen and Governors*, Sydney, 1973, Leslie Rees discusses his work in *The Making of Australian Drama*, Sydney, 1973 and Eunice Hanger gives an appreciation of *Sydney Delivered* in *Southerly*, vol. 24 (1964).

ALEXANDER BUZO, b. 1944. Playwright. His published plays include: *The Front Room Boys*, in *Plays*, ed. Graeme Blundell, Ringwood, Vic., 1970, *Macquarie*, introd. by Katharine Brisbane and preface by Manning Clark, Sydney and London, 1971, *Three Plays: Norm and Ahmed: Rooted: The Roy Murphy Show*, introd. by Katharine Brisbane, Sydney and London 1973, *Coralie Lansdowne Says No*, preface by Ken Horler, Sydney and London, 1974, *Tom*, Sydney, 1975, *Martello Towers*, prefaces by John Sumner and Richard Wherrett, comments by the author and Maria Triaca, Sydney and London, 1976, and *Norm and Ahmed*, Sydney, 1976. His unpublished plays include: 'The Revolt' (1967), 'Batman's Beach-head' (1973), and

447

'Makassar Reef' (1978). The following are informative interviews: (with David Sparrow) *Script, Screen and Stage*, vol. 4, 5 (1971), and (with Victoria Duigan) *National Times*, 29 January–3 February 1973. The most lengthy study of Buzo's plays to date is Terry Sturm's analysis of his dramatic technique, *Southerly*, vol. 35 (1975). J. G. Baxendale and J. S. Ryan describe his background and career in *ADHSJP*, No. 17 (1974), and in the same issue J. S. Ryan writes on *Macquarie*. Two general articles which include discussion of Buzo are those by Roslyn Arnold in *Southerly*, vol. 35 (1975), and Margaret Williams in *Meanjin*, vol. 31 (1972). Leslie Rees in an appendix to *The Making of Australian Drama*, Sydney, 1973, gives a full account of official reactions to the first production of *Norm and Ahmed* in 1968.

DAVID CAMPBELL, 1915–79. Poet. His collections of poetry include: *Speak With the Sun*, London, 1949, *The Miracle of Mullion Hill*, Sydney, 1956, *Poems*, Sydney, 1962, *Selected Poems 1942–1968*, Sydney, 1968, enlarged edn with preface, Sydney, 1973, *The Branch of Dodona and Other Poems, 1969–1970*, Sydney, 1970, *Devil's Rock and Other Poems, 1970–1972*, Sydney, 1974, *David Campbell Reads From His Own Work*, St. Lucia, 1975, *Deaths and Pretty Cousins*, Canberra, 1975, and *Words With a Black Orpington*, Sydney, 1978. He has also published two collections of short stories: *Evening Under Lamplight*, Sydney, 1959, and *Flame and Shadow*, St. Lucia, 1976. The latter includes *Evening Under Lamplight* and adds eight wartime stories. Studies of his poetry include those by: Vivian Smith, *Southerly*, vol. 25 (1965), Leonie Kramer, *Quadrant*, vol. 13, 3 (1969), and James McAuley's, *A Map of Australian Verse*, 1975. Graeme Kinross Smith's profile in *Westerly*, no. 3 (1973) is informative, and Kevin Hart conducts an interview in *Makar*, vol. 11 (1975).

MARCUS CLARKE, 1846–81. Novelist and journalist. His novels and tales include: *Long Odds*, Melbourne, 1869, republished as *Heavy Odds*, London, 1896, *Old Tales of a Young Country*, Melbourne, 1871, reprinted as a facsimile edn with introd. by Joan E. Poole, Sydney, 1972, *Holiday Peak and Other Tales*, Melbourne, 1873, and his best known work, *His Natural Life*, Melbourne, 1874. This last, originally serialized in the *Australian Journal*, 1870–72, before revision for publication as a book, was first titled *For the Term of His Natural Life*, in an 1882 edition. The serial version has been published twice, in 1929, ed. Hilary Lofting, and in 1970, ed. Stephen Murray-Smith. The 1874 version has been regularly reprinted, the most significant recent editions being those edited or introduced by L. H. Allen, London, 1952, F. H. Mares, Penrith, NSW, 1968, George Ivan Smith, Sydney, 1969, and Brian Elliott, Cremorne, NSW, 1975. Clarke's remaining works of fiction are: *'Twixt Shadow and Shine*, Melbourne, 1875, *Four Stories High*, Melbourne, 1877, *The Mystery of Major Molineux and Human Repetends*, Melbourne, 1881. *Sensational Tales*, Melbourne, 1886, and *Chidiock Tichbourne, or the Catholic Conspiracy*, London, 1893. *The Peripatetic Philosopher*, Melbourne, 1869, is a collection of essays, and Clarke also wrote several dramatic pieces. Early collections of his work include: *The Marcus Clarke Memorial Volume*, ed. Hamilton Mackinnon,

Melbourne, 1884, and *The Austral Edition of the Selected Works of Marcus Clarke*, ed. Hamilton Mackinnon, Melbourne, 1890. *A Marcus Clarke Reader*, ed. Bill Wannan, Melbourne, 1963, is a useful selection but has been replaced by the more extensive *The Portable Marcus Clarke*, ed. Michael Wilding, PAA, St. Lucia, 1976. L. T. Hergenhan has also edited an important selection, including much material republished for the first time, titled: *A Colonial City: High and Low Life. Selected Journalism of Marcus Clarke*, St. Lucia, 1972. The best bibliography so far is S. R. Simmons, *Marcus Clarke: An Annotated Check List 1863–1972*, ed. with additions by L. T. Hergenhan, SAB, Sydney, 1975. Michael Wilding, in a review of Simmons's check list, *ALS*, vol. 8 (1977), lists important additional items. The standard biography is Brian Elliott's *Marcus Clarke*, Oxford, 1958, the most substantial critical study is Michael Wilding's *Marcus Clarke*, AWW, Melbourne, 1977, and there is also a multiplicity of essays. Several of these concentrate on the use of historical sources in *His Natural Life*: L. L. Robson in *ALS*, vol. 1 (1963) has covered the historical veracity of some of the novel's major events, Decie Denholm explores the accuracy of the picture of Port Arthur in *ALS*, vol. 4 (1969), and in *Historical Studies*, vol. 14 (1970), H. J. Boehm in *ALS*, vol. 5 (1971) deals with the origins of some of the novel's characters and events, Bruce Nesbitt in *ALS*, vol. 5 (1971), explores Clarke's use of historical material and the possibility of plagiarism, a possibility that Joan Poole discounts in *ALS*, vol. 6 (1974), and J. V. Barry in *The Life and Death of John Price*, Melbourne, 1964, deals with his picture of Price as Maurice Frere. The structure of the novel has also received attention: R. G. Howarth's essay in *Southerly*, vol. 15 (1954), is one of the first attempts to uncover the novel's thematic design, L. T. Hergenhan in *ALS*, vol. 2 (1965) discusses the novel's themes of redemption and corruption in *Southerly*, vol. 29 (1969), Annette Stewart in *ALS*, vol. 6 (1974) compares the revised and serialized versions, Barry Argyle in *IAN* makes a detailed study of its themes, H. J. Boehm in *JCL*, vol. 7 (1972) uncovers a coherent thematic statement, and J. F. Burrows discusses the role of melodrama in *Southerly*, vol. 34 (1974). Michael Wilding has contributed substantially to Clarke studies: besides his selection and monograph *supra*, and a general appreciation of *His Natural Life* in *AE*, he has broken new ground with three essays: on *Chidiock Tichbourne*, *ALS*, vol. 6 (1974), on *Old Tales of a Young Country*, *Southerly*, vol. 33 (1973), and on the short stories, *BBB*. L. T. Hergenhan makes a general study of *His Natural Life* in *Meanjin*, vol. 31 (1972), describes its contemporary reception in *Southerly*, vol. 31 (1971), the circumstances of its English publication in *BBB*, and Clarke's response to the Australian landscape in *Quadrant*, vol. 13, 4 (1969). Joan Poole, the author of a significant MA thesis on Clarke, discusses the attitude to Christianity in his fiction, *ALS*, vol. 6 (1973), and the changes in Maurice Frere's wife in the revised version of *His Natural Life*, *ALS*, vol. 4 (1970). Other essays include Eric Irvin's description of his dramatic work, *ALS*, vol. 7 (1975), S. R. Simmons's study of the background of the writing of *Long Odds*, privately printed, 1946, and F. H. Mares's general appreciation, *L of A*, (1964).

VICTOR DALEY, 1858–1905. Poet. *At Dawn and Dusk*, Sydney, 1898, is the only selection published in his lifetime. Although much is still un-collected later selections include: *Poems*, Edinburgh, [1908], *Wine and Roses*, ed. with a memoir by Bertram Stevens, Sydney, 1911, and a collec-tion of satiric verse, *Creeve Roe*, ed. Muir Holburn and Marjorie Pizer, with a foreword by E. J. Brady, Sydney, 1947. Useful commentaries on his work include the biographical and critical notice by A. G. Stephens, *Victor Daley*, Sydney, 1905, and essays by Brian Elliott in *Singing to the Cattle*, Melbourne, 1947, F. T. Macartney in *ALE*, and H. J. Oliver in *Meanjin*, vol. 10 (1951). A. W. Jose in *The Romantic Nineties*, Sydney, 1933, and G. A. Wilkes in *Arts*, vol. 1 (1958), reprinted *ALC*, discuss his place in the 'eighteen nineties'.

ELEANOR DARK, b. 1901. Novelist. Her novels include: *Slow Dawning*, London, 1932, *Prelude to Christopher*, Sydney, 1934, *Return to Coolami*, London, 1936, *Sun Across the Sky*, London, 1937, *Waterway*, London, 1938, *The Timeless Land*, London, 1941, *The Little Company*, Sydney, 1945, *Storm of Time*, Sydney and Toronto, 1948, *No Barrier*, Sydney, 1953, and *Lantana Lane*, London, 1959. The most substantial study of her novels, A. Grove Day's *Eleanor Dark*, TWAS, Boston, 1976, includes extensive bio-graphical material and a comprehensive bibliography. In addition, there are two bibliographical check-lists, both by Hugh Anderson and both in *Biblionews*, vol. 7, 9 (1954), and 2nd series, vol. 3, 2 (1969). Jean Devanny's *Bird of Paradise*, Sydney, 1945, includes an informative interview, and a more recent one is with Kylie Tennant, *SMH*, 14 February 1974. Critical essays include those by: Eric Lowe, *Meanjin*, vol. 10 (1951), G. A. Wilkes, *Southerly*, vol. 12 (1951), and John McKellar, *Southerly*, vol. 9 (1948). Humphrey McQueen in *Hemisphere*, vol. 17, 1 (1973) makes a fresh appreciation of her novels in the face of current neglect.

FRANK DALBY DAVISON, 1893–1970. Novelist. His writings include the novels: *Forever Morning*, Sydney, 1931, *Man-Shy*, Sydney, 1931, *Children of the Dark People*, Sydney, 1936, *Dusty*, New York and Sydney, 1946, and *The White Thorntree*, limited edn, Melbourne, 1968, reprinted 2 vols, Sydney, 1970; the collections of short stories: *The Woman at the Mill*, Sydney, 1940, and *The Road to Yesterday*, Sydney, 1964; and an account of the Australian Light Horse in Palestine in the 1914–18 War, *The Wells of Beersheba*, Sydney, 1933. He gives an account of his writing of *The White Thorntree* in *Southerly*, vol. 29 (1969). The most substantial study to date is Hume Dow's *Frank Dalby Davison*, AWW, Melbourne, 1971, although additional biographical information is contained in John Hetherington's *Forty-Two Faces*, 1962, in an interview conducted by John Barnes, *Westerly*, no. 3 (1967), and in the accounts by Owen Webster, *Overland*, no. 44 (1970), and Graeme Kinross Smith, *Westerly*, no. 4 (1974). Owen Webster also deals with his early life and writing in *The Outward Journey*, Canberra, 1978. H. P. Heseltine, in an article in *Meanjin*, vol. 27 (1968), surveys the whole of his fiction, including his last, controversial novel. Other articles on *The White Thorntree* include those by G. A. Wilkes in *Southerly*, vol. 29 (1969) and John Barnes in *Westerly*, no. 1 (1971).

BRUCE DAWE, b. 1930. Poet. His collections include: *No Fixed Address*, Melbourne, 1962, *A Need of Similar Name*, Melbourne, 1965, *An Eye for a Tooth*, Melbourne, 1968, *Beyond the Subdivisions*, Melbourne, 1969, *Heat-Wave*, Bulleen, Vic., 1970, *Bruce Dawe Reads From His Own Work*, St. Lucia, 1971, *Condolences of the Season*, Melbourne, 1971, *Just a Dugong at Twilight*, Melbourne, 1975, and *Sometimes Gladness: Bruce Dawe. Collected Poems 1954–1978*, Melbourne, 1978. Craig McGregor's *In the Making*, 1969, includes a useful interview. The most substantial study to date is Basil Shaw's *Times and Seasons*, Melbourne, 1974, which contains selected verse, a biography, bibliography, and essays on his work. Other essays include those by: Philip Martin, *Meanjin*, vol. 25 (1966), John M. Wright, *Westerly*, no. 1 (1974), John Hainsworth, *Southerly*, vol. 36 (1976), Chris Wallace-Crabbe, *Meanjin*, vol. 35 (1976), John Wallis, *Checkpoint*, no. 6 (1970), and Andrew Deacon, *MUM*, (1959).

CLARENCE (MICHAEL) JAMES DENNIS, 1876–1938. Poet. He is best known for: *The Songs of a Sentimental Bloke*, Sydney, 1915, and *The Moods of Ginger Mick*, Sydney, 1916. Selections which appeared after his death include: *Selected Verse*, sel. and introd. by A. H. Chisholm, Sydney, 1950, and *Random Verse*, sel. by his wife, Margaret Herron, Melbourne, 1952. Biographical accounts include Margaret Herron's *Down the Years*, Melbourne, 1953, and Ian F. McLaren's *C. J. Dennis: His Life and Work*, Melbourne, 1961. A. H. Chisholm's *The Making of a Sentimental Bloke*, Melbourne, 1946, reprinted London, 1976, with the title, *C. J. Dennis, His Remarkable Career*, is a mainly biographical study. *The World of the Sentimental Bloke*, comp. Barry Watts, Sydney, 1976, includes selections from Dennis's writing as well as various appreciations. Alexander Porteous in *ALS*, vol. 1 (1964), makes a thorough study of his critical reception, Rosemary Wighton discusses his editorship of *The Gadfly, Australian Letters*, vol. 4,3 (1962), reprinted *The Vital Decade*, Melbourne, 1968, K. S. Inglis in 'The Anzac Tradition', *Meanjin*, vol. 24 (1965) discusses the transformation of Ginger Mick at Gallipoli, and Brian Elliott writes on his individual quality in *Southerly*, vol. 37 (1977).

ROSEMARY DOBSON, b. 1920. Poet. Her collections include: *Poems*, Mittagong, privately printed, 1937, *In a Convex Mirror*, Sydney, 1944, *The Ship of Ice*, Sydney, 1948, *Child With a Cockatoo*, Sydney, 1955, *Rosemary Dobson*, sel. and introd. by the author, AP, Sydney, 1963, *Cock Crow*, Sydney, 1965, *Rosemary Dobson Reads From Her Own Work*, St. Lucia, 1970, *Selected Poems*, Sydney, 1973, and *Over the Frontier*, Sydney, 1978. Important statements by Miss Dobson about her poetry are included in an interview with John Thompson, *Southerly*, vol. 28 (1968), and in a published lecture, *Southerly*, vol. 33 (1973). The last two also include biographical information. Graeme Kinross Smith's profile, *Westerly*, no. 3 (1974) includes an extensive discussion of her life and art. At the beginning of her career, Rosemary Dobson's preoccupation with painting frequently led to her being charged with artificiality, see the criticisms by H. M. Green in his *A History of Australian Literature*, Sydney, 1962, Patricia Excell in *Meanjin*, vol. 10 (1951), and A. D. Hope in a review,

Meanjin, vol. 14 (1955). Hope has since reversed this earlier criticism in his essay in *Quadrant*, vol. 16,4 (1972), reprinted *NC*, and other essays on the nature of her preoccupation with art include those by: David Campbell, *Southerly*, vol. 17 (1956), Stuart Lee, *Quadrant*, vol. 9,4 (1965), and two studies by Robyn S. Heales, *ALS*, vols. 6 (1974) and 7 (1975). J. F. Burrows, in *Southerly*, vol. 30 (1970), surveys her poetry including the first collection, *Poems* (1937), and some uncollected verse. Other appreciations include Leonie Kramer's in *Poetry Magazine*, no. 2 (1968), and two essays by James McAuley, one in *ALS*, vol. 6 (1973), reprinted *The Grammar of the Real*, Melbourne, 1975, and the other in *A Map of Australian Verse*, 1975.

LOUIS ESSON, 1879–1943. Playwright. His published plays include: *Three Short Plays* [*The Woman Tamer, Dead Timber,* and *The Sacred Place*], Melbourne, 1911, *The Time is Not Yet Ripe*, Melbourne, 1912, reprinted Sydney, 1973, ed. Philip Parsons, *Dead Timber and Other Plays* [includes *The Drovers*], London, 1920, *The Southern Cross and Other Plays* [*Mother and Son,* and *The Bride of Gospel Place*], introd. by Hilda Esson, Melbourne, 1946, and *The Woman Tamer*, Sydney, 1976. *Andeganora* is included in *Best Australian One-Act Plays*, Sydney, 1937. His unpublished plays include: 'The Battler, or Digger's Rest' (1922), 'Australia Felix' (1926), 'Shipwreck' (c.1928), and 'Vagabond Camp' (c.1928). In *Australian Quarterly*, vol. 11,2 (1939) and in *Fellowship* (1921), reprinted *Adult Education*, vol. 9,4 (1965), Esson describes the influence of W. B. Yeats and the Irish National Theatre on his subsequent co-founding of the 'Pioneer Players'. Vance Palmer's *Louis Esson and the Australian Theatre*, Melbourne, 1948, is a memorial volume consisting of a selection of Esson's letters with commentary. Evaluations of his drama include those by: Keith Macartney in *Meanjin*, vol. 6 (1947), Leslie Rees in *The Making of Australian Drama*, 1973, and Margaret Williams in *Drama*, AWW, Melbourne, 1977. David Walker in *Meanjin*, vol. 31 (1972), and in *Dream and Disillusion*, Canberra, 1976, gives an account of his literary nationalism.

ROBERT DAVID FITZGERALD. b. 1902. Poet. His collections of poetry include: *The Greater Apollo: Seven Metaphysical Songs*, Sydney, privately printed, 1927, *To Meet the Sun*, Sydney, 1929, *Moonlight Acre*, Melbourne, 1938, *Heemskerck Shoals*, Lower Fern Tree Gully, Vic., 1949, *Between Two Tides*, Sydney, 1952, *This Night's Orbit*, Melbourne, 1953, *The Wind at Your Door*, Cremorne, NSW, 1959, *Southmost Twelve*, Sydney, 1962, *R. D. FitzGerald*, sel. and introd. by the author, AP, Sydney, 1963, *Forty Years' Poems*, Sydney, 1965, *R. D. FitzGerald Reads From His Own Work*, St. Lucia, 1971, and *Product*, Sydney, 1977. FitzGerald has also written numerous literary essays and reviews, including a study titled *The Elements of Poetry*, Brisbane, 1963, and a book of essays, *Of Places and Poetry*, St. Lucia, 1976, and has edited selections of Hugh McCrae's letters and of Mary Gilmore's poetry, *q.v.* There are the following interviews: (with John Thompson) *Southerly*, vol. 27 (1967), and (with Craig McGregor) *SMH*, 7 August 1965. The most substantial study to date, A. Grove Day's *Robert D. FitzGerald*, TWAS, New York, 1974, is a comprehensive biography, making references to numerous unpublished letters, and including a bibliography. Further biographical material can be found in Nancy Keesing's reminiscences, *Overland*, no. 25 (1962–63), and in the profile by Graeme Kinross Smith, *ALS*, vol. 7 (1976). A bibliography of FitzGerald prepared by J. Van Wageningen and P. O'Brien, appeared in 1970 and is supplemented annually in the *Index to Australian Book Reviews*. The checklist by Hugh Anderson, *ALS*, vol. 4 (1970) should also be consulted. At the beginning of his career, FitzGerald's reputation stood high. T. Inglis Moore's essay in *Six Australian Poets*, Melbourne, 1942, is an accurate reflection of his standing at that time. Since then estimates of his work have been considerably revised, and in particular the quality of his thought has come under attack. The essays by H. J. Oliver, *Meanjin*, vol. 13 (1954), reprinted *ALC*, by Vincent Buckley, *Essays in Poetry*, 1957, and by Judith Wright, *PIAP*, are all critical of this aspect. Several critics have defended his work, however, including Hugh Anderson, *Southerly*, vol. 19 (1958), F. H. Mares, *Southerly*, vol. 26 (1966), Terry Sturm, *Landfall*, vol. 20 (1966), and G. A. Wilkes, *Southerly*, vol. 27 (1967). An analysis of the issues involved is made in Leonie Kramer's 'R. D. FitzGerald— Philosopher or Poet?', *Overland*, no. 33 (1965). Other general essays include those by: John Lloyd, *Makar*, no. 20 (1964), and Douglas Stewart, *L of A* (1964), reprinted *TCALC*. There are also several specialist essays, including two on the significance of his experience in Fiji: A. Grove Day, *Meanjin*, vol. 24 (1965), and D. Petersen, *LiNQ*, vol. 4,3/4 (1975). Terry Sturm has considered the influence of A. N. Whitehead, *Southerly*, vol. 29 (1969), and K. M. Cantrell has analysed some elusive passages in 'Essay on Memory', *Southerly*, vol. 30 (1970).

STELLA MILES FRANKLIN, 1879–1954. Novelist. Her novels include: *My Brilliant Career*, Edinburgh, 1901, *Some Everyday Folk and Dawn*, Edinburgh, 1909, *Old Blastus of Bandicoot*, London, 1931, *Bring the Monkey*, Sydney, 1933, *All That Swagger*, Sydney, 1936, and *My Career Goes Bung*, Melbourne, 1946. *Pioneers on Parade*, Sydney, 1939, was written in collaboration with Dymphna Cusack. She also wrote an account of her first ten years, *Childhood at Brindabella*, Sydney, 1963, a critical study of Australian literature, *Laughter, Not for a Cage*, Sydney, 1956, with Kate Baker, a biography of Joseph Furphy, *q.v.*, and six novels under the pseudonym 'Brent of Bin Bin'. The most comprehensive study to date, especially useful as biography, is Marjorie Barnard's *Miles Franklin*, TWAS, New York, 1967, revised and enlarged, Melbourne, 1967. Bruce Sutherland has provided supplementary material in his account of her years in America, *Meanjin*, vol. 24 (1965), and another biographical source is the tribute published after her death 'by some of her friends', Melbourne, 1955. Although David Martin, in a valedictory appreciation, *Overland*, no. 2 (1954-55), reprinted *AOM*, and in his recollection of their last meeting , *Overland*, no. 62 (1975), confidently looks forward to a revival of her reputation, other critics are not so sanguine. Appraisals of her work include P. R. Stephensen's CLF Lecture (1959), Ray Mathew's monograph, *Miles Franklin*, AWW, Melbourne, 1963, and two essays by Arthur Ashworth, *Southerly*, vols. 9 (1948), and 12 (1951). Bibliographical material is included in Marjorie Barnard's and Ray Mathew's studies *supra*, and in Walter Stone, 'Miles Franklin: Biography and Bibliography', *Miles Franklin's Manuscripts and Typescripts*, Berkelow's Catalogue no. 47, Sydney [1962].

JOSEPH FURPHY ('Tom Collins'), 1843–1912. Novelist. His major novel is *Such is Life*, Sydney, 1903, second edn, with preface by Vance Palmer, Melbourne, 1917, and an abridged edn London, 1937. Of the numerous reprints since then the most useful are those introd. by John Barnes, 1968, and by F. H. Mares, 1970. *Rigby's Romance*, originally included in *Such is Life*, and first serialised in the *Barrier Truth*, 1905-1906, was published in Melbourne, 1921, severely edited and with a preface by A. G. Stephens. The serial version has since been published twice, introd. by R. G. Howarth, 1946, and introd. by G. W. Turner, 1971. *The Buln-Buln and the Brolga*, also originally part of *Such is Life*, was published in Sydney, 1948, introd. by R. G. Howarth, and in 1971, introd. by Kevin Gilding. *The Poems of Joseph Furphy*, ed. K[ate] B[aker], with a preface by Bernard O'Dowd, appeared in Melbourne, 1916. Of the several bibliographical essays, Walter W. Stone's *Joseph Furphy: An Annotated Bibliography*, SAB, Cremorne, NSW, 1955, is the most substantial, and a supplement to the secondary material is Nina Lebedewa's check-list in *ALS*, vol. 3 (1967). Although the definitive biography has yet to be written, the study by Miles Franklin, in assoc. with Kate Baker, *Joseph Furphy: The Legend of a Man and his Book*, Sydney, 1944, contains much original information, and there are several briefer studies, such as John Barnes's monograph, *Joseph Furphy*, GA, Melbourne, 1967, and the profile by Graeme Kinross Smith in *Westerly*, no. 4 (1975). Furphy's reputation did not begin to establish itself until the 1940s, when several criticisms of *Such is Life*, concerned mainly with its structure, began to appear. Furphy himself, in an anonymous review of the novel, *Bulletin*, 30 July 1903, reprinted *WIA*, had gone some way towards undermining the notion that the novel was a formless panorama. Four critics, in particular, made major contributions in this area: A. K. Thomson in *Meanjin*, vol. 2,3 (1943), H. J. Oliver in *Southerly*, vol. 5,3 (1944), A. G. Mitchell in *Southerly*, vol. 6,3 (1945), reprinted *TCALC*, and A. D. Hope in *Meanjin*, vol. 4 (1945), reprinted *AN* and *NC*. Later criticisms that have consolidated these findings include: Clive Hamer in *Southerly*, vol. 12 (1951), John Barnes in *Meanjin*, vol. 15 (1956), reprinted *AN* and *ONG*, and in his monograph, *Joseph Furphy*, AWW, Melbourne, 1963, 2nd edn 1979, and Brian Kiernan in *Quadrant*, vol. 6,3 (1962). Three essays deal with the history of Furphy's reputation: Douglas Dennis in *Australian Quarterly*, vol. 36,4 (1964), G. A. Wilkes in *The Teaching of English*, no. 6 (1965), and Cecil Hadgraft in *ALS*, vol. 7 (1966). In addition, there are several essays on specialist topics: Clive Hamer considers his 'Christian philosophy' in *Meanjin*, vol. 23 (1964), Chris Wallace-Crabbe examines his realism in *Quadrant* vol. 5,2 (1961), reprinted *ALC*, and his 'masculine strength' in *LC&N*, reprinted and revised *MOB*. Brian Kiernan has written a further three major essays, in *Meanjin*, vol. 23 (1964), in *ALS*, vol. 1 (1963), reprinted *AN*, and in *ISN*. K. A. McKenzie has examined Furphy's knowledge of Shakespeare and the Bible, *ALS*, vol. 2 (1966). Other essays include those by: A. A. Phillips in *Meanjin*, vol. 14 (1955), reprinted *AT*, 1958, revised 1966, F. H. Mares in *Australian Quarterly*, vol. 34,3 (1962), H. J. Oliver in *L of A* (1964 and 1976), Nina Knight in *Southerly*, vol. 29 (1969), Barry Argyle in *IAN*, F. Devlin Glass in *AE*, Judith Rodriguez in *ALS*, vol. 7 (1973), and John Barnes in *BBB*.

MARY GILMORE, 1865–1962. Poet. Her collections of verse include: *Marri'd and Other Verses*, Melbourne, 1910, *The Passsionate Heart*, Sydney, 1918, *The Wild Swan*, Melbourne, 1930, *The Rue Tree*, Melbourne, 1931, *Under the Wilgas*, Melbourne, 1932, *Battlefields*, Sydney, 1939, *The Disinherited*, Melbourne, 1941, *Pro Patria Australia*, Sydney, 1945, *Selected Verse*, Sydney, 1948, enlarged edn Sydney, 1969, *Fourteen Men*, Sydney, 1954 and *Mary Gilmore*, sel. and introd. by R. D. FitzGerald, AP, Sydney, 1963. She also published a collection of essays: *Hound of the Road*, Sydney, 1922, and two books of reminiscences: *Old Days: Old Ways*, Sydney, 1934, and *More Recollections*, Sydney, 1935. Biographical information is contained in *Mary Gilmore: A Tribute*, by T. Inglis Moore, Dymphna Cusack, Barry Ovenden and Walter Stone, Sydney, 1965, in Sylvia Lawson's *Mary Gilmore*, GA, Melbourne, 1966, in W. H. Wilde's *Three Radicals*, AWW, Melbourne, 1969, and also in his essays on her 'hidden years' 1902–12, *Meanjin*, vol. 32 (1973), and *National Times*, 6–11 May 1974, and in Graeme Kinross Smith's profile, *Hemisphere*, vol. 20,9 (1976). Her years in Paraguay are described by Gavin Souter in *A Peculiar People*, Sydney, 1968. Kylie Tennant assesses her achievement in *Westerly*, no. 3 (1963), as do A. G. Mitchell and Judith Wright in separate essays in *Overland*, no. 4 (1955), F. H. Mares in *Southerly*, vol. 25 (1965), and W. H. Wilde in *Three Radicals*, *supra*. Other general appreciations include those by R. D. FitzGerald in *Australian Quarterly*, vol. 11,4 (1939), and *Meanjin*, vol. 19 (1960), and T. Inglis Moore in *Southerly*, vol. 10 (1949).

ADAM LINDSAY GORDON, 1833–70. Poet. Collections published in his lifetime include: *The Feud: A Ballad*, Mount Gambier, SA, 1864, *Ashtaroth: A Dramatic Lyric*, Melbourne, 1867, *Sea Spray and Smoke Drift*, Melbourne, 1867, another edn with preface by Marcus Clarke, Melbourne, 1876, and *Bush Ballads and Galloping Rhymes*, Melbourne, 1870. Later editions include: *Poems of the late Adam Lindsay Gordon*, the 'copyright' edn with preface by Marcus Clarke, Melbourne, 1880, *Poems of Adam Lindsay Gordon*, ed. with introd. by Frank Maldon Robb, London, 1912, and *Adam Lindsay Gordon*, ed. Brian Elliott, Melbourne, 1973. Of the numerous biographies the most notable are: J. Howlett-Ross ed. *The Laureate of the Centaurs*, London, 1888, *Adam Lindsay Gordon and His Friends in England and Australia*, by Douglas Sladen and Edith Humphris, London, 1912, and the memorial volume, *Adam Lindsay Gordon: the Life and Best Poems of the Poet of Australia*, also by Douglas Sladen, London, 1934. Edith Humphris produced a more extensive account in *The Life of Adam Lindsay Gordon*, London 1934. *The Last Letters 1868–1870, Adam Lindsay Gordon to John Riddoch*, ed. Hugh Anderson, Melbourne, 1970, illuminates his last years. Geoffrey Hutton's *Adam*

Lindsay Gordon, London, 1978, is a critical biography. Gordon's high reputation lasted for a short time after his death, but thereafter gradually declined. Francis Adams wrote the first appraisal in *Melbourne Review*, vol. 10 (1885), although he recanted his criticism in a later essay, *Centennial Magazine*, vol. 2 (1890). Other earlier criticisms include those by: Oscar Wilde, *Pall Mall Gazette* (1889), Joseph Furphy, *Bulletin*, 9 February 1895, J. W. L., *Alma Mater*, no. 2 (1900), and A. G. Stephens in his 1918 preface to Gordon's poems, and in the *Bookfellow*, 1 November 1912. Leonie Kramer in *ALS*, vol. 1 (1963), surveys the fluctuations of Gordon's reputation, and the general critical issues they illuminate, and Brian Elliott in his 1973 selection *supra* has provided a good introduction. There are also two recent substantial studies: C. F. MacRae's *Adam Lindsay Gordon*, TWAS, New York, 1968, strongly criticised by Leonie Kramer in *ALS*, vol. 5 (1971), and W. H. Wilde's *Adam Lindsay Gordon*, AWW, Melbourne, 1972.

RODNEY HALL, b. 1935. Poet. His collections of poetry include: *Penniless Till Doomsday*, London, 1962, *Forty Beads on a Hangman's Rope*, limited edn, Newnham, Tas., 1963, *Eye-witness*, Sydney, 1967, *The Autobiography of a Gorgon*, Melbourne, 1968, *The Law of Karma*, Canberra, 1968, *Heaven, In a Way*, St. Lucia, 1970, *Rodney Hall Reads 'Romulus and Remus'*, St. Lucia, 1970, *A Soapbox Omnibus*, St. Lucia, 1973, *Selected Poems*, St. Lucia, 1975, and *Black Bagatelles*, St. Lucia, 1978. He has also written two novels: *The Ship on the Coin*, St. Lucia, 1972, and *A Place Among People*, St. Lucia, 1975, and a study of an Australian poet, *J. S. Manifold*, St. Lucia, 1978. The following are informative interviews: (with Warwick Dalton), *Australian*, 27 July 1968, (with Martin Duwell and N. J. MacLeod), *Makar*, vol. 10,1 (1974), and he discusses his work in *The Creative Artist at Work*, ed. W. R. Lett, Sydney, 1975. Thomas Shapcott appraises his verse in *Makar*, vol. 5,1 (1969).

FRANK HARDY, b. 1917. Novelist and short story writer. His writings include the novels: *Power Without Glory*, Melbourne, 1950, reprinted with introd. by Jack Lindsay, London, 1968, *The Four Legged Lottery*, London and Melbourne, 1958, *The Outcasts of Foolgarah*, Melbourne, 1971, and *But the Dead are Many*, London, 1975, and the collections of short stories: *The Man from Clinkapella*, Melbourne, 1951, *Legends from Benson's Valley*, London, 1963, revised and expanded with the title, *It's Moments Like These*, Melbourne, 1972, and *The Yarns of Billy Borker*, introd. by Clement Semmler, Sydney, 1965. He has also written an account of the controversy surrounding *Power Without Glory* in *The Hard Way*, London and Sydney, 1961, a social commentary on the aborigines of the Northern Territory, *The Unlucky Australians*, Melbourne, 1968, several unpublished plays, and an account of a visit to the Soviet Union, *Journey into the Future*, Melbourne, 1952. Of the numerous interviews, the most substantial are those with Tony Morphett, *Quadrant*, vol. 11,1 (1967), and with Bruce Molloy, *ALS*, vol. 7 (1976). In 'Environment and Ideology in Australian Literature', *Lit. Aust.*, he reflects on literary trends and his own preoccupations. He is included in John Hetherington's *Forty-Two Faces*, 1962. Fred Wells in *Quadrant*, vol. 13,2 (1969) outlines the history of his connection with the Communist Party. Appreciations of the literary quality of his work include those by: David Martin in *Meanjin*, vol. 18 (1959), and Clement Semmler in *The Art of Brian James*, St. Lucia, 1972. John Docker in *Arena*, no. 41 (1976) studies *But the Dead are Many*.

CHARLES HARPUR, 1813–68. Poet. Not all Harpur's work was published in his lifetime, and criticism has been greatly hampered by the corrupt state of his manuscripts, and by the lack of a definitive edition. Works published in his lifetime include: *Thoughts. A Series of Sonnets*, Sydney, 1845, first publ. in Duncan's *Weekly Register*, 1843–45, *Songs of Australia, First Series*, [Sydney, c. 1850], *The Bushrangers, a Play in Five Acts, and Other Poems*, Sydney, 1853, *A Poet's Home*, a broadsheet, Sydney, 1862, *A Rhyme*, Braidwood, NSW [c.1864], and *The Tower of the Dream*, Sydney, 1865. The later collection, *Poems* [ed. H. M. Martin], Melbourne, 1883, is by no means the definitive edition, as C. W. Salier reveals in his discussion of Martin's large-scale emendations, *Southerly*, vol. 12 (1951). Salier has also edited Harpur's love poetry, *(Rosa) Love Sonnets to Mary Doyle*, Melbourne, 1948, and two recent selections include: *Charles Harpur*, sel. and introd. by Donovan Clarke, AP, Sydney, 1963, and *Charles Harpur*, ed. Adrian Mitchell, Melbourne, 1973. J. Normington-Rawling's biography, *Charles Harpur, An Australian*, Sydney, 1962, is the most comprehensive to date, although additional information is provided in Marcel Aurousseau's review, *Meanjin*, vol. 22 (1963). There is no specialist bibliography as yet, although Normington-Rawling's study *supra* contains a useful listing. C. W. Salier, one of the earliest of Harpur's critics, has contributed various essays and textual studies, including a 'Pre-Centenary Note', *Australian Quarterly*, vol. 15,4 (1943), and discussions of Harpur's learning, *ibid.*, vol. 19,1 (1947), of *Thoughts. A Series of Sonnets* (1845), *ibid.*, vol. 17,3 (1945), of his translations from the *Iliad*, *Southerly*, vol. 7, (1946), and aspects of his connection with Kendall, *Southerly*, vol. 9 (1948). Donovan Clarke's survey of Kendall's correspondence, *ALS*, vol. 1 (1964), also throws light on the relationship. Elizabeth Perkins has explored Harpur's influence on Kendall, *ALS*, vol. 5 (1972), and also Emerson's influence on Harpur, *ALS*, vol. 6 (1973). In the same volume of *ALS*, Leon Cantrell discusses his reading of Marvell. Judith Wright has extended appreciation of Harpur with her monograph, *Charles Harpur*, AWW, Melbourne, 1963, 2nd revised edn, 1977, and with her study in *PIAP*. Other comparative studies are J. Normington-Rawling's essay on his significance, *Quadrant*, vol. 7,1 (1963), and A. D. Hope's 'Three Early Australian Poets', *NC*. Elizabeth Perkins in *ALS*, vol. 7 (1976), considers an early, untypical short story, Eric Irvin describes the contemporary reception of his unstaged play, *The Bushrangers*, in 'Australia's "First" Dramatists', *ALS*, vol. 4 (1969), and V. C. Mishra in *Southerly*, vol. 36 (1976) makes a study of his literary reputation to 1900.

ELIZABETH HARROWER, b. 1928. Novelist. Her novels, all published in London, include: *Down in the City*, 1957, *The Long Prospect*, 1958, *The Catherine Wheel*, 1960, and *The Watch Tower*, 1966. Her short stories contributed to periodicals and anthologies, are listed in R. G. Geering's comparative study of her work, *Recent Fiction*, AWW, Melbourne, 1974. John Hetherington includes a profile in *Forty-Two Faces*, 1962. Articles on her novels include those by R. G. Geering, *Southerly*, vol. 30 (1970), and [Max Harris], *Australian Letters*, vol. 4,2 (1961).

GWEN HARWOOD, b. 1920. Poet. Her collections of poetry include: *Poems,* Sydney, 1963, *Poems/Volume Two*, Sydney, 1968, and *Selected Poems*, Sydney, 1975. She has also written two libretti for operas composed by Larry Sitsky: *The Fall of the House of Usher*, (1965), and *Lenz* (1974). *Quadrant*, vol. 19,7 (1975) includes an interview with John B. Beston, and she discusses her work in *The Creative Artist at Work*, ed. W. R. Lett, Sydney, 1975. Douglas Dennis and A. D. Hope discuss her verse in an interchange of essays: Douglas Dennis, *Quadrant*, vol. 13,2 (1969), A. D. Hope, *ALS*, vol. 5 (1972), reprinted *NC*, and Douglas Dennis, *ALS*, vol. 6 (1973). John B. Beston considers her treatment of artists and academics in *Quadrant*, vol. 18,3 (1974), Norman Talbot makes an extensive, general study in *ALS*, vol. 7 (1976), and R. F. Brissenden gives an appreciation in *Southerly*, vol. 38 (1978). Other essays on her poetry include those by: David Moody, *Meanjin*, vol. 22 (1963), and Chris Wallace-Crabbe, *Meanjin*, vol. 28 (1969), reprinted *MOB*.

WILLIAM GOSSE HAY, 1875–1945. Novelist. He wrote six novels, all published in London: *Stifled Laughter*, 1901, *Herridge of Reality Swamp*, 1907, *Captain Quadring*, 1912, *The Escape of the Notorious Sir William Heans*, 1919, reprinted Melbourne, 1955, with essays by R. G. Howarth and E. Morris Miller, *Strabane of the Mulberry Hills*, 1929, *The Mystery of Alfred Doubt*, 1937, as well as a collection of short stories and essays, *An Australian Rip Van Winkle*, London, 1921. Biographical material is contained in Fayette Gosse's monograph, *William Gosse Hay*, AWW, Melbourne, 1965, and in J. H. M. Abbott's essay, *Southerly*, vol. 13, (1952). Hay was virtually ignored until F. Earle Hooper aroused interest in his work with an address to the English Association (Sydney branch) in October 1944. Miss Hooper also contributed a memoir, and made an analysis of the technique of *The Escape of Sir William Heans*, both in *Southerly*, vol. 7 (1946), and a study of the background of *Herridge of Reality Swamp, Southerly*, vol. 15 (1954). Although large claims have been made for Hay, his literary standing is still subject to critical debate. R. G. Howarth in his introductory essay, *supra*, reprinted from *Australian Quarterly*, vol. 26,2 (1954), and in his essay on the novel's technique, *Southerly*, vol. 7 (1946), praises his moral preoccupations and style. Critics who have discounted these claims include: Frederick T. Macartney in *ALE*, John Barnes in *L of A* (1964 and 1976), and Barry Argyle in *IAN*. Thelma Herring in *Southerly*, vol. 26 (1966) traces the influence of Hawthorne and Meredith, although L. T. Hergenhan in an article in *Southerly*, vol. 27 (1967), regards this approach as misleading. An earlier attempt to come to terms with Hay's singularity is Brian Elliott's essay in *Singing to the Cattle*, Melbourne, 1947. Clive Hamer, a supporter of Hay's work, compares *The Escape of Sir William Heans* with other convict novels in *Southerly*, vol. 18 (1957), and another essay on the same theme is J. C. Horner's in *THRA*, vol. 15,1 (1967). P. D.

Edwards in *BBB* throws light on some of the novel's ambiguities. Hay's standing as a historical novelist, supported by R. G. Howarth and F. Earle Hooper *supra*, has been assessed at length by I. D. Muecke in *ALS*, vol. 2 (1965). Muecke also considers Hay's unfinished novel, 'The Return of Robert Wasterton' in *South Australiana*, vol. 7 (1968).

SHIRLEY HAZZARD, 1931. Novelist. Her writings include three novels: *The Evening of the Holiday*, London, 1966, *People in Glass Houses*, London, 1967, and *The Bay of Noon*, Boston and London, 1970, a collection of short stories, *Cliffs of Fall*, London, 1963, and a commentary on the United Nations, *Defeat of an Ideal*, London and New York, 1973. Two introductions are John Colmer's essay in *Meanjin*, vol. 29 (1970), and R. G. Geering's study in *Recent Fiction*, 1974.

XAVIER HERBERT, b. 1901. Novelist. His novels include: *Capricornia*, Sydney, 1937, *Seven Emus*, Sydney, 1959, *Soldiers' Women*, Sydney, 1961 and *Poor Fellow My Country*, Sydney, 1975. He has also published a collection of short stories, *Larger Than Life*, Sydney, 1963, and an autobiographical work *Disturbing Element*, Melbourne, 1963. There have been several reprints of *Capricornia* including a paperback edn with introd. by L. T. Hergenhan, Sydney, 1972. Of Herbert's numerous articles about his life and work, the most illuminating are: 'Autobiographette', *Publicist*, no. 24 (1938), 'I Sinned Against Syntax', *Meanjin*, vol. 19 (1960), 'How *Capricornia* was Made', *Bulletin*, 8 March 1961, reprinted *Observer*, 18 March 1961, 'The Agony—and the Joy', *Overland*, no. 50/51 (1972), 'The Writing of *Capricornia*', *ALS*, vol. 4 (1970), and (on his last novel) 'The Signing of the Peace Treaty', *Australian*, 29 March 1975. There are interviews (with Patricia Rolfe) in *Bulletin*, 5 January 1974, and (with Jillian Robertson) in *Bulletin*, 19 October 1963, and a profile by John Hetherington in *Forty-Two Faces*, 1962. The most substantial critical study to date is H. P. Heseltine's monograph, *Xavier Herbert*, AWW, Melbourne, 1973. Three major essays on *Capricornia* have also appeared: Vincent Buckley's study in *Meanjin*, vol. 19 (1960), reprinted *ALC*, and Brian Kiernan's, *ALS*, vol. 4 (1970), reprinted in a revised form, *ISN*, and Laurie Clancy's, *Meanjin*, vol. 34 (1975). The two latter qualify Buckley's view. Apart from Heseltine's work *supra*, little has been written on *Soldiers' Women*, or, as yet, on the massive *Poor Fellow My Country*. Provisional assessments of the latter, however, are made by H. P. Heseltine in *Meanjin*, vol. 34 (1975), Don Grant in *Overland*, no. 65 (1976), Laurie Clancy in *Southerly*, vol. 37 (1977), and David Kelly in *Overland*, no. 67 (1977).

DOROTHY HEWETT, b. 1923. Poet and playwright. Her collections of verse include: (with Merv. Lilley) *What About the People!* [Brisbane, 1961], *Windmill Country*, Melbourne, 1968, and *Rapunzel in Suburbia*, Sydney, 1975. Her published plays include: *The Chapel Perilous*, introd. by Aarne Neeme, preface by Sylvia Lawson, Sydney, 1972, *Bon-Bons and Roses for Dolly. The Tatty Hollow Story. Two Plays*, introd. by Arthur Ballet, Sydney and London, 1976, *This Old Man Comes Rolling Home*, introd. by Jack Beasley with a note by Merv. Lilley, Sydney and London, 1976, *The*

Golden Oldies, Hecate, vol. 2,2 (1976), *The Beautiful Mrs Portland, Theatre-Australia*, vol. 1,4 and 5 (1976). Her unpublished plays include: 'Time Flits Away Lady' (1941), and the musicals: 'Catspaw' (1974) 'Joan' (1975) and *Pandora's Cross* (1978). She has also written a novel of factory life, *Bobbin Up*, Melbourne, 1959. In *Zeitschrift fur Anglistik und Americanistik*, Leipzig, vol. 15 (1967), she reflects on her life and writing career, and the following are informative interviews: (with Kevon Kemp) *National Times*, 4–9 September 1972 and 30 September–5 October 1974, (with Barry Eaton) *Theatre-Australia*, vol. 1,4 (1976), and (with Pip Porter) *Hecate*, vol. 3,1 (1977). Appraisals of her work include: Bruce Williams's review of *Windmill Country*, *Westerly*, no. 4 (1968), Brian Kiernan's critique of her poetry and plays in *Overland*, no. 64 (1976), Bruce Williams's exposition of her poetry in the same volume, Carole Ferrier's detailed survey in *Lip*, Carlton, Vic., 30 October 1976, Alan van der Poorten's general appreciation in *Theatre-Australia*, vol. 1,4 (1976), and Hal Colebatch's review of *Rapunzel in Suburbia* in *Westerly*, no. 3 (1975). Jean Whitehead in *Westerly*, no. 1 (1971), and Reba Gostand in *BBB* write on *The Chapel Perilous*, Margot Luke considers *Bon-Bons and Roses for Dolly* in *Westerly*, no. 4 (1972), and 'Catspaw' in 'Perth Festival Drama 1974', *Westerly*, no. 1 (1974).

JACK HIBBERD, b. 1940. Playwright. His published plays include: *Just Before the Honeymoon, Komos*, vol. 2 (1969), *White with Wire Wheels* and *Who?* in *Plays*, ed. Graeme Blundell, Ringwood, Vic., 1970, *A Stretch of the Imagination*, introduced by the author, preface by Margaret Williams, Sydney, 1973, *Dimboola: A Wedding Reception Play* (bound with John Powers, *The Last of the Knucklemen*), Ringwood, Vic., 1974, *Three Popular Plays*, [which includes *One of Nature's Gentlemen, A Toast to Melba*, and the *Les Darcy Show*], Melbourne, 1976, *Memoirs of a Carlton Bohemian, Meanjin*, vol. 36 (1977). His unpublished plays include: 'Three Old Friends' (1967), 'Brainrot' (1968), 'Klag' (1970), 'Customs and Excise', later 'Proud Flesh' (1970), 'Aorta' (1971), 'Captain Midnight, V.C.' (1972), and 'Peggy Sue' (1974). *Lot's Wife*, 16 September 1974 includes an interview, conducted by Andrew Knight and John Alsop, and useful analyses include those by Alrene Sykes in *BBB* and Peter Pierce in *ALS*, vol. 8 (1978).

ALEC DERWENT HOPE, b. 1907. Poet and critic. His collections of verse include: *The Wandering Islands*, Sydney, 1955, *Poems*, London, 1960, *A. D. Hope*, sel. by Douglas Stewart, introduced by the author, AP, Sydney, 1963, *Collected Poems 1930–1965*, Sydney, 1966, 2nd edn titled *Collected Poems 1930–1970*, introduced by Leonie Kramer, Sydney, 1972, *New Poems 1965–1969*, Sydney, 1969, *Dunciad Minor*, Melbourne, 1970, *A. D. Hope Reads From His Own Work*, St. Lucia, 1972, *Selected Poems*, Sydney, 1973, *A Late Picking*, Sydney, 1975, and *A Book of Answers*, Sydney, 1978. He has also published several scholarly studies and collections of essays including: *The Cave and the Spring*, Adelaide and San Francisco, 1965, 2nd edn, Sydney, 1974, *A Midsummer Eve's Dream*, Canberra, 1970, *The Literary Influence of Academies*, Sydney, 1970, *Native Companions*, Sydney, 1974, *The*

Pack of Autolycus, Canberra, 1978, *The New Cratylus*, Melbourne, 1979, and studies of Henry Kendall and Judith Wright, *q.v.* A bibliography by Patricia O'Brien, Adelaide, 1968, reviewed by Leon Cantrell, *ALS*, vol. 5 (1971), and supplemented annually in the *Index to Australian Book Reviews*, since 1968, has been superseded by Joy Hooton's bibliography, AB, Melbourne, 1979. There are the following interviews (with Desmond O'Grady) *Observer*, 12 November 1960, (with John Thompson) *Southerly*, vol. 26 (1966), and (with Craig McGregor) *In the Making*, 1969. Additional important statements by Hope about his poetry include: his introduction to *A.D. Hope, supra*, and 'How It Looks to the Cow', *Idiom*, no. 7 (1967). His poetry was slow to win a general audience. Critics of his work include Vincent Buckley, James McAuley and R. F. Brissenden. Vincent Buckley wrote the earliest extended criticism in *Direction*, vol. 1,4 (1955), reprinted and revised in his *Essays in Poetry*, 1957. McAuley's contributions include an essay, *Quadrant*, vol. 5,4 (1961), reprinted *ALC*, a study in his *A Map of Australian Verse*, 1975, and reminiscences in *Quadrant*, vol. 20,4 (1976). R. F. Brissenden has written three major essays: an interpretation of 'The Double Looking Glass', *ALS*, vol. 6 (1974), a discussion of the role of the academy in his development, *L of A* (1976), and an appreciation of *New Poems, Southerly*, vol. 30 (1970). Leonie Kramer has also made a substantial study in her *A. D. Hope*, AWW, Melbourne, 1979. Other important essays are S. L. Goldberg's review of *The Wandering Islands, Meanjin*, vol. 16 (1957), and William Walsh's chapter in *A Manifold Voice*, London and New York, 1970. W. A. Suchting analyses the theme of isolation in his poetry, *Meanjin*, vol. 21 (1962), G. A. Wilkes makes a general survey of his preoccupations, *Australian Quarterly*, vol. 36, 1 (1964), Gustav Cross discusses his vision of the artist, *L of A* (1964), Judith Wright explores the duality of his world view in *PIAP*, and Barry Argyle analyses the nature of his wit, *JCL*, no. 3 (1967) reprinted *RCL* Dorothy Green discusses his versatility, *Adult Education*, vol. 12,2 (1967), Chris Wallace-Crabbe in *Meanjin*, vol. 26 (1967), reprinted *MOB*, explores his concept of the creative way, and Edwin Webb deals with the resolution of dualities in his verse, *Southerly*, vol. 32 (1972), and *JCL*, vol. 6 (1971). Harry Heseltine discusses his achievement in *New Poems, Meanjin*, vol. 29 (1970), Suzanne Graham explores his treatment of myth, *ALS*, vol. 7 (1975), and Vivian Smith discusses several poems in detail, *SMH*, 12 June 1973. John Docker deals with his image of woman in *Arena*, no. 22 (1970), and in *ACE*, and Ross Mezger studies his treatment of the grotesque in *Southerly*, vol. 36 (1976).

DAVID IRELAND, b. 1927. Novelist. His novels include: *The Chantic Bird*, London, 1968, reprinted with introd. by Adrian Mitchell, Sydney, 1973, *The Unknown Industrial Prisoner*, Sydney, 1971, *The Flesheaters*, Sydney, 1972, *Burn*, Sydney, 1974, and *The Glass Canoe*, Melbourne, 1976. He has also published a play, *Image in the Clay*, preface by Norman McVicker, St. Lucia, 1964. There are the following interviews: (with Frank Moorhouse) *Bulletin*, 22 July 1972, and (with Brian Dale) *National Times*, 1–6 January 1973. The most substantial critical study so far is Adrian Mitchell's 'Paradigms of Purpose: David Ireland's Fiction', *Meanjin*, vol. 34 (1975).

GEORGE JOHNSTON, 1912–70. Novelist. His major novels include: *The Darkness Outside*, London, 1959, *Closer to the Sun*, London, 1960, *The Far Road*, London, 1962, *The Far Face of the Moon*, New York, 1964 and his most well-known, semi-autobiographical trilogy: *My Bother Jack*, London, 1964, *Clean Straw for Nothing*, London, 1969, and *A Cartload of Clay*, Sydney, 1971. There are the following interviews: (with Sandra Hall) *Bulletin*, 26 October 1968 and 23 August 1969, and (with Clifford Tolchard) *Walkabout*, vol. 35,1 (1969). There is an article by his wife, Charmain Clift, in *POL*, no. 9 (1969). Apart from reviews, the most notable of which is by F. H. Mares on *My Brother Jack*, *Southerly*, vol. 24 (1964), there are only two major essays: A. E. Goodwin's study of the unifying motifs of his trilogy, *ALS*, vol. 6 (1973), and Geoffrey Thurley's evaluation of *My Brother Jack*, *Ariel*, vol. 5,3 (1974).

HENRY KENDALL, 1839–82. Poet. The main collections of poetry published in his lifetime include: *Poems and Songs*, Sydney and London, 1862, *Leaves from Australian Forests*, Melbourne, 1869, and *Songs from the Mountains*, Sydney and London, 1880. *Poems of Henry Clarence Kendall*, Melbourne, 1903, sel. with memoir and notes by his son, Frederick C. Kendall, is an extensive selection and the basis of two recent collections, both titled *Leaves from Australian Forests*, AC, Hawthorn, Vic., 1970, and SAC, Adelaide, 1975. Of the other recent collections, *The Poetical Works of Henry Kendall*, ed. T. T. Reed, Adelaide, 1966, is the most comprehensive and bibliographically informative, although *Henry Kendall*, ed. Leonie Kramer and A. D. Hope, Melbourne, 1973, is a well-balanced selection including poems, prose and letters. Other collections are: *Selected Poems of Henry Kendall*, ed. T. Inglis Moore, Sydney, 1957, and *Henry Kendall*, sel. and introd. by T. Inglis Moore, AP, Sydney, 1963. Although there is as yet no specialist bibliography, several listings have been published including Iris Burke's 'Draft List of the Prose Writings', *Foreshadowings*, Sydney, 1963, and bibliographies by T. Inglis Moore, *Biblionews*, vol. 10,2 (1957), and by W. H. Wilde in his study, *Henry Kendall*, TWAS, Boston, Mass., 1976. Although most Kendall editions contain biographical information, the most valuable sources, T. T. Reed's D. Litt. thesis, Adelaide, 1953, and Donovan Clarke's M. A. Thesis 'A Critical Edition of the Letters of Henry Kendall', Sydney, 1959, remain unpublished. Clarke has published two articles based on his thesis, however, in *ALS*, vol. 1 (1964) and vol. 2 (1966) and T. T. Reed's short study, *Henry Kendall: A Critical Appreciation*, Adelaide, 1960, includes valuable biographical material. Although early Kendall criticism concentrated on his lyrics, recent studies have emphasised his narrative, elegiac and satiric verse, see the introductions to their Kendall editions by A. D. Hope and T. Inglis Moore, *supra*, the comprehensive study by W. H. Wilde, *supra*, and A. D. Hope's lecture, *Henry Kendall: A Dialogue with the Past*, Sydney, 1971. Several critics have studied the connection between Harpur and Kendall including: C. W. Salier in *Southerly*, vol. 9 (1948), Elizabeth Perkins in *ALS*, vol. 5 (1972), and Judith Wright in *PIAP*, and *L of A* (1964 and 1976). General studies include Donovan Clarke's analysis of his imagery and the fluctuations of his reputation, *Australian Quarterly*, vol. 29,4 (1957) and vol. 30,1 (1958),

Judith Wright's appreciations *supra*, A. C. W. Mitchell's analysis of his imagery and poetic themes, *ALS*, vol. 4 (1969), and A. D. Hope's comparative study, 'Three Early Australian Poets', *NC*.

THOMAS KENEALLY, b. 1935. Novelist. His novels include: *The Place at Whitton*, London, 1964. *The Fear*, Melbourne, 1965, *Bring Larks and Heroes*, Melbourne, 1967, *Three Cheers for the Paraclete*, Sydney, 1968, *The Survivor*, Sydney, 1969, *A Dutiful Daughter*, Sydney, 1971. *The Chant of Jimmie Blacksmith*, Sydney, 1972, *Blood Red, Sister Rose*, London, 1974, *Gossip from the Forest*, London, 1975, *Season in Purgatory*, London, 1976, and *A Victim of the Aurora*, London, 1977. He has also written several plays: *Halloran's Little Boat* (1966, published Ringwood, Vic., 1975), 'Childermas' (1968), and 'An Awful Rose', (1972). Articles by Keneally on his work include: 'The Novelist's Poison', *Australian Author*, vol. 1,4 (1969), 'Origin of a Novel' [on *The Survivor*], *Hemisphere*, vol. 13,10 (1969), and 'Doing Research for Historical Novels', *Australian Author*, vol. 7,1 (1975). Of the numerous interviews with Keneally, the most informative are those with Craig McGregor, *In the Making*, 1969, and with John B. Beston, *WLWE*, vol. 12 (1973). J. S. Ryan has supplied further biographical details in *ADHSJP*, no. 15 (1971/72). Although there is no full scale study of Keneally's fiction as yet, there are several substantial essays: Kerin Cantrell in *Southerly*, vol. 28 (1968), and L. J. Clancy in *Meanjin*, vol. 27 (1968), study his early novels, Robert Burns in *ALS*, vol. 4 (1969), and in *DOAF*, considers his distinctive qualities, and R. G. Geering contrasts his development with that of Randolph Stow in *Recent Fiction*, 1974. John B. Beston considers his treatment of the theme of freedom in *ALS*, vol. 5 (1972), and in *Makar*, vol. 7,2 (1971), and analyses the play 'An Awful Rose' in *Southerly*, vol. 33 (1973). Brian Kiernan discusses *Bring Larks and Heroes* in *Southerly*, vol. 28 (1968), revised in *ISN*, F.C. Molloy explores the significance of its Irish background in *ALS*, vol. 7 (1976), and Michael Wilding evaluates *Three Cheers for the Paraclete* in *Southerly*, vol. 29 (1969). Brian Kiernan in *Meanjin*, vol. 31 (1972) appraises *The Chant of Jimmie Blacksmith*, Keneally's most favourably received novel so far, Terry Sturm discusses its treatment of Australian racism in *Southerly*, vol. 33 (1973), W. S. Ramson considers its strengths and weaknesses in *AE*, and Helen Daniel explores its exposure of white society in *Southerly*, vol. 38 (1978).

PETER KENNA, b. 1930. Playwright. His published plays include: *The Slaughter of St. Teresa's Day*, introd. by Philip Hickie and preface by Cyril Pearl, Sydney, 1972, *A Hard God*, introd. by John Bell and preface by Katharine Brisbane, Sydney, 1974, *Mates* [in *Drag Show*], Woollahra, NSW, 1977, and *Three Plays by Peter Kenna: Talk to the Moon, Listen Closely, Trespassers Will be Prosecuted*, Sydney, 1977. His unpublished plays include: 'Muriel's Virtues' (1966), and the radio and television plays, 'Julie Was', 'Shameless Hussies' and 'Goodbye, Gloria, Hello'. Kenna has recently supplemented *A Hard God* with two other plays, 'Furtive Love' and 'An Eager Hope' (both 1978), to form a trilogy, 'The Cassidy Album'.

There are the following interviews: (with Lenore Nicklin) *SMH*, 11 January 1975, and (with Katharine Brisbane) *National Times*, 14–19 June 1976.

HENRY KINGSLEY, 1830–76. Novelist. His novels of Australian interest, all published in London, include: *The Recollections of Geoffry Hamlyn*, 1859, *The Hillyars and the Burtons: A Story of Two Families*, 1865, reprinted as facsimile edn with introd. by Leonie Kramer, Sydney, 1973, *The Boy in Grey*, 1871, and *Reginald Hetherage*, 1874. His collections of stories also of Australian interest include: *Tales of Old Travel Re-Narrated*, 1869, *Hetty and Other Stories*, 1871, and *Hornby Mills and Other Stories*, 1872. Bibliographical information is contained in W. H. Scheuerle's study, *The Neglected Brother: A Study of Henry Kingsley*, Tallahassee, Florida, 1971, in S. M. Ellis, *Henry Kingsley 1830–1876, Towards a Vindication*, London, 1931, in John Barnes's monograph, *Henry Kingsley and Colonial Fiction*, AWW, Melbourne, 1971, and in several of the critical essays listed below. Recently Kingsley's Australian years have been subjected to more detailed analysis and in particular, the veracity of certain early commentaries, has been examined. Important analyses of this nature include those by: Brian Elliott in *ALS*, vol. 3 (1968), John Barnes in *Meanjin*, vol. 30 (1971), Hugh Anderson in *ALS*, vol. 4 (1969), J. S. Ryan in *ADHSJP*, no. 19 (1976), and J. S. D. Mellick, in *ALS*, vol. 6 (1973) and vol. 7 (1976). *Geoffry Hamlyn* has always attracted most critical attention. Marcus Clarke in his preface to *Long Odds* (1869), and Rolf Boldrewood in *Old Melbourne Memories* (1884), praised the novel, although Joseph Furphy in *Such is Life* (1903) was caustically critical. Recent studies, which recognise the minor nature of Kingsley's work, and deal with the novel in a more neutral manner, include J. C. Horner's analysis of its Australian setting, *ALS*, vol. 1 (1963), also studied by Rosilyn Baxter in *ALS*, vol. 4 (1970), L. T. Hergenhan's study of its contemporary reception, *ALS*, vol 2 (1966), Barry Argyle's general appreciation, *IAN*, G. A. Wilkes's explanation of its literary survival, *Southerly*, vol. 32 (1972), revised for *AE*, and Julian Croft's discussion of cultural division, *ALS*, vol. 6 (1974). Of the more general studies, the most substantial single critical work so far is John Barnes's monograph, *supra*, although W. H. Scheuerle's study also *supra* contains some new material.

EVE LANGLEY, 1908–1974. Novelist. Her novels include: *The Pea Pickers*, Sydney, 1942, and *The White Topee*, Sydney, 1954. Hal Porter describes his meetings with her in *London Magazine*, vol. 5,6 (1965) and in *The Extra*, Melbourne, 1975, and Helen Frizell discusses her life and work in *SMH*, 26 July 1975. Douglas Stewart writes extensively on *The Pea Pickers* in *The Flesh and the Spirit*, Sydney, 1948, and other contemporary assessments include those by Frank Dalby Davison in the *Bulletin*, 23 October 1940, and Norman Lindsay in the same journal, 3 June 1942.

RAY LAWLER. b. 1921. Playwright. His plays include: *Summer of the Seventeenth Doll*, London and New York, 1957, *The Piccadilly Bushman*, London, 1961, and *The Doll Trilogy*, Sydney, 1978, which includes two companion pieces to the *Doll: Kid Stakes* and *Other Times*. His un-published plays include: 'The Unshaven Cheek' (1963), and 'The Man Who Shot the Albatross' (1971). Useful articles on his work are those by R. F. Brissenden, *Texas Quarterly*, vol. 5 (1962), P. H. Davison, *Southerly*, vol. 23 (1963), Alexander Porteous, *ALS*, vol. 3 (1967), and Jack Hibberd, *Meanjin*, vol. 36 (1977). In *The Making of Australian Drama*, Sydney, 1973, Leslie Rees discusses the *Doll's* reception in Australia and overseas.

HENRY LAWSON, 1867–1922. Poet and short story writer. Lawson's major collections of verse and prose published in his lifetime include: *Short Stories in Prose and Verse*, Sydney, 1894, *In the Days when the World Was Wide and Other Verses*, Sydney and London, 1896, *While the Billy Boils*, Sydney, 1896, *On the Track*, Sydney, 1900, *Over the Sliprails*, Sydney and London, 1900, *Verses Popular and Humorous*, Sydney and London, 1900, *Joe Wilson and His Mates*, Edinburgh, 1901, *Children of the Bush*, London, 1902, and *When I Was King and Other Verses*, Sydney, 1905. Since his death there have been numerous editions of his work. Colin Roderick's *infra* super-sede the first major verse and prose collection, 1925 and 1935 respectively. Cecil Mann's prose collection, *The Stories of Henry Lawson*, 3 vols, Sydney, 1964, includes material not previously available, but its text has come under criticism see Dennis Douglas, *ALS*, vol. 2 (1966). Roderick's collected prose edition, 2 vols, Sydney, 1972, includes *Short Stories and Sketches 1888–1922* (vol. 1) and *Autobiographical and Other Writings 1887–1922* (vol. 2). His edition of Lawson's collected verse appeared in 3 vols, organized by date of composition, Sydney, 1967–69. Roderick is also the editor of *Henry Lawson, Letters 1890–1922*, Sydney, 1970. Popular selections of Lawson's work are numerous. The most comprehensive is Brian Kiernan's *Henry Lawson*, PAA, St. Lucia, 1976. Other representative selections include: *Selected Stories*, ed. Brian Matthews, Adelaide, 1971, *Henry Lawson's Australia*, ed. Alan Brissenden, Hawthorn, Vic., 1970, *The World of Henry Lawson*, comp. Walter W. Stone, Dee Why West, NSW, 1974, and *The Bush Undertaker and Other Stories*, ed. Colin Roderick, Sydney, 1970. There are various bibliographical studies: *An Annotated Bibliography of Henry Lawson*, Sydney, 1951, by George Mackaness is a detailed guide to the works published in Lawson's lifetime, and there are two listings by Walter W. Stone: *Henry Lawson: A Chronological Checklist of his contributions to 'The Bulletin', 1887–1924*, SAB, 2nd edn, Sydney, 1964, and 'Henry Lawson and *The Boomerang*, a Check-List', *Biblionews*, vol. 2,10 (1949). Bruce Nesbitt's notes on Lawson's contributions to the *Bulletin*, 1887–1900, *Biblionews*, 2nd series, vol. 2,1 (1967), corrects and supplements Stone's earlier listing. H. F. Chaplin has described his important private collection, which contains material not available elsewhere, in *Henry Lawson*, SAB, Surry Hills, NSW, 1974, and the Roderick editions *supra* also contain bibliographical information. Although there is a mass of information on Lawson's life, much of it anecdotal, no definitive, scholarly biography has yet been written. *Henry Lawson, The Grey Dreamer*, by 'Denton Prout', Adelaide, 1963, is an interesting, general study, although it lacks scholarly documentation, Manning Clark offers a portrait in *In Search of Henry Lawson*, Melbourne, 1978, Judith Wright's

Henry Lawson, GA, Melbourne, 1967, is a useful introduction, and the studies by Arthur Phillips, TWAS, New York, 1970, and by Stephen Murray-Smith, AWW, Melbourne, 1962, 2nd edn, 1975, provide analyses of the facts. Brian Matthews's critical study, *The Receding Wave. Henry Lawson's Prose*, Carlton, Vic., 1972, is also an interpretation of Lawson's decline. His years in New Zealand have been covered comprehensively by W. H. Pearson in *Henry Lawson Among Maoris*, Canberra and Wellington, 1968, and in a subsequent article, *ALS* vol. 4 (1969), in a series of articles in *ALS* by Rollo Arnold: vols. 3 (1968), 4 (1969) and 4 (1970), and by Rosilyn Baxter in the same journal, vol. 5 (1971). Colin Roderick has written extensively on Lawson's life, both in his various editions and elsewhere: three articles in *JRAHS*, vols. 45 (1960) and 46 (1961) subsequently reprinted, Sydney, 1960 and 1961, and vols. 53 (1967) and 55 (1969), describe his formative, later and middle years. In *Southerly*, vol. 24 (1964), Roderick deals with his Norwegian forbears, and in *Meanjin*, vol. 27 (1968), with his relationship with Hannah Thornburn. A useful, though not comprehensive, guide to secondary material is Colin Roderick's bibliography, in his anthology, *Henry Lawson Criticism 1894–1971*, Sydney, 1972. Although Roderick in *Henry Lawson, Poet and Short Story Writer*, Sydney, 1966, and in 'Lawson the Poet', *BBB*, and Stephen Murray-Smith in his monograph *supra*, argue the case for Lawson's poetry, other modern critics give pre-eminence to his prose. A. A. Phillips has written two essays 'Henry Lawson as Craftsman', *Meanjin*, vol. 7 (1948), reprinted *AT* (1958), and *TCALC*, and 'Henry Lawson Revisited', *Meanjin*, vol. 24 (1965), reprinted *AT* (1966), and *AN* as well as his 1970 study, *supra*. H. P. Heseltine provides interpretations of Lawson's treatment of mateship in *Quadrant*, vol. 5,1 (1960–61), and in 'Australian Image 1) the Literary Heritage', *Meanjin*, vol. 21 (1962), reprinted *TCALC*. A. D. Hope deals with his craftsmanship in *NC*, and compares him with Steele Rudd in *Meanjin*, vol. 15 (1956), reprinted *AN*, and revised for *NC*. Other essays on Lawson's craftsmanship include Livio Dobrez on some of his stories, *ALS*, vol. 7 (1976), and Chris Wallace-Crabbe on the Joe Wilson sequence, *ALS*, vol. 1 (1964), reprinted *AN* and *MOB*. General essays include those by: F. M. Todd, *Twentieth Century*, vol. 4,3 (1950), reprinted *ALC*, T. Inglis Moore, *Meanjin*, vol. 16 (1957), Desmond O'Grady, *Southerly*, vol. 18 (1957), reprinted *AN*, H. J. Oliver, *L of A* (1964), G. A. Wilkes, *Southerly*, vol. 25 (1965), and Brian Matthews, *BBB*.

NORMAN LINDSAY, 1879–1969. Artist and novelist. His writings include the novels: *A Curate in Bohemia*, Sydney, 1913, *Redheap*, London, 1930 (banned in Australia till 1958 but published in New York, 1930, with the title *Every Mother's Son*), *The Cautious Amorist*, New York, [1932], *Saturdee*, Sydney, 1933, *Pan in the Parlour*, New York, [1933], *Age of Consent*, New York and London, 1938, *The Cousin from Fiji*, Sydney, 1945, *Halfway to Anywhere*, Sydney, 1947, and *Rooms and Houses*, Sydney, 1968; the children's novel: *The Magic Pudding*, Sydney, 1918; the autobiographies: *Bohemians of the Bulletin*, Sydney, 1965, *The Scribblings of an Idle Mind*, Melbourne, 1966, and *My Mask*, Sydney, 1970. His attitudes to life, art, and literature are expressed in *Creative Effort*, Sydney, 1920, *Hyperborea*,

London, [1928], *Madam Life's Lovers*, London, [1929], and in numerous
uncollected essays, many of them contributed to the *Bulletin*. An important bibliographical study is Harry F. Chaplin's annotated listing of his
collection of Lindsay's books, manuscripts and autograph letters, Sydney,
1969, and bibliographies are also included in Hetherington's biography
and Stewart's memoir *infra*. John Hetherington has contributed the most
substantial, if not definitive, biography in his study, authorized by
Lindsay, *Norman Lindsay, The Embattled Olympian*, Melbourne, 1973, and
other sources include the numerous reminiscences by members of his
family, as well as Douglas Stewart's reflections on his last three decades in
Norman Lindsay. A Personal Memoir, Melbourne, 1975. Jack Lindsay has
written two important articles on his father's life and work in *Meanjin*,
vol. 29 (1970) and vol. 33 (1974). A great deal has been written on the
influence of Lindsay's aesthetic theories, especially as presented via the
journal *Vision* (1923–4). An interchange of essays on the subject between
Jack Lindsay, Kenneth Slessor, and Norman Lindsay appears in *Southerly*,
vol. 13 (1952) and vol. 14 (1953), supplemented by Slessor's essay in
Southerly, vol. 16 (1955). Judith Wright in *PIAP* is critical of the *Vision*
movement, as is Vincent Buckley in his essay, 'Utopianism and Vitalism',
Quadrant, vol. 3,2 (1958–9), reprinted *ALC*. Nigel Jackson, on the other
hand, in *Quadrant*, vol. 13,2 (1969), and Douglas Stewart in *Quadrant*, vol.
19,4 (1975), defend its quality and influence. Brian Kiernan in *Criticism*,
AWW, Melbourne, 1974, presents a balanced survey, and Humphrey
McQueen analyses its socio/political implications in *Westerly*, no. 4 (1975).
Other allied essays on Lindsay's aesthetic theories are John Docker's
study of *Creative Effort*, *ALS*, vol. 6 (1973), reprinted and revised in *ACE*,
Jack Allison's analysis of his concern with futurity in the same work,
Meanjin, vol. 29 (1970), and his general interpretation of his ideas in
Drylight (1967). By contrast, there are few critical appreciations of
Lindsay's fiction. The most substantial study, John Hetherington's
Norman Lindsay, AWW, Melbourne, 1961, 2nd edn, 1962, 3rd edn, 1969, is
sympathetic but cursory. Other essays include Douglas Stewart's
personal appreciation of the novels in *Southerly*'s Lindsay number, vol.
20,1 (1959), C. H. Hadgraft's discussion of his treatment of youth,
Southerly, vol. 12 (1951), and D. R. Burns's of his treatment of sex, *Meanjin*,
vol. 32 (1973), reprinted *DOAF*, Kerin M. Day's thorough analysis of the
novels' persistent preoccupations, *AE*, and Jack Lindsay's survey of their
characteristic qualities, *BBB*.

JAMES MCAULEY, 1917–76. Poet and critic. His collections of verse
include: *Under Aldebaran*, Melbourne, 1946, *A Vision of Ceremony*, Sydney,
1956, *James McAuley*, ed. and introd. by the author, A P Sydney, 1963,
Captain Quiros, Sydney, 1964, *Surprises of the Sun*, Sydney, 1969, *James
McAuley Reads From His Own Work*, St. Lucia, 1970, *Collected Poems
1936–1970*, Sydney, 1971, *Music Late at Night*, Sydney, 1976, and *A World of
Its Own*, Canberra, 1977. Besides numerous uncollected essays, his critical
and scholarly studies include: two essay collections, *The End of Modernity*,
Sydney, 1959, and *The Grammar of the Real*, Melbourne, 1975, a study of
C. J. Brennan, *q.v.*, a general study of Australian poetry, *The Personal*

Element in Australian Poetry, Sydney, 1970, and a critical, bibliographical survey, *A Map of Australian Verse*, Melbourne, 1975. The following are important interviews: (with Desmond O'Grady) *Observer*, 29 October 1960, and (with John Thompson) *Southerly*, vol. 27 (1967), and he discusses his work in *A Map of Australian Verse supra*. The most substantial critical study to date is Vivian Smith's monograph, *James McAuley*, AWW, Melbourne, 1965, 2nd edn, 1970, a revised and extended version of his earlier CLF lecture, Canberra, 1964. Vincent Buckley has contributed two essays: an analysis of his classicism, *Essays in Poetry*, 1957, reprinted *ALC*, and a general appreciation, *Westerly*, no. 3 (1960). Leonie Kramer discusses his use of traditional literary forms in a CLF lecture, Canberra, 1957, gives a general survey of his life and work in *Quadrant*, vol. 20,11 (1976) a review of his collected poems, *Bulletin*, 29 May 1971, and an exegesis and assessment of *Captain Quiros*, *Southerly*, vol. 25 (1965). A. D. Hope considers the epic qualities of *Captain Quiros* in *Twentieth Century*, vol. 19 (1964), reprinted *NC*, and Judith Wright in *PIAP* studies the effect of McAuley's convictions on his work. Essays that deal with shifts in his development include David Bradley's study, *L of A* (1964), revised *L of A* (1976), R. F. Brissenden's appreciation of his response to despair, *Southerly*, vol. 32 (1972), Chris Wallace-Crabbe's analysis of division in his work, *Meanjin*, vol. 30 (1971), reprinted *MOB*, and the delineation of three stages by Livio Dobrez, *Southern Review*, Adelaide, vol. 9 (1976). John Docker discusses his social, political and aesthetic ideas in *Arena*, no. 26 (1971), and Carmel Gaffney gives an appraisal of his late work in *Southerly*, vol. 36 (1976). A tribute by fellow poets is offered in *Poems in Honour of James McAuley*, Hobart, 1978.

HUGH McCRAE, 1876–1958. Poet. His collections of poetry include: *Satyrs and Sunlight: Silvarum Libri*, Sydney, 1909, *Colombine*, Sydney, 1920, *Idyllia*, Sydney, 1922, *Satyrs and Sunlight* [collected poetry], London, 1928, *The Mimshi Maiden*, Sydney, 1938, *Poems*, Sydney, 1939, *Forests of Pan*, sel. by R. G. Howarth from poems not previously reprinted in *Satyrs and Sunlight*, Brisbane, 1944, *Voice of the Forest*, Sydney, 1945, *The Best Poems of Hugh McCrae*, ed. R. G. Howarth, Sydney, 1961, and *Hugh McCrae*, sel. and introd. by Douglas Stewart, AP, Sydney, 1966. McCrae also published a play, *The Ship of Heaven*, Sydney, 1951, and a selection of stories and anecdotes, *Story-Book Only*, Sydney, 1948 (which also reprints the reminiscences *My Father and My Father's Friends*, Sydney, 1935, and an abridged edn, of the light-hearted annals, *The Du Poissey Anecdotes*, Sydney, 1922). R. D. FitzGerald has edited a collection of his letters, Sydney, 1970. There are several bibliographical studies, the most substantial being H. F. Chaplin's description of his holdings of the McCrae family's writings, *A McCrae Miscellany*, SAB, Sydney, 1967. Chaplin's later listing, *Norman Lindsay*, Sydney, 1969, also contains relevant material, and George Mackaness discusses editions of McCrae's writings in *Bibliomania*, Sydney, 1965. Biographical accounts, important for an understanding of McCrae's historical position, include: Norman Lindsay's reminiscences in *My Mask*, Sydney, 1970, and *Bohemians of the Bulletin*, Sydney, 1965, John Hetherington's account of his relationship with Lindsay in *Norman Lindsay*, Melbourne, 1973, and Norman Cowper's essay in *Southerly*, vol. 19 (1958), reprinted in FitzGerald's edition of letters *supra*. The nature of his contemporary reputation can be gauged by the tone of Norman Lindsay's and Kenneth Slessor's appreciations in the issue of *Southerly*, dedicated to McCrae, vol. 17,3 (1956). This issue also contains essays by Douglas Stewart, A. R. Chisholm, O. N. Burgess, R. G. Howarth and Lionel Lindsay. R. G. Howarth has contributed a further series of appreciations, all in *Southerly*: vols 6,1 (1945), 10 (1949), 15 (1954), and 18 (1957), and T. Inglis Moore has written on his work in *Six Australian Poets*, 1942, in *Australian Quarterly*, vol. 17,1 (1945), in *Prometheus* (1958), and in *Meanjin*, vol. 17 (1958). Both R. D. FitzGerald and Douglas Stewart have defended McCrae's historical and literary importance: FitzGerald's appreciations appear in *Australian Quarterly*, vol. 11,4 (1939), in *Meanjin*, vol. 17 (1958), and in his introduction to the letters, *supra*. Stewart's *apologia* is in *Southerly*, vol. 22 (1962), reprinted in *Hugh McCrae*, 1966, *supra*. Other essays include Judith Wright's attempt to define the reasons for what she sees as his immaturity in *PIAP*, and John Webb's exploration of the dark element in his verse, *ALS*, vol. 6 (1973). For other critics, however, McCrae's talent seems too slight for serious consideration, see the reviews by Philip Martin in *Quadrant*, vol. 6,2 (1962), John Peacock in *Poetry Magazine*, no. 2 (1962), and Evan Jones in *Prospect*, vol. 5,1 (1962).

KENNETH MACKENZIE ('SEAFORTH MACKENZIE'), 1913–54. Poet and novelist. His writings include the novels: *The Young Desire It*, London, 1937, reprinted Sydney, 1963, with foreword by Douglas Stewart, *Chosen People*, London, 1938, *Dead Men Rising*, London, 1951, *The Refuge*, London, 1954, and the verse collections: *Our Earth*, Sydney, 1937, *The Moonlit Doorway*, Sydney, 1944, *Selected Poems*, sel. and introd. by Douglas Stewart, Sydney, 1961, and *Poems*, ed. with introd. by Evan Jones and Geoffrey Little, Sydney, 1972. Mackenzie discusses his verse in *Southerly*, vol. 9 (1948), and a 'Seaforth Mackenzie' issue of *Westerly*, no. 3 (1966), includes some prose and poetry published for the first time, although much remains unpublished as Diana Davis's guide in *ALS*, vol. 4 (1970) establishes. Diana Davis has also written two biographical accounts, in *Westerly*, no. 3 (1966), and *ALS*, vol. 3 (1968). The most substantial critical study to date is Evan Jones's *Kenneth Mackenzie*, AWW, Melbourne, 1969. Although Jones gives preeminence to Mackenzie's poetry, other critics have concentrated on his fiction: Marjorie Barnard in *Meanjin*, vol. 13 (1954), finds his novels divide into spontaneous and artificial works, Peter Cowan, on the other hand, traces a linear progression in his work, *Meanjin*, vol. 24 (1965), Donovan Clarke sees him as a novelist of alienation, *Southerly*, vol. 25 (1965), and R. G. Geering takes issue with some of Clarke's findings and discusses Mackenzie's narrative technique, *Southerly*, vol. 26 (1966). Studies of his poetry include Dorothy Hewett's survey in *Westerly*, no. 4 (1972), and Evan Jones's article, *Australian Quarterly*, vol. 36,2 (1964).

FREDERIC MANNING, 1882–1935. Novelist and poet. Although Manning published three volumes of verse and a collection of prose pieces, *Scenes and Portraits*, London, 1909, he is best remembered for his novel, *Her Privates We*, London, 1930, which appeared first in a limited and unexpurgated edition titled *The Middle Parts of Fortune*, London, 1929. For both editions Manning used the pseudonym 'Private 19022'. Information on his life can be found in William Rothenstein's *Men and Memories*, London, 1932, and *Since Fifty*, London, 1939, and in an essay by C. Kaeppel in *Australian Quarterly*, vol. 7, no. 26 (1935). Useful critical appreciations include those by Edmund Blunden in his introduction to the 1964 edn, of *Her Privates We*, Bernard Begonzi in *Heroes' Twilight*, London, 1965, and J. D. Pringle in *On Second Thoughts*, Sydney, 1971, reprinted *AE.* L. T. Hergenhan discusses his work and its contemporary reception in *Quadrant*, vol. 6,4 (1962), and the attitudes that inform *Her Privates We* in *Quadrant*, vol. 14,4 (1970). H. M. Klein discusses the same novel in detail in *ALS*, vol. 6 (1974), and in *JCL*, vol. 12 (1977), as does C. N. Smith in *The First World War in Fiction*, ed. H. M. Klein, London, 1976.

DAVID MARTIN, b. 1915. Novelist and poet. His major writings include the novels: *The Young Wife*, London, 1962, *The Hero of Too*, Melbourne, 1965, *The King Between*, Melbourne, 1966, also published as *The Littlest Neutral*, New York, 1966, *Where a Man Belongs*, Melbourne, 1969, and *Frank and Francesca*, Melbourne, 1972; the verse collections: *From Life: Selected Poems*, with a foreword by Mary Gilmore, Sydney, 1953, *Poems of David Martin 1938–1958*, Sydney, 1958, *Spiegel The Cat*, Melbourne, 1961, *The Gift: Poems 1959–1965*, Brisbane, 1966, and *The Idealist*, Brisbane, 1968; and an account of his travels in Australia, *On the Road to Sydney*, Melbourne, 1970. Commentaries by Martin on his life and work include a reply to A. A. Phillips *infra*, 'Apologia without Apology', *Meanjin*, vol. 20 (1961), 'David Martin on David Martin', *Southerly*, vol. 31 (1971), and '3 Homes Rules My Life', *Walkabout*, vol. 38,1 (1972). John Hetherington includes a portrait in *Forty-Two Faces*, 1962, and Martin's article on contemporary Australian novelists, 'Among the Bones', *Meanjin*, vol. 18 (1959), indirectly reveals his own conception of the novel. Apart from reviews the only substantial critical studies are A. A. Phillips's general survey, *Meanjin*, vol. 20 (1961), and an appreciation by Nancy Keesing, *Overland*, no. 63 (1976).

PETER MATHERS, b. 1931. Novelist and short story writer. His writings include the novels: *Trap*, Melbourne, 1966, and *The Wort Papers*, Melbourne, 1972, and several uncollected short stories. Articles in which he comments on his life and work include 'Pittsburgh Identity: 0000000621', *Overland*, no. 39 (1968), and 'Extractions', *Southerly*, vol. 31 (1971). Craig McGregor's *In the Making*, 1969, and Laurence Collinson's 'Seeing Mathers Subjectively', *Overland*, no. 35 (1966–67) contain further information. Two essays on *Trap* are Robert Burns's comparative study of the 'underdog-outsider', *Meanjin*, vol. 29 (1970), and the general interpretation by Vincent Buckley, *Ariel*, vol. 5,3 (1974). Other articles include L. J. Clancy's on *Trap*, *Meanjin*, vol. 25 (1966), and on *The Wort Papers*, *Meanjin*, vol. 33 (1974), and Betty L. Watson's exploration of recent satiric novels, *English in Australia*, no. 18 (1971).

FRANK MOORHOUSE, b. 1938. Short story writer. His collections of stories include: *Futility and Other Animals*, Sydney, 1969, *The Americans, Baby*, Sydney, 1972, *The Electrical Experience*, Sydney, 1974, *Conference-Ville*, London, 1976, and *Tales of Mystery and Romance*, London, 1977. There are interviews with David Osborne, *National Times*, 1–6 July 1974 and with Jim Davidson, *Meanjin*, vol. 36 (1977), and Brian Kiernan provides background notes on his literary and political preoccupations in *Overland*, no. 56 (1973). Essays on his work include Don Anderson's study of his discontinuous narratives, *Southerly*, vol. 36 (1976), Carl Harrison-Ford's comparison of his approach with that of Michael Wilding, *Southerly*, vol. 33 (1973), and Thomas Keneally's appreciation of *The Electrical Experience*, *National Times*, 3–8 February 1975.

LES(LIE) A(LLAN) MURRAY, b. 1938. Poet. His collections include: (with Geoffrey Lehmann) *The Ilex Tree*, Canberra, 1965, *The Weatherboard Cathedral*, Sydney, 1969, *Poems Against Economics*, Sydney, 1972, *Lunch & Counter Lunch*, Sydney, 1974, *Selected Poems. The Vernacular Republic*, Sydney, 1976, *Ethnic Radio*, 1977, and *The Boys Who Stole the Funeral*, Sydney, 1979. *The Peasant Mandarin*, St. Lucia, 1978, is a collection of prose pieces. In 'The Human Hair-Thread', *Meanjin*, vol. 36 (1977), Murray discusses his work and thought. There is an interview with Robert Gray in *Quadrant*, vol. 20, 12 (1976) and Graeme Kinross Smith gives a biographical profile in *Westerly*, no. 3 (1980). Essays on his work include those by: Dianne Ailwood, *Southerly*, vol. 31 (1971), Gary Catalano, *Meanjin*, vol. 36 (1977), Christopher Pollnitz, *Southerly*, vol. 40 (1980) and 41 (1981), and Michael Sharkey, *Overland*, no. 82 (1980).

JOHN SHAW NEILSON, 1872–1942. Poet. His verse collections include: *Heart of Spring*, Sydney, 1919, *Ballad and Lyrical Poems*, Sydney, 1923, *New Poems*, Sydney, 1927, *Collected Poems*, ed. R. H. Croll, Melbourne, 1934, *Beauty Imposes*, Sydney, 1938, *Unpublished Poems*, ed. James Devaney, Sydney, 1947, *Shaw Neilson*, sel. and introd. by Judith Wright, AP, Sydney, 1963, *Witnesses of Spring: Unpublished Poems*, ed. Judith Wright, and sel. by Judith Wright and Val Vallis from material assembled by Ruth Harrison, Sydney, 1970, *The Poems of Shaw Neilson*, ed. with introd. by A. R. Chisholm, Sydney, 1965, revised and enlarged edn, 1973. *Southerly*, vol. 17,1 (1956), a Neilson number, includes some previously unpublished material. Hugh Anderson has produced the most substantial bibliography: *Shaw Neilson: An Annotated Bibliography and Checklist 1893–1964*, SAB, Sydney, revised edn, 1964, and another valuable listing is Harry F. Chaplin's *A Neilson Collection*, SAB, Sydney, 1964. Due to the corrupt state of Neilson's manuscripts, a definitive text has not yet appeared, and that of *Witnesses of Spring supra*, has been criticized as unreliable. Studies of his manuscripts by Ruth Harrison, J. F. Burrows and Clifford Hanna are described in a series of essays in *ALS*, vol. 3 (1968), and *Southerly*, vols. 32

(1972), 33 (1973) and 35 (1975) H. J. Oliver has also described the manuscripts' revelation of a more versatile Neilson in *Southerly*, vol. 17 (1956).
The question of A. G. Stephens's editorship is discussed by Hugh
Anderson and L. J. Blake in their biography *infra*, by H. J. Oliver in his
essay *supra*, and in his monograph, *Shaw Neilson*, AWW, Melbourne,
1968, by Hugh Anderson in *Biblionews*, vol. 9,8 (1956), and in *Meanjin*, vol.
10 (1951), and by J. F. Burrows in one of the most professional studies of
the manuscripts, *Southerly*, vol. 32 (1972). There are two substantial
biographies: James Devaney's *Shaw Neilson*, Sydney, 1944, and *John Shaw
Neilson* by Hugh Anderson and L. J. Blake, Adelaide, 1972. The former,
less scholarly, objective and detailed than the latter, is nevertheless still
valuable for its first-hand appreciations. Devaney has added to his recollections in an interview in *Makar*, vol. 8,2 (1972). Also essential are
Neilson's autobiographical notes, first published in full and introduced
by Nancy Keesing, Canberra, 1978. The most substantial critical work is
H. J. Oliver's monograph *supra* and essays include those by Judith
Wright, *Quadrant*, vol. 3,4 (1959), reprinted *ALC*, and revised for *PIAP*,
James McAuley, *ALS*, vol. 2 (1966), reprinted *RCL*, and *The Grammar of
the Real*, 1975, and Clifford Hanna, *ALS*, vol. 5 (1972). A. R. Chisholm has
contributed substantially to Neilson studies: as well as his edition of the
poems and introduction *supra*, he has written on Neilson's metaphysic,
Southerly, vol. 17 (1956), reprinted *TCALC*, and on his celtic quality,
Meanjin, vol. 21 (1962). Other essays include Annette Stewart's analysis of
'The Orange Tree', *ALS*, vol. 5 (1971), Douglas Dennis's study of his
imagination in the same volume, Hugh Anderson's appreciation of his
complex lyric impulse, *Southerly*, vol. 17 (1956), T. Inglis Moore's study in
Six Australian Poets, 1942, and the general appreciations by James
McAuley in *A Map of Australian Verse*, 1975, and by A. D. Hope, *NC*.

BARRY OAKLEY, b. 1931. Novelist and playwright. His writings include the
novels: *A Wild Ass of a Man*, Melbourne, 1967, *A Salute to the Great
McCarthy*, Melbourne, 1970, *Let's Hear it for Prendergast*, Melbourne,
1970; and the plays: *Witzenhausen, Where Are You?*, first published
Meanjin, vol. 26 (1967), included in *6 One-Act Plays*, St. Lucia, 1970,
Bedfellows, introd. by Brian Kiernan, Sydney and London, 1975, *The Feet of
Daniel Mannix*, introd. by Leonard Radic and postscript by the author,
Sydney, 1975, *A Lesson in English*, first publ. *English in Australia*, no. 8 (1968),
Sydney and London, 1976, and *Scanlan*, *Meanjin*, vol. 37 (1978); and the
short stories: *Walking Through Tigerland*, St. Lucia, 1977. His unpublished
plays include: 'From the Desk of Eugene Flockhart' (1967), 'It's a
Chocolate World' (1971), and 'Beware of Imitations' (1973). In 'On Being
a Writer in Australia', *Dissent*, no. 29 (1972), revised in *Westerly*, no. 3
(1975), he humorously describes his youth and writing career, and there
are interviews (with Victoria Duigan) *National Times*, 8–13 January 1973,
and (with Andrew Knight and John Alsop) *Lot's Wife*, 26 August 1974.
Betty L. Watson's 'Barry Oakley and the Satiric Mode', *ALS*, vol. 7 (1975)
is an appreciation.

BERNARD O'DOWD, 1866–1953. Poet. His writings include the verse
collections: *Dawnward?*, Sydney, 1903, *The Silent Land and Other Verses*,

Melbourne, 1906, *Dominions of the Boundary*, Melbourne, 1907, *The Seven Deadly Sins*, Melbourne, 1909, *The Bush*, Melbourne, 1912, *Alma Venus! and Other Verses*, Melbourne, 1921, *The Poems of Bernard O'Dowd* [title on spine, *Collected Poems of Bernard O'Dowd*], Melbourne, 1941, and *Bernard O'Dowd*, sel. and introd. by A. A. Phillips, AP, Sydney, 1963; the aesthetic manifesto *Poetry Militant*, Melbourne, 1909, and the essay collection, *Fantasies*, Melbourne, 1954. Hugh Anderson has compiled a comprehensive bibliography, *Bernard O'Dowd (1866–1953)*, SAB, Sydney, 1963. There are two substantial studies: the 'official' biography, by Victor Kennedy and Nettie Palmer, Melbourne, 1942, and Hugh Anderson's *Bernard O'Dowd*, TWAS, New York, 1968, revised and enlarged edn, with title, *The Poet Militant: Bernard O'Dowd*, Melbourne, 1969. Although O'Dowd's work has more interest for the social and literary historian than for the critic, there are several studies of his verse including T. Inglis Moore's analysis in *Six Australian Poets*, 1942, assessments of his strengths and limitations by F. M. Todd in *Meanjin*, vol. 14 (1955), reprinted *AN*, and by Judith Wright in *PIAP*, W. H. Wilde's overview in *Three Radicals*, 1969, E. Morris Miller's examination of his early writings, *Meanjin*, vol. 8 (1949), and S. E. Lee's survey of his fugitive verse, *Southerly*, vol. 14 (1953). The importance and meaning of *The Bush* have been explored in separate essays by A. R. Chisholm and Hugh Anderson in *Southerly*, vol. 14 (1953), and by E. Morris Miller in *Diogenes*, no. 3 (1957). Studies of his social and cultural importance include those by: Vance Palmer in *The Legend of the Nineties*, 1954, A. A. Phillips in *AT* (1958 and 1966), G. A. Wilkes in 'The Eighteen Nineties', *Arts*, vol. 1 (1958), reprinted *ALC*, Vincent Buckley in 'Utopianism and Vitalism', *Quadrant*, vol. 3,2 (1959), also reprinted *ALC*, and Humphrey McQueen in *A New Britannia*, Ringwood, Vic., 1970. A. A. Phillips takes issue with this last assessment in *Meanjin*, vol. 30 (1971).

VANCE PALMER, 1885–1959. Novelist, short story writer and critic. His major novels are: *The Man Hamilton*, London, 1928, *Men Are Human*, London, 1930, *The Passage*, London, 1930, *Daybreak*, London, 1932, *The Swayne Family*, Sydney, 1934, *Legend for Sanderson*, Sydney, 1937, *Cyclone*, Sydney, 1947, and the trilogy, *Golconda*, Sydney, 1948, *Seedtime*, Sydney, 1957, *The Big Fellow*, Sydney, 1959. His collected short stories include: *The World of Men*, London, 1915, *Separate Lives*, London, 1931, *Sea and Spinifex*, Sydney, 1934, and *Let the Birds Fly*, Sydney, 1955. *The Rainbow-Bird and Other Stories*, sel. by A. Edwards, Sydney, 1957, is a collection of reprints. Palmer's socio-literary criticism includes: *National Portraits*, Sydney, 1940, enlarged edn, Melbourne, 1954, *The Legend of the Nineties*, Melbourne, 1954, and *Intimate Portraits and Other Pieces*, sel. by H. P. Heseltine, Melbourne, 1969. Of his numerous plays only a few have been published: *The Black Horse and Other Plays* [*The Prisoner, Travellers* and *Telling Mrs. Baker*], Melbourne, 1924, *Ancestors*, in *Best Australian One-Act Plays*, Sydney, 1937, and *Hail Tomorrow*, Sydney, 1947. Unpublished plays include: 'A Happy Family' (1915), and 'Prisoner's Country' (1960). He also published two collections of poetry, and critical studies of A. G. Stephens, Louis Esson and Frank Wilmot *q.v.* Vivian Smith has edited the

Letters of Vance and Nettie Palmer 1915–1963, Canberra, 1977, and the National Library has published a guide to its holdings of Vance and Nettie Palmer's papers, Canberra, 1973. A checklist of the Palmers' books and articles, by C. M. Hotinsky and Walter Stone, is included in *Meanjin*'s Palmer issue, vol. 18,2 (1959), and David Walker's *Dream and Disillusion*, 1976, also includes a comprehensive bibliography. There are two substantial studies of his life and work: H. P. Heseltine's *Vance Palmer*, St. Lucia, 1970, and Vivian Smith's *Vance and Nettie Palmer*, TWAS, Boston, 1975. Vivian Smith has also written a shorter appreciation, *Vance Palmer*, AWW, Melbourne, 1971, and studies of the Palmers' work and pre-occupations 1938–48 in *BBB*, and of their literary journalism in *ALS*, vol. 6 (1973). General appreciations include the essays by T. Inglis Moore, Brian Fitzpatrick, John Barnes, Russel Ward, Jack Lindsay, and others in *Meanjin*'s Palmer issue *supra*, and D. R. Burns's comparison of his novels and short stories, *ALS*, vol. 6 (1974), reprinted *DOAF*. David Walker in *Meanjin*, vol. 35 (1976) and in *Dream and Disillusion, supra*, makes an extensive reassessment of the nature and impact of his socio-literary ideas. Studies of his novels include C. H. Hadgraft's general evaluation, *Southerly*, vol. 10 (1949), John McKellar's analysis of their limitations, *Southerly*, vol. 15 (1954), A. D. Hope's appreciation of their individual quality, *Southerly*, vol. 16 (1955), expanded and revised in *NC*, and David Walker's adverse assessment in *Dream and Disillusion, supra*. Leslie Rees in *The Making of Australian Drama*, 1973, and Keith Macartney in *Meanjin*, vol. 18 (1959), deal with his plays, and A. A. Phillips in the same volume, reprinted *AT* (1966) writes on his short stories.

ANDREW BARTON PATERSON, 1864–1941. Poet. His writings, all published in Sydney, include the verse collections: *The Man From Snowy River*, 1895, *Rio Grande's Last Race*, 1902, *Saltbush Bill, J.P.*, 1917, *The Collected Verse of A. B. Paterson*, 1921 (which reprints the three preceding volumes and has in turn been reprinted numerous times, the most useful being that of 1951, with introd. by F. T. Macartney), and *The Animals Noah Forgot*, 1933; the fiction: *An Outback Marriage*, 1906, *Three Elephant Power and Other Stories*, 1917, and *The Shearer's Colt*, 1936; and the autobiographical sketches, *Happy Dispatches*, 1934. He also edited a collection of ballads, *Old Bush Songs*, Sydney, 1905. More recent collections include Clement Semmler's edition of his prose: *The World of 'Banjo' Paterson*, Sydney, 1967, and Walter Stone's edition of verse and prose: *The Best of Banjo Paterson*, Sydney, 1977. Semmler's *The Banjo of the Bush* and especially Lorna Ollif's study *infra* contain extensive bibliographies, and another checklist by Walter Stone lists his contributions to the *Bulletin* to 1902, *Biblionews*, vol. 10,12 (1957). A series of articles by Paterson on his life, *SMH*, 4 February–4 March 1939, and an interview with Bernard Espinasse in *Table Talk*, 31 January 1896, are illuminating. Clement Semmler has contributed extensively to Paterson studies with the major biography, *The Banjo of the Bush*, Melbourne, 1966, 2nd edn, St. Lucia, 1974, and shorter studies in the GA series, Melbourne, 1967, and AWW series, Melbourne, 1965, revised edn, 1972, as well as discussions of his place in the 1890s, *Southerly*, vol. 24 (1964), and of his similarities with Kipling, *Australian Quarterly*, vol. 39,2 (1967), reprinted *The Art of Brian James*, 1972. Apart from numerous essays and books on the 'Waltzing Matilda' question, studies of Paterson have concentrated mainly on his significance as a bush balladist of the 1890s, rather than on his work in its own right. Brian Elliott in *Singing to the Cattle*, Melbourne, 1947, discusses both his verse and prose, John Manifold in *Overland*, no. 1 (1954) and no. 2 (1954–5), reprinted *AOM*, and in *Who Wrote the Ballads?*, Sydney, 1964, discusses his significance in the bush ballad tradition, Judith Driscoll in *ALS*, vol. 5 (1971) defends 'A Man From Snowy River', Bruce Nesbitt in an essay in the same volume 'Literary Nationalism and the 1890s', discusses the famous *Bulletin* interchange between Lawson and Paterson, Gavin Long in *Meanjin*, vol. 23 (1964), writes on his uncollected poems and casts further light on the *Bulletin* debate, and H. P. Heseltine in an essay in the same volume, reprinted *AN*, discusses his significance as a figure of folk-culture. Lorna Ollif's study, *Andrew Barton Paterson*, TWAS, New York, 1971, is a competent work.

HAL PORTER, b. 1911. Short story writer, novelist, playwright and poet. His writings include the short story collections: *A Bachelor's Children*, Sydney, 1962, *The Cats of Venice*, Sydney, 1965, *Mr. Butterfry and Other Tales of New Japan*, Sydney, 1970, *Selected Stories*, sel. with introd. by Leonie Kramer, Sydney, 1971, and *Fredo Fuss Love Life*, Sydney, 1974; the novels: *A Handful of Pennies*, Sydney, 1958, *The Tilted Cross*, London, 1961, reprinted with introd. by Adrian Mitchell, Adelaide, 1971, and *The Right Thing*, Adelaide, 1971; the verse collections: *The Hexagon*, Sydney, 1956, *Elijah's Ravens*, Sydney, 1968, and *In An Australian Country Graveyard and Other Poems*, Melbourne, 1974; the autobiographies: *The Watcher on the Cast-Iron Balcony*, London, 1963, *The Paper Chase*, Sydney, 1966, and *The Extra*, Melbourne, 1975; and the local history: *Bairnsdale: Portrait of an Australian Country Town*, Melbourne, 1977. Three of his plays have been published: *The Tower* in *Three Australian Plays*, Ringwood, Vic., 1963, *The Professor*, London, 1966, and *Eden House*, Sydney, 1969. A bibliography, compiled by J. H. Finch, Adelaide, 1966, is extensively reviewed by Michael Wilding, *ALS*, vol. 3 (1967), and supplemented by Mary Lord, *ALS*, vol. 4 (1970). The *Index to Australian Book Reviews* has annually listed material by and on Porter since 1965. Articles in which Porter discusses his work include: 'That Certain Book: Beyond Whipped Cream and Blood', *Bulletin*, 28 April 1962, and 'Answers to the Funny, Kind Man', *Southerly*, vol. 29 (1969), and the following are informative interviews: (with Patricia Rolfe) *Bulletin*, 14 December 1963, (with Erika Feller) *Farrago*, 9 May 1969, (with Libby Booth) *Farrago*, 21 June 1974, (with Craig McGregor) *In the Making*, (1969), and (with Mary Lord) *ALS*, vol. 8 (1978). Biographical accounts include John Hetherington's essay in *Forty-Two Faces*, 1962, and Graeme Kinross Smith's profile, *ALS*, vol. 7 (1975). The most substantial critical study to date is Mary Lord's introduction, *Hal Porter*, AWW, Melbourne, 1974. R. G. Geering in four essays in *Southerly*, discusses his autobiographies, vols 27 (1967) and 36 (1976), gives a general appreciation of his individual quality, vol. 24 (1964), and analyses the role of melodrama in *Mr. Butterfry* and *The Right Thing*, vol. 33 (1973). Other essays include Robert Burns's analysis of his treatment of time, *Meanjin*, vol. 28 (1969), and his discussion of his extravagant style in *DOAF*, R. A. Duncan's study of his fiction's absurdist elements, *Meanjin*, vol. 29 (1970), John Barnes's comparison of his stories with those of White and Cowan, *Meanjin*, vol. 25 (1966), Mary Lord's analysis of his comic technique, *ALS*, vol. 4 (1970), L. T. Hergenhan's interpretation of *The Tilted Cross* in *Southerly*, vol. 34 (1974), and A. C. W. Mitchell's of *The Right Thing* in *Ariel*, vol. 5,3 (1974). Essays on his drama include Kerin Cantrell's assessment of *The Professor*, *Southerly*, vol. 27 (1967), and Reba Gostand's analysis of *The Tower*, *ALS*, vol. 6 (1973).

PETER PORTER, b. 1929. Poet. His collections of poetry include: *Once Bitten, Twice Bitten*, Lowestoft, Suffolk, 1961, (with Kingsley Amis and Dom Moraes) *Penguin Modern Poets 2*, Harmondsworth, 1962, *Poems Ancient and Modern*, Lowestoft, Suffolk, 1964, *A Porter Folio: New Poems*, London, 1969, *The Last of England*, London, 1970, *After Martial*, London, 1972, *Preaching to the Converted*, London, 1972, (with Arthur Boyd) *Jonah*, London and Melbourne, 1973, *Peter Porter Reads From His Own Work*, St. Lucia, 1974, *Living in a Calm Country*, London, 1975, and *The Cost of Seriousness*, London, 1978. Autobiographical essays include: 'A Land Fit for Conservatives', *TLS*, 30 July 1971, 'Living in London', *London Magazine*, n.s. vol. 13,2 (1973), and 'Brisbane Comes Back', *Quadrant*, vol. 19,6 (1975). There are the following interviews: (with Peter Orr) *The Poet Speaks*, London, 1966, (with Dennis Douglas) *Overland*, no. 44 (1970), (with Philip Martin) *Quadrant*, vol. 18,1 (1974), and (with Nancy Gordon and Elaine Lindsay) *Issue*, vol. 4,14 (1974).

ROSA CAMPBELL PRAED. 1851–1935. Novelist. Of her many novels the following, all published in London, are the most notable: *An Australian Heroine*, 1880, *Policy and Passion*, 1881, *The Head Station*, 1885, *Miss Jacobsen's Chance*, 1886, *The Romance of a Station*, 1889, *Outlaw and Lawmaker*, 1893, *Mrs. Tregaskiss*, 1895, *Nulma*, 1897, *Fugitive Anne*, 1903 *The Ghost*, 1903, *The Maid of the River*, 1905, *The Lost Earl of Ellan*, 1906, *The Luck of the Leura*, 1907, *Opal Fire*, 1910, *Lady Bridget in the Never Never Land*, 1915, and *Sister Sorrow*, 1916. Both *Australian Life: Black and White*, 1885, and *My Australian Girlhood*, 1902, deal with her reminiscences of Australia. Colin Roderick's semi-fictional account of her life and work, *In Mortal Bondage*, Sydney, 1948, is the most substantial to date, and expands his earlier essay in *Southerly*, vol. 8 (1947). Other essays include Desmond Byrne's early but indispensable study in *Australian Writers*, London, 1896, Clive Hamer's comparative consideration in *ALS*, vol. 2 (1965), and Brian Elliott's general appreciation in *Commonwealth Literature*, ed. John Press, London, 1965.

KATHARINE SUSANNAH PRICHARD, 1883–1969. Novelist and short story writer. Her writings include the novels: *The Pioneers*, London, 1915, *Black Opal*, London, 1921, *Working Bullocks*, London, 1926, *The Wild Oats of Han*, Sydney, 1928, *Coonardoo*, London, 1929, *Haxby's Circus*, London,

1930, *Intimate Strangers*, London, 1937, *Subtle Flame*, Sydney, 1967, and the gold-fields trilogy, *The Roaring Nineties*, London, 1946, *Golden Miles*, Sydney, 1948, and *Winged Seeds*, London and Sydney, 1950; the stories: *Kiss on the Lips and Other Stories*, London, 1932, *Potch and Colour*, Sydney, 1944, *N'goola and Other Stories*, Melbourne, 1959, *Happiness: Selected Short Stories*, Sydney, 1967; the verse collections: *Clovelly Verses*, London, 1913, and *The Earth Lover*, Sydney, 1932; the plays: *Brumby Innes*, Perth, 1940, republished with *Bid Me to Love*, ed. Katharine Brisbane, Sydney and London, 1974, and *Pioneers* in *Best Australian One-Act Plays*, Sydney, 1937; and the autobiography, *Child of the Hurricane*, Sydney, 1963. A selection of her writings, titled *On Strenuous Wings*, ed. Joan Williams, was published in Berlin, 1965. In 'Some Perceptions and Aspirations', *Southerly*, vol. 28 (1968), Miss Prichard discusses her work, and in *Why I Am a Communist*, Sydney, 1957, her political convictions. Ric Throssell's biography, *Wild Weeds and Wind Flowers*, Sydney, 1975, includes a bibliography, and Hugh Anderson has compiled a checklist, *Biblionews*, vol. 12,3 (1959), extended *ibid*, 7 (1959). Ric Throssell, K. S. Prichard's son, has produced the most extensive though not the definitive biography, *supra*, and the most substantial critical study to date is Henrietta Drake-Brockman's *Katharine Susannah Prichard*, AWW, Melbourne, 1967. There are also numerous essays, although here critical opinion is sharply divided about her fiction, especially her gold-fields trilogy. Jack Beasley in *The Rage for Life*, Sydney, 1964, Muir Holburn in *Meanjin*, vol. 10 (1951), and Aileen Palmer in *Overland*, no. 12 (1958) and no. 13 (1958), unreservedly praise her social realism and response to the Australian environment. Jack Lindsay in *Meanjin*, vol. 20 (1961) makes a biased survey of her fiction, as Ellen Malos points out in *Meanjin*, vol. 22 (1963). Richard Sadlier, on the other hand, in *Westerly*, no. 3 (1961), and A. D. Hope in *NC* find her novels simplistic and contrived. The extent of the critical division is revealed by the diverse reactions in *Overland*, no. 44 (1970) to Dorothy Hewett's assessment of her weaknesses, 'Excess of Love', *Overland*, no. 43 (1969–70). Other essays include G. A. Wilkes's assessment of the peaks and troughs of her achievement in *Southerly*, vol. 14 (1953), S. Murray-Smith's analysis of division in her work, *L of A*, (1964), H. P. Heseltine's historical evaluation, *Westerly*, no. 2 (1968), and the discussion of her major themes by Ellen Malos, *ALS*, vol. 1 (1963). Jane Sunderland discusses her studies of women in *Hecate*, vol. 4,1 (1978), and Margaret Williams reviews the first production of *Brumby Innes* in 1972, *Meanjin*, vol. 32 (1973).

'HENRY HANDEL RICHARDSON' (ETHEL F. L. ROBERTSON), 1870–1946. Novelist. Her writings include the novels: *Maurice Guest*, London, 1908 (other edns include 1922 with preface by Hugh Walpole, and 1965 with preface by A. N. Jeffares), *The Getting of Wisdom*, London, 1910, (another edn, 1968 with introd. by Leonie Kramer), the trilogy *Australia Felix*, London, 1917, *The Way Home*, London, 1925, and *Ultima Thule*, London, 1929, revised omnibus edn, with title *The Fortunes of Richard Mahony*, London, 1930, (other edns include 1968 with introd. by G. A. Wilkes, and 1971 with introd. by Leonie Kramer), and *The Young Cosima*, London, 1939; the unfinished autobiography *Myself When Young*, London, 1948;

and the short stories *The End of a Childhood and Other Stories*, London, 1934. She also translated J. P. Jacobsen's *Niels Lyhne*, titled *Siren Voices*, London, 1896, and B. Björnson's *Fiskerjenten*, titled *The Fisher Lass*, London, 1896. K. J. Rossing has edited the *Letters of Henry Handel Richardson to Nettie Palmer*, Uppsala, 1953, and *Southerly*, vol. 23,1 (1963) includes several important uncollected articles, stories and notes. Bibliographies include Gay Howells's *Henry Handel Richardson, 1870–1946*, Canberra, 1970, Verna D. Wittrock's annotated listing of secondary material, *English Literature in Transition (1880–1920)*, vol. 7,3 (1964), and the guide to her papers held by the National Library, Canberra, 1975. A great deal has been written on Miss Richardson's life: Nettie Palmer's study, *Henry Handel Richardson*, Sydney, 1950, is still one of the most balanced accounts, and the collection of reminiscences, *Henry Handel Richardson. Some Personal Impressions*, ed. Edna Purdie and Olga M. Roncoroni, Sydney, 1957, remains a valuable record. Dorothy Green's major study, *Ulysses Bound*, Canberra, 1973, combines criticism and psychologically interpretative biography, and Leonie Kramer's monograph, *Myself When Laura*, Melbourne, 1966, explores the combination of fact and fiction in *The Getting of Wisdom*. There are several substantial critical studies including those by Nettie Palmer and Dorothy Green *supra*, Vincent Buckley's monograph, *Henry Handel Richardson*, AWW, Melbourne, 1961, 2nd edn, 1970, and W. D. Elliott's *Henry Handel Richardson*, TWAS, Boston, 1975. An early influential essay is that by J. G. Robertson, Richardson's husband, published with *Myself When Young*, 1948. Critics have concentrated mainly on the Mahony trilogy, especially on its organization, style and relation to fact. General appreciations include those by A. N. Jeffares in *JCL*, no. 6 (1969), reprinted *RCL*, Brian Kiernan in *ISN*, and A. K. Thomson in *Meanjin*, vol. 26 (1967). Leonie Kramer's *A Companion to Australia Felix*, Melbourne, 1962, is a useful guide, and her other work includes: *Henry Handel Richardson and Some of her Sources*, Melbourne, 1954, essays in *Melbourne Critical Review*, no. 3 (1960), and in *L of A* (1964 and 1976), and a monograph in the GA series, Melbourne, 1967. Jennifer Dallimore in *Quadrant*, vol. 5,4 (1961), reprinted *ALC*, criticizes the trilogy's lack of cohesion, a criticism that is accepted but modified by Brian Kiernan in *Southerly*, vol. 29 (1969), and Leonie Kramer, in her various studies *supra*, discusses her use of sources and factual material and the quality of her writing. F. H. Mares in *Meanjin*, vol. 21 (1962), Dorothy Green in her 1973 study *supra*, and in *Henry Handel Richardson 1870–1946: Papers Presented at a Centenary Seminar*, Canberra, 1972, and W. M. Maidment, in a review of Jennifer Dallimore's essay, *Southerly*, vol. 24 (1964), defend the novels' unity and shaping vision. Two essays on the novels' unifying motifs and patterning are those by Elizabeth Loder in *Southerly*, vol. 25 (1965), and Kenneth Stewart in *AE*. Barry Argyle in *IAN* discusses the trilogy's epic qualities and its place in the Australian tradition. A number of studies have concentrated on the trilogy's relation to fact: Leonie Kramer's 1954 study, *supra*, stands out and Dorothy Green's *Ulysses Bound, supra* includes a sustained investigation of the facts of Walter Richardson's life. Other explorations include three essays in *Meanjin*, vol. 29 (1970) by Kenneth Stewart, by Alan Stoller and

478

R. H. Emmerson, and by M. A. Clutton-Brock, and Kenneth Stewart has made further investigations in *ALS*, vol. 4 (1970), *Teaching History*, vol. 4,3 (1970), and *Southerly*, vol. 33 (1973). Alan Stoller and R. H. Emmerson expand their theory in *Papers Presented at a Centenary Seminar, supra*. Studies of the trilogy's general historical background include S. B. Liljegren's *Ballarat and the Great Gold Rush According to the Richard Mahony Trilogy*, Uppsala and Copenhagen, 1964, and Weston Bate's 'From Gravel Pits to Green Point' in *Papers Presented at a Centenary Seminar, supra*. *Maurice Guest* has also attracted considerable attention: A. D. Hope's analysis of the influence of Nietzsche, *Meanjin*, vol. 14 (1955), reprinted *TCALC*, and *NC*, is criticized by Dorothy Green in *Ulysses Bound, supra*, and modified by Brian Kiernan, Kenneth Stewart and Elizabeth Loder *infra*, and by Anthony J. Palmer in *ALS*, vol. 5 (1972). Elizabeth Loder analyses the novel's themes and assesses its quality in *Balcony*, no. 4 (1966), and discusses the influence of other writers, especially that of Jacobsen in *Southerly*, vol. 26 (1966), Dennis Douglas deals extensively with the novel in *Maurice Guest: Henry Handel Richardson*, Melbourne, 1978, and Elizabeth Odeen, in her detailed work, *Maurice Guest: A Study*, Austin, Texas, 1963, outlines its method, and place in Richardson's work. Kenneth Stewart analyses the novel and its dependence on *Niels Lyhne* in *ALS*, vol. 5 (1972), and Brian Kiernan in *Southerly*, vol. 28 (1968), and *ISN*, analyses its nature and quality. Apart from the major studies, *The Young Cosima* has received little attention: Richardson's source books for the novel, held in the library of the University of Tasmania, are catalogued by D. H. Borchardt, Melbourne, 1973, and her transformation of the material is outlined by L. A. Triebel in *Australian Letters*, vol. 5,1 (1962).

JOHN ROMERIL, b. 1945. Playwright. His published plays include: *Chicago, Chicago*, in *Plays*, ed. Graeme Blundell, Ringwood, Vic., 1970, *I Don't Know Who to Feel Sorry For*, introd. by Graeme Blundell, preface by Margery M. Morgan, Sydney and London, 1973, and *The Floating World*, with comment by Allan Ashbolt and Katharine Brisbane, Sydney and London, 1975. His unpublished plays include: 'A Nameless Concern' (1968), 'Kitchen Table' (1968), 'Mrs. Thally F' (1971), 'Rearguard Action' (1971), 'Bastardy' (1972), 'And the Beast' (1972), 'He Can Swagger Sitting Down' (1972), 'The Golden Holden' (1975), and (with John Timlin) 'The Dudders' (1976).

'STEELE RUDD' (ARTHUR HOEY DAVIS), 1868–1935. Novelist and short story writer. His numerous works of fiction include: *On Our Selection*, Sydney, 1899, *Our New Selection*, Sydney, 1903, *Sandy's Selection*, Sydney, 1904, *Back at Our Selection*, Brisbane, 1906, *Stocking Our Selection*, Sydney, 1909, and *Green Grey Homestead*, Sydney, 1934. Hugh Anderson has provided a check-list of his stories contributed to the *Bulletin*, 1895–1932, *Biblionews*, vol. 11,5 (1958), and Steele Rudd's son, Eric Davis, has written the most substantial biography, *The Life and Times of Steele Rudd*, Melbourne, 1976, as well as an essay on his father's comic gift, *JRHSQ*, vol. 9,1 (1969–70). Of the numerous appreciations of Rudd's work, the few that are of any depth, include the studies by Vance Palmer in *Over-*

land, no. 15 (1959), reprinted *Intimate Portraits*, 1969, by Brian Elliott in *Singing to the Cattle*, 1947, A. D. Hope's 'Steele Rudd and Henry Lawson', *Meanjin*, vol. 15 (1956), reprinted *AN* and extensively revised in *NC*, and Van Ikin's 'Steele Rudd as Failed Artist', *Southerly*, vol. 36 (1976). Eric Irvin in *Quadrant*, vol. 20,1 (1976), discusses the success of the dramatized version of *On Our Selection*.

KENNETH SLESSOR, 1901–71. Poet. His writings include the verse selections: *Thief of the Moon*, privately printed, Sydney, 1924, *Earth-Visitors*, London, 1926, *Cuckooz Contrey*, Sydney, 1932, *Darlinghurst Nights and Morning Glories*, Sydney, [1933], *Five Bells*, Sydney, 1939, *One Hundred Poems 1919–1939*, Sydney, 1944, and *Poems*, Sydney, 1957, 2nd paperback edn, 1972 with introd. by Clement Semmler and notes by the author; and the prose collection: *Bread and Wine*, Sydney, 1970. Slessor discusses his work in 'Writing Poetry the Why and the How', *Southerly*, vol. 9 (1948), reprinted *Critical Essays on Kenneth Slessor*, ed. A. K. Thomson, Brisbane, 1968, and the following are important interviews: (with Desmond O'Grady) *Observer*, 17 September 1960, and (with John Thompson) *Southerly*, vol. 26 (1966), reprinted *Considerations*, Sydney, 1977. The most substantial biographical study is Douglas Stewart's memoir, *A Man of Sydney*, Melbourne, 1977, and other reminiscences include those of his brother, Robert C. Slessor, in *Southerly*'s Slessor memorial number, vol. 31,4 (1971), R. D. FitzGerald, in *ALS*, vol. 5 (1971), and Hal Porter in *The Extra*, Melbourne, 1975. There are several substantial critical studies including Herbert C. Jaffa's *Kenneth Slessor*, TWAS, New York, 1971, Max Harris's monograph Melbourne, 1963, and Graham Burns's study, AWW series, Melbourne, 1975. An introduction written for a foreign audience, is Clement Semmler's monograph in the 'Writers and Their Work' series, London, 1966. Some of the most stimulating criticisms are in essay form, several of them collected, with an extensive bibliography in *Critical Essays*, *supra*. Particularly important are: Vincent Buckley's consideration of his romanticism, *Meanjin*, vol. 11 (1952), reprinted in *Essays in Poetry*, 1957, Douglas Stewart's appreciations of his poetry in *The Flesh and the Spirit*, Sydney, 1948, and in *Meanjin*, vol. 28 (1969), and of his prose in *Southerly*, vol. 35 (1975), the last two reprinted in *A Man of Sydney*, *supra*. James McAuley analyses four poems in *Quadrant*, vol. 17,1 (1973), reprinted *The Grammar of the Real*, 1975, considers some of the poems rejected for *One Hundred Poems*, *Southerly*, vol. 33 (1973) and gives general appreciations in *A Map of Australian Verse*, 1975 and in *Considerations*, 1977. Other essays include: Charles Higham's appreciation, *Quadrant*, vol. 4,1 (1959–60), reprinted *ALC*, A. D. Hope's explanation of the poetry's survival, *Bulletin*, 1 June 1963, reprinted *NC*, Frederick T. Macartney's examination of his technique, *Meanjin*, vol. 16 (1957), A. C. W. Mitchell's exploration of his cult of the grotesque, *ALS*, vol. 1 (1964), A. K. Thomson's extensive introductory essay in *Critical Essays supra*, the appreciations by Leonie Kramer and L. A. C. Dobrez in *Southerly*, vol. 37 (1977), R. G. Howarth's analysis of sound in his poetry, *Southerly*, vol. 16 (1955), reprinted *TCALC*, Vivian Smith's study of ambivalence in his work, *Southerly*, vol. 31 (1971), reprinted *Considerations*, 1977, and Chris

Wallace-Crabbe's analysis of his use of language, *L of A* (1964 and 1976). Judith Wright in *PIAP* dwells at length on Slessor's nihilism, as does William Grono in a review, *Westerly*, no. 4 (1966). In addition, there are essays on specific poems: Julian Croft considers 'Five Visions of Captain Cook' in two essays in *ALS*, vol. 4 (1969), and his conclusions are modified by Alan Frost in *ALS*, vol. 4 (1970), and by Gerald McCallum in *ALS*, vol. 5 (1971). Croft also studies Slessor's treatment of time in 'Five Bells', *ALS*, vol. 5 (1971), and in 'Captain Dobbin', and 'Out of Time', *Southerly*, vol. 31 (1971), and combines and revises three of the above studies in an essay in *Considerations*, 1977. Norman Lindsay's influence has also been a favourite topic, discussed by several of the above studies, and see Norman Lindsay, *supra*. *Critical Essays, supra*, reprints several articles on the topic, and other essays include T. L. Sturm's corrective study, *Southerly*, vol. 31 (1971), and John Docker's cultural interpretation, *ACE*. Douglas Stewart in *Quadrant*, vol. 19,4 (1975), reprinted *A Man of Sydney, supra*, further explores the background of Slessor's involvement with *Vision*.

CATHERINE HELEN SPENCE, 1825–1910. Novelist. Her novels, published in London, include: *Clara Morison*, 1854, *Tender and True*, 1856, *Mr. Hogarth's Will*, 1865, and *The Author's Daughter*, 1868. Her last novel, *Gathered In*, serialized in Australia 1881–2, was first published in book form in 1977, introduced by B. L. Waters and G. A. Wilkes. *An Agnostic's Progress*, published anonymously in 1884, is a re-working of Bunyan's *The Pilgrim's Progress* to fit her own religious beliefs, and *An Autobiography*, Adelaide, 1910, reprinted 1975, deals with her experiences and aspirations. A bibliography, compiled by E. J. Gunton, Adelaide, 1967, is a useful guide to her work. Further information on her life and reform work can be found in Jeanne F. Young's study, *Catherine Helen Spence*, Melbourne, 1937, and in Janet Cooper's *Catherine Spence*, GA, Melbourne, 1972. Frederick Sinnett in 'The Fiction Fields of Australia', 1856, gives a warm appreciation of *Clara Morison*, and other useful essays include Susan Eade's introduction to a reprint of the same novel, Adelaide, 1971, and the general appreciations of her literary achievements by Jennifer Wightman in *Meanjin*, vol. 33 (1974), and John Barnes in *Henry Kingsley and Colonial Fiction*, AWW, Melbourne, 1971. R. B. Walker traces the development of her Utopian ideas in *ALS*, vol. 5 (1971), and her connection with South Australian politics in *Australian Journal of Politics and History*, vol. 15 (1969).

CHRISTINA STEAD, b. 1902. Novelist. Her writings include the novels: *Seven Poor Men of Sydney*, London, 1934, reprinted with introd. by R. G. Geering, Sydney, 1965, *The Beauties and the Furies*, London and New York, 1936, *House of all Nations*, London and New York, 1938, *The Man Who Loved Children*, New York, 1940, reprinted with introd. by Randall Jarrell, New York, 1965, *For Love Alone*, New York, 1944, reprinted with introd. by Terry Sturm, Sydney, 1973, *Letty Fox: Her Luck*, New York, 1946, reprinted with introd. by Meaghan Morris, Sydney, 1974, *A Little Tea, A Little Chat*, New York, 1948, *The People with the Dogs*, Boston, 1952, *Dark Places of the Heart*, New York, 1966, reprinted with title *Cotters'*

England, London, 1967, *The Little Hotel*, London and Sydney, 1973, and *Miss Herbert (The Suburban Wife)*, New York, 1976; and the stories: *The Salzburg Tales*, London, 1934, reprinted with introd. by Ian Reid, Sydney, 1974, and *The Puzzleheaded Girl*, New York, 1967. A bibliography by Rose Marie Beston, *WLWE*, vol. 15 (1976), is a detailed guide to her work. In 'A Writer's Friends', *Southerly*, vol. 28 (1968), Christina Stead discusses her life and work, her attachment to the short story in *Kenyon Review*, vol. 30,4 (1968), and in *Twentieth Century Authors*, ed. S. J. Kunitz and H. Haycraft, New York, 1942, she outlines the influences on her writing. There are the following interviews: (with Jonah Raskin) *London Magazine*, n.s. vol. 9,11 (1970), (with Greeba Jamison) *Walkabout*, vol. 36,2 (1970), (with Ann Whitehead) *ALS*, vol. 6 (1974), and (with John B. Beston) *WLWE*, vol. 15 (1976). Biographical accounts include those by Graeme Kinross Smith, *Westerly*, no. 1 (1976), and John B. Beston, *WLWE*, vol. 15 (1976). The two most susbstantial critical studies are both by R. G. Geering, one in the AWW series, Melbourne, 1969, and the other, written earlier, TWAS, New York, 1969, both extensively discussed by Michael Wilding in a review, *ALS*, vol. 4 (1970). Miss Stead's work, slow to win recognition at first, enjoyed a renaissance in the 1960s, especially after Randall Jarrell's introduction to *The Man Who Loved Children*, *supra*. Amongst recent critical studies this novel has attracted the most attention: Graham Burns in *Critical Review*, no. 14 (1971) considers its moral design, Pauline Nestor in the same journal, no. 18 (1976), analyses the central character's development, Dorothy Green in *AE* gives a general appreciation, and Terry Sturm in *Cunning Exiles*, ed. Don Anderson and Stephen Knight, Sydney, 1974, discusses the experimental realism of both this novel and others. *Seven Poor Men of Sydney* has also been extensively analysed: Anthony Miller assesses its strengths and weaknesses in *Westerly*, no. 2 (1968), Grant McGregor explores the historical dimension, and Judith Barbour the representation of the sublime in *Southerly*, vol. 38 (1978), Tony Thomas explores the sombre world-view of both this novel and *The Salzburg Tales* in *Westerly*, no. 4 (1970), Dorothy Green provides an interpretation of its nature and design in *Meanjin*, vol. 27 (1968), Brian Kiernan in *ISN* describes the radical response to Australian society in both this novel and in *For Love Alone*, Michael Wilding gives an analysis of the style and themes in the same two novels, *Southerly*, vol. 27 (1967), and D. R. Burns in *DOAF* considers their response to the harsh Australian environment. Susan Higgins interprets *For Love Alone* in *Southerly*, vol. 38 (1978) and in the same volume R. G. Geering considers *The Little Hotel* and *Miss Herbert*. Other general appreciations include: Clement Semmler in *L of A* (1976), Elizabeth Hardwick in *A View of My Own*, London, 1964, and Joan Lidoff in *Southerly*, vol. 38 (1978).

ALFRED GEORGE STEPHENS, 1865–1933. Critic and Editor. Much of his critical writing, published mainly in the *Bulletin*, the *Bookfellow*, the *Commonwealth* and other journals, remains uncollected. His collected criticism includes: *The Red Pagan*, Sydney, 1904, Vance Palmer's general selection in *A. G. Stephens: His Life and Work*, Melbourne, 1941, and Leon

Cantrell's *A. G. Stephens: Selected Writings*, Sydney, 1978. Stephens also published poetry, drama, essays, a novel, critical studies of Kendall, Brennan, and Daley, *q.v.*, and edited or introduced numerous selections and anthologies. Vance Palmer's study *supra* is still the main biographical work, although there are several anecdotal accounts such as the character sketches by Hugh McCrae and Clement Hansen in *Southerly*, vol. 8 (1947). A number of critical essays concentrate on his influence and role in the 1890s including those by: Leon Cantrell in *BBB*, S. E. Lee in *L of A* (1964 and 1976), Bruce Nesbitt in *ALS*, vol. 5 (1971), and H. P. Heseltine in *ALS*, vol. 1 (1963). Others dealing with his qualities as a critic include Brian Kiernan's general appreciation in *Criticism*, 1974, T. Inglis Moore's assessments of his influence in *Prometheus* (1956), and in *Texas Quarterly*, vol. 5,2 (1962), and John Barnes's appreciation in *Meanjin*, vol. 27 (1968). S. E. Lee analyses his critical *credo* in *ALS*, vol. 1 (1964), and Gillian Whitlock discusses his internationalist range in *ALS*, vol. 8 (1977). The effects and style of his literary editing are frequently discussed, particularly in studies of McCrae, Barcroft Boake and Neilson, *q.v.*, and see the general essay by S. E. Lee in *Southerly*, vol. 24 (1964). W. M. Maidment in 'A. G. Stephens and the *Gympie Miner*', *Southerly*, vol. 24 (1964), discusses his earliest extant writing.

DOUGLAS STEWART, b. 1913. Poet, playwright and critic. His collections of verse include: *Green Lions*, Auckland, 1936, *The White Cry*, London, 1939, *Elegy for an Airman*, Sydney, 1940, *Sonnets to the Unknown Soldier*, Sydney, 1941, *The Dosser in Springtime*, Sydney, 1946, *Glencoe*, Sydney, 1947, *Sun Orchids*, Sydney, 1952, *The Birdsville Track*, Sydney, 1955, *Rutherford*, Sydney, 1962, *Douglas Stewart*, sel. and introd. by the author, AP, Sydney, 1963, *Collected Poems 1936–1967*, Sydney, 1967, *Douglas Stewart Reads From His Own Work*, St. Lucia, 1971, and *Selected Poems*, Sydney, 1973. He has also written the following verse plays: *Ned Kelly*, Sydney, 1943, *The Fire on the Snow [and] The Golden Lover: Two Plays for Radio*, Sydney, 1944, *Shipwreck*, Sydney, 1947, *Four Plays* [includes all the foregoing], Sydney, 1958, and the part verse, part prose play, *Fisher's Ghost*, Sydney, 1960; a collection of short stories: *A Girl with Red Hair*, Sydney, 1944, a book of fishing and other reminiscences: *The Seven Rivers*, Sydney, 1966; two collections of critical essays: *The Flesh and The Spirit*, Sydney, 1948, and *The Broad Stream*, Sydney, 1975; a collection of lectures broadcast in 1977, *Writers of the Bulletin*, Sydney, 1977; and memoirs of Norman Lindsay and Kenneth Slessor, *q.v.* There are the following interviews: (with Desmond O'Grady) *Observer*, 1 October 1960, (with Arthur Ashworth) *Poetry Magazine*, no. 5 (1966), and (with John Thompson) *Southerly*, vol. 27 (1967), reprinted *Considerations*, 1977. There are two substantial studies of his work: Nancy Keesing's *Douglas Stewart*, AWW, Melbourne, 1965, 2nd edn, 1969, and Clement Semmler's *Douglas Stewart*, TWAS, New York, 1974. Essays on his drama include those by: J. F. Burrows in *Southerly*, vol. 23 (1963), Leslie Rees in *The Making of Australian Drama*, 1973, H. J. Oliver in *Texas Quarterly*, vol. 5,2 (1962), and A. A. Phillips (on *Ned Kelly*) in *Meanjin*, vol. 15 (1956), reprinted *AT* (1958). David Bradley in *Westerly*, no. 3 (1960) gives an adverse criticism. There are several essays on Stewart's poetry, of which the most outstanding are: R. D. FitzGerald's study of the motifs in his work, *The Elements of Poetry*, Brisbane, 1963, James McAuley's analysis of his achievement, *L of A* (1964, revised 1976), Vivian Smith's appreciation of his individual quality, *Meanjin*, vol. 26 (1967), A. A. Phillips's analysis of his craftsmanship, *Meanjin*, vol. 28 (1969), and Leonie Kramer's study of the duality of his vision, *Southerly*, vol. 33 (1973). The essays by FitzGerald, Smith, Phillips and Leonie Kramer are all reprinted in *Considerations*, 1977. James McAuley also included a chapter on Stewart's work in his *A Map of Australian Verse*, 1975.

LOUIS STONE, 1871–1935. Novelist. His major novel is *Jonah*, London and Sydney, 1911, re-issued Sydney, 1965, with introd. by Ronald McCuaig. His other novel, *Betty Wayside*, London, 1915, is a lesser work. He also wrote several short stories and plays. The most substantial critical study is H. J. Oliver's monograph, *Louis Stone*, AWW, Melbourne, 1968, which expands Oliver's earlier essay in *Meanjin*, vol. 13 (1954). Dorothy Green considers *Jonah*'s cinematic qualities in *ALS*, vol. 2 (1965), reprinted *AN*.

RANDOLPH STOW, b. 1935. Poet and novelist. His writings include the novels: *A Haunted Land*, London, 1956, *The Bystander*, London, 1957, *To the Islands*, London, 1958, *Tourmaline*, London, 1963, *The Merry-Go-Round in the Sea*, London, 1965, and *Midnite*, Melbourne, 1967; and the verse collections: *Act One*, London, 1957, *Outrider*, with paintings by Sidney Nolan, London, 1962, *A Counterfeit Silence*, Sydney, 1969, and *Randolph Stow Reads From His Own Work*, St. Lucia, 1974. He has also written the libretti for two musical compositions by Peter Maxwell Davies: 'Eight Songs for a Mad King' (1971), and 'Miss Donnithorne's Maggot', (1974). A bibliography by Patricia O'Brien, Adelaide, 1968, is supplemented annually in the *Index to Australian Book Reviews*, and Rose Marie Beston has supplied another check-list in *Literary Half-Yearly*, vol. 16,2 (1975). Biographical accounts include John Hetherington's in *Forty-Two Faces*, 1962, and John B. Beston's in *Literary Half-Yearly*, vol. 16, 2 (1975). There are the following interviews: (with Anna Rutherford and Andreas Boelsmand) *Commonwealth Newsletter*, Aarhus, [1974], and (with John B. Beston) *WLWE*, vol. 14 (1975). Ray Willbanks has written the most substantial study of his work, *Randolph Stow*, TWAS, Boston, 1978. G. K. W. Johnston provides an introduction to his novels in *Meanjin*, vol. 20 (1961), and in the same volume, Vincent Buckley compares his preoccupations with those of Patrick White. Thomas Keneally in *Australian Author*, vol. 1, 4 (1969) suggests that Stow is over-concerned with form, and David Martin in 'Among the Bones', *Meanjin*, vol. 18 (1959), finds a dichotomy between realism and symbolism in his work, a theme that is expanded in Leonie Kramer's essay, *Southerly*, vol. 24 (1964). O. N. Burgess, on the other hand, in *Australian Quarterly*, vol. 37, 1 (1965), and Jennifer Wightman, in an extensive study, *Meanjin*, vol. 28 (1969), regard his work as more unified. A. D. Hope, in an essay, *AE*, gives a fresh interpretation of Stow's philosophical preoccupations as an answer to Leonie Kramer's objections *supra*, although L. T. Hergenhan takes issue with both Leonie Kramer and Hope in his analysis of *To the Islands*,

Southerly, vol. 35 (1975). Geoffrey Dutton in *JCL*, no. 1 (1965), reprinted *RCL*, explores a major theme in his work, the search for permanence and Alice Oppen in *Southerly*, vol. 27 (1967), interprets the progression of his vision. William H. New concentrates on his theme of individuality in *Critique*, vol. 9,1 (1967), R. G. Geering in *Recent Fiction*, 1974, compares his work with Keneally's, and Anthony J. Hassall in *Meanjin*, vol. 32 (1973), and Adrian Mitchell in *Opinion*, vol. 12,3 (1968), write on *The Merry-Go-Round in the Sea*. Apart from reviews, his poetry has attracted less attention: Philip Martin considers his first collection in *Twentieth Century*, vol. 12 (1958), Brandon Conron reviews *A Counterfeit Silence* in *Ariel*, vol. 1,4 (1970), and John B. Beston considers his love poetry in *ACLALS Bulletin*, no. 5 (1977).

KYLIE TENNANT, b. 1912. Novelist. Her writings include the novels: *Tiburon*, Sydney, 1935, *Foveaux*, London, 1939, *The Battlers*, London and New York, 1941, *Ride on Stranger*, Sydney, London and New York, 1943, *Time Enough Later*, New York, 1943, *Lost Haven*, New York and Melbourne, 1946, *The Joyful Condemned*, London and New York, 1953, expanded version with title *Tell Morning This*, Sydney, 1967, and *The Honey Flow*, London and New York, 1956; and the short stories: *Ma Jones and the Little White Cannibals*, London, 1967. She has also published an autobiographical memoir, *The Man on the Headland*, Sydney, 1971, a biography of H. V. Evatt, Sydney, 1970, and a play about Alfred Deakin, *Tether a Dragon*, Sydney, 1952. John Hetherington in *Forty-Two Faces*, 1962, and Graeme Kinross Smith in *Westerly*, no. 1 (1975) have written biographical accounts. The most substantial critical study is Margaret Dick's *The Novels of Kylie Tennant*, Adelaide, 1966, and other essays include Dorothy Auchterlonie's appreciation, *Meanjin*, vol. 12 (1953), T. Inglis Moore's analysis of her strengths and weaknesses, *Southerly*, vol. 18 (1957), reprinted *TCALC*, and Xavier Pons's interpretation of *The Battlers*, *ALS*, vol. 6 (1974).

CHRIS WALLACE-CRABBE, b. 1934. Poet and critic. His verse collections include: *The Music of Division*, Sydney, 1959, *In Light and Darkness*, Sydney, 1963, *The Rebel General*, Sydney, 1967, *Where the Wind Came*, Sydney, 1971, *Selected Poems*, Sydney, 1973, *Chris Wallace-Crabbe Reads From His Own Work*, St. Lucia, 1973, and *The Foundation of Joy*, Sydney, 1976. He has also written a collection of critical essays, *Melbourne or the Bush*, Sydney, 1974, and edited another, *The Australian Nationalists*, Melbourne, 1971. There are the following interviews: (with R. A. Simpson) *Poetry Magazine*, no. 3 (1966), (with Brian Kiernan) *Australian*, 13 November 1971, and (with Thomas Shapcott) *Makar*, vol. 13, 3 (1978). E. A. M. Colman in *Westerly*, no. 1 (1969), and Peter Steele in *Meanjin*, vol. 29 (1970) have written on his poetry.

JUDAH WATEN, b. 1911. Novelist and short story writer. His writings include the novels: *The Unbending*, Melbourne, 1954, *Shares in Murder*, Melbourne, 1957, *Time of Conflict*, Sydney, 1961, *Distant Land*, Melbourne, 1964, *Season of Youth*, Melbourne, 1966, and *So Far No Further*, Mt. Eliza,

Vic., 1971; the short story collections, *Alien Son*, Sydney, 1952, and *Love and Rebellion*, Melbourne, 1978; and an autobiographical account of a return journey to Russia, *From Odessa to Odessa*, Melbourne, 1969. Waten discusses his life and work in 'My Two Literary Careers', *Southerly*, vol. 31 (1971), and his childhood in 'A Child of Wars and Revolutions', *Southerly*, vol. 33 (1973). Further information is provided in John Hetherington's study in *Forty-Two Faces*, 1962, and in a biographical sketch by John Morrison, *Overland*, no. 11 (1958). Articles on his fiction include David Martin's comparative study, *Meanjin*, vol. 18 (1959), reprinted *ONG*, and A. D. Hope's appreciation of *The Unbending*, *NC*.

FRANCIS WEBB, 1925–73. Poet. His verse collections include: *A Drum for Ben Boyd*, with illustrations by Norman Lindsay, Sydney, 1948, *Leichhardt in Theatre*, Sydney, 1952, *Birthday*, Adelaide, 1953, *Socrates*, Sydney, 1961, *The Ghost of the Cock*, Sydney, 1964, *Collected Poems*, with a preface by Sir Herbert Read, Sydney, 1969, enlarged by inclusion of 'Early Poems 1942–1948', Sydney, 1977, and *Francis Webb Reads From His Own Work*, St. Lucia, 1975. Some uncollected poems are included in *Poetry Australia*'s 'Francis Webb (1925–1973) Commemorative Issue', no. 56 (1975), as well as a bibliography and some biographical material. Critics have been slow to come to terms with the arresting nature of Webb's work. Douglas Stewart's reviews, *Bulletin*, 19 May 1948 and 18 June 1952, and Vincent Buckley's study in *Meanjin*, vol. 12 (1953), the first appreciations of any length, were not followed by any significant work until 1961 when Chris Wallace-Crabbe's CLF lecture, *Order and Turbulence*, reprinted *MOB*, was published. Since then there have appeared major interpretative essays by: Elizabeth Feltham, *Quadrant*, vol. 6,2 (1962), H. P. Heseltine, *Meanjin*, vol. 26 (1967), James Tulip, *Southerly*, vol. 29 (1969), and Vincent Buckley, *Quadrant*, vol. 14,2 (1970). Webb's death stimulated a series of reassessments, of which the most well-researched are those by W. D. Ashcroft in *Southerly*, vol. 34 (1974), *Meanjin*, vol. 33 (1974), *ALS*, vol. 7 (1975), *Poetry Australia*, no. 56 (1975), and *Hemisphere*, vol. 20,8 (1976). Other essays at this time include the appreciations by Rosemary Dobson in *ALS*, vol. 6 (1974), and H. P. Heseltine in *Meanjin*, vol. 33 (1974). The most substantial body of criticism, however, is contained in *Poetry Australia*'s commemorative issue *supra*, which includes besides those items already mentioned, appreciations and reminiscences by Rosemary Dobson, A. D. Hope, James Tulip, Vincent Buckley, R. F. Brissenden, Chris Wallace-Crabbe, Michael Griffith, Craig Powell and others.

PATRICK WHITE, b. 1912. Novelist, short story writer and playwright. His writings include the novels: *Happy Valley*, London, 1939, *The Living and the Dead*, London and New York, 1941, *The Aunt's Story*, London and New York, 1948, *The Tree of Man*, New York, 1955, *Voss*, London and New York, 1957, *Riders in the Chariot*, London and New York, 1961, *The Solid Mandala*, London and New York, 1966, *The Vivisector*, London and New York, 1970, *The Eye of the Storm*, London, 1973, and *A Fringe of Leaves*, London, 1976; the collected short stories, *The Burnt Ones*, London and New York, 1964, and *The Cockatoos*, London, 1974; the verse

486

collections, *Thirteen Poems* [1929 or 1930] and *The Ploughman and Other Poems*, Sydney, 1935, and *Four Plays* [*The Ham Funeral, The Season at Sarsaparilla, A Cheery Soul,* and *Night on Bald Mountain*], introd. by H. G. Kippax, London, 1965, and *Big Toys*, Sydney, 1978. His unpublished plays include: 'Bread-and-Butter Women' (1935), 'The School for Friends' (1935?), and 'Return to Abyssinia' (1946). In 'The Prodigal Son', *Australian Letters*, vol. 1,3 (1958), reprinted *The Vital Decade*, 1968, White discusses his preoccupations and relationship with Australia, and the following are important interviews: (with Craig McGregor) *In the Making*, 1969, and (with Thelma Herring and G. A. Wilkes) *Southerly*, vol. 33 (1973). Alan Lawson's comprehensive bibliography, *Patrick White*, AB, Melbourne, 1974, has superseded Janette Finch's earlier listing, Adelaide, 1966, which is supplemented annually in the *Index to Australian Book Reviews*. Leon Cantrell in *ALS*, vol. 6 (1974), and Michael Wilding in *ALS*, vol. 3 (1967), have supplied further bibliographical details. As well as a multiplicity of essays, of which only a few can be listed here, there are several substantial critical studies, including: the introductions by Geoffrey Dutton, AWW, Melbourne, 1961, 4th edn, 1971, and R. F. Brissenden, 'Writers and Their Work' Series, London, 1966, Barry Argyle's *Patrick White*, Edinburgh, 1967, F. W. Dillistone's *Patrick White's Riders in the Chariot*, New York, 1967, G. A. Wilkes's edition of essays from *Southerly*, *Ten Essays on Patrick White*, Sydney, 1970, Bernard Hickey's *Aspects of Alienation in James Joyce and Patrick White*, Roma, 1971, Patricia A. Morley's *The Mystery of Unity*, St. Lucia and Montreal, 1972, Ingmar Björksten's introduction from a European point of view, *Patrick White: epikern fran Australien*, Stockholm, 1973, transl. Stanley Gerson, St. Lucia, 1976, J. R. Dyce's *Patrick White as Playwright*, St. Lucia, 1974, Peter Beatson's interpretation, *The Eye in the Mandala*, London, 1976, and William Walsh's two studies, *Patrick White's Fiction*, Hornsby, NSW, 1977, and *Patrick White: Voss*, London, 1976. General essays include R. F. Brissenden's early evaluation, *Meanjin*, vol. 18 (1959), and three appreciations by Brian Kiernan in *ISN*, in *Cunning Exiles*, 1974, and in *L of A* (1976). H. P. Heseltine analyses his style in *Quadrant*, vol. 7,3 (1963), and both A. A. Phillips in *Meanjin*, vol. 24 (1965), and John McLaren in *ALS*, vol. 2 (1966), reprinted *TCALC*, criticise his symbolism. An important corrective study is Alan Lawson's survey of his critical reception in Australia, *Meanjin*, vol. 32 (1973). J. F. Burrows and Thelma Herring write on *The Aunt's Story* in *Southerly*, vols. 26 (1966) and 25 (1965) respectively, and John B. and Rose Marie Beston have made more specific studies of the novel in *Ariel*, vol. 3,4 (1972), in *JCL*, vol. 9,3 (1975), and (by John B. Beston only) in *Quadrant*, vol. 15,5 (1971). Important articles on *The Tree of Man*, include those by: Vincent Buckley in *Twentieth Century*, vol. 12 (1958), reprinted *ALC*, G. A. Wilkes in *Southerly*, vol. 25 (1965), Manfred MacKenzie in *Meanjin*, vol. 25 (1966), A. K. Thomson in the same volume, A. P. Riemer in *Southerly*, vol. 27 (1967), J. F. Burrows in *Southerly*, vol. 29 (1969), and Leonie Kramer in *AE*. *Voss* is the subject of essays by: Ian Turner in *Overland*, no. 12 (1958), reprinted *AOM*, R. P. Laidlaw in *Southern Review*, Adelaide, vol. 4 (1970) and Dorothy Green in *AE*. There are also four studies in *Southerly* by James McAuley, vol. 25 (1965), G. A. Wilkes, vol. 27 (1967), Peter Beatson, vol. 30 (1970), and Veronica Brady, vol. 35 (1975). The following deal mainly with *Riders in the Chariot*: Marcel Aurousseau in *Meanjin*, vol. 21 (1962), Sylvia Gzell in *ALS*, vol. 1 (1964), J. F. Burrows in *Southerly*, vol. 25 (1965), Leonie Kramer in *Quadrant*, vol. 17,3 (1973), and Susan Moore in *Southerly*, vol. 35 (1975). The following are studies of *The Solid Mandala*: A. A. Phillips in *Meanjin*, vol. 25 (1966), Thelma Herring in *Southerly*, vols. 26 (1966) and 28 (1968), G. A. Wilkes in *Southerly*, vol. 29 (1969), and William Walsh in a combination of two previously published articles in *RCL*. *The Vivisector* is the subject of the following: Richard N. Coe in *Meanjin*, vol. 29 (1970), Thelma Herring in *Southerly*, vol. 31 (1971), John B. Beston in *ALS*, vol. 5 (1971), Terry Smith in *Meanjin*, vol. 31 (1972), George Turner in *Overland*, no. 50/51 (1972), John Docker in *Southerly*, vol. 33 (1973), reprinted *ACE*, and R. F. Brissenden in *AE*. Articles on *The Eye of the Storm* include those by: Veronica Brady in *Westerly*, no. 4 (1973), Dorothy Green in *Meanjin*, vol. 32 (1973), Leonie Kramer in *Quadrant*, vol. 18,1 (1974), and Rose Marie Beston in *WLWE*, vol. 13 (1974). White's short stories are studied by: Jack Lindsay in *Meanjin*, vol. 23 (1964), J. F. Burrows in *Southerly*, vol. 24 (1964), Andrew Taylor in *Overland*, no. 31 (1965), John Barnes in *Meanjin*, vol. 25 (1966), Anthony J. Hassall in *Southerly*, vol. 35 (1975), and R. J. B. Wilson in *BBB*. Numerous articles have been written on his plays, including: the general studies by R. F. Brissenden in *Meanjin*, vol. 23 (1964), reprinted *ONG*, Roger Covell in *Quadrant*, vol. 8,1 (1964), Thelma Herring in *Southerly*, vol. 25 (1965), J. F. Burrows in *ALS*, vol. 2 (1966), and Dennis Douglas in *BBB*; and the specific studies of *The Ham Funeral* by Andrew Taylor in *Meanjin*, vol. 32 (1973), John Tasker in *Meanjin*, vol. 23 (1964), Elizabeth Loder in *Southerly*, vol. 23 (1963), and J. J. Bray in *Meanjin*, vol. 21 (1962). In addition, Keith Macartney interprets *A Cheery Soul*, *Meanjin*, vol. 23 (1964), David Bradley comments on *The Season at Sarsaparilla*, *Meanjin*, vol. 21 (1962), and Axel Kruse analyses *Night on Bald Mountain*, *Southerly*, vol. 35 (1975). L. T. Hergenhan speculates on 'Return to Abyssinia' in *ALS*, vol. 7 (1976).

MICHAEL WILDING, b. 1942. Short story writer, novelist and critic. His short story collections include: *Aspects of the Dying Process*, St. Lucia, 1972, *The West Midland Underground*, St. Lucia, 1975, *Scenic Drive*, Sydney, 1976, and *The Phallic Forest*, Sydney, 1978. His novels include: *Living Together*, St. Lucia, 1974, and *The Short Story Embassy*, Sydney, 1975. Information is contained in an interview with Rudi Krausmann, *Aspect*, (Spring 1975), and Carl Harrison-Ford in *Southerly*, vol. 33 (1973) compares his short stories with those of Frank Moorhouse.

DAVID WILLIAMSON, b. 1942. Playwright. His published plays include: *Don's Party*, introd. by John Clarke, preface by H. G. Kippax, Sydney, 1973, *The Removalists*, ed. Sylvia Lawson, Sydney, 1972, *The Coming of Stork. Jugglers Three. What If You Died Tomorrow*, introd. by the author, Sydney and London, 1974, *The Department*, introd. by Rodney Fisher, Sydney and London, 1975, *A Handful of Friends*, introd. by Rodney Fisher, Sydney, 1976, and *The Club*, Sydney, 1978. In *Meanjin*, vol. 33 (1974) Williamson describes his intentions in *The Removalists*, and the following are informative interviews: (with Dave Jones) *Cinema Papers*, January, 1974, and (with Meryl Tobin) *Westerly*, no. 2 (1975). Critical essays include: Brian Kiernan's survey of his development, *Southerly*, vol. 35 (1975), Roslyn Arnold's analysis of his drama's aggressive vernacular in the same volume, Margaret Williams's interpretation of his use of stereotypes, *Meanjin*, vol. 31 (1972), and her general survey in *Drama*, 1977, and Rose Marie Beston's analysis of sexual antagonisms in *Jugglers Three*, *Refractory Girl*, no. 4 (1973).

FRANK WILMOT 'FURNLEY MAURICE', 1881–1942. Poet. His collections, all published in Melbourne, include: *Some Verses*, 1903, *Some More Verses*, 1904, *Unconditioned Songs*, 1913, *To God: From the Weary Nations*, 1917, *The Bay and Padie Book*, 1917, *Eyes of Vigilance*, 1920, *Ways and Means*, 1920, *Arrows of Longing*, 1921, *The Gully and Other Verses*, 1929, *Odes for a Curse-Speaking Choir!*, 1933, *Melbourne Odes*, 1934, and *Poems by Furnley Maurice (Frank Wilmot)*, sel. by Percival Serle, 1944. Hugh Anderson's bibliography and criticism, Melbourne, 1955, is a helpful guide, although David Walker's *Dream and Disillusion*, Canberra, 1976, lists supplementary material. Substantial studies of his work and aspirations include those by David Walker in *Dream and Disillusion supra*, and by W. H. Wilde in *Three Radicals*, AWW, Melbourne, 1969, Vance Palmer's tribute *Frank Wilmot (Furnley Maurice)*, Melbourne, 1942, and F. T. Macartney's *Furnley Maurice (Frank Wilmot)*, Sydney, 1955. Vance Palmer discusses the chief features of his work in *Australian Quarterly*, vol. 14, 2 (1942) T. Inglis Moore surveys his achievement in *Southerly*, vol. 12 (1951), and John Heuzenroeder considers his preoccupations in *Meanjin*, vol. 33 (1974).

JUDITH WRIGHT, b. 1915. Poet and critic. Her writings include the verse collections: *The Moving Image*, Melbourne, 1946, *Woman to Man*, Sydney, 1949, *The Gateway*, Sydney, 1953, *The Two Fires*, Sydney, 1955, *Birds*, Sydney, 1962, *Judith Wright*, sel. and introd. by the author, AP, Sydney, 1963, *Five Senses*, Sydney, 1963, *The Other Half*, Sydney, 1966, *Collected Poems 1942–1970*, Sydney, 1971, *Alive: Poems 1971–72*, Sydney, 1973, *Judith Wright Reads From Her Own Work*, St. Lucia, 1973, *Fourth Quarter*, Sydney, 1976, and *The Double Tree: Selected Poems 1942–1976*, Boston, 1978; the short story collection, *The Nature of Love*, Melbourne, 1966; the collected critical essays, *Preoccupations in Australian Poetry*, Melbourne, 1965, and *Because I was Invited*, Melbourne, 1975; and a history of her family, *The Generations of Men*, Melbourne, 1959. She has also written studies of Harpur, Lawson and Neilson, *q.v.*, and several books for children. The following are important interviews: (with John Thompson) *Opinion*, vol. 9,2 (1965), reprinted *Southerly*, vol. 27 (1967), and (with Craig McGregor) *In the Making*, 1969. Taped interviews are also included in W. N. Scott's study *infra*. An incomplete bibliography by P. O'Brien and E. Robinson, Adelaide, 1968, is supplemented annually in the *Index to Australian Book Reviews*, and by Hugh Anderson's review, *ALS*, vol. 3 (1968). A. D. Hope's *Judith Wright*, AWW, Melbourne, 1975, is the most comprehensive critical study, W. N. Scott's *Focus on Judith Wright*, St. Lucia, 1967, includes invaluable background information, and A. K. Thomson's edition *Critical Essays on Judith Wright*, Brisbane, 1968, reprints several major studies. Two leading critics of her poetry are R. F. Brissenden and James McAuley: Brissenden has written a general appreciation, *Meanjin*, vol. 12 (1953), reprinted *ALC*, an extensive review of *Five Senses*, *Australian Quarterly*, vol. 36,1 (1964), reprinted *TCLAC*, and a consideration of her later poetry in *Considerations*, 1977. McAuley analyses several poems in *ALS*, vol. 3 (1968), reprinted in *The Grammar of the Real*, 1975, and gives a more general interpretation in *A Map of Australian Verse*, 1975. Other essays include: Vincent Buckley's critical survey, *Essays in Poetry*, 1957, T. Inglis Moore's definition of her metaphysical quest, *Meanjin*, vol. 17 (1958), reprinted *ONG*, Terry Sturm's analysis of continuity in her work, *Southerly*, vol. 36 (1976), G. A. Wilkes's appreciation of her later poetry, *Southerly*, vol. 25 (1965), Rodney Hall's interpretation of her themes, *L of A* (1976), and R. I. Scott's consideration of her world-view, *Southerly*, vol. 17 (1956), Max Harris's essay in *L of A* (1964), Donald Davie's evaluation in *Considerations*, 1977, Adrian Mitchell's analysis of her limitations in the same volume, Bruce Bennett's interpretation of her moral position, *Westerly*, no. 1 (1976), and Chris Wallace-Crabbe's comparison of her work with that of Elizabeth Bishop in *Westerly*, no. 1 (1978). Richard Wilson writes on her short stories in *ALS*, vol. 1 (1963).

NOTES

INTRODUCTION

1 Samuel Lorenzo Knapp, *American Cultural History 1607–1829*, intro. and index by Richard Beale Davis and Ben Harris McClary. Facsimile edn. *Lectures on American Literature* (1829), Florida, 1961, p. 36.
2 Charles Darwin, 'Journey Across the Blue Mountains to Bathurst in January, 1836', *Fourteen Journeys Over the Blue Mountains in New South Wales 1813–41*, ed. George Mackaness, Sydney, 1965, p. 233.
3 Vance Palmer, *The Legend of the Nineties*, Melbourne, 1954, p. 55.
4 Brian Elliott, *The Landscape of Australian Poetry*, Melbourne, 1967, p. 29.
5 'Furnley Maurice', 'National Poetry', *Romance*, Melbourne, 1922, p. 25.
6 Vance Palmer, 'An Australian National Art' (1905), *The Writer in Australia 1856–1964*, ed. John Barnes, Melbourne, 1969, p. 169.
7 H. G. Turner and A. Sutherland, *The Development of Australian Literature*, London, 1898, p. 24.
8 Leon Cantrell, ed., 'Introduction', *A. G. Stephens Selected Writings*, Sydney, 1978, p. 3.
9 A. G. Stephens, 'Australian Literature II' (*Bookfellow*, 1907), in Cantrell, p. 91.
10 Palmer, in Barnes, p. 169.
11 Rex Ingamells, 'Conditional Culture' (1938), in Barnes, p. 249.
12 Judith Wright, *Preoccupations in Australian Poetry*, Melbourne, 1965, p. xxi.
13 Wright, p. 79.
14 Ingamells, in Barnes, p. 254.
15 E. A. Badham, 'An Australian School of Literature', *Cosmos*, April 30, 1895, p. 417.
16 Sydney Long, 'The Trend of Australian Art Considered and Discussed' (1905), *Documents in Art and Taste in Australia: The Colonial Period 1770–1914*, ed. Bernard Smith, Melbourne, 1975, p. 267.
17 Frederick Sinnett, 'The Fiction Fields of Australia', in Barnes, p. 11.
18 David Walker, *Dream and Disillusion*, Canberra, 1976, p. 206.

FICTION

1 Watkin Tench, *A Narrative of the Expedition to Botany Bay*, 3rd edn., London, 1789, p. 113.
2 Watkin Tench, Preface to *A Complete Account of the Settlement at Port Jackson in New South Wales* (1793); repr. in Tench, *Sydney's First Four Years*, ed. L. F. Fitzhardinge, Sydney, 1961, pp. 127–8.
3 Charles Rowcroft, *Tales of the Colonies*, London, 1843, vol. 1, p. 98.
4 *Settlers and Convicts*, by an Emigrant Mechanic, ed., C. M. H. Clark, Melbourne, 1953, p. 32.
5 *Ibid.*, p. 88.
6 *Ibid.*, pp. 180–1.
7 *Catherine Helen Spence: An Autobiography*, ed. Jeanne F. Young, Adelaide, 1910, p. 97.
8 Catherine Helen Spence, *Clara Morison*, with introduction by Susan Eade, Adelaide, 1971, p. 70.
9 Marcus Clarke, preface to *Long Odds*, Melbourne, 1869.
10 Henry Kingsley, *The Recollections of Geoffry Hamlyn*, Cambridge, 1859, vol. 2, p. 145.
11 Rolf Boldrewood, *Old Melbourne Memories*, Melbourne, 1884; 1896, p. 172.
12 Kingsley, *The Recollections of Geoffry Hamlyn*, vol. 2, p. 1.
13 *Ibid.*, vol. 2, p. 51.
14 'Charles Dickens', *Marcus Clarke*, ed. Michael Wilding, St. Lucia, 1976, p. 632.
15 *Ibid.*, 'Review: *The Luck of Roaring Camp*', p. 637.

491

16   Rolf Boldrewood, *Robbery Under Arms*, London, 1889, p. 1.
17   *Ibid.*, p. 37.
18   Norman Lindsay, Introduction to Edward Dyson, *The Golden Shanty: Short Stories*, Sydney, 1963, p. vii.
19   'Tom Collins', *Such is Life*, Sydney, 1903, p. 1.
20   Miles Franklin, *Laughter, Not for a Cage*, Sydney, 1956, p. 149.
21   Henry Handel Richardson, *Maurice Guest*, London, 1922, p. 6.
22   *Ibid.*, p. 18.
23   Henry Handel Richardson, 'Some notes on my books', *Southerly*, 1, 1963, p. 14.
24   Henry Handel Richardson, *The Young Cosima*, London, 1939, p. 254.
25   William Gosse Hay in a letter to Miss F. Earle Hooper, cited by R.G. Howarth, Introduction to *The Escape of the Notorious Sir William Heans*, Melbourne, 1955, p. x.
26   Havelock Ellis, *Views and Reviews: a selection of uncollected articles 1884–1932* (First Series: 1884–1919), London, 1932, p. 175. Originally in *Weekly Critical Review*, Sept. 17, 1903.
27   Miles Franklin, *All That Swagger*, Sydney, 1947, p. 417.
28   Frederic Manning, Prefatory Note, *Her Privates We*, London, 1930.
29   Leonard Mann, *Flesh in Armour*, Melbourne, 1932, p. 134.
30   Vance Palmer, 'An Australian National Art', *Steele Rudd's Magazine*, January 1905; reprinted in John Barnes, ed., *The Writer in Australia: A Collection of Literary Documents 1856–1964*, Melbourne, 1969, pp. 168–9.
31   Katharine Susannah Prichard in a letter to Henrietta Drake-Brockman, quoted in Drake-Brockman, 'Katharine Susannah Prichard: the colour in her work', *Southerly* 4, 1953, p. 214.
32   P. R. Stephensen, 'The Foundations of Culture in Australia', 1935; reprinted in John Barnes, *op. cit.*, p. 206.
33   Frank Dalby Davison, 'Return of the Hunter', *The Woman at the Mill*, Sydney, 1940, p. 200. Reprinted in *The Road to Yesterday: Collected Stories*, Sydney, 1964.
34   Xavier Herbert, 'The Writing of *Capricornia*', *Australian Literary Studies*, May 1970, p. 212.
35   Xavier Herbert, *Larger than Life: Twenty Short Stories*, Sydney, 1963, p. x.
36   Kylie Tennant, 'The Development of the Australian Novel', Commonwealth Literary Fund lecture, Canberra, 1958, p. 11.
37   Ann Whitehead, 'Christina Stead: An Interview', *Australian Literary Studies*, May 1974, p. 232.
38   Jonah Raskin, 'Christina Stead in Washington Square', *London Magazine*, February 1970, p. 77.
39   See Sue Higgins, '*For Love Alone*: A Female Odyssey?' *Southerly*, 4, 1978, p. 430.
40   Martin Boyd, 'Preoccupations and Intentions', *Southerly*, 2, 1968, p. 86.
41   Craig McGregor, 'Patrick White', *In the Making*, Melbourne, 1969, p. 218.
42   Stow has published *Visitants* (1979) since this went to press. Other substantial books to appear are Patrick White, *The Twyborn Affair* (1979); David Ireland, *A Woman of the Future* (1979); Peter Cary, *War Crimes* (1979), and Thomas Keneally, *Confederates* (1979).
43   Vance Palmer, 'Fiction chronicle', *Meanjin*, 4, 1958, p. 433.
44   Hal Porter, 'Beyond whipped cream and blood', *Bulletin*, 28 April, 1962, p. 66.
45   'Peter Mathers', in Craig McGregor, *op. cit.*, p. 39.

DRAMA

1   F. C. Brewer, *The Drama and Music of New South Wales*, Sydney, 1892, p. 95.
2   Despatch to Henry Dundas, 10 March, 1794.
3   David Collins, *An Account of the English Colony in New South Wales*, London, 1798, p. 448. Lieutenant-Colonel Collins was Judge-Advocate and Secretary of the Colony from the foundation of the settlement to 1796.
4   Watkin Tench, *A Complete Account of the Settlement at Port Jackson in New South Wales*, London, 1793, p. 25.
5   See *Ralph Rashleigh* [1845], Sydney, Angus and Robertson, 1952, Chapters XII and XIV (especially, pp. 95–6).
6   *The Australian*, 14 October, 1845.
7   Eric Irvin, *Theatre Comes to Australia*, University of Queensland Press, 1971, p. 42.
8   *Ibid.*, p. 46.
9   *Sydney Gazette*, April, 1828, cited in Paul McGuire, *The Australian Theatre*, Melbourne, O.U.P., 1948, p. 14.

10   *Theatre Comes to Australia, op. cit.,* p. 33.
11   See Peter Cunningham, *Two Years in New South Wales,* London, 1827, Vol. I, p. 53.
12   *The Australian,* 28 November, 1844.
13   *The Drama and Music of New South Wales, op. cit.,* p. 7.
14   See Helen Oppenheim, 'The Author of *The Hibernian Father*: An Early Colonial
     Playwright', *Australian Literary Studies,* December, 1966; Albert B. Weiner, 'The
     Hibernian Father: The Mystery Solved', *Meanjin* 4, 1966; Helen Oppenheim, '*The
     Hibernian Father*: Mysteries Solved and Unsolved', *Australian Literary Studies,* June, 1967;
     Eric Irvin, 'Australia's "First" Dramatists', *Australian Literary Studies,* May, 1969; Roger
     Covell, Introduction to *The Currency Lass,* Sydney, The Currency Press, 1976.
15   *The Australian,* 28 June, 1845.
16   Colonial Secretary's Correspondence, New South Wales Archives, 44/3673.
17   Colonial Secretary's Correspondence, New South Wales Archives, 43/6965.
18   The manuscript of *Jemmy Green,* along with that of another play, *The Grahame's
     Vengeance,* and a convict novel, *Ralph Rashleigh,* came to light in 1920, although
     Tucker's authorship was not established until the 1950s, by Colin Roderick. It is not
     known whether *Jemmy Green* was ever performed at Port Macquarie. See Colin
     Roderick's Introduction and Appendices to *Jemmy Green in Australia,* Sydney, Angus
     and Robertson, 1955.
19   Colonial Secretary's Correspondence, New South Wales Archives, 45/5515.
20   *The Sydney Morning Herald,* 29 July, 1844.
21   *Ibid.,* 26 December, 1844.
22   *The Australian,* 29 January, 1845.
23   *The Sydney Morning Herald,* 24 March, 1845.
24   *Ibid.,* 27 December, 1845.
25   Eric Irvin has noted (Introduction, Walter Cooper, *Colonial Experience,* Sydney, The
     Currency Press, 1979, p. xi) that between 1834 and 1914 nearly six hundred Australian
     plays are known to have been performed, of which barely one hundred have survived.
     Given the relative smallness of Australia's population, this seems a substantial figure,
     but it represents per year an average of only about seven plays compared with the
     hundreds of overseas plays.
26   *The Drama and Music of New South Wales, op. cit.,* p. 17.
27   For a detailed account of Cooper's life and work see Eric Irvin's Introduction to
     Colonial Experience (The Currency Press, Sydney, 1979).
28   For an informed critical discussion of Darrell's work, and a list of his plays (sixteen in
     all) known to have been performed in Australia, see Margaret Williams (ed.), *The
     Sunny South,* Sydney, The Currency Press, 1975.
29   For a detailed discussion of Dampier's life and work, see John Rickard, 'Alfred
     Dampier: An Actor-Manager in the "Land of Romance"', *Komos,* March, 1973.
30   For an account of some of the earliest critiques of commercial theatre in Australia, in
     The Lone Hand and elsewhere, see Leslie Rees, 'Rallying Calls for an Indigenous
     Australian Drama' (Chapter VI of *The Making of Australian Drama,* Sydney, Angus and
     Robertson, 1973).
31   Letter to Leslie Rees, quoted in *The Making of Australian Drama,* Sydney, Angus and
     Robertson, 1973, p. 266.
32   Margaret Williams, *Drama* (Australian Writers and their Work series), Melbourne,
     O.U.P., 1977, p. 3.
33   For a detailed discussion of Gregan McMahon's relations with the commercial and
     repertory theatres, see M. M. Morgan and D. Douglas, 'Gregan McMahon and the
     Australian Theatre', *Komos* 2, 1969; 4, 1972; March, 1973; and Allan Ashbolt, 'Courage,
     Contradiction and Compromise: Gregan McMahon, 1874–1941', *Meanjin* 3, 1978.
34   Leslie Rees, *The Making of Australian Drama, op. cit.,* p. 484; and see Mona Brand, 'New
     Theatre Movement', *Theatre Australia,* October, November, 1978.
35   Letter to Vance Palmer, 8 June, 1921, in Vance Palmer, *Louis Esson and the Australian
     Theatre,* Melbourne, Georgian House, 1948, p. 40.
36   *Louis Esson and the Australian Theatre, op. cit.,* p. 34.
37   *Ibid.,* p. 49.
38   David Walker, *Dream and Disillusion: A Search for Australian Cultural Identity,* Australian
     National University Press, 1976, Chapter I.
39   *Louis Esson and the Australian Theatre, op. cit.,* p. 69.
40   *Ibid.,* p. 52.

41 The programme did not eventuate, but it provided the stimulus for Esson to write *The Drovers*, and Palmer's *The Prisoner* was also to be included. (See *Louis Esson and the Australian Theatre*, pp. 16–19.)

42 Gregan McMahon compared the play with the work of Eugene O'Neill, and tried unsuccessfully to arrange a production under the commercial sponsorship of Tait's. Esson saw it as a 'terribly daring play', offering a challenge to 'Repertory or any other audience', 'the type of play the Pioneers should have done' (*Louis Esson and the Australian Theatre*, pp. 90–1). Its first performance in 1972 was a co-production by the Australian Performing Group and the Nindethana (Aboriginal) Theatre at the Pram Factory Theatre in Melbourne.

43 For a biographical account of Prichard's visit to this region, see Ric Throssell, *Wild Weeds and Wind Flowers, The Life and Letters of Katharine Susannah Prichard*, Sydney, Angus and Robertson, 1975, Chapter 5.

44 See Jonathan Shaw's Introduction to *The Touch of Silk*, Sydney, The Currency Press, 1974, for a detailed account of its stage and radio history. It was first produced by Frank Clewlow for the Melbourne Repertory Theatre in 1928, and subsequently by the Brisbane and Adelaide Repertory Theatres and by Sydney's brief-lived Turret Theatre (in 1929). Sydney's New Theatre staged it in 1939, and the play received fifteen separate A.B.C. radio productions between 1938 and 1957.

45 See Margaret Williams, *Drama, op. cit.*, pp. 14–15.

46 For a survey of the main achievements of Australian radio drama, see Leslie Rees, *The Making of Australian Drama, op. cit.*, pp. 154–210.

47 'The Playwright in Australia', *Australian Theatre Year I* (1955–56), pp. 9, 27.

48 Although written for the stage, the play's first performance was a ninety-minute radio version in 1942. Its first stage performance was at May Hollinworth's small, repertory-style Metropolitan Theatre in Sydney, and it subsequently had numerous amateur and repertory revivals. (See, especially, A. A. Phillips's account of the production planned by Dolia Ribush, 'Dolia Ribush and the Australian Theatre', and 'The Australian Romanticism and Stewart's Ned Kelly', in *The Australian Tradition*, Melbourne, F. W. Cheshire, 1958, Chapters VI and VII.) In 1956 the play was chosen as the successor of *Summer of the Seventeenth Doll* by the Elizabethan Theatre Trust, and received a full-scale professional production.

49 Author's Note, *Khaki, Bush and Bigotry: Three Australian Plays* (ed. Eunice Hanger), University of Queensland Press, 1968, pp. 26–7.

50 Initially recommended for performance at the Festival of Adelaide, its Board of Governors rejected the play on the grounds that it would be offensive to the Returned Services League. Its first performance was by an amateur group in Adelaide in 1960, and a full Trust-supported professional production was mounted in Sydney in 1961, under the direction of Robin Lovejoy.

51 For an exemplary account of the origins and development of the oldest of the professional theatres established in the 1950s, the Melbourne Theatre Company (originally, the Union Theatre Repertory Company)—and especially of the kinds of support it gave to new Australian drama—see Geoffrey Hutton, *It Won't Last a Week: The First Twenty Years of the Melbourne Theatre Company*, Melbourne, Sun Books, 1975.

52 The circumstances of *The Ham Funeral's* performance in 1961 after it had been rejected by the Governing Board of the Adelaide Festival of Arts, gave renewed impetus to a growing body of critical complaint about the conservatism and timidity of the Elizabethan Trust, its unwillingness to give active support to work which might be unusual, experimental, or unprofitable. For an account of this and other debates about subsidization policies in the 1960s, see H. G. Kippax's Introduction to *Four Plays* by Patrick White (Melbourne, Sun Books, 1967), and his chapter, 'Drama', in *Australian Society, A Sociological Introduction* (eds. A. F. Davies and S. Encel, Revised Edition, Melbourne, F. W. Cheshire, 1970).

53 See John Romeril, 'Street Theatre', *Arena* 20, 1969.

54 Jack Hibberd, 'How Marvellous Melbourne Came to Life', *Theatre Australia*, August, 1977, p. 37.

55 Postscript, *The Feet of Daniel Mannix*, Sydney, Angus and Robertson, 1975, p. 84.

56 Interview with John Romeril, *Meanjin* 3, 1978, p. 303.

57 See Graeme Blundell, Introduction, *I Don't Know Who To Feel Sorry For*, Sydney, The Currency Press, 1973, p. 9.

58 *Ibid.*, p. 9.

59 Jack Hibberd, Notes in the APG programme for the 1970 Perth Festival.
60 Jack Hibberd, Introduction, *Three Popular Plays*, Collingwood, Outback Press, 1976, p. 5.
61 See Jack Hibberd, Introduction, *A Stretch of the Imagination*, Sydney, The Currency Press, 1973, p. vi.
62 Interview with Craig McGregor, *National Times*, 24–29 October, 1977, p. 39.
63 Interview, *Honi Soit* 8, 1976, p. 12.
64 Alexander Buzo, Notes in the APG programme for the 1970 Perth Festival.
65 'Buzo: one step further', Alexander Buzo interviewed by Richard Zachariah, *Sunday Australian*, 4 June, 1972.

POETRY

1 W. H. Auden, 'The Cave of Making (in Memoriam Louis MacNeice)', *About the House*, London, Faber, 1966, p. 20.
2 A. D. Hope, Introduction, *Henry Kendall*, ed. Leonie Kramer & A. D. Hope, Melbourne, 1973, pp. xvi–xvii.
3 Elizabeth Perkins, 'Towards Seeing Minor Poets Steadily and Whole', *Bards, Bohemians, and Bookmen: Essays in Australian Literature*, ed. Leon Cantrell, St Lucia, University of Queensland Press, 1976, p 54.
4 Barcroft Boake, *Where the Dead Men Lie and Other Poems*, With Memoir by A. G. Stephens, London, Angus and Robertson, 1913, p. 200.
5 Brian Elliott, 'The Colonial Poets', *The Literature of Australia*, ed. Geoffrey Dutton, Penguin, 1964, pp. 244–245.
6 G. A. Wilkes, Introduction, *Poems (1913)*, Facsimile Edition, Sydney University Press 1972, p. 5.
7 Frank Kermode, 'Christopher·Brennan', *The Vital Decade: Ten Years of Australian Art and Letters*, selected by Geoffrey Dutton and Max Harris, Melbourne, Sun Books, 1968, p. 12.
8 Noel Macainsh, 'Christopher Brennan's Wanderer', *Quadrant*, February, 1980, p. 59.
9 James Devaney, *Shaw Neilson*, Sydney, Angus and Robertson, 1944, pp. 197–198.
10 Rex Ingamells, Introduction, *Jindyworobak Review 1938–1948*, Melbourne, Jindyworobak, 1948, p. 20.
11 *ibid.*, p. 25.
12 James McAuley, *A Map of Australian Verse*, Melbourne, Oxford University Press, 1975, pp. 201–202.
13 Nancy Keesing, *Douglas Stewart*, Melbourne, 1965, p. 31.
14 A. D. Hope, *Australian Literature 1950–1962*, Melbourne University Press, 1963, p. 1.
15 *ibid.*, pp. 3–4.
16 Bruce Dawe's statement in *Contemporary Poets*, London, St James Press, 1973, p. 275.

INDEX

A

Absurdism, 169, 215, 236, 239, 252, 260–261, 351
An Account of the English Colony in New South Wales, 29
Achurch, Janet, 222
The Acolyte, 166–167
Across the Sea Wall, 157–158
The Actors: An Image of the New Japan, 160
Actresses' Franchise League, 222
Adams, Francis, 294, 305, 318
Adamson, Robert, 423
An Address to the Inhabitants of the Colonies, established in New South Wales and Norfolk Island, 27
Adelaide Repertory Theatre, 212
Aestheticism, Aesthetic movement, 9, 218, 298, 312, 318, 323, 337, 349, 355, 402, 410
The Afterlife of Arthur Cravan, 265
'Agamemnon', *see* Burn, David
Age of Consent, 142
Akhurst, W. M., 198, 199
Alien Son, 130
Alive, 399
All for Gold, 198, 201
All That Swagger, 103, 104
Alma Venus, 309, 389
And the Big Men Fly, 244
Anderson, Ethel, 129
Angry Penguins, 370
Angry Penguins, 368, 370, 371, 383
Anoli: the Blind, 207, 222
An Anzac Muster, 316
A.P.G., *see* Australian Performing Group
Arcady and Other Places, 417–418
Archibald, J. F., 10
Are You Ready, Comrade?, 224
Art Nouveau, 320, 325, 328
Art Theatres, 207
Ashtaroth, 290

Astley, Thea, 110, 166–167, 168, 172
Astley, William, ('Price Warung') 54, 75–76, 98
At Dawn and Dusk, 319, 320–321
At Least You Can Say You've Seen It, 240
Augustan, 3, 288, 382
The Aunt's Story, 20, 21, 131, 149–150, 242
Australasia, 288, 310
Australia, 106
Australia Felix, 90, 92
Australia: Her Story, 129
The Australian, 179, 185
Australian Drama Nights, 210, 213, 222
Australian Literature Society, 138
Australian Performing Group, 212, 246–247, 248, 249–250, 251, 252, 253, 254, 255, 256
Authors' Theatre, 207

B

A Bachelor's Children, 158, 160
Badham, E. A., 14
Bail, Murray, 167, 171
Bailey, Bert, 209
Ballantyne, Gina, 369
The Bandit of the Rhine, 188
Banfield, E. J., 142
Barrier Truth, 79
Barrington, George, 32
Barton, G. B., 8
The Battlers, 213
Baylebridge, William, 272, 316–318, 320
Baynton, Barbara, 75
The Bay of Noon, 165
Bean, C. E. W., 305
Beasley, Jack, 130
Beaver, Bruce, 361, 415, 416, 418, 421, 422, 423, 426
Becke, Louis, 142, 303
Bedfellows, 244, 247
The Beginnings of an Australian Literature, 7, 289

Belfield, Francis, 194
Bell, John, 247, 256
Bell's Life in Victoria, 291
Beloved Son, 165
Berry, Premier Graham, 199
Betty Can Jump, 247
Betty Wayside, 99
Between Two Tides, 366
Beware of Imitations, 247, 250
Beynon, Richard, 207, 232, 233, 234, 244
Big Toys, 168, 243–244
Birds, 399
The Birdsville Track, 402, 404, 405, 406
Black Cargo, 131
The Black Horse, 221
The Black Opal, 117
Blackman, Charles, 338
Blair, Ron, 236, 241, 248
Bleak Dawn, 207, 221
Bleak Dawn and Other Plays, 221
Blight, John, 410
Blood Red, Sister Rose, 168
Blundall, Graeme, 247
Boake, Barcroft, 292, 294, 305, 318, 319
Bobbin Up, 131
Boddy, Michael, 236, 247, 248
Bohemians of the Bulletin, 324
'Boldrewood, Rolf' (Thomas Alexander Browne), 6, 7, 48, 53, 60–64, 68, 96, 99, 203
Bonanza, 126
Bon Bons and Roses for Dolly, 264
The Bookfellow, 350
The Book Lover, 313
Bourke, Governor Richard, 185
Boyd, Arthur, 19, 392, 393
Boyd, Martin ('Martin Mills'), 13, 18, 21–22, 67, 84, 114, 123, 131, 138–146
The Boy in Grey, 53
The Boy in the Bush, 107
The Boys in the Island, 157–158
Brady, E. J., 305
Brand, Mona, 211
Bread and Wine, 323
The Breaking of the Drought, 198
Brennan, Christopher, 9–10, 227, 279, 298, 307, 309, 315, 316, 318, 320, 324, 327–338, 348, 351, 361, 380, 383, 416, 418, 419, 426
'Brent of Bin Bin', *see* Franklin, Miles
Brereton, John Le Gay, 330, 349
Brewer, F. C., 175, 188, 195
The Bride of Gospel Place, 214, 217, 218

Bring Larks and Heroes, 168, 169, 246
Brisbane, Governor Thomas, 184
The Broad Arrow, 43
Brodney, Spenser, 220
Brooksbank, Anne, 265
Browne, T. A., *see* 'Boldrewood, Rolf'
Brumby Innes, 117, 207, 222, 223
Buckley, Vincent, 315, 390, 415, 416, 417–419, 420, 421, 423, 424, 426
The Bulletin, 9, 10, 11, 59, 67, 68–69, 73, 74, 75, 76, 77, 78, 83, 99, 100, 116, 142, 322, 323, 340, 404, 410, 411
The Buln-Buln and the Brolga, 79, 81
Burn, 170
Burn, David ('Agamemnon'), 175, 178–183, 187, 188, 189, 193, 225, 227
The Burnt Ones, 153, 243
Burstall, Betty, 236, 246
The Bush, 309–310, 314, 389
Bush Ballads and Galloping Rhymes, 293
Bush ballads, songs, 298–302, 410
The Bushranger of Van Dieman's Land, 37, 41
The Bushrangers (Burn, D.), 178, 179, 181–183
The Bushrangers (Harpur, C.), 188, 195
The Bushrangers (Melville, H.), 188
The Bushrangers and Other Poems, 277
Bush Studies, 75
But the Dead are Many, 130
Buvelot, Louis, 279
Buzo, Alexander, 8, 236, 239, 244, 246, 248, 252, 259–263
The Bystander, 154

C

Café La Mama Theatre (Melbourne), 236, 246
Cambridge, Ada, 66, 67
The Camp, 348
Campbell, David, 1, 16, 22, 302, 370, 400, 404, 408–410, 414, 421, 425, 426
Campion, Sarah, 126, 129
Capricornia, 34, 118, 123–126
Captain Quadring, 97
Captain Quiros, 276, 310, 366, 384, 386, 387–389, 390
Carboni, Rafaello, 56
The Cardboard Crown, 143, 144
Carey, Peter, 171
Casey, Gavin, 129
The Cassidy Album, 238, 239
The Catherine Wheel, 164

The Cats of Venice, 160, 161
The Cautious Amorist, 142
The Chantic Bird, 169–170
The Chant of Jimmie Blacksmith, 169
The Chapel Perilous, 226, 239, 264
'The Characteristics of Australian
    Poetry', 296
A Cheery Soul, 153, 243
Cherry, Wal, 233
Chevalier, Nicholas, 279
Chicago, Chicago, 251, 252
Chidley, 265
Chisholm, A. R., 334
Chisholm, Caroline, 27
The Chocolate Frog, 266
The Christian Brothers, 241
*Clara Morison: a Tale of South Australia
    During the Gold Fever*, 44–47
Clark, Manning, 19
Clarke, John, 256
Clarke, Marcus, 3, 6, 7, 20, 43, 47, 50,
    52, 52, 54–60, 64, 69, 75, 98, 99, 274,
    293
Clarke, Mrs, 187
Clewlow, Frank, 225
The Cliffs of Fall, 165
Clift, Chairman, 163
The Club, 258–259
Coast to Coast, 128
Cobb, Chester, 108
*The Cockatoos: Shorter Novels and
    Stories*, 153
Collected Poems (Neilson, J. S.), 339
Collins, David, 29, 176
'Collins, Tom', *see* Furphy, Joseph
Colonial Experience, 200–201
'The Colonial Poets', 295–296
Colonial Times (Hobart), 33
The Coming of Stork, 246, 256
Commercial theatre, 183–188, 194,
    195–197, 207–210, 248
Community Playhouse (Sydney), 210
*A Complete Account of the Settlement at
    Port Jackson*, 29
Compton, Jennifer, 248
Conditional Culture, 368
Confessions of a Beachcomber, 142
*Contemporary Portraits and Other
    Stories*, 167
The Convict, 55
Coonardoo, 117, 118–119
Cooper, Walter, 198, 199–201, 203
Coppin, George, 187
Coralie Lansdowne Says No, 244, 262

Cotters' England, 137
Couvreur, Mrs. Jessie, *see* 'Tasma'
Cove, Michael, 248
Cowan, Peter, 129
Craig, Alexander, 414
Creative Effort, 349
Croll, R. H., 339
Cuckooz Contrey, 354
Cunningham, Peter, 185
The Cupboard Under the Stairs, 164
The Currency Lass, 188, 189–191, 246

D

Daley, Victor ('Creeve Roe'), 14, 74,
    274, 298, 303, 306, 307, 312, 318,
    319–322, 323, 324, 328
'Daly, Rann' *see* Palmer, Vance
Dampier, Alfred, 197, 198–199, 201,
    202–204, 208, 247
Dampier, Lily, 250
Dann, George Landen, 211, 212, 221
Dark, Eleanor, 8, 19, 103, 121–122
Darling, Governor Ralph, 184–185
Darrell, George, 175, 197, 198, 199,
    201–202, 203, 235
Davis, Arthur Hoey, *see* 'Rudd,
    Steele'
Davison, Frank Dalby, 69, 107, 111,
    120–121, 126, 314
Dawe, Bruce, 15, 322, 415, 417, 419–422,
    424, 425
Dawnward?, 308
*Day of My Delight: An
    Anglo-Australian Memoir*, 141
Days of Disillusion, 108
Dead Men Rising, 122
Dead Timber, 213, 217
De Groen, Alma, 248, 265
Dennis, C. J., 99, 100, 106, 272
The Department, 258–259
De Rullecourt, or Jersey Invaded, 179
Devaney, James, 339, 340, 346, 369
*The Development of Australian
    Literature*, 9
Dibdin, Charles, 189
A Difficult Young Man, 140, 143, 145
Dimboola, 246, 254, 255
Disturbing Element, 125
Dobson, Rosemary, 323, 410, 426
'The Doll', *see Summer of the
    Seventeenth Doll*
The Doll Trilogy, 239
Dominions of the Boundary, 309
Don's Party, 244, 246, 256–257, 258–259

The Dosser in Springtime, 403–404
Dowling, Robert, 283
Down in the City, 164
Down Under, 265
The Drama and Music of New South Wales, 175
Dramatic Company for the Production of Australian Plays, 201
Dransfield, Michael, 423, 425
The Drovers, 214, 215–217
Dusty, 120
Dyson, Edward, 75, 99, 305

E

An Eager Hope, 239
The Earthquake Shakes the Land, 225
Earth Visitors, 354
Eden House, 159
Edens Lost, 165
The Education of Young Donald, 163
Eldershaw, Barnard, 103
Elegy for an Airman, 402, 403
Elijah's Ravens, 159
Elizabethan Theatre (Sydney), 232
Elizabethan Theatre Trust, 232, 233, 245, 248
Elliott, Brian, 295, 297
Ellis, Havelock, 102, 107, 111
Ellis, R. Kyndon, 296
Ellis, Robert, 236, 247, 265
The Elocution of Benjamin Franklin, 241
The Emigrant Family, 39, 41
'An Emigrant Mechanic' *see* Harris, Alexander
The End of a Childhood and Other Stories, 95
Ern Malley, *see* Malley, Ern
The Escape of the Notorious Sir William Heans (and the mystery of Mr Daunt): A Romance of Tasmania, 97–98
Essay on Memory, 310, 363–364, 365
Essays in Poetry, Mainly Australian, 417
Esson, Louis, 77, 114, 198, 204, 206, 210, 211, 212, 213–220, 221, 222, 226, 231, 232, 234, 236, 238, 239, 244, 253, 393
Evans, George Essex, 298, 305, 318
The Evening of the Holiday, 165
An Excursion to Port Arthur in 1842, 178
Excuse I, 240
The Extra, 162–163
The Eye of the Storm, 21, 121, 147, 153–154
Eyes of Vigilance, 313

F

Fact'ry 'Ands, 99
Farquar, George, 176
Farrell, John, 298
Farwell, George, 211
The Fat Man in History, 171
Favenc, Ernest, 118
Fawcett, George, 199
The Feet of Daniel Mannix, 247, 250–251
The Felonry of New South Wales, 38
The Feud, 290
'The Fiction Fields of Australia', 15, 45
Field, Barron, 28, 31, 275
Film, 74, 111, 197, 198, 204, 207–208, 209, 248
The Fire on the Snow, 225, 227, 403, 406
'The Firm', *see* Williamson, J. C.
First Fruits of Australian Poetry, 275
The Fisher Lass, 84, 89
Fitton, Doris, 211, 212, 223, 230
FitzGerald, R. D., 1, 8, 16, 227, 272, 287, 310, 361–367, 369, 383, 394, 397, 403, 411, 417
Flesh in Armour, 109
The Flesheaters, 169–170
The Floating World, 247, 251, 252–253
Foiled, or Australia Twenty Years Ago, 200
The Forger's Wife, 43
For Love Alone, 132, 136–137
For Love and Life, 203
For the Term of His Natural Life, see His Natural Life
The Fortunes of Richard Mahony, 10, 53, 83, 84, 86, 90, 91–94, 95
'The Foundations of Culture in Australia', 120
Fountains Beyond, 212, 221
Franklin, Miles ('Brent of Bin Bin'), 69, 84, 96, 100–104, 105, 106, 111, 116, 314
Fredo Fuss Love Life, 160
A Fringe of Leaves, 21, 153–154
The Front Room Boys, 246, 259, 261
Furphy, Joseph ('Tom Collins'), 10, 12, 21, 39, 47, 59, 63, 67, 68, 76–83, 85, 89, 96, 102, 109, 127, 128, 134, 172, 215, 220, 297, 308, 320, 393
Furtive Love, 239
Fuss, 200
'The Future Australian Race', 60

G

The Gateway, 397–398
Gay, William, 298
Gellert, Leon, 348
The Generations of Men, 408
Geoffry Hamlyn, see The Recollections of
 Geoffry Hamlyn
Geoghegan, Edward, 188–193m 194,
 199, 203, 235, 246
George, Keith, 214
The Getting of Wisdom, 84, 88–90
Gifford, Kenneth, 367–368
Gilbert, Kevin, 425
Gillies, Max, 247
Gilmore, Mary, 106, 111, 306, 311–312,
 316, 322, 323, 393
The Glass Canoe, 170
Glover, John, 279
Going Home, 265
Golconda, 114–116
Golden Builders and Other Poems, 418
The Golden Lover, 225, 227, 403
Gordon, Adam Lindsay, 6, 14, 106,
 274, 289–295, 301, 319, 411
Gossip From the Forest, 168
Gould, William, 278
Gray, Oriel, 211
Gray, Robert, 424
The Greater Apollo: Seven Metaphysical
 Songs, 362
The Great Man, 222
The Great South Land, 310, 366, 369
Green, H. M., 299, 403
Green Lions, 402–403, 406
The Gully and Other Verses, 313
Gum Tops, 369
Gunn, Mrs Aeneas, 99

H

'The Habit of Irony: Australian Poets
 in the Fifties', 414–415
Hadgraft, Cecil, 297, 340
Hail Tomorrow, 221, 238
Half-Crown Bob and Tales of the
 Riverine, 76
Hall, Rodney, 418
Halloran's Little Boat, 168, 246
The Ham Funeral, 148, 241–242
Hancock, Keith, 106
A Handful of Friends, 244, 259
A Handful of Pennies, 161
The Happy Land, 199
Happy Valley, 148
A Hard God, 239

Hardy, Frank, 76, 130
Harlequin Jack Spratt; or The Fire Fiend,
 and the Fairy of the Evening Star, 194
Harpur, Charles, 5, 6, 13, 20, 188, 195,
 225, 227, 272, 274, 277–281, 282, 283,
 289, 292, 295, 319, 426
Harris, Alexander ('An Emigrant
 Mechanic'; 'A Working Hand'), 28,
 31, 36, 38–42
Harris, Max, 369–370
Harrower, Elizabeth, 164, 165, 166, 168
Hart-Smith, William, 369, 370, 410
Harwood, Gwen, 415, 416, 418, 421,
 422, 423, 426
Hatfield, William, 107
A Haunted Land, 154–155
Hay, William Gosse, 43, 96–99, 100,
 105
Hazard, 200
Hazzard, Shirley, 165–166, 168
Heemskerk Shoals, 365, 366
Herbert, Xavier, 18, 48, 76, 107,
 123–126
The Hermit in Van Diemen's Land, 33
Her Privates We, 108–109
Heseltine, Harry, 293, 303
Hewett, Dorothy, 131, 226, 236, 239,
 263–265
The Hexagon, 159
Hibberd, Jack, 234–236, 239, 241, 246,
 247, 249–250, 252, 253–256
The Hibernian Father, 192, 193
The Hidden Bole, 363–263, 365
The Hillyars and the Burtons, 7, 49, 50,
 51–54
His Natural Life, 3, 7, 20, 52, 55–59, 198,
 199, 202
A History of Australia, 19
A History of Australian Literature, 299
Hollinworth, May, 223, 232
Holt, Bland, 197, 199, 216
Hope, A. D., 1, 16, 22, 274, 275, 285, 288,
 302, 322, 323, 338, 345, 367, 371–383,
 385, 393, 398, 400, 411, 414, 415, 416,
 417, 418, 420, 421, 426
Hopgood, Alan, 244
Hopkins, Francis R. C., 198, 201
Horler, Ken and Lilian, 247
Horne, Donald, 163
Horne, Richard Hengist, 286
House of All Nations, 132
How Does Your Garden Grow, 266
Hudson, Flexmore, 369–370
Human Toll, 75

Humphries, Barry, 240–241, 371
Hunter, John, 29, 176

I

I Don't Know Who to Feel Sorry For,
  246, 251, 252, 253
Idriess, Ion, 107
An Imaginary Life, 171
In An Australian Country Graveyard
  and other poems, 159
Independent Theatre (Sydney), 211,
  212, 230
Ingamells, Rex, 12, 13, 14, 310, 366,
  367–369, 393
Inheritors, 107
Intimate Strangers, 119, 121
Ireland, David, 167, 168, 169–170
Irvin, Eric, 185
Isn't It Pathetic at His Age, 240
It's Harder for Girls, 129

J

Jack, 266
Jack and the Beanstalk; or Harlequin
  Ogre, 194
Jackey Jackey, or the Australian
  Bushranger, 193
Jack Shepherd, 193
James, G. P. R., 55
James, John Stanley ('Julian Thomas',
  The Vagabond'), 60
Jane Street Theatre (Sydney), 245, 247,
  248, 256
Jemmy Green in Australia, 192, 200
Jephcott, Sydney, 298, 308
The Jindyworobaks, 12, 14, 111,
  367–370, 371, 383
Jindyworobak, Towards an Australian
  Culture, 368
Johnno, 171
Johnson, Rev. Richard, 27
Johnston, George, 84, 90, 157, 163, 171
Jonah, 99–100
Jones, Evan, 414, 415, 416
The Joss Adams Show, 265
Journal of a Voyage to New South Wales,
  28
Just a Show, 240

K

Kanga Creek: An Australian Idyll,
  107–108
Kangaroo, 104–105, 107, 117
Keesing, Nancy, 299

Kendall, Henry, 5, 13, 14, 274, 277,
  281–289, 290, 292, 295, 296, 310, 312,
  319, 393, 426
Keneally, Thomas, 8, 90, 110, 167,
  168–169, 172, 245, 246
Kenna, Peter, 207, 219, 232–233, 234,
  238, 239
Kid Stakes, 239
A Kindness Cup, 167
King, Governor Philip Gidley, 176
King, Morton, 187
Kingsley, Henry, 6, 7, 10, 47–54, 59,
  60, 61, 64, 65, 68, 69
Knowles, Conrad, 187, 188, 189
Knox, George, 296
Koch, Christopher, 122, 157–158,
  171–172
Kodadad and his Brothers, 200

L

Laird, J. T., 348
La Mama Theatre (Melbourne), 212,
  236, 246–247, 252
Lambert, George W., 321
The Lame Dog Man, 165
The Landscape of Australian Poetry, 297
Landtakers, 107
Lang, John, 43
Lang, John Dunmore, 27, 28, 312
Langley, Eve, 126–127, 129
Langton tetralogy, 21, 138, 143–145
Larger Than Life, 123–124
The Last Days of Pompeii, 193
The Last of the Knucklemen, 266
A Late Picking, 383
Lawler, Ray, 163, 204–207, 211, 217,
  219, 231, 232, 233, 234, 239, 244
Lawrence, D. H., 104–105, 107, 117, 118,
  407
Lawson, Henry, 9–10, 11, 12, 15, 19, 41,
  59, 64, 69–74, 76, 99, 100, 106, 128,
  215, 220, 297, 301, 302–305, 306, 312,
  321, 337, 340, 347
Lawson, Will, 393
Lazar, John, 187, 189, 193, 194
Leakey, Caroline, 43
Leaves from Australian Forests, 281,
  283–285
The Legend of King O'Malley, 247,
  248–249, 250
The Legend of the Nineties, 4, 11–12, 69,
  220
Lehmann, Geoffrey, 418, 422, 426
The Lemon Farm, 141–142

The Les Darcy Show, 250, 255
A Lesson in English, 250
Let's Hear it for Prendergast, 167
Levey, Barnett, 183–186, 187, 188
The Life and Death of Captain Cook, 203
Life in Sydney; or The Ran Dan Club, 192
Light, 296
Lindsay, Jack, 225
Lindsay, Joan, 122
Lindsay, Norman, 75, 105–106, 111, 142, 225, 227, 324, 349, 351, 352, 362, 364, 410
Literature in New South Wales, 8
Literature Society of Melbourne, 306
The Little Company, 122
The Little Hotel, 137
Little theatre movement, 207, 212, 223, 245–248
Livermore, Reg, 241
The Living and the Dead, 149
Locke-Elliott, Sumner, 165, 211, 230–231, 233
Lone Hand, 105, 198
Long, Gavin, 128
Long, Sid, 14
Longford, Raymond, 208
The Long Prospect, 166
Loreda, 178
Lovejoy, Robin, 233
Love Redeemed, 317
Lucinda Brayford, 21, 138, 139–140, 142–143, 144
The Lucky Streak, 245, 252
Lurie, Morris, 167, 168

M

Macainsh, Noel, 316, 338, 414
Macartney, Frederick, T., 306
McAuley, James, 1, 16, 18, 22, 272, 274, 276, 287, 310, 338, 366, 369, 370, 383–392, 398, 400, 414, 416, 417, 418, 421, 425, 426
McCombie, Thomas, 193
McCrae, Hugh, 111, 225, 298, 303, 307, 312, 316, 322–326, 345, 349, 403
McCuaig, Ronald, 323
McCullough, Colleen, 107
McDonald, Roger, 424
McInnes, Graham, 163
Mackellar, Dorothea, 373
Mackenzie, Kenneth ('Seaforth Mackenzie'), 121, 122–123, 323, 410

Macky, Stewart, 213, 214
McLachlan, J. R., 193
McMahon, Gregan, 210, 212, 213
McNeil, Jim, 248, 265–266
Maconochie, Alexander, 38
Macquarie, 239, 261–262
Mad, Bad and Dangerous to Know, 241
The Magic Pudding, 106
Makassar Reef, 244, 262, 263
Malley, Ern, 317, 370–371, 383
Malouf, David, 171, 322, 422, 425, 426
The Man From Chicago, 246
The Man From Snowy River, 304
The Man Hamilton, 113
Manifold, John, 302, 408, 415
Mann, Leonard, 109, 369
Manning, Frederic ('Private 19022'), 108–109, 111
Man-Shy, 120
The Man Who Loved Children, 132, 134, 135–136
A Map of Australian Verse, 414
Marshall, Alan, 107, 129
Martello Towers, 244, 262–263
Martens, Conrad, 279
Martin, Arthur Patchett, 7, 283, 289
Martin Beck, 39
Martin, David, 130, 131
Marvellous Melbourne (Dampier, A.), 198, 203–204, 247
Marvellous Melbourne (Hibberd, J., Romeril, J.), 247, 249–250, 251
Mary Stuart, 179
Masters in Israel, 417
Mathers, Peter, 167, 168
'Maurice, Furnley', *see* Wilmot, Frank
Maurice Guest, 84–88, 91, 95
Meale, Richard, 424
Melbourne Literary Club, 350
Melbourne Odes, 313
Melbourne Repertory Theatre, 212, 213
Melville, Henry, 188
The Memoirs of James Hardy Vaux, 31–32
Meredith, George, 187
The Merry-go-round in the Sea, 156–157
The Middle Parts of Fortune: Somme and Ancre, 108
Midnite: The Story of a Wild Colonial Boy, 156
Miles, Peter, 369
Milgate, Rodney, 245
'Mills, Martin', *see* Boyd, Martin

The Miner's Right, 203
Miscellanies in Prose and Verse, 27
Miss Herbert (The Suburban Wife), 137
'Mo', *see* Rene, Roy
Mo Burdekin, 126
Modern Australian Literature, 310
Montefiore, J. L., 189
The Montforts, 138
Moore, Tom Inglis, 285, 316
Moore, William, 210, 213, 222
Moorhead, Alan, 128
Moorhouse, Frank, 170–171, 172
More Recollections, 106
Moreton Miles, 317
Morrison, John, 130, 131
Mother and Son, 214, 218–219, 221
The Moving Image, 392–395, 398
Mr Butterfry and other Tales of New Japan, 160
Mr Moffatt, 108
Mrs Pretty and the Premier, 214
Much Else in Italy, 141, 146
Mudie, Ian, 369
Mudie, James, 38
Murdoch, Walter, 111, 369
Murray, Les, 19, 20, 314, 400, 417, 418, 420, 421, 422, 424, 425, 426
My Brilliant Career, 100, 102–103
My Brother Jack, 157, 163, 171
My Career Goes Bung: Purporting to be the Autobiography of Sybylla Penelope Melvyn, 102–103
Myself When Young, 90
The Mystery of Alfred Doubt, 98

N

Nagel, Charles, 189
Narrative of an Overland Journey . . . to Macquarie Harbour, 178
A Narrative of the Expedition to Botany Bay, 29
National Institute of Dramatic Art (N.I.D.A.), 245, 248
National Notes, 316, 317
'National Poetry', 350
Ned Kelly, 225, 227–229, 403
Negro Vengeance, a Tale of the Barbadoes, 194
Neild, James E., 199
Neilson, John Shaw, 11, 74, 298, 306, 311, 316, 319, 322, 323, 337, 338–348, 349, 408, 426

Nesbitt, Francis, 187, 189
A New Crime; or 'Andsome 'Enery's Mare's Nest, 200
New Theatre movement, 207, 211, 212, 221, 224, 236
A Nice Night's Entertainment, 240
N.I.D.A., *see* National Institute of Dramatic Art (N.I.D.A.)
Nietzsche in Australia, 316
Night on Bald Mountain, 243
Niland, D'Arcy, 107
Nimrod Street Theatre (Sydney), 245, 247–248, 256
The Nineties, 9–10, 11–12, 16, 20, 69, 74, 76, 82, 100, 103, 106, 111, 115, 128, 142, 204, 208, 286, 294, 297, 298–302, 307, 308, 312, 318–320, 322–323, 324, 327–328, 330, 339, 348, 349, 355, 414
Nobel Prize, 154
No Fixed Address, 419
Nolan, Sidney, 19, 370–371, 392, 393, 408
Norm and Ahmed, 246, 259, 260, 261
Normington-Rawling, J., 277
Nowra, Louis, 236, 248
Nuns in Jeopardy, 141, 142

O

Oakley, Barry, 167, 168, 236, 244, 246, 247, 250–251
O'Dowd, Bernard, 298, 305–311, 314, 316, 320, 322, 323, 325, 361, 362, 367, 380, 389
O'Flaherty, Eliza (Winstanley, Eliza), 189
O'Flaherty, H. C., 189, 192
Ogilvie, W. H., 305, 340
Old Bush Songs, 304
Old Days, Old Ways, 106
The Old Familiar Juice, 266
Old Melbourne Memories, 60
Old Tote Theatre (Sydney), 245, 247, 248, 256
The One Day of the Year, 163, 207, 231–232, 233, 253
One of Nature's Gentlemen, 246, 254
On Our Selection, 74, 209
Other Banners, 348–349
Other Times, 239
Our First Lieutenant, 179, 180–181
Our New Selection, 74
Outbreak of Love, 67, 143, 144

P

Page, Geoff, 424

Palmer, Nettie, 111, 112, 114, 128, 306, 310, 349, 350, 392, 426

Palmer, Vance ('Rann Daly'), 4, 5, 7, 11–12, 18, 69, 75, 107, 111–116, 117, 119, 120, 125, 129, 142, 160, 211, 213, 214, 217, 218, 219, 220–221, 226, 238, 244, 274, 302, 305, 306, 312, 314, 321, 348, 349, 361, 368, 369, 392, 400

Pandora's Cross, 264–265

The Paper Chase, 162

Parade Theatre, 256

'Parker, Leslie' see Thirkell, Angela

The Passage, 114–115, 368

Passenger, 168

The Past Within Us, 138

Paterson, Andrew Barton ('The Banjo'), 6, 12, 15, 64, 99, 272, 291, 292, 301, 302–303, 304–305, 324, 340, 426

The Patterns of Australian Culture, 297

The Pea Pickers, 126–127

Peggy Sue, 247, 254

Penalty Clause, 212

The Penguin Book of Modern Australian Verse, 415

Penton, Brian, 103, 107

People in Glass Houses, 1686

The People's Journal, 39

Perceval, John, 370

'The Peripatetic Philosopher', 60

Perkins, Elizabeth, 294

Perry, John, 203

Petty, Bruce, 251

Phillip, Governor Arthur, 27, 30, 176

Picnic at Hanging Rock, 122

Pioneer Players, 114, 210, 213–214, 222, 367

The Pioneers, 116, 222

Poems (1913), 328–338, 419

Poems and Songs, 282

Poetry and Morality, 417

Poetry and the Sacred, 417

'Poetry Militant: An Australian Plea for the Poetry of Purpose', 306–308, 309

Poetry of the Nineties, 318, 328

Policy and Passion: a novel of Australian Life, 64–66, 68

The Pommy Cow, 126

Poor Fellow My Country, 48, 125–126

Porter, Hal, 8, 18, 127, 131, 158–163, 172, 211, 244, 371

Porter, Peter, 422

Powers, John, 266

Power Without Glory, 130

Praed, Rosa Campbell, 7, 64–66, 67–68, 83, 109

Pram Factory Theatre (Melbourne), 212, 246–247, 249–250

Prelude to Christopher, 121

Prichard, Katharine Susannah, 18, 69, 105, 107, 111, 116–120, 121, 125, 206, 211, 212, 214, 219, 222–223, 306, 321, 349

Prince of Wales Theatre (Sydney), 195

'Private 19022' see Manning, Frederic

'The Prodigal Son,' 90, 104

Q

Quare Fatisgasti, 291

The Queen's Love, 179, 181

Queen's Theatre (Adelaide), 186

Queen's Theatre Company, 194

Queen's Theatre Royal (Melbourne), 186

Quintus Servinton, A Tale Founded upon Incidents of Real Occurrence, 33–34

R

Radio, 207, 208, 209, 210, 224, 225, 403, 412

Ralph Rashleigh, 42–44

Realist Writers, 130, 158

Rebel Chief, 194

Rebel Smith, 220

The Recollections of Geoffry Hamlyn, 7, 47–54

The Recruiting Officer, 176

Redheap, 106

Reed, Bill, 236

Reedy River, 213

Rees, Leslie, 225

A Refined Look at Existence, 245

The Refuge: A Confession, 122–123

Regulus, 179

The Removalists, 238, 246, 256–257, 258, 266

Rene, Roy ('Mo'), 208

Repertory Theatre movement, 207, 210–214, 223, 224

Retribution; or, The Drunkard's Curse, 194

Retrospect, 138

Return to Coolami, 121

Reverses, 199

Richardson, Henry Handel, 10, 53,
    83–96, 98, 100, 105, 132, 329
Rickards, Harry, 199
Riders in the Chariot, 21, 152–153
Rigby's Romance, 79–81, 172
The Right Thing, 161–162
Riley, Patrick, 189
The Road to Gundagai, 163
Robbery Under Arms, 7, 34, 49, 53,
    61–64, 198, 203
Roberts, Tom, 305, 321
Robinson, Michael Massey, 272, 275
Robinson, Roland, 369, 370, 402, 404
'Roe, Creeve' *see* Daley, Victor
Roland, Betty, 207, 211, 212, 219,
    223–225
Romance, 350
The Romantics, 3, 281, 288
Romeril, John, 236, 246–247, 249,
    251–253, 256, 264
Rooms and Houses, 105
Rooted, 259, 260–261
Roper, J., 279
Ross, Major Robert, 31
Ross's Poems, 422
Rowcroft, Charles, 28, 31, 34–38, 41
Royal Victoria Theatre (Hobart), 186,
    187
Royal Victoria Theatre (Sydney), 186,
    188, 189, 191, 193, 194, 199
'Rudd, Steele' (Arthur Hoey Davis),
    74–75, 209, 217
Rusty Bugles, 230–231
Rutherford, 404, 406

S

The Sacred Place, 213
*St. George and the Dragon; or, Harlequin
    and the Seven Champions of
    Christendom*, 194
A Salute to the Great McCarthy, 167
Saturdee, 106
Satyrs and Sunlight, 323
Savery, Henry ('Simon Stukeley'), 31,
    33–34, 37, 38, 43
Scandal of Spring, 141
Scott, Archdeacon Thomas Hobbes,
    184
The Scout, 198, 203
Sculthorpe, Peter, 424
Searle, James, 245, 252
*The Season at Sarsaparilla: A Charade of
    Suburbia*, 242–243
Sea Spray and Smoke Drift, 291

Seedtime, 114
*Settlers and Convicts, or Recollections of
    Sixteen Years' Labour in the
    Australian Backwoods*, 28, 38–41
The Seven Deadly Sins, 309
Seven Poor Men of Sydney, 132, 134–135
Seymour, Alan, 163, 207, 211, 219,
    231–232, 233, 234, 244, 253
Shapcott, Thomas W., 361, 418
The Shifting Heart, 207, 232, 233
Shipwreck, 225, 227
Short Stories (Porter, H.), 160
Short Stories in Prose and Verse
    (Lawson, H.), 70
Sidaway, Robert, 176
The Silent Land, 309
Simmons, Joseph, 187, 189
Simpson, Colin, 128
Simpson, Helen, 103
Simpson, R. A., 416, 425
A Single Flame, 141
Sinnett, Frederick, 15, 45, 47
Siren Voices, 84
Six Australian Poets, 316
Skinner, Mary Louisa (Molly), 107
Sladen, Douglas, 289, 290
The Slaughter of St. Teresa's Day, 207,
    232–233
Slessor, Kenneth, 1, 227, 274, 285, 312,
    313, 315, 316, 323, 350–362, 365–366,
    367, 394, 411, 426
Smith, James, 199
Smith, Vivian, 414
Soldiers' Women, 125
The Solid Mandala, 21, 152
Somers, Thomas, 198, 203
Songs from the Mountains, 281, 286–288
Songs of a Campaign, 348
Songs of the Sentimental Bloke, 99
Sonnets to the Unknown Soldier, 402,
    403
Souter, D. H., 302
The Southern Cross, 212, 214, 219, 238
Speak With the Sun, 408, 410
Spears, Steve J., 241, 248
Spence, Catherine Helen, 44–47,
    66–67, 69
Stead, Christina, 16, 84, 108, 114, 123, 131,
    132–138, 146, 158, 164, 172, 271, 422
Stephens, Alfred George, 11, 23, 74,
    294, 318, 319, 322, 339
Stephens, James Brunton, 283, 288,
    296, 298, 305, 373
Stephensen, P. R., 120

Stewart, Douglas, 1, 16, 17, 207, 211, 219, 225–229, 236, 299, 302, 315, 323, 361, 370, 383, 400–408, 410, 412, 414, 416
Stewart, Harold, 370, 424
Stivens, Dal, 129
Stone, Louis, 99–100, 106
Stow, Randolph, 19, 83, 117–118, 122, 154–157, 158, 415, 425
A Stranger and Afraid, 164
Streeton, Arthur, 305, 321
Street Theatre, 246
A Stretch of the Imagination, 234–235, 241, 247, 254–255
Struck Oil, 196
'Stukeley, Simon' *see* Savery, Henry
Such is Life, 10, 11, 34, 59, 69, 76–82
Summer of the Seventeenth Doll, 204, 205–207, 217, 225, 231, 232, 233–234, 239, 264
Sumner, John, 233, 237, 240
Sun and Shadow, 200
The Sunny South, 201–202, 203
Sun Orchids, 404, 405
Surprises of the Sun, 390, 426
Sutherland, Alexander, 9, 294
The Sweatproof Boy, 265
Sydney Delivered, 178, 179, 180
Sydney Gazette, 184
Sydney Monitor, 185, 188
Sydney Repertory Theatre, 212
The Sydney University Review, 296
Symbolist movement, 9, 222

T

Tait, J. and N., 208, 212
Tait's Magazine, 193
Tales of the Colonies; or The Adventures of an Emigrant, 28, 34–38, 41
Tales of the Convict System, 75
Tales of the Early Days, 75
Tales of the Isle of Death, 75
Tales of the Old Regime, 75
'Tasma' (Couvreur, Mrs. Jessie), 66–67, 69, 83
The Tatty Hollow Story, 264
Taylor, Andrew, 423
Television, 207–210, 248
Tell Us About the Turkey, Joe, 129
Tench, Captain Watkin, 29–31, 32, 176–177
Tennant, Carrie, 210, 223
Tennant, Kylie, 107, 129–130

Testimony to the Truth; or, the Autobiography of an Atheist, 39
Theatre Royal (Hobart), 186
Theatre Royal (Melbourne), 195
Theatre Royal (Sydney), 185–186, 187, 188
Thiele, Colin, 369
Thief of the Moon, 354
Thirkell, Angela ('Leslie Parker'), 109–111, 163
This Great City, 203
This Old Man Comes Rolling Home, 264
Thomas, Evan Henry, 188
'Thomas, Julian' *see* James, John Stanley
Thornton, R. K. R., 318, 319, 328
Thoughts: a Series of Sonnets, 277
Three Cheers for the Paraclete, 110
The Tilted Cross, 158, 161
Time Given, 391
The Time Is Not Yet Ripe, 213, 214–215, 218, 236, 239
The Timeless Land, 19, 121
The Tins and Other Stories, 129
A Toast to Melba, 247, 250, 255
Tom and Jerry; or Life in London, 192
Tomholt, Sydney, 207, 211, 220, 221–222
Tompson, Charles, 4–6, 274, 276
To the Islands, 154–155
To the West, 203
The Touch of Silk, 207, 212, 223–225
Tourmaline, 156, 157
The Tower, 244
The Tower of the Dream, 280
The Tragedy of Donohue, 188
Transit of Cassidy, 165
Transported for Life, 201
Trap, 167
The Trapper, 198, 203
The Tree of Man, 20, 150–151
The Triad, 222
Tribune, 311
Trio, 354
Trooper to the Southern Cross, 109–110
True Love, or The Interlude Interrupted, 191
'The Trust' *see* Elizabethan Theatre Trust
Tucker, James, 31, 37, 38, 42–44, 177, 192, 200
Turner, Ethel, 99
Turner, George, 164–165

Turner, Henry Gyles, 9
Turner, W. J., 321, 422
XXI Poems Towards the Source, 336
Twenty-Three, 131
The Two Fires, 397–398

U

Ullathorne, William Bernard, 27, 38
Ultima Thule, 90, 94
Uncle Piper of Piper's Hill: An Australian Novel, 66–67
Under Aldebaran, 384, 386
Union Theatre Repertory Company (Melbourne), 237, 240, 244
The Unknown Industrial Prisoner, 169

V

'The Vagabond' *see* James, John Stanley
The Vagabond Papers, 60
Vaux, James Hardy, 31–32, 33, 34, 37, 38, 41, 43, 44
Verse (Brennan, C. J.), 329–330
A Victim of the Aurora, 169
Vindication of Van Dieman's Land, 178
Vision, 349, 350, 354, 361, 367
A Vision of Ceremony, 386, 389
The Vivisector, 21, 147, 153–154
Voices of the Night, 203
Von Guerard, Eugene, 279
Voss, 17, 20, 150, 151–152, 154, 155, 412
Voyager Poems, 17

W

Walch, Garnet, 198, 199
Walker, David, 218
Walker, Kath, 425
Walking Through Tigerland, 167
Wallace-Crabbe, Chris, 414–415, 420, 422, 423, 425
The Wandering Islands, 371, 378
Ward, Russel, 311
'Warung, Price' *see* Astley, William
A Waste of Shame, 164
The Wasters, 214
The Watcher on the Cast-Iron Balcony, 162, 163
The Watch Tower, 164
Waten, Judah, 130
Water Under the Bridge, 165
Watson, E. L. Grant, 118
The Way Home, 90

Webb, Francis, 370, 400, 411–413, 415
The Well-Dressed Explorer, 166
Wentworth, William Charles, 19, 28, 274, 276, 287, 288, 310
What If You Died Tomorrow, 244, 258, 259
When Blackbirds Sing, 139, 143, 144
Wherrett, Richard, 247
White, John, 28, 29
White, Patrick, 1, 16, 17, 19, 20–21, 22, 90, 100, 104, 110, 121, 123, 128, 131, 133, 146–154, 155, 157, 158, 166, 168, 172, 211, 222, 226, 236, 241–244, 263, 271, 371, 380, 398, 416
The White Cry, 402, 403
The White Thorntree, 121
White Topee, 127
White With Wire Wheels, 246, 254, 256
Whitworth, R. P., 199
Who?, 246, 254
Why They Walk Out, 141
A Wild Ass of a Man, 167
Wilding, Michael, 170–171
Wilful Murder, 203
Wilkes, G. A., 330
Williams, Margaret, 210
Williams, Victor, 369
Williamson, David, 230, 236, 238, 244, 246, 248, 251, 252, 256–259, 266
Williamson, J. C. ('The Firm'), 196, 208
Williamson, Maggie, 196
Wilmot, Chester, 128
Wilmot, Frank ('Furnley Maurice'), 5, 312–315, 316, 322, 323, 340, 350, 416, 425
Wilson, Thomas, 189
Wine and Roses, 320, 321
Winstanley, Eliza, 187, 189
The Witch of Hebron, 280–281
Witzenhausen, Where Are You?, 250
The Woman Tamer, 213, 217, 218
Woman to Man, 395, 398
Women's Group (within the Australian Performing Group), 247, 254
Woolls, William, 27
Workers' Art Guild (Perth), 214, 222
Working Bullocks, 117–118
'A Working Hand' *see* Harris, Alexander
A World of Its Own, 391
The World's Flesh, 417
The Wort Papers, 167
The Wreck of the Dunbar, 203

Wright, Judith, 1, 5, 8, 12–13, 16, 19, 20, 23, 274, 277, 279, 311, 317, 326, 338, 341, 361, 370, 379, 383, 384, 392–400, 404, 408, 411, 412, 414, 416, 420, 426
Wyatt, Joseph, 186, 187

Y
The Year of Living Dangerously, 157, 171–172

The Young Cosima, 91, 94–96
The Young Desire It, 122
Young Man of Talent, 164
The Young Wife, 131

Z
Zisca the Avenger, 194